Transactions of the Royal Historical Society

FIFTH SERIES

40

LONDON 1990

British Library Cataloguing in Publication Data

Transactions of the Royal Historical Society.
—5th series, vol. 40 (1990)
1. History—Periodicals
I. Royal Historical Society
905 D1

ISBN 0-86193-124-6

Made and printed in Great Britain by Butler & Tanner Ltd, Frome and London

CONTENTS

TRANSACTIONS OF THE
ROYAL HISTORICAL SOCIETY

PRESIDENTIAL ADDRESS

by F. M. L. Thompson

ENGLISH LANDED SOCIETY IN THE TWENTIETH CENTURY

I PROPERTY: COLLAPSE AND SURVIVAL

READ 17 NOVEMBER 1989

THE death rattle of the landed order, like the death knell of capitalism, has been clearly heard dozens of times over the last hundred years and more. Yet there is a suspicion that the sounds have been mis-heard or misinterpreted, for collapse and decomposition have never followed the symptoms of sickness and crisis. The Churchill family have played their part in crying 'wolf'. In 1885 the 8th Duke of Marlborough, reflecting on 'the organised agitation against the present ownership of land', asserted that 'were there any effective demand for the purchase of land, half the land of England would be in the market tomorrow'.[1] He had inside information, the Blenheim estate being heavily indebted. A generation later his son, the 9th Duke, having helped stave off disaster by marrying Consuelo Vanderbilt, wrote in his turn to *The Times*. Under the heading 'Old Order Doomed' and the shock of the 1919 Budget, with its 'confiscatory' increase in death duties to a rate of 40 per cent on estates of £2 million and over, he stated that '[the] fortresses of territorial influence it is proposed to raze in the name of social equality' and forecast that 'the new tax must make it impossible for the heirs of these men—[the landed magnates]—to carry on the tradition'.[2] Whether the heirs have carried on the tradition is debatable, but it is indisputable that in 1989 his grandson, now the 11th Duke, is still seated in Blenheim Palace, surrounded by an estate of 11,500 acres. That may be no more than half the acreage owned by his great-grandfather but it is nevertheless a very large estate, and a principal reason for placing the

[1] Letter to *The Times*, 8th Duke of Marlborough, 3 Oct. 1885.
[2] Letter to *The Times*, 9th Duke of Marlborough, 19 May 1919.

11th Duke among the 200 wealthiest people in Britain. It is not the sole reason: the art collection at Blenheim is extremely valuable, and marrying the divorced first wife of the Greek shipowner, Aristotle Onassis, may have been a help.[3]

A junior branch of the Churchill family was much involved in creating the atmosphere which the landed classes felt was choking them to death. Winston Churchill was a warm supporter of the 1909 Budget whose new land taxes were perceived by the landed classes as a swingeing populist attack on themselves. The main proposal was to levy one fifth of the future unearned increment in the value of land, where the increase in value was attributable to external and publicly financed developments, and agricultural land was exempt from the new tax. 'Such is the increment tax', Winston wrote in 1909, 'about which so much chatter and outcry are raised at the present time, and upon which I will say that no more fair, considerate, or salutary proposal for taxation has ever been made in the House of Commons.'[4] He was a member of the Government which virtually doubled the rate of death duties in 1919, was a member of a later Government which in 1940 effectively wiped out the advantages of creating private estate companies as a means of tax avoidance, and presided over the Government which raised the maximum rate of death duties from 50 per cent to 65 per cent in the course of the Second World War.[5] Yet the landed aristocracy and the property press were united in denouncing death duties, from their introduction in 1894 onwards, as vicious, vindictive, and partisan instruments deliberately designed to destroy inherited estates and inherited wealth and humble the pride and pomp of ancient families. Winston, having done his bit to increase the power of this scourge, professed to regret its apparent effect in undermining the power and prestige of the old landed families. At a wartime by-election in 1944, famous at the time, the Marquess of Hartington, eldest son of the 10th Duke of Devonshire, stood for the Cavendish family seat of West Derbyshire and was defeated. The fact that Hartington was a characteristically unpolitical soldier who remarked in one of his campaign speeches that the nationalisation of the coal mines had not been a success, this anticipating events by three years and a general election, was not helpful, but his failure was a clearcut defeat for the Chatsworth territorial influence which had

[3] *Sunday Times Supplement: Britain's Rich, The Top 200*, 2 April 1989, 62. The data in this guide are undoubtedly not entirely reliable, but the size of the Marlborough estate is corroborated in R. Perrott, *The Aristocrats: A Portrait of Britain's Nobility and their Way of Life Today* (1968), 153.

[4] W. S. Churchill, *Liberalism and the Social Problem* (1909), 329–30.

[5] Rates of death duties are most easily accessible in *Whitaker's Almanack* (various editions), normally under the heading 'Estate Duty'.

been undisputed in Derbyshire for centuries. Churchill recognised it as such, and the result cast 'a pall of the blackest gloom' over him as he contemplated the passing of the traditional political order and the unreliability and ingratitude of the democracy.[6]

This highly condensed and selective piece of family history neatly illustrates four strands in the story of the landed classes in the present century. The loss of prestige and influence, and with it the passing of the artistocratic life style. The imposition of taxes on inherited wealth, and the understandable fear that these were directed at landed wealth in particular. The break-up of estates and a steep decline in territorial possessions. And, in spite of all this, the survival of a group of large and very wealthy landowners into the 1990s, most of them members of a long-established landed aristocracy with roots in the eighteenth century and earlier, and most of those, like the dukes of Marlborough, members of the landed nobility. The family history also hints at a fifth strand: the fact that the taxation which has either crippled the landed interest or frightened it away from its land has been imposed, maintained, or increased indifferently by Liberal, coalition, Conservative, and Labour governments. From the 1880s onwards the landed interest had learned to regard radicals, Liberals, single-taxers, and socialists as distinctly unfriendly and probably dangerous. They were identified as the enemy, and if they were allowed to reach office it was only to be expected that they would inflict vicious taxes and other anti-landowner measures. The Conservative party, on the other hand, was long taken to be little more than the political expression of the landed interest. That may well have ceased to be so by 1900. Still, the Tories were the only political friends the landowners had. When the Tories failed to reverse the anti-landowner taxes, and not merely failed to do so for more than sixty years after 1919 but also on occasion even gently tightened the screw, the old guard of the landed interest could have been forgiven for feeling 'with friends like that who needs enemies.'

At the very least this failure of the post-1919 Conservative party, or of any post-1919 Conservative governments or Chancellors before Nigel Lawson, to behave as the champions or protectors of traditional landed interests cannot fail to have impressed the landed aristocracy as hurtful, bewildering, or perverse. Those of the landed classes who did remain active in politics and who held office, of whom there were quite a number, no doubt both understood and accepted the reasons of principle and expediency which made it impossible for Conservative governments to appear to discriminate in favour of a class that was

[6] J. Colville, *The Fringes of Power. Downing Street Diaries, 1939–55* (1985), 474, quoted by M. Beard, *English Landed Society in the Twentieth Century* (1989), 86.

generally thought to be wealthy and privileged. The less political and less personally ambitious majority of the landed aristocracy and gentry, on the other hand, may have understood those reasons but drawn the conclusion that since they had been driven onto the sidelines of political life, and since no amount of effort on their part was ever going to put the clock back, there was little point in spending much energy, let alone money, in supporting either the party or a prominent public life. Labour governments could normally be relied upon to be beastly to landowners, raising death duties (1929, 1946, 1949), abolishing tax avoidance devices (1969), or inventing fiendish new taxes with which to torment inherited wealth (1975), and when Labour ran true to form in this way the Tory adrenalin of the landed classes flowed strongly. Labour, however, was also responsible for friendly acts, such as the introduction of a lower rate of death duties for agricultural land in 1929, the enlargement of this concession in 1949, and above all for the friendliest measure of the twentieth century, the 1947 Agriculture Act. Such conflicting signals may well have added to the confusion of the landed classes and convinced many of the futility of party politics.

Whatever the reasons the withdrawal symptoms are clear. In the 1910 Parliament about 40 per cent of the M.P.s were members of landed society, either landowners or the sons of landowners; since 1945 the proportion has fluctuated around 5 per cent. In 1910, in somewhat exceptional circumstances, between a third and half of the hereditary peers attended sittings of the House of Lords fairly frequently; in the 1980s hereditary peers, apart from the politically dedicated, the office-holders, and those so impoverished that the collection of the daily attendance allowance is a matter of moment, are rarely to be seen in the House. In the traditional strongholds of the shires the retreat has been equally marked, and is possibly more significant. It can be convincingly argued that the disappearance of the landed aristocracy from the parliamentary scene is a straightforward result of a loss of power, influence, and social relevance, and simply records their ejection from the political machinery by the business, professional, and working-class groups with control of voting power, and thus their descent into political obscurity. In the counties, however, the office of lord lieutenant has become more and more honorific and ceremonial; lords lieutenant have no serious executive functions, and only a vestigial influence as a channel for suggesting names for inclusion in the commission of the peace. What the job requires is a figure who commands the respect of the county as a social leader, who has the time and money to take an interest in local enterprises and charities, and the presence to preside over local occasions with appropriate dignity. With growing calls to receive visiting royals and to perform opening ceremonies of schools, hospitals, bridges, bypasses, motorways, factories, and occasionally universities, demands which have increased particularly since 1945, it might have been expected that the call for the services of the landed aristocracy as lords lieutenant, as the most readily identifiable pool of dignified and county-based talent available, would have been well maintained. There was no room for it to have increased, since traditionally all lords lieutenant had been members of the titled landed aristocracy, a situation reflected in the pre-1914 world where, in 1910, 39 of the total of 43 lords lieutenant of English counties and 28 of the 33 in Scotland were landed noblemen or landed baronets of long standing; in Wales a certain displacement of the essentially Anglican landed elite had already set in, and no more than 7 of the 12 lords lieutenant were drawn from that group.[7] After the First World War this tradition began to be eroded in England and Scotland as well, and since the Second World War, despite the general popularity of pomp and archaic ceremonial, it has virtually collapsed. By the early 1970s no more than 15 of the English lords lieutenant (swollen in total number to 46 with the subdivision of some counties) were the heads of old-established landed families holding hereditary titles, and the titular county leadership was dominated by retired generals, naval commanders, and succesful businessmen. In Scotland tradition was a little more regarded, with nearly half of these posts still in the hands of the old guard, but Wales completely repudiated its resident aristocracy and had no peers amongst its lords lieutenant in 1973 and no more than three baronets of long standing. The situation remains much the same at the end of the 1980s, and can be considered to have stabilised with a greatly reduced but still surviving aristocratic presence.[8]

In other positions of local authority the aristocrats were perhaps positively thrust aside, precisely because power was at stake and party machines and country electorates ceased to be willing to entrust it to hereditary landowners. Just beore 1914 the still relatively new county councils numbered, in England and Wales, 15 peers and 7 baronets among their chairmen, well over one-third of the total. By 1973 less than 10 per cent of the county council chairmen were landowners with hereditary titles, with a fractionally higher proportion in Scotland and none at all in Wales; at the end of the 1980s there are none in any of the three countries.[9] Thus a century after the elective principle, and in its train party politics, were introduced into county government in 1888, the fears voiced at that time that it was a revolutionary measure

[7] *Whitaker's Almanack* (1911 edn.).
[8] *Whitaker's Almanack* (1973 and 1988 edns.).
[9] *Whitaker's Almanack* (1973 edn.).

which would deprive the landed aristocracy of its age-old control of the counties have been realised.[10]

Yet it is not altogether clear that this was the result of a revolution from below successfully deposing a ruling class and stripping it of power, not through anything so dramatic as the barricades but through the ballot box, and through a gradual but unrelenting erosion of its wealth. It is possible that the landed aristocracy have not so much suffered a series of defeats in political and economic battles as beaten a retreat, in moderately good order, from a series of untenable positions. In some cases, indeed, they may have been deprived of the leadership of county councils against their will; but in the majority of counties that have remained consistently true blue over the decades the vanishing aristocrats have not been elbowed aside, they have simply lost interest. Lord lieutenancies could, presumably, have continued to be theirs for the asking, at least in all but a handful of heavily urbanised and unusually egalitarian counties. When Northumberland can continue to turn to its Duke, Durham to Lord Barnard of Raby Castle, Lincolnshire to the Earl of Ancaster, Gloucester to the Duke of Beaufort, or Sussex to the Duke of Norfolk, it cannot be seriously contended that Berkshire or Buckinghamshire, Cumberland or Lancashire, Northamptonshire or Oxfordshire were by the 1970s literally denuded of eligible and presentable dukes and earls. In fact all those counties had a fairly liberal supply, but were served by a variety of gentrified majors and company directors. When Hertfordshire turned to a major-general for its lord lieutenant, or Derbyshire to a worthy local baronet, it seems likely that the current Marquess of Salisbury or Duke of Devonshire were opting out rather than being overlooked; or at the very least they were expressing a view that the lord lieutenancy was not of key importance to their public image or social standing.

This suggests voluntary withdrawal from public life rather than eviction. Withdrawal, in a military sense, implies the retreat of a depleted and outnumbered force to some redoubt where it may hope to regroup and continue resistance. This may not be an appropriate metaphor for the twentieth-century manœuvres of the landed battalions, although much of the writing about them has used the language of conflict, attack, defence, defeat, in describing the decline of the landed aristocracy.[11] Decline there has certainly been, in territorial

[10] J. P. D. Dunbabin, 'Expectations of the new County Councils, and their realization,' *Historical Journal*, viii (1965); R. J. Olney, *Rural Society and County Government in Nineteenth-Century Lincolnshire* (Lincoln, 1979), 135–40.

[11] Summarised by Heather A. Clemenson, *English Country Houses and Landed Estates* (1982), 212–15. See also Beard, *English Landed Society*, 119–21, or Perrott, *Aristocrats*, chap. 1, for statements of the pessimistic position on aristocratic decline.

possessions. But in some ways it is better to think of the landed aristocracy as having gone into self-liquidation as a social group, and not as a dwindling and embattled band reduced to a mere remnant of its Victorian glory by the ceaseless batterings of taxation, wars, and political democracy.

The social cohesion of the group had never been complete. Newcomers had always been able to gain entry into landed society, and members of established landed families had always to some extent been open to recruiting new blood and money by marrying outside their own circle. The Victorian and pre-Victorian landed aristocracy of titled landowners and untitled landed magnates was not a closed caste. Nevertheless, while not a watertight or bloodtight caste it was emphatically a social group or social elite with a clear set of prevailing or normative standards and values, expressed in a way of life and a way of marrying. It was precisely because the group's conventional marriage patterns were so clearly established that the not infrequent exceptions, whether to bankers' daughters in the 1820s or to American girls in the 1890s, were instantly visible and attracted copious social comment. From the later eighteenth century, and probably earlier, through to 1914 at least half the marriages of titled landed aristocrats were to daughters of titled landed families; a further quarter were to daughters of the landed gentry, Anglican clergymen, or military officers, all members of landed society and its fringes. No more than a quarter of these marriages were to the daughters of commoners who were outside the direct circle of British landed society. These others included the foreign counterparts of British landed and military families, as well as businessmen, men of the professions, and civil servants. This pattern was exclusive, but not rigourously exclusive, and it was not rigidly unchanging over the nineteenth century; there was a noticeable loosening of the conventions in the 1890s and a slight increase in the influx of non-artistocratic, non-landed, stock. But in 1914 there was every chance that three out of every four peeresses encountered would have been of noble and landed families themselves.[12]

By the mid-1970s no more than one out of every four peeresses—defined as the wives of those holding titles created before 1900, who are roughly equivalent to the traditional landed aristocracy—were themselves daughters of titled landed families. The proportion was only slightly larger among those at the apex of the peerage. In 1975

[12] Maureen E. Montgomery, *Gilded Prostitution: Status, money, and transatlantic marriages, 1870–1914* (1989), Tables 5.1 and 5.2, 89–91. See also F. M. L. Thompson, 'Aristocracy, Gentry, and the Middle Classes in Britain, 1750–1850,' in Adolf M. Birke and Lothar Kettenacker, eds., *Burgertum, Adel und Monarchie* (Munich, 1989), Appendix 1, 33.

there were 24 duchesses, outside the royal family, and 9 divorced duchesses—these, it may be noted, were the remains of the broken marriages of no more than 6 dukes. Thirteen of these 33 duchesses were the daughters of titled families; one of those 13 came from a whisky peerage given to the head of Dewar's in 1916, but the other 12 came from families of some standing in the peerage and on the land. Thus in the traditional fashion the Duchess of Northumberland was the daughter of the 8th Duke of Buccleuch, and the Duchess of Sutherland the daughter of the 8th Duke of Northumberland. Intermarriage among the great clans had, however, become a minority practice. The majority of the duchesses, almost two-third of them, were socially diverse and miscellaneous in their origins. Not one came from a landed gentry family, although the six army officers' daughters and the lone clergyman's daughter were no doubt gentrified in upbringing and perhaps in family connections. The rest, while not exactly a cross-section of the population which a dustman stood as much chance of encountering as a duke, were a cross-section of a cosmopolitan society of position and wealth, not of birth and lineage: they were the daughters of businessmen, of American and French businessmen and society figures, widows of bankers, and divorcees.[13] A sample of 227 marriages of peers of all ranks who were alive in 1975 and whose titles dated from before 1900 shows, in addition to the 24 per cent of the wives who were daughters of titled families, only 4 per cent who were daughters of landed gentry families and 1 per cent who were clergymen's daughters; 14 per cent were the daughters of military or naval officers, 2 per cent were daughters of families in the professions, 12 per cent were daughters of foreigners who probably themselves had a variety of social and occupational positions, and 42 per cent had fathers who were simply unclassified and unlisted commoners.[14]

It would be idle to speculate on the social origins of this great pool of peeresses which comprised more than two-fifths of the total, and for present purposes it is not necessary to contemplate the laborious genealogical research that might trace their fathers' occupations and status. The essential point is that they all had social opportunities for meeting and mixing rather intimately with the nobility and more purposefully with the eldest sons of peers, which was the stage at which most marrying happened, and that they were all non-landed

[13] *Who's Who* (1975 edn.) and *Burke's Peerage* (1970 edn.).

[14] *Who's Who* (1975 edn.) and *Burke's Peerage* (1970 edn.), sample of all peers with pre-1900 titles under letters A, B, C, and S: there were 179 peers in this group, roughly a quarter of the total peerage of pre-1900 creations. Of these, 16 were unmarried; the 163 who had ever married had contracted 227 marriages.

or at least did not belong to families which had inherited land. This specification points towards the upper middle class of business, the professions, or the arts (for example, the 7th Marquess of Anglesey married, in 1948, the daughter of the playwright and novelist Charles Morgan), who had the manners, wealth, and tastes, perhaps including country tastes, to behave as pseudo-gentry, but it does not exclude other social backgrounds for the peerage wives. There were many reasons for their evident ability to mix with and marry the nobility, and underpinning them all, at a personal level, should no doubt be placed a virtually complete relaxation of all former social and parental restraints on the freedom of aristocratic men to marry anyone they fancied. It would be interesting to know whether the men married for love, money, affection, shared interests, ambition, the prospect of useful family connections, or other reasons, but such knowledge would not affect the main conclusion to be drawn from the new marriage pattern of the mid-twentieth century. This is that rank and birth had almost ceased to matter in the social contacts out of which marriages blossomed. The society columns of the quality press and society magazines like the *Tatler* continued for obvious reasons to make more of titled engagements and weddings than of ordinary run-of-the-mill matches, because hereditary titles retained some glamour and snob-appeal. But the somewhat fragmented and sometimes hectically itinerant social life which had replaced the organised and institutionalised marriage market of the season in Victorian London had become non-aristocratic, which is not the same thing as saying that it had become classless. From one point of view one could say that girls from a great variety of family backgrounds had penetrated the circles frequented by the sons of the nobility. The alternative viewpoint discloses the sons of the nobility setting aside consciousness of their status and simply forming part of whichever upper-class set appealed to their tastes and their pockets, within which they might find a partner, whose membership of a titled or landed family had become a matter of indifference.

All these indicators—of office, political and public activity, county position, and marriage—have quite rightly been interpreted as symptoms of the decline of the landed classes. That decline, in turn, has usually been linked with the break-up of landed estates, the destruction of country houses, and the general erosion of the economic base of the landed aristocracy, on the simple but understandable ground that loss of social and political position has followed a loss of wealth. There is a good deal of truth in this. There is also a good deal of truth in reversing the causal relationship and arguing that a loss of wealth, so far as it has resulted from taxation policies, has followed a prior loss of social and political position. Neither argument is wholly satisfactory, because what has happened since the First World War is that the eclipse of social and political position has been only a little short of total, while the loss of wealth has been far from uniformly dire, maybe catastrophic in some cases but negligible in others. The landed aristocracy as a class has disappeared, but landed estates have not. That is an exaggeration, as in several counties the county gentry still retain a definite and distinct social status and presence, most readily detectable in the hunting field and at hunt balls. The landed aristocracy, however, has ceased to regard itself, and has ceased to be regarded, as a distinct and separate national or metropolitan class. It has dropped out of political discourse and is not noticed in social comment or in analyses of social structure.[15] Individual members of the group have merged almost anonymously into the layer of the upper middle class appropriate to their income and personal inclinations, or have withdrawn into a secluded and private social life; while in the world of high politics those who choose to perform in the company of the life peers, who are mainly retired or failed professional politicians seasoned with a sprinkling of businessmen, journalists, and academics, do so as political animals not as representatives of a class. The class, which before 1914 had an exceptionally high profile as it felt itself to be besieged by Lloyd George's demagoguery and menaced by his land valuation, has performed an astonishing vanishing trick. This has been so effective that most people believe that the landed aristocracy has vanished from the public consciousness because it has been obliterated, apart from a few harmless survivors who act as caretakers for sundry parts of the national heritage. In fact, because it has been so adroit in being self-effacing, while at the same time exploiting the popular addiction to nostalgia, it is alive and well in the 1980s.

The landed aristocracy became practically invisible as a class in the course of the half century or more following the First World War, while individual landed aristocrats continued to exist and sometimes to flourish, in rather the same way as the French nobility ceased to exist as a social order some half a century or more earlier, although individual French noblemen continued to be wealthy and often very influential. The reasons were broadly similar. Perceiving that the order or class had become politically and ideologically doomed, individuals preferred the path of self-preservation and individual survival to the heroics of a futile collective defence of privileges that had become indefensible. In the years between 1906 and 1914 the British landed aristocracy attempted precisely such a collective defence. This

[15] J. Scott, *The Upper Classes: Property and Privilege in Britain* (1982): from 1914 the 'landed aristocracy' ceases to be used as a distinct socio-political category, and is replaced by 'the business classes'; see especially chap. 7.

was most vociferously and belligerently obvious in the resistance to the 1909 Budget and the Parliament Act, and Lord Willoughby de Broke's marshalling of the backwoodsmen was a para-military operation. Arguably the ruthless class politics continued right up to August 4th 1914, with the wrangles over Irish Home Rule and the whole tactic of keeping Ireland at the centre of the stage being, from the aristocratic point of view, a diversionary exercise in damage limitation designed to forestall further instalments of undesirable rural and land legislation from the Liberal government. War substituted a national enemy for the class enemy, and indeed the politician the aristocrats loved to hate became their best friend and repealed his own 1909 land taxes in 1920. The diehards stood down, and were never again mobilised as a parliamentary land defence force. When the disintegration of the landed classes, long threatened, seemed to be happening at a headlong pace with the massive land sales which started in 1919, this was treated as an event in the property market scarcely appropriate for political comment or protest. The 'great betrayal' of the repeal of the Corn Production Act in 1921 was a political action, but it too aroused no aristocratic revolt: the immediate victims of this abrupt and dishonest cancellation of guaranteed agricultural prices were the farmers, and it was they who received the *trinkgeld* which the government paid out for breaking the promises it had renewed as recently as twelve months before.[16] But this return to free trade pulled the rug from under agricultural rents and initiated a slide in both rents and land values; it was as dramatic in its way as the repeal of the Corn Laws, and its effects were a great deal more instantaneous.

The landed interest remained mute in 1919–21 and has remained mute ever since at the level of public debate and the great issues of the day, retreating to the hideout of a pressure group—the Central Landowners Association of 1907, renamed the Country Landowners Association in 1949—which was effective on technical, mainly fiscal, issues, but kept clear of making any parade of class solidarity; and otherwise confining itself to individual and unco-ordinated grumbles and apologetic murmurs of protest. Since 1919 the group attitude, indeed, has been one of *sauve qui peut*. The group, if it can still be called one, has sat on its hands and done nothing while watching unfortunate individual members go to the wall, the colonies, or the dogs. Its answer to the problem of impoverished noblemen or landless gentry has been to ignore them if they have been incapable of looking after themselves, and to accept them as social equals if they have succeeded in finding

[16] Edith H. Whetham, *The Agrarian History of England and Wales*, VIII, *1914–1939* (Cambridge, 1978), 139–41.

other means of keeping decently afloat after parting with their estates. The inherent individualism of this stance, as well as confirming that the landed aristocracy went into voluntary self-liquidation as a class, suggests that the financial and property disasters of the unfortunates may have been regarded more as the misfortunes of particular accident-prone individuals than as the extreme cases of a general malaise affecting the entire aristocratic body.

For the vanishing trick has been more than mere illusion, it has not been just a conjuring trick. Territorial empires have been dismantled, estates have been broken up, and landed families have disappeared: there have been plenty of real casualties in the struggle for the survival of the fittest. As might be expected, the greatest losses have been experienced by the gentry. Given the comparatively small size of their estates, in the 1,000–10,000 acre bracket, when an accumulation of debts, family charges, income and super taxes, or death duties forced any sale of land they were likely to force the sale of the entire estate. There were about 4,000 landed gentry in the 1880s. The 1937 edition of *Burke's Landed Gentry* also listed about 4,000 families, but something like one-third of them were landless, in most cases having been parted from their land during the lifetime of the then current head of the family. In the preface to the 1952 edition, which listed about 4,500 families, the editor observed that while in 1937 'perhaps a third of the entries were of families which no longer owned land; in the present edition this proportion may have risen to half.'[17] This implies that something of the order of 1,300 landed gentry, of families of varying degrees of antiquity, sold up in the inter war years, and a further 1,000 during the Second War and its immediate aftermath. Unsurprisingly *Burke's Landed Gentry* announced that it had ceased to be a register of the untitled landowners, which is what it had always aimed to be before 1914, and had become a hybrid pedigree book listing genealogies but also any of the newly-landed who wished to claim admittance. No similar problem of how to handle landless peers troubled the editors of *Burke's Peerage*, since hereditary titles continued until male heirs gave out and this register had never imposed any property qualification. Indeed, in the high noon of the landed aristocracy in the 1880s no more than 250 peers and baronets were large landowners, with estate of 10,000 acres or more; about 350 peers owned smaller properties, including 55 who had less than 2,000 acres apiece and a dozen or so who were completely landless.[18] It is difficult to discover

[17] *Burke's Landed Gentry* (1952 edn.), Preface (by L. G. Pine), xvii.

[18] F. M. L. Thompson, *English Landed Society in the Nineteenth Century* (1963), 28–9, 56–62. J. Bateman, *The Great Landowners of Great Britain and Ireland* (1878 edn.), 463–71. (1883 edn.), 499–500.

how many of these 500 landowning peers of the 1880s have descendants a hundred years later who are still landowners. One guess, based on a fair amount of investigative journalism, put the number at 350 in 1968, implying that perhaps one-third had become landless.[19] The remaining two-thirds, it is well known, did not retain anything like the extent of land that their Victorian forebears had commanded, and the story of the dispersal of parts of their inheritance is scattered in the reports of the property press over the last 70 years.

Serious selling of parts of great estates began in the last three or four years before 1914. The main motives were financial, either to liquidate loss-making investments or to switch from low-income land into higher-income stocks and shares. This did not prevent some of the prominent sellers making a little additional political capital out of their transactions: Walter Long, the leading political squire in the Commons and Conservative front-bench man on agriculture, claimed in 1910 that he was being forced to sell a large part of his Wiltshire estate because of the hostility of the Government towards large landowners and the threat of confiscatory taxes.[20] The great avalanche of selling, however, came after the end of the First World War. It has been estimated that between the end of 1918 and the end of 1921 something between six and eight million acres changed hands in England and Wales; a few million more could certainly be added for Scotland, since this was the time when the Duke of Sutherland started the process of reducing the family's enormous but almost worthless estates of over 1.3 million acres in Sutherland and Ross to their present more modest size of 158,000 acres.[21] Selling continued throughout the rest of the inter-war years, but not at the same frantic pace, and it seems to have become no more than sporadic and personal. There was a second, less concentrated, and smaller wave of selling after the Second World War, lasting from 1945 into the 1950s; and a steady trickle of large estate sales has continued since. It is impossible to quantify the total volume of land sales in the twentieth century, there being no central register and no public record of land transactions and no better source than the somewhat idiosyncratic and selective reporting of the property press. A guess at the order of magnitude might suggest that at least ten million acres of aristocratic and gentry

[19] Perrott, *Aristocrats*, 182.

[20] *The Times*, 24 Sept. 1910, 8. Long also claimed that 'those of us who did not possess other sources of income' are obliged to sell land. This was mendacious: he was a director of the Great Western Railway and chairman of Bath Breweries, and owned property in Canada.

[21] *The Times*, 4 Jan. 1919, 11; *Estates Gazette*, 4 Jan. 1919, 10. The price realised on the sale of 137,342 acres in 1919, £1.46 an acre, was not as derisory as it seems, since it amounted to about 30 years' purchase.

land in England and Wales were sold between 1910 and 1980. The group owned between them 18.5 million acres at the start of the process, in 1883, so that if this estimate is anywhere near the mark the survivors now control half, or rather less than half, the former aristocratic territory.

If half one's life is over it sounds as though death and oblivion are close at hand, and if half one's life is yet to come a long if not indefinite future stretches ahead. Maybe that is the position which the traditional landed families have reached after 70 years away from the centre of power, and maybe no further explanation is needed for the apparently curious way in which this state of affairs is habitually described in the sombre or sentimental tones of decline, decay, disaster, ruin, dispersal of estates, dissolution of the traditional structure of rural society, and the disappearance of ancient families. These global estimate are certainly consistent with the only systematic and detailed analysis of changes in landownership since 1880 which has yet been undertaken, that by Heather Clemenson. Taking a sample of 124 aristocratic landowners (with estates of 10,000 acres and upwards) and 376 of the greater gentry (with estates between 3,000 and 9,999 acres) from 1880 she tracked down their descendants in 1980 through questionnaires and interviews, and found that 65 per cent of the aristocratic families still owned estates of at least 1,000 acres, 29 per cent of them estates of more than 10,000 acres; while no more than 38 per cent of the gentry families had estates of at least 1,000 acres and only 19 per cent of them estates of over 3,000 acres. Overall her conclusion was that 52 per cent of the 1880 landed families had descendants in 1980 who owned some land, but only 44 per cent still possessed estates of at least 1,000 acres.[22] The 1979 *Report* of the Royal Commission on the Distribution of Income and Wealth broadly supported these conclusions, although making the sharp, but unheeded, observation that 'the paucity of comprehensive up to date information on land-ownership is remarkable'. The *Report* endorsed estimates that 6 million acres of agricultural land in England and Wales were held in privately-owned estates of 5,000 acres or more, that is less than 1,200 individuals owned one-quarter of English farmland.[23] The total land area of England and Wales was half as much again as the farmland area, when the space occupied by mountain and heath too rough even to be included in the 'rough grazing' category of the agricultural returns, as well as the area of towns, industries, and other non-agricultural

[22] Clemenson, *Landed Estates*; her findings are summarised in Tables 7.1, 7.2, and 7.3, 119–22.

[23] *Royal Commission on the Distribution of Income and Wealth*, Report No. 7, July 1979 [Cmnd. 7595, 1979–80], 6.26–6.28, 152.

uses, are added in. It may be assumed that these late twentieth-century large landowners, like their Victorian predecessors, owned amongst them extensive tracts of this non-agricultural land, some of them vast and worthless except as sporting estates, some of them small and extremely valuable, for although large landowners have long been in retreat from the position of urban landlords they are far from having evacuated it altogether. It is safe to say, therefore, that the 1,200 large landowners of the 1980s possess rather more than 6 million acres in total. They can be broadly compared with the 1,688 large landowners of the 1880s who owned about 14 million acres, but in estates measured from a lower threshold of 3,000 acres; or with the more rarified group of roughly 1,000 owners of estates of 6,000 acres and upwards which was estimated to own around 8 million acres in England and Wales in the 1880s.[24]

These global estimates are sufficiently imprecise and vague to permit us to believe either that the structure of landownership has barely altered at all in the last hundred years, or that the dominion of the large landowners has shrunk perceptibly but not catastrophically. The estimates are, however, sufficiently robust to make it plain that there has been no revolution in landownership. The picture of the contemporary Scottish scene reinforces that conclusion. Scotland has always tended to produce mammoth estates of low monetary value, so great is the proportion of the country occupied by mountains, moors, and forests. Hence great shooting and stalking estates, measured in hundreds of thousands of acres, have a special propensity to remain great sporting estates when they change hands, so that the experience of dispersal and subdivision, although not the experience of selling itself, is inherently likely to have been different from that in England. Thus it is perhaps not surprising that despite the fact that the largest Scottish estate, that of the Sutherlands, has shed well over a million acres since the 1880s, large estates still remain dominant. In the 1880s three-quarters of the entire country was in the hands of 476 estates; in the 1970s about half was encompassed by no more than 546.[25] In Ireland alone of the countries of the United Kingdom all

[24] Bateman, *Great Landowners* (1883 edn.), 515. Norton, Trist and Gilbert, 'A Century of Land Values: England and Wales' (1889), reprinted in E. M. Carus-Wilson, ed., *Essays in Economic History*, III (1962), 128. Bateman, *Great Landowners* (1878 edn.), 472, produced a table of 'the distribution of the area of the United Kingdom among the great landowners themselves, divided into six classes.' There was a total of 2,512 owners of estates of over 3,000 acres; in Class VI, the holders of between 3,000 and 6,000 acres there were 1,014 owners. There were thus 1,498 holders of estates of over 6,000 acres in the U.K. The ratio of holders of all estates of over 3,000 acres, U.K.: England and Wales, was 2,512:1,688, and at the same ratio there would have been 1,003 holders of estates of over 6,000 acres in England and Wales alone.

[25] *R.C. Distribution of Income and Wealth*, 6.26, 152, citing J. McEwan, *Who Owns*

the sources and all observers agree that there has been a complete revolution in landownership and landholding in the last hundred years, thanks to land purchase measures, political changes, and the near total collapse of landed society: in the 1880s half the country was owned by the aristocracy and larger gentry with estates of 3,000 acres and upwards, and in the 1980s virtually none.[26]

During the debates on Irish Home Rule and Irish land purchase one of the anxieties was that it might come to be argued that what was good for Ireland and the Irish people was also good for the mainland, or more prosaically that Irish measures would inexorably become precedents for British measures, which would subvert property rights and lead to expropriation and the downfall of country-house living, quite apart from other minor irritations like local parliaments. One of the advantages of Irish independence, little as it may have been appreciated at the time by the Unionist gentry, was that it effectively insulated Britain, politically and institutionally, from any backwash from the Irish land question. It may also have been one of the reasons for the abrupt disappearance of the land reform campaigners from the British political scene after the First World War, when their cause and their programme, shifting from 'free trade in land' to land value taxation, had lain near the heart of radical politics for the best part of a hundred years. The collapse was closely connected with the remodelling of British politics caused by the rise of Labour and the decline and disintegration of the Liberal party. Land reform had always been a radical-liberal issue, a cause that attracted free-trade intellectuals, nonconformists who were anti-Anglican and anti-landowner, and the independent self-educated workingman who disliked and distrusted inherited wealth and privilege. Some of the pre-war land reformers gravitated towards the Labour party, but their concerns had never been regarded as more than peripheral by trade unionists or party theologians; so they were welcomed as mildly interesting and harmless left-wing cranks, not as heavy reinforcements to be used in serious political battles. Hence Labour governments, to

Scotland? (Edinburgh, 1977). Scottish estates of 3,000 acres and upwards, in the 1880s, have been counted from individual entries in Bateman, *Great Landowners* (1878 edn.). By excluding the essentially English (and a very few Welsh and Irish) landowners who chanced to own a handful of acres in Scotland, but including the more seriously Anglo-Scottish landowners who had large estates in each country, this total is smaller than the 491 great landowners who were noted by Bateman as having some land in Scotland (he listed 375 as having their estates solely in Scotland), 473.

[26] Bateman, *Great Landowners* (1878 edn.), 476–7. It was nevertheless asserted in 1958 that in spite of the small size and greatly reduced numbers of surviving estates, enough of the Old Ascendancy gentry remained to make a society of their own 'as much divorced from the governing class as is the old noblesse in France': Preface to *Burke's Irish Landed Gentry* (1958 edn.), xix–xxi.

humour their faddists, brought in measures to tax land values in 1931, 1947, and 1976, measures exceeded in their immensely boring complexity only by the rapidity with which Conservative governments repealed them and by the deafening silence with which the public greeted their comings and their goings. Unearned increment, betterment, development levy, and community value, were not words which ever fired the mass electorate with any detectable enthusiasm; but they were words which small property owners and householders with potential building sites in their gardens, as well as large landowners and developers, found chilling. This was convenient for the larger landowners, who were spared the blow of any serious and efficient system of land taxation without the need to put up any dangerously conspicuous defence on their own account, and who profited greatly from the windfall gains of very high development values particularly in the 1960s and 1970s.[27]

Thus English, Scottish, and Welsh landowners were never put through either the mincing machine of Irish-style land reform or the shredder of land value taxes designed to strip out externally-generated capital appreciation. Instead they were by and large left alone by governments to cope with the same general conditions of taxation, and of economic opportunity, as any other section of the population; or, more accurately, when there was any discrimination it was likely to be in their favour, as with lower rates of death duty on agricultural land than on other forms of property, and as with subsidies for agriculture and forestry. They did not appear to manage very well under these 'neutral' conditions. The reports of the break-up of estates in the press were so incessant, and the predictions and announcements of the collapse of the old landed order so loud and so frequent, that erstwhile land campaigners from the heroic days of Henry George's single tax, yellow vans, or the People's Budget, could have been excused for retiring into inactivity on the grounds that the battle was already being won with other weapons. The chorus accompanying the avalanche of land sales between 1919 and 1921 is well-known, with *The Times* and the *Estates Gazette* declaring in unison 'England is changing hands' and that 'a revolution in landowning' was in progress.[28] Lord Strabolgi, a landless Labour peer (holding a title which against his Fabian principles his father had perversely suc-

[27] Out of a large literature on pre-1914 land reform and land tax matters much the best discussion, theoretical and empirical, is in Avner Offer, *Property and Politics, 1870–1914* (Cambridge, 1981), especially chaps. 16, 19, and 22. See also, F. M. L. Thompson, 'Land and politics in England in the nineteenth century,' *ante*, xv (1965); R. Douglas, *Land, People, and Politics: A History of the Land Question in the United Kingdom, 1878–1952* (1976). For a latter-day land-taxer see Peter Hall, *London 2001* (1989), 190–6.

[28] Cited in Thompson, *Landed Society*, 330–2.

ceeded in reviving in 1916 after it had been in abeyance since 1788) believed that this revolution had really happened by the 1930s. 'We have accomplished a silent revolution in England since 1914', he wrote in 1933. 'A whole class, the landed aristocracy, has been wiped out. The country gentry have gone.'[29] He was mistaken, but not alone in his view. In fact almost as Strabolgi was writing this the editor of the 1937 edition of *Burke's Landed Gentry* was confident that the country gentry 'was, and still is, an important class', and viewed the recent flood of estate sales with an amazing, Olympian, detachment: 'the reign of George V', he thought, 'witnessed no more than an acceleration of that process of disintegration and renewal which has affected the landed gentry as a class from before the time of the Norman Conquest.'[30] Four decades later the introduction of the capital transfer tax in 1975, replacing death duties by a supposedly unavoidable tax on all transfers of property whether by gift or inheritance, provoked similar predictions of imminent collapse. 'The results of the capital transfer tax will be the break-up of a land pattern which has existed for a thousand years', ran one comment; and the Country Landowners' Association produced a pamphlet on *The Future of Landownership* which claimed that there was none, and that the break-up of the remaining traditional landed estates had been made inevitable.[31] By 1984 capital transfer tax was gone and death duties were back, under the new name of inheritance tax; in 1989 the thousand-year old land pattern was still in existence, somewhat dented and battered to be sure but little more battered than it had been 15 years earlier.

The landed interest and its supporters have become so addicted to 'crying wolf' that it is a wonder they have not lost all credibility with the rest of the public. Public opinion, however, so far as there can be said to have been one at all since those pre-1914 days when the 'land monopoly' and aristocratic privilege were headline news, has been fed with plenty of hard, if anecdotal and selective, evidence of the decline of individual great landowners and the collapse of old landed families, and has been offered little evidence of their continued survival. Great and famous estates have indeed been sold in quantity, and it would be easy to compose a lengthy roll-call of properties which were once household names that have been on the transfer list at some point since 1918. It would range from parts of the Arundel estate in Sussex to the Dunrobin estate in Sutherland, and quite apart from the great

[29] J. M. Kenworthy [Lord Strabolgi], *Sailors, Statesmen and Others* (1933), 48–9, cited by D. Cannadine, *The Decline of the British Landed Establishment* (forthcoming, 1990).

[30] *Burke's Landed Gentry* (1937 edn.), Preface, xv, xxiii.

[31] G. R. Judd, 'Capital taxation and the farmer,' *Estates Gazette*, 5 April 1975, 35; C. L. A. *The Future of Landownership* (1976), 8: cited by Clemenson, *Landed Estates*, 114, 213.

selling wave of 1919–21 would run through the alphabet from the Marquess of Anglesey parting with Beaudesert land in 1932 to the Duke of Westminster selling Melton Constable in 1957.[32] There are indeed plenty of landless peers of the older, pre-1900, creations, bereft of great houses or acres and living in rather modest addresses in Kensington, or Hove, or living more exotically in exile in villas in France or bungalows in Kenya. Some of these were tax exiles, many had been forced by death duties to sell the family estates. The 11th Duke of Leeds illustrates both positions. Parts of the family estates had already been sold before he succeeded his father in 1927, but the sale of the major block of the Hornby Castle estate in 1930 was linked to the need to pay the death duties. He then went to live as a tax exile in Jersey and a villa at Cap Martin, continuing to sell off land from time to time, most notably in 1953 when a large sale fell neatly and maybe not without connection between his two divorces in 1948 and 1955. He had three wives but no children, and when he died in 1963 was succeeded as 12th Duke by an Osborne cousin, a diplomat who had been British Minister to the Vatican during the Second World War and who continued to live in Rome, unmarried, until he died a year later whereupon the title became as extinct as the family estates.[33]

The Leeds story is in fact a warning against assuming that all landless peers are simply the products of crippling death duties without other complications. Two peers were singled out in 1967 as being entirely without land. One, the 15th Earl of Huntingdon, belonged to a family which had never been anything but Irish landowners, a background which may have helped him in his career as an artist and author but one which made the fate of the family estates subject to the Irish exception. The second was the 10th Earl of Breadalbane, descendant of very substantial Scottish landowners who had over 400,000 acres in the 1880s (of no great value, though the £58,000 rental was not insignificant). This might seem to be a straightforward instance of ruin through bad luck, with earls dying in 1922 and 1923. Large blocks of the core estate, however, had been sold in 1921, before any deaths; and a great deal more was sold in 1936, when the 9th Earl still had 23 years to live. It seems probable that the disintegration and dissipation of the Breadalbane estates was more connected to the circumstance that two of the earlier twentieth-century earls either had no surviving sons, or were unmarried, being succeeded by a nephew and by a distant cousin respectively, but leaving closer descendants in the female line.[34]

[32] *Estates Gazette*, 22 Oct. 1932, 592; 9 Nov. 1957, 603.

[33] *Estates Gazette*, 11 Jan. 1930, 46; 1 Aug. 1953, 129. *Burke's Peerage* (1959 edn.), *Who was Who*, VI, 1961–70.

[34] Perrott, *Aristocrats*, 153, 154. *Estates Gazette*, 1 Jan. 1921, 31 Dec. 1921, 8 Jan. 1936, 225. *Burke's Peerage* (1959 edn.).

The separation of titles from estates through the failure of direct male heirs is not a twentieth-century invention. The suggestion is that it may well have become more common, partly as a consequence of the general reduction in family size, but mainly because increased personal control over the disposition of family estates coupled with the waning of aristocratic class feeling may have made the heads of landed families set less store than formerly on passing some land to distant male heirs to titles, at the expense of their daughters. Thus, as a straw in the wind, the 6th Earl Grey, descendant of Grey of the Reform Bill, no longer owns Howick; he is a quantity surveyor, the son of a trooper in the Canadian army, and he succeeded his cousin in 1963. Howick is in the hands of the 2nd Baron Howick of Glendale, who on inspection turns out to be the son of Sir Evelyn Baring, of the bank, and Lady Mark Cecil Grey, daughter of the 5th Earl Grey, who took the title of Howick in 1960 presumably because it was already settled that the house and lands would be inherited by Lady Mary. Burghley House is no longer lived in by a marquess of Exeter. When the 6th Marquess, the Olympic hurdler, died in 1981 his brother, who inherited the title, was already well-established in British Columbia with no wish to return to England. The house was made over to the Burghley House Preservation Trust, and with the income from the 10,000 acre estate in and around Stamford to sustain it, along with the tourist takings, is occupied and cared for by Lady Victoria Leatham and her family, one of the 6th Marquess's four daughters: a kind of private, family, National Trust arrangement, one could say. Or one could take Wrotham Park in Hertfordshire, the home of the Byng family since the time of the Admiral who was executed on his quarter deck before he had finished building the house. The house is no longer occupied by an earl of Strafford (the title taken by a later Byng who was a Peninsula War hero and had a Wentworth grandmother), since on the death of the 6th Earl in 1951 the title passed to a nephew while the house and estate went to one of his daughters, who herself resumed the name of Byng after her divorce. The Wrotham Park estate, in 1989, is almost exactly the same size as it was in 1883, about 5,000 acres, having shed the site of Heathrow Airport and some building land in Borehamwood and Potters Bar in the interval.[35]

It is impossible to say how many of today's landless peers are the offspring of such broken families where title and estate have become separated, but it is clear that they are not in themselves evidence that

[35] *Burke's Peerage* (1970 edn.). *Guide to Burghley House* (Stamford, 1989). Ex inf. Julian Michael Byng, Wrotham Park.

the family estates no longer exist. Landless gentry are another matter. With no hereditary titles to cloud the issue in the social registers, it is safe to assume that when, in *Burke's* formula, an entry is made for 'Arkwright, formerly of Hampton Court, Hereford' or for 'Bevan formerly of Trent Park, Hertfordshire', the original family estates have gone. Often the entry states when: before 1935 in the first case, and in 1909 in the second, when Trent Park was bought by Sir Edward Sassoon. The two thousand or more landed gentry who disappeared thus between 1914 and the 1950s were not an army of ghosts or straw men. But it is worth quoting the views of Hugh Montgomery-Massingberd, in his editorial preface to the last, 1972, volume of *Burke's Landed Gentry*: 'Up to 1914 a strict requirement of landed property was enforced [for inclusion in the register] and if a family sold its estates the pedigree was ejected from the book. For example, of the families included in 1863 at least 50 per cent had disappeared by the 1914 edition.'[36] His opinion would seem to be that in the rest of the twentieth century the landed gentry have experienced nothing out of the ordinary, just a normal rate of natural wastage.

That seems an extremely complacent view, at variance with common sense let alone with the rhetoric of preservationists. It does not seem to sit easily, either, beside the story of the country house in the twentieth century, a story which has received much publicity and which forms the point of the greatest public awareness of the rise and demise of landed society. A famous exhibition in 1975 counted more than 600 country houses in Britain that had been destroyed, abandoned, ruined, or demolished since 1920, over 200 of them in the single decade of the 1950s.[37] In addition many had been converted to other uses, as schools, hotels, offices, institutions of various kinds, local government offices, not to mention zoos and fun centres. The rest, as far as the public could see, had been made over into heritage museums, either run privately by the owners as caretakers, or by the National Trust under its Country House Scheme started in 1937. Country houses which were still used as normal aristocratic residences, and which were not open to the public, had become virtually invisible. The disappearance of country houses is of course associated with the disappearance of landed families, but it is not solely associated with that. In particular cases, perhaps in very many particular cases, country houses ceased to be viable after 1918 for the basic financial reason that after-tax incomes, depressed both by high tax rates and

[36] *Burke's Landed Gentry* (1937 edn.), Arkwright and Bevan; vol. III (1972 edn.), Preface, ix.

[37] Roy Strong, Marcus Binney, and John Harris, eds., *The Destruction of the Country House* (1974), especially 15–100, 188–92.

by agricultural rents that remained low until the mid-1960s, could not meet the rising costs of maintenance. The more general reason for their loss of viability, however, was that they became social white elephants. They were designed to be run by large households of domestic servants, and the technical reason for their abandonment was the difficulty, amounting to near impossibility after 1939, of continuing to find servants in sufficient quantity. Above all, they were designed as the stage settings for lives of public display of the aristocratic presence, fountains of honour, hospitality, paternalism, and local power. The self-liquidation of the aristocracy as a class abolished the need for the public display, and with it the need to keep up the stage set. One effect has been the miniaturisation of country houses by the demolition of superfluous and mainly Victorian wings, particularly marked since 1945, in an effort to cut the costs of staffing and upkeep. The more radical effect has been the abandonment and probably demolition of the original house and the retreat of the family into a much smaller dower house or farmhouse, or if those did not suit, into a completely new country house built for twentieth-century private aristocratic lives. It is well-known that the 4th Duke of Westminster demolished the vast, many-turreted and much iron-columned, Alfred Waterhouse masterpiece of Eaton Hall between 1961 and 1963, and that the 5th Duke of Westminster built the new Eaton Hall between 1971 and 1973, which has been termed 'the most ambitious Modern house in England' and which could also be described in Caroline idiom as the most conspicuous squashed stump in the country.[38] As this was the work of the wealthiest individual in Britain it may be thought an untypical example. Nevertheless, the architectural historian John Martin Robinson has described and listed no less than 232 new country houses 'built since the Second World War, largely by old-established landowners wishing to continue a traditional way of life on their estates.'[39] The replacement rate, it would seem, has just about kept pace with the demolition rate; it would certainly be unwise to equate the destruction of a pre-1914 country house with the disappearance either of the family which lived in it or the landed estate which supported it.

What has happened since the First World War is something far short of the collapse or catastrophe which has been over-dramatised by many commentators. Certainly every landed estate that survives in the 1980s in the hands of its traditional owners is smaller than it was a century ago. Even the 9th Duke of Buccleuch, reputedly the largest private landowner in Britain today, has no more than a quarter

[38] J. M. Robinson, *The Latest Country Houses* (1984), 136–42.
[39] Robinson, *Country Houses*, 6, 197–234.

of a milion acres to set alongside the 450,000 which the 6th Duke had in 1883.[40] In fact most large landowners who had sensible financial advisers undertook more or less extensive restructuring of their investment portfolios, especially in the boom conditions of the land market in 1919–21 but also at intervals since then. The object was to get out of land, except for the central estates considered to be the family heartland, and into higher-yielding securities which were thought to have better prospects of capital stability or growth. It may well be that those who were too lazy or ignorant to unload land either in the first rush or at the very low land prices of the later 1920s and the 1930s, were not the foolish ones, if they or their families survived to see the astonishing rise in land prices in the 1960s and 1970s which wafted land from £60 an acre in 1945 to £2,000 an acre in the early 1980s.[41] High taxation of income may well have made it difficult to make ends meet at the top of the wealth scale and have led to scaling down of living standards, and possibly to some selling of land; but there were considerable tax advantages in owning land and particularly in both owning and farming it, and many landowners far from selling were induced to become large-scale farmers after 1945. It hardly needs to be said that death duties became a voluntary tax for the wealthy: indeed the preferential treatment of agricultural land meant that there was a cult of buying landed estates, switching out of other securities, as the accountants' recipe for preparing for death.

None of the motives for selling landed estates which are conventionally cited turn out to have been compellingly strong. One circumstance which has not yet been investigated was divorce, a costly business in legal expenses and in alimony. Aristocrats did not necessarily indulge in divorce with any more gay abandon than the population at large, but the very frequency of divorce in their ranks in the twentieth century is in itself an indication of the extent to which they came to behave like any other group in society, and abandoned the primacy of loyalty to the family and its inheritance. At the financial level it remains to be established whether divorce among the wealthy meant the splitting-up of estates as well as the splitting-up of marriages. A possible pointer is that when the 11th Duke of Argyll had his second divorce, in March 1951, in an undefended action on the grounds of his adultery in a hotel in Sussex, an announcement of the sale of part of the Inveraray estate followed in November 1951. After his third divorce, in 1963, however, the Duchess agreed to pay the costs, having figured in a compromising photograph with an anonymous and head-

[40] *Sunday Times, Britain's Rich*, 40, claimed he is 'Europe's largest private landowner.'
[41] *Report of the Committee of Inquiry into the Acquisition and Occupancy of Agricultural Land* [the Northfield Report] [Cmnd. 7599, 1979], 92–7.

less naked man who had been positively identified as not the Duke. There is no evidence of any land sales at that time.[42] This would have satisfied the Victorians, at least, that no such thing as landed society as they understood it any longer existed. But while the society has vanished it is equally certain that there are many dukes, marquesses, earls, viscounts, barons, and plain gentry around in the 1980s who are a great deal more than mere curators of museums, caretakers of stately homes, or guardians of heritage parks.

[42] *The Times*, 12 March 1951, 4; 17 Nov. 1951, 8; 27 Feb. 1963, 6; 2 March 1963, 5; 6 March1963, 6; 15 March 1963, 7; 3 May 1963, 14; 9 May 1963, 7; 15 May 1963, 8.

THE COMPARATIVE STUDY OF MEMORIAL PREACHING

By David d'Avray

READ 27 JANUARY 1989

ANYONE who has attended an academic memorial service or a funeral has directly experienced the tradition of memorial preaching. I define this largely, and include any sermon about a dead person not a saint, whether or not it was given at a service linked to burial. I have not included purely secular addresses, though they are closely related.[1] The subject lends itself to comparative treatment because memorial preachers of different periods have tried to bring out the significance of a person's life and death in the light of the religious and other values of the society to which both preacher and deceased belong. This provides the common basis without which comparative history is uninstructive.

The history of memorial preaching is not a neglected subject. A whole institute is devoted to the study of *Leichenpredigten* in early modern Germany,[2] and its director, Rudolf Lenz, has done much to bring together scholars working on different areas and periods of the genre's history.[3] The following essay is a raid by small privateer, attached informally to a large fleet, into waters that the main force has not yet visited.

The Marburg institute analyses its texts with the help of a sophisticated questionnaire, designed to elicit information bearing on many

[1] The relation needs to be elucidated, especially where the early renaissance period is concerned. John M. McManamon's excellent *Funeral Oratory and the Cultural Ideals of Italian Humanism* (Chapel Hill and London, 1989) is not much concerned with this particular problem.

[2] The Forschungsstelle f. Personalschriften, at the Philipps-Universität Marburg.

[3] See *Leichenpredigten als Quelle historischer Wissenschaften* (i, Vienna, ii and iii, Marburg, 1975–84), ed. R. Lenz. For bibliography on the whole history of funeral and memorial preaching, see Lenz, *Leichenpredigten, Eine Bestandsaufnahme. Bibliographie und Ergebnisse einer Umfrage* (Marburger Personalschriften-Forschungen Bd. 3; Marburg, 1980). An attempt to bring this up to date would be out of place here, but the following deserve special mention: W. Kierdorf, *Laudatio funebris. Interpretationen und Untersuchungen zur Entwicklung der römischen Leichenrede* (Meisenheim am Glan, 1980) (Prof. M. Crawford drew my attention to this); S. Powell and A. J. Fletcher, '"In die sepulture seu trigintali": the Late Medieval Funeral and Memorial Sermon', *Leeds Studies in English*, new series, xii (1981) pp. 195–228; J. M. McManamon, 'Innovation in Early Humanist Rhetoric: the Oratory of Pier Paolo Vergerio the Elder', *Rinascimento*, second series, xxii (1982), 3–32, and *Funeral Oratory* (cited above, note 1).

sorts of history. Here I will ask one rather abstract-sounding question bearing on a particular sort of history, akin to the history of portraiture. The question is about parts and wholes: what is the relation which unifies the elements of a memorial sermon in a given period, and how far does it change over time?

One sort of unifying principle, in a portrait or in a memorial sermon, is the unique individuality of the person who has died. A sermon preached by E. W. Benson on James Prince Lee (d. 1869), the first bishop of Manchester, is a good example of this principle in action.[4] It leaves a strong impression of a powerful personality. 'Have any wondered . . . at a certain dread of sympathy, a certain look which held the expression of it towards himself in check? Was it not that the unceasing struggle between the strong will and the unequal frame was so nearly balanced that there was an unconscious sense that the needful tension might too easily be relaxed beyond the possibility of restoration . . . ?'[5] 'How he hated finesse in daily life, how impossible he found it to tread circuitous paths, or to walk with those who did! If ever his judgement of a character was warped, it was because he could allow for any fault but that. The ashy paleness of his forehead, the severe pain that its lines expressed if even a lad brought him an untrue tale, we remember it well.'[6] It is actually a sympathetic portrait, but it aims at realism in depicting Lee's individuality. Though a few morals are drawn at the end,[7] this is a representation, not of a churchman like others only better, not of an ideal type, but of a person different from anyone else.

The question of when this sense of distinctness becomes a common feature of the genre is an important question, but neither I, nor, so far as I know, anyone else, has yet succeeded in answering it. 'Realism' and 'Individuality' trigger associations with Burckhardt and the Italian Renaissance, but I would be surprised if there are many Renaissance orations comparable to the sermon on Lee.[8]

The funeral sermon given by Pietro da Castelleto O.E.S.A. in 1402 on one of Burckhardt's despotic individualists, Giangaleazzo Visconti, seems more like a pattern of relatively abstract virtues than a likeness

[4] Edward White Benson, D.D., SALPISEI, *A Memorial Sermon preached after the death of the Right Reverend James Prince Lee, D.D. . . . in his parish church of Heaton Mersey, Manchester* (London and Manchester, 1870).

[5] Benson, 7–8.

[6] Benson, 9.

[7] Benson, 19–20.

[8] McManamon's *Funeral Oratory* (cited above note 1) is concerned with ideas about roles rather than with the verbal depiction of individuality, which deserves further study. His invaluable 'Finding List' of renaissance funeral orations would facilitate such an investigation.

of his individual personality, and it may serve as a foil to the previous example.[9] Pietro works his way through Giangaleazzo's Faith, Hope, Charity, Justice, Fortitude, Temperance, Prudence, Piety, Mercy, 'Magnificence', Intelligence, and Humility. The section on Prudence is really a little disquisition on the joys of the world and on heaven,[10] much of the section on 'Magnificence' is taken up with an extraordinary genealogy, in which Giangaleazzo's ancestry is traced back to Venus and her father Jove,[11] and the section on intelligence is largely taken up with the *Ubi sunt?* topos,[12] but the other sections are indeed a description of the great man's goodness and achievements. Each virtue, however, is so to speak a pigeon-hole which Pietro fills with more or less relevant remarks. This is not to say that the sermon is dry. The twelve virtues are held together before the mind by a strong visual image (that of a crown with four rays, each with three stars). The point is that the general categories are not combined in such a way as to give a unified impression of Giangaleazzo's character.

It is tempting to present generality and individuality as opposite poles, but this conceptual scheme is too simple. There was another way of limiting emphasis on individuality, viz., by giving as much or more space to other themes, which would normally have some kind of relation to the man or the fact of his death, but which would not in themselves have much to do with his individual personality, or indeed with the virtues he embodied.

We therefore need a second foil to the memorial sermon on James Prince Lee. Bishop John Fisher's funeral sermon on King Henry VII of England will serve.[13] The first part is directly concerned with

[9] The sermon is printed in *Rerum Italicarum Scriptores*, ed. L. Muratori, xvi (Milan, 1730), cols. 1038–1050. Cf. McManamon, 'Innovation ...', 20 and note 2; he points out that the sermon is 'thematic': i.e., not 'classicizing' in the new humanist manner which he analyses in this article.

[10] Muratori, xvi, col. 1043. Pietro says that Giangaleazzo showed his prudence by distinguishing between the good things of this world, and the things above the heavens, and inferring that '... *si carcer Mundi hujus pulcher est, patria, civitas, & domus qualis est?*' The immediately preceding description of the joys of this life is so eloquent as to make the argument (whether or not Giangaleazzo expressed it) a not ineffective way of conveying the idea of heaven. I have the impression that the real focus of Pietro's attention moved away from Giangaleazzo's virtues when developing this point.

[11] Muratori, xvi, cols 1046–8. The section also lists Giangaleazzo's distinguished relations from great dynasties of his own time; and tells Milan and Pavia that they should show gratitude (for all he had done to restore their greatness) by their obedience to his successors. Dynastic greatness seems to be the general theme of the section; obviously it was not unrelated to virtue.

[12] Muratori, xvi, cols 1048–9: e.g. '*ubi sunt Caesares atque Reges ... Ubi nunc satellites armati ...*'?

[13] I have used a copy in the British Library, press mark C. 25. k. 6, inc. 'This sermon folowynge was compyled & sayd in the Cathedrall chyrche of saynte Poule ... the body beynge present of the moost famouse prynce kynge Henry the .vii. ...' (Wynkyn

Henry's life, especially the last period of it, but the second tries to persuade the listener to feel compassion and pray for him on account of '... the paynfull greuaunces of deth that he felte in his body /... the ferefull remembraunce in his soule of the Jugement of god /... the myserable vanytees of his lyfe wherin he founde but payne and trauayle /... the lamentable crye to god for helpe and socour.'[14] Though the *function* of this part relates to the king,[15] its content does not include very much about his qualities and personality, and could without too many modifications be turned into a miniature treatise on the difficulty of dying. In the same way, the third part of the sermon, designed to comfort the listeners, is a fairly general discussion of salvation and the afterlife of the saved.[16] At one point special mention is made of Henry's humility before death, but, taken as a whole, this part of the sermon is not about Henry as a distinctive personality *or* Henry as a living norm of virtue.

I have argued that concentration on individual character can be limited either by reduction to a set of general virtues, or by the introduction of other topics. These two types of limitation are not incompatible; indeed we find them both in Fisher's sermon on Henry VII. If Henry's personality is subordinated to other themes in the second and third parts of the sermon, in the first part it is broken up into a generalised pattern of virtue. After a succinct list of qualities and achievements of a worldly sort (dismissed as transitory)[17] Fisher lists four proofs that Henry met a virtuous end: '... a true tournynge of his soule from this wretched worlde unto the loue of almyghty god.... a fast hope & confydence ... in prayer.... a stedfast byleue of god and of the sacramentes of the chyrche.... a dylygent askynge of mercy in the time of mercy':[18]—faith, hope, and charity, and asking

de Worde; London, 1509). The sermon is discussed at length in William S. Stafford, 'Repentance on the Eve of the English Reformation: John Fisher's Sermons of 1508 and 1509', *Historical Magazine of the Protestant Episcopal Church*, liv (1985), 297–338 (I am grateful to Maria Dowling, who has in hand a study of Fisher, for making a copy of this article available to me).

[14] Fisher, fo. 12^r (I ignore the numbers in the book, which are not consecutive folio numbers). This is from the summary at the end of the sermon. The section in question is on fos. 6^r–8^v.

[15] It is extended to all Christian souls: 'And or we procede ony ferder of our psalme let vs here deuoutly and affectually saye for his soule and all crysten soules euery of vs one pater noster.' Fisher, fo. 8^v.

[16] The main headings are summarised on fo. 12^r: '.../fyrst for that he hath so mercyfull a lorde and god/seconde for that he is taken in to his tuicyon and custody/thyrde for that he is now delyuered from so many perylles/fourth for that he shall from hens forwarde contynue in the gracyous fauour of almyghty god....'

[17] Fisher, fo. 2^v.

[18] Fisher, 3^v.

for mercy, especially in Lent.[19] There is nothing unconventional about the schema, nor, probably, was it Fisher's intention to depict a personal style of goodness.

Up to this point I have been concerned to illustrate forms or concepts useful for analysis, and have not attempted to characterise periods. A bird's eye view of the whole history of funeral preaching in the West[20] would be premature, though the converging work of several scholars may make it possible before too long. This general history *en devenir* should include sections on Ambrose, the early Middle Ages;[21] the genre of the thirteenth and fourteenth centuries, so different from that of late Antiquity; the humanist revival of the classical *oratio funebris*;[22] the influence of this approach north of the Alps;[23] the distinctive German tradition which Luther seems to have begun;[24] on France, on England, and so forth.

It may be possible to obtain a few of the advantages of this future synthesis more quickly and economically by comparing the memorial preaching of two quite different periods within the same broad tradition. This will not tell us for certain what happened in between, but should convey a more acute sense of what was historically specific in the memorial preaching of the two periods.[25] I have chosen to concentrate on the (earlier) fourteenth, and on the eighteenth centuries. For the later period I will confine myself to France.[26] (In the earlier period funeral and memorial sermons were written down in Latin, and thus belong to an international world of culture.)

[19] For the reference to Lent see Fisher, fo. 5^{v}.

[20] On the Byzantine East see A. Sideras, 'Byzantinische Leichenreden. Bestand, Prosopographie, zeitliche und räumliche Distribution, literarische Form und Quellenwert', in Lenz, *Leichenpredigten* iii, 17–49 (summarising Sideras's own unpublished Habilitationsschrift.

[21] On late Antiquity and the earlier Middle Ages see F. Jürgensmeier, 'Die Leichenpredigt in der katholischen Begräbnisfeier', in Lenz, *Leichenpredigten* i, 122–45, at 125–9.

[22] McManamon, 'Innovation ...' cited above (note 3) and *Funeral Oratory*, cited above, (Note 1).

[23] See Th. Woltersdorf in Greifswald, 'Zur Geschichte der Leichenreden im Mittelalter', *Zeitschrift für praktische Theologie*, vi (1884), 359–365 (I am grateful to Martin Camargo for procuring a xerox of this for me), and Verdun L. Saulnier, 'L'Oraison funèbre au XVIe siècle', *Bibliothèque d'Humanisme et Renaissance* x (1948), 124–57.

[24] See e.g. R. Lenz, 'Leichenpredigten—Eine Quellengattung', *Blätter für deutsche Landesgeschichte* 111. Jahrgang (1975), 15–30.

[25] I have attempted something similar in 'The Gospel of the Marriage Feast at Cana and Marriage Preaching in France', in *The Bible in the Medieval World: essays in memory of Beryl Smalley*, ed. K. Walsh and D. Wood (Studies in Church History. Subsidia 4; Oxford, 1985), 207–24 (comparing the thirteenth and seventeenth centuries).

[26] For a good introduction to the genre in this period, see J. McManners, *Death and the Enlightenment. Changing Attitudes to Death among Christians and Unbelievers in Eighteenth-century France* (Oxford, 1981), 288–91.

Since I want to concentrate on forms of thought, there is not space to say much about the processes of transmission here, but a couple of points should be born in mind. In the earlier period many memorial sermons appear to have been preserved in only one manuscript; in the 'classical age', many were published (and these are the ones I have used). The sermons from the medieval period are frequently if not generally abridged in their written transmission;[27] the printed early modern ones are finished literary productions. In the earlier period the principal conscious intention may have been to provide models for later preachers, whereas in the later period the intention may have been to edify the reading public in an aesthetically pleasurable way (and perhaps to please some important people). But this last contrast may be too sharp. In both periods those who wrote down and reproduced the sermons probably had a sense that they were transmitting something of religious and cultural value. They may have obscurely realised that efforts to fit a person's history into a wider view of the world, to make religious sense of the lives of powerful men, might have a more than transient interest, to more than one sort of reader.

What follows must be by way of illustration rather than systematic demonstration. To stay within bounds I will confine myself to sermons in memory of kings, and content myself with three medieval examples and three from the eighteenth century; after which I will suggest how the contrast which they illustrate can be more firmly grasped with the help of a different sort of comparative analysis.

We may begin with a sermon on the death of Philip V of France, who died in 1322, by his relative Juan d'Aragon, son of King Jaime II of Aragon and Archbishop of Toledo.[28] There is nothing in the structure of the sermon to suggest that the personal life or political achievements of the king are central to its message; indeed, in the obviously abridged version that has survived to us, there is nothing about them at all.[29]

The main points—expressed in the form of divisions and scriptural quotations, as was normal in the period—seem to be as follows. Philip's

[27] For the evidential value of abridged sermons, see d'Avray, *The Preaching of the Friars. Sermons diffused from Paris before 1300* (Oxford, 1985), 129, 172.

[28] On Juan d'Aragon see J. Ernesto Martinez Ferrando, *Jaime II de Aragon. Su vida familiar* (2 vols.) (Consejo Superior de Investigaciones científicas, Escuela de Estudios Medievales, Estudios ix and x; Barcelona, 1948), i, 141–151. I have so far been unable to obtain Ignacio de Janer, *El patriarca Don Juan de Aragon, su vida y sus obras (1301–1334)* (Tarragona, 1904), which, to judge by entry no. NJ 0042366 in the U.S. National Union Catalogue, was printed in only 100 copies.

[29] The sermon survives in Valencia Cathedral MS. 182 fo. 128vb–129ra; it is no. 257 under Johannes de Aragon in J. B. Schneyer, *Repertorium d. lateinischen Sermones des mittelalters für die Zeit von 1150–1350* (Münster Westfalen, 1969–) iii, 314.

death was a fulfilment of divine will; it was an escape from disaster in the world; it meant the attainment of eternal happiness.[30] Christ took Philip away from the mire of the corruption of (?original) sin through justifying grace; from the war of hostile temptation through the grace that gives help; from the pit of the affliction of punishment through glorifying grace.[31] These ideas are then reinforced with scriptural quotations, which Juan had no doubt developed at length in the original sermon, and which a preacher using the schema as a model would also have known how to expand.

It would be misleading to suggest that medieval sermons in memory of kings show no sense of political realities. The next example, a sermon on the death of Philip IV 'the Fair' of France (d.1314) by the Florentine Dominican Remigio de' Girolami, begins by explaining that the king of France is most powerful (*potentissimus*) in five ways: with respect to the breadth (*latitudinem*) of his kingdom; to the great size of the population, to the valour of its knights (*militie strenuitatem*); to overflowing wealth (*opulentie ubertatem*),[32] and to his, the king's, position at the top of the hierarchy (*praesidentie sublimitatem*), since he has the kings of England, Navarre, and Apulia beneath him, since they hold land from him, and no kings above him.[33]

This glorification of the French monarchy is balanced, however, and its significance transformed, by the second part of the sermon, which is about mutability and transitoriness. Remigio notes that Philip was scarcely fifty years old when he died, and he gives a cross-reference to a sermon on the death of pope Clement V,[34] and more

[30] '*Spiritus domini rapuit Philippum et inuentus est in Azoto* Act. viii° (40). Tria describuntur: diuine uoluntatis adimplecio: *Spiritus domini*; mundane calamitatis euasio: *rapuit Philippum*; superne felicitatis adepcio: *et inuentus est in Azoto*.' Valencia MS 182 fo. 128vb.

[31] His language may be more theologically technical than my translation suggests: 'Rapuit eum Christus de: luto criminalis corrupcionis per graciam iustificantem; bello hostilis temptacionis per graciam adiuvantem; puteo penalis affliccionis per graciam glorificantem.' Valencia MS. 182 fo. 128vb.

[32] The sub-section includes some remarks about Philip's character: '... fuit pulcher in corpore et in anima, quia abstinens, quia elemosinarius, quia auditor officii et predicationum, quia habebat semper confessorem specialem &c. Item fuit verus et taciturnus in sermonibus, mansuetus in moribus: exemplum de domina provinciali que vocavit eum mutum; et iustus in expeditionibus seu operibus.' G. Salvadori and V. Federici, 'I Sermoni d'Occasione, le Sequenze e i Ritmi di Remigio Girolami Fiorentino', in *Scritti vari di Filologia: A Ernesto Monaci gli scolari. 1876–1901* (Rome, 1901), 455–508, at 492. The emphasis on the king's pious practices and taciturnity hits the mark, but the allusion to his mildness is surprising (E. Panella tells me that he and another have in hand an edition and study of this and the other *de diversis* sermons.)

[33] Salvadori and Federici, 492.

[34] This must be the sermon on the text *Omnis potentatus brevis vita* (Eccli. 10: 11), Schneyer, *Repertorium* v, 94, no. 453. The sermon is in Florence Nazionale Conv. soppr. MS.G.4.936, fos. 379va–381va.

specifically to a passage in it about the text 'Man, born [of a woman, living for a short time, is filled with many miseries. Who cometh forth like a flower, and is destroyed, and fleeth as a shadow, and never continueth in the same state.]'[35] The exposition in the sermon on Clement is extended, and Remigio may have had in mind a part of it which emphasises the brevity of human life.[36] Remigio says that the preacher should add how 'man' should be understood as the king of kings, according to Genesis 1 verse 26: 'Let him have dominion [over the fishes of the sea, and the fowls of the air, and the beasts, and the whole earth, and every creeping creature that moveth upon the earth.'] Remigio explains this by adding that the lion is the king of beasts, the eagle the king of birds, etc.,[37] the implication being that in ruling all these creatures man is a king of kings. This makes a connection with his remarks about Philip as king of kings. Though the precise workings of Remigio's mind are not easy to follow, the general effect is to narrow the gap between his message about Philip and his message about man in general. Perhaps the idea is to show that his remarks about the emptiness of power are relevant to everyone, not just to kings. In the remainder of this highly compressed sermon he uses Valerius Maximus to make a point about the cares, dangers, and miseries of royal power,[38] compares worldly power to a shadow, and, using Acts 8 verse 40 as a springboard, manages to touch on mortal sin, venial sin, charity, hell, purgatory, and paradise.[39]

Thus the second part of Remigio's sermon neutralises or rather alters the receiver's interpretation of the apparently enthusiastic remarks about Philip the Fair's power in the first half. Not that he criticizes Philip's record as such. I can detect no trace of critical allusion to his actions against Boniface VIII and the Templars.[40] His message is about other things, however, as well as Philip.

[35] In the sermon on Philip (Salvadori and Federici, 492), he merely says 'expone sicut expositum est supra de papa Clemente super eodem temate illud Iob .xiii.: "Homo natus" &c ...', but the passage is in fact from chapter 14; the whole of the first two verses are expounded in the sermon on Clement (Florence Naz. Conv. soppr. MS. G.4.936 fos. 380vb–381va).

[36] The passage beginning '3° quantum ad uiuendi modicitatem, quia bre(uis) u(iuit) t(empore) ...' and ending '"Momentaneum est omne quod finem habet."' (fo. 381ra).

[37] Salvadori and Federici, 492.

[38] 'et addas exemplum Valerii lib. .vii. de rege subtilis iudicii, ...' Salvadori and Federici, 492; the reference seems to be to Lib. VII cap. II, 5 p. 329 (*Valerii Maximi Actorum et Dictorum Memorabilium Libri Novem ed. C. Kempf (Teubner; Leipzig, 1888), p. 329*).

[39] 'item quomodo dicitur Act. .viii. quod Philippus inventus est in Azoto, quod interpretatur incendium: est enim incendium in vita ista peccati mortalis et venialis et caritatis; et est incendium in alia, scilicet inferni quod redditur primo, et purgatorii quod redditur secundo, et paradisi quod redditur tertio. ...' (Salvadori and Federici, 492–3).

[40] Cf. above note 32.

The third medieval example is a sermon on the death of Edward I of England (d.1307).[41] This time the general message precedes the particular case. The text is a slightly adapted version of Psalm 74 verse 9; in its modified form it reads: '[?He] *leaned down from this to that, but the dregs of it are not emptied; all the sinners of the earth shall drink from it.*' The image never comes into sharp focus in the sermon, but it is full of movement. To judge by the immediate context in the Psalms, it involves a 'cup of strong wine full of mixture'; the subject of '*Inclinauit se ...*' at the start of the text might be a person holding the cup, but might even be the cup itself, in which case a free translation might be: '*It is tipped this way and that ...*'

After applying the text to preaching itself, in a section that we may pass over, the preacher tells us that 'in this same text it can be made clear to us what the human condition is like (*humane nature condicio*) and we can say that the human condition is expressed in a twofold way in the text. Firstly, with respect to its mutability'—here the '*Inclinavit se ...*' clause is cited. 'Secondly, with respect to the inevitability of death, when it is added: *but the dregs of it are not emptied; all the sinners of the earth shall drink from it.*[42]

He then proceeds to give a brief explanation of the whole problem of death: how it was a feature of human nature from its first creation that it should be variable and mutable, changing from health to illness, from joy to sadness, and from life to death; how before the Fall it was preserved by a gift of grace from this mutability, but lost the immunity by disobedience; how Christ's passion and death restored the possibility of the Beatific Vision, but did not exempt man from death, sickness, etc. Finally he explains that just as Christ had to drink the dregs of the Passion, so too must all sinners drink the dregs of the Lord, that is, death (this is linked up with the Pauline idea that Christ 'emptied himself').[43]

The last part of the sermon applies the same images of leaning or tipping this way and that, and of drinking the dregs, to Edward himself. According to the preacher the mutability and variability of

[41] In Rome, Angelica MS.158, fos. $157^{rb}/^{vb}$. Since space is limited, and I hope to discuss this and other sermons on Edward fully elsewhere without too much delay, I will merely give folio references, without transcriptions, to the passages I translate or paraphrase in the text. For a brief description of the whole manuscript and its contents, see B. Ministeri, 'De Augustini de Ancona, O.E.S.A. (†1328) Vita et Operibus', *Analecta Augustiniana* xxii (Typis Polyglottis Vaticanis, 1952), 7–56, 148–262, at 225 and 226–31. Schneyer, *Repertorium* i, 374, lists the *de mortuis* collection to which this sermon belongs under Augustinus Triumphus de Ancona, but there is not much evidence for such an attribution: see Ministeri, 225.

[42] fo. 157rb.

[43] fo. $157^{rb}/^{vb}$.

human nature can be seen in him. He 'never knew how to remain passive (*quiescere*)', and '*leaned down from this to that*, crossing from England to Spain, being knighted there with honour, ... travelling right through Outremer (*partes ultramarinas*), warring down the enemies of Christ mightily there, sometimes also to Wales, sometimes to Flanders, sometimes to Scotland, sometimes to Gascony, setting out himself with his people, enlarging and augmenting his realm.'[44]

The preacher continues his not unperceptive sketch of Edward for a while, then goes on to his death: 'he has now drunk those dregs which all we sinners must drink.'[45] Though the days of man are short, however, Edward 'saw many and various conditions in temporal things, and all of them, by the grace of God, he passed through with honour, in respect of the body, and with recompense in respect of the soul, for always he passed through these temporal things defending the faith, raising up the poor, casting down the proud (*depressione superborum*) and advancing the humble ...'[46] Shortly afterwards the sermon is brought to a close.

The sermon thus contains a panegyric on Edward, but it cannot be reduced to a panegyric, since the miniature treatise on change and death in the history of salvation is an independent and no less prominent part of the sermon. There are indeed memorial sermons from this period where the greatness of the dead person takes up most of the sermon, but normally the plan, as opposed to its execution, can suggest a different balance, comparable to that of our three examples. If one moves from sermons in memory of kings to model funeral and memorial sermons in general, this tendency to tie together praise of the dead person's christian virtue with religious ideas that are not of the same sort becomes more evident still.

In the France of Louis XIV and XV,[47] by contrast, the norm seems to have been to orientate all the parts of the initial division towards the life of the deceased on this side of the grave (including, it should be noted, the last days or hours). We may begin with a sermon on James II of England, preached at Saint Germain-en-Laye in 1702 by Antoine Anselme.[48]

It is about his faith, which is described as the virtue which especially

[44] fo. 157vb.

[45] fo. 157vb.

[46] fo. 157vb.

[47] Here I should admit that my investigation has been far less systematic, though the findings are so uniform as to give me confidence in the conclusions.

[48] On Anselme, see *Dictionnaire de Biographie Française*, ii (Paris, 1936), cols. 1429–30. For convenience I have used the edition of the sermon in J. P. Migne, *Collection intégrale et universelle des orateurs sacrées* tome xxi (Paris, 1845), cols. 179–203.

characterises (*fait le caractère dominant*)[49] of this king, and which follows him step by step in the principal circumstances of his life: before he ascended the throne, when he was on the throne, and after he had left the throne. The division into parts is based on this distinction between three periods of his life. (1) 'Before ascending the throne, he embraced the faith and was its conquest.' (2) 'On the throne, he worked to re-establish the faith, and was its hope.' (3) 'Off the throne, he suffered for the faith and was its victim.'[50]

The first part[51] describes James's ancestry, his troubles in consequence of the English Civil War, his military training, his exploits as Admiral after the Restoration, his conversion to Catholicism, that of his wife, and, finally, of his brother Charles II. The second part[52] is an account of his reign and deposition. It is interesting as an effort to explain in religious terms the defeat of a Catholic king, when it had seemed that the faithful had everything to hope from his reign. The third part[53] is mainly about James's holy life and death in exile (Anselme also urges England to submit to James's son, and the refugees not to lose heart).

Even from this highly compressed summary, it will have become clear that Anselme's sermon on James II includes a good deal of narrative, a lot more than in medieval memorial sermons so far as one can judge from the form in which these survive. Though it is not a general rule for the parts to be in chronological sequence, as they are in Anselme's sermon, it seems to have been common in our second period to bring in substantial segments of detail about events.

In the remaining two examples the narrative detail will be taken as read. We will only show how the individual parts are related. This is not hard to do since it was the practice to set out the structure of the sermon explicitly at the beginning.[54]

In a sermon on the death of Louis XIV, Thomas-Bernard Fellon[55] says that the king was characterised, firstly, by a glory which God had reserved for him to raise him above all the monarchs of the earth, and secondly, by a glory consecrated by a sincere piety which knew

[49] col. 181.

[50] col. 181. I have transposed from the present continuous.

[51] cols. 181–189.

[52] cols. 189–196.

[53] cols. 196–203.

[54] This practice may go back to the thirteenth century; but in the Middle Ages it was closely linked to the citation and interpretation of scriptural authorities, which can make the course of the sermon hard to guess from the division.

[55] On Fellon see the *Dictionnaire de biographie française*, xiii (Paris, 1975), cols. 974–5. I have read it in a *Recueil de plusieur oraisons funebres de Louis XIV, Roy de France, etc.* 2 vols. (1716) B.L. Press Mark 236. b. 30.

how to bring it back constantly to God.[56] Thus Louis was 'A king above all kings, through the unprecedented glory with which God filled his reign', and 'A king above the glory of his reign, by the constant piety which made him refer all this glory to God.'[57]

The third eighteenth century example is the *oraison funèbre* by Denis-Xavier Clément[58] on the death of Stanislas Leszczyński (d. 1766)[59] who twice acquired and twice lost the crown of Poland. His history had a happy ending, for the king of France married his daughter, and afterwards gave him the Duchy of Lorraine.[60] The division of Clément's sermon is not so different from that of Fellon's on Louis XIV: 'Here then we have a hero, whose heroism the world cannot mistake or deny: [this is the] subject of the first point. But he is a hero whose whole glory belongs to religion, [which is the] subject of the second point.'[61] Clément then describes in detail Stanislas's vicissitudes, his enlightened rule in Lorraine, and his dedication to the Catholic faith.

Thus our eighteenth century examples are divided into parts which cumulatively present the qualities, gifts, and virtues manifested by the life of the deceased. Each part deals with something about the king that was worthy of admiration. The blocks which are put together to make the sermon—and I am speaking of ideas, not of the rhetorical surface structure—are in this sense homogenous.

In the medieval examples, especially the second two, the preachers also present the kings' lives as objects of admiration, but other parts of their sermons deal with religious ideas which are distinct from the kings' greatness and/or goodness. Yet there is at least one important principle of unity, well below the rhetorical surface, which relates the different ideas in medieval memorial sermons. In medieval, as indeed in eighteenth-century Catholicism, the idea of a man's death was a sort of ideological junction from which direct lines went out to points in the ideological system relatively distant one from another: in one direction to the set of ideas connected with human goodness in this life; in another to beliefs about the origins of death: to the significance of the Fall and the state of human nature before it; in another to the whole range of ideas associated with the afterlife; and so on. Whereas eighteenth century *oraisons funèbres* tend to concentrate on one sector (goodness in this life, taking that in a wide sense), medieval memorial sermons tend to bring to the surface connections between different

[56] I paraphrase from *Recueil*, i, 147–8.
[57] *Recueil*, i, 148.
[58] On Clément, see *Dictionnaire de Biographie Française*, viii (Paris, 1959) col. 1438.
[59] I have used the text in Migne, *Or. sacr.* lv, cols. 489–510.
[60] N. Davies, *God's Playground. A History of Poland* (Oxford, 1981), i, 508.
[61] Migne, *Or. sacr.*, lv, at 491.

sectors. Because the connections were already more or less implicit in the system of belief, the sermons hold together.

One could end there. Nevertheless it is worth adumbrating a way of taking the analysis further by refining the concept of genre. We have been looking at representative examples of a medieval and a later genre or form—both subsets of the wider genre or form of memorial preaching. Recent reflections on the notion of genre may therefore have something useful to tell us.

Instead of regarding genres as fixed and perpetual types, or rejecting the notion of genre altogether, it has been suggested that we define genres in terms of the expectations that works initially arouse.[62] This seems sensible. One can watch ten minutes of a Hollywood film from the nineteen-thirties and guess that it will have a happy ending; or, in a different genre from the same period, that the little Caesar will meet a violent end. Or, to take a different sort of example, a fifteenth century Italian expected an altarpiece to narrate scripture clearly, to impress the narrated matter on the mind, and perhaps also to do credit to the donor or donors.[63]

It should be added that according to the theory to which I have alluded, the works that really matter are those which sooner or later—the historical dimension is crucial—change the genre's 'horizon of expectation'.[64] In what follows I will gratefully pervert the theory by leaving precisely these works out of consideration.

If the concept of a 'horizon of expectation' can be accepted, it is hard to object to the idea of a horizon of hopes, or to a definition of genre as a 'set of expected objectives or ends'—which texts within the genre achieve with varying degrees of success. For even if all concerned are in accord about the rules of the game, not every member of the genre achieves the same score.

In consequence it would seem that a gap between 'is' and 'ought' is part of the structure of any genre. In the minds of conventional writers and readers, or preachers and listeners, the 'ought' has all the virtues of previous texts in the genre, but, if possible, to a higher degree, and without any elements (or lacunae) that interfere with the effects that members of the genre are supposed to bring about. Moreover the 'ought' could include the further idea that a new sermon

[62] H. R. Jauss, 'Literaturgeschichte als Provokation der Literaturwissenschaft', reprinted in *Rezeptionsästhetik. Theorie und Praxis*, ed. R. Warning (Munich, 1975), 126–62, at 130–33.

[63] On these and other functions of a fifteenth century altarpiece see M. Baxandall, *Patterns of Intention. On the Historical Explanation of Pictures* (New Haven and London, 1985), 106.

[64] Jauss, 'Literaturgeschichte . . .', 133–6.

should not only try to fufil the expectations or rather hopes raised by its evident membership of the genre, but also do this in a way different enough to avoid the duplication of existing texts.

In short, genres are teleological: which is to say that one cannot claim to have understood their structure if one ignores the trajectory of the 'is' towards the 'ought'. Genres are social and historical, so we cannot leave the understanding of them to literary scholars. But to trace the trajectory, and form a notion of the genre's objectives, historians will have to engage in evaluative practices of a kind that they have preferred to leave to literary critics, and old fashioned critics at that. Of course the purpose of the exercise is not the same in the two cases; for historians, it is to understand a special sort of social structure from the inside.

Evaluative comparisons between different texts of the same genre and period are one way of assessing the trajectory, and bringing out the structure of the genre in each period more clearly. We may start by comparing the sermon on Edward I summarised above with another which immediately follows it in the same manuscript.[65] The sermons will be called *Inclinauit* and *In uirtute* respectively, after their first words.

As an embodiment of its genre the sermon already examined, *Inclinauit*, is notably successful in at least two respects. To begin with, it casts its doctrinal net wide, taking in the history of human nature in its connection with change, death, and Christ, and relating this to the virtues and death of Edward. Secondly, this pattern of ideas is reinforced by a strong appeal to the sense and the imagination. The image of leaning this way and that holds the attention because it is full of movement, and the image of dregs might have a more than visual impact, since it might elicit taste images.

On the other hand, *Inclinauit* by itself would not give an adequate impression of the genre's possibilities. The image of leaning this way and that, though full of movement, seems undefined, out of focus. After many readings, I am still not quite sure whether it is meant (in this sermon) to be an image of a cup, or a person, or both. At the level of ideas, the parallelism which unites the general discussion of change and death and the section devoted to Edward himself does not quite work. In the general section, change and death are described in distinctly negative terms, as being a result of the Fall; and it is emphasised that they are common to all men. When one comes to the corresponding passage on Edward, the change and variety of his life is described in a positive, almost admiring tone; and the preacher

[65] Sermon on the text *In uirtute tua, domine* ... (Ps. 20: 1), Rome, Angelica MS. 158 fo. 158ra/^{b}.

indicates that it was something especially characteristic of the man. There is thus an asymmetry between the section on the human condition in general and the section on Edward. This is a weakness because the analogy between the sections is evidently meant to help hold the sermon together.[66]

In uirtute helps us to see how tight the bond between the elements of a sermon in this genre might be. Its parts are firmly linked by an idea which successfully makes the awkward connection between the description of worldly success and the assumption that the dead man has earned happiness in heaven: 'Just as some men's punishment (*pena*) ... is initiated here in the present life, and in the future one it is increased and augmented—like that of Pharaoh, who in this life was smitten with many plagues as a foretaste (*insinuacionem*) of future punishment—so too the joy and happiness of certain men begins ... in the present life, and is completed ... in the future one. We firmly believe that one of these was the Lord king whose exequies we are celebrating now. His happiness ... is expressed in the text ...: Firstly with respect to its beginning in this temporal life ... Secondly, with respect to its summit (*terminacionem*) in the future eternal life ...'[67] It will be noted that the idea is reinforced by the apt 'converse exemplum' of Pharaoh and the plagues, which would have been a stimulus to imagery in the minds of an audience familiar with Old Testament stories. On the other hand, *In uirtute* has a narrower doctrinal range than *Inclinauit*, and as it stands it does not give us such a good idea of the direct appeal to the imagination which was possible within the genre.

The two sermons both possess the features of the medieval genre in some degree, but in each case the intensity, as it were, is uneven. When one can say in which respect each embodies a feature of the genre to a higher degree, one has a better—above all a more concrete—sense of what the genre was aiming at. It is the same if we look at sermons on the death of Louis XIV; and the evaluative method brings out the contrasts with the medieval genre in a concrete way.

The section on the *oraison funèbre* in an eighteenth century work on preaching says that the preacher should praise more for the edification of his listeners than for the glory of his hero.[68] One finds somewhat

[66] The symmetry might have been restored if the preacher had argued in the general section that mutability, though a penalty of sin, can be turned to the good as a medium in which virtue is exercised.

[67] Rome, Angelica MS. 158, fo. 158ra. The happiness in this life is taken by the preacher to include God's help when Edward was in danger, as well as divine help in his spiritual growth.

[68] V. Houdry, *La Bibliothèque des prédicateurs*, xxii ('*contenant l'eloquence chrétienne dans l'idée et dans la pratique*') (Lyons, 1741), 243. On p. 241, however, he says that 'C'est qu'une Oraison funebre n'est que pour la gloire des morts, & pour le plaisir des vivans;

similar sentiments in a sermon on the death of Louis XIV preached in the cathedral of Metz by the Abbé Favier,[69] who says that the preacher's concern should be more with piety and religion than with his political exploits.[70] He says this, however, after he has devoted the first two parts of his sermon to military and political achievements respectively. It is not an outright internal contradiction: for instance, in his patriotic account of the military history of the reign he argues that Louis fought for justice,[71] and that he cared more for the happiness of his peoples and the tranquillity of Europe than for military success;[72] but at the end of the sermon he admits that Louis, when dying, had scruples about the motives behind his wars, which weakens the attempt to keep the parts in harmony. On the basis of this sermon alone one might fail to appreciate how far it was possible to unify a sermon about someone like Louis within the rules of the genre.[73]

It might be argued that this kind of underlying tension was inescapable in the genre, but it was possible to harmonize the elements to a greater extent. One example is a sermon by Edmé Mongin given in the chapel of the Louvre in the presence of members of the Academie Française.[74] He impressionistically describes Louis's military successes[75] and his fostering of the sciences and arts, and of commerce[76] then points out that his civil achievements had their recompense in fame and honour, and that his victories were due in part to fortune and to his armies. If one makes a great merit of his good fortune, one would have to make a crime of his ill-fortune (*disgraces*). True, he met them with great steadfastness; but kings are always to some extent cushioned personally against disaster.[77] It is at death that one sees what a man is made of. If you can find within yourself and in

---

c'est là sa principale, & presque son unique fin ...'. The earlier remark should presumably be interpreted in the light of the later one, but there is still a certain tension within his account of the *oraison funèbre*, perhaps because of disagreements about its ends.

[69] *Recueil*, ii, 287–346.

[70] 'Quelques hautes idées que puissent nous donner d'un Roi ses Vertus militaires ou politiques, la rapidité de ses Conquêtes ou la sagesse de son Gouvernement; nous ne sçaurions être autorisez à le louër dans la Chaire de verité que la Pieté et la Religion n'ayent relevé l'éclat & la Majesté de son Trone.' *Recueil*, ii, 328–9 (and the passage which follows).

[71] *Recueil*, ii, 304–5.

[72] *Recueil*, ii, 307.

[73] *Recueil*, ii, 345.

[74] *Recueil*, ii, 139–80.

[75] *Recueil*, ii, 151–3.

[76] *Recueil*, ii, 153–5.

[77] *Recueil*, ii, 155–6.

your courage the resources to sustain yourself, when abandoned by everything, and in the 'debris general de vôtre puissance', that is a glory which really belongs to you. It is a glory which as it were makes manifest and develops the whole soul, and which, showing it in all its force, casts a new lustre over the actions of your entire life.[78]

The second part of Edmé's sermon deals not only with the way he met his death, which is described in detail towards the end, but with all the achievements which can be presented by the preacher as specifically christian and a preparation for death. He argues, for instance, that God permitted Louis to suffer the defeats of his later years and the death of his children to prepare in him the qualities of patience and courage which Louis would show when he came to meet death.[79]

The elements of Edmé's sermon are not in perfect accord, and it would be possible to show, by comparison with other *oraisons funèbres* (I am thinking in particular of those of the bishop of Valence[80] and Massillon[81]) how the sermon's internal unity could have been increased. Though space does not permit this, I would suggest that more of this sort of comparison would further enhance our sense of the trajectory of the genre.

There is no need to restate elaborately the general conclusion that in eighteenth century *oraisons funèbres* the constituent elements are held together by mutual resemblance: they all relate to praiseworthy features of the dead king's life; whereas medieval memorial sermons make manifest the connections between heterogeneous doctrines. These are not absolute laws, only approximate generalisations. It goes without saying that the intermediate period needs to be mapped (though some of the questions we should ask about it may have been clarified *per accidens*), and that each genre needs to be studied in the wider social context of its period; but *abstrahere non est mentiri.* The confrontation and evaluation of individual texts within each genre represents a different kind of comparative method, which may be used, as here, as a handmaid of the usual one, though the two are in principle independent of one another. The evaluative comparisons leave the conclusions formally untouched, but they should enhance out understanding of what the genres were trying to achieve, by avoiding confusion between the 'is' and the 'ought' of each form. When we

[78] I paraphrase and abridge *Recueil*, 156–7.

[79] *Recueil*, ii, 174.

[80] *Recueil*, 181–246, esp. 187–8 and 203–4.

[81] I have used the text in *Oraisons funèbres choisies de Mascaron, Bourdaloue, La Rue et Massillon*, (Paris, 1802) (no editors name on title page), 291–351.

critically compare one sermon with another, we enter more fully into the states of mind of the preachers and the publics who created the genres.

BODIN AND THE DEVELOPMENT OF THE FRENCH MONARCHY

By Richard Bonney

READ 3 MARCH 1989

THE 'history of ideologies' is now very much the vogue since Professor Quentin Skinner's fine study on *The foundations of modern political thought.*[1] Whether or not one agrees with all aspects of his interpretation of Bodin—and Dr Parker might argue that it fails to draw out sufficiently the moral philosopher inside the jurist,[2] while Professor Rose might prefer to stress the Judaizing tendencies of the theorist as a central preoccupation[3]—it is a testament to the decisive impact made by Skinner on the history of political thought that no-one has challenged his new and radical approach. It is no part of the purpose of this paper to do so. Indeed, an understanding both of Bodin's predecessors and of the ideological conflict of the 1570s which influenced the drafting of the *Six bookes of a commonweale* (the title given to the *République* by its first English translator, Richard Knolles) is fundamental before any appreciation of the theorist can be made free from distortion. It is no use at all asserting that Bodin started from scratch, even on the issue of sovereignty, where he made his most original contribution.[4] Bodin himself minimized his originality, basing his commentary on the powers historically enjoyed by French kings. The French king had traditionally regarded his authority as that of *princeps legibus solutus*, as an absolute ruler above the law. If the French king had been unable to do those things described by Bodin, in the view of that author, 'il n'estoit pas Prince souverain'.[5] Bodin also

[1] For his discussion of Bodin, Skinner, *The foundations of modern political thought. II. The Age of Reformation* (Cambridge, 1978), 284–301. A recent study of French political thought consciously adopts at least a history of ideologies veneer, but is disappointing on Bodin: N.O. Keohane, *Philosophy and the state in France. The Renaissance to the enlightenment* (Princeton, NJ 1980), 67–82.

[2] D. Parker, 'Law, society and the state in the thought of Jean Bodin,' *History of political thought*, ii (1981), 253–85.

[3] P.L. Rose, *Bodin and the great God of nature* (Geneva, 1980). Also idem, 'Bodin's universe and its paradoxes: some problems in the intellectual biography of Jean Bodin', *Politics and society in Reformation Europe*, ed. E.I. Kouri and T. Scott (1987), 266–88.

[4] See R.J. Bonney, *L'absolutisme* (Paris, 1989), chapter one.

[5] J. Bodin, *Les six livres de la république* ... (Paris, 1583, repr. Darmstadt, 1977), 154. Idem, *The six bookes of a commonweale*, trans. R. Knolles (1606), ed. K.D. McRae (Harvard, Mass., 1962), 107. A. Esmein, 'La maxime *princeps legibus solutus est* dans

noted the contribution of the canon lawyers of the Middle Ages to the development of his political theory and remarked that Pope Innocent IV was he who best understood the nature of sovereignty.[6]

The history of ideologies, therefore, helps us to place a political thinker of the stature of Bodin in his context. The reservation that one might have about this approach, however, is whether it necessarily helps us to understand or to estimate the significance of a thinker such as Bodin in the longer term. It is not merely that there is a difficulty with the 'snapshot' presentation of a particular political theorist in his historical context, which arises when he is divorced from his followers: the significance of Bodin in the seventeenth century cannot be assessed without a full study of Loyseau, Le Bret and Domat in France, which is still awaited. The differences between Bodin's influence on them and on other thinkers such as Grotius and Hobbes[7] has never been analyzed systematically and needs to be taken into account. A second and more important difficulty is that we cannot assume that the 'true' historical legacy of a theorist such as Bodin will appear simply by studying the debt owed by subsequent political theorists to Bodin in the context of their times. This paper seeks to argue that one or two central ideas of a key political thinker are so seminal that they prove decisive in the political arena itself, and not just in the relatively abstract world of political thought. The nature of politics in a given country can become consciously and unconsciously moulded as a result of the gradual, insidious, long-term impact of a seminal idea.

Such, it will be contended, is the significance of Bodin's discussion of the role of the commissioner and the distinction he makes between the commission and the office for the later development of the French monarchy and what, for want of a better term, is frequently referred to as 'absolutism' in France. It used to be assumed by virtually all historians that Bodin's new conception of sovereignty was crucial to this development. However, what one might call the 'revisionist' school of French historians is now beginning to question the significance of Bodin's theory *tout court*. The most recent exponent of this line of reasoning suggests that 'the notion of legislative sovereignty had much less significance both in theoretical discourse and in legal practice than has frequently been supposed; nor was the influence of

l'ancien droit public français', *Essays in legal history . . .*, ed. P. Vinogradov [Vinogradoff] (Oxford, 1913), 205.

[6] Bodin, *République*, 132–133. Idem, *Commonweale*, ed. McRae, 92. The Papal origins of the theory and practice of absolute sovereignty have recently been stressed by Professor Prodi: P. Prodi, *The Papal prince. One body and two souls: the Papal monarchy in early modern Europe*, trans. S. Haskins (Cambridge, 1988).

[7] Although King has made a start in considering Bodin's influence on Hobbes: P. King, *The ideology of order. A comparative analysis of Jean Bodin and Thomas Hobbes* (1974).

Roman law on monarchical absolutism as clear-cut as some authorities suggest'.[8] Dr Parker maintains that 'as one expression of the need to create stability out of instability or as a means of legitimizing the regime, the concept of legislative sovereignty is comprehensible; but as an explanation of how the system really worked, and on whose behalf, it is inadequate'.[9] Taking the examples of the post-Bodin jurist Cardin Le Bret and Jean Domat, it is argued that in the seventeenth century 'the concept of legislative sovereignty effectively disappeared or, at least, was subsumed within an essentially traditional world-view'.[10] Dr Parker's reading of Cardin Le Bret is clearly at variance with that presented later in this paper; but the fundamental difficulty with the 'revisionist' viewpoint is that it is much more effective in its depiction of the limitations on royal freedom of action—for example, in the crown's dealing with the *Parlements*—than it is in its analysis of the strength of (in English constitutional terminology) the royal prerogative, notably in the powers accorded to provincial intendants and other royal commissioners. On this latter point, either the explanation provided by the 'revisionists' is impressionistic[11] or silence prevails.[12] To remedy this unjustified neglect, the principal discussion in this paper will not be concerned with the arguments of the 'revisionists', but rather to re-examine the traditionalists' line, which stresses the importance of Bodin's new conception of sovereignty for the development of French absolute monarchy.

These historians have almost invariably argued their case without explaining the process by which such sovereignty might be exercised.[13]

[8] D. Parker, 'Sovereignty, absolutism and the function of the law in seventeenth-century France', *Past and Present* cxxii (1989), 36–74, at p. 71.

[9] *Ibid.*, 72.

[10] *Ibid.*, 48.

[11] Relatively short shift is given to the intendants of Louis XIV in R. C. Mettam, *Power and faction in Louis XIV's France* (Oxford, 1988), 211–17. Something of the flavour of this account is provided by the opening remark to this section of the book at p. 211: 'There are a number of reasons why the *intendants* could not have been the cornerstones of "absolutism" that some old-fashioned historians have maintained them to be.' The present author is embarked on a detailed study of the intendants during the personal rule of Louis XIV.

[12] There is no mention of the provincial intendants in Parker, 'Sovereignty, absolutism and the law'. At p. 65, in the context of the *grands jours* of Auvergne, he comments that 'justice by commission of this sort, cutting across all vested interests, was perhaps as near to absolutism in the popular sense as the crown ever got'.

[13] There have been some exceptions, notably at the Munich conference on Bodin: R. Polin, 'L'idée de République selon Jean Bodin', *Jean Bodin. Proceedings of the international conference on Bodin in Munich*, ed. H. Denzer (Munich, 1973), p. 349; also *ibid.*, p. 469: in the discussion, Freund asserted that the development of the commission was 'fondamental pour toute pensée politique postérieure', while Derathé noted that the distinction between *officier* and *souverain* was 'plus importante, plus développée dans la littérature postérieure que chez Bodin'.

But it will be argued that the importance of Bodin's discussion lay as much in the process of issuing royal commissions as in the concept of sovereignty. As early as 1919, Otto Hintze had drawn attention to Bodin as offering 'the first theoretical discussion' of royal commissions; 'it apparently became as basic to the French administrative law of the *ancien régime*', Hintze wrote, 'as was his theory of sovereignty to constitutional law . . .'—a distinction between administrative and constitutional law with which few historians would now agree.[14] However, apart from an oblique reference to 'magistrates and commissioners',[15] Professor Skinner does not discuss royal commissions at all; neither does Professor Keohane, who nevertheless argues that Bodin's ideas 'were crucial for the development of absolutism in France'.[16] Professor Franklin did mention commissions in 1973, it is true, and noted that Bodin was apparently 'oblivious' to the idea that 'it would be technically legitimate for a king to circumvent the courts by attributing functions to commissioners'[17]—but even this would seem to be rather less than a complete discussion of the significance of Bodin's theory.

It is a curious omission on the part of modern commentators, because if we compare Bodin with his two most important predecessors in the sixteenth century, Claude de Seyssel[18] and Guillaume Budé,[19] this issue provides one of the most striking contrasts in their writings. The earlier theorists were silent on the powers of royal commissioners; Bodin not only discusses them, but characteristically provides a definition:[20]

> An Officer therefore is a publike person, who hath an ordinarie charge by law limitted vnto him. A Commissioner is a publike person, but with an extraordinaire charge limited vnto him, without law, by vertu of commissi[on] onely.

Richard Knolles's translation is not as elegant as the French original; nor is it entirely accurate. Under the office-holder's powers, he substitutes 'law' for *édit*, while in the original French there is no mention of law at all in the context of the commissioner. We must therefore

[14] O. Hintze, 'The commissary and his significance in general administrative history: a comparative study', *The historical essays of Otto Hintze*, ed. F. Gilbert (New York, 1975), 281–2.

[15] Skinner, 300.

[16] Keohane, 81.

[17] J. H. Franklin, *Jean Bodin and the rise of absolutist theory* (Cambridge, 1973), 99–100.

[18] C. de Seyssel, *La monarchie de France* [1515], ed. J. Poujol (1961).

[19] G. Budé, *De l'institution du prince* [1518] (repr. 1547; facsimile repr., Farnborough, 1966).

[20] Bodin, *République*, 372. *Idem, Commonweale*, ed. McRae, A77, 278.

necessarily quote the French original and then the translation which we would propose:

> L'Officier est la personne publique qui a charge ordinaire limitée par edict [*sic*]. Commissaire, est la personne publique qui a charge extraordinaire, limitée par simple commission.

> The office-holder is a public person who has an ordinary function limited by edict. The commissioner is a public person who has an extraordinary function, limited by a simple commission.

In Book III, chapter 2 of the *République*, ('Des Officiers & Commissaires'), Bodin proceeded to distinguish different types of commissions, citing examples from ancient Rome, and noting that commissions tended to develop into offices. However, for our purposes his two most important comments concerned the nature of the commissioner's powers and the distinction between them and the powers of the office-holder. Commissions were almost invariably addressed to office-holders, but Bodin argued (to quote Knolles) that 'an officer in the qualitie of an officer, cannot be also a commissioner, for the self same charge limited vnto him by his office'.[21] In his view, 'the ordinary hearing of the cause is to be preferred before the commission, even as the qualitie of the officer is to be preferred before the qualitie of the Commissioner; and the acts of the officers [are] more assured than the acts of the Commissioners.'[22] Commissions might be issued in different forms, but whatever type of commission was issued, it 'is directed with power and authoritie to heare and proceed in the cause; either without appeal, or else with appeal reserved vnto the sovereign prince ... as sometime [a] commission is given out for the instruction of the affaires, or proceedings, vnto the definitive sentence exclusively or inclusively, saving the execution thereof, if appeal be made'.[23] In Bodin's view, the essential elements of the commission were the right to hear cases without appeal (or with appeal reserved to the sovereign), periodicity and revocability; offices, on the contrary had 'a continuance perpetuall [*sic*]'. It therefore followed:[24]

> the power of an officer besides that it is ordinarie, it is also better authorised, and larger than is a commissioner's, & that is it for which the Edicts and lawes leave many things to the consciences and discretions of the Magistrats [*sic*]: who indifferently applie and interpret the lawes according to the occurrents & exigence of the causes presented: Whereas Commissioners are otherwise bound,

[21] Bodin, *République*, 380. *Idem, Commonweale*, ed. McRae, 284.
[22] *Ibid.*
[23] Bodin, *République*, 381. *Idem, Commonweale*, ed. McRae, 285.
[24] Bodin, *République*, 387–8. *Idem, Commonweale*, ed. McRae, 289.

and as it were tyed vnto the verie words of their commission, and especially where question is of the affaires of state ...

It is clear from Bodin's discussion of the powers of the commissioner that he was indulging in an historical survey: 'orderly proceeding required that wee should before speake of Commissioners, then of officers; for that they were before any lawyers or Officers established ...'[25] Bodin was clearly influenced by Louis XI's so-called 'law of irremovability' (*loi d'inamovibilité*), promulgated in 1467: '... ordinary offices and charges by the prince once lawfully bestowed', runs Knolles's translation, 'cannot from them on whom they are so bestowed be againe taken, except they have committed some criminall cause ...'[26] Since office-holders were permanently established, in Bodin's view their authority was likely to be 'more assured'. Bodin as we have seen also had a high opinion of Pope Innocent IV as 'hee that of others best knew the lawes of maiestie or soveraigntie' and of the canon lawyers who stated that 'the Pope can neuer bind his owne handes'.[27] He was thus almost certainly aware of a distinction made by the canon law between *officium* and *dignitas*, and of papal practice which had distinguished between a commission of a delegate judge who was named (*facta personae*) and one who was not (*facta dignitati*): the canon law dictum had been that 'a delegation made to the Dignity without expressing a proper name passes on to the successor'; in contrast, a named delegation was necessarily temporary and lapsed with the death of the appointee.[28] Bodin clearly thought in terms of the named delegation which lapsed with the death or revocation of the appointee.

Subsequent theorists, notably Charles Loyseau, writing in *Cinq Livres du Droit des Offices* (1609), echoed Bodin's arguments that the office-holder's powers were ordinary ones and thus capable of extension, whereas a commissioner had extraordinary powers which were limited.[29] The fact that the commissioner had 'no assured rank' ('point de rang asseuré') in the social hierarchy was of great importance to

[25] Bodin, *République*, 392–3. *Idem, Commonweale*, ed. McRae, 293.

[26] Bodin, *République*, 393. *Idem, Commonweale*, ed. McRae, 293. The ordinance of 21 October 1467 stated that 'désormais nous ne donnerons aucun de noz offices, s'il n'est vaquant par mort ou par résignation faicte de bon gré et consentement du résignant, dont il apperre [*sic*] duement, ou par forfaicture préalablement jugée et déclarée judiciairement et selon les terms de justice, par juge compétent ...': *Ordonnances des rois de France de la troisième race*, ed. C. E. J. P. Pastouret et al. (1820), xvii. 26.

[27] Bodin, *République*, 132–3. *Idem, Commonweale*, ed. McRae, 92.

[28] E. H. Kantorowicz, *The king's two bodies. A study in medieval political theology* (Princeton NJ, 1957), 384–6.

[29] C. Loyseau, *Cinq livres du droit des offices* (1613 edn.), 570. For Loyseau's importance as a theorist: H. A. Lloyd, 'The political thought of Charles Loyseau, 1564–1627', *European Studies Review*, xi (1981), 53–82.

Loyseau, who was preoccupied with questions of honour and status.[30] Thus if an office-holder and a commissioner found themselves both with powers to judge the same case, the commissioner should be the one to give way.[31] This was a significant and far-reaching attempt to limit the independence of the government from its permanent officials. But Loyseau went still further, and argued that the commissioner should publish his commission in the locality. If he did not do so, then no-one was obliged to recognise or obey him because his powers were unknown.[32] Acceptance of the principle of publicity would have given the local law court the opportunity to criticize the powers contained in the commission and to make representations to the king's council. But it was not generally accepted.

The most important French theorist of the next generation was Cardin Le Bret, whose treatise *De la souveraineté du roy* (1632) marked a decisive change in the prevailing theory about the nature of the powers of the royal commissioner. (Le Bret was a former intendant, and was half-way through a distinguished career as a councillor of state when he published his *magnum opus*.)[33] He reversed the priorities of Bodin and Loyseau. The power to grant commissions was 'a right of sovereignty' ('un droit de souveraineté');[34] indeed, 'to confer commissions to whomseover they wish[ed was] one of the principal rights of the sovereign authority of kings'.[35] The commissioner had supremacy over the local office-holders because he represented 'more particularly the person of the prince'—in this respect, Le Bret cited the canon law maxim *omnis delegatus maior est ordinario in re delegata*.[36] Finally, since the person chosen as commissioner would often be a councillor of state, he would bring to his commission 'the prerogatives of the rank and precedence which is owed to this status (qualité) . . .'[37] By the third decade of the seventeenth century, therefore, Le Bret had overturned the arguments of Bodin and Loyseau, without losing or altering their central preoccupation with sovereignty. Le Bret continued to stress that the power to issue royal commissions was an emanation of the king's undivided legislative sovereignty. Thus during the Fronde, at a time when Le Bret himself was the *doyen* of the council

[30] For Loyseau: H. A. Lloyd, 'The political thought of Charles Loyseau, 1564–1627', *European Studies Review* xi (1981), 53–82. *Idem*, *The state, France and the sixteenth century* (1980).

[31] *Ibid.*, 571.

[32] *Ibid.*, 569.

[33] G. Picot, *Cardin Le Bret, 1558–1655, et la doctrine de la souveraineté* (Nancy, 1948).

[34] C. Le Bret, *De la souveraineté du roy* (1632), 149.

[35] *Ibid.*, 160.

[36] *Ibid.*, 151.

[37] *Ibid.*, 160.

of state, a decree was issued on 18 February 1652 which annulled the commission conferred by Gaston d'Orléans on Talon and Le Secq, *trésoriers de France* at Caen 'to carry out the function of intendants'—such powers could be granted only by the king himself and the *trésoriers* were warned that if they attempted to usurp such authority as intendants they would be guilty of treason.[38]

While the extension of the concept of treason during Richelieu's ministry was one of Le Bret's more notorious achievements,[39] the idea that the power to issue commissions emanated from the king's undivided legislative sovereignty although voiced by Le Bret seems to have originated with Bodin. Bodin, of course, was drawing on the medieval distinction between the king's 'retained' and his 'delegated' justice; there had undoubtedly been royal commissioners of various types, including *maîtres des requêtes* on circuit-tour, in the later Middle Ages.[40] However, the extant evidence suggests that royal commissions of *intendant* or *surintendant de justice*, the true precursors of the intendants of the seventeenth century, were few and far between before the publication of Bodin's *Six bookes of a commonweale* in 1576: perhaps a dozen commissions survive from the period before 1577, the earliest being the power of Pierre de Panisse as intendant of justice in Corsica, which was issued on 24 August 1556.[41] In other words, Bodin is unlikely to have had much knowledge of the practical difficulties facing royal commissioners before he advanced his theory.

It is thus a curious irony that the influence of Bodin extended into an area which it would have been virtually impossible for him to have envisaged. There was no 'system' of intendants—provincial officials empowered by royal commissions—prior to the late 1630s and it was not until the ruling of 22 August 1642 that the principle of one

[38] *Arrêts du conseil du roi. Règne de Louis XIV. Inventaire analytique des arrêts en commandement. I. 20 mai 1643–8 mars 1661*, ed. M. Le Pesant (1976), no. 1630. A[rchives] N[ationales] E 1698 no. 35 and E 1700 no. 26, 18 Feb. 1652.

[39] R. E. Giesey, L. Haldy, J. Millhorn, 'Cardin Le Bret and lese majesty', *Law and history review*, iv (1986), 23–54.

[40] G. Dupont-Ferrier, 'Le rôle des commissaires royaux dans le gouvernement de la France, spécialement du xive au xvie siècle', *Mélanges Paul Fournier* (1929), 171–84, Bonney, *Political change in France under Richelieu and Mazarin*, 102.

[41] It has long been established that this was the earliest commission: G. Hanotaux, *Origines de l'institution des intendants des provinces* (1884), 10. More recently: M. Antoine, 'Institutions françaises en Italie sous le règne de Henri II: gouverneurs et intendants, 1547–1559', *Mélanges de L'école française de Rome* xciv (1982), 815–18. For the 1560s: Bonney, *Political change*, 140. For Sade de Mazan in 1577: D.J. Buisseret, 'Les précurseurs des intendants du Languedoc', *Annales du Midi*, lxxx (1968), 87–88. Professor Antoine has discovered a number of new commissions from the period before 1577. However, most of these are not of *intendants de justice*, although the individuals appointed may be regarded as their functional precursors: M. Antoine, 'Genèse de l'institution des intendants', *Journal des savants* (1982), 283–317, especially 291–7.

intendant de la justice, police et finances per *généralité* (or fiscal district) was established. It was the powers conferred by their commissions and the supplementary decrees and rulings of the council on these powers which completely altered the nature of royal administration in France and gave Bodin's discussion, with the subsequent interpretation of Le Bret, a posthumous significance. What had started as an historical argument had now become a matter of great contemporary relevance, due to the progressive extension of the intendants' powers by royal commission and the refusal of the king's council to permit registration of these powers in the sovereign courts.[42] As the number of tasks assigned to the intendants increased, so it was recognized that their capacity for fulfilling them was hindered by the enormous geographical areas over which some had responsibility; it was even suggested that 'to keep a province properly controlled by this method ... it would be necessary to have as many intendants as there are *élections* (that is to say, lesser fiscal districts)'—that 170-odd intendants were needed rather than 22 to keep France effectively administered.[43]

There was never any prospect of such expansion; but it is clear that relatively early on the intendants were relying increasingly on subordinate officials whom they had appointed (*subdélégués*). Sometimes the power of *subdélégation*, a crucial development in the French monarchy of the *ancien régime*,[44] had been conferred on the intendant by his commission[45] or by a specific decree of the council;[46] but this was certainly not always the case, and there is at least a suggestion that the intendant sometimes exceeded his powers in this matter, even under Richelieu and Mazarin, by, for example, allowing his subdelegates to carry out judicial prosecutions.[47] Some of the subdelegates served successive intendants for long periods of time and provided continuity in provincial administration—thus Jean Anoul, a *juge royal* at Uzès, was a faithful servant of the intendants of Languedoc from 1630 to 1661. By the 1660s, significant powers were being conferred by the intendants on their *subdélégués* in certain areas of responsibility, for example in the general investigation into titles of nobility (*recherche de noblesse*). Following a decree of the council on 25 February 1666, Claude Pellot, the intendant of Guyenne, drew up

[42] R. J. Bonney, *Political change in France under Richelieu and Mazarin, 1624–1661* (Oxford, 1978), 135–59, 244–5.

[43] Bonney, *Political change in France under Richelieu and Mazarin*, 46–7, 72–4, 237, 453–5.

[44] M. Antoine, *Le dur métier du roi. Études sur la civilisation politique de la France d'ancien régime* (1986), 61–80.

[45] Bonney, *Political change in France under Richelieu and Mazarin*, 146, 149, 155, 275.

[46] *Ibid.*, 272.

[47] *Ibid.*, 249–50.

general instructions for his subdelegates, which emphasised the political sensitivity of the investigation and outlined the procedure to be adopted in the hearings. It is perfectly clear from the extant documentary evidence that it was the subdelegates, and not the intendant himself, who dealt with these cases. They provided him with a dossier on each nobleman and advised the intendant on whether the claim to nobility should be accepted or rejected. The intendant simply acted upon their advice, either by signing an *ordonnance de maintenu de noblesse*, or, in the case of a false claim to nobility, a standard ordinance which was printed with blank spaces for the names of the subdelegate and the name of the *roturier* who had sought fiscal exemption to be filled in by hand.[48]

Given the growing amount of business imposed by the central government on the intendants, it is not surprising that such methods were adopted. By the end of Louis XIV's reign, an intendant such as Basville in Languedoc had used his thirty-three years in office to build up a network of some twenty-two subdelegates.[49] This was certainly one of the more elaborate examples, but it merely serves to illustrate a problem of which Colbert was well aware. The Roman law principle was perfectly clear: *delegatus non potest subdelegare*; a commissioner could not empower a subdelegate without having been given prior authorisation by a royal commission.[50] In 1645, the king's council confirmed this principle in a case concerning the intendancy of Poitou. René I Voyer d'Argenson, the intendant, obtained a decree of the council empowering his son, René II, to act as subdelegate for the recovery of the king's taxes in the *élections* of Saintes and Cognac. However, René I had not been able to confer on his son the power to investigate crimes of tax rebellion 'since this authority derived solely from His Majesty's power'. This power was granted in a subsequent decree of the council.[51]

This was an unusual case of subdelegation, and d'Argenson was no doubt particularly careful to clear the lines of authority, since the powers were being attributed to his own son. Colbert contended that later intendants had been much less scrupulous,[52] and in the penultimate year of his ministry (1682), he demanded details of the

[48] A[rchives] D[épartementales du] Gers (Auch) C 362, printed ordinance of Pellot, 15 Apr. 1666; his instructions to subdelegates, 12 June 1666; his undated printed ordinance concerning Barthélémé Carrère, drawn up on the report of his subdelegate, Pierre Chadebert, an *avocat* in the *Parlement* of Toulouse.

[49] Bonney, *Political change in France under Richelieu and Mazarin*, 428.

[50] Antoine, *Le dur métier du roi*, 69.

[51] AN E 199^{b}, fo. 146, 15 Feb. 1645.

[52] For Colbert's hostility to subdelegates: J. Ricommard, 'Les subdélégués des intendants au xviie et xviiie siècles', *L'information historique* xxiv (1962–3), 144–5.

extent of delegated responsibilities in each of the intendancies. One of the clearest answers was given by Poncet de la Rivière, intendant at Bourges. He did not use the word sovereignty, but there can be no doubt that it was what he was talking about:[53]

> ... you order me to assume jurisdiction only in those matters where the king has given me the power, and not to appoint permanent subdelegates, merely using them for specific matters when I cannot be present in person. You will permit me to inform you, Monsieur, that I have always acted in this way, that I have given no judgement in matters beyond my competence, and that I have never issued a commission of subdelegate. I only empower people to hold preliminary hearings in specific cases (*pour l'instruction de chaque affaire particulière*) when I cannot be present in person. As a result, I have no subdelegate who judges without appeal in matters concerning my authority. They can scarcely in truth be called subdelegates, since they are only empowered for particular cases when I send them to hold preliminary hearings, or to obtain further information on matters where I have received a complaint. But since people empowered in this way sometimes increase their authority, as I have observed on more than one occasion, you will kindly favour me, Monsieur, with the jurisdiction over any judgements which may follow ... Since I have had the honour to serve in the provinces [as intendant], I have made it a cardinal principle to carry out all my functions without the help of others, so that I have always been in a position to give account of what it was that I had done ...

A similar denial of any generalized power of subdelegation was made by Marle, the intendant at Riom,[54] while at Pau, duBois du Baillet was reluctant even to use his predecessor's subdelegate without official approval.[55] Whatever the actual practice in the provinces, the intendants knew their Bodin and Le Bret and, as we might expect, in their answers to Colbert they studiously avoided any statement which might be interpreted as undermining royal sovereignty.

The question is whether or not later ministers undermined this balance, firstly by the creation of permanent offices for *subdélégués* during the war of the Spanish Succession, and secondly by the establishment in certain provinces of permanent general subdelegations (*subdélégués-généraux*). The first matter is usually dismissed as a temporary fiscal expedient resulting from the war: the *subdélégués* were established as office-holders in April 1704, and the measure was

[53] AN G^7 124, 20 June 1682.
[54] AN G^7 101, 19 July 1682.
[55] AN G^7 112, 18 Aug. 1682.

revoked in August 1715; thereafter, there was no further attempt to repeat the experiment in the *ancien régime*.[56] The edict of creation made it clear:[57]

> ... the ministry of these officials has become so important and their functions so extensive, that we have judged it necessary to invest those who henceforth exercise them with a character which gives them the prominence and authority necessary for the good functioning of their duties with more honour and impartiality ...

The government appeared to have swung full circle by accepting the argument of Bodin and Loyseau that office-holders had more permanency and a higher social status than temporary commissioners. However, if the comments of the intendant of Amiens are at all representative, even the windfall that the government expected from the sale of these offices was not as great as it might have hoped—by 1710 the subdelegates were declared to be in greater need of revenues than to be burdened with new taxes: they were not the wealthy local office-holders the government had sought to appoint.[58] The long-term political disadvantages of the introduction of venality must have been clear and, as has been seen, the decision was reversed with the coming of peace in 1715.

The general subdelegation is more interesting, because it became a permanent feature of the *ancien régime*.[59] The first commission as *subdélégué-général* was issued on 14 January 1702 to the sieur Basset in Dauphiné;[60] two others were issued before 8 November 1704, when a similar commission was issued to Saint-Macary in Béarn: the Dauphiné and Béarn examples are alike in that both conferred an acting intendancy on an individual during the absence abroad of the previously commissioned provincial intendant. Méliand, who had been appointed intendant of Béarn in April 1704, served simultaneously for five years as intendant there and in Catalonia; but this was a device to permit him to hold two salaries, the salary as intendant of the army being insufficient to cover his real costs.[61] At the provincial estates of 1706, St-Macary, the *subdélégué-général* or acting intendant, ran into conflict because he had appointed as his *subdélégué* the syndic

[56] Antoine, *Le dur métier du roi*, p. 76 and the articles by J. Ricommard there cited, notably, 'L'édit d'avril 1704 et l'érection en titre d'office des subdélégués des intendants', *Revue historique*, 195 (1945), 24–35, 123–39.

[57] C. V. E. Boyer de Sainte-Suzanne, *L'administration sous l'ancien régime. Les intendants de la généralité d'Amiens (Picardie et Artois)* (1865), 583.

[58] AN G^7 92, 8 Sept. 1710. There had been difficulty in finding purchasers in Béarn as late as 1706: AN G^7 117, 5 Oct. 1706.

[59] Antoine, *Le dur métier du roi*, 125–79.

[60] *Ibid.*, 130, 169–70.

[61] AN G^7 116, 24, 25 Nov. 1704. AN G^7 118, 20 Jan. 1710. AN G^7 119, 8 Mar. 1711.

of the province. The acting intendant alleged that the two posts were not incompatible, and the controller-general agreed; but this was clearly not the view of the province's representatives. Although called a subdelegate-general, St-Macary as acting intendant had appointed his own subdelegate despite the Roman law maxim *delegatus non potest subdelegare*. However, the controller-general did not take St-Macary to task for having done so.[62] Nevertheless, with the possible exception of this incident, St-Macary seems to have been scrupulous in the exercise of his powers. On Méliand's return as intendant in 1709, St-Macary's authority should have come to an end: but did it do so if the intendant did not return to the province itself, but went straight to Versailles? St-Macary asked the ministers to settle the issue.[63] Despite the apparent oddity of the general subdelegation, which became increasingly common in the eighteenth century as a device to permit the absence of the intendant from the province, it led to no undermining of the notion of sovereignty, as the creation of offices for subdelegates in 1704 had done, albeit potentially.

Indeed, contrary to Colbert's fears, the evidence suggests that the intendants and acting intendants (*subdélégués-généraux*) of Louis XIV never became possessed of sovereign powers in their own right except in specific instances where the crown had given prior authorisation. Much has been written about the development of French absolutism, and even about the drafting of decrees of the council,[64] but few commentators have focused attention on the intendants' own drafting of decrees (*projets d'arrêts*), empowering them to deal with a specific case often without appeal. The draft decree was sent to the minister, often the controller-general, for approval, together with the various documents justifying the need for such a specific additional power.[65] In one sense, this process may be seen as the monarchy relying more than hitherto on the local initiative of the intendant; but in an equally important sense, the procedure enshrined Bodin's principle of undivided legislative sovereignty residing in the king, even if it was exercised on his behalf by the ministers, and the council in this case. The king's sovereignty remained undivided: the intendant was merely his agent in specific delegated matters. Furthermore, authorization by these decrees of the council was personal to the intendant: if a change of intendants occurred before the final sentence was pronounced by the tribunal over which he presided, the new appointee was careful to

[62] AN G^7 117, 5 Oct. 1706: 'luy ayant donné cette commission ...'.

[63] AN G^7 118, 20 Aug. 1709.

[64] Most recently, a distinguished study by A. N. Hamscher, *The conseil privé and the Parlements in the age of Louis XIV: a study in French absolutism* (Transactions of the American Philosophical Society, lxxvii, 1987).

[65] AN G^7 92, 22 Dec. 1710. This carton has several examples.

obtain a decree transferring authority in the case to him (*arrêt de subrogation*).[66] This was the Bourbon monarchy's equivalent to the Papacy's *facta personae* which we encountered earlier.

Moreover, the evidence suggests that most intendants were prudent, and took care to obtain the requisite prior authorisation for their actions. When they did not seek it, their judgements might be called into question by the minister. Carré de Montgeron received a commission on 16 September 1705 as intendant of Berry which empowered him, among other duties, to 'investigate carefully any exactions, misappropriation, violence and malversation which may have been carried out in financial matters in the said province, and to proceed against the offenders by judgement of last resort and without appeal'. Although the intendant recognised that normally he should have requested a specific decree of attribution in a case involving financial corruption in the *brigade des gabelles* at Épineuil, the intendant warned the accused that the case was being heard without appeal and commenced procedures against them. He did so not because he wished to arrogate sovereignty for himself, but because he had only one witness in the case, who lived thirty leagues away and wanted to return home. If the witness had left the province, then the case would have fallen. The minister nevertheless denounced Montgeron's actions and warned him that the accused in the case might have grounds for a civil action against him. In a reply couched in diplomatic language, the intendant remained quite unrepentant. He enclosed a copy of the appropriate passage from his commission, cited above, and commented that the council had in any case chosen to support his action by subsequently granting an *arrêt d'attribution*. His words are significant for our purposes:[67]

> I well know that it is common practice to request specific decrees each time some matter arises which requires investigation, and which will result in a prosecution. But these do not render null and void legal procedures which have been begun by the intendant as a result of the powers confered by his commission, unless these decrees mention the fact ...

Thus as late as 1707 Bodin—as reintepreted by Le Bret—was alive and kicking in Berry, with an assertion by the intendant of the fundamental right of the commissioner to adjudge without appeal, notwithstanding all the practical constraints of political prudence

[66] AN G[7] 127, 19 Jan. 1709. Foullé de Montargis, the new intendant, sent a draft decree with the appropriate power based on those granted to Montgeron, his predecessor, in the case, but with a simple substitution of names.

[67] AN G[7] 127, 18 May 1707.

during the war of the Spanish Succession, and above all the desire not to offend the superior courts which were helping to contribute towards the war effort. Although Montgeron was replaced as intendant in the late summer of the following year, there is no evidence that he was recalled in disgrace. On the contrary, he was transferred to the intendancy of Limousin—neither promotion nor demotion. The intendant, not the minister, had won the argument. However, what the intendant could not do was to overrule the decision of the majority of judges in such cases without appeal, even when he felt that the sentence was too lenient or, as happened in Berry in 1714, too severe.[68]

The case has been argued in this paper that Bodin left a posthumous legacy to the French monarchy, in a concept of the royal commission that in turn permitted the development of the idea of subdelegation. The distinction between the commission and the office, which was first made by Bodin, was fundamental for the later development of the French monarchy and made it, if not unique, distinctive in comparison with its European counterparts, where no such definition had been made. If we take the example of the Spanish Habsburg union of crowns, in 1581 and 1592 Philip II swore to uphold the privileges respectively of Portugal and Aragon and in 1652 Philip IV did so with regard to Catalonia, notwithstanding previous acts of rebellion within these kingdoms. Not until after the establishment of the new Bourbon dynasty were the privileges of the outlying Iberian kingdoms revoked (in 1707), while in 1713 the Catalans still demanded the confirmation of their privileges even though they were in rebellion. They received a stony reply from Philip V's representatives, who echoed Bodin's words that it was not for a king's subjects to treat with their prince.[69] Contractual monarchy was finally dead, and it is symptomatic of Philip V's government that intendants on the French model were introduced after 1711.[70] But the earlier concessions to rebels had served to emphasise the Habsburgs' conception of a contractual monarchy.

However, although the formal introductions of intendants was not made until 1711, there had been precursors in Castile under Habsburg rule. Officials with powers resembling those of the later intendants (*jueces de comisión*) may have been appointed already in the fifteenth century to deal with particular cases. They seem to have been used rather more frequently in the 1590s, although as yet no commission has been found. Their first extensive employment, however, was during

[68] AN G^7 128/130, 16 Aug. 1714.

[69] AN G^7 508, 21 June 1713.

[70] H. Kamen, *The war of succession in Spain, 1700–15* (1969), 115 and references at n. 104, and 390.

Olivares's ministry (1622–43), but even so the powers of the commissioners were restricted in crucial respects,[71] while those of the existing law courts in the localities actually grew in the course of the seventeenth century: 'centralized justice collapsed', it has been said, 'and the settlement of disputes reverted to the community.[72] An example of the restricted powers accorded to royal commissioners in Castile is provided by the 60-day commission granted by Philip IV on 11 July 1627 to Juan de Morales to serve in Jerez de la Frontera, with appeals from his decision to be heard only by the council of finance (*Consejo de Hacienda*).[73] What a curious document it is from the perspective of a French historian! It was issued only six years before some of the most wide-ranging French commissions of intendant, which included considerable powers of prosecution; if there was a time limit on the French intendants, by the 1630s and 1640s it was a three-year and not a 60-day rule.[74] The Spanish commission was, in contrast, an exceptional delegation of closely circumscribed powers—it was desirable that Morales should carry out his delegated tasks in less than 60 days if possible. His commission illustrates Bodin's argument that commissioners were 'tyed vnto the verie words of their commission': Morales was empowered to act in a specific case concerning the tax arrears of Jerez de la Frontera for the years 1611 to 1625. In so far as he had any jurisdiction in Cadiz, Sanlucar de Barrameda and Puerto de Santa Maria, it was merely with respect to this specfic case. In contrast, French commissions, even as early as that of Pierre de Panisse in 1556, were not tied to a specific lawsuit or fiscal problem, but contained general powers as *intendant de la justice*, and later *intendant de la justice, police et finances*; as has been seen, specific attributions of authority were granted separately by decrees of the council.

How are we to explain this discrepancy between Bourbon and Habsburg governing practice in the late 1620s and early 1630s? Clearly, the highly developed conciliar structure in Castile, which was considerably in advance of its French equivalent in the sixteenth century, was an important reason. At its inception, the Habsburg system had been more sophisticated than its counterparts elsewhere,

[71] The author is grateful to Professor Juan Gelabert of the University of Cantabria (Santander) for communicating this information in a letter of 25 November 1988, and for commenting on this article in draft form.

[72] I. A. A. Thompson, 'The rule of the law in early modern Castile', *European history quarterly*, xiv (1984), 221–34, esp. at p. 222. R. L. Kagan, *Lawsuits and litigants in Castile, 1500–1700* (Chapel Hill, NC, 1981).

[73] The author is grateful to Professor Gelabert for sending a copy of this commission in a letter of 20 November 1987. The source is Archivo General de Simancas (Valladolid), Consejo y Juntas de Hacienda, legajo 671.

[74] Bonney, *Political change in France under Richelieu and Mazarin*, 49, 146.

and this may have served to impede subsequent administrative innovation; however, the system failed to evolve and to address itself in the seventeenth century to a new fundamental requirement, the mechanism of contact between the periphery and the centre.[75] Habsburg Spain was stable, it has been said, 'because it was largely self-governing, not because it was governed by an absolute monarchy'.[76] Indeed, in Spain the conciliar structure itself was part and parcel of the contractual nature of monarchy, and served as a limitation on the absolute power of the king[77]—this helps explain the opposition to Olivares's reforming plans and his use of *juntas* composed of his supporters. Doubtless also Philip IV was anxious to avoid alienating the *Cortes* of Castile, which until 1664 enjoyed significant fiscal powers.[78]

Nevertheless, one suspects that the crucial reason for the lack of Castilian intendants on the French model in the lifetime of Philip IV is the absence in Spanish political thought of any real theoretical discussion of the nature and extent of the commission itself. Bodin's ideas failed to make an impact in Spain, except in the diluted form of Botero's *Reason of state*[79] and Justus Lipsius's *Six bookes of politickes or civil doctrine*,[80] which did not discuss the commission. Spanish political thought after Bodin remained contractualist, and free from his central preoccupation with the issue of unlimited legislative sovereignty.[81] It is true that one of its leading theoreticians, Francisco Suárez, categorically dismissed the view that it was possible for the community 'to retain essential power itself', and 'merely to delegate this power to its prince'. On the contrary, he argued, the ruler was not the delegate but the 'proper owner' of his powers; ultimately, the prince was *legibus solutus*, free from the coercive power of the positive laws. On the other hand, according to Suárez, it was lawful for the community to resist its prince, even to kill him, if it had no other means

[75] Kamen, *op. cit.*, 37.

[76] H. Kamen, *Spain in the later seventeenth century, 1665–1700* (1980), 17.

[77] B. Cárceles, 'The constitutional conflict in Castile between the council and the Count-Duke of Olivares', *Parliaments, estates and representation*, vii (1987), 51–9.

[78] C. Jago, 'Habsburg absolutism and the Cortes of Castile', *American historical review*, lxxxvi (1981), 307–26. I. A. A. Thompson, 'Crown and Cortes in Castile, 1590–1665', *Parliaments, estates and representation*, ii (1982), 29–45. Idem, 'The end of the Cortes of Castile', *Parliaments, estates and representation*, iv (1984), 125–33.

[79] G. Botero, *The reason of state* [1589], ed. and trans. P. J. and D. Waley (1956).

[80] J. Lipsius, *Six bookes of politickes or civil doctrine* [1589], trans. W. Jones [1594] in *The English experience*, 287 (Amsterdam/New York 1970).

[81] B. Hamilton, *Political thought in sixteenth-century Spain. A study of the political ideas of Vitoria, De Soto, Suárez and Molina* (Oxford, 1963). G. Lewy, *Constitutionalism and statecraft during the golden age of Spain: a study of the political philosophy of Juan de Mariana, SJ* (Geneva, 1960).

of preserving itself. The right of self-preservation could 'by no covenant be relinquished'.[82]

There was a considerable difference between a relatively cautious absolutism in theory and a much more cautious exercise of power in practice in Spain. In 1622, the president of the council of Castile reminded the king that 'the origin of monarchies was derived from the common approval and election by the people, giving the sovereign power to [one person as a result of an agreement and under conditions], ... in order for him to undertake to maintain [a just power], which is the origin and foundation of peace.'[83] Not surprisingly, the Habsburg monarchs reflected this tradition. It was Philip II who had stated that 'the community was not created for the prince, but rather ... the prince was created for the community'.[84] His successors did not depart greatly from this dictum. Philip IV was reminded by the count of Peñaranda that 'it is the people who raise up and give power to kings for their own defence and preservation ... God did not create kingdoms for the defence of kings but kings for the good of kingdoms'.[85] As Dr Thompson has demonstrated, not only had the king of Castile customarily taken an oath in the *Cortes* to maintain the royal patrimony and to confirm the customs, privileges and liberties of the cities—Philip II, Philip III and Philip IV all did so soon after their accession[86]—but also they had agreed to 'mutual, reciprocal and obligatory' contracts with the *Cortes* which went far beyond petitions of subjects to their king and made the grant of additional taxation conditional on the fulfilment of the contract. In 1642, it was recognised that the *Cortes* had been offered by the crown certain conditions as a 'pact and obligation' and that if these were not honoured then the towns would be freed from contributing to the agreed increases in taxation; on another occasion, it was judged 'very dangerous ... to break with the cities and the ancient custom of these kingdoms'.[87] This was an ascending theory of sovereignty, and a practice of government, which was light years away from Jean Bodin's descending theory, that 'the principall point of soveraigne maiestie, and absolute power, ... consist[s] in giving laws vnto the subiects in generall, without their consent ...'[88]

[82] Skinner, vol. ii., 177–8, 182–4.

[83] Cárceles, *op. cit.*, 56.

[84] H. G. Koenigsberger, 'The statecraft of Philip II', *European studies review*, i (1971), 3.

[85] R. A. Stradling, *Philip IV and the government of Spain, 1621–1665* (Cambridge, 1988), 301.

[86] Thompson, 'The end of the Cortes of Castile', 126.

[87] Thompson, 'Crown and Cortes in Castile', 34–5, 42.

[88] Bodin, *Republique*, 142. *Idem, Commonweale*, ed. McRae, 98.

When writing his *Foundations of modern political thought*, Professor Skinner expressed the hope that by situating the work of the leading political thinkers in 'the more general social and intellectual matrix out of which their works arose' a history of political theory 'with a genuinely historical character' might arise. This would then provide 'a clearer understanding of the links between political theory and practice'.[89] This paper has suggested that the methodology which Professor Skinner advocates, 'the history of ideologies', can at best provide only one half of the answer. A better understanding of the ideas and the ideologists, in his words, 'on what questions they were addressing and trying to answer, and how far they were accepting and endorsing, or questioning and repudiating, or perhaps even polemically ignoring, the prevailing assumptions and conventions of political debate'[90] is certainly necessary. But it is not enough in itself. To achieve the ultimate objective, 'a clearer understanding of the links between political theory and practice', something else is necessary. This is not merely to establish when the foundations were completed for a new concept of the state as 'an omnipotent yet impersonal power'[91] but to ascertain precisely how such a new concept might have been translated into practice. In other words, so far there has perhaps been too great a concentration on the ideology and the ideologists and not enough on the mechanisms by which their ideas were put into effect. Hence the emphasis in this paper, which has been less about Bodin and more concerned with the development of the French monarchy. It remains to be seen whether this methodology will meet with general approval, or be considered an anachronistic exercise of viewing that which the beholder wishes to view. If the legitimacy of the exercise is accepted, then clearly the methodology will have to be refined, although it is by no means clear that a single methodology would be appropriate to the possible impact of all types of political ideas. But what is clear is that political thought can no longer be regarded as a sacrosanct and isolated activity, followed by a few historians with a minority specialist interest, but which is devoid of any importance or relevance to the scholarly pursuits of the majority. And if the history of ideologies has been criticised as insufficient, we may nevertheless be grateful to its leading exponent for having laid the ghost of a narrow, and ultimately sterile, textualist approach which the majority of historians could ignore with impunity.

89 Skinner, vol. i., x, xi, xiii.

90 *Ibid.*, vol. i., xiii.

91 *Ibid.*, vol. ii, 355–6, 358. For the application of this development to France: H. A. Lloyd, *The state, France and the sixteenth century* (1980).

PARLIAMENT AND THE SHAPING OF EIGHTEENTH-CENTURY ENGLISH SOCIAL POLICY

by Joanna Innes

READ 21 APRIL 1989

THIS paper provides a preliminary and exploratory account of some of the ways in which eighteenth-century parliaments helped to shape English social policy.[1] At the heart of this study lie a body of measures, several hundred strong, which came before Parliament in the course of the eighteenth century. These were general rather than local measures, applying to the country as a whole. They dealt with such matters as the relief and regulation of the poor, repression of vice (variously conceived), handling of insolvent (and therefore perhaps imprisoned) debtors, and prevention and punishment of crime.

It is not, I think, generally recognised quite how many measures of this kind were introduced into and considered by Parliament in the course of the eighteenth century. It is true that a substantial proportion of these measures failed: perhaps something of the order of half the total. But several hundred secured the assent of both Houses, and were ultimately promulgated as statutes.

One might have thought that historians would have been moved to enquire into various aspects of the history of this substantial body of laws and projected laws. It is true that some of the questions one might want to ask are most naturally asked of particular measures or groups of measures: questions about why *this* measure at *this* time? But other sorts of questions also suggest themselves, of a more general nature. Thus, what sorts of considerations led people to suppose that problems they perceived were best addressed by legislation? and when it had been decided that legislation should be sought, how were measures of this kind drawn up? and by whom? who introduced such bills into Parliament? how did Members of Parliament set about assessing their merits? and what sorts of considerations determined their success or failure?

Special interest attaches to these questions because, during the

[1] I have received helpful comments and advice on this paper from people too numerous to mention. I am however especially indebted to John Beattie, David Eastwood, Paul Langford, Paul Slack and above all to John Styles, for their sustained interest and encouragement.

eighteenth century, measures of this kind were not, in general, promoted by ministers, or men representing the interests, or acting under the direction of, departments of state—as they had at least sometimes been in earlier centuries, and as they would increasingly commonly be in subsequent centuries. Measures of the sort that we are concerned with were, during the eighteenth century, usually introduced into Parliament by backbenchers. We have here then a body of *general* laws or projected laws, shaping public policy in matters of quite general concern, not (in most cases) evidently serving any organised sectional interest—and yet somehow emerging from the floor of the House, and finding their way, or not finding their way, through Parliament by means that are profoundly obscure.

The object of this paper is to shed some light on these obscure processes—and in this way to add to our understanding of the nature of eighteenth-century English government, and of course (because this is the nature of the subject) to our understanding of the ways in which social issues and social interests were constituted in eighteenth-century England.[2]

Why has this subject not attracted more attention from other historians? And what sort of work *have* they undertaken that bears, in some fairly immediate way, upon it?

Among historians of an earlier generation, Beatrice and Sidney Webb, in terms of their knowledge and the nature of their interests, were undoubtedly best placed to open up an enquiry of this kind. Ironically, however, the Webbs have almost certainly done more than most to deter historians from embarking on any such study.

The Webbs were clearly well aware that eighteenth-century parliaments produced large quantities of legislation bearing on questions of social policy. In the more policy-oriented volumes of their *History of English Local Government*—that is, in their histories of the poor law, prison management and so forth—they provide long and detailed surveys of eighteenth-century statute law.[3] Indeed, they explicitly comment on the sheer volume of Parliament's output. In their history

[2] I exclude all discussion of local bills from this paper not because they are irrelevant to my concerns, but simply because, in a short paper, there are limits to what one can take on. In fact, local issues were very often considered in terms of general *principles*, and ideas generated in the context of local discussions were often subsequently imported into national legislation (and vice versa). Furthermore, the same people were often involved in promoting and refining both sorts of measure. In a fuller discussion, the relation between local and national measures would certainly merit attention I cannot give it here.

[3] S. and B. Webb, *The History of Liquor Licensing in England* (London, 1903), *The Story of the King's Highway* (London, 1913), *English Prisons under Local Government* (London, 1922), *English Poor Law History. Part I. The Old Poor Law* (London, 1927).

of the *Old Poor Law*, they observe that, during the eighteenth and early nineteenth centuries, Parliament produced 'fourscore or so' acts relating to the relief and regulation of the poor, above and beyond the 'hundred or more' local acts which it sanctioned during the same period, laying down rules for the relief of the poor in particular districts.[4]

However, although they recognised that Parliament was active in this sphere, the Webbs expressed very strong reservations about the quality and significance of its activity. Their most serious—that is, most forcefully asserted—charge was that this great mass of legislation was essentially inconsequential: it had next to no effect on the way in which the country was governed in practice.[5] The reason for this, in the Webbs' account, was that the central executive element of English government (that is, the main departments of state) had so tenuous a hold on magistrates, constables, parish officers and so forth—the sorts of men to whom it should have fallen to execute these laws—that they were effectively unable to determine how these men operated. In fact, according to the Webbs, there was not even any comprehensive system for diffusing knowledge of new laws: 'Parliament might pass a law, but it was nobody's business even to communicate the fact to such local authorities as existed.'[6]

If laws had no effect—or an extremely uneven and imperfect effect—it perhaps matters relatively little what their content may have been, except insofar as this provides an index to contemporary aspirations. In fact, however, the Webbs were also unimpressed by the *substance* of most such legislation. How did they account for its poor quality? It appears that they thought that the root of the problem lay in deficiencies in procedures for initiating and handling such bills. Bills of this kind, they noted, were commonly introduced (and presumably drafted) by backbenchers. Such men, they seem to have felt, lacked the *sort* of experience of government that might have equipped them to devise effective measures. Nor, in the absence of any well-developed political science, could such 'amateur legislators' compensate for their lack of practical experience by private study.[7]

The Webbs made no serious attempt to explain why backbenchers should have promoted general laws, or to determine how they went about formulating measures. Nor did they identify these as possibly interesting questions to pursue.

[4] Webbs, *Old Poor Law*, 149.

[5] See e.g. Webbs, *English Prisons*, 25–30; *Old Poor Law*, 99–100, 149–50.

[6] Webbs, *English Prisons*, 29.

[7] For the phrase 'amateur legislators', see *King's Highway*, 75. The issue is not very systematically explored in the Webbs' writings, but see also *English Prisons*, 27–9, 41, 73–5; *Old Poor Law*, 425–7.

The Webbs' *History*—a product of the early part of this century—dominated thinking about many aspects of eighteenth-century English government for several decades. During the past fifteen to twenty years historians of the eighteenth century have broken free of their influence, and opened up many new lines of enquiry. Breaking free of the Webbs has meant, among other things, developing more respect for the skill and effective power of the men who ruled eighteenth-century England.

Especially germane to our purpose are those recent studies which suggest that the whole question of Parliament's role in shaping social policy is worth opening up. In this connection, we might cite first recent work on Parliament itself. Until quite recently, studies of eighteenth-century parliaments commonly focussed on the making and breaking of ministries, nature of party conflict, construction of systems of political influence and the like. Little attention was paid to what we might term the 'business side' of Parliament: to its role in vetting government financial programmes, or to almost any part of its legislative activities, bar a few constitutional and other such controversial measures. By contrast, during the past few years historians have homed in on such topics with a vengeance (as a glance at any issue of the journal *Parliamentary History* will reveal). Sheila Lambert must be given credit for leading the way, with her study of the drafting and processing of private bills, *Bills and Acts*, and her monumental compilation, the House of Commons Sessional Papers of the Eighteenth-Century.[8] A sense that the parliaments in this period were institutions in which serious and complex business was transacted by serious men emerges clearly from all her work. More recently, a stream of articles have traced the careers, in and out of Parliament, of particular bills, and explored the legislative activities of particular M.P.s. Most studies of this kind have focussed on backbenchers. In this historiographical context, the Webbs' low estimate of backbenchers' legislative capacity loses some of its plausibility, though the question posed here—how did backbenchers go about devising and promoting general measures bearing on questions of social policy?—has not, as yet, been more than fragmentarily illuminated.[9]

[8] S. Lambert, *Bills and Acts* (Cambridge, 1971); *House of Commons Sessional Papers of the Eighteenth Century* (145 vols., Wilmington, Dela, 1975–6). O. C. Williams, *The Clerical Organization of the House of Commons 1661–1850* (Oxford, 1954) is a useful older study; see also P. D. G. Thomas, *The House of Commons in the Eighteenth Century* (Oxford, 1971), D. Rydz, *The Parliamentary Agents* (London, 1979), and M. R. Julian, 'English Economic Legislation 1660–1714' (unpubl. M.Phil. thesis, L.S.E., 1979), chs. 1–2. D. Lieberman, *The Province of Legislation Determined* (Cambridge, 1989), 13–28 provides a useful overview of a shifting historiography.

[9] Studies particularly relevant to this paper include E. P. Thompson, *Whigs and Hunters. The Origins of the Black Act* (London, 1975); J. Styles, 'Embezzlement, Industry

Other recent work has dramatically recast our picture of the character and dynamics of what the Webbs termed 'local government' (a term they imported into the eighteenth from the nineteenth century): that is, of the complex network of often part-time and unpaid office holders who carried out the work of government at all but the very highest level. According to the Webbs, during the eighteenth century a great gulf yawned between the central executive and local government. It was because they believed in this gulf that they found it hard to see how acts of parliament could have been more than imperfectly implemented. Recent studies suggest that their account was at fault in at least two significant ways.

First, they underestimated the extent to which there *were* institutionalised links between central government and the localities. Here, a key part was played, in the eighteenth as in earlier centuries (if not in precisely the same way) by the High Court judges, who not only heard civil cases from all over the kingdom in their courts, but also, twice a year, changed their hats and went off around the country on Assize circuits. Service as circuit judges not only brought these men into contact with magistrates and other local officers; in this capacity, they also carried out an important part of the work of government in their own persons, inasmuch as they presided over almost all trials for serious crimes (that is, hanging crimes).[10]

---

and the Law in England 1500–1800', in M. Berg, P. Hudson and M. Sonenscher, ed. *Manufacture in Town and Country before the Factory* (Cambridge, 1983); P. B. Munsche, *Gentlemen and Poachers. The English Game Laws 1671–1831* (Cambridge, 1981); J. M. Beattie, 'London Crime and the Making of the English Criminal Law, 1689–1718', in L. Davison et al. ed. *Reform and Regulation. The Debate over Social and Economic Problems in England 1689–1750* (forthcoming); P. Clark, 'The Mother Gin Controversy in the Early Eighteenth Century,' *supra* 5th series, xxxviii (1988), 63–84; J. V. Beckett, 'A Back-Bench MP in the Eighteenth Century: Sir James Lowther of Whitehaven', *Parliamentary History*, i (1983), 79–97; D. Hayton, 'Sir Richard Cocks: the Political Anatomy of a Country Whig', *Albion*, xx (1988), 221–46, and 'Moral Reform and Country Politics in the Late Seventeenth Century House of Commons', *Past and Present* (forthcoming, 1990). Two studies which shed more general light on the behaviour of MPs as legislators are T. K. Moore and H. Horwitz, 'Who Runs the House? Aspects of Parliamentary Organization in the late Seventeenth Century', *Journal of Modern History*, xliii (1971), 205–27, and P. Langford, 'Property and "Virtual Representation" in Eighteenth-Century England', *Historical Journal*, xxxi (1988), 83–115.

[10] The high court/circuit judges figure remarkably little in the Webbs' study of *The Parish and the County* (London, 1906). Among modern studies, J. Cockburn, *A History of English Assizes 1558–1714* (Cambridge, 1972), is primarily concerned with the pre-Revolutionary period, as is A. Fletcher, *Reform in the Provinces. The Government of Stuart England* (New Haven, 1986). No general study of their role in 18th cent. government exists, but see C. Brooks, 'Interpersonal Conflict and Social Tension: Civil Litigation in England 1640–1830', in *The First Modern Society*, A. L. Beier, D. Cannadine and J. Rosenheim, ed. (Cambridge, 1989); J. M. Beattie, *Crime and the Courts in England 1660–1800* (Oxford, 1986) and N. Landau, *The Justices of the Peace 1676–1760* (Berkeley, 1984).

If on the one hand the Webbs underestimated the strength of institutional links between locality and centre, on the other hand, recent work also suggests, they underestimated the strength and significance of *extra*-institutional links: that is, of informal, social and cultural ties. They seem to have assumed that perhaps even county magistrates, and certainly constables, parish officers and the like, lived for the most part in a narrowly-bounded social world, such that issues that might trouble Parliament were very much less likely to trouble them. This does not seem a plausible picture. It is doubtful it would do as an account of what England was like in the seventeenth century; still less will it do as an account of what it was like in the newspaper-reading, book-club subscribing, party-politically-conscious eighteenth century. Why should local officeholders not being harassed by civil servants have taken the trouble to implement new laws? Often they did so, surely, because they shared the concerns that had prompted Parliament to pass them in the first place.[11]

The Webbs recognised that eighteenth-century parliaments were producing large numbers of laws relating to the treatment of the poor, vagrants, criminals and so forth. But, having little respect for the legislative capacities of backbenchers, and doubting that such laws could have had much impact in practice, they appear not to have thought the processes—formal and informal—by which such laws were produced worthy of study. Recent writing suggests that their scepticism on both counts may have been exaggerated. This being so, we can open our enquiry in good heart.

The discussion which follows has two main parts. The first puts the case for regarding the sorts of measures we will be concerned with here as significant—in two rather different senses. First, it will be noted that they constituted a non-trivial proportion of all measures laid before Parliament and acts passed by Parliament. Secondly, we will cite some examples of acts that not only were ambitious in scope but also in practice made a substantial impact. Some measures that fall within the scope of our enquiry were trivial in content and insignificant in practice. But, *pace* the Webbs, this cannot be said of them all.

The second part of our discussion takes as its starting point the proposition that general measures dealing with matters of social policy were, in the eighteenth century, most commonly the work of back-

[11] See Landau for J.P.s involvement in national political conflict. The extent of political consciousness lower down the social scale remains the subject of dispute. N. Rogers, *Whigs and Cities* (Oxford, 1989), affirms its wide reach, though with qualifications. D. Vaisey ed. *The Diary of Thomas Turner 1754–65* (Oxford, 1984) presents us with a one-time local officer the breadth of whose reading suggests wide horizons.

benchers. A series of questions arise. Is this true? what can have motivated backbenchers to act in this way? and how might an eighteenth-century backbencher set about trying to frame and promote a measure intended to affect the conduct of government throughout the land?

We must be wary of exaggerating the significance of numbers. Some bills occupied many M.P.s for many hours; some passed quickly through small committees and thin houses. Some acts affected thousands of lives; some none. Any attempt to categorise legislation entails making a multitude of more or less arbitrary judgments. Counting bills and acts nonetheless offers us one way of putting our concerns in perspective.

All the figures that follow are approximate, but are probably of the right order of magnitude.[12] Between 1690 and 1790, some 15,000 bills were laid before Parliament. Of these, about four-fifths ultimately issued as statutes; about one in five failed. The class of bills we want to count can be defined partly by elimination, partly by positive definition. Categories of bill we are *not* concerned with include all private and local measures; all fiscal, military and naval measures; all constitutional and religious measures; all forms of economic regulatory legislation. The widest definition of the category of measures that do concern us would include all measures relating to civil or criminal law, or civil administration, not included in one of the categories above.[13] Between 1690 and 1790, about 1,000 bills of this kind were laid before Parliament. Bills of this kind had a higher than average propensity to fail: only about 500 of this 1,000 reached the statute book.

Both our 1,000 bills and our 500 acts were fairly evenly distributed over time. Parliament considered about ten measures of this kind every year, and passed about five.[14] By contrast, numbers of bills and acts in many other categories increased over time. The growth in the number of bills processed owed much to the increasing size of the

[12] John Styles of the University of Bristol, Julian Hoppit of the University of London and I have recently obtained a grant from the Leverhulme Trust to finance research on English legislation 1660–1800. The estimates cited here derive from preliminary surveys, which we should be able to refine when the project is complete. I am grateful to Sheila Lambert for having supplied us with copies of her own working notes, from which these estimates have been in part compiled. All totals are however my own.

[13] Many other bills had a social policy *dimension*, which would entitle them to consideration in a more broadly conceived study. For the purposes of this paper, I have adopted a relatively narrow definition of my subject matter.

[14] Somewhat more acts were passed in years of peace than in years of war, however: no doubt because war-related business always tended to squeeze other matters off the agenda.

government's annual fiscal programme; even more to Parliament's increasing willingness to deal with a large flow of local and private measures. Simple arithmetic tells us that our category of bills and acts must have represented a declining *proportion* of the total: in fact making up about 1 in 10 of all acts at the beginning of the century, 1 in 50 at the end. (The fractions would be larger if the same calculation were made in terms of bills, but the trend would be the same.)

Given fairly constant absolute numbers, there seems no reason to read these trends as evidence of declining parliamentary interest in questions of domestic government. Furthermore, though the number of measures we are talking about was not large, nor were they so few as to warrant dismissal as exceptional items on the parliamentary agenda. The case from numbers alone cannot—and need not—be made more strongly than that.

How ambitious might such measures be in substance? And now significant *were* they in effect? Probably the most ambitious measures falling within the scope of our enquiry were proposals for the comprehensive reform of the poor laws. Attempts to replace the Elizabethan poor laws with a whole new scheme of legislation were made in the 1690s and first decade of the eighteenth century; in the 1730s, 1750s and over several decades in the later eighteenth century, culminating in the 1780s.[15] Bills drafted on these occasions were ambitious in the sense that they were intended more or less comprehensively to supersede a complex mass of existing legislation, *and* in the sense that they proposed to summon into being a whole new tier of administration. Characteristically, these bills anticipated important elements of the Poor Law Amendment Act of 1834, inasmuch as they proposed to create new administrative districts and establish Boards of Guardians. None of these bills passed both Houses, although some major reform bills did pass the Commons.[16]

A complex mix of factors appear to have operated against these bills, but an important stumbling block was almost certainly the proposal to establish new kinds of local authority, a project fraught with troubling political implications, quite apart from its other dis-

[15] Webbs, *Old Poor Law*, 112–14, 126, 265–70, 170–1, 273. S. Macfarlane, 'Studies in Poverty and Poor Relief in London at the end of the Seventeenth Century' (unpubl. D.Phil. thesis, Oxford, 1982), 263–76, and T. Hitchcock, 'The English Workhouse. A Study in Institutional Poor Relief in Selected Counties 1696–1750' (unpubl. D.Phil. thesis, Oxford, 1985), ch. 2 supply fuller accounts of late 17th–18th cent. efforts.

[16] Thus Sir Humphrey Mackworth's 1704 and 1706 bills, and Thomas Gilbert's 1765 bill all passed the Commons, but failed in the Lords.

advantages.[17] Although many *local* bills calling into being new forms of local authority secured the approval of Parliament during the eighteenth century, very few successful general measures even went so far as to create new forms of local officer. Most of the measures we are considering bestowed new powers upon or modified the existing powers of extant public officers and bodies: Commissioners of Gaol Delivery, Justices of the Peace, constables, overseers of the poor and the like.

To pass from the comprehensive reform of the poor laws to even the most ambitious of successful acts is to come down a notch or two on the scale of ambition. Nonetheless, it is not hard to find examples of acts that not merely *set out* to bring about significant changes in the way government operated, but which actually had this effect.

Drawing on the work of John Beattie, we might cite first certain acts relating to the punishment of crime.[18] At the end of the seventeenth and in the first two decades of the eighteenth century, Parliament passed a number of acts providing for new ways of dealing with men and women convicted of clergyable (that is, non-capital) felonies: a sizeable proportion of all convicts. In 1699, an act laid down that men and women claiming benefit of clergy should no longer be branded in the hand, as theretofore, but instead in the face. In 1707, on the grounds that this measure had made the rehabilitation of convicts impossible, Parliament revoked its former order and suggested instead that convicts might be imprisoned in houses of correction. Finally, in 1718, Parliament decided to authorise the transportation of clergied felons.[19]

Quarter Sessions and Assize records suggest that all these acts were speedily acted upon. Thus, at the end of the seventeenth century, there is evidence in many Quarter Sessions records that counties were investing in new branding equipment (commonly described by county clerks as 'engines' for 'burning' criminals)[20]—and, in the aftermath of the 1707 act, we find keepers of houses of correction complaining of

[17] E.g. T. Andrews, *An Enquiry into the Causes of the Encrease and Miseries of the Poor of England* (London, 1738), 8; [T. Gray], *Considerations on Several Proposals lately made for the Better Maintenance of the Poor* (London, 1751), 11, 22–5; *An Impartial Examination of a Pamphlet Intitled, Considerations* ... (London, 1752), 19.

[18] Beattie, *Crime and the Courts*, chs. 9–10. Examples cited here are all drawn from ch. 9.

[19] 10 Will. 3 c. 12; 6 Ann. c. 9; 6 Geo. I c. 23. All references to acts follow *Statutes of the Realm* numeration. Dates cited in the text are those of the year (N.S.) in which the act passed.

[20] Northamptonshire Record Office, Quarter Sessions, Treasurer's Accounts 1 (1669–1746), 1700; Northumberland Record Office, QSO 3, Easter 1700. Such 'engines' cost £3–4.

the trouble and expense involved in housing convicts.[21] True, it seems to have taken a few years for counties to gear themselves up to organise convict transportation. But within five years, transportation had been established as the dominant form of punishment for clergyable felonies, a position it was to retain for more than half a century.[22]

Other examples of relatively ambitious and consequential legislation might be cited in connection with the practice of imprisonment for debt. In the 1720s, Parliament passed a number of acts, designed to alleviate the most troubling consequences of this practice. Orders were given for the break-up of the remaining, already illicit, debtors' sanctuaries. At much the same time, pre-trial arrests for sums of less than 40s were prohibited, and procedures were devised for the release of people imprisoned following court judgments. Tables specifying prison fees were ordered to be drawn up and displayed in every prison; and Parliament also provided a sum of money to buy out the mortgagees of the Fleet prison, and return the prison to public ownership. (The long-term consequences of early Stuart privatisation had come to be judged intolerable.)[23]

It is not easy to gauge the impact of these measures on creditors' appetite for imprisoning debtors, since this period witnessed a secular decline in the frequency with which most forms of civil action were employed.[24] The Vexatious Arrests Act—prohibiting arrests for the smallest debts—may however have contributed to this decline, and this series of acts did more demonstrably have other effects. Commitments for debt in the metropolis, previously out of all proportion to commitments elsewhere, fell precipitately, and were never to return to their previous disproportionate size; several small metropolitan debtors' prisons went out of business; tables of fees were drawn up

[21] J. M. Innes, 'Prisons for the Poor: English Bridewells 1555–1800', in *Labour, Law and Crime*, ed. F. Snyder and D. Hay (London, 1987), 90.

[22] First references to arrangements made for convict transportation commonly appear in Quarter Sessions Order Books in the early 1720s. For the practice in its heyday, see Beattie, *Crime and the Courts*, 506–13, 518–19, 538–48, 560–5; R. Ekirch, *Bound for America. The Transportation of British Convicts to the Colonies 1718–75* (Oxford, 1987).

[23] Relatively little has been published on the practice of imprisonment for debt, but see generally J. M. Innes, 'The King's Bench Prison in the Later Eighteenth Century: Law, Order and Authority in a London Debtors' Prison', in J. Brewer and J. Styles ed. *An Ungovernable People* (London, 1981), 251–61 and P. Haagen, 'Eighteenth-Century Society and the Debt Law', in S. Cohen and A. Scull ed. *Social Control and the State* (Oxford, 1983), 222–47. The reform measures of the 20s have nowhere been comprehensively explored, but see R. L. Brown, 'The Minters of Wapping: The History of a Debtors' Sanctuary in Eighteenth-Century East London', *East London Papers*, xiv (1972), 77–86; L. F. Church, *Oglethorpe: A Study of Philanthropy in England and Georgia* (London, 1932), ch. 3. The acts in question are 9 Geo. 1 c. 28; 11 Geo. 1 c. 22; 12 Geo. 1 c. 29; 2 Geo. 2 c. 22.

[24] Brooks, esp. 365–6.

and displayed in prisons up and down the country—large numbers of them were still to be seen when John Howard made his tour of the prisons fifty years later; and the buying out of the Fleet mortgagees decisively altered structures of power in the major London debtors' prisons.[25]

Or consider the case of vagrancy. In this connection, the most consequential piece of legislation was probably the 1700 Vagrant Removal Costs Act, which shifted responsibility for financing the removal of vagrants from the parish to the county.[26] This Act took speedy effect throughout the country. In the course of the next few decades, its more profound implications gradually became apparent, as Justices of the Peace, made more sensitive to the vagrancy problem by the fact that they were now paying the bills, developed new systems for their removal, often involving the transfer of much of the work to a small number of vagrant contractors.[27]

Finally, the Workhouse Act of 1723 provides an interesting instance of a permissive act which appears nonetheless to have had a significant effect: perhaps partly simply because it served to publicise certain ideas about the potential of workhouses.[28] The decade preceding the passage of the Act had seen a number of influential new workhouse foundations, but after the passage of the Act, a trickle turned into a powerful current. Within fifteen years, there were probably relatively few market towns or populous industrial parishes which had not at least experimented with the establishment of a workhouse.

The Webbs, as we have noted, believed that the character of eighteenth-century government should have made it difficult to implement legislation. Drawing on recent historiography, we have already argued that their assessment of the situation may have been too pessimistic. The examples of relatively ambitious and consequential legislation cited lend support to this case.

But this question merits pursuing a little further. What mechanisms *were* at work, when relatively ambitious legislation was reasonably effectively translated into practice in the eighteenth century? Certainly not the same mechanisms in every case. In some instances, the high court judges, whether acting in their ordinary judicial capacity, or as circuit judges, played a crucial role. We have already argued that it was a deficiency of the Webbs' analysis that they did not make more allowance for the part played by these men. The judges, for

[25] E. Burford, *In the Clink* (London, 1977), 63–5; J. Howard, *State of the Prisons in England and Wales* (Warrington, 1777); Innes, 'King's Bench Prison', 271 and n. 62.

[26] 11 Will. 3 c. 18.

[27] Webbs, *Old Poor Law*, 378–87.

[28] 9 Geo. 1 c. 7. Hitchcock now provides the fullest survey of responses to the act.

example, certainly played a crucial part in securing the implementation of new penal legislation. This they were well placed to do, presiding, as they did, over the conduct of the most serious criminal trials. As we shall see, it may have been standard practice for judges to be consulted in advance before new penal laws were introduced. Against this background, it is scarcely surprising to find them rapidly availing themselves of new laws in the courtroom. Local authorities then had to find the wherewithal to execute these sentences.

It is clear that, in the seventeenth century, circuit judges sometimes brought pressure to bear on local magistrates to make them implement legislation. It was also not unknown for them to act in this way in the eighteenth century—though the fact that all the examples I can cite relate to the upkeep of prisons *may* indicate that, by this date, they operated in this way only in a limited and particular range of contexts. In Essex, in the 1780s, a storm of protest broke out when a circuit judge imposed a fine on the county for failure to comply with a recent statute requiring them to provide a sick room in the county gaol. (Most other counties had promptly complied with the Act.) The local bench contested the judge's right to act in this way, and a fierce legal battle ensued, which terminated inconclusively.[29] This was however not the only instance of a county being fined for failure to maintain its gaol adequately, and not every such fine was contested.[30] It may well be too that, in a much greater number of cases, circuit judges succeeded in persuading local authorities to act, without resorting to coercion (indeed, part of the Essex Justices' complaint was that they had not initially been approached in a more informal way).[31]

Some eighteenth-century statutes were implemented because of the actions of men who might be described as agents of the central executive. In these cases, the Webbs were mistaken because they underestimated this executive's power and reach. But the Webbs' excessive pessimism about the effectiveness of eighteenth-century government and significance of eighteenth-century statute law stemmed also from their tendency to overrate the importance of institutional machinery of this kind. Local authorities very often appear to have complied with new laws simply because they took it for granted that it was their responsibility to do so, or perhaps because (as presumably in the case of the 1723 Workhouse Act) they felt that national legislation effectively addressed their needs.

Local officials may sometimes have been influenced by the know-

[29] R. E. Negus, 'The Jurisdiction of Judges of Assize to Fine a County', *Essex Review*, xxxxvii (1938), 57–67.

[30] E.g. Westmorland Record Office WQ/O 8, 1765 passim.

[31] Negus, 59.

ledge that, if they did not punctiliously conform to law, they laid themselves open to legal actions at the hands of ordinary citizens. In Middlesex in the 1720s and 1730s, rural ratepayers, angered by the size of the contributions they were asked to make towards the cost of removing vagrants (essentially, they argued, an inner-city problem) succeeded in overturning a series of rates the county had not managed to impose in sufficiently unimpeachably legal a fashion. In this case the problem was not so much that the county had failed to pay due heed to legislation, as that existing laws were insufficiently clearly drafted. Middlesex Justices could nonetheless find no way out of the corner they had been backed into but via an application for a new law (the result of their efforts being the procedurally important County Rates Act of 1739).[32] Though it has certain idiosyncratic features, this example does suggest some reasons why local authorities may have thought it necessary to pay meticulous regard to certain sorts of statute law.

It would certainly be wrong to suggest that either simple conformist instincts, or sympathy with the aims of the legislature, or pressure exerted from either above or below between them ensured that all eighteenth-century statutes were promptly and punctiliously observed. Dozens of examples could be cited of eighteenth-century statutes which were either unevenly enforced or indeed altogether ignored.[33] However, it would equally be wrong to suppose that the nature of eighteenth-century government determined that acts were highly unlikely to be implemented. A more discriminating account of the weaknesses of eighteenth-century English government should be capable of explaining why different acts were observed in very differe-nt degrees.

This part of this discussion has concentrated chiefly on demonstrating that some measures of the sort that concern us were very ambitious, and that some were both relatively ambitious and consequential. In the context of the historiography, this seems to be the case that needs to be made. It is not suggested, however, that all our measures were of this kind. To correct the balance, let us close this section by considering a narrowly conceived bill.

In 1723, William Lowndes, who happened to be Secretary to the Treasury, but was also (and in this context more significantly) a resident of Buckinghamshire and Justice of the Peace for the county,

[32] 12 Geo. 2 c. 29. Lambert, *Sessional Papers*, xv. 171–322; *Commons Journals*, xxiii. 217–18, 289–90.

[33] For example, I agree with the Webbs (*English Prisons*, 29) that an act of 1744 ordering Quarter Sessions to appoint two Justices to visit and report on county houses of correction was not generally observed (although many counties did operate more informal supervisory systems).

brought into the Commons a bill proposing to alter the established manner of raising money for the building and repair of gaols. According to Sir Edward Knatchbull, who moved successfully for the bill's rejection, this bill should never have been put forward as a general measure at all, since it related only to a 'contest... in Buckinghamshire ... who should pay the tax, landlord or tenant'. It had been brought in as a public bill only to 'save the charges of a private one ... and so it was rejected nem. con.'.[34]

Trivial or ambitious, effective or not—who introduced such bills into Parliament, and how did they go about framing and promoting measures of this kind?

The Webbs observed that their promoters were commonly backbenchers—an arrangement which they clearly felt left much to be desired. Their basic observation was well-founded. However, by no means every bill emerged from this source, nor in many other cases does 'backbencher' without qualification constitute an adequate characterisation of the man involved.

Both at the beginning and at the end of our period, officers of the central government played some part in drafting and promoting measures relating to the poor, though in neither case was this involvement long sustained. In the late 1690s and first decade of the eighteenth century, the Board of Trade—a body established by royal commission in 1696—was charged by both Crown and Parliament with responsibility for reviewing current arrangements for relieving and regulating the poor, devising new policies, and embodying them in draft laws.[35] However, the Board's interest in such matters did not persist beyond the earliest years of the new century. When the Board's abolition was proposed (and carried) in 1782, one of its members, refusing to defend its record of service, observed in the Commons that, in relation to 'the state of the poor and the method of employing them ... he naturally looked ... (as the public at large did)' to the backbench reformer Thomas Gilbert, 'who on that subject he considered as the only board of trade he knew of'.[36]

In the 1790s, against a background of war and harvest crisis, the

[34] *The Parliamentary Diary of Sir Edward Knatchbull*, ed. A. N. Newman (London, 1963), 18.

[35] I. K. Steele, *Politics of Colonial Policy* (Oxford, 1968), describes the establishment of the board, and provides a (selective) account of its development. For the Board and poor law policy, see Macfarlane, 263–76; Hitchcock, ch. 2. The Webbs' brief account of these matters focusses chiefly on John Locke's proposals to the Board: *Old Poor Law*, 109–12. The Board's proposals did not win parliamentary assent, and indeed, according to one member, led to their being lampooned as a 'Commission of Chimerical Affairs' (G. Jacobsen, *William Blathwayt* (New Haven, 1932), 335).

[36] *Parliamentary History*, ed. W. Cobbett (36 vols., London, 1806–20), xxi. 250.

supposedly deficient state of the poor laws attracted the attention of the Prime Minister, who introduced an (unsuccessful) amending bill in 1796.[37] During these troubled years, leading magistrates represented to the Home Office their desire that ministers should sponsor legislation to coordinate local action, and the newly-founded Board of Agriculture explored the practicability of some particular schemes mooted.[38] Central agencies however once more did not maintain their interest when the immediate crisis was thought to have passed.

Officers of the central government intermittently played a part in promoting measures relating to criminal justice. The Law Officers of the Crown, for example, were sometimes active in this way. In 1717/18, it was the Solicitor General of the day who piloted the Transportation Act through the Commons. Sixty years later, his successor brought in one of the measures designed to cope with the collapse of the transportation system in consequence of the American War.[39]

The Secretaries of State played little part in promoting general domestic legislation before the 1780s. When their offices were reorganised in 1782, however, and the distinct roles of Foreign and Home Secretary established, the Home Secretary quickly came to the fore in promoting certain measures against crime. In 1783, for instance, 'Mr Secretary Townshend' laid two bills before Parliament intended, he said, to improve the police of the metropolis (although the bills were formally national in scope). One proposed to extend the vagrancy laws to cover new categories of suspicious persons; the other proposed that receiving goods obtained by burglary or highway robbery should be made a capital offence.[40]

Central government officers might play a part in formulating legislation even when they did not themselves introduce it. Private members promoting legislation sometimes sought prior advice either from Law Officers, from judges, or indeed from ministers. Members

[37] J. Ehrman, *The Younger Pitt. The Reluctant Transition* (London, 1983), 471–6. T. Ruggles, *History of the Poor* (2 vols., London, 1793), i. pp. vi–vii implies that as early as the late 1780s, public rumour had it that the minister intended to take the matter on, and that meanwhile he 'discountenanced the indigested schemes of private individuals'.

[38] D. Eastwood, 'Governing Rural England: Authority and Social Order in Oxfordshire 1780–1840' (unpubl. D.Phil. thesis, Oxford, 1985), 85. For the Board of Agriculture, Webbs, *Old Poor Law*, 174; R. Mitchison, *Agricultural Sir John. The Life of Sir John Sinclair of Ulbster 1754–1835* (London, 1962), ch. 11. On governmental responses to poverty in the 1790s, see also R. Wells, *Wretched Faces. Famine in Wartime England 1793–1801* (Gloucester, 1988), Part 3.

[39] Beattie, *Crime and the Courts*, 503; *Commons Journals*, xxxix. 963.

[40] *Parliamentary History*, xxiii. 364–5. R. R. Nelson, *The Home Office 1782–1800* (Durham N.C., 1969), charts the early history of the office from an administrative point of view, but is not helpful on the Home Secretary's parliamentary role.

not competent to draft bills for themselves might seek the advice of experienced parliamentary draftsmen, but it seems to have been fairly common for members to consult Law Officers or judges. The correspondence of Lloyd Kenyon, successively Attorney General, Master of the Rolls and Lord Chief Justice of the King's Bench, provides several examples of applications of this kind.[41]

There is some evidence that it was expected that Law Officers and judges should be consulted about certain kinds of bill. When in 1786, William Wilberforce brought a bill into Parliament to authorise the handing of the bodies, not of murderers alone (as was already the practice), but of a wide range of executed felons over to the surgeons for dissection, he was denounced in the House of Lords by Lord Loughborough (then Lord Chief Justice of Common Pleas) for not having followed the usual course and consulted the judges first. According to Loughborough, it was an established custom that all bills relating to criminal justice and its execution should be submitted to the opinion of the judges in the first instance. (In fact, according to Wilberforce's sons, the bill had been drawn up by the Solicitor General, corrected by the Attorney General, and communicated to one of the judges, who had promised to lay it before the rest of the Bench. In their account, Loughborough's criticisms were essentially the product of political pique.)[42]

Bills dealing with the administration of civil or criminal laws which failed in the Commons on their first introduction were sometimes later reintroduced in an amended form in the Lords, whence they passed successfully through all the usual stages, to emerge ultimately as acts.[43] The object of their removal to the Lords seems to have been to allow at least some of the judges to play a formal part in shaping their progress at an early stage. Judges were sometimes formally asked to draft bills on subjects on which it was proving difficult to formulate satisfactory laws. In the early eighteenth century, after several sessions of effort to devise a new poor law that would prove generally acceptable had failed to bear fruit, the House of Lords requested the judges

[41] *HMC* Kenyon, 511, 541; see also City of London Record Office, Rep 95, 189v (Dec. 1690); *Monthly Review*, lxii (1780), 315. Bishop Porteus in his notebook for 1781 (Lambeth Palace Lib. MS. 2099, 20–2) provides a very full account of the series of consultations with magistrates, lawyers, judges and legal officeholders he undertook before introducing a new Sabbatarian bill in that year.

[42] *Parliamentary History*, xxvi. 195–202; R. I. and S. Wilberforce, *Life of William Wilberforce* (5 vols., London, 1838), i. 114–15. See also Lord Hardwicke's strong objections to the introduction of the 1758 Habeas Corpus Bill without adequate consultation with the judges (again an objection with a political edge to it); P. C. Yorke ed. *Life and Correspondence of Philip Yorke, Earl of Hardwicke* (3 vols., Cambridge, 1913), iii. 12.

[43] Thus the act which ultimately passed as 6 Ann. c. 9.

to draft some appropriate measure. Their draft, produced in the following session, in fact proved no more able to command assent than earlier bills had been.[44]

Law Officers and judges were consulted because of their legal expertise—and no doubt also because a bill was unlikely to flourish in the face of their determined opposition.[45] Ministers were probably consulted in some cases because their opposition likewise might sink a bill. There were certainly cases in which ministerial opposition spelt the end of proposed domestic measures. In 1754, the Prime Minister, Henry Pelham, asked the Earl of Hillsborough not to persist with a bill for the radical reform of the poor laws Hillsborough was then promoting, on the ground that it might produce 'similar clamours to that raised against the Jew Bill, then recently repealed'.[46] Hillsborough, a loyal supporter of the government, compliantly abandoned his scheme. In 1782, a bill for the preservation of game was lost when the fall of the North government brought the Marquis of Rockingham and his friends to power. When the bill came up for its second reading, Rockingham's Attorney General 'rose and pointed out the several restraints the bill imposed as intolerable in a free government'. Its promoter promptly offered to withdraw the measure.[47]

Measures of the kind we are considering were sometimes heralded in the King's Speech.[48] Such august expressions of support for at least an attempt to attack a particular problem might seem to betoken ministerial involvement, and probably this was often the case. However, it may not always have been so: the monarch may sometimes have been approached through non-ministerial channels. In 1712, for example, members of the Society for Promoting Christian Knowledge considered asking Mr Auditor Harley (admittedly the brother of the Prime Minister) to ask the Queen to recommend a bill against duelling from the throne 'least,' (as it was observed) 'for want of this

[44] *Lords' Journals*, xvii. 506a.

[45] I have as yet found little evidence that the bishops were much involved, or were often especially consulted, in connection with legislation of this kind, though this is a topic that would bear more investigation. For some traces of their activity, see (for Archbishop Tenison) Lambeth Palace Library MS 640, 221 (a reference I owe to Steve Macfarlane), and W. O. B. Allen and E. McClure, *Two Hundred Years: the History of the S.P.C.K.* (London, 1898), 25; (for Bishop Porteus), R. Hodgson, *Life of the Right Reverend Beilby Porteus* (London, 1813), and Porteus' notebooks, Lambeth Palace Library MS. 2099–2100.

[46] *Parliamentary History*, xviii. 629. For Hillsborough's bill, see Webbs, *Old Poor Law*, 269, for the Jew Bill, T. W. Perry, *Public Opinion, Propaganda and Politics in Eighteenth-Century England* (Cambridge, Mass. 1962).

[47] *Parliamentary Register*, ed. J. Debrett (45 vols., London, 1781–96), vii. 210.

[48] E.g. *Commons Journals*, xiii. 1; xxvi. 298; xxxix. 5.

Precaution, the Bill should undergoe the same fate wth the last'.[49]

It becomes clear that not all measures that concern us were promoted by backbenchers, and even those that were might come before Parliament with some sort of official blessing. It is nonetheless true that the majority were introduced by private members.[50] Yet we must be careful not to overstate the 'amateur' status of these men. Many were notably experienced parliamentarians. In a very useful and suggestive article, published in the *Journal of Modern History* in 1971, T. K. Moore and Henry Horwitz examined the characteristics of the men most active in the Commons in two sessions in the mid-1690s.[51] On this basis of this work, they suggested that we should distinguish between two sorts of active M.P. Some, the more familiar sort, spoke frequently in debate, struck partisan attitudes, and aspired to and were often successful in securing political office. But they also identified a second, less familiar sort of activist: often a rather older man, sitting for a county or open borough, distinguished above all by the frequency with which he brought in legislation, or by his service on drafting and second reading committees. The two sorts of activism were not mutually exclusive.[52] But the basic point—that even among backbenchers, a group of leaders may be distinguished from a group of followers—clearly holds true throughout the eighteenth century.

It must be stressed, furthermore, that while even active backbenchers could not speak and act with the authority of ministers, they often could speak with another sort of authority, which, in certain circumstances and for certain purposes, might give them more weight than a mere minister could hope to command. Their authority might derive from their acknowledged expertise in a field they had made the object of special study: certainly in the later eighteenth century there were men who made themselves experts on such topics as the criminal law or weights and measures.[53] Or alternatively, they might speak with authority derived from extensive practical experience of

[49] *Correspondence and Minutes of the S.P.C.K. relating to Wales 1699–1740*, ed. M. Clement (Cardiff, 1932), 53–4. The Queen did in fact commend the measure, which however did not pass. For her speech, see *Commons Journals*, xvii. 278.

[50] An impressionistic judgment, which the research project described n. 12 will make it possible to test and endow with some precision.

[51] Moore and Horwitz, 'Who Runs the House?'

[52] Sir George Yonge, for example, who was for a time the Younger Pitt's Secretary at War, also frequently displayed an interest in issues of domestic government, in ways that seem to arise from his West Country experience. L. Namier and J. Brooke ed. *History of Parliament. The House of Commons 1754–90* (3 vols., London, 1964), iii. 673–3, fails to mention these interests.

[53] For penal reformers, L. Radzinowicz, *History of English Criminal Law* (5 vols., London, 1948–86), Part 2. For Sir John Riggs Miller's campaign to reform weights and measures, West Yorkshire Record Office, QD 1/218 (copy of circular letter); *Parliamentary Register*, xxvii. 395–403.

local government, a form of experience few ministers could claim. It seems to have been widely assumed in eighteenth-century parliaments (and not unreasonably) that there were a range of questions to which active magistrates were best qualified to speak. Very striking evidence to this effect is provided by a letter written in 1799 to the President of the Board of Agriculture, by a lawyer whose advice the President had sought in connection with a bill for the better upkeep of highways he wished to bring before Parliament. As well as offering detailed comments on the bill, the lawyer urged the President not to bring in the bill himself, on the grounds that 'it would be presumptuous in a man ... who has never acted as a Justice of the Peace to undertake [such] a measure in its commencement ...'[54]

What considerations moved men not officers of the central government to bring in general measures bearing on domestic government? In some instances such men seem to have been acting essentially as good constituency M.P.s: the bills they brought in were intended to combat problems arising in their own neighbourhoods. We have already mentioned two bills with origins of this kind: to wit, the Buckinghamshire Gaol Rate Bill, and the County Rates Bill of 1739, which had its origins in difficulties experienced by Middlesex Justices. The two criminal bills introduced by the Home Secretary in 1783 similarly arose out of metropolitan experience. Some local problems *could* not be tackled by purely local legislation: criminal laws, for example, had always to be national in scope.[55]

Not every general measure arose out of particular local problems, however. To explain what other than experience in their neighbourhoods might motivate men to act, it may be helpful to pay some regard to the rhetoric many of them used, and (in a certain sense at least) accept the claim so many of them made, that they were motiv-

[54] Somerset Record Office, Hancock MSS DD/HC, box 6E, W. Dickinson to Lord Somerville, 1 Feb. 1799. I owe this reference to John Styles. What is probably being suggested in this case is that a private member might be asked to bring in a bill with official origins. This may have been common practice, complicating still further the task of distinguishing official and unofficial effort. [E. Jones], *Observations on the Scheme before Parliament for the Maintenance of the Poor* (Chester, 1776), 22n, suggests that the Judges 'caused' a bill to 'be brought in' abolishing the Elizabethan statutory requirement that every cottage built should have at least four acres of land to it (for most purposes already a dead letter, the old statute had provided the basis for a recent malicious prosecution). In fact this bill was introduced into the Commons by a private member, a Mr Cator.

[55] See also Norfolk Record Office C/S2/7, Fakenham sessions, January 1716/7, suggesting a bill to facilitate the prosecution of horsetheft. H. Zouch, *Hints respecting the Public Police* (London, 1786), 4, notes West Riding Justices' desire for legislation against nightpoaching (an issue also of concern to Norfolk justices: see Munsche, 25–6). For a case-study and discussion, Beattie, 'London Crime'.

ated by a desire to promote the public good. The point is not that such claims sufficiently explain the *content* of measures proposed. 'The public good' is an essentially contested concept, and every measure we are concerned with embodied some highly particular, eminently contestable vision of what this good might consist in. However, this rhetoric may help illuminate the forces impelling particular individuals to act. Some men who distinguished themselves by promoting general measures were men the general tenor of whose lives suggests that they were governed by a strong sense of public duty—sometimes founded in powerful religious convictions (a point interestingly developed by David Hayton in a forthcoming essay).[56] More cynically, we might observe that one sort of parliamentary career strategy entailed persistent dedication to promoting 'improvements' in law and local government. Men who acted in this way might hope for public acclaim. 'His name should be written in letters of gold,' pronounced Sir Gregory Page Turner of the poor law reformer Thomas Gilbert in 1788.[57] But it was also possible to hope for more material recompense. Gilbert himself had been more materially rewarded for his parliamentary labours a little earlier in the same decade, when he had secured appointment as Chairman of Ways and Means: a post carrying a handsome salary.[58]

Neither support for nor opposition to particular measures of social policy necessarily reflected other political commitments in this period. But neither was activity of this kind always politically innocent. Opposition M.P.s might promote such measures partly in order to gain credit for themselves among backbenchers: by presenting themselves as devotees of the public good, they might hope to dramatise their own merits as against those of tax-squandering ministers. In the Parliament of 1727–34, opponents of Walpole made great play of the need for reform in the nation's legal institutions. Their efforts bore various fruits, including not only some of the acts relating to imprisonment for debt mentioned earlier, but also the act which finally established English, rather than Latin, as the sole language of the law.[59] In the 1770s and 80s, the interest some Rockinghamite and

[56] Hayton, 'Moral Reform'.

[57] *Parliamentary Register*, xxii. 277.

[58] Namier and Brooke, ii. 499–501. For other legislative initiatives of Gilbert's, see Webbs, *King's Highway*, 73, 121; G. Best, *Temporal Pillars* (Cambridge, 1964), 217. Sometimes it was not M.P.s themselves, but their constituents who were full of zeal for the public good. See *Parliamentary History*, xxxvi. 1060; *Parliamentary Register*, xxiii. 105–6.

[59] Research on the parliament of 1727–34, undertaken for a University of Leicester Ph.D. by Andrew Hanham, now of the History of Parliament Trust, should do much to illuminate these machinations. Some aspects of the law reform movement of this period are briefly discussed in G. Aylmer, 'From Office-Holding to Civil Service: the Genesis of Modern Bureaucracy,' *supra* 5th ser., xxx (1980), 99–102.

Chathamite M.P.s displayed in the reform of the criminal law may similarly have had a political edge to it.[60]

Some M.P.s who set out to promote general measures seem almost to have drawn their causes out of a hat. But others' concern arose out of their prior involvement with voluntary societies formed to promote particular forms of social or moral improvement. Societies of this kind commonly devoted most of their efforts to an immediate assault on social problems. But when their leaders became convinced that new legislation might help them to attain their ends, they might also turn their attention towards Parliament. If there were M.P.s among their number, these men were of course likely to be asked to bring in appropriate bills. Otherwise, some prominent figure judged likely to be sympathetic would be approached.

The earliest society I have identified as being active in promoting legislation in this way was the Society for the Promotion of Christian Knowledge, the S.P.C.K., founded in 1698. Bills promoted by the S.P.C.K., some of which were successful, some of which were not, included bills for the repression of blasphemy, debauchery and duelling (as previously mentioned), and for the provision of religious services in prisons.[61] It was noted in 1708 that the Society hoped that 'as soon as the Legislature can find leisure to attend to so difficult a work', some steps might be taken to further the general provision of education for the poor, but apparently Parliament never enjoyed sufficient leisure to turn its mind to this task.[62]

At the end of the century, the Society for the Enforcement of His Majesty's Proclamation against Vice and Immorality, or Proclamation Society, defined its brief as widely as the S.P.C.K. It promoted bills relating to prisons, vagrants, liquor licensing, apprenticeship and the observance of the Sabbath.[63] Other societies had narrower aims. The Thatched House Society for the Relief of Small Debtors, for example, founded in 1772, operated initially as a charity,

[60] Debates on the criminal law in the early 1770s are best traced in the Cavendish diaries. J. Wright ed. *Sir Henry Cavendish's Debates of the House of Commons* (2 vols., London, 1841–3) and British Library, Egerton MSS 215–63; thereafter in the *Parliamentary History* and *Parliamentary Register*, though these may be supplemented by reports from a variety of newspapers and diaries. J. Brewer, 'The Wilkites and the Law 1763–74', in Brewer and Styles, is of related interest. See esp. 160–1, 163.

[61] For blasphemy and debauchery, G. V. Portus, *Caritas Anglicana, or an enquiry into ... religious etc. societies ... 1678–1790* (London, 1912), 61, 66. *S.P.C.K. and Wales*, 83 ff, 93 notes activity in relation to duelling and prisons. See also Hitchcock, 115–27; Clark, 74–7.

[62] J. Chamberlayne, *Magnae Britanniae Notitia* (London, 22nd ed., 1708), 276.

[63] J. M. Innes, 'Politics and Morals: the Reformation of Manners Movement in Later Eighteenth-Century England', in E. Hellmuth, ed. *The Transformation of Political Culture in Late Eighteenth-Century England and Germany* (Oxford, forthcoming, 1990), esp. 96–7.

supplying funds to buy insolvent but worthy debtors out of prison. But experience acquired by investigating the cases of such debtors persuaded its leaders that existing law was seriously defective. Accordingly Lord Beauchamp, one of the Society's Vice Presidents, brought several bills into Parliament to amend the law.[64]

Certain difficulties might have been expected to confront backbenchers who set about trying to formulate general laws to guide the operations of government. How could such men inform themselves adequately about the current state of practice? And how could they feel confident that the regulations they proposed would be acceptable, practicable and effective? In fact, under eighteenth-century conditions, difficulties such as these did not confront backbenchers alone. Such ministers as took an interest in questions of social policy also characteristically had little in the way of staff to research problems and explore the relative merits of various forms of remedy for them—although, in the case of measures relating to the administration of criminal or civil law, judges and experienced lawyers were presumably quite well placed to diagnose problems and suggest solutions.

Private members proposing ambitious pieces of legislation—bills designed comprehensively to overhaul the poor laws, for example—often publicly professed their sense of their unfitness for the task confronting them.[65] Their modest disclaimers were no doubt in part conventional gestures, and in part devices to help them cope gracefully with criticism. But to some extent such protestations must be taken at face value. Private members probably did often feel ill-equipped to devise and bring to fruition major legislative projects.

One possible strategy for a man in these circumstances was to trust that his own deficiencies might be compensated for by the expert advice he might procure in the course of the parliamentary process. He might seek to have even the substance of his measure largely supplied for him by others. Thus, an M.P. might approach an experienced lawyer—a public officeholder or otherwise—with only the vaguest notion of what he wanted to accomplish, trusting to the lawyer's practical experience and expert knowledge to flesh out the

[64] The best account of the Thatched House society and Beauchamp's legislative efforts is P. Lineham, 'The Campaign to Abolish Imprisonment for Debt in England 1750–1840' (unpubl. M.A. thesis, Canterbury N.Z., 1974), 89–101, 110–11, 135–41. See also D. Owen, *English Philanthropy 1660–1960* (Cambridge, Mass., 1964), 63–5; the several *Reports* of the Society, and *Parliamentary History*, xx. 1395–1406. For an initiative undertaken somewhat further down the social scale, see an interesting series of efforts by friendly societies to combine to obtain legislation securing their position, *Manchester Journal*, 23 Jan. 1779; *York Courant*, 21 Nov. 1786; *St James Chronicle*, 31 July, 9 Oct., 18 Nov. 1790 (I owe these latter references to Peter Clark).

[65] E.g. *HMC* Townshend, 376; *Parliamentary Register*, xxii. 211.

scheme for him.[66] Alternatively, the would-be progenitor of a measure might feel it within his reach to produce the outline of a scheme, but bring it into Parliament with very little commitment to the details of his own plan, in the hope that it might be hacked into more promising shape in committee, or indeed on the floor of the House.[67]

Contemporary comment suggests what one might anyway suppose, that debates on bills of the kind we are concerned with were not on the whole very well attended. But that is not to say such bills might not be subjected to well-informed, wide-ranging and probing criticism. Discussion seems often to have been dominated by lawyers and experienced magistrates; sometimes other M.P.s who took a special interest in or had made a special study of some matter might take an active part. A mere handful of such men might provide a very effective vetting team. At the committee stage especially, they might take a bill in hand and very substantially recast it.[68]

These eighteenth-century parliamentary processes are difficult to penetrate. Committee minutes were by and large destroyed in the fire of 1834, and newspapers very rarely carried reports of debates on such matters before the 1770s. It is possible to gain some insights into the character of discussion, however, from parliamentary diaries, correspondence, and newspaper reporting *from* the 1770s. Pamphlets sometimes make at least passing reference to discussions in Parliament, and something can be inferred from the study of successive versions of bills, when these survive. What the scanty surviving evidence does suggest is that it would be a mistake to suppose from the sparseness of the sources alone that well-informed and critical debate was not taking place.

One example will illustrate the form a critical intervention might take. The parliamentary diary of William Hay, M.P. for Seaford (Sussex) under Walpole, includes among its entries some accounts of speeches made by Hay.[69] One of these sets out his views on a bill laid before Parliament in 1733, which proposed to make the offence of 'assault with intent to rob' (not previously defined as a distinct form of assault) punishable by transportation. By Hay's own account, his criticisms of the bill were wide-ranging and vigorous. He argued that it would be difficult to prove the intent; that the bill would

[66] E.g. *HMC* Kenyon, 511, Peter Davies to Lloyd Kenyon.

[67] Thomas Gilbert, for instance, showed himself very willing to modify his original notions substantially in the light of discussion.

[68] For the role Joseph Jekyll, Master of the Rolls, played in recasting William Hay's poor law reform bills, see [Hay], *Remarks on the Laws Relating to the Poor with Proposals for their Better Employment* (London, 1751), p. v.

[69] Northamptonshire Record Office, Hay MSS L (C) 1732–3. For the speech cited here, see L (C) 1732, entry for 13 March 1733/4.

consequently open the way to malicious prosecutions; that it was improper to make assault with intent to rob a transportable offence, when assault with intent to maim, ravish or murder were not so; and that in any case, fine or imprisonment—the punishments currently available in cases of assault—were more appropriate than transportation, in part because they could be more precisely calibrated to the severity of the offence. This is a striking fragment because almost no other accounts of parliamentary debates on bills relating to criminal justice survive from before the 1770s, and it has sometimes been supposed that such bills were not critically scrutinised before that date.[70] However, it seems unlikely that Hay's intervention was unique in kind. Hay was Chairman of East Sussex Quarter Sessions, a senior and experienced magistrate. His views may well have been heard with respect. The bill did not pass.

Bills might be scrutinised in the light of the knowledge and experience Members of Parliament could bring to bear. But certain formal steps could also be taken to enhance the stock of knowledge at Parliament's disposal. Select committees might go on investigatory trips (to London debtors' prisons, for example) or people might be summoned to testify.[71] It has been said of those examined by nineteenth-century select committees that they were usually pre-selected to prove a case. My impression is that in the eighteenth century this might have been defended as appropriate practice. The object of summoning people was as often as not to demonstrate the need for legislation: so witnesses might have been summoned by a court of law, in the expectation that their evidence would support one side of a case. Thus, when 'Mr Secretary Townshend' was trying to persuade the Commons of the need to strengthen police powers is dealing with suspicious persons, in 1783, 'two patroles and a thieftaker' were summoned to the bar of the House, to testify that they had recently taken up people in the night with offensive weapons on them.[72]

As well as or instead of calling people to testify, Parliament might call for information in writing. In the first half of the eighteenth century, it was standard practice for Parliament to call for accounts and papers in connection with not only political and diplomatic, but also fiscal and economic questions. During the second half of the century, it became increasingly common for Parliament to call for the systematic compilation of data to inform its discussions of social

[70] For fuller discussion, J. M. Innes and J. Styles, 'The Crime Wave: Recent Writing on Crime and Criminal Justice in Eighteenth-Century England', *Journal of British Studies*, xxv (1986), 420–30.

[71] E.g. *Knatchbull Diary*, 88, 89. A painting by Hogarth, depicting a debtor giving evidence before the 'Gaol Committee', is held by the National Portrait Gallery.

[72] *Parliamentary Register*, x. 65.

policy.[73] Thus, in 1751, Parliament launched an enquiry through Quarter Sessions into expenditure on the relief of the poor and removal of vagrants; in 1765, sheriffs were asked to return lists of prisoners for debt in every county, with details of the claims made against them, and in 1776, Parliament first attempted the collection of certain criminal statistics. Collecting data in such cases was commonly a matter of asking the relevant official to compile retrospective statistics from his records, and the returns secured were usually fairly comprehensive.

Though Parliament might take steps to inform itself, it might also find information, and opinions, thrust upon it. Those who felt that proposed legislation impinged upon their interests might petition Parliament, have printed 'Cases' distributed to members, or even retain counsel to put their case at the bar of the House. Among the sorts of measures we are concerned with, those which bore upon the practice of imprisonment for debt were by far the most likely to provoke such representations. Court and prison officials, creditor interests and imprisoned debtors themselves all repeatedly employed one or more of these techniques to press their views upon legislators.[74]

The law relating to imprisonment for debt was also the subject of lively pamphlet debate from as early as the mid-seventeenth century.[75] Pamphlet debate on the pros and cons of the poor laws, and ways in which Parliament might amend them, took its rise from the late 1670s.[76] A pamphlet debate on criminal law and punishment was rather slower in taking shape. Although miscellaneous pamphlets appeared earlier, a real debate can scarcely be said to have developed before the 1770s.[77] By that time, pamphlets were no longer the only or chief medium through which such debates were pursued. Essays on these topics were also carried in magazines, and sometimes in newspapers.[78]

[73] Lambert, *Sessional Papers*, i. 54–71, provides the best general account of Commons' practice in calling for accounts and papers. Her volumes i–ii list all accounts and papers requested.

[74] E.g. *HMC* House of Lords MSS 1695–7, 396–409; *The Case of the Mortgagees of the Office and Fees of Office, of Marshal of the Marshalsea of the Court of King's Bench* (nd [1753]) (BL: 357 d 10/45); *Parliamentary History*, xx. 1395–9. For examples relating to the poor laws, *Proposals for the Better Management of the Affairs of the Poor* (nd, [169?])—a four-page pamphlet, apparently written for distribution to M.P.s, of which a copy survives in the Clark Library, Los Angeles; E. E. Butcher ed. *Bristol Corporation of the Poor* (Bristol, 1932), 117.

[75] D. Veall, *The Popular Movement for Law Reform 1640–60* (Oxford, 1970), 142–51.

[76] Pamphlets by Sir Matthew Hale, Sir Josiah Child, Thomas Firmin and others, adumbrating many of the issues which would inform discussion over succeeding decades, were all published within a few years during the late 1670s and early 1680s.

[77] Radzinowicz, i. Part 3; Beattie, *Crime and the Courts*, 548–59, 569–73, 585–6.

[78] Daniel Defoe repeatedly attacked early 18th cent. poor law reform proposals in

By no means all essays and pamphlets which dealt with these topics placed parliamentary action at the centre of their concerns. But a strikingly large number did. Many addressed themselves to specific measures currently or recently under consideration by Parliament. Many pamphlets were dedicated, either to Parliament or the House of Commons as a whole, or to specific M.P.s. The growth of a wider public debate around questions of social policy reflects the development of a historically-specific kind of 'public opinion', associated with a particular sort of media infrastructure. But the part Parliament played in shaping this development, by providing both issues for discussion and an audience that seemed worth addressing ought not to be ignored.

From the beginning of the eighteenth century, and indeed from a much earlier date, M.P.s had no doubt been in the habit of seeking opinions from friends, acquaintances, neighbours, constituents and other interested parties as to the merits and limitations of measures they were currently considering.[79] Bills were sometimes printed to facilitate their circulation to a wider audience. When William Hay was promoting poor law reform in the 1730s, he claimed that his object in encouraging the Commons to discuss the report of a committee he had chaired was 'that Gentlemen might know the Sense of the House, and afterwards consult their neighbours in the country in order for a Bill another Sessions'.[80]

In the last few decades of the century, some M.P.s attempted to extend and to systematise such forms of consultation. Thomas Gilbert was especially remarkable for his efforts in this vein in connection with *his* campaign for the reform of the poor laws, pursued from the mid 1760s through to the late 1780s. Gilbert ultimately failed to obtain the comprehensive reform he sought. But this was certainly not for want of effort to ascertain what sorts of reform men experienced in and knowledgeable about local government might judge practicable and desirable.

---

his *Review* (Hitchcock, 39), as well as writing an important pamphlet on the subject. The Manchester magistrate T. B. Bayley, who published a series of letters commenting on Gilbert's poor law reform proposals in the *London Chronicle* Jan.–Apr. 1787, commented in the first of these (Jan. 25–7), that he thought he could better gain the attention of the public by writing for a newspaper than by publishing a pamphlet.

[79] See, for example, for various forms of consultation undertaken by Edmund Burke, in connection with a bill he had drafted to punish the plunderers of wrecks. T. W. Copeland ed. *Correspondence of Edmund Burke* (9 vols., Cambridge, 1958–70), iii. 140–1, 145, 222, 258.

[80] N'hants RO, L (C) 1733, entry for 2 May 1735. In 1736, the Commons ordered that Hay's bill be printed in sufficient numbers to supply all members: *Commons Journals*, xxii. 717. Hitchcock, 244 notes that the S.P.C.K. distributed copies of Hay's bill to their corresponding members.

Gilbert developed his consultative techniques as he went along. By the late 1780s, he had brought them to a high pitch of elaboration. His procedure by this point was to begin by circulating an outline of his current reforming scheme as widely as possible, especially among active magistrates, with a request for comments. He then introduced a bill towards the end of the parliamentary session, and had it printed, so that it might circulate in the country during the summer. Magistrates were invited to consider the bill at Quarter Sessions or some special meeting, and to make their opinion known.[81] It is clear that such meetings were held in several counties on several occasions during the 1760s, 70s and 80s.[82] Gilbert then brought a version of the bill amended in the light of comments received before Parliament in the next session. It should be stressed that Gilbert did amend his original scheme of the 1760s very considerably in the light of critical comments elicited in these various ways.

At the end of the 1780s, the Proclamation Society adopted a rather different approach to systematising consultation with experienced magistrates. They invited every county bench to nominate two from among their number as delegates to attend a convention to be held in London in the spring of 1790, where certain legislative schemes were to be considered. Most counties did nominate delegates, and the convention was duly held. The Society's executive committee laid two proposals for bills—one dealing with prisons, one with vagrants—before the assembled magistrates, and amended their proposals in the light of the magistrates' comments. Both bills were laid before Parliament, and both ultimately passed, though only in a further amended (and in one case, very much further amended) form. A second conference was planned for 1791, and several counties also nominated delegates to attend this, but, for some reason as yet unclear, the second convention never met.[83]

Reviewing the question of whether or not eighteenth-century legislation bearing on general questions of social policy was implemented, in an earlier part of this discussion, we observed that the Webbs may have overstated the need for a strong executive. Consideration of the ways in which such legislation was *generated* prompts a similar reflection. Although officers of the central executive played some part in shaping such legislation, very often the initiative was taken by backbenchers. A considerable number of general measures were

[81] T. Gilbert, *Heads of a Bill for the Better Relief and Employment of the Poor* (Manchester, 1786); *A Plan of Police, and Objections ... Stated and Answered* (1786); *Considerations on the Bills for the Better Relief and Employment of the Poor &c &c Intended to be Offered to Parliament this Session* (London, 1787).

[82] E.g. *York Courant*, 12 Dec. 1786, 23 Jan. 1787.

[83] Innes, 'Politics and Morals', 94–5.

initiated in this way, critically assessed, and amended in the light of criticisms received. The ways in which the need for legislation was ascertained, and its appropriateness evaluated, were no doubt rather rough and ready: these procedures were not indeed without their contemporary critics.[84] However, the procedures adopted were more sophisticated than might have been imagined. It is unclear that, had officers of the central executive more consistently taken a directing role, the outcome would have been vastly different—or indeed that *any imaginable* eighteenth-century central executive department would have been much better placed to undertake these tasks.

To conclude, let us reflect on the implications of this account in two sorts of general context. First, we might ask how this account might be fitted into a more chronologically extended survey of the changing ways in which English social policy has been shaped. During the late sixteenth and early seventeenth centuries—and indeed even into the later seventeenth century—the Privy Council clearly played some part (and at periods perhaps a predominant part) in shaping social policies. Acts of Parliament bearing on questions of social policy passed throughout this period may have been little more than the instruments the Council used to achieve its ends—although at least some seem to have been spontaneously generated within Parliament, and in every case the laying of a bill before Parliament gave men with experience of local government or with ideas on the subject a chance to speak their piece and to influence the character of measures.[85]

It has sometimes been supposed that when the Privy Council withdrew from the field, Parliament lost its sense of direction in these matters, or used its power only for very narrowly-conceived and sectional ends: that is, chiefly to protect the property claims of the landed gentry.[86] The Webbs' account can be fitted quite well into this sort of story. This situation began to change (this sort of account may go on) only in the late-eighteenth and early-nineteenth centuries. Change at that date was partly a result of pressures exerted on existing arrangements by social and economic change, but also had to do with

[84] E.g. B. White, *An Inquiry into the Management of the Poor* (1767), 64, suggested that instead of laws relating to 'public manners' being introduced 'casually ... by any public spirited member, a standing committee should be appointed for that great and important service'. (I owe this reference to Donna Andrew.)

[85] G. Elton, *The Parliament of England 1559–1581* (Cambridge, 1986); P. Slack, *Poverty and Policy in Tudor and Stuart England* (London, 1988), ch. 6, esp. 117; C. Russell, *Parliaments and English Politics 1621–1629* (Oxford, 1979), 35–48, esp. 45 ff.

[86] E.g. U. Q. R. Henriques, *Before the Welfare State* (London, 1979), 4 ff. See also the passages cited by Lieberman, 6, 28.

the rise, from the later eighteenth century, of a new species of public figure: the humanitarian reformer—Gilbert and Wilberforce being specimens of the type; and also, a little later in the day, with the appearance of reform-minded administrators, as represented pre-eminently by Edwin Chadwick.[87]

In contrast to the account just sketched, the account provided in this paper suggests that the early and mid-eighteenth century cannot be dismissed as a mere caesura. As the executive relaxed its grasp on social policy, Parliament, to a limited but not insignificant extent, assumed a directing role. Nor can this role adequately be characterised as consisting of no more than a set of reflex actions by landed gentlemen concerned to defend the social status quo. There is a story still to be told about when and how Parliament came to take on the part it was playing even at the beginning of our period (perhaps this story might be called 'The Winning of the Initiative by the House of Commons'?).

Looking to the other end of the story: developments *during* the eighteenth century should be seen as having provided the matrix out of which developments at the end of the century were to emerge. The humanitarian reformers of the late eighteenth century were not a new species of men, even though they had some distinctive attributes. Rather they were the latest representatives of a line of backbench activists. When, in the late eighteenth century, the executive, chiefly in the form of the Home Office, began to take more responsibilities upon itself, it took over certain practices pioneered by Members of Parliament: for example, the compilation of criminal statistics as an aid to policy making.[88]

If the lines along which effective responsibility for shaping social policy developed have been misrepresented, this is surely because many historians have followed the Webbs in assuming that significant social policy must be devised and implemented by a powerful executive. Once we modify this assumption, we can tell the story differently.

A second general issue to be considered concerns the relation between the aspects of government treated here and other forms of state power. In his recent book, *Sinews of Power*, John Brewer has explored those late seventeenth and early eighteenth-century governmental developments which made possible England's rise to great power status.[89] The eighteenth-century English state is misrepresented, Brewer observes, when it is portrayed as a weak state, for in

[87] O. Macdonagh, *Early Victorian Government 1830–1870* (London, 1977), ch. 1.

[88] Nelson, 61–2.

[89] J. Brewer, *Sinews of Power. War, Money and the English State 1688–1783* (London, 1989).

fact in terms of its ability to mobilise money and military force, it was notably effective: quite as effective as any of the absolutist states. It might be thought that the argument presented here represents the other side of coin from Brewer's, and in a sense this is so: in both cases it is urged that we should be wary of underestimating the capacities of eighteenth-century English government.

However, the arguments are also significantly distinct. John Brewer is concerned above all to trace the growing power of the executive element in English government, as manifested above all in its ability to mobilise money and military force. This paper has explored ways in which government was able to function fairly effectively *even without* the executive playing a large part. If both the executive and, in certain respects, the legislative components of eighteenth-century English government were somewhat more effective than has always been allowed, those two circumstances may be no more than contingently related. In this connection it would no doubt be illuminating to develop some comparisons between England and other eighteenth-century European states. But that is an exercise for another occasion.

THE BARONIAL CONTEXT OF THE ENGLISH CIVIL WAR

The Alexander Prize Essay

By J. S. A. Adamson

READ 19 MAY 1989

WHEN rebellion broke out in England in 1642, the political nation had been, for over a decade, obsessed with medieval precedent and its gothic past. Practices and institutions which had seemed defunct revived, during the 1630s, into new and sometimes controversial life. Trial by combat was reintroduced in appeal of treason in 1631,[1] and confirmed by the judges in 1637 as a legitimate legal procedure even in disputes of property;[2] in 1636 a bishop was appointed to the Lord Treasurership for the first time since the reign of Edward IV;[3] in 1639 England went to war without the summons of a Parliament for the first time since 1323;[4] and the following year the Great Council of Peers met, for the first time since the reign of Henry VIII,[5] to deal with a revolt of the Scottish nobility. At Court, the king was encouraging a gentleman of his Privy Chamber, Sir Francis Biondi, in his labours on a massive survey of the baronial struggles in England from Richard II to Henry VII—a work which, when it appeared in 1641 as *The Civill Warres of England*, was shortly to be endowed with a profoundly ironic topicality.[6]

This essay is an attempt to understand how the contemporary fascination with precedent influenced English politics during a decade in which rebellion affected all three of Charles I's monarchies. It

[1] College of Arms, Arundel MS LIV (Procs. in the Court of Chivalry, 1631–2); Bodleian Lib., MS Additional c. 79 (notes of the trial of Lord Reay); P. H. Hardacre, 'The Earl Marshal, the Heralds, and the House of Commons, 1604–41', *International Review of Social History* ii (1957), 106–25; H.M.C., *Mar and Kellie MSS* (1904), 184–192.

[2] Cambridge University Lib., Add. MS 7569 (misc. 17th cent. papers), ff. 41–3; *Claxton v. Lilburne*, printed in J. Rushworth, *Historical Collections* (8 vols, 1680–1701), ii. 788–90.

[3] William Juxon was appointed Lord Treasurer in 1636; the last bishop to hold the office was William Grey, bishop of Ely, who was Lord Treasurer 1469–70.

[4] C. S. R. Russell, *The Fall of the British Monarchies* (Oxford, forthcoming).

[5] Bodleian Lib., MS Tanner 91, f. 187 (historical notes, *c.* 1640).

[6] Sir Giovanni Francesco Biondi, *An History of the Civill Warres of England, betweene the two Houses of Lancaster and Yorke* (2 vols, 1641–6).

seeks to address two central questions: how did the contemporary preoccupation with medieval precedent affect the terms in which the aristocratic leadership in the civil war defined their conduct and comprehended their experience? And, in particular, how did the attempt to find historically validated solutions to the problem of the 'evil counsels' of Charles I—a problem which was itself defined in medievalised terms—affect the nobility's choice of political options in that decade of civil war?

The definition of the conflict in terms of a baronial war was not one confined to the particular outlook of the parliamentarian nobility. The king set up his standard at Nottingham, not against his Parliament, but against the 'late rebellion of the Earl of Essex': so his August ultimatum to Parliament declared; so royal pronouncements reiterated throughout 1643.[7] Whatever the truth of this as the *casus belli*, at the outset of the war Essex was widely regarded both as the leader and the personification of the parliamentarian cause.[8] Essex's ascendancy as parliamentarian commander-in-chief entailed a concentration, in the hands of a single individual, of political and military power within the kingdom which had not been seen since the early sixteenth century. It brought with it not only an aristocratic reaction against this over-mighty subject, but also, in its wake, a profound change in the English nobility's attitude to its military tradition—the tradition in which the power and obligations of the nobility were nowhere more honourably exemplified than in the profession of arms and in the command of armies in the field.

I

It is, of course, a commonplace that in early modern England history was the tutor of politics.[9] History provided the frame of reference within which the dilemmas of the present could be compared and

[7] See the king's proclamation of 9 Aug. 1642; and his offer of pardon to the rebels at Edgehill, 24 Oct. 1642: *An exact collection of all remonstrances* ([Husbands's collection], 1643), 503–7, 673; cf. the king's proclamation of 27 Oct. 1642, ibid., 675–7. *Two speeches spoken by the earl of Manchester, and Jo. Pym* ([13 Jan.] 1642[3]), 9.

[8] Essex's role in the parliamentarian war effort is discussed below, 105–16.

[9] Cf. Barnabe Barnes, *Fovre books of offices: enabling privat persons for the speciall seruice of all good princes* (1606), 168. Degory Whear, *Relectiones hyemales, de ratione et methodo legendi utrasque historias* (Oxford, 1637). Whear was Pym's tutor at Oxford; and the first edition of the work, in 1625, was dedicated to William, 3rd earl of Pembroke: (1625 edn), sig. ¶2. See aso, D. R. Woolf, 'Change and continuity in English historical thought, c. 1590–1640', (unpublished D. Phil. thesis, University of Oxford, 1983); *idem*, 'The true date and authorship of Henry, Viscount Falkland's *History of the life, reigne, and death of King Edward II*', *Bodleian Library Record* xii (1988), 440–52; K. Sharpe, *Sir Robert Cotton* (Oxford, 1979). *English historical scholarship in the 16th and 17th centuries*, ed. Levi Fox (Publ. of the Dugdale Soc., Oxford, 1956). Pauline Croft, 'Annual Parliaments

contrasted with the experience of the past, and whence remedies and solutions could be sought. It was, affirmed Richard Greenway, the translator of Tacitus, 'as well as a guide, an image of mans present estate, [and] a true and lively patterne of things to come'.[10] Though classical reference forms a regular source of analogy in early seventeenth-century political discourse, (and comparisons between Charles I and Tiberius or Caligula were commonplace), it was not Livy and Tacitus who enjoyed the greatest literary vogue during the early years of the Long Parliament, but works recounting the baronial crises of fourteenth- and fifteenth-century England.

In the years 1640–9, publication on English medieval history reached a peak for the seventeenth century which was not to be approached again until the years of the Exclusion Crisis. With public interest heightened by the revolt of the Scottish nobility in 1639—a revolt unequivocally baronial in organization, if religious in professed intent—publishers responded with a flood of histories, discourses and annals, chronicling the reigns from Henry III to the defeat of Richard III. This was the period of 'the civill warres of England', as the earl of Monmouth termed it in 1641.[11] Moreover, much of this body of publication was dedicated to, or undertaken by the friends and clients of, those peers who were associated with the 'commonwealth party' in the House of Lords during the early years of the Long Parliament, and subsequently with the parliamentarian cause: with Essex, Warwick, Pembroke and Saye. Nor should this be surprising; for it was these peers who, in advocating a restoration of the medieval great offices of state, stood most to gain from a revived, baronial view of the nobility's role as a counterpoise to the arbitrary powers of kings. In the three years between 1641 and 1643 there were no less than 15 large-scale histories of the period of the Wars of the Roses,[12] and a large number of shorter works and extracts from the Parliament Rolls.[13]

---

and the Long Parliament', *BIHR* 59 (1986), 167. L. L. Peck, *Northampton: patronage and policy at the Court of James I* (1982), chapter 6.

[10] The work's printer, Richard Whitaker, was associated with Saye's faction in the House of Lords: for his relations with Saye, see V. Malvezzi, *Discovrses upon Cornelius Tacitus* (1642), sig. A2, ep. ded. from Whitaker to Saye.

[11] Biondi, *The Civill Warres of England*, title page and sig. a.2.

[12] Esp. Sir Thomas More, *The Historie of the Pitifvll Life, and unfortunate death of Edward the fifth* (1641); Sir Robert Cotton, *A Short View of the Long Life and Reigne of Henry the Third* (1641); J[ohn] T[russell], *A Continuation of the Collection of the History of England ... being a Compleat History of the begining and end of the Dissention betwixt the two houses of York and Lancaster* (1641); Sir Francis Bacon [Viscount St Alban], *The Historie of the reigne of King Henry the Seventh* (1641); Sir Richard Baker, *A chronicle of the kings of England* (1643); cf. George Buck, *The History of the Life and Reign of Richard the Third* (1646), dedicated to the earl of Pembroke, and reprinted in 1647.

[13] Sir John Hayward, *The History of the Life and Raigne of Henry the Fourth* (1642), one

Parliament's *Nineteen Propositions*—the rejection of which was the immediate catalyst for its decision to raise an army[14]—were steeped in, and informed by, this heightened awareness of the medieval past. It was an awareness most strikingly evident in the provisions for the re-establishment of the ancient 'great officers of the kingdom': the Lord High Steward and the Constable of England. These were to be restored, not as ceremonial functionaries, appointed for specific occasions, but as permanent officers of the realm wielding the full range of powers enjoyed by (or attributed to) their medieval predecessors.[15] The *Nineteen Propositions* legislated for a revolution in government: a separation of the spheres of the king's household and the commonwealth's government. Repudiated was the system of government in which intimacy of attendance on the king, rather than noble birth and status within the commonwealth, determined the efficacy of a counsellor's advice;[16] in place of government by Privy Chamber or Bedchamber was to be a baronial council, dominated by the magnates and great officers of state.[17] Its intended effect was, as the king correctly understood, 'to depose both our self and our posterity'.[18]

How was this virtual deposition to be achieved? The table of precedence listed in the *Propositions* is here highly significant. The first officers of the kingdom were to be the Lord High Steward of England, and the Lord High Constable—offices which had been claimed, respectively, by the earl of Essex's step-grandfather, Leicester, and his

---

of many works republished in the 1640s with its original (1599) dedication to the 2nd earl of Essex. Thomas Merke, bishop of Carlisle, *A Pious and Learned Speech delivered in the High Court of Parliament, 1 H[enry] 4* [1642]—a work reprinted during the Exclusion Crisis, and again in 1689 (Wing, M 1826–7, S 4868A). For extracts from the Parliament Rolls, see, E.G., *The Bloody Parliament in the Raigne of an unhappy Prince* ([9 Feb.] 1643), printing part of the Parliament Roll for 10 Ric. II. For the printing of the medieval tract of the Steward see, *Certaine Observations tovching the two great Offices of the Seneschalsey . . . and High-Constableship of England* (17 Oct. 1642). Bracton had been reprinted in 1640: Henricus de Bracton, *De Legibus et Consuetudinibus Angliae Libri Quinque* (1640).

[14] *CJ* ii. 668–9; *LJ* v. 204–6. Cf. B.L., Add. MS 33374 (Jones of Gellilyfdy papers), ff. 19v–20.

[15] There had not been a regular High Steward of England (to be distinguished from the domestic office of Steward of the Household) since the death of the duke of Clarence at the battle of Beaugé in 1421: L. W. Vernon Harcourt, *His Grace the Steward and Trial of Peers* (1907), 191. The nature of the powers the Lord Steward was intended to enjoy by the framers of the *XIX Propositions* is discussed below.

[16] David Starkey, 'Court history in perspective', in *idem*, ed., *The English Court: from the Wars of the Roses to the Civil War* (1987), 1–24.

[17] *LJ* v. 97–9; S. R. Gardiner, *The Constitutional Documents of the Puritan Revolution 1625–1660* (3rd edn, Oxford, 1906), 250–4.

[18] Charles I, 'Answer to the *XIX Propositions*', printed in Rushworth, v. 728–32. *LJ* v. 97; Gardiner, *Constitutional Documents*, 251.

father, the 2nd earl.[19] After these two revived medieval officers[20] ranked the Lord Chancellor, the Lord Treasurer, the Privy Seal, Earl Marshal, Lord Admiral, Warden of the Cinque Ports, Chief Governor of Ireland, Chancellor of the Exchequer, the Master of the Wards, and the two Secretaries of State. These officers, nominated by Parliament, were to be the representatives of the 'commonwealth' within the Council.[21] The king still had free nomination of the officers of his household—the Lord Great Chamberlain, the Steward and Chamberlain of the Household, and the other domestic officers; and these could still be sworn of the Council. But as the Council was to have a maximum number of 25, it was the 13 'officers of state' who, in any full Council meeting, would always constitute a majority of one. Here was a reassertion of the role of the Lords Appellant[22] in checking monarchical power, their authority now founded not on the medieval power-base of retainers-in-arms, but on the legislative authority of a Parliament in which the nobility and gentry cohered. From this perspective, Parliament was, in Henry Parker's phrase, 'the admirable Councell of Aristocracy'.[23]

These propositions, sent from the Lords and later approved by the Commons, were carefully constructed to locate their radical redefinition of the powers of the crown within an ancient, and thus legitimizing, historical tradition. The figure of twenty-five, as the maximum for the new Privy Council, was hardly coincidental; it identified the new Council with the tradition of the 'twenty-five persons from all the peers of the kingdom' described in the *Modus Tenendi Parliamentum*, the most widely circulated of all the medieval parliamentary texts in early Stuart England.[24]

[19] I am grateful to Professor Wallace MacCaffrey for a discussion of the 2nd earl of Essex's claim to the Constableship. In the late 1590s (when Essex made his claim to this office and the Earl Marshalship), as in 1642, it was an office which (possessing vice-regal powers) would have been of particular importance in the event of the monarch's death.

[20] These two great offices were omitted from the table of precedence in Henry VIII's Act of Proclamations: 31 Hen. VIII, c. 8, § 4.

[21] Gardiner, *Constitutional Documents*, 251 (*XIX Propositions*, § 2).

[22] A. Tuck, *Crown and Nobility 1272–1461* (1985), 191–8.

[23] [Henry Parket], *Observations upon some of his Majesties late Answers and Expresses* (1642), 24. Parker's *Observations* were written in response to the king's *Answer to the XIX Propositions*. For Parker's links with the circle which drafted the propositions, see J. S. A. Adamson, 'The *Vindiciae Veritatis* and the political creed of Viscount Saye and Sele', *Historical Research* lx (1987), 60–1.

[24] 'Modus Tenendi Parliamentum', § xvii; printed in N. Pronay and J. Taylor, *Parliamentary Texts of the Later Middle Ages* (Oxford, 1980), 87; the text is common to both the 'A' and 'B' recensions of the Latin *Modus*. For the earl of Arundel's copy, College of Arms, Arundel MS XLI. A copy of the *Modus* is the first item listed as having been found in Saye's study when it was searched for seditious and subversive papers at the conclusion of the Short Parliament: Bodleian Lib., MS Tanner 88*, f. 115. As

Two questions here arise. What powers did the framers of the *Nineteen Propositions* intend the Steward and Constable to possess? And why was it that these offices, so prominent in the agenda of 1642, disappear from lists of officers of state in the parliamentary peace terms proposed after 1645? To the second of these questions I hope to suggest an answer later in this paper; first, let us take the question of their powers.

It was of course from amongst the authors of the propositions—from the circle of Northumberland, Essex, Saye,[25] Pembroke, Mandeville and Brooke—that the Parliament was most likely to appoint such officers. (Indeed, Pembroke had been already nominated to the Lord Stewardship of the Household by the Commons in August 1641.)[26] Perhaps the clearest indication of their future intentions may be gleaned from a tract published in October 1641, a week before the battle of Edgehill, under the aegis of Essex and Mandeville. It has been possible to trace the manuscript from which this tract was printed, which was MS Titus C I in the Cottonian Library.[27] Cotton had scrupulously recorded the removal of manuscripts from his library—in particular the removal of a series of tracts in 1630, when the library was sealed on the orders of the Privy Council, by Mandeville's father, the Lord Privy Seal, the 1st earl of Manchester.[28]

---

most legally literate members of the Long Parliament would have been aware, these twenty-five, summoned by the Steward, the Constable and the Earl Marshal, had power to deal with political crises—where 'there is discord between the king and some magnates', or where there was a division within the peerage ('Modus', ed. Pronay and Taylor, 87). Similar passages attributing particular significance to twenty-five men chosen from the Parliament appear in the medieval *Treatise on the Steward*, versions of which were almost as widely circulated as the *Modus* itself: B.L., Cotton MS Vespasian B VII, f. 100 (for other copies, bound with the *Modus*: Cotton MS Nero C I, ff. 1–5v; Landsdowne MS 522, ff. 6v–7v). Other treatises on the Steward, Marshal and Constable frequently accompanied copies of the *Modus*: B.L., Cotton MS Domitian A XVIII, ff. 15v–22 (*Modus*), ff. 23–35 ('Officium Marescalli et Constabularii Anglie'). B.L., Add. MS 32097 (William Lambarde's copies of 15th century treatises), ff. 13–21. Harcourt, *Steward*, 164–7; Pronay and Taylor, *Parliamentary Texts*, 27n.

[25] Scottish R.O., Hamilton MS, GD 406/1/1658: Saye to Hamilton, 3 June 1642: the reason for Saye's omission from the drafting committee was that he was suffering from 'a feavorish distemper' and was not well enough to attend the House; as his letter to Hamilton indicates, the propositions clearly expressed his own aspirations for the settlement of the kingdom.

[26] Christ Church Muniment Room, Oxford, Nicholas Box (Evelyn collection): earl of Pembroke to Edward Nicholas, 29 Nov. 1641. *LJ* iv. 355.

[27] B.L., Cotton MS Titus C I; the 'emperor system' for the classification of the Cottonian Library was not introduced until after Cotton's death in 1631, though it appears to have been operative by 1639: C. G. C. Tite, 'The early catalogues of the Cottonian Library', *British Library Journal* vi (1980), 148.

[28] B.L., Harl. MS 6018 (1621 catalogue of the Cotton Lib.), ff. 178, 184: the volume is listed as 'A booke of collections of many things concerning the office of the steward, Constable, and especially the Marshall of England' (f. 184).

Amongst these papers, which included Fortescue's treatise 'de dominio politico et regali',[29] was this Titus manuscript, and a collection of antiquarian tracts. Thereafter the Titus manuscript remained at Manchester House and was not returned until after the Civil War. Intended as a polemical work, it reflects the attitudes of Essex's and Mandeville's circle within the Lords to the authority and jurisdiction of the great officers of state.[30]

The treatise attributed to the Steward and Constable quasi-regal powers.[31] Citing a 'an old booke of Parchmine' once in the possession of Recorder William Fleetwood—the fourteenth-century *Treatise on the Steward*—the tract printed in 1642 argued that the Steward's jurisdiction was 'immediately after the *King*, to oversee and governe the whole Kingdome of *England*, and all the Offices of the Justice ... in all times both of Peace and Warre'.[32] Yet that which spoke most pertinently to the circumstances of 1642 was the power of the Steward and Constable to prosecute the king's 'evill Counsellours'.[33] If, after admonishment, the king would not rid himself of any who was reputed 'amongst the people ... to bee an evill Counsellour to the King', the two great officers of state possessed almost unlimited powers.

> Then for the Weale Publick it is lawfull for the Steward, Constable of *England*, noble men and other of the Commonaltie of the Realme, with Banner in the Kings name displayed to apprehend such Counsellour[s] as common enemie to the King and the Realme.[34]

Thus, when Parliament sent its *Nineteen Propositions* to the king in the summer of 1642, the peers at Westminster had a clear perception of the nature and extent of the powers they were seeking to revive: by

[29] B.L., Harl. MS 6018, f. 184.

[30] B.L., Cotton MS Titus C I. These papers, presented to the Society of Antiquaries, were almost certainly the source of the copies made for the earl of Northumberland (Alnwick Castle, Northumberland MSS 541–2). For Hakewill's employment in antiquarian research by the earl of Northumberland during the early 1640s, see Kent Archives Office, De L'Isle MS U 1475/A 98 (Northumberland's general account for 1640; a stray from the Alnwick archives). The notes on 'The Office and Jurisdiction of the Constable and Marshall of England' [c. 1640s], drawn from 'Mr [Francis] Thynns Collectio[n]' (Bodleian Lib., MS Tanner 91, ff. 186–9) derive from a later copy of the treatises in Cotton MS Titus C I.

[31] B.L., Cotton MS Titus C I (Antiquaries' tracts), ff. 26–32; printed as *Certaine Observations touching the two great Offices of the Seneschalsey ... and High Constableship of England* (17 Oct. 1642). It was printed for Laurence Chapman, a stationer later associated with the publication of the *Scotish Dove*.

[32] *Certaine Observations*, sig. B[r–v].

[33] *Certaine Observations*, sig. B2.

[34] *Certaine Observations*, sig. B2[v].

October 1642 (when this tract appeared), Parliament's new Lord General, Essex, was already asserting his claim to the Constableship.[35]

In the context of October 1642, publication of the treatise on the medieval great officers[36] was part of a political campaign, directed by Essex, to confer upon himself protectoral rank and power. Giustiniani, the Venetian Ambassador (whose informants in the House of Lords included Feilding and Holland), had reported in mid-September that Essex was resisting requests that he advance against the king because 'he is anxious to induce Parliament to declare him [High] Constable of England first, and to grant him despotic powers

[35] Christ Church Muniment Room, Oxford, Nicholas Box (Evelyn collection): Pembroke to Nicholas, 29 Nov. 1641. There was little doubt as to who would be the incumbents of the offices. The earl of Pembroke, whose household vied in size and splendour with the royal Court, had been nominated by the Commons to the Lord Stewardship as early as August 1641: *LJ* iv. 355. On the size of Pembroke's household see [George] Sedgwicke, autobiographical narrative, printed in J. Nicholson and R. Burn, *History and Antiquities of the counties of Westmorland and Cumberland* (2 vols, 1777), i. 296: '[Pembroke's] family [*sc.* household] in London was for the most part about 80, in the country double that number'. Sedgewicke was Pembroke's man-of-business at London and one-time assistant to Michael Oldisworth as secretary to the earl. Pembroke's palace at Wilton was conceived on a scale larger than any building attempted by any monarch since Henry VIII.

[36] Cf. B.L., Cotton MS Vespasian C XIVB, ff. 98–101v. The treatise published by Mandeville and Essex was possibly one of a series prepared for Essex's father in 1597, when the 2nd earl was pressing his claim to the Constable's office, by the antiquary, Francis Thynne; cf. Peck, *Northampton*, 241n. It is possible that Robert Bowyer's collection of notes on 'Honor and Armes', made in 1598, which examined at length the powers of the Constableship, was prepared in connexion with this claim: B.L., Add. MS 12191 (Bowyer's notes), ff. 117–125. In advancing his claim to the Constableship in 1642, Essex was aided by the common identification, advanced in official and unofficial polemic alike, between the crusade against Charles I's evil counsellors, and the attacks on Edward II's favourite, Piers Gaveston, and the parliamentary assault on the evil counsellors of Richard II in 1388. The association first gained currency during the attack on Strafford in 1641: see 'The Earle of Strafford Characterized', [March] 1641: Strafford's favour with the king was thought to 'have beene purchased and bought from the peoples affections at a higher price then all the Privadoes of Edw. the Second, or Rich[ar]d the 2[n]d, for that this onely man [Strafford] hath cost and lost the King and Kingdome more trasure and loyalty then Pierce of Gaveston, the Two Spencers, and Marques of Dublin [in 1387–8] did ever cost their masters, being put together'. Bodleian Lib., MS Rawlinson D 924 (misc. papers), f. 139v. This letter seems to have been widely circulated in MS; for a contemporary copy see Kent A.O., Foulis MS U 1886/L 26. The Lords' committee that drafted the resolution declaring in 1642 that the king intended to make war on Parliament, accompanied their votes with extracts from the Parliament Rolls of 11 Richard II (justifying the Constable's proceedindgs against evil counsellors), and 1 Henry IV (confirming Richard's deposition): *LJ* v. 76–7. The committee which drafted these resolutions consisted of Northumberland, Essex, Mandeville, Saye, Brooke, Holland, Leicester and Paget. It was Northumberland who characteristically, on 16 May 1642, reported to the House that before proceeding further in answering the king's messages, precedents should be searched. *LJ* v. 66.

for conducting the war, as well as to negotiate and conclude the [agreement] with the king'.[37] It was as part of these attempts to define Essex's role in the war in terms of the Constableship that his allies published the tract on the great officers—including the translation of the medieval tract on the Steward—in the week before Essex encountered the king at Edgehill.

As the earl of Essex, likened to, and armed with the powers of, the High Constable, marched out with his army to do battle with an enemy characterised, in equally gothic terms, as the king's evil counsellors, the war of 1642 seemed to some at Westminster disconcertingly like a barons' war. Contributing powerfully to this perception was the manner in which the conflict had escalated over the summer, and the nobility's expectations as to how the contest was to be resolved once battle was joined.

II

Throughout the country, over the summer and autumn of 1642, rival peers vied with each other for control of the kingdom's arsenals and its places of military strength. Lord Brooke confronted the earl of Northampton in Warwickshire;[38] Lord Fairfax the earl of Cumberland in Yorkshire; Pembroke the marquess of Hertford in Wiltshire; peers—either as parliamentarian Lords Lieutenant or as royalist Commissioners of Array—sought to rally support and outmanoeuvre opponents in a series of trials of local strength. Public perceptions of the opening of the war were dominated, not simply by the clash of 'parliamentarian' and 'royalist', but by a series of localized aristocratic struggles for regional control. With a third of the English nobility leading armies in the field[39]—a figure comparable with the baronial conflicts of the fourteenth and fifteenth centuries—it was the battles of barons and viscounts, marquesses and earls, that dominated published (and contemporary private) accounts of the war. A contemporary diarist entered his account of Edgehill, not as a battle between king and Parliament, but between 'the king and the Earle of Essex'.[40] In the pamphlets and newsbooks which related the fighting, the national conflict was particularised in titles such as *Lord Falkland's encounter with the Earl of Essex's Forces before Worcester*, or the *Trve relation of the late fight betweene the Earle of Manchesters Forces and the Marquesse of Newcastles*

[37] Giustiniani to the Doge and Senate, 18 Sept. 1642: *Calendar of State Papers, Venetian, 1642–3* (1925), 154.

[38] Thomas Johnsons, *Some speciall passages from Warwickshire* ([Aug.] 1642), 1–5 (B.L., E 109/3).

[39] J. B. Crummett, 'The Lay Peers in Parliament, 1640–44' (D. Phil. dissertation, Manchester, 1972), appendix XIV.

[40] Bodleian Lib., MS Rawlinson D 141 ('Certaine memorable accidents', anon.), 47.

Forces.[41] Forces were referred to by the name of their aristocratic commanders even more often than as 'Cavaliers' or the 'Parliament's forces'. Lord Falkland crowed over his 'encounter with the Earle of Essex Forces before *Worcester*';[42] accounts of major battles, such as the first battle of Newbury in 1643, where the earls of Caernarvon and Sunderland and Lord Falkland met their deaths, inevitably stressed the combatants' rank and status, and the peers' personal engagement in battle. The way the war was conducted, and reported, in the years before the creation of the New Model Army in 1645, threw the military role of the nobility into high relief.

The opening of the civil war, then, suggested obvious parallels with the baronial conflicts of the past. These parallels were emphasized in the rhetoric in which parliamentary and royalist pronouncements were cast: in the royalist enemy characterised as 'evil counsellors', and in a parliamentarian party cast as the abettors of a 'rebellion of the earl of Essex'. Thus, even at the battle of Edgehill, the king could offer free pardon 'to both officers and soldiers', 'verily believing that many of his Subjects, who are now in actual Rebellion against him, are ignorant against whom they fight'.[43] In the conduct of the war, the perception of the conflict as a baronial war had its correlative in the chivalric code by which the fighting was engaged. Nowhere was this more strikingly apparent than in the issuing of challenges to personal combat and to trial by battle. Even before the battle of Edgehill, when royalist and parliamentarian forces had already mobilised in Warwickshire, Lord Brooke offered, to 'avoyde the profusion of bloud', that he and his royalist opponent, the earl of Northampton, 'might try the quarrell by the sword in single combat'.[44] According to Edward Howard, son of the royalist earl of Berkshire and an officer in the king's army, a similar scene was enacted by the earl of Lindsey, the king's commander in chief, in the opening stages of the battle of Edgehill. And early in 1643, the royalist earl of Newcastle challenged Lord Fairfax to trial by battle, self-consciously evoking 'the Examples of our Heroicke Ancestors'.[45]

[41] *A true relation* (1643), relates a fight which took place on 11 Oct. 1643.

[42] *A letter sent from the Lord Falkland ... vnto the ... earle of Cvmberland* (York, 30 Sept. 1642), sig. A2.

[43] Proclamation, 23 Oct. 1642: *The Parliamentary or Constitutional History of England* (24 vols, 1751–62), xi. 471, (hereafter, *Old. Parl. Hist.*). The proclamation was intended to be read by the Clarencieux herald before Essex's army on the day of the battle.

[44] Bodleian Lib., MS Eng. hist. e. 240, 35–6; printed as 'The Genealogie, Life and Death of the Right Honourable Robert Lord Brooke', ed. P. Styles, *Miscellany I* (Publications of the Dugdale Society, Oxford, 1977), 178. The 'Genealogie' was written in 1644 by Thomas Spencer, a chaplain who had served in the household of the 2nd Lord Brooke. See also the contemporary account of the incident in *Englands losse and lamentation occasioned by the death of ... Lord Brooke* ([9 Mar.] 1642[3]), sig. A2v.

[45] Edward Howard, *Carololoiades, or, the Rebellion of Forty One* (1689), 37. (I owe this

The archaic formalities of the challenge to combat testify to a perception, shared by the principal participants, that the war was taking place within a tradition of aristocratic conflict—or, from the king's perspective, of aristocratic rebellion[46]—a tradition which dictated the combatants' code of behaviour.[47] Clarendon, a hostile witness, was convinced that Essex's sense of chivalry would have prevented him from joining battle at Edgehill had he realised the king was present in the field.[48] To Essex, the adversary was not the person of the king, but his fellow Privy Councillors amongst the nobility who, he held, had persuaded the king to tyrannous courses of action.[49] It was to vindicate himself against these opponents, while observing the clause in his commission to preserve the safety of the king's person, that Essex returned to the expedient of trial by battle in July 1643. Then, in what was perhaps the most gothic moment of the civil war, Parliament's commander-in-chief proposed that the war be determined by a single, set-piece battle, on condition that the king absented himself from the field.[50]

---

reference to Mr John Sutton.) *A Declaration of . . . the Earle of Newcastle* ([?] Feb. 1642[3]), p. 9. The challenge was, in effect, a formal accusation of treason, a process that had been employed before the king himself at the trial by battle of Lord Reay in 1631, a trial at which Lindsey presided as High Constable of England. This gave particular significance to the king's choice of Lindsey as commander-in-chief, as Lindsey's adversary at Edgehill in Oct. 1642, Essex, had claimed the Constableship only the month before. Essex was to be opposed by an earl of equal distinction who had already held, on the *king's* terms, the very office which Essex was seeking to claim. For Reay's trial, College of Arms, Arundel MS LIV (Procs. in the Court of Chivalry, 1631–2); Bodleian Lib., MS Additional c. 79. Cf. also, Sir George Clark, *War and Society in the Seventeenth Century* (Cambridge, 1958), chapter 2 'The Analogy of the Duel'.

[46] *Old. Parl. Hist.*, xi. 471.

[47] Challenges to combat were not, however, confined to officer peers. For a challenge from Sir William Balfour's son to a royalist officer in Col. Lunsford's regiment: *A copy of a letter from his Excellencie, Robert Earle of Essex* ([Sept.] 1642), 2–3 (B.L., 100.b.22). John Lilburne, an officer in Essex's army who also thought of the war in profoundly historical terms, issued a challenge to the royalist court martial which condemned him in November 1642. Demanding a sword, Lilburne challenged Prince Rupert and the earls Rivers and Northampton, 'telling them he desired to die in single opposition, man to man, with any there'. Lilburne knew the precedents well: his father, Richard Lilburne, had caused consternation to Justice Berkeley at the Durham sessions in 1638, when he arrived with a champion 'in Array', 'who cast his Gantlet into the Court', to offer trial by battle with a Durham neighbour with whom he had a long-standing property dispute, Rushworth, ii. 788–90; for the background to the case: P. Gregg, *Free-born John: a biography of John Lilburne* (1961; 1986 edn), 72–3.

[48] Edward Hyde, earl of Clarendon, *The History of the Rebellion*, ed. W. D. Macray (6 vols, Oxford, 1888), ii. 355–6 (Bk vi, § 79n). Propaganda issued on Essex's behalf throughout the war repeatedly emphasised his chivalric behaviour: see, for example, *The earle of Essex his desires to the Parliament* (13 Aug. 1642), 3.

[49] Cf. William Bridge, *A sermon preached unto the voluntiers of the City of Norwich* (30 Jan. 1642[3]), 17–18.

[50] Essex to Speaker Lenthall, 9 July 1643: printed in W. B. Devereux, *Lives and Letters*

These challenges to combat cannot be understood outside the contemporary political and historical culture which informed the opening stages of the civil war. The *locus classicus* for the challenge to trial by battle was the challenge issued in 1398 by Henry of Lancaster to Richard II's 'evil counsellor', the duke of Norfolk—accounts of which were published on the eve of Essex's rebellion of 1601,[51] and again in 1641, 1642 and 1643. In most versions, the challenge to trial by battle was accompanied by an account of Bolingbroke's denunciation of the evil counsellors of Richard II. Sir John Hayward's version—republished in 1641, again in two further editions in 1642, and widely plagiarized—gives the essence of the charge. Bolingbroke launched

> into [a] complaint, how the King regarded not the Noble Princes of his bloud and Peeres of the Realme, and by extremities used to some, discouraged the rest from intermedling in any publique affaires; how instead of these, hee was wholly governed by certaine new-found and new-fangled favorites, vulgar in birth, corrupt in qualities, having no sufficiency either of councell for peace, or of courage for warre.[52]

This was an indictment of the king's disregard for the counsels of his nobility which spoke directly to the framers of the *Nineteen Propositions*. Although it went through three editions during 1641–42, it had first appeared in 1599 under the patronage of the 2nd earl of Essex. Then it had been read as a thinly veiled attack on the dominance of Cecil.[53] When it was reprinted in 1642, on the eve of the second Essex rebellion, Henry of Lancaster's accusation had a similar contemporary force: as a protestation of the nobility's right to govern the counsels of the king.

So the challenges to combat issued by Brooke, Lindsey and Essex in the first years of the civil war were part of a political and chivalric culture in which the challenger identified himself with virtuous counsel, and with the nobility's 'just rights'. Only in this context do the opening moves of the battle of Edgehill, or Essex's offer of trial by battle in 1643, cease to be eccentric anachronisms and attain a coherence as part of a political culture which comprehends such diverse phenomena in Caroline England as the revival of trial by combat and

of the Devereux, Earls of Essex (2 vols, 1853), ii. 367–9. V.F. Snow, *Essex the Rebel* (Lincoln, Nebraska, 1970), 371–2.

[51] On Hayward and the circle of the 2nd earl of Essex, M. E. James, 'At the crossroads of the political culture: the Essex revolt, 1601', in *idem, Society, Politics and Culture: Studies in early modern England* (Cambridge, 1986), 418–23.

[52] Sir John Hayward, *The History of the Life and Raigne of Henry the Fourth* (1642 edn), 90–6.

[53] James, 'At the crossroads of the political culture', 420. Cecil claimed Hayward's history was intended to make 'this time seem like that of Henry IV, to be reformed by him [Essex] as by Henry IV' (*ibid.*, citing *Cal. State Papers, Domestic, 1598–1601*, 555).

the Great Council of Peers, the literary vogue for medieval history, and the proposals for the re-creation of the great medieval offices of state.

III

It is against this background that the figure of Essex needs to be reassessed: the soldier-turned-statesman whose role as protector of the commonwealth during the first half of the 1640s was to create so influential a precedent for Oliver Cromwell in the succeeding decade. It was natural in a kingdom habituated to personal monarchy that the alternative to government by Charles I should be thought of in terms of a figure endowed with quasi-monarchical powers. The appointment of a *custos regni*, such as had governed during the minority of Henry VI,[54] had been suggested as early as 1641.[55] Various forms of protectoral office—from the *custos regni* of 1641, the 1642 Captain-Generalship, and the Governorship of the King's Children of 1645—were suggested, and tried, to fill the vacuum in the exercise of monarchical power. Essex's commission of appointment as commander-in-chief in 1642 created him Captain-General, an office linked with protectoral or vice-regal rank.[56] The king, for one, did not miss the significance of Essex's title: in a proclamation significantly entitled 'for the suppressing of the present Rebellion under the Command of Robert Earle of Essex', the king declared that Essex 'hath assumed unto himself those Titles [sc. the Captain-Generalship]', and begun to execute 'those Powers and Authorities which are inconsistable with Our Soveraignty'.[57]

Public protocol reinforced this identification of Essex's Captain-Generalship with constabular or protectoral rank. From his appointment as Captain-General, Essex (who stood in precedence after such ancient titles as those of the 10th earl of Northumberland or the 10th earl of Kent), assumed a status which out-ranked all the other peers

[54] J. S. Roskell, 'The office and dignity of Protector of England, with special reference to its origins', *EHR* lxviii (1953), 194.

[55] P.R.O., SP 81/51/2, f. 215: the elder Sir Henry Vane thought that a *custos regni* would be appointed before the king's departure for Scotland in the summer of 1641.

[56] The two most famous of his predecessors in the office were Lord Protector Somerset (created 'Locumtenens [Regis] ac Capitaneus Generalis pro Guerris et Bellis' in 1548) and, in the 1580s, the earl of Leicester—with whose supposed monarchical ambitions Essex was frequently associated. Thomas and Leonard Digges, *An Arithmetical Warlike Treatise named Stratiotikos* (1590), sig. Aij (ep. ded to Leicester), and chapter xxiii: 'The Lord General', esp. 305, 307, 315; the first edition appeared in 1579. Roskell, 'The office and dignity of Protector', 229.

[57] *An exact collection* (1643), 504 (proclamation of 9 Aug. 1642); *Stuart Royal Proclamations Vol. II: Royal Proclamations of King Charles I, 1625–1646*, ed. James F. Larkin (Oxford, 1983), 791.

in Parliament. Moreover, members of the House of Commons were required to make the utterly baronial undertaking 'to live and die with the earl of Essex' in this cause.[58] From 11 August 1642, this oath to Essex became as much a test for membership of the House of Commons as the oaths of allegiance and supremacy had been before the outbreak of the war.[59] The oath was, strictly, an oath of fealty. From Essex's point of view, as his later conduct demonstrated, the oath brought the Lords and Commons close to being his liege men.[60] '*Vive le Roy et Essex*, God save the king and Essex', Lord Robartes claimed in September 1642, would henceforth be the Commons' cry.[61] Lord Robartes's suggestion that Essex's name would be joined in the traditional royal acclamation—as '*Vive le Roy et Essex*'—takes on heightened significance when placed beside the protocol and civic ceremonial that attended the Captain-General.[62] Alone amongst the parliamentarian commanders before 1645 was Essex distinguished by the honorific title 'His Excellency'. Alone of the commanders during the civil war, Essex was permitted to stage 'triumphs': state entries into the City on his return from successful campaigns.[63]

Essex's entry into the City after Edgehill, in November 1642, was explicitly modelled on Charles I's royal entry in November of the previous year. Just as at the king's entry, Essex was received by the City dignitaries outside the City walls, where after speeches and homage from the City fathers, he entered London by Moorgate,[64] tracing the route to Guildhall, and then on to Whitehall, that had been followed by the king only twelve months before.[65] As on that

[58] *CJ* ii. 668–9; *LJ* v. 206, 208.

[59] *CJ* ii. 715 for the resolution; for examples of the oath being tendered to M.P.s, *CJ* ii. 741, 743, 755–6, 765, 767, 774, 784, 787, 802, 810, 822, 832, 874.

[60] When relations between the Lord General and Parliament became strained, Essex was quick to remind the Commons of their solemn undertaking to adhere to him as leader and protector of the parliamentary cause. The terms of the oath to Essex were frequently reiterated in parliamentarian propaganda, particularly after such crises as Waller's plot, in June 1643: *A Declaration of the Lords and Commons ... setting forth the Several Plots* ([5 June] 1643), 16 (B.L., E 105/5).

[61] *The Resolution of ... the Earle of Essex his Excellence* ([9 Sept.] 1642), 2–4, 5 (B.L., 100 b. 21).

[62] Robert Codrington, *The Life and Death of the illustrious Robert, Earle of Essex* (1646), 14; on the traditional royal processional route through the City, D. M. Bergeron, *English Civic Pageantry 1558–1642* (1971), 118–21; and *idem*, 'Charles I's royal entries into London', *Guildhall Miscellany* iii (1970), 91–7. Corporation of London R.O., MS 86.5 (Accounts of extraordinary disbursements of the Chamber, c. 1640–60).

[63] Codrington, *Life of Essex*, 38.

[64] For the king's entry in 1641, *The Subjects Happinesse, and the Citizens Joy* (1641), sig. A2; *Ovatio Carolina* (1641); Robert Withington, *English Pageantry: an historical outine* (2 vols, Cambridge, Mass., 1918–20), i. 238–9. For Essex's triumphal entries of 1642–4, the place of meeting outside the walls was either Finsbury Fields or Moorfields.

[65] Devereux, ii. 360; *LJ* v. 441.

occasion, the streets were thronged with spectators; and on his arrival at Westminster Essex was presented with formal addresses, congratulatory verses,[66] and a royal gift of £5,000—actually paid—by the Commons.[67]

Much of the language used in the parliamentarian propaganda of 1642–3 describes Essex in terms of almost religious reverence.[68] Devout but simple souls in the garrison of Wallingford in 1643 placed credence in reports that Essex was the returned Saint John the Baptist.[69] And so unparallelled was Essex's place in history, Daniel Evance thought in 1646, that future patriotic Englishmen would even train their parrots to 'prate great Essex's name'.[70]

The civic pageantry attending Essex's second formal entry into the City in September 1643, after the Gloucester campaign, made his claim to vice-regal status still more bluntly. Essex was acclaimed by the City Militia forces at their formal review in Finsbury Fields.[71] This time, however, Essex did not go to Whitehall to receive the thanks of Parliament. In a carefuly orchestrated and highly significant change of procedure, now it was the members of the two Houses and their Speakers who gave attendance in the presence chamber at Essex House—not the earl who attended the Houses at Westminster. At Essex House, the Speaker presented humble addresses before the victorious Lord General as before a king. After homage from the two Houses, 'the Mayor and Aldermen of London came in their scarlet gowns to him,' Whitelocke noted, 'and highly complemented him, as

[66] For the presentation of congratulatory verses as part of Charles I's formal entry in 1641: Withington, *English Pageantry*, i. 238–9.

[67] *A Continuation of Certaine Speciall and Remarkable Passages* (4–11 Nov. 1642), 4 (B.L., E 127/3); for the payments, B.L., Add. MS 5497 (Parliamentary papers, 1642–9), f. 56r–v. Compare the gift presented to Charles I in November 1641: Corporation of London R.O., City Cash Book 1/4, ff. 146v–8.

[68] The congratulatory ode which marked Essex's and Warwick's return to London in November 1642 claimed that henceforth 'children shall rejoyce/In their first language, and the common voyce/Shall be to chaunt soft Hymnes and pleasant layes/To Noble Essex and brave Warwicks praise'. *London's Ioyfull Gratulation and Thankfull Remembrance for their Safeties* ([11 Nov.] 1642), 7 (B.L., E127/1).

[69] *The Journal of Sir Samuel Luke*, ed. I. G. Philip (3 vols, Oxfordshire Rec. Soc., 1950–3), i. 76.

[70] Daniel Evance, *Justa Honoraria: or, Funeral Rites in honour to the Great Memorial* (1646), 14. John Wild thought that if Essex had died in ancient Rome, he would have been deified: J. W[ild], *An Elegie upon the Earle of Essex's Funerall* ([29 Oct.] 1642), B.L., E 359/11.

[71] *Merc. Civicus*, no. 18 (21–28 Sept. 1643), 141; Bodleian Lib., MS Rawl. D. 141, 'Certaine memorable accidents', 150–1. On this occasion the troops were reported to have declared their undertaking to serve Essex personally 'when soever his Excellence (their Heroick Generall) should command their service': Codrington, *Life of Essex*, 38; for the attendance of the Lord Mayor and aldermen at Temple Bar: *ibid.* See also, G. A. Raikes, *The History of the Honourable Artillery Company* (2 vols, 1878–9), i. 128.

the Protector of them and their fortunes'.[72] The only parallels for such homage from the two Houses were royal. And regal ceremonial on a scale of unparallelled magnificence and self-consciously archaic pomp attended Essex's funeral at Westminster Abbey in October 1646: the parliamentary contribution alone was £5,000.[73] The only comparable display in recent memory had been the royal funeral of James I in 1625.[74] No contemporary could have failed to notice the obvious political claim symbolized in these exhibitions of vice-regal status and power.

For such was the power which Essex claimed: the power of a medieval Constable, or the unlimited commission of a Roman dictator. In January 1643, three months after he had claimed the Constableship, Essex again declared—through his secretary, Henry Parker—the extent of the power he sought. 'As our dangers now are', wrote Parker, 'it would bee good for us to adde more power to the Earle of *Essex* ... for till I see him lookt upon, and served as a temporary Dictator, and the bounds of his Commission to bee only this, *ne quid detrimenti capiat Respublica cavere*,[75] I shall never think the Parliaments safety sufficiently provided for'.[76] This classical political vocabulary encoded Essex's claims to protectoral, vice-regal authority, and became an increasingly important element in the Lord General's propaganda after the triumphal entry into London in September 1643. The Latin account of Essex's victories, issued with the authority of the House of Lords in 1644 and directed to a European

[72] Mount Stuart, Rothesay (Isle of Bute), MS 196 D. 13 (Diary of Bulstrode Whitelocke), f. 63v; most of this account is also to be found in B.L., Add. MS 37343 (Whitelocke's Annals), ff. 275v–6. The capitalization of 'Protector' is, perhaps, revealing. The wearing of scarlet gowns by the Lord Mayor and aldermen was also the traditional form of apparel for the reception of the king: John Taylor, *Englands Comfort, and London Ioy* (1641).

[73] *LJ* viii. 490, 507, 508, 533, 540–2.

[74] P.R.O., LC 2/6 (Lord Chamberlain's dept., accounts of James I's funeral), f. 1v. The total cost of James's funeral was £16,520—a total which included the cost of hanging the interiors of the principal royal houses near London with mourning cloth, and providing mourning clothes for the members of the royal household. Essex's funeral was on a par—in terms both of cost and magnificence—with the royal funerals of the early seventeenth century. On the importance of Essex's funeral, see the perceptive remarks of Miss Sheila Lambert, 'The opening of the Long Parliament', *Historical Journal*, xxvii (1984), 286–7.

[75] This was the so-called 'ultimate decree' of the Roman Senate: cf. Cicero, *Pro Milone*, xxvi. 70.

[76] [Henry Parker], *The Contra-replicant, his Complaint to His Majestie* [31 Jan. 1643], 19. Cf. Richard Vines, *The Hearse of the Renowned ... Robert, Earle of Essex* ([29 Oct.] 1646), 30–1: 'You ... looked out for a *Dictator*', Richard Vines reminded both Houses in Essex's funeral sermon, 'and happily pitcht your eye and choyce upon this man'; (delivered 22 Oct. 1646).

audience, spoke pointedly of Essex as 'Robertus, Supremus Imperator'.[77]

Regal ceremonial and a classical rhetoric of unlimited civil and military power did not pass without provoking a nervous reaction amongst Essex's erstwhile equals in the House of Lords. Essex, no longer *primus inter pares*, but now recognizing no equal but the king, posed a classically baronial problem: that of the over-mighty peer attempting to dominate politics in an acephalous kingdom. As Essex's ascendancy brought in its train an aristocratic reaction against the extent of his authority, the nature of the problem recommended a series of equally baronial solutions. The first clear signs of misgivings had appeared after Essex's triumphant return to London in September 1643, when the two Houses and the City fathers had given attendance in person at Essex House. Within a week of that act of homage it had been proposed that the duke of Gloucester, the king's youngest son, then in the custody of Parliament, should be appointed 'Constable of England by Ordinance of Parliament, and then Menage the warre in his Name'.[78]

The aristocratic reaction of that September was, however, nugatory in comparison to the furore of January 1644, when both Houses of the royalist Parliament at Oxford petitioned Essex to mediate a peace.[79] Presented to Essex on 30 January, the petition's form was as significant as its content. Unlike previous approaches to Essex on this subject, it was not simply a letter, but a formal Address of the Parliament, engrossed on parchment;[80] those who petitioned for his mediation included the Prince of Wales and the duke of York, and all the peers and commons of the Oxford Parliament. As with the Westminster Parliament's addresses at Essex House, the only precedents for such formal, engrossed addresses from the two Houses of a Parliament were submissions to a Protector or to a reigning king.[81]

For the Lord General's fellow peers at Westminster, acknow-

[77] *Descriptio rerum guestarum in expeditione, quam suscepit illustrissimus heros, Robertus Comes Essexiae, Supremus Imperator* ([14 April] 1643 [*recte* 1644]), title page; Sir Philip Stapilton, the commander of Essex's body-guard was termed the Tribune of the Praetorian Guard, the imperial bodyguard: *ibid.*, 5. The Lords' order for its publication is dated 1 November 1643: *ibid.*, sig. E[1]. For the English original, see *A true relation of the late expedition* (1643), B.L., E 70/10.

[78] Kent Archives Office, Sackville MS U 269/C 267/19: the earl of Bath to the countess of Bath, 1 Oct. 1643.

[79] Text printed in *Old Parl. Hist.*, xiii. 59–61, 73–77; for Essex's reply, addressed to the earl of Forth, 30 Jan. 1644: Devereux, ii. 390. *The Copy of his Excellency the Earle of Forth's letter to the Earle of Essex* (Oxford, 7 March 1644), 1–5.

[80] B.L., Add. MS 37343 (Whitelocke's Annals), f. 286r–v. Whitelocke, who claimed to have been consulted by Essex for advice as to how to reply, described the document as 'a parchement rowle' (*ibid.*, f. 286r).

[81] Devereux, ii. 390.

ledgement of Essex's protectoral status by loyal parliamentarians was one thing; acknowledgement by a royalist Parliament at Oxford quite another. Peers such as the earl of Northumberland and Viscount Saye and Sele, who themselves hoped to exercise a formative influence on the terms for peace, felt most acutely the threat of Essex's ascendancy. Their response was almost immediate. Two days after Essex received the Oxford Parliament's supplication, Saye introduced into the House of Lords a radical new bill intended to usurp Essex's supremacy of command.[82] Exploiting the Scots' hostility towards an English Captain-General who claimed jurisdiction over the deployment of their forces, Saye put forward his proposal to concentrate executive power in a Committee of *Both* Kingdoms, a powerful executive to be composed of a small contingent of English parliamentarians, meeting with the Commissioners of Scotland.[83] Henceforth, the Committee would be empowered 'to order and direct whatsoever doth or may concern the managing of the war' and 'whatever may concern the peace of his Majesty's dominions'[84]—the two areas of policy which Essex had sought to appropriate as his proprietary concerns.[85]

[82] For the test of this first bill: *CJ* iii. 504; printed in Gardiner, *Constitutional Documents*, 273–4; the bill pointedly gives the earl of Northumberland precedence (as a 10th earl) over Essex, who should otherwise have outranked all other peers as Captain-General. For Essex's precedence, B.L., Add. 37343 (Whitelocke's Annals), f. 285v. The establishment of the committee is discussed in W. Notestein, 'The establishment of the Committee of Both Kingdoms', *American Historical Review* xvii (1911–12), 477–95, where the authorship of the bill is ascribed to the younger Vane (*ibid.*, 482). Notestein offers no evidence to support this assertion; and there is no reason to suppose that Saye, who introduced the bill, was not also its draftsman. *LJ* vi. 405; *CJ* iii. 384; *Merc. Aulicus* 7th week (11–17 Feb. 1644), 828 (B.L., E 35/27).

[83] B.L., Add. MS 37343 (Whitelocke's Annals), f. 287v: the English contingent was to consist of 7 lords and 14 members of the Commons, to be 'a joint Councell'. The question of the committee's size was controversial; 'the fewnes of the number', Whitelocke observed, 'distasted many who were left out'. The nobility was disproportionately well represented on the committee, for although the English contingent was composed according to the usual ratio for parliamentary committees (two Commons to one peer), peers predominated amongst the Scottish Commissioners; the effect at meetings was to make the overall ratio of peers to Commons much closer to one-to-one than one-to-two. The proposal for such a joint committee first emerged in Saye's circle in a positional paper drafted by Saye's nephew, Henry Parker, in the summer of 1642. Its publication, in a limited edition of 50 copies, was paid for by Sir John Danvers; and the proposal was presented to the marquess of Hamilton in June 1642. See H[enry] P[arker], *The Generall Junto, or the Councell of Union* (1642), and Thomason's MS note to his copy, B.L., 669 f. 18/1; and Sir John Danvers to Hamilton, 1 July 1642: Scottish R.O., Hamilton MS GD 406/1/1700.

[84] *CJ* iii. 504. B.L., Harl. MS166 (D'Ewes's diary), f. 7.

[85] The Committee of Both Kingdoms supplanted the authority of the (exclusively English) Committee of Safety, a Committee which was staffed by Essex's household men, and which acted as an extension of his commissariat. SP 28/261–262 (Cttee of Safety papers); many of these papers are in the hand of Henry Parker, who doubled

Yet one who had tasted such power was not so easily to be tamed. Throughout the campaigning season of 1644, Essex showed a lofty disregard to the new Committee's orders and remonstrations. His own political objectives remained as they had been in 1642: the rescuing of the king from his 'evil counsellors'; and pursuit of a negotiated peace, a peace which comprehended moderates at Oxford—such as Dorset and his own brother-in-law, Hertford—in the membership of a reformed Privy Council.[86] These political principles dictated his military strategy. So long as he could dominate the terms of the settlement as commander-in-chief, the purpose of war was not to inflict a crushing military defeat on the king's forces, but merely to secure a strategic superiority whereby both sides would not only have to reach a compromise, but have to reach a compromise in which Essex was architect of the peace.[87] Ironically, Essex's claim to vice-regal status rendered him far more acceptable to Charles I as a party to negotiation than the institution of Parliament for which he had so adamant a contempt. In November 1643, shortly before the presentation of the Oxford Parliament's Address, Charles confided to the duke of Richmond that while he could never do business with a Parliament, he would deal with Essex or with none at all.[88]

It was against this background that the king made a second overture for peace, in August 1644, again acknowledging Essex's role as mediator between himself and Parliament. Addressing himself in terms almost of equality, Charles invited Essex to join forces with him to impose a settlement that guaranteed Essex's dominance of the future government. The king was scarcely exaggerating when he

---

as secretary to the Committee of Safety and secretary to the earl of Essex. Denzell Holles and Sir John Meyrick, two of Essex's staunchest supporters in the Commons, were conspicuously absent from the ranks of the new Committee of Both Kingdoms, even though they had formerly served on the Committee of Safety. For the lame duck existence of the Committee of Safety after February 1644, see P.R.O. (Kew), WO 47/1 (Ordnance Office, entry bk of orders 1644–5), 8, 14, 26, 35; Holles continued to attend the Committee of Safety's meetings throughout 1644: e.g., *ibid.*, 35, 40, 57.

[86] B.L., Add. MS 18980 (Prince Rupert corr., 1642–3), f. 60: Sir Edward Nicholas to Prince Rupert, 11 May 1643. William Salt Library, Stafford, Salt MS 509: Essex to Prince Rupert, 22 June 1643. (I owe this last reference to Dr David Smith, of Selwyn College, Cambridge.)

[87] Cf. the peace initiative proposed by Essex after his triumphant return from the Gloucester campaign in September 1643, when his political stock was at its highest. Through his secretary, Henry Parker, Essex advocated the disbandment of both armies, and a readmission of moderate royalist councillors (such as his brother-in-law, Hertford), to the parliamentary deliberations on the settlement of the kingdom: [Henry Parker], *The Oath of Pacification: or a forme of Religious Accommodation* (1643), 22, 29–30.

[88] Leeds Castle, Kent, Fairfax MS, unfol.: duke of Richmond and Lennox to Rupert, 12 Nov. [1643].

wrote: 'you have at this time in your power to redeeme your country and the crown, and to obleidge your King in the highest degree, ... Such an oppertunitie as, perhaps, Noe subiect before you euer had, or after you shall haue'.[89] United, their power would be irresistable. And should anyone be so foolhardy as to oppose this alliance, the king added with characteristically sinister philanthropy, 'Wee will make them happie, by Godds blessing, euen against their wills'.[90]

It is here, at Lostwithiel in August 1644, that the origins of the Self-Denying Ordinance—the final phase of the aristocratic reaction against Essex in both Houses—are to be found. Essex's decision to advance into the west towards the king's army had been against the expressed instructions of the Committee of Both Kingdoms, to which Essex was now nominally subordinate.[91] Misgivings as to Essex's military objectives were now heightened by the prospect that he might accept Charles's offer and turn against the Scots.[92] 'This with other things', Saye declared in 1646, 'then laid the foundation in mens hearts of that resolution, which soon after was put in execution, to new Model the Army, and put the Command into other hands'.[93] To those who had been the promoters of the alliance with the Scots—to Saye, Northumberland, St John and the younger Vane—the disaster of Essex's army in the west-country was Parliament's Cannae; but it was also a providential reprieve: had Essex been in a position of strength in August 1644 that would have guaranteed his personal bargaining position with the king, a conjunction of the boundlessly ambitious Essex and a king who had offered him 'all possible meanes of assurance to the publique and to his own perticular if he would consent vnto it'[94] seemed all too close and terrible a possibility.

So the problem posed at Westminster by Essex was not simply military; indeed, the memory of his brilliant victories at Gloucester the previous year had not yet been effaced. Essex posed a political problem: the baronial problem of a noble with a military power-base, claiming protectoral or constabular rank, exercising a corresponding

[89] B.L., Add. MS 27402 (Misc. historical papers), f. 79: Charles to Essex, from Liskeard, 6 Aug. 1644.

[90] *Ibid*; cf. Prince Maurice and others to Essex, 8 Aug. 1644: Devon R.O., Seymour MS 1392 M/L 16/1644/54.

[91] *CJ* iii. 504.

[92] B.L., Add. MS 27402 (Misc. historical papers), f. 80. The bearer of the king's letter, John Richard, explained to Essex that the offer was made for '[the] common end of preseruing this Kingdom from a Conquest by the Scotts, and from vtter ruine and desolation'. John Richard would have been familiar to Essex as he was in the household of the earl's brother-in-law, the marquess of Hertford, and seems to have acted as Hertford's man-of-business at London: Longleat, Seymour Papers, Box V, f. 30.

[93] [Viscount Saye and Sele], *Vindiciae Veritatis* (1654), 52.

[94] B.L., Add. MS 27402 (Misc. historical papers), f. 80: summary by John Richard of what was said at the presentation of the king's offer to Essex, 7 Aug. 1644.

authority, and heedless of the instructions even of Parliament itself. It is in this context that the origins and effect of the military reforms of the winter of 1644–5—the famous Self-Denying Ordinance, the creation of the New Model Army, and the appointment of Sir Thomas Fairfax as Lord General—need to be re-examined.

The principal object of the Self-Denying Ordinance—the chief instrument of these reforms, removing members of both Houses from civil and military command—was widely perceived to be the dismissal of the earl of Essex.[95] As with the bill to establish the Committee of Both Kingdoms, one of the principal moving spirits behind this ordinance was Viscount Saye. On 9 December 1644, he moved in the Lords for the resolution for 'self-denial'—that all members of both Houses should give up the civil and military offices that had been conferred since the outbreak of the war; that day, almost certainly by prior arrangement, Zouch Tate, then chairman of the Committee for the Lord General's Army, moved the same motion in the House of Commons.[96]

If the Self-Denying Ordinance and the replacement of Essex by Sir Thomas Fairfax as Lord General solved the military aspect of this problem, it did not solve the political problem caused by the protectoral status Essex had claimed, and been accorded, particularly within the capital. (Even in May 1646, more than a year after his enforced resignation as Captain-General, he was presiding at the general muster of the City forces as commander-in-chief, despite the absence of any statutory authority for such a role.)[97] The attempted solution to this aspect of the problem was a second piece of legislation—introduced at the same time as the Self-Denying bill, and clearly part of the same process of reform[98]—elevating the 10th earl of Northumberland to the Governorship of the King's Children, and giving him the status of Lord Protector in all but name. Northumberland, the senior peer attending the House of Lords, was to have free choice of any of the royal residences;[99] was to have custody

[95] Essex, *A Paper Delivered into the Lords House . . , at the offering up of his Commission* (1645), 3 [*recte* 5].

[96] John Vicars, *Magnalia Dei Anglicana. Or Englands Parliamentary-Chronicle* (1646), 74–5; for Saye's involvement in the management of the legislation, *ibid.*, 130, and [Saye], *Vindiciae Veritatis*, 53. *CY* iii. 718.

[97] Bodleian Lib., MS Clarendon 28, f. 40v: newsletter, 21 May 1646.

[98] Vicars, *Magnalia Dei Anglicana*, 127–30. The conference on Fairfax's officer-list, approval of which made the creation of the New Model almost inevitable, was on 18 March 1645; Northumberland's appointment was approved by the Lords on the same day. Bodleian Lib., MS Tanner 60, f. 86 (report on the custody of the king's children); P.R.O., SP 16/511/62. *LJ* vii. 277, 317.

[99] P.R.O. (Kew), AO 1/2429/79 (Surveyor of the Works, decl. acc., 1647–8). Northumberland chose to reside in St James's Palace; his appartments were at the west end of the queen's chapel. *CJ* iv. 270.

of the dukes of Gloucester and York, and Princess Elizabeth;[100] and he was to take precedence over all others peers—including, now, the deposed earl of Essex—in the protocol of the house of Lords.

The vice-regal figure of Essex was to be supplanted by a figure, resident at St James's, of even more explicit vice-regal pretensions.[101] With the establishment of this Court at St James's[102] came the revival of the Board of Green Cloth to oversee expenditure in Northumberland's state household,[103] and a spate of appointments to vacant Household offices in which Northumberland's own household servants acquired offices in the reconstituted royal Household at Whitehall and St James's. Northumberland's Gentleman of the Wardrobe, Lancelot Thorneton, for example, acquired the title of Clerk of the Robes and Wardrobe to the king in 1646.[104] The following year Northumberland spent the staggering sum of £3,077 on what his accountant modestly described as 'a rich Coach'—a magnificently ornamented coach drawn by six coach horses—nominally for the duke of York, but used by Northumberland in his journeys from St James's Palace to the Parliament.[105]

If the elevation of the earl of Northumberland represented the baronial solution to the problem of the status claimed by Essex, the intimate connexion between the political and military aspects of that solution was epitomized in the new prominence assumed by Robert Scawen, Northumberland's secretary and the steward of Syon House, as chairman of the Army Committee[106]—the standing committee

[100] Bodleian Lib., MS Tanner 60, f. 86. House of Lords R.O., M[ain] P[apers] 14/4/45, f. 80; *CJ* iv. 270.

[101] Alnwick Castle, Northumberland MS O. I. 2(f): Northumberland to Hugh Potter, 23 Dec. 1646; Northumberland MS O. I. 2(g): the earl to Potter, 22 Dec. 1646. P.R.O., SP 16/513, f. 64 (notes made by Northumberland, *c.* 7 Feb. 1646).

[102] *The History of the King's Works*, ed. H. M. Colvin, iv (1982), 241–252; v (1976), fig. 21 (facing 247), for a plan of the palace. The palace had been extensively ornamented by Charles I: the king's collection of antique sculpture was housed there, and Van Dyck's 1633 equestrian portrait of Charles I hung at the end of the gallery.

[103] P.R.O., SP 16/539/300 (investigation into the accounts of Cornelius Holland, Clerk of the Green Cloth to the Prince, 2 Aug. 1645); SP 16/515/84.

[104] Petworth House, Sussex, MS 629; P.R.O., SP 28/251/1, f. 343v. *LJ* viii. 663, 680.

[105] Alnwick Castle, Northumberland MS U. I. 6, Gen. acc. 1646–7: 'for a rich Coach and sett of Coachhorses'. A royalist writer who saw the coach in April 1647 described it as a costly 'French Embrodered Coach [with] 6 excellent Coach horses'; it was also used by the royal children for drives in Hyde Park: Bodleian Lib., MS Clarendon 29, f. 165.

[106] P.R.O. (Kew), WO 47/1 (Ordnance Office, entry bk of orders 1644–5), 245 (order signed by Scawen); for Scawen's activities in general see, ibid., 211–345. Claydon House, Bucks., Verney MS: Henry Verney to Sir Ralph Verney, 17 April 1645. For Essex's reconciliation with the Scots—perhaps the most remarkable *volte face* associated with the coup—see, H.L.R.O., Willcocks MS 1: Essex to Manchester, 23 March 1645; and Dr Williams's Lib., MS 24.50 (Juxon diary), f. 37v.

charged with overseeing the financial and logistical supply of the army, and with maintaining relations with its new commander-in-chief, Sir Thomas Fairfax.[107] Not surprisingly, much of Scawen's work was undertaken from his master's houses: from Northumberland's state residence of St James's;[108] from his newly acquired Suffolk House;[109] or, as during the army negotiations of autumn 1647, from Syon House.[110] As the recent work of Dr Starkey has emphasised,[111] the functions of the 'household' and of the bureaucracy of the state were intimately linked in early modern England; to this the government erected by the nobility during the English civil war was no exception.

Thus the new-modelled army was not to provide Gardiner's janizaries of the 'puritan revolution'; nor was it—as has been argued—a balanced and essentially apolitical response to the military misfortunes of 1644.[112] Military disaster in the west, and Cromwell's suspiciously timely feud with the earl of Manchester,[113] provided the occasion for reform. But the palace coup of 1645—the coup which installed Northumberland in St James's Palace and demoted Essex,

[107] P.R.O. (Kew), WO 47/1 (Ordnance Office), 211–345. The committee was occasionally referred to as the Committee for the Army and Contracts (WO 47/1, 291). Scawen gradually supplanted Zouche Tate (chairman of the other army committee in January 1645), who was in ailing health: *CJ* iv. 26. As usual in the parliamentarian bureaucracy, the most effective members of the administrative committees were the nobility's men-of-business. Thomas Pury senior, who occasionally deputised for Scawen as chairman of the committee, was a client of (and later executor to) the earl of Pembroke, and intimately connected with the Saye-Northumberland interest which had pushed through these political and military reforms. For Pury, see also SP 28/257 (Army Cttee papers), unfol.; SP 28/28/4, f. 309; SP 16/514, f. 15; for his connection with Pembroke: Sheffield Central Lib., Elmhirst MS 1352/11; Elmhirst MS 1360, f. 6; with Salisbury: Hatfield, A. 44/8; he gave evidence on behalf of Nathaniel Fiennes at his trial in 1644: W. Prynne and C. Walker, *A true and full relation of the prosecution ... of Nathaniel Fiennes* (1644), sig. Aa2v. Pury also served on the vestry of the parish of St Martin-in-the-Fields, a body that was stacked with the clients of the parish's chief inhabitants, Northumberland, Pembroke and Salisbury: Westminster Public Lib., MS F 2517, f. 22.

[108] P.R.O. (Kew), AO 1/2429/79 (Surveyor of the Works, decl. acc., 1647–8).

[109] Bodleian Lib., MS Tanner 60, f. 214: Scawen to Sir John Potts, from Suffolk House (later renamed Northumberland House), 17 July 1645. For Scawen's powers of patronage as chairman of the committee: Silvanus Taylor to Scawen, 12 June 1645: SP 28/30/4, f. 389.

[110] *CJ* v. 298; Pury served as his second in the Commons: *CJ* v. 308. See also Scawen's accounts for the parliamentary commissioners to the army, 8 June–29 Sept. 1647: P.R.O., E 351/1275 (Pipe Office, decl. acc.).

[111] Starkey, 'Court history in perspective', 1–24.

[112] Cf. M. A. Kishlansky, *The Rise of the New Model Army* (Cambridge, 1979), 26–51.

[113] P.R.O., SP 16/503, ff. 140–182: depositions relating to Cromwell's accusations against the earl of Manchester; Dr Williams's Library, MS 24.50 (Juxon diary), ff. 24v, 27v–28, 31, 33. *Mercurius Britanicus*, no. 52 (30 Sept.–7 Oct. 1644); *ibid.*, no. 60 (2–9 Dec. 1644); *CJ* iii. 703–4.

the claimant of the Constableship, to the earls' benches in the House of Lords—was merely the culmination of a conservative aristocratic reaction to the phenomenon of Essex which had its origins in the peers' first nervous reaction to the vice-regal status he had successfully claimed in his 'triumph'—the triumph of a self-styled 'Supremus Imperator'—back in September 1643. The makers of this coup in the Lords were, almost to a man, the scions of Tudor Privy Councillors: Salisbury, Nottingham, Howard, Pembroke, North; or those whose claim to be *consiliarii nati* was even more ancient: men such as Northumberland, Kent, Dacre and Saye. Their ideas for a blue-print for the future government were to find expression in Saye's projected settlement of 1647.[114]

The political and baronial causes of the coup affected both the choice of Essex's successor, and the terms upon which he assumed his command. Fairfax inherited Essex's honorific as 'his Excellency'; but otherwise he entered upon an office radically transformed. There was to be no fealty sworn to the new commander-in-chief; no ceremonial entries into the capital at the conclusion of successful campaigns. Following on the towering and charismatic figure of Essex, invested with the mystique of Leicester and the martyred 2rd earl, Fairfax—the scholarly soldier, apparently lacking in either interest or acumen for politics—seemed an able and maleable choice. Indeed, after Essex, Fairfax's mediocrity in politics commended him to the Saye-Northumberland interest at Westminster no less than his distinction in the field. This recipient of Essex's military office was, moreover, a loyal upholder of the Percy interest in his native Yorkshire, and a friend of the earl of Northumberland—upon whom the political mantle snatched from Essex had so recently been cast.[115]

Nothing witnesses to the transformation of the status of the Lord Generalship so clearly as the change in the ceremonial and civic ritual

[114] *LJ* vii. 276–7; 297. I am grateful to Professor Hugh Trevor-Roper for a discussion on this point. J. S. A. Adamson, 'The English nobility and the projected settlement of 1647', *Historical Journal* xxx (1987), 567–602.

[115] Leeds Castle, Kent, Fairfax MS, unfol.: Northumberland to Ferdinando, Lord Fairfax, 9 Dec. 1644 (from York House). 'I am informed by my officers in the North', Northumberland wrote, '[that] your Lo[rdshi]p is pleased to afford them your countenance and protection vpon all occations in my businesses.' For the strength of Northumberland's ties with the Fairfaxes, see also: Alnwick Castle, Northumberland MS O. I. 2(f): Northumberland to Hugh Potter, 14 Jan. 1645; for their long standing: Christ Church, Oxford, Muniment Room, Nobility Letters (Evelyn coil.) I, f. 99: 1st Lord Fairfax to Northumberland, 26 Jan. [no year, but 1630s]. For Sir Thomas Fairfax's consultations at Syon House, on 31 July 1647, before the army's march on London: *A narrative by John Ashburnham of his attendance on King Charles the First* (2 vols., 1830), ii. 92; *The memoirs of Edmund Ludlow*, ed. C. H. Firth (2 vols, Oxford, 1894), i. 162; Hatfield, Accounts, Box L/1.

that attended its two incumbents. Essex's formal entries into the City were characterised, as we have seen, by vice-regal ceremonial, second only to that which attended the king at his entry into the City in November 1641. Until Essex's removal from command in 1645, these entries were annual events.[116] Fairfax's treatment was otherwise. Up to Pride's Purge, the Lord General was permitted only one formal entry into the City. In August 1647, after the abortive 'Presbyterian' coup of July, he made a triumphal entry into the City at the head of his troops, returning the Speakers to the two Houses and the Saye-Northumberland peers, to whom in large measure he owed his command, to an unrivalled dominance of the House of Lords. The symbolism of the procession was highly significant. Fairfax entered, not as Charles I and Essex had done, riding a charger—the formal equestrian entry of a Renaissance *triumphator*—but riding in a domestic coach, as the prelude to a magnificent cavalcade of the peers in their coaches, led by Northumberland in his magnificent new state coach.[117]

The political meaning of such a change in the civic ceremonial associated with the Lord Generalship was not lost on contemporaries. It was 'such a deep dissembled ceremony', observed one M.P., 'that no man but saw through it, and did beleeve, with reason, that the *Members* brought his Excellency to the Parliament, and not he them'.[118] When Essex received the thanks of Parliament in 1643, the two Houses had waited on him in person at Essex House; when Fairfax received thanks from the Speakers, it was normally by post. Essex had at times seemed Parliament's master; Fairfax, for the moment at least, seemed its employee—a circumstance which sharpened the point of Presbyterian taunts that the New Model was 'a mere mercenary army'.

Changed too were the conventions by which the war was to be fought. Gone were the self-conscious evocations of baronial wars: the challenges to combat, the oath 'to live and die' with the Lord General, the chivalric scruples over the safety of the person of the king. The new war of 1645 was to be professionalised and efficient, fought to victory by an able general, apparently innocent of political

[116] Even after Essex's disastrous western campaign of 1644, his return to London was attended by considerable ceremonial. He made a formal entry on 27 Sept. accompanied by two regiments, and was met by the sheriffs of the City and a delegation of chief citizens: L. C. Nagel, 'The Militia of London, 1640–9' (Ph.D. dissertation, University of London, 1982), 206.

[117] Bodleian Lib., MS Clarendon 30, f. 32: Sir Edward Forde to [Lord Hopton?], 9 Aug. 1647; *Perfect Occurrences of Every Daie Iournall*, no. 52 (6–13 Aug. 1647), 210–11 (B.L., E 518/17). Almost to a man, the peers who comprised that procession were the same group that had effected the deposition of Essex and the military reforms of 1645.

[118] G. S. [Giles Strangeways?], *A Letter from an Ejected Member of the House of Commons to Sir Jo: Evelyn* (16 Aug. 1648), 11.

ambition—to a victory which left power with an oligarchic faction at Westminster, not with a Lord General with aspirations to constabular rank.

With a redefinition of the purpose of war went a repudiation of the two great military offices of state: the Stewardship and the Constableship, the two offices which had outranked all others in the propositions of 1642. From the preparation of the Uxbridge Propositions, formulated contemporaneously with the military reforms over the winter of 1644–5, the Stewardship and Constableship were dropped from the list of the offices of state. Henceforth, the two senior officers of state would be the Chancellorship (already exercised as if in commission by the allies of the Saye-Northumberland group),[119] and the Lord Treasurership, to which Saye openly aspired.[120] Amongst the old nobility and their Commons allies at Westminster, the experience of what might be termed the baronial phase of civil war—during the years 1642–4—had provoked an oligarchic reaction. For this group at Westminster, their political power base was to be, even more emphatically than before, the control of place, patronage, and the effective working of their parliamentary 'interests' in the two Houses.

The redefinition of the political function of the army was embodied in the new commission to Fairfax as Lord General. Passed, against the staunch opposition of Essex's faction in the Lords,[121] the new commission omitted any reference to 'saving the safety of the King's person', which had been the touchstone of Essex's baronial conception of the war as a crusade against evil and papist counsellors. The war that was renewed in 1645 was to be fought, as Charles had long since perceived, to reduce him to the status of 'a Doge of Venice'.[122] The peers who effected the political coup of 1645 were fighting a war, in Lord Brooke's phrase, 'to reduce [the king] to a necessity of granting'.[123] There was more than a little truth in the charge of the royalist ballad-monger that

[119] H.L.R.O., MP 10/11/45, f. 38; *CJ* iv. 477, 599, 634. P.R.O. (Kew), AO 1/361/15. See also the draft in Northumberland's hand of a proposed list of Commissioners of the Great Seal: H.L.R.O., MP 24/12/46, f. 78; *LJ* viii. 626. For the earl of Kent's activities as Commissioner of the Great Seal, see Bedfordshire R.O., Lucas MS L 29/27/1. After the death of the earl of Bolingbroke in 1646, the earl of Salisbury joined Kent as the other peer in commission, further strengthening the influence of the Saye-Northumberland group: H.L.R.O., MP 3/7/46; *LJ* viii, 410.

[120] Bodleian Lib., MS Dep. c. 170 (Nalson papers xvi), ff. 181v, 193. Kent Archives Office, De L'Isle MS, U 1475/C 114/21: Sir John Temple to the earl of Leicester, 22 July 1641.

[121] *LJ* vii. 277; Kishlansky, *New Model Army*, 47.

[122] Scottish R.O., Hamilton MS GD 406/1/10492: Charles I to Hamilton, 25 June 1638. Bodleian Lib., MS Clarendon 34, f. 17.

[123] Lord Brooke, *Two Speeches made in the House of Peers* (1642/3), 6 (B.L., E 84/35).

You must have places and the Kingdomes sway,
The King must be a Ward to your Lord *Say*.[124]

The power-base of the nobility that displaced Essex was not to be the ability to mediate a settlement through the dominance of personal military command (one of the traditional roles of the nobility), but through the command of a complex patronage machine, in Parliament and in the bureaucracy of the state; through the triumph of an aristocratic oligarchy buttressed by an obedient and effective military force. Throughout the years 1646–7, it was the Saye-Northumberland group in the House of Lords, and their allies in the Commons, who fought most doggedly to oppose the disbandment of the army they had themselves 'new-modelled'.[125] The ancient military power base of the nobility, personal command of armies in the field—a power base upon which Essex had effectively built in the early years of the war—was effectively dismantled in England after 1645.

During the 1650s it was also dismantled literally. The passing of the 'military age' of the nobility was starkly symbolized by the demolition and slighting of castles throughout the country, enforced during the years immediately after the second civil war.[126] Castles such as Basing, Raglan, Warwick and Belvoir—the fortified bastions of the medieval nobility—had proved to be of dangerously contemporary use in England's most recent experience of civil war.[127]

By the reign of Charles II, a radically different attitude to military power and military service held sway among the nobility. Peers continued to hold at least nominal posts of command; but more for the lucrative trade in commissions this afforded than for zeal for martial honour in the field. After the great causes of the early seventeenth century—the heroic campaigns of Maurice of Nassau or of Gustavus Adolphus—the prospect of service in Bombay or Tangiers simply did not have the same cachet.[128] When, in 1688, the nobility again found it necessary to depose a king, it imported a foreign army to do its work. In little more than a generation there had been a profound change in the nobility's attitude to military command.[129] In 1640, as

[124] *Sampsons Foxes Agreed to Fire a Kingdom* (Oxford, [22 June] 1644), 7 (B.L., E 52/6).

[125] See especially the Lords' divisions of 4 March 1647 and 27 May 1647: *LJ* ix. 56–7, 207; Worcester College, Oxford, Clarke MS XLI, f. 137: [Gilbert Mabbot?] to Fairfax, [27 May 1647, or shortly thereafter].

[126] M. W. Thompson, *The Decline of the Castle* (Cambridge, 1987), 138–57, and appendix 3, 'Parliamentary demolition, proposed or executed, 1642–60', 179–85.

[127] Their destruction is recorded in detail in P.R.O., E 317 (Commonwealth, surveys).

[128] John Childs, *The Army of Charles II* (1976), 19, 23, 28–46, 115–51.

[129] During the 1620s and '30s, it was claimed, a generation of the peerage had sought service in foreign wars—against Spain in the Low Countries, and in the campaigns of the Thirty Years War—seeking the martial glory which was seen as the proper complement of the noble estate. 'At that time', Essex's biographer, Robert Codrington,

in 1340, generalship of armies in the field had been seen as the natural concomitant of noble status; by 1700, it had become the forlorn last choice of the noble younger son too stupid to find another more lucrative career.

Of course there were exceptions. Eminent military command remained a route of entry into the peerage for General Monck as for General Haig. Even after the Restoration, a few peers of ancient lineage continued to make their careers in war. Aubrey de Vere, 20th earl of Oxford, was a professional soldier into the reign of William III.[130] But he was a lone survivor of that antediluvian generation which had gone in search of martial honour in the Low Countries before the civil war.[131] Dodo-like, he lumbered on to the opening of the eighteenth century; but with his death in 1703, his illustrious and indigent title became extinct. Yet the martial tradition he represented had long since predeceased him. And, in the feudal ceremonial of 1646, amid the regal pomp attending the obsequies of the Captain-General of England's last baronial war, it had had its fitting interment.

---

wrote in 1646, 'the Netherland ... was the Schoole of honour for the Nobility of England in the service of Armes.' Codrington, *Life of Essex*, 8–9.

[130] Arthur Collins, *Historical Collections of the Noble Families* (1752), 276–82. His cousin, the 18th earl, had been Essex's companion-in-arms against Spínola in the 1620s. Cambridge University Lib., Add. MS 33 (Arthur Wilson's 'Observations'), ff. 9v–10.

[131] Collins, *Historical Collections*, 276–7.

THOMAS HOBBES ON THE PROPER SIGNIFICATION OF LIBERTY

The Prothero Lecture

By Quentin Skinner

READ 5 JULY 1989

I

'CIVIL philosophy', Hobbes declares in an oft-quoted boast at the start of *De Corpore*, is a science 'no older ... than my own book *De Cive*.'[1] As Hobbes explains in *De Cive* itself, and later in *Leviathan*, the failure of all previous efforts has simply been due to their 'want of method.'[2] The method hitherto followed, especially in the universities, has been to rely on the authority of selected writers and books.[3] The universities, indeed, have come to rely so heavily on one particular writer that their teachings no longer deserve to be called philosophy, but merely Aristotelity.[4] This approach, however, is nothing but 'a signe of folly', one that is 'generally scorned with the name of Pedantry.'[5] The only scientific way of proceeding is to follow the methods of geometry, which requires its practitioners to 'begin at settling the significations of their words'.[6] Only by this means can we hope to avoid the insignificant speech of the Schoolmen, and thereby lay the foundations for a genuine science of political life.[7] For 'the foundation of all true Ratiocination is the constant Signification of words.'[8]

As Hobbes turns to employ this approach in *Leviathan*, there is no

[1] Thomas Hobbes, 'Elements of Philosophy. The First Section. Concerning Body' in *The English Works*, ed. W. Molesworth, (11 vols. 1839–45), Vol I, ix. The Latin version, *De Corpore*, was first published in 1655; the English translation appeared in 1656. See H. Macdonald and M. Hargreaves, *Thomas Hobbes: A Bibliography* (1952), 41–2.

[2] Thomas Hobbes, *Leviathan*, Penguin Classics edn., ed. C.B. Macpherson (Harmondsworth, 1985), 114, Cf also 261. All subsequent references to *Leviathan* are to this edition, except for fn. 112, *infra*. I have retained the original spelling, but dropped Hobbes's copious italicisation. I have also felt free to modernise his punctuation where this helps to bring out more clearly my interpretation of his text.

[3] *Leviathan*, 106. Cf also 132, 307–8.

[4] *Leviathan*, 688.

[5] *Leviathan*, 117. Cf. also 112–13.

[6] *Leviathan*, 105.

[7] *Leviathan*, 105, 113.

[8] *Leviathan*, 428.

case in which he is so anxious to insist on his own definition, and to argue that all others are dangerously misleading, as he is in explicating the concept of liberty. It is striking, moreover, that his anxieties on this score increased as he progressively refined his theory of the state. In *The Elements of Law*, originally circulated in 1640, he voices no such concern and fails even to supply a formal definition of liberty. Only in *De Cive*, first published in 1642, does he formulate the basic definition on which he later relies.[9] Even at this stage, moreover, he still alludes only glancingly to the dangers of misunderstanding the term, while his application of his own formula is not entirely free from ambiguity.[10] By the time he came to publish *Leviathan* in 1651, however, all such equivocations had been removed, and the meaning of liberty had come to be one of his central themes. Not only does he devote a special chapter to discussing the liberty of subjects, but he constantly emphasises the importance of establishing 'the proper signification of the word', what it 'signifieth properly', its 'proper and generally received meaning', and how to understand it 'in the proper sense'.[11]

These developments prompt two questions, both of which I shall seek to answer in the final section of these remarks. Why does Hobbes become increasingly preoccupied by the idea of liberty? And why does he become increasingly anxious to insist that, as *Leviathan* puts it, 'it is an easy thing for men to be deceived' by its 'specious name'?[12] Before we can address these issues, however, we obviously need to be sure that we have understood what Hobbes means by liberty itself. This is a topic on which his commentators seem to me to have cast a considerable amount of darkness. So I shall first consider this purely

[9] Thomas Hobbes, *De Cive: The Latin Version*, ed. H. Warrender (Oxford, 1983), 167. For the corresponding passage in *The Elements of Law*, which lacks the formal definition, see Thomas Hobbes, *The Elements of Law*, ed. F. Tönnies with an Introduction by M. M. Goldsmith (1969), 134. As several scholars have recently argued, the English translation of *De Cive* issued in March 1651 is almost certainly not by Hobbes, despite Warrender's assertions to the contrary. See H. Warrender, 'Editor's Introduction' in Thomas Hobbes, *De Cive: The English Version* (Oxford, 1983), 4–8. Compare the scepticism voiced in M. M. Goldsmith, 'Picturing Hobbes's Politics: the Illustrations to *Philosophical Rudiments*', *Journal of the Warburg and Courtauld Institutes*, xliv (1981), 232–37, and the references there to earlier expressions of doubt. For further doubts see Noel Malcolm, 'Citizen Hobbes', *The London Review of Books*, 18–31 October, 1984, 22. The point is also taken up in Richard Tuck, 'Warrender's *De Cive*', *Political Studies*, xxxiii (1985), 308–15, esp. at 310–12. Since the 1651 translation is of such doubtful standing—and indeed makes use of a political vocabulary partly at odds with the one Hobbes generally employs when writing in English—I have preferred to make my own translations from Warrender's edition of the Latin test.

[10] For these ambiguities see the references given *infra* in fns. 183 and 184.

[11] See *Leviathan*, respectively at 189, 261, 262, 264.

[12] *Leviathan*, 267.

textual problem, before turning to the more contextual and historical questions in which I am principally interested.

II

When Hobbes first introduces the topic of human freedom in *Leviathan*, it is in connection with his discussion of 'the right of nature' in Chapter XIV. This he defines as 'the liberty each man hath to use his power as he will himself for the preservation of his own nature.'[13] This freedom or liberty[14], he at once stresses, must be defined in negative terms. The presence of liberty is always marked, that is, by the absence of something else. Specifically, it is marked by 'the absence of externall Impediments.'[15] And by 'impediments' Hobbes means anything that can hinder a man from using his powers 'according as his judgment and reason shall dictate to him.'[16]

This analysis is subsequently taken up and elaborated at the start of Chapter XXI, at which point Hobbes presents his formal definition of what it means to be a free man. 'A FREE-MAN is he that, in those things which by his strength and wit he is able to do, is not hindered to do what he has a will to.'[17] As this makes clear, Hobbes sees two essential elements in the concept of human freedom. One is the idea of possessing an underlying power or ability to act. As Hobbes had already observed in Chapter XIV, it is in relation to 'a man's power to do what hee would' that we speak of his being or not being at liberty.[18] The other is the idea of being unimpeded in the exercise of such powers. As Hobbes explains later in Chapter XXI, the freedom of a man 'consisteth in this, that he finds no stop in doing what he has the will, desire or inclination to do.'[19]

Hobbes's basic doctrine can thus be very simply summarised. He

[13] *Leviathan*, 189. Note that, because Hobbes equates human freedom with the freedom of a man, and because I am seeking to explicate his views, I have felt obliged to follow his usage. But I should not like it to be thought that this is an equation I accept.

[14] As Hobbes makes clear at the start of Chapter XXI of *Leviathan*—where he speaks (p. 261) of what 'LIBERTY, or FREEDOM, signifieth'—he makes no distinction of meaning between the two terms. I have followed him in using them interchangeably.

[15] *Leviathan*, 189.

[16] *Leviathan*, 189.

[17] *Leviathan*, 262.

[18] *Leviathan*, 189. Cf. also the earlier discussion of power in Chapter X, especially Hobbes's definition of 'The POWER of a man' as 'his present means to obtain some future apparent Good', 150.

[19] *Leviathan*, 262. The point is foreshadowed in the discussion of deliberation in Chapter VI. See especially 127, where Hobbes claims that deliberation is so called 'because it is a putting an end to the Liberty we had of doing or omitting according to our own Appetite or Aversion.'

already hints as much at the start of Chapter XIV of *Leviathan*,[20] but he says so most clearly at the end of *The Questions concerning liberty, necessity and chance*, his final reply to Bishop Bramhall on the problem of free will. A free agent is he who, in respect of his powers or abilities, 'can do if he will and forbear if he will.'[21]

As Hobbes recognises, however, this analysis is not yet a very illuminating one. We still lack an account of the kinds of limitations on human action that can count as impediments. To put the point another way, we still lack a criterion for distinguishing between inherent limitations upon our powers themselves, and positive constraints upon our freedom to exercise or forbear from exercising our powers in accordance with our will and desires.

Turning to this further theme at the start of Chapter XXI, Hobbes distinguishes two ways in which a man's freedom may be said to be hindered or impeded. The first is common to human and inanimate bodies.[22] It occurs when an agent encounters 'the opposition of some externall body' which operates in such a way that the agent is tied—or, as Hobbes also says, is bound[23]—so that 'it cannot move but within a certain space'.[24] Hobbes has just laid it down that to be free is to be unimpeded from doing or forbearing from doing something. But these are cases in which the agent is impeded from doing something. An action within his powers is rendered physically impossible of performance. It follows that such agents 'are not at Liberty to move in such manner as without those externall impediments they would.'[25]

The other way in which a man can be hindered from using his powers at will is considered in the same passage. This happens when he is physically bound or obliged to act in a particular way by the

[20] See *Leviathan*, 189, where 'right' is defined in terms of 'liberty to do or forbeare'. See also the earlier account of deliberation as the means by which we put an end to our liberty 'of doing or omitting'. Cf. fn. 19, *supra*.

[21] See Thomas Hobbes, *The Questions Concerning Liberty, Necessity and Chance* (1656), 301. Cf. also Hobbes's opening formula, 28–9. For the complete bibliography of Hobbes's debate with Bramhall, see Macdonald and Hargreaves, *Hobbes*, 37–41.

[22] See *Leviathan*, 261–2 and 660. At 261 Hobbes even claims that the concept of liberty can be applied to inanimate bodies (his own example being a body of water) 'no less' than to rational creatures. If he means by this that the concept can be applied in exactly the same way, this would seem to be a slip: for his definition of human freedom makes essential reference to the idea of the will. In his *Questions Concerning Liberty*, Hobbes explicitly distinguishes human freedom from wider notions of free action when he observes that 'I understand compulsion to be used rightly of living creatures only', 209. For Hobbes's view of compulsion, cf. fn. 26, *infra*.

[23] *Leviathan*, 189, 191.

[24] *Leviathan*, 261. Hobbes also speaks in the same passage (262) of the agent being 'restrained'. Cf. also 359, 401.

[25] *Leviathan*, 262.

operation of an irresistible external force.[26] Hobbes assumes that, if we are to describe a man as free, we must not only be able to say that he is free to act; we must also be able to say that, if he acts in a certain way, then he performs his action freely, in that he 'may refuse to do it if he will.'[27] If, by contrast, he cannot forbear from acting, then his action will not be that of 'one that was free.'[28] As Hobbes had already noted in his preliminary discussion in Chapter XIV, 'obligation and liberty are in one and the same matter inconsistent.'[29]

This second type of impediment might seem to be of merely residual significance, especially as Hobbes largely confines himself to illustrating it with such simple instances as that of the man who is 'led to prison by force.'[30] But in fact the category of actions we cannot forbear from performing is of considerable theoretical importance for Hobbes, since he takes it to be the means of defining two forms of human bondage.

One is that of slavery. According to Hobbes's analysis, both in *De Cive* and *Leviathan*, the lack of liberty suffered by slaves is not simply due to the fact that they are 'kept in prison or bonds'.[31] It is also due to the fact that 'their labour is appointed to them by another' in such a way that their bodies 'are not in their own power'.[32] A slave is thus defined as someone whose lack of freedom is due in part to the fact that he is, literally, a bondsman: someone who is bound or forced to act, and is not at liberty to forbear from acting.[33]

[26] Note that Hobbes distinguishes, with a fair degree of consistency, between being 'forced' and being 'compelled'. I am compelled if my will is coerced. I am forced if it is rendered physically impossible for me to forbear from acting in a certain way. For Hobbes, compulsion is compatible with liberty, although force is not. See especially the discussion in *Questions Concerning Liberty*, 199–200, 208–9, 216–17. This point is well brought out in A.G. Wernham, 'Liberty and Obligation in Hobbes', *Hobbes Studies*, ed. Keith C. Brown (Oxford, 1965), 117–39, at 123.

[27] *Leviathan*, 262.

[28] *Leviathan*, 262.

[29] *Leviathan*, 189.

[30] See *Questions Concerning Liberty*, 216–17. Hobbes earlier uses the same example in *Elements of Law*, 63. The reason the category may appear residual, even empty, is that Hobbes sometimes speaks as though an action we cannot forbear from performing cannot be treated as an action: it is a case in which we are acted upon, not a case in which we act. See for example the discussion in *Questions Concerning Liberty*, 209, 216–17. But the implication—that all actions are free by definition—is one that Hobbes elsewhere rejects. See, for example, *Leviathan*, 263, where he lays it down that it is only 'actions which proceed from the will' that 'proceed from liberty'.

[31] *Leviathan*, 255.

[32] *Leviathan*, 667.

[33] See *Leviathan*, 667 for the explicit distinction between 'the service of Bondmen' and of 'a voluntary Servant'. Except for discussing enslavement as a result of conquest in war, however, Hobbes does not explain how such bondage can arise. His discussion of slavery is perhaps somewhat in tension with his stress on the implications of human equality. On this point see further fn. 71, *infra*.

The other way in which human freedom is similarly forfeited is among those who admit God's providence. This too is stressed both in *De Cive* and *Leviathan*, although in this case the earlier analysis is the fuller one. God's power, to those who recognise it, must appear as irresistible.[34] It follows that when God issues a command to those who believe in him—for example through the Scriptures, which many believe to be the word of God—then 'they cannot forbear from obeying him.'[35] They are tied or bound to obey in such a way 'that their bodily liberty is forfeited.'[36] As Hobbes summarises in Chapter XLV of *Leviathan*, all religious believers 'are God's slaves.'[37]

The whole of Hobbes's analysis thus depends on his initial distinction between power and liberty. An agent forfeits his liberty if an external force renders him either powerless to act or powerless not to act in some particular way. The distinction is I think clear, but is nevertheless worth underlining. For as Hobbes himself stresses, it is all too easy for the two concepts to become confused.[38] The danger arises from the fact that, if we follow a Hobbesian analysis, we are bound to say of a man who is capable of exercising the power to act in some particular way that he is also at liberty to act in that way. In this case, the man's power and liberty amount to the same thing. This being so, there is a temptation to add—as Hobbes notes in his reply to Bramhall[39]—that if a man analogously lacks the power to act, he must also lack the liberty.

This is certainly a temptation to which 'negative' theories of liberty have regularly fallen prey in the twentieth no less than in the sev-

[34] See *De Cive: The Latin Version*, 221, and cf. *Leviathan*, 397.

[35] *De Cive: The Latin Version*, 223: 'non potest non obedire'. For a valuable discussion of this difficult passage, see Robert Orr, 'Thomas Hobbes on the Regulation of Voluntary Motion' in *Lives, Liberties and the Public Good*, ed. George Feaver and Frederick Rosen (1987), 45–60, at 58–9. Orr interprets Hobbes as claiming that, although fear of our fellow-men does not take away our liberty, fear of God does. Even in this passage, however, what Hobbes seems to be saying is that it is our fatalistic disbelief in our capacity to resist God's power which forces us to obey and so takes away our liberty. If we turn, moreover, to the corresponding passage in *Leviathan* (397), we find all reference to fear deleted. Hobbes is now clear that the believer is forced to obey simply by the fact that God appears as an irresistible force. Orr is surely right to point out, however, that there is something strange about this argument. As we have seen, Hobbes holds that liberty can only be taken away by external impediments to motion. It is clear that God's omnipotence will constitute such an impediment if it is a fact. But it is not clear how it can be said to do so if it is merely believed to be a fact. For further discussion of the passage from *De Cive*, see M. M. Goldsmith, *Hobbes's Science of Politics* (New York, 1966), 111–13 and Appendix 4.

[36] *De Cive: The Latin Version*, 223: 'libertas ... corporeis tollitur'.

[37] *Leviathan*, 668.

[38] See *Leviathan*, 262 and cf. *Questions Concerning Liberty*, 211.

[39] *Questions Concerning Liberty*, 209–11.

enteenth century.[40] But as Hobbes rightly observes, it may or may not make sense to claim that an agent who lacks power also lacks liberty. It will not make sense where the impediment to motion lies 'in the constitution of the thing itself.'[41] To take Hobbes's own example, a man 'fastned to his bed by sickness' lacks the power to move, but it makes no sense to say that he also lacks the liberty.[42] The reason he cannot be said to be unfree is that nothing is impeding him from moving; he is simply incapable of movement. This contrasts with the predicament of someone 'imprisoned or restrained with walls.'[43] His plight is similar to that of the sick man in that he is unable to leave. But the sick man would still be unable even if the prison doors were to be opened, whereas the prisoner is only unable because the doors remain locked. He possesses an underlying power or ability to leave which has been 'taken away' from him.[44] So while the sick man merely lacks ability, the prisoner lacks freedom.

If this interpretation is sound, it is worth adding that Hobbes's theory of human freedom seems to have been rather widely misunderstood. Hobbes is often singled out as the classic exponent of what is sometimes called the pure negative theory of liberty.[45] He is claimed, that is, to hold the view that an individual is unfree if and only if his doing of some particular action has been rendered impossible.[46] But this appears to be untrue to Hobbes's analysis in two distinct ways. Although Hobbes agrees that an agent may be said to lack freedom if an action within his powers has been rendered impossible, he does not think that this is the only way in which unfreedom can be produced.[47] The agent will also lack freedom if he is tied or bound to act in such a way that he cannot forbear from acting. The other misunderstanding is that, even if no one is rendering it impossible

[40] See, for instance, C. W. Cassinelli, *Free Activities and Interpersonal Relations* (The Hague, 1966), 28, for a contrasting discussion of an example very similar to the one Hobbes considers in *Leviathan*, 262. Felix Oppenheim, *Political Concepts: A Reconstruction* (Chicago, 1981), 87, gives a good criticism of Cassinelli's analysis.

[41] *Leviathan*, 262.

[42] *Leviathan*, 262. Cf. also *Questions Concerning Liberty*, 211.

[43] *Leviathan*, 262.

[44] See Hobbes's initial formula in *Leviathan*, 189, and cf. the summary in *Questions Concerning Liberty*, 285.

[45] See Michael Taylor, *Community, Anarchy and Liberty* (Cambridge, 1982), 142. As a paradigm of the pure negative theory Taylor cites Hillel Steiner, 'Individual Liberty', *Proceedings of the Aristotelian Society*, lxxv (1974–75), 33–50.

[46] This is to allude to the definition given by Steiner, *Aristotelian Society*, 1974–75, 33. I formerly accepted this interpretation of Hobbes's theory myself. See Quentin Skinner, 'Il concetto inglese di libertà', *Filosofia Politica*, iii (1989), 77–102, at 83–5.

[47] As appears to be assumed, for example, in J. P. Day, 'Individual Liberty' in *Of Liberty*, ed. A. Phillips Griffith (Cambridge, 1983), 17–29, where Hobbes's analysis is treated as though he is concerned only with being free and unfree to act.

for an agent to act in a given way, it still does not necessarily follow for Hobbes that the agent is free to perform the action concerned.[48] This is because, as we have seen, the action in question may still be beyond the agent's powers. It is true that, given the lines along which Hobbes analyses the concept, he might be willing to admit that the agent is free to try to perform the given action—although Hobbes does not in fact pronounce upon that question at any point. But what is certain is that, for Hobbes, the question of whether the action is one that the agent is or is not free to perform simply does not arise.

Rather than being an instance of the pure negative theory of liberty, Hobbes's analysis serves to suggest that there may be something amiss with the theory itself. To state it in its positive and most widely accepted form, the theory holds that a man is free unless an action within his powers has been subjected to 'preventing conditions.'[49] This formulation certainly avoids the awkwardness of claiming that a man remains free to perform actions that are beyond his powers. But it still appears to confuse the general concept of social freedom with the more specific notion of being free to act.[50] It overlooks the possibility that a man's lack of freedom may derive not from being unfree to act, but rather from being unable to act freely.[51]

III

So far I have presented Hobbes's theory of human freedom as a simple and unambiguous one. But it must be admitted that this interpretation faces a difficulty. It is a difficulty, moreover, that has caused many of Hobbes's commentators to conclude that his theory is not only more

[48] As appears to be assumed, for example, in M. M. Goldsmith, 'Hobbes on Liberty', *Hobbes Studies*, ii (1989), 23–39, who claims (24) that according to Hobbes 'to be unfree is to be restrained from acting as one wishes to act'. This implies that we remain free so long as no one restrains us from performing an action we may wish to perform. As we have seen, however, Hobbes's view is that, if the action in question is beyond our powers, the question of freedom does not arise. Nevertheless, Goldsmith's article seems to me very valuable, especially for its emphasis on the coherence of Hobbes's views about liberty, and I regret that it only appeared after the text of my own lecture had been completed and delivered.

[49] See for example the classic essay by Gerald C. MacCallum, 'Negative and Positive Freedom', *Philosophy, Politics and Society*, Fourth Series, ed. Peter Leslett, W. G. Runciman and Quentin Skinner (Oxford, 1972), 174–93, at 176.

[50] See the excellent discussion of this point in Oppenheim, *Political Concepts*, 83–84.

[51] This distinction is well drawn, however, in F. S. McNeilly, *The Anatomy of Leviathan* (1968), 171. See also J. W. N. Watkins, *Hobbes's System of Ideas* (1965), 120–22, and the valuable remarks on unfree action in D. D. Raphael, 'Hobbes' in *Conceptions of Liberty in Political Philosophy*, ed. Z. Pelczynski and John Gray (1984), 27–38, at 30.

complicated than I have been implying, but is also seriously confused.[52]

The main grounds for this accusation are furnished by the range of examples Hobbes uses to illustrate his theory at the start of Chapter XXI. One of the cases he considers is that of a free gift. 'When we say a Guift is free', he maintains, 'there is not meant any liberty of the Guift, but of the Giver, that was not bound by any law or Covenant to give it'.[53] Hobbes's point is that the agent is free in the sense of being able to act freely as opposed to being bound or forced to act. But his chosen instance seems to presuppose a view much broader than I have so far been suggesting of the range of ties that can properly be said to take away our liberty to forbear from acting. As well as the purely physical constraints of slavery, he now appears to include not merely the bonds of law, but also of our own promises.

A further example Hobbes discusses in the same passage is that of freedom of speech. 'When we speak freely', the freedom we exercise 'is not the liberty of voice or pronunciation, but of the man, whom no law hath obliged to speak otherwise than he did.'[54] Here Hobbes is making the contrasting point that the agent is free in the sense of being free to act as opposed to being prevented. But again he appears greatly to expand his sense of the range of ties that are capable of stopping us from acting, and hence of taking away our liberty. As well as the purely physical bonds on which he initially concentrated, he now appears willing to include the bonds of law as another such potential impediment.

In the light of such examples, it is easy to see how the accusation of inconsistency arises. Hobbes first defines freedom as the absence of purely physical hindrances. But he then seems to allow that our liberty can also be limited by legal and moral ties. By passing, as one critic has put it, 'from physical impediments to obligations' as his criterion of unfreedom, he leaves his analysis muddled and confused.[55]

[52] For the accusation that Hobbes's discussion of liberty is confused, see for example J. Roland Pennock, 'Hobbes's Confusing "Clarity"—the Case of "Liberty"' in *Hobbes Studies*, ed. Brown, 101–16, at 102, 116; A. G. Wernham, 'Liberty and Obligation in Hobbes' in *Hobbes Studies*, ed. Brown, 117–39, at 120–21; David P. Gauthier, *The Logic of Leviathan* (Oxford, 1969), 62, 65–6; Ralph Ross, 'Some Puzzles in Hobbes' in *Thomas Hobbes in his Time*, ed. Ralph Ross, Herbert W. Schneider and Theodore Waldman (Minneapolis, 1974), 42–60, esp. at 55–6; and Raphael, 'Hobbes' in *Conceptions of Liberty* ed. Pelczynski and Gray, 30–34. But for a valuable defence of Hobbes's consistency see W. von Leyden, *Hobbes and Locke: The Politics of Freedom and Obligation* (1982), 32–50, esp. 45–50; See also the article by Goldsmith cited in fn. 48, *supra*.

[53] *Leviathan*, 262.

[54] *Leviathan*, 262.

[55] McNeilly, *Anatomy of Leviathan*, 171. Similar criticisms are advanced by several of the commentators cited in fn. 52, *supra*. Note that, although *Leviathan* contains an extensive discussion of the concept of unfreedom, Hobbes at no point uses that word.

I cannot myself see, however, that these criticisms are justified. Consider first Hobbes's contention that we are tied or bound by our covenants and promises. It is certainly true that he speaks as if the act of promising, and thus of laying aside a right, prevents me from acting contrary to my word. I am said to be 'obliged or bound, not to hinder those to whom such Right is granted.'[56] He also speaks as though a promise or covenant can similarly tie or bind me to act. 'If I covenant to pay a ransom' I am said to be 'bound by it'; 'If I be forced to redeem my self from a Theefe by promising him mony' I am said to be 'bound to pay'.[57] Moreover, Hobbes also supplies an unambiguous account of the means by which these ties operate. It is a law of nature, as the start of Chapter XV declares, 'That men performe their Covenants made.'[58] And we are bound to obey the laws of nature. Not only are we 'commanded' and 'forbidden' by their dictates,[59] but they also 'bind to a desire they should take place.'[60] It is the laws of nature, in short, that tie or bind us to keep our covenants and promises.

Hobbes is no less clear, however, that these ties cannot be said to limit our liberty in the proper signification of the word. The laws of nature, as he repeatedly affirms, are 'improperly' called laws.[61] They are no more than 'dictates of Reason'[62], or 'habits of the mind'[63], which 'reason suggesteth' are 'conducive to peace.'[64] When we say, therefore, that we are tied or bound by these laws, this is only to say that, if we desire peace and defence, we are bound or obliged to follow the dictates of our reason. For it is reason which supplies us with 'theorems concerning what conduceth to the conservation and defence' of ourselves.[65] Such bonds as these, however, cannot genuinely restrict our liberty. As Hobbes has explained, such limitations can only derive from the natural strength of external impediments. But as Hobbes almost wistfully puts it, these bonds have no strength 'from

[56] *Leviathan*, 191.
[57] *Leviathan*, 198.
[58] *Leviathan*, 201.
[59] For these formulae see *Leviathan* respectively at 189 and 190.
[60] *Leviathan*, 215.
[61] *Leviathan*, 216–17. Cf. also 314.
[62] *Leviathan*, 216. Cf. also 190, 205, 320.
[63] *Leviathan*, 330.
[64] *Leviathan*, 188. Cf. also 314.
[65] *Leviathan*, 217. By now it is perhaps unnecessary to add that this understanding of what Hobbes means by being 'bound' serves to cast considerable doubt on the interpretation offered in H. Warrender, *The Political Philosophy of Hobbes* (Oxford, 1957). For my own latest comments on this hardy perennial of Hobbes scholarship, see Quentin Skinner, 'Warrender and Skinner on Hobbes: A Reply', *Political Studies*, xxxvi (1988), 692–5.

their own nature', for 'nothing is more easily broken than a man's word.'[66] They neither have the power to 'bridle' us from acting as ambition, avarice and anger dictate.[67] Nor do they have the power to force us to act and so 'keep men to their promises.'[68] They leave us, in short, in full possession of our liberty.

Hobbes admittedly adds that, although the force of words is 'too weak to hold men', there are two possible 'helps to strengthen it.' One is 'a Feare of the consequence of breaking our word'; the other 'a Glory or Pride in appearing not to need to breake it.'[69] However, it is Hobbes's contention that, in the case of covenants and promises, neither of these auxiliary strengths can be brought to bear. No reliance can be placed on pride. For this presupposes 'a Generosity too rarely found to be presumed on, especially in the pursuers of Wealth, Command or sensual pleasure, which are the greatest part of Mankind.'[70] But nor can we rely on fear. There is no reason to feel alarm at the consequences of failing to keep my promises unless I have good grounds for fearing either the wrath of God or of my fellow-men. But there is no reason to entertain a sufficient fear of my fellow-men. For 'Nature hath made men so equall' that they will have just as strong a reason for feeling intimidated by me.[71] Nor does the fear of being punished by God supply a rational person with a sufficient motive for keeping his promises. Any rational person is bound to confess that God is completely incomprehensible.[72] This being so,

[66] *Leviathan*, 192. Yet Hobbes does say, in discussing his example of a free gift (262), that it will be free if the giver 'was not bound by any law or covenant to give it.' The addition of the words 'or covenant' appears to be a slip. The liberty of the giver can certainly be bound by law, in that the law constrains our liberty as subjects. But it cannot similarly be constrained by his own covenants, which are but words, and in the absence of Laws are 'of no strength to secure a man at all.' Cf. *Leviathan*, 223. But Hobbes's consistency can be rescued if we take him to be referring to just those cases in which a promise or covenant can be legally enforced.

[67] *Leviathan*, 196.

[68] *Leviathan*, 200. Cf. also 231.

[69] *Leviathan*, 200.

[70] *Leviathan*, 200. As Michael Oakeshott in particular has emphasised, however, Hobbes at this point leaves open the possibility that pride can be 'moralized', and thus that justice and the pursuit of glory need not be incompatible. See Michael Oakeshott, *Hobbes on Civil Association* (Oxford, 1975), esp. 119–25; For the place of 'generous natures' in Hobbes's theory, see also Keith Thomas, 'The Social Origins of Hobbes's Political Thought', *Hobbes Studies*, ed. Brown, 185–235, esp. 202–7.

[71] For the natural equality of men, see *Leviathan*, 183. For the fact that this will tend (in the absence of compulsive laws) to militate against our keeping of our promises, simply because no sufficient 'inequality of power' will appear, see 200. But if 'Nature hath made men so equall' as Hobbes here argues, how can one man get another so completely into his power as to enslave him? Hobbes does not directly address this point.

[72] This point is constantly reiterated. See *Leviathan*, 167, 171, 403–4, 430. This does

there can be 'no natural knowledge of man's estate after death, much less of the reward that is then to be given to breach of faith.'[73] Nor does it alter the case that the Scriptures appear to promise us punishments after death for failing to abide by our word. For while we may believe, yet we cannot possibly know, that the Scriptures are indeed the word of God.[74] It follows that, for all we know, there may be no such punishments. And it follows from this—at least if we reject Pascal's wager, as Hobbes here implicitly does—that 'covenants, without the sword, are but words, and of no strength to secure a man at all.'[75]

A similar set of considerations applies if we turn to Hobbes's account of the manner in which human laws may be said to act as a tie or bond. Again, there can be no doubt that Hobbes repeatedly speaks in this way. The force of law is capable of binding men from acting, as when it serves 'to tie their hands from rapine and revenge.'[76] It is also capable of obliging them to act, as in the case where 'Subjects are bound to uphold whatsoever power is given to the Soveraign.'[77] But again, the question is whether these bonds can be counted as impediments to liberty in the proper signification of the word.

To grasp Hobbes's answer, we need to begin by making a cardinal distinction that he himself draws in the passage of Chapter XXI of *Leviathan* immediately following the one on which I have so far concentrated. On the one hand, there is the idea of liberty as he has so far been considering it, the idea of 'naturall liberty, which only is properly called liberty.' But on the other hand, we also need to take note of a distinct concept which he now introduces for the first time, a concept which he labels 'the Liberty of Subjects'.[78]

---

not mean, of course, that Hobbes disbelieves in God, although it does mean that he sharply distinguishes knowledge from mere belief. Cf. fn. 74, *infra*, and William B. Glover, 'God and Thomas Hobbes', *Hobbes Studies*, ed. Brown, 141–68.

[73] *Leviathan*, 206. Cf. also 130. This dismissal of the fear of God as a rational ground for obedience was still exceptional. See David Wootton, 'The Fear of God in Early Modern Political Theory', Canadian Historical Association *Historical Papers, 1983*, 56–80.

[74] For this claim see *Leviathan*, 425, 614. For the fact that we also cannot hope to receive any supernatural revelation of God's will, cf. 331–3. Hobbes thus distances himself—as in the discussion at 395–8—from the claim that we can acquire knowledge of an omnipotent God. Cf. the valuable discussion in R. J. Halliday, Timothy Kenyon and Andrew Reeve, 'Hobbes's Belief in God', *Political Studies*, xxxi (1983), 418–33.

[75] *Leviathan*, 223. For a sharply contrasting account of the relationship between God's law and political obligation, see F. C. Hood, *The Divine Politics of Thomas Hobbes* (Oxford, 1964), esp. 85–90, 135–7.

[76] *Leviathan*, 238. On the capacity of laws to bind or restrain us from acting, see also 388, 701.

[77] *Leviathan*, 334. On the capacity of laws to oblige or constrain us to act, see also 591, 700.

[78] *Leviathan*, 263.

There is no doubt that the force of law serves to limit our liberty as subjects. To say that someone is a subject is to say that he has covenanted to give up the condition in which we all naturally find ourselves, the condition of 'meer Nature' in which 'every man holdeth this Right, of doing any thing he liketh.'[79] But to say that the state of nature can be defined as a condition in which everyone can do as they please is to say that it is a state in which, apart from our obligation to obey the laws of nature, there can be no legal obligations at all. The state of nature is simply defined as a state of lawlessness, a condition in which we are free from the binding force of any agreed human laws. But this is to say that there is a sense in which the state of nature must be a condition in which there is 'a full and absolute Libertie in every Particular man.'[80] There is therefore a sense in which, in agreeing to give up our natural condition, we must be deciding to give up a form of liberty. By covenanting to become subjects of a Commonwealth, we agree to regulate our behaviour according to its civil laws. 'But Civil Law is an Obligation, and takes from us the Liberty which the Law of Nature gave us. Nature gave a Right to every man to secure himselfe by his own strength, and to invade a suspected neighbour by way of prevention; but the Civil Law takes away that Liberty'.[81]

It is the fulcrum of Hobbes's theory of the Commonwealth to insist on the rationality of giving up this freedom from any obligation to obey human laws. Because everyone in the state of nature enjoys this freedom, and because 'nature hath made men so equal' in power and strength,[82] the state of nature can only be described as a condition of liberty in the most paradoxical sense. It can equally well be described as a condition in which we all enjoy an equal liberty to master and enslave our neighbours, while they enjoy the same liberty 'to make themselves Masters' of our own 'persons, wives, children and cattell' if they can.[83]

Nevertheless, there remains a sense in which liberty is forfeited when we covenant to become the subjects of a Commonwealth.[84] To

[79] *Leviathan*, 183, 188, 190.

[80] *Leviathan*, 266. Cf. also 207, 212, 240, 273, 395.

[81] *Leviathan*, 334–5. Cf. also 240.

[82] *Leviathan*, 183–4.

[83] *Leviathan*, 184–5; cf. also 264.

[84] As *Leviathan*, 315 puts it, 'the Right of Nature, that is, the naturall Liberty of man, may by the Civill Law be abridged and restrained; nay, the end of making Lawes is no other but such Restraint'. But this summary could perhaps be misleading. As Hobbes has already argued (263), to speak of natural liberty is only to speak of the absence of external impediments. But this is not the form of liberty that defines the state of nature. What characterises that state is freedom from the obligation to obey any human laws.

live as a subject is, by definition, to live in subjection to law.[85] To speak of the liberty of a subject is thus to speak of nothing more than 'the silence of the Law.'[86] If there are 'cases where the Soveraign has prescribed no rule, there the Subject hath the liberty to do or forbeare according to his own discretion.'[87] But where the law enjoins or forbids a certain course of action, there the subject is tied or bound to act or forbear from acting as the law and sovereign command.[88]

As Hobbes makes clear at the outset, however, these considerations apply only to the liberty of subjects. It remains to ask whether these considerations also apply to liberty in the proper signification of the word. For only in that case will it be justifiable to claim that Hobbes's exposition is confused.

Before turning to that question, it is important to note that Hobbes allows one exception even to his doctrine that the form of liberty characteristic of the state of nature is cancelled by our obligation to obey the civil laws. The exception is grounded on the fact that, when I convenant to take upon myself the bonds of a subject, 'the motive and end for which this renouncing and transferring of Right is introduced is nothing else but the security of a man's person in his life and in the means of so preserving life as not to be weary of it.'[89] It follows that, if 'the end of obedience is protection', there must be certain natural rights—and hence liberties of action—that 'can by no Covenant be relinquished.'[90] Specifically, I cannot consistently agree to relinquish my freedom to act in protection of my life and bodily liberty. For my sole aim in agreeing to the Covenant was to assure a better protection for precisely those rights than I could ever have hoped to achieve by my own unaided efforts in the free but warlike condition of mere nature.[91]

However, the main point on which Hobbes wishes to insist is that, even in those cases where the liberty of the state of nature is undoubtedly abridged by our obligation to obey the civil laws, this does nothing to limit our liberty in the proper signification of the word.

[85] For this point see *Leviathan*, 273, 356, 367.

[86] *Leviathan*, 273. Apart from the exception constituted by 'the true Liberty of a Subject' (268), which 'can by no covenant be relinquished' (272). On this point see *infra*, fns. 90 and 91.

[87] *Leviathan*, 271.

[88] Hence Hobbes defines a crime (*Leviathan*, 336) as 'the Committing (by Deed or Word) of that which the Law forbiddeth, or the Omission of what it hath commanded.'

[89] *Leviathan*, 192. Cf. also 254, 272.

[90] *Leviathan*, 272.

[91] For this claim see *Leviathan*, 199, and cf. also 337. For the range of things that a subject, 'though commanded by the Soveraign' may 'without Injustice refuse to do', see 268–71.

Hobbes of course intends this conclusion to seem a paradoxical one. But the paradox can readily be resolved if we turn to the account he gives of the distinctive ways in which any system of law operates to ensure the obedience of those subject to it. There are two separate routes, according to Hobbes, by which a citizen can come to feel the force of a law and decide to obey it. First, all rational persons will, *ex hypothesi*, recognise that obedience is in their interests. For the basic aim of law is to seek peace by protecting life and liberty, and these are the goals that all rational persons seek above all. So the liberty of such agents to act as their judgment and reason dictate will not in the least be infringed by their obligation to obey the law. The dictates of their reason and the requirements of the law will prove to be one and the same.

This expresses a traditional view about the compatibility of law and liberty, one that John Locke was classically to restate a generation later in his *Two Treatises of government*. 'Law in its true notion is not so much the Limitation as the direction of a free and intelligent Agent to his proper interests.' Locke draws the inference that, when we submit to the direction of such laws, this will constitute an expression rather than a restriction of our liberty. 'That ill deserves the Name of Confinement that hedges us in only from Bogs and Precipices.'[92] This is not merely a doctrine that Hobbes appears to endorse, but one that he enunciates in the form of a simile later echoed by Locke with remarkable closeness. 'The use of Lawes', as Hobbes puts it in discussing the office of the sovereign in Chapter XXX, 'is not to bind the People from all Voluntary actions, but to direct and keep them in such a motion as not to hurt themselves by their own impetuous desires, rashnesse, or indiscretion, as Hedges are set, not to stop Travellers, but to keep them in the way.[93]

As Hobbes stresses, however, this is not the reason why the generality of men obey the law, moved as they are by mere considerations of wealth, command or sensual pleasure. The only mechanism by which they can be brought to obey is by making them more terrified of the consequences of disobedience.[94] As we have seen, there is admit-

[92] John Locke, *Two Treatises of Government*, ed. Peter Laslett, Student Edition (Cambridge, 1988), II, para. 57, page 305.

[93] Hobbes puts the point in this way in the course of discussing the extent to which laws are necessary. See *Leviathan*, 388. But the argument is a corollary of his earlier contention that we are bound by reason to obey the laws of nature. Cf. esp. 215.

[94] Hobbes occasionally seems to allow, however, that there can also be a more direct mechanism: a citizen may be physically forced to act by an authorised agent of the commonwealth. For passages in which this seems to be envisaged, see *Leviathan*, 196, where the 'common Power' of the state is said to be capable of compelling by force, and 269, where the sovereign is described as authorising assault.

tedly no hope of employing this device outside the confines of the commonwealth. Covenants without the sword are but words, and of no strength to secure a man at all. But if a 'visible Power' is erected 'to keep them in awe, and tie them by fear of punishment', then there is every prospect of compelling them both to act in line with their obligations and at the same time to forbear from acting as partiality, pride and revenge would otherwise dictate.[95]

It is of course true that, where the mechanism of using fear to produce obedience works successfully, a subject will elect not to exercise his powers or abilities in various ways. The whole purpose of assigning the right of punishment to sovereigns is 'to forme the wills' of subjects in just this way.[96] Hobbes's point, however, is that this does nothing to take away the continuing power or ability of a subject to act as his will and desires dictate. 'The Consent of a Subject to Sovereign Power' is such that 'there is no restriction at all of his own former natural liberty.'[97]

To see how Hobbes can consistently defend this crucial conclusion, we need only recall his account of the means by which we are alone capable of forfeiting our liberty in the proper signification of the word. An external impediment must intervene in such a way that we are either stopped from acting or forced to act contrary to our will and desires. But neither fear nor any other passion of the soul can possibly count as such an impediment. Rather, a man who acts out of fear performs his action because he wills or desires to avoid various consequences which, he fears, will otherwise befall him. Of such a man we may certainly say that he acts as he does because his will has been 'formed' or 'compelled'.[98] But to compel someone's will is only to cause him to have a will or desire to act other than the will or desire for the sake of which he would otherwise have acted. When such a person acts, it will still be because he possesses the will or desire to act in precisely the way in which he acts. It follows that, even if the cause of his will is fear, the actions he performs out of fear will still be free actions.

To illustrate this argument, Hobbes takes the familiar example originally put forward by Aristotle at the start of Book III of the *Nicomachean Ethics*, the example of a man who 'throweth his goods into

[95] *Leviathan*, 223. Cf. also 343, 355.
[96] *Leviathan*, 227.
[97] *Leviathan*, 269.
[98] Because Hobbes distinguishes between bodily coercion, which takes away liberty, and coercion of the will, which does not, he has no objection to describing threats of punishment as coercing and compelling us to act, while insisting that the resulting actions will nevertheless be freely performed. For his invocation of this vocabulary, see *Leviathan*, 196, 202, 362, 594, 670.

the Sea for feare the ship should sink.'[99] The man certainly acts out of fear; so we may say if we like that he felt compelled to act. But as Hobbes grimly adds—challenging Aristotle's analysis[100]—'he doth it nevertheless very willingly, and may refuse to do it if he will: it is therefore the action of one that was free.'[101]

Hobbes's basic argument is thus that 'Feare and Liberty are consistent'.[102] It follows that, if we speak of being tied or bound by the laws, we cannot be speaking of natural ties, but only of artificial or metaphorical ones. Hobbes himself seems anxious to underline this point, for he proceeds to describe the artificial character of these bonds in a grotesque piece of imagery at odds with his usual expository style. 'As men for the atteyning of peace, and conservation of themselves thereby, have made an Artificiall Man, which we call a Commonwealth, so also have they made Artificial Chains, called Civill Lawes, which they themselves, by mutuall covenants, have fastned at one end to the lips of that Man or Assembly to whom they have given the Soveraigne Power; and at the other end to their own Ears.'[103]

Hobbes is alluding here to Lucian's version of the fable of Hercules. According to Lucian, the ancient Gauls thought of Hercules as a venerable and exceptionally prudent orator, and symbolised his gifts of persuasion by picturing him as drawing men along by fetters attached at one end to his tongue and at the other end to his followers' ears.[104] Hobbes's original readers might perhaps have been surprised to come upon this sudden classical flourish, especially as Hobbes himself boasts in his Review and Conclusion that he has deliberately left *Leviathan* unencumbered with any such conventional references to ancient authorities.[105] But Hobbes would undoubtedly have expected his original readers both to recognise his allusion and to grasp its relevance, especially as Lucian's claim that men can be 'led by the ears' had already become a favourite *topos* among humanist writers on rhetoric by the end of the sixteenth century.[106] For Hobbes, the moral of the

[99] *Leviathan*, 262. For Aristotle's discussion see *The Nicomachean Ethics*, 1110a.

[100] According to Aristotle, *Ethics*, 1110a, the action is 'mixed': voluntary and yet in a sense involuntary.

[101] *Leviathan*, 262. Hobbes makes the same point in his *Questions Concerning Liberty*, 199, 208.

[102] *Leviathan*, 262. Cf. *Questions Concerning Liberty*, 209.

[103] *Leviathan*, 263–4.

[104] See Lucian, 'Heracles' in *Lucian*, ed. and trans. A. M. Harmon, 8 vols., Vol. I (1913), 65.

[105] *Leviathan*, 726–7.

[106] See for example the reference to those who are 'subjects à estre menez par les oreilles' in Michel de Montaigne, *Essaies*, ed. Jean Plattard, 6 vols. (Paris, 1946), II, 55, and Montaigne's further reference to the same *topos* at II. 230 in the course of his discussion of oratory. Cf. the claim that 'with his golden chaine/The Orator so farre mens harts doth bind' in Sonnet LVIII of Philip Sidney, 'Astrophel and Stella' in *The*

story seems clear. On the one hand, the artificial chains by means of which we are persuaded to obey the law are of course sufficient to bind us as subjects. For the category of 'subject' is itself an artificial one, the product of that indispensable piece of political artifice, the Covenant, from which political obligation can alone be derived.[107] But on the other hand, these chains 'in their own nature' are 'but weak'. They can only be made to hold 'by the danger, though not by the difficulty of breaking them.'[108] We retain our natural liberty, in short, to break through what Hobbes later calls the cobweb laws of our country whenever we choose.[109]

I cannot see, therefore, that there is any serious inconsistency in Hobbes's theory of human freedom. He does not contradict himself by first saying that liberty can only be constrained by external impediments and later that it can also be constrained by laws. Rather one can summarise his argument by observing that liberty on the one hand, and civil law on the other, belong for Hobbes to different spheres. Liberty belongs to the sphere of nature, the sphere in which everyone has an equal right, and thus a liberty, 'to use his own power, as he will himselfe, for the preservation of his own Nature'.[110] This liberty can only be constrained by ties or bonds which are themselves natural—that is, physical—in character. But civil law belongs to the sphere of artifice, the sphere in which, as Hobbes's Introduction explains, 'by Art is created that great Leviathan, called a Common-wealth, or State, (In latine Civitas) which is but an Artificial Man'.[111] There is of course a sense in which the laws of the Commonwealth may be said to limit our liberty as subjects, since we may feel sufficiently frightened of the consequences of disobeying them to feel tied or bound by their commands. But the ties in this case are purely artificial in character. They leave entirely unimpaired our natural liberty to make use of our powers as we please. Summing up at the end of Chapter XXI, Hobbes spells out this crucial implication as unambiguously as possible: 'generally all actions which men doe in Common-wealths for feare of the law are actions which the doers had liberty to omit.'[112]

Complete Works, ed. Albert Feuillerat, Vol. II (Cambridge, 1922), 241–301, at 265. Lucian's image of Hercules appears as Emblem CLXXXI in Andreae Alciati, *Emblemata*, cum commentariis Claudii Minois [et al.] (Padua, 1621), 751.

[107] On the artificial character of the Covenant, see *Leviathan*, 226, and cf. the Introduction, 81.

[108] *Leviathan*, 264.

[109] *Leviathan*, 339.

[110] *Leviathan*, 189.

[111] *Leviathan*, 81.

[112] Here I quote from the first edition of *Leviathan* (1651), 108, since this sentence is garbled in the Macpherson edition.

IV

I have now tried to lay out what I take to be Hobbes's view about the proper signification of liberty. But I am far from supposing that I have said enough to enable his theory to be fully understood. As I indicated at the outset, it remains to explain why he should have been so anxious to insist that this explication of the concept is the only possible one. Having followed the account he gives, it now becomes possible to rephrase that initial question more pointedly. Why should Hobbes have been so anxious to insist on such a restricted analysis of the circumstances in which we can legitimately claim that our liberty has been infringed?

The basic answer is I think that Hobbes had a profound philosophical motive for drawing the boundaries of unfreedom in such a narrow way. On the one hand, a major concern of *Leviathan* is to explore the relationship between liberty and political obligation. Hobbes accordingly stands in need of a firm criterion for distinguishing between free and unfree actions. But on the other hand, Hobbes is a determinist. He cannot allow that anyone is ever free to will or not to will. To be free is to be unimpeded from moving according to one's will or desire. But since the will itself 'is not subject to Motion', it cannot be 'subject to Impediment.'[113] It follows that 'from the use of the word Freewill, no liberty can be inferred to the will, desire or inclination' in any instance at all.[114]

It might seem that this leaves Hobbes with an insuperable difficulty. But by adopting the precise view of human freedom I have outlined, he is able to frame an elegant solution to it. On the one hand, he is able to maintain that the will is never free, always determined. 'Every act of mans will, and every desire and inclination proceedeth from some cause', so that 'to him that could see the connexion of those causes, the necessity of all mens voluntary actions would appeare manifest.'[115] But on the other hand, he is able to mark a clear distinction between free and unfree actions. A man remains free provided that no external impediment obstructs him from acting according to his will or desire. He only ceases to be free if he is impeded in such a way that his will (which is itself caused) no longer functions as the cause of his actions.

As Bishop Bramhall acutely remarked, Hobbes is here reviving an essentially stoic vision of the compatibility between liberty and necessity.[116] The effect is to enable him to speak of human freedom in

[113] *Leviathan*, 262. Cf. *Questions Concerning Liberty*, 29.

[114] *Leviathan*, 262. Cf. *Questions Concerning Liberty*, 289.

[115] *Leviathan*, 263.

[116] Modern commentators have been inclined to credit Hobbes with the invention of

a manner wholly consistent with his determinism. An agent's will is never free; but where an agent is unimpeded from acting at will, we may nevertheless speak of free action. As Samuel Pepys noted in his *Diary* for 20 November 1661, the solution is 'very shrewd'.[117]

As well as his metaphysical commitments, however, Hobbes had at least two powerful reasons of a political nature for wishing to draw the boundaries of unfreedom in a restricted way It is clear in the first place that he felt an urgent need to respond to the dangers he had come to associate with the classical republican theory of liberty espoused by so many of his fellow-countrymen. This attitude reflects perhaps the sharpest change of direction we encounter at any point in the evolution of Hobbes's political thought.[118] In *The Elements of Law* Hobbes had basically accepted the classical republican case, arguing that 'liberty in a commonwealth' can only be said to be truly secured 'in the popular state or democracy.'[119] Aristotle is warmly praised for having stressed this insight: he 'saith well' that 'the ground or intention of a democracy is liberty'.[120] In the *De Cive*, however, Hobbes had already begun to change his mind. Aristotle's contention that 'in the case of a Commonwealth governed by its own citizens liberty can simply be assumed' is now dismissed as a vulgar speech, and Aristotle is criticised 'for following the custom of his time in confusing dominion with liberty'.[121] By the time he published *Leviathan*, moreover, Hobbes had come to have a new and far graver reason for wishing to repudiate the classical republican theory of liberty. He had come to believe that 'by reading of these Greek and Latine Authors, men from their childhood have gotten a habit (under a false shew of Liberty) of favouring tumults, and of licentious controlling the actions of their Sovereigns'.[122] One of the results, he now feels convinced, has been the civil war itself. The outcome of being 'made to receive our opinions concerning the Institution, and Rights of Common-wealths from Aristotle, Cicero' and other defenders of popular states has been 'the effusion of so much blood, as I think I may truly say, there never was

his 'compatibilist' doctrine. See for example Raphael in *Conceptions of Liberty*, 30. But Cf. Bramhall's comments on Hobbes's evident debt to the stoics, quoted by Hobbes in his *Questions Concerning Liberty*, 192–4, 195–7.

[117] Samuel Pepys, *The Diary*, ed. Robert Latham and William Matthews (11 vols. 1970–83), ii, 217.

[118] A point excellently brought out in Gauthier, *Logic of Leviathan*, 145–6.

[119] *Elements of Law*, 169–70.

[120] *Elements of Law*, 170.

[121] *De Cive: The Latin Version*, 176: 'Aristoteles ... consuetudine temporis libertatem pro imperio nominans. Lib. 6. *Politicorum*, cap.2. *In statu populari libertas est ex suppositione. Quod vulgo dicunt.*'

[122] *Leviathan*, 267.

anything so deerly bought, as these Western parts have bought the learning of the Greek and Latine tongues.'[123]

According to the exposition Hobbes now gives in Chapter XXI, the classical republican theory of liberty may be said to embody two false and seditious elements. One is the claim—which Hobbes again quotes from Aristotle's *Politics*—that 'in democracy, Liberty is to be supposed'; for 'tis commonly held that no man is Free in any other government.'[124] The other is the connected doctrine that Greece, Rome and modern republics are worthy in some special sense to be described as 'free Commonwealths', whereas 'all manner of Commonwealths but the Popular' can be dismissed as tyrannies.[125]

Faced with these contentions, which he now regards as so dangerous, what Hobbes does is to deploy his distinctive analysis of liberty in such a way as to try to show that both these claims are arbitrary and absurd. This is obvious, he thinks, in the case of the inflammatory contention 'that the Subjects in a Popular Common-wealth enjoy Liberty; but that in a Monarchy they are all Slaves.'[126] As Hobbes has explained in Chapter XXI, to speak of the liberty of subjects is only to speak of the silence of the law. But all Commonwealths have laws, and no subject is free of them. 'They that live under a monarchy' may deceive themselves into thinking otherwise. But we never encounter this illusion among those who actually live under popular governments. For as Hobbes adds in his most forbidding tones, 'they find no such matter.'[127]

No less absurd, on the analysis Hobbes now gives, is the idea of 'free Commonwealths', the idea 'whereof there is so frequent and honourable mention' in Greek and Roman writings on statecraft.[128] Given that freedom merely consists in the absence of impediments,

[123] *Leviathan*, 267, 268. Cf. also 369, 698–99. The charge is reiterated in *Behemoth*, ed. F. Tönnies with an Introduction by M.M. Goldsmith (1969), 3, 23. See also R. MacGillivray, 'Thomas Hobbes's History of the English Civil War: A Study of *Behemoth*', *Journal of the History of Ideas* xxxi (1970), 179–98. James Harrington sought in *Oceana* (1656) to revive the classical theory of liberty—especially as enunciated by Machiavelli in his *Discorsi*—in direct opposition to Hobbes's account. See James Harrington, 'Oceana' in *The Political Works of James Harrington*, ed. J.G.A. Pocock (Cambridge, 1977), esp. pp. 161–3. For the Machiavellian account itself, and for Hobbes's attack on it, see Quentin Skinner, 'The Idea of Negative Liberty: Philosophical and Historical Perspectives' in *Philosophy in History*, ed. Richard Rorty, J.B. Schneewind and Quentin Skinner (Cambridge, 1984), 193–221.

[124] *Leviathan*, 267. Cf. also 369.

[125] *Leviathan*, 698. Cf. also 266.

[126] *Leviathan*, 369. But for a contrasting explanation of Hobbes's rejection of this belief, see Richard Tuck, *Hobbes* (Oxford, 1989), 47.

[127] *Leviathan*, 369.

[128] *Leviathan*, 266. Hobbes also mocks the absurdity of 'free states' in *Behemoth*, ed. Tönnies, 164.

the only sense that can be assigned to this concept is that such commonwealths must be free to act as they will or desire. But this form of natural liberty is obviously common to all states that are 'not dependent on one another', each of which 'has an absolute Libertie to doe what it shall judge' to be 'most conducing to their benefit.'[129] It makes no sense, therefore, to speak as though some particular types of commonwealth can uniquely be described as 'free states'. 'Whether a Common-wealth be Monarchicall or Popular, the Freedome is still the same.'[130]

By the time Hobbes completed *Leviathan* between 1649 and 1651, however, he had also come to have a far more immediately political reason for wishing to insist on his distinctive analysis of liberty. By doing so, he was able to suggest an answer to the most vexed question of conscience that had arisen during those very years: the question of whether the new government of the Commonwealth 'without a king or House of Lords' could be lawfully obeyed.[131]

No sooner had the Rump Parliament and its Council of State settled themselves in power in February 1649[132] than they found their legitimacy questioned on all sides. The most vehement denunciations came of course from surviving royalists. But the most dangerous opposition came from a number of groups that had hitherto supported the parliamentary cause. Among these, the most intransigent were the Levellers. But by far the most numerous were those who remained loyal to the authority of Parliament as it had been constituted before its purge by the army leadership in December 1648.

Both these latter groups attacked the government from the same basic standpoint. They agreed that, because liberty is a birthright, any regime must derive its legitimacy from a voluntary act of submission on the part of its own subjects. With the Levellers this took the form of a demand that the new government should receive its powers from a formal Agreement of the People.[133] But among the leading writers in

[129] *Leviathan*, 266.

[130] *Leviathan*, 266.

[131] The formula used in the Oath of Engagement which, by an Act of 2 January 1650, all males over the age of eighteen were required to take. For the oath, and extracts from the Act, see *Divine Right and Democracy: An Anthology of Political Writing in Stuart England*, ed. David Wootton (Harmondsworth, 1986), 357–8. For the definitive survey of the associated pamphlet literature, see John M. Wallace, 'The Engagement Controversy 1649–1652: An Annotated List of Pamphlets', *Bulletin of the New York Public Library*, lxviii (1964), 384–405. See also Margaret Sampson, '"A Question that hath non-*plust* many": the right to private property and the "Engagement Controversy", 1648–1652' (M.A., University of Sussex, 1979.)

[132] For the settlement and creation of the Council see Blair Worden, *The Rump Parliament* (Cambridge, 1974), 177–85.

[133] The Levellers issued their third and final *Agreement* in May 1649. For the document

support of Parliament—such writers as Edward Gee, Edmund Hall, William Prynne, Nathaniel Ward and many others—there was no less emphasis on the claim that any regime which can lawfully call on the allegiance of its citizens must originate (as the anonymous author of *The Grand Case of Conscience* put it) in 'the generall consent of the major part of the people.'[134]

As both groups went on to argue, however, the government of the Rump lacked any such basis in consent. The Levellers concentrated on the fact that, with its 'long plotted Council of State erected', as John Lilburne put it, the army leadership now 'threateneth tyranny.'[135] More sweepingly, the protagonists of Parliament declared that the entire sequence of events from Pride's Purge to the execution of the king and the abolition of the House of Lords lacked any vestige of consent and hence of legality. As William Prynne declared, the new Commonwealth has been 'forcibly and treasonably erected' by sheer military strength, 'without consent of Kingdome, People or Parliament'.[136]

Having fought for their liberty against the tyranny of Charles I, the people of England have thus been rewarded with a new form of slavery. John Lilburne's major pamphlet of February 1649 is actually entitled *Englands New Chains Discovered.* Scarcely less violent is the language of the tracts written in support of summoning a new Parliament. Nathaniel Ward affirms that 'I believe, while the Parliament of England are the armies Servants, the People of England shall be very Slaves.'[137] William Prynne even feels able to congratulate the late King Charles I for his prophetic insight in seeing that the army would 'subject both King and People, Lawes and Liberties' and 'bring them into perpetuall slavery and bondage.'[138]

There can therefore be no duty to obey the new government. It owes its position, Edmund Hall maintains, to 'bare possession, without any right'. But this 'gives no true title to any power', and no basis in

itself, together with commentary, see *The Levellers in the English Revolution*, ed. G. E. Aylmer (New York, 1975), 159–68.

[134] Anonymous, *The Grand Case of Conscience Stated* (n.p., n.d.) (Thomason copy, British Library, gives date of 22 June 1649), 14.

[135] John Lilburne, *Englands New Chains Discovered* and *The Second Part of Englands New Chains Discovered* in *The Leveller Tracts, 1647–53*, ed. W. Haller and G. Davies (repd. Gloucester, Mass., 1964), 157–70 and 172–89, at 165, 167. For the authorship and circumstances of composition, see *Levellers*, ed. Aylmer, 142.

[136] [William Prynne], *Summary Reasons against the New Oath and Engagement* (n.p., 1649), 3, 13. For a discussion of the tract, and attribution to Prynne, see William Lamont, *Marginal Prynne* (1963), 187–8.

[137] [Nathaniel Ward], *Discolliminium* (1650), 53. For the attribution to Ward see Wallace, 'Engagement Controversy', 398.

[138] Prynne, *Summary Reasons*, 6.

consequence for obligation.[139] Edward Gee goes even further, stressing the positive duty of disobedience. The new government has come to power by sheer force, in the manner of a conquering party usurping a lawfully established form of sovereignty.[140] But 'the right and title of Sovereignty is not built upon possession'; it can only be built 'upon the people's consent.'[141] Such 'violent intrusion into, and possession of the Seat of Authority gives no right to it, and consequently neither draws allegiance after it, nor evacuates it in relation to another.'[142] To yield obedience to such a conquering and usurping power is in consequence unlawful, and cannot be justified.[143]

Among supporters of the Rump, the initial response to these outbursts was partly a concessive one. They admitted that the new government was perhaps illegal in its origins, but argued that it ought nevertheless to be obeyed as a power ordained of God.[144] In the course of 1650, however, a much more positive line of defence emerged. A number of writers began to claim that, even though the government may have acquired its powers only as a consequence of the army's victory, this ought not to be regarded as impugning either its legitimacy or its title to allegiance.

This suggestion appears to have originated with Anthony Ascham,[145] but was soon taken up in an even more forthright style by such publicists as George Wither and especially Marchamont Nedham. The point on which they all agree is that conquest is simply one of the means (and historically the most usual means) by which political authority comes to be lawfully acquired.[146] Bodin and Grotius

[139] [Edmund Hall], *Lazarus's Sores Licked* (1650), 3. For the attribution to Hall see Wallace, 'Engagement Controversy', 401.

[140] [Edward Gee], *An Exercitation Concerning Usurped Powers* (n.p., 1650), 5–7, using the pretence that he is describing 'a nation in America'. For the attribution to Gee, see Wallace, 'Engagement Controversy', 394–5. For a yet more explicit reference to the new government as 'a conquering party', see *Grand Case*, 7.

[141] Gee, *Exercitation*, 11–12.

[142] Gee, *Exercitation*, 13. For the same claim see Prynne, *Summary Reasons*, 12 and Ward, *Discolliminium*, 8.

[143] Gee, *Exercitation*, 9. For the same conclusion see *The Grand Case*, 7, 9 and Prynne, *Summary Reasons*, 3.

[144] For the development of this position see John M. Wallace, *Destiny his Choice* (Cambridge, 1968), 43–7, 51–6 and Quentin Skinner, 'Conquest and Consent: Thomas Hobbes and the Engagement Controversy' in *The Interregnum: The Quest for Settlement 1646–1660*, ed. G. E. Aylmer (1972), 79–98.

[145] On Ascham see Wallace, *Destiny his Choice*, 30–41, 45–8, 53–8 and Richard Tuck, *Natural Rights Theories: Their Origin and Development* (Cambridge, 1979), 116–17, 123–4, 152–4.

[146] For this claim see [George Wither], *Respublica Anglicana* (1650), 42. (For the attribution see Wallace, 'Engagement Controversy', 401.) See also Marchamont Nedham, *The Case of the Commonwealth of England, Stated*, ed. Philip A. Knachel (Charlottesville, 1969), 15–29. A similarly forthright argument had earlier appeared anonymously in *The Constant Man's Character* (1650), 64–70.

had already developed this case, as had a number of likeminded writers in England, including John Hayward, Alberico Gentili and Calybute Downing.[147] Nedham not only quotes both Bodin and Grotius,[148] but proceeds to apply their doctrine (in defiance of common law sentiment)[149] directly to the history of England, claiming that William I and Henry VII both founded their dynasties on the right of conquest.[150]

It is thus a misconception, Nedham argues in the course of his attack on Gee, to suppose that 'only a call from the people' can 'constitute a lawful magistracy'.[151] This forgets that a king may 'by right of war lose his share and interest in authority and power, being conquered'. When this happens, 'the whole right of kingly authority' is 'by military decision resolved into the prevailing party.' This in turn means that 'what government soever it pleases them next to erect is as valid *de jure* as if it had the consent of the whole body of the people.'[152] 'For the sword creates a title for him or those that bear it, and installs them with a new majesty of empire, abolishing the old.'[153] As Richard Saunders more succinctly puts it in the title of a sermon published shortly afterwards, 'plenary possession makes a lawful power'.[154]

Hobbes's view of political obligation in *Leviathan* has sometimes been assimilated to that of these defenders of *de facto* powers.[155] While there are important similarities, however, this interpretation overlooks the fact that, in the basic premises of his political theory, Hobbes stands much closer to Prynne, Gee and other such enemies of the

[147] For the development of arguments about conquest see Quentin Skinner, 'History and Ideology in the English Revolution', *Historical Journal*, viii (1965), 151–78 and especially Johann P. Sommerville, 'History and Theory: The Norman Conquest in Early Stuart Political Thought', *Political Studies*, xxxiv (1986), 249–61.

[148] Nedham, *Case*, cites Bodin, 32, Grotius, 39.

[149] For common law hostility to conquest theory, see J. G. A. Pocock, 'The Ancient Constitution Revisited' in *The Ancient Constitution and the Feudal Law: A Reissue with a Retrospect* (Cambridge, 1987), esp. 42–55, 293–305.

[150] Nedham, *Case*, 25–9, 48–50.

[151] Nedham, *Case*, 37.

[152] Nedham, *Case*, 36. Cf. also 40.

[153] Nedham, *Case*, 38.

[154] Richard Saunders, *Plenary Possession makes a Lawful Power* (1651). (Thomason copy, British Library, gives date of 28 July.)

[155] I originally argued for this interpretation myself. See the article cited *Supra*, fn. 144 and also, more fully, Quentin Skinner, 'Thomas Hobbes et la défense du pouvoir "de facto"' *Revue philosophique*, xcix (1973), pp. 131–54. Some of the best recent scholarship on *Leviathan* has continued to uphold this point of view. See for example David Johnston, *The Rhetoric of Leviathan* (Princeton, 1986), 208; see also, more fully, Deborah Baumgold, *Hobbes's Political Theory* (Cambridge, 1988), 124–33.

Rump. He agrees that our natural condition is one of 'full and absolute Libertie.'[156] He agrees that, because 'all men equally are by Nature Free', there can be 'no Obligation on any man which ariseth not from some Act of his own'.[157] Finally, he agrees in consequence that conquest and victory can never in themselves yield any 'right of dominion over the vanquished' nor any obligation on the part of the conquered.[158] The reason is that, where someone submits merely as a result of being 'overcome', their obedience will be due to the fact that they have been 'put into prison or chains' and have found it impossible not to submit.[159] As we have seen, however, to be physically forced into submission in this way is, for Hobbes, to be in the condition not of a subject but a slave.[160] If, by contrast, a man's obligation is to be that of a true subject, it is indispensable that his submission should take the form of an act of free consent. Right and obligation can never be derived simply from conquest or victory.[161]

The significance of Hobbes's intervention in the debates about the Commonwealth government is not best captured, therefore, by seeing him essentially as a defender of *de facto* power. The importance of his argument stems rather from the characteristically ironic form in which it is couched.[162] Hobbes accepts the premises of the Rump's leading enemies, but he seeks to show that the wrong conclusions have been drawn from them. Above all, he seeks to show that those who believe the government to be imposing a new form of bondage have simply failed to understand the proper signification of liberty.

In mounting this case, Hobbes develops two distinct lines of attack. The more general is aimed at those who, as he puts it, are clamouring for liberty and calling it their birthright.[163] Given his analysis of human freedom, Hobbes now feels able to dismiss these claims as

[156] *Leviathan*, 266.

[157] *Leviathan*, 268.

[158] *Leviathan*, 255–6.

[159] *Leviathan*, 256.

[160] A point Hobbes subsequently corroborates in his Chapter on Crimes by saying (p. 339) that, although in all places and all ages 'Actions have been authorised by the force and victories of those that have committed them', such actions have in all cases been unjust.

[161] See *Leviathan*, 721, on the mistake of those who seek to 'justify the War by which their power was at first gotten, and whereon (as they think) their Right Dependeth'.

[162] Several leading arguments in *Leviathan* are presented in a form that Renaissance rhetoricians, following Quintilian, described as dispositionally ironic: familiar premises are adopted, but surprising conclusions are then shown to follow from them. For Quintilian's discussion of this form of irony, see *Institutio Oratoria*, Book IX, II. 44–6.

[163] For these phrases see *Leviathan*, 264, 267. For evidence about the clamour for liberty, see Keith Lindley, 'London and popular freedom in the 1640s' in *Freedom in the English Revolution*, ed. R.C. Richardson and G.M. Ridden (Manchester, 1986), 111–50.

totally confused. Suppose we take it, he says, that what these agitators are demanding is 'liberty in the proper sense', that is, 'freedome from chains and prison'. Then it is 'very absurd for men to clamour as they doe' for this form of freedom, since they manifestly enjoy it.[164] But suppose, he goes on, we instead take them to be calling for liberty in the sense of 'exemption from laws'—what Hobbes has been describing as the liberty of subjects. To ask for complete freedom in this sense is no less absurd. For this is to demand a return to the state of nature. And as Hobbes has already shown, to call for this is to call in effect for slavery, since it is to ask for that form of liberty 'by which all other men may be masters' of our lives.[165]

Hobbes reserves his most detailed criticisms, however, for those who had been arguing about the rights of conquest. He mainly focuses on this issue in the Review and Conclusion of *Leviathan*, where he complains that 'divers English books lately printed' make it evident that no one has understood the concept properly.[166] But it is in Chapter XX that he first takes up the question of 'Dominion acquired by Conquest or victory in war', and is thus led to examine the predicament of a man who, finding his sovereign vanquished, submits to his conqueror in order 'to avoyd the present stroke of death'.[167]

The first point Hobbes makes specifically about the liberty of a man in such a situation is that he is free to submit. If 'his life and corporall Libertie' are given to him 'on condition to be Subject to the Victor, he hath Libertie to accept the condition'.[168] Here in turn Hobbes has two claims to make. The first, which he takes for granted, is that such a man is free in the fundamental sense that nothing is stopping him. Although Hobbes observes in his Conclusion that such impediments can certainly arise, the only instance he mentions is that of someone prevented from submitting by the fact of being abroad at the time when his country is conquered.[169] Hobbes's other and principal point is that such a man is also free as a subject. He is under no legal or moral obligation not to submit. The reason is that our obligations as subjects depend, as we have seen, upon our sovereign's capacity to protect us. If our sovereign is conquered, we lose any such protection and the commonwealth is dissolved. We thereupon cease to be subjects, and each of us is left 'at liberty to protect himselfe by such courses as his own discretion shall suggest unto him.'[170]

[164] *Leviathan*, 264.
[165] *Leviathan*, 264.
[166] *Leviathan*, 719.
[167] *Leviathan*, 255.
[168] *Leviathan*, 273.
[169] *Leviathan*, 721.
[170] *Leviathan*, 375. Cf. also 272–3, 345.

In his Review and Conclusion Hobbes clarifies and expands this account of 'when it is that a man hath the liberty to submit'.[171] He reiterates that 'for him that hath no obligation to his former Soveraign but that of an ordinary Subject', the moment comes 'when the means of his life is within the Guards and Garrisons of the Enemy'.[172] But he now adds the highly topical observation that, if the man is not merely a subject but a soldier in a civil war, the case becomes more complicated. 'He hath not the liberty to submit to a new Power as long as the old one keeps the field, and giveth him means of subsistence'. For in that case 'he cannot complain of want of Protection'. But as soon as that fails, he too is at liberty to 'seek his Protection wheresoever he has most hope to have it, and may lawfully submit himself to his new Master.'[173]

The other point Hobbes makes specifically about the liberty of a man in this predicament is also brought out in Chapter XX, but is particularly underlined in the Review and Conclusion. It is that such a man is not merely free to submit; if he submits, he will also be acting freely.

Here again Hobbes has two points to make. The first and obvious one is that such a man will be acting freely in the legal sense. He is clearly under no legal obligation to submit, since his predicament is such that he has no legal obligations at all. But Hobbes's main point—and the heart of his eirenic reply to the enemies of the Commonwealth—is that such a man will also be free according to the proper signification of the word. If he submits, his act will be that of a free man voluntarily consenting to a new sovereign power.

To see how Hobbes arrives at this central conclusion, we need only recall the conditions that would have to be met before it could properly be claimed that such a man's freedom of action has been infringed. He would have to be physically tied or bound to submit in such a way that he could not forbear from submitting. As we have seen, this is of course a possible way of inducing submission. It describes the manner in which a slave, someone 'not trusted with the libertie of his bodie,' is forced to obey.[174] It is Hobbes's principal aim, however, to establish that this is not the position of the man who submits to a conqueror in order to avoid imprisonment or death. The reason is that this describes the predicament of a man who, unlike the slave, is offered a condition of submission, and is thus at liberty to accept or

[171] *Leviathan*, 719, referring the reader back to the discussion in Chapter XXI.

[172] *Leviathan*, 719.

[173] *Leviathan*, 720.

[174] *Leviathan*, 273. Cf. also 256, 720.

refuse that condition 'if hee will'.[175] He is not forced to submit by being 'beaten and taken'; on the contrary, 'he commeth in and submitteth to the Victor' on condition that 'his life and the liberty of his body' are spared.[176]

Hobbes's fundamental contention is thus that the man he is describing is someone who, far from being forced to submit, freely consents to the terms of his own submission and thereby enters into a covenant with a new sovereign.[177] 'Having liberty to submit to him, he consenteth either by expresse words or by other sufficient sign to be his Subject.'[178] He may thus be said to 'contract with the Victor, promising Obedience for Life and Liberty.'[179] Hobbes's reason for treating it as an error to suppose that plenary possession makes a lawful power is thus that 'it is not therefore the Victory that giveth the right of Dominion over the Vanquished, but his own Covenant.'[180]

In relating his theory of liberty to the debates about the Commonwealth government, Hobbes appears to have acted with full self-consciousness. The best evidence lies in the fact that his conclusions are based not just on a clarification but a revision of his earlier arguments. In the *Elements of Law* he still espouses the orthodox position that *Leviathan* repudiates, contrasting the position of a man who 'submitteth to an assailant for fear of death' with that of someone who makes a 'voluntary offer of subjection'.[181] In *De Cive* the discussion is more ambiguous, and undoubtedly begins to move in the direction

[175] *Leviathan*, 720.

[176] *Leviathan*, 255–6.

[177] *Leviathan*, 719. But if the man submits only on condition that his life and liberty are spared, this would appear to make the victor a party to the covenant. This would be contrary to Hobbes's basic contention (p. 230) that 'he which is made Soveraigne maketh no Covenant with his Subjects beforehand'. This contention raises no problems in the case of what Hobbes calls (p. 228) 'commonwealth by institution'. For the form taken by the Covenant in such cases is simply that each prospective subject agrees with everyone else who shall be sovereign. Ever since Pufendorf stressed the point, however, critics have complained that Hobbes contradicts himself when he comes to what he calls (p. 228) 'commonwealth by acquisition', and thus to the relationship of victor and vanquished. For in this case he explicitly states (p. 252) that the subjects covenant not with each other but with 'him they are afraid of'. Hobbes's consistency can be rescued, however, if we interpret him as saying not that the conqueror covenants to allow life and liberty to those he has vanquished, but merely that he accepts their covenant by allowing them life and liberty, while remaining free from any obligation to respect these terms. This point is excellently brought out in Gauthier, *Logic of Leviathan*, 114–15.

[178] *Leviathan*, 719.

[179] *Leviathan*, 721.

[180] *Leviathan*, 255–6.

[181] *Elements of Law*, 127.

later taken up in *Leviathan*.[182] But Hobbes still makes a distinction between states 'founded on contracts and on mutually given faith' and states 'acquired by power and natural force.'[183] Only in the former case is he prepared to say that the *civitas* has been 'founded on the consent of many men' who have 'willingly submitted themselves'.[184]

In *Leviathan*, by contrast, he unequivocally insists that, when a man submits to a conqueror to avoid the present stroke of death, his act of submission is the willing act of a free man. As a result, he is able to make a novel and dramatic intervention in the debate about conquest and allegiance. As we have seen, many enemies of the Rump had argued that, because the new commonwealth government was founded on conquest and usurpation, it lacked any basis in consent and condemned the people of England to a state of enslavement. Many of its defenders had retorted that, although the government had doubtless been imposed without consent, the fact of its being founded on an act of conquest gave it a just title to be obeyed. By contrast with both these positions, Hobbes suggests that there is no need to invoke the supposed rights of conquerors in order to vindicate the present duty of allegiance. By deploying his distinctive analysis of liberty, he is able to insist that the concepts of conquest and consent are not in the least incompatible in the way that all parties to the debate had hitherto supposed.

This in turn enabled Hobbes to draw the polemical conclusion in which he is clearly most interested. Since the act of submitting to a conqueror is based on consent and expressed in a covenant, a man who submits in this way cannot possibly be described as a slave—as the Levellers and supporters of Parliament were both trying to claim. Rather he must be acknowledged to be a true subject with an absolute duty of obedience. The conclusion is first drawn at the end of the Chapter on the liberty of subjects. If a man 'hath his life and corporall Libertie given him, on condition to be subject to the Victor, he hath Libertie to accept the condition, and having accepted it is the subject of him that took him.'[185] The suggestion that such a man has no obligation to obey, on the grounds that he has merely been compelled to submit out of fear, is scornfully dismissed at the end of the Chapter on the dissolution of commonwealths as nothing but a 'fraudulent

[182] Especially in clearly stating that conquest and consent are at least potentially compatible. See *De Cive: The Latin Version*, 160.

[183] *De Cive: The Latin Version*, 160 contrasting the case of a civitas 'pactis & fide mutuo data . . . inita est' with a civitas 'quae acquiritur potentia & viribus naturalibus'.

[184] *De Cive: The Latin Version*, 160: only the civitas founded 'pactis & fide mutuo data' can be described as founded 'multorum consensione' by men acting 'volentes'.

[185] *Leviathan*, 273.

pretence'.[186] Finally, the basic argument is triumphantly reiterated in the closing pages of the Review and Conclusion. A man who finds himself conquered is at liberty to 'submit himself to his new Master' and 'may do it lawfully, if hee will. If therefore he doe it, he is undoubtedly bound to be a true Subject: for a Contract lawfully made, cannot lawfully be broken.'[187]

ACKNOWLEDGMENTS. For commenting on drafts of this lecture I am extremely grateful to Raymond Geuss, Susan James, James Tully and Austin Woolrych.

[186] *Leviathan*, 375.
[187] *Leviathan*, 720.

REFLECTIONS ON ENTREPRENEURSHIP AND CULTURE IN EUROPEAN SOCIETIES

By Sidney Pollard

READ 23 SEPTEMBER 1989

THE theme which I have been asked to consider refers to the whole of Europe, but the terms on which it has been defined made it clear that the focus of interest was still to lie in Britain. I shall bear that focus in mind.

After a brief review of the debate relating to entrepreneurship and culture in Britain in the late Victorian and Edwardian period, the period with which I shall be more specifically concerned, and a similarly cursory examination of the role of entrepreneurship in economic theory and in the writings of economic historians in recent decades, I shall turn to the main theme, entrepreneurship and its cultural setting in the decades before World War I in the rest of Europe. A return to the British problem will complete the paper.

I

The most specific connection between the British economic retardation after the Second World War and the cultural environment has been made by Martin J. Wiener. A British tradition going back at least to the middle of the nineteenth century, he alleged, exalted the rustic life, romanticised past, non-industrial ages and looked down upon money making, especially in an industrial environment. The Public Schools in particular, increasingly patronised by the middle classes, spread the gentlemanly ideal and bore much of the responsibility for the irresistible 'gentrification of the industrialist'. His book, which appeared in 1981,[1] received widespread attention, not least on the part of the media. For them it had everything: it was well written, it was extremely one-sided, and it knocked the establishment. These, however, are not qualities that will necessarily commend themselves to academic readers, and the reception of the book by the profession has been less than enthusiastic, in part precisely because of its lack of balance.[2] Nevertheless, in its emphasis on the decline of British

[1] Martin J. Wiener, *English Culture and the Decline of the Capitalist Spirit 1850–1980* (Cambridge, 1981).

[2] E.g. the review by W. Ashworth in the *Ec.H.R.*, 2nd ser., xxxiv (1981), 659–60.

entrepreneurship about the last quarter of the nineteenth century it has fitted into a respectable view, well-established in the literature,[3] and as such must be taken seriously.

It cannot be denied that in the period under review, the social prestige, and with it presumably the influence upon the national culture, of the industrial entrepreneur stood at a very low ebb. The top financial and commercial bourgeoisie of the City of London had clearly separated itself out from the rest of the entrepreneurial class, intermingling socially and culturally with the nobility and gentry to form a single ruling elite. This left the mainly provincial industrialists out in the cold and politically without influence.[4]

Nevertheless, the issue is by no means clear-cut. Thus some of the phenomena described then were by no means new. Even before the onset of the industrial revolution Adam Smith had noted that 'merchants are commonly ambitious of becoming country gentlemen'.[5] Other alleged entrepreneurial failures of the late Victorian era, such as the habit of sons of businessmen to leave the trade, and the neglect of science and innovation, were found in the early nineteenth century also,[6] when no one would dream of accusing the British of lacking entrepreneurship. Individual examples can usually be found for anything.

[3] David S. Landes, *The Unbound Prometheus* (Cambridge, 1969), 326–58; A. L. Levine, *Industrial Retardation in Britain 1880–1914* (New York, 1967); D. C. Coleman, 'Gentlemen and Players', *Ec.H.R.*, 2nd ser. xxvi (1973), 92–116; D. H. Aldcroft, 'Technical Progress and the British Entrepreneur', *Business History*, viii (1966) 122–39; idem, 'The Entrepreneur and the British Economy, 1870–1914', *Ec.H.R.*, 2nd ser. xvii (1964–5), 113–134, and the literature cited there. In recent years Aldcroft's views have become rather less critical: 'The Economy, Management and Foreign Competition' in: Gordon Roderick and Michael Stephens, eds., *Where Did We Go Wrong?* (Lewes, 1981), 13–31. Also see H. W. Richardson, 'Retardation in Britain's Industrial Growth, 1870–1913', in: Derek H. Aldcroft and Harry W. Richardson, eds., *The British Economy 1870–1939* (1969), 101–25.

[4] There is a large literature. E.g. Geoffrey Ingham, *Capitalism Divided? The City and Industry in British Social Development* (1984); Youssef Cassis, *Les Banquiers de la City à l'époque Edouardienne* (Geneva, 1984); Michael Lisle-Williams, 'Merchant Banking Dynasties in the English Class Structure', *British Journal of Sociology*, xxxv (1984), 333–62; José Harris and Pat Thane, 'British and European Bankers 1880–1914: an Aristocratic Bourgeoisie?', in Pat Thane et al., eds., *The Power of the Past: Essays for Eric Hobsbawm* (Cambridge, 1984); Sidney Pollard, *Britain's Prime and Britain's Decline*, (1989), chapter 4.

[5] Quoted in R. H. Campbell and R. G. Wilson, ed., *Entrepreneurship in Britain 1750–1939* (1975), 28.

[6] Peter L. Payne, 'Industrial Entrepreneurship and Management in Great Britain', in *Cambridge Economic History of Europe*, vii (Cambridge 1978), 180–230; *idem, British Entrepreneurship in the Nineteenth Century* (1974), 25–6; Donald Coleman and Christine MacLeod, 'Attitudes to New Techniques: British Businessmen, 1800–1950', *Ec.H.R.*, 2nd ser., xxxix (1986), 588–611.

There are also other reasons for doubt. Thus it can be shown that there was no shortage of enterprising and innovating businessmen in the later Victorian years in such new mass consumer goods industries (a category in which Britain was said to lag particularly badly) as soap, chocolates, cigarettes, newspapers, margarine, bicycles and patent medicines. In several of these they were leading the world. Others were building up holiday resorts, residential suburbs and local transport systems.[7]

These were mostly newer consumer goods in which the richer British economy might be expected to do well. But even in the older staple industries in which British entrepreneurs were alleged to have failed, they have lately been found, mostly by American and German economic historians, on the contrary, to have acted rationally and sensibly to make the most of their given market and technical opportunities. Thus the iron and steel masters have been rehabilitated by McCloskey, Hyde, Temin and Wengenroth,[8] the cotton masters by Sandberg, Saxonhouse and Wright, among others,[9] engineers and armaments producers by Harrison, Saul and Trebilcock,[10] while no one ever doubted that British shipbuilders were the world's most successful.[11]

Nor has the thesis of the neglect of education and science by entrepreneurs in Britain remained unscathed. German universities and technical colleges (but only they, together possibly with the Swiss) may indeed have been ahead of the British but then they were catching up, at best, as far as their technologically relevant teaching was

[7] Charles Wilson, 'Economy and Society in Late Victorian Britain', *Ec.H.R.*, 2nd ser. xviii (1965), 183–98; W. Ashworth, 'The Late Victorian Economy', *Economica*, xxxiii (1966), 17–33; A. E. Musson, *The Growth of British Industry* (1978), Chapter 8.

[8] D. N. McCloskey, *Economic Maturity and Entrepreneurial Decline* (Cambridge, Mass., 1973) and *idem*, *Enterprise and Trade in Victorian Britain* (1981); Charles K. Hyde, *Technological Change and the British Iron Industry 1700–1870* (Princeton, 1977), p. 189; Peter Temin, 'The Retardation of the British Steel Industry 1880–1913', in: Henry Rosovsky ed., *Industrialization in Two Systems* (New York, 1966), 140–55; Ulrich Wengenroth, *Unternehmensstrategien und technischer Fortschritt. Die deutsche und die britische Stahlindustrie, 1865–1895* (Göttingen 1986).

[9] Lars G. Sandberg, *Lancashire in Decline* (Columbus, 1974); Gary R. Saxonhouse and Gavin Wright, 'New Evidence on the Stubborn English Mule and the Cotton Industry, 1878–1920', *Ec.H.R.*, 2nd ser., xxxvii (1984), 507–19.

[10] S. B. Saul, 'The Market and the Development of the Mechanical Engineering Industry in Britain, 1860–1914', *Ec.H.R.*, 2nd ser. xx (1967), 111–30; A. H. Harrison, 'The Competitiveness of the British Cycle Industry 1890–1914', *Ec.H.R.*, 2nd ser. xxii (1969), 287–303; Clive Trebilcock, *The Vickers Brothers, Armaments and Enterprise 1854–1914* (1977).

[11] S. Pollard, 'British and World Shipbuilding, 1890–1914: A Study in Comparative Costs', *Journal of Economic History*, xvii (1957), 426–44; Hugh B. Peebles, *Warshipbuilding on the Clyde* (Edinburgh, 1987). Also, in general, Lars Sandberg, 'The Entrepreneur and Technical Change', in: Roderick Floud and Donald McCloskey, eds., *The Economic History of Britain since 1700* (2 vols., Cambridge, 1981), i. 99–119.

concerned, with the existing practice in British industries. By the end of the century, when the practical experience of the leading firms had to be supplemented, in one high-tech industry after another, by formal training, Britain developed her academic teaching with astonishing rapidity.

Chairs and fellowships in science and even in engineering were founded in the older Scots and even the ancient English universities: Cambridge gained three Nobel prizes in physics within five years, between 1904 and 1908. Beside London, eleven civic universities and colleges were founded, and may be looked upon as counterparts to the rising German technical universities. Imperial College, established 1907, was not far behind its model, the T.U. at Charlottenburg, while the National Physical Laboratory had by 1914 overtaken its rival, the Physikalisch-Technische Reichsanstalt in Berlin in several respects. Polytechnics in London, and technical and evening classes in the provinces multiplied remarkably rapidly in the early years of this century. In student numbers, it is true, the Germans were still ahead, but increases in Britain were breathtaking: the cumulative total of English graduates in science and technology rose from 127 in 1870 to 1447 in 1890 and to 14,330 in 1910, or 113-fold in forty years.[12] These comparisons were made, as always, with the very best abroad. Other countries, with the possible exception of the United States, were far behind both Britain and Germany.

There remain the public schools, corrupters of youth, 'irrelevant' for business, according to David Ward, diverting promising middle-class sons towards the values and career hopes of a landed class which was traditionally idle or at most destined to rule at home or in the Empire.

> They facilitated the transmission of the culture of the landed and gentry classes to the industrial classes, a culture which virtually ignored the economic life of the country ... they produced a haemorrhage of talent and perhaps of capital in the older industries which could not be made good. This goes some way to explain the poor performance of these industries in the 1870's.[13]

Such sentiments could be multiplied many times over from the literature. Yet even here some doubts remain. For did not the German elite schools, the 'classical Gymnasien', look down their noses at modern studies, just like their English counterparts, and did not the German entrepreneurs of that period, deservedly admired by their

[12] Pollard, *Britain's Prime*, chapter 3, and literature cited therein.

[13] David Ward, 'The Public Schools and Industry in Britain after 1870', *Journal of Contemporary History*, ii (1967), 47, 52.

contemporaries, have as their most admired qualities 'creativeness and dynamic, courage and originality, initiative and capacity for leadership'[14]—precisely the qualities fostered by the public schools? Moreover, it was the leading financiers, not the industrialists, who had passed through the public schools, and no one has as yet accused them of lack of enterprise.[15] The industrialists sent at most their sons there in our period, they themselves had enjoyed a less privileged education. Their performance between 1870 and 1914 could therefore not have been affected by what went on in Eton and Harrow.[16]

We therefore have something of a puzzle. Over against the near unanimity about the failure of entrepreneurship and a declining industrial spirit, we have the reality of numerous flourishing, expanding, innovative industries; we have much the highest industrial productivity and national income per head in Europe, we have economic growth and a rapid increase of exports, though both at a lower rate than in the peak years before 1873, and at a lower rate than in some other countries. We have a tertiary sector, including shipping, banking and insurance[17] which dominated the world as never before, and in which there was clearly no lack of enterprise. Under those conditions it is indeed conceivable that one or other firm might go under for lack of enterprise at the top, but it is hard to believe that there were not others eagerly waiting their chance to take their place. After all, this was no backward economy waiting for a breath of modernity from the outside. In the words of Harry Richardson, 'it is necessary to explain why the economy which produced the most dynamic entrepreneurs in the first half of the nineteenth century produced the most inefficient in the second'.[18]

Before proceeding further, it might be advisable to look briefly at the concept of entrepreneurship itself.

[14] Jürgen Kocka, *Unternehmer in der deutschen Industrialisierung* (Göttingen, 1975), 111. [Transl. S.P.].

[15] Coleman, 'Gentlemen', 111; T. W. Bamford, *Rise of the Public Schools* (1967), 253.

[16] This point is developed in an unpublished dissertation at Bielefeld University, Hartmut Berghoff, *Englische Unternehmer 1870–1914, Eine Kollektivbiographie führender Wirtschaftsbürger in Birmingham, Bristol und Manchester* (1989).

[17] Barry Supple, 'Aspects of Private Investment Strategy in Britain', in: Herman Daems and Herman van der Wee, eds., *The Rise of Managerial Capitalism* (Louvain, 1974), 89 ff.; also Charles Morazé, *The Triumph of the Middle Classes* (New York, 1968), pp. 491 ff.

[18] Richardson, 'Retardation', 114.

II

What do we mean by entrepreneurship, and what do we expect from it? If we turned to mainstream economics, we would look in vain for an answer. It would, on the contrary, be true to say that in the basic structure of neoclassical economics, entrepreneurship does not figure at all. In a tradition going back to Adam Smith and much strengthened by Ricardo, economic relationships are explained by quantities and prices, and by supply and demand reacting on each other without an explicit human will. Human agents within the economy, buyers, sellers, workers, managers, will behave as expected, in the expected proportions, given the correct stimuli.[19]

There is, however, a second tradition, going back to Richard Cantillon, the Irish merchant trading in France in the first half of the eighteenth century, and to Jean-Baptiste Say, which has a role for the entrepreneur, as the organiser, coordinator, decision-maker in a business. In a further development of the concept, he also determines its strategy, its direction and its purpose,[20] implying, at the least, a not quite automatic reaction to market signals. The entrepreneur would also have to lay out the costs of inputs in anticipation of later sales and profits, and this involved risk and uncertainty. This provides a second function for the entrepreneur, as risk bearer, conjointly with the organising and controlling function, an aspect first examined thoroughly by Frank H. Knight.[21]

It is evident that we have here in a particularly acute form the central problem of all the social sciences, which try to predict the behaviour of people in the mass of whom each may be presumed to be different and to have some free will as to his actions.[22] For it is in

[19] E.g., Mark Casson, *The Entrepreneur. An Economic Theory* (Oxford, 1982), 9–11; Hugh G. J. Aitken, 'The Problems of Entrepreneurial Freedom', *Explorations in Entrepreneurial History*, I (April 1949), 1–2; Fritz Redlich, 'Toward an Understanding of an Unfortunate Legacy', *Kyklos*, 19 (1966), 709–18; Joseph A. Schumpeter, 'Economic Theory and Entrepreneurial History', in: Hugh G. J. Aitken, ed., *Explorations in Enterprise* (Cambridge, Mass., 1967), 48.

[20] Schumpeter, 'Economic Theory'; Fritz Redlich, 'The Origin of the Concepts of "Entrepreneur" and "Creative Entrepreneur"', *Explorations in Entrepreneurial History*, I (Feb. 1949), 1–2; Guido Turin, *Der Begriff des Unternehmers* (Zürich, 1948); W. N. Parker, 'Entrepreneurship, Industrial Organisation, and Economic Growth', *Journal of Economic History*, xiv (1954), 380–400; Arthur H. Cole, 'The Stone that the Builders Rejected ...', *Tradition*, xiii (1968), 106; Wolfgang Zorn, 'Typen und Entwicklungskräfte deutschen Unternehmertums im 19. Jahrhundert', *Vierteljahrschrift für Sozial- und Wirtschaftsgeschichte*, xliv (1957), 57–77; J.-B. Say, *A Treatise on Political Economy* (New York, 1964) [1st ed. 1803], 329.

[21] Frank H. Knight, *Risk, Uncertainty and Profit* (1948) [1st ed. 1921].

[22] Sidney M. Greenfield and Arnold Strickton, 'Entrepreneurship and Social Change: Toward a Populational Decision-Making Approach', in: S. M. Greenfield et al., eds., *Entrepreneurs in Cultural Context* (Albuquerque, 1979), 329–50.

the nature of entrepreneurial theory to assume that some people are different, and are capable of affecting others in a crucial way, down, in extreme cases, to altering the rules by which they all operate. In principle this is incompatible with the notion that people behave regularly and comformably to some rules. At the least, it requires a search for regularity among the irregular, of orderliness among those who break the order.

The problem is that not only do order and control sit uneasily together with risk, the other entrepreneurial function; it is also that both fit badly into a science which, like neoclassical economics, is built up on the varying relationships between the three factors of production, land, labour and capital. At one level of abstraction, enterprises will behave exactly according to their factor endowment and market position; at a lower level, the mediation of economic agents whose action can make a difference, becomes a necessary object of enquiry. In the early years of this century economists tried to get over this by developing 'entrepreneurship' as a fourth factor of production (Marshall called it 'organization'),[23] but this, in turn, was an awkward fit, rather like time as a fourth dimension. In most versions entrepreneurship was placed above the other three:

> Enterprise stands on a different footing from, and above, the other productive factors ... It alone is productive, the other three being simply forces set in motion ... The Enterpriser is the only direct creator of purchasing power.[24]

A very much higher value even than this was given to the entrepreneur by Schumpeter. In a work first completed in 1911, Schumpeter's entrepreneur does not appear simply as manager or organiser of a routine business, no matter how large. He is the innovator, the practical introducer of something new. The innovation might be a new product or process, new markets opened, new sources or types of supplies developed, or a new form of organisation.[25] Schumpeter made the entrepreneur not only responsible for all human progress, but also for the cyclical form of development of modern capitalist societies.

The entrepreneur, in other words, moved things forward by cre-

[23] Alfred Marshall, *Principles of Economics* (8th ed., 1946), 136–9, 220 ff.

[24] F. B. Hawley, *Enterprise and the Productive Process* (New York, 1907), quoted in Campbell and Wilson, 72; Fred Rogers Fairchild, Edgar Stevenson Furniss, Norman Sydney Buck, *Elementary Economics* (New York, 1928), 40–1; N. S. B. Gras, 'Capitalism, Concepts and History', in: Frederick C. Lane and Jelle C. Riemersma, eds., *Enterprise and Technical Change* (1953), 69.

[25] Joseph A. Schumpeter, *The Theory of Economic Development* (New York, 1961) [1st ed. 1911]; also his 'Creative Response in Economic History', *Journal of Economic History*, vi (1947), 149–59; article 'Unternehmer' in *Handwörterbuch der Staatswissenschaften* (1928), viii. 476–87; *Capitalism, Socialism and Democracy* (New York, 1942).

ating change. He was the disturber of the peace, the destroyer of existing values ('creative destruction'), the exception. Fritz Redlich and others later developed the concept a little further,[26] without detracting from its essential power.

Clearly, not every type of society would form an equally favourable breeding ground and field of action for the Schumpeterian entrepreneur. Had late Victorian Britain become a society less receptive than others to the innovator? If economics is to help us in finding the entrepreneurial culprit in Victorian Britain, it will have to be the Schumpeterian variety rather than the neoclassical; for the latter concept has no room, other than sheer irrationality, for entrepreneurial failure.

III

For economic historians it is much harder than it is for theorists to ignore reality and the entrepreneur. Nevertheless it would be true to say that those in the profession who hold most clearly to the precepts of theory, which at present means above all the practitioners of what has come to be known as the New Economic History, essentially follow their preceptors also in this. Listen to the words of Jonathan Hughes who in other respects has much sympathy for them:

> In my speciality, economic history, individual persons tend to figure so little in the work that it is almost a triumph if a person's name can be woven into the statistical and analytical historical tapestry ... If the configuration of the market forces favour monopoly, a monopolist will appear and monopolize. If not, then *no* monopolist can succeed. There is no room for initiative.

Against this, he maintained that

> we cannot assume that change has come automatically from the 'masses' and the 'forces of history'. There are no 'masses'. There are only individuals. There are no 'forces of history', only human action ... Men make economic change. The American economy is the sum product of the acts of individuals.[27]

[26] Fritz Redlich, 'The Business Leader as a 'Daimonic' Figure', *American Journal of Economics and Sociology*, xii (1952–3), 163–78 and 288–99; also his 'Origin', 3 ff.; and his *Der Unternehmer* (Göttingen, 1964), 77, 172–7, 230 ff. A. H. Cole, 'An Approach to the Study of Entrepreneurship', *Journal of Economic History*, vi, Supplement (1946), 1–15; Richard V. Clemence and Francis S. Doody, *The Schumpeterian System* (New York, 1966) [1st ed. 1950].

[27] Jonathan Hughes, *The Vital Few, American Economic Progress and Its Protagonists* (1973) [1st ed. 1966], pp. viii–ix, 2.

The argument is of course almost as old as the hills. In this debate, the neoclassical economic historians have never had it all their own way, and in more recent decades the study of entrepreneurship as an economic force has been much benefited by the foundation in 1948 of the Centre for Entrepreneurial History in Harvard, which after ten years' existence left behind it a large number of publications, a journal which is still flourishing, and much influential thought on the nature of entrepreneurship and its influence on growth and economic progress.[28]

Harvard was only one, if possibly the most productive source of the large body of opinion, as well as of literature, in the field of economic history which places the responsibility for the success of an economy, and particularly its capacity for change and progress, on the shoulders of the entrepreneur. There was, of course, no agreement how far this could outweigh the objective factors of an adverse cultural tradition, with all its many facets, of poor resources, of a structure made rigid by the interrelatedness of factors such that important decisions are beyond the powers of a single entrepreneur,[29] of a misleading information flow, of possible monopoly gain, or the many other influences impinging on the entrepreneur.

Only Schumpeter believed that the true entrepreneur could overcome all these obstacles by his very opposition to the existing circumstances, at least by moving one step at a time, and indeed the Harvard Centre was much influenced, though indirectly, by Schumpeter as well as by Talcott Parsons' sociology.[30]

Its work was affected also by the lessons drawn from American aid to less developed countries. The dispatch of capital, of equipment and of skilled labour was found not to have been enough to lift a country out of its traditionalism; something that might be called 'entrepreneurship' was evidently still missing before it could be set on a growth path.[31]

The link to contemporary problems revealed by this example did not always lead to happy results. One of the Centre's most controversial theses was to hold her poor entrepreneurship responsible in

[28] Cole, 'The Stone', 107 ff. Hugh G.J. Aitken, 'Entrepreneurial Research: The History of an Intellectual Innovation', in: Aitken, *Explorations*, 3–19.

[29] This, clearly, was of considerable importance in Britain, as part of the heritage of the 'early start'. A large literature has followed the early studies of that phenomenon: M. Frankel, 'Obsolescence and Technical Change in a Maturing Economy', *American Economic Review*, xlv (1955), 296–319; Charles P. Kindleberger, 'Obsolescence and Technical Change', *Bulletin of the Oxford University Institute of Statistics*, 23 (1961), 281–97.

[30] Thomas C. Cochran, '"Role and Sanction" in American Entrepreneurial History', in: Aitken, *Explorations*, 93–112.

[31] John E. Sawyer, 'The Social Basis of the American System of Manufacturing', *Journal of Economic History*, xiv (1954), 361–79; Greenfield et al., *Entrepreneurs*, 9.

large part for the slow economic development in France in the nineteenth century.[32] The French economy was in bad shape at the time, and its slow growth a reasonable topic. Since then it has recovered quite remarkably, the assumption of slow growth has been much modified, and the French entrepreneur has been at least partly rehabilitated. It is now, of course, the turn of the British entrepreneur.

IV

It is time now to turn to the core of this paper: entrepreneurship in the rest of Europe in the decades before World War I, seen in its cultural context. How far were continental entrepreneurs, and above all the industrialists, attracted by the aristocratic embrace, the wish to leave industry as soon as possible when they had accumulated sufficient wealth, to take up the life style of the landed classes?

Let us begin with Germany, for only the German entrepreneurs, at least in the iron and steel industries, in chemicals, electricals, in instruments and in the formation of cartels (but in no other significant fields) could be said to have shown enterprise and commercial success superior to the British. Was their country's culture more favourable to them than British culture to their counterparts?

At one level the answer is simple. German historiography of this period has in recent years been dominated by the debate about the German 'Sonderweg'.[33] As they ask themselves the agonising question how a presumed civilised nation in the middle of Europe could have fallen for Hitler, German historians are bound to look for something that was different in Germany that could explain that exceptional disaster. One answer which has found widespread support is the notion of a German deficit of *Bürgerlichkeit*, particularly in our period, the years of the Kaiserreich. *Bürgerlichkeit* is not easy to translate. It contains an element of civic sense; but in the main, it means middle class values. Germany under the Kaiser, the story runs, suffered

[32] John E. Sawyer, 'Strains in the Structure of Modern France', in: Edward M. Earle, ed., *Modern France* (Princeton, 1951), 293–312; David S. Landes, 'French Entrepreneurship and Industrial Growth in the Nineteenth Century', in: Barry S. Supple, ed., *The Experience of Economic Growth* (New York, 1963), 340–53; Rondo Cameron, 'Economic Growth and Stagnation in France, 1815–1914', *Journal of Modern History*, xxx (1958), 1–13; Claude Fohlen, 'Entrepreneurship and Management in France in the Nineteenth Century', *Cambridge Economic History of Europe*, vii (Cambridge 1978), 347–81.

[33] An excellent balanced summary of the debate will be found in Jürgen Kocka, 'German History before Hitler: The Debate about the German Sonderweg', *Journal of Contemporary History*, xxiii (1988), 3–16. Also his introduction: 'Bürgertum und bürgerliche Gesellschaft im 19. Jahrhundert', in Kocka, ed., *Bürgertum im 19, Jahrhundert, Deutschland im europäischen Vergleich*, 3 vols. (Munich, 1988), i. 11–67.

the fatal combination of a powerful industrial base governed by an unregenerate landed-militarist-bureaucratic elite which, far from being democratised by the modernisation of the economy, imposed its own traditionalist authoritarian values on the industrial middle classes. In one form or another, this failure of liberal middle class values to establish themselves has been a dominant theme among modern German historians. Curiously enough, it needed the work of two British historians, Blackbourn and Eley who assigned a much higher weight to the role of bourgeois values in the Wilhelmine Reich—not least by comparison with Britain—to point out that the contrast may possibly have been drawn too starkly. This is also confirmed by recent statistical enquiries.[34]

There had been some middle-class assertions of power in parts of Germany up to and including the revolution of 1848, 'The most able, the most vigorous citizens were called upon to govern', David Hansemann had said in the Rhenish provincial Landtag in 1843, 'factory owners as much as landowners.[35] Even then, the more progressive regions like the Rhineland and Westphalia were put down by the reactionary Prussian bureaucracy in a manner unknown in Britain.[36] In the years thereafter, and particularly in consequence of the methods by which the Empire was united under Bismarck, the middle classes, including the industrialists, were seen to be only too eager to subordinate themselves to Prussian militarist and aristocratic values. True, as Kaelble stressed,[37] to call this a deficit in *Bürgerlichkeit* made sense only in comparison with the western European nations, and ignored the differing experiences of Baden, Wurttemberg, Bavaria, the Hanse cities and even parts of the Rhineland. But the doctrine of the 'feudalized bourgeoisie' or even of a 'bourgeois-aristocratic neofeudalism',[38] of the pathetic weakness of the entrepreneurs

[34] David Blackbourn and Geoff Eley, *The Peculiarities of German History* (Oxford, 1984) [Original German edition 1980]. Also see Hartmut Kaelble, 'Wie feudal waren die deutschen Unternehmer im Kaiserreich?' in: Richard Tilly, ed., *Beiträge zur quantitativen vergleichenden Unternehmensgeschichte* (Stuttgart, 1985), 148–71.

[35] Cited in Hans-Peter Helbach, 'Berliner Unternehmer in Vormärz und Revolution 1847–1848', in: Otto Büsch, ed., *Untersuchungen zur Geschichte der frühen Industrialisierung vornehmlich im Wirtschaftsraum Berlin/Brandenburg* (Berlin, 1971), 419. [Transl. S.P.]. Also see Wolfgang Zorn, 'Das deutsche Unternehmerportrait in sozialgeschichtlicher Betrachtung', *Tradition*, vii (1962), 90–2, and Friedrich Zunkel, *Der rheinisch-westfälische Unternehmer 1834–1879* (Cologne, 1962), 66, 89.

[36] E.g., Frank B. Tipton, Jr., *Regional Variations in the Economic Development of Germany in the Nineteenth Century* (Middletown, Conn., 1976), 146–7.

[37] Hartmut Kaelble, 'Französisches und deutsches Bürgertum', in Kocka, *Bürgertum*, i. 108.

[38] Eckart Kehr, *Economic Interest, Militarism and Foreign Policy* (Berkeley, 1977), 104, 119. Also, Ralf Dahrendorf, *Society and Democracy in Germany* (1968).

as against the massed phalanx of the landed nobility together with the army, the bureaucracy and even the learned professions, has not been shaken.

Actually, the tradition of the social and cultural weakness of the German middle classes, particularly the industrial entrepreneurs, is an old one. It goes back to Sombart and Michels, to name but the most prominent ancestors. In the past forty years, Michels had written in 1910,

> we could observe a process, advancing with tremendous speed, of the absorption of the young industrial middle classes by the aristocracy of birth. The German middle classes were well on the way to be feudalized ... Those who have become rich know no higher ambition than to be absorbed as fast as possible by the upper class.

A successful entrepreneurial family, he thought, would rarely last longer than two generations: the attractions of an alternative life style were too great.[39] And here is Sombart, in 1909:

> There never was a chance to form a ruling class with an alternative ideal to that of our 'Gentilhommery'. It has remained the highest aim of our middle classes to become Junkers, to gain a title and to assume, as far as possible, gentrified patterns of thought and knightly airs ...
>
> As soon as members of the upper middle classes have made their money, they try to forget their origins and to merge with the nobility or at least with the feudal landed gentry. The capitalist enterprise which had provided the family fortune is sold off; sons and grandsons buy themselves into landed property, opt for primogeniture, marry into titled families, let their sons serve with guards regiments ... and would not dream of letting any of them be brought up in a commercial firm.[40]

Such comments could be multiplied many times over, and were at least as common as Wiener's evidence about England. It need hardly be stressed that the romantic and romanticising literature of which he makes so much, which praises the contemplative rural life as against the money-grabbing pursuits of the modern industrial city, exerted a much more powerful influence in Germany than in Britain. After all, much of the English literature on this theme drew its inspiration from the German. Of particular interest in this connection is the

[39] Robert Michels, *Zur Soziologie des Parteiwesens in der modernen Demokratie* (Stuttgart, 1970), 16. [1st ed. 1910] [Transl. S.P.]. Also his *Umschichtungen der herrschenden Klasse nach dem Kriege* (Stuttgart and Berlin, 1934), 43.

[40] Werner Sombart, *Die deutsche Volkswirtschaft im neunzehnten Jahrhundert* (Berlin, 1909), 508 [Transl. S.P.].

international comparisons made by the Germans about their cultural context. For the ideal against which this unsatisfactory German bourgeois performance is set, namely, a society suffused with bourgeois-democratic values, was represented by France and, above all, by Britain. Surely, the debate is full of ironies. Nothing like the Prussian–German rule by the nobility and the top bureaucrats could be found in Britain, according to Michels, and Kocka has stressed that the British middle classes had a much better starting position than the German. Kaelble noted that Prussian landowners were even keener than the British to keep their sons out of industry, and Palmade judged that the compromise between the ruling elites went far more in favour of the aristocracy in Germany than in Britain.[41] Far from having a more favourable cultural environment, the informed debate about the German entrepreneur concerns itself with the question of how far he was disadvantaged.

France appears in quite a different light in the literature. There the nobility never quite recovered from the blows of the Revolution, though we know now that its decline in economic power and political influence was much less marked in the first half of the nineteenth century, the age of the *notables*, than had once been thought.[42] In the latter part of the century, however, French culture was more middle-class dominated, and the French bourgeoisie had more power and self-confidence than probably any other in Europe—with the possible exception of the Swiss, in whose country 'capital-rich entrepreneurs . . . lorded it with their modern enterprises (industry, railways, banks, insurance companies) over the masses as well as over politics'.[43] 'It was with the Second Empire' wrote Palmade 'that the great masters of industry assumed a social importance and a place of merit as supreme representatives of the capitalist world.' 'A kind of "industrial nobility", of whom the ironmasters were the prototype, had come into its own with the diminishing importance of landed property', according to Tom Kemp. And, finally, Adeline Daumard: 'La société francaise apparaissait essentiellement comme une société bourgeoise.'[44]

[41] Robert Michels, *Probleme der Sozialphilosophie* (Leipzig, 1914), 167–8; Kocka, 'Bürgertum', 67–8; H. Kaelble, 'L'evolution du recruitement du patronat comparé a celles des États-Unis et de la Grande-Bretagne depuis la revolution industrielle', in: Maurice Lévy-Leboyer, ed., *Le patronat de la seconde industrialisation* (Paris, 1979), 20–1; Guy Palmade, ed., *Das bürgerliche Zeitalter* (Frankfurt/M., 1975), 170; Jeffrey Herf, *Reactionary Modernism: Technology, Culture and Politics in Weimar and the Third Reich* (Cambridge, 1984), chapter 1.

[42] Thomas D. Beck and Martha W. Beck, *French Notables* (New York, 1987).

[43] Albert Tanner, 'Bürgertum und Bürgerlichkeit in der Schweiz', in: Kocka, ed., *Bürgertum*, i. 200, [Transl. S.P.].

[44] Guy P. Palmade, *French Capitalism in the Nineteenth Century* (Newton Abbot, 1972),

Even as regards France, however, Michels was not entirely convinced. 'For the past hundred years', he wrote, 'it is the wish of those who have acquired riches in France to acquire a historic country house, which alone can give a social cachet to their property.' Even though the nobility did not exist officially, the bourgeoisie was trying to enter it and be accepted by it by sporting an appropriate life style.[45]

According to Roger Price, top financiers had to have a 'château with a park and woods for hunting in a department close to Paris', while 'the dream of most business and professional men had continued to be to make enough money to purchase land and adopt the less demanding life of a *rentier*'.[46] A recent study found that in a Paris directory of 1901, only 2% of entries were of top business men, and in the equivalent of *Who's Who* of 1908, only 9.3%.[47]

However, the problem with all this is that precisely in the country in which the controllers of large businesses enjoyed exceptional prestige, social approval and political power, entrepreneurship was found to have been weak and conservative. We have noted above the views of the Harvard Centre. Although it had to be somewhat modified later,[48] the essential critique remains, and the French entrepreneur is judged to have been inferior to the British and certainly inferior to the German.

French enterprises lived in a 'world of a multitude of small rival businessmen, fighting for a limited market' (Caron); Bergeron similarly noted the small size and traditionalist attitude of French businesses, though he also saw some advantages in family firms, and thought they might still have some access to outside capital. Palmade considered that the French entrepreneur had less fighting spirit than the British: he was 'cautious, tried to make do with his own capital, to renew his machines as little as possible', and he 'looked with horror on the international competition foreshadowed by the commercial treaty of 1860'.[49]

152; Tom Kemp, *Economic Forces in French History*, (1971), 182; Adeline Daumard, 'La bourgeoisie et les classes dirigeantes', in: Fernand Braudel and Ernest Labrousse, eds., *Histoire économique et sociale de la France* (Paris, 1970–82), iv. 51. Also ibid., iii. 946; Kaelble, 'Französisches', 113, 124; Louis Bergeron, *Les capitalistes en France (1780–1914)*, (Paris 1978). 163.

[45] Michels, *Umschichtungen*, 50 [Transl. S.P.]. Also his *Probleme*, 157–8.

[46] Roger Price, *A Social History of Nineteenth-Century France* (1987), 99.

[47] Christophe Charle, 'L'image sociale des milieux d'affaires d'après Qui êtes-vous?' in: Lévy-Leboyer, *Patronat*, 278 ff.

[48] Rondo Cameron and Charles E. Freeman, 'French Economic Growth. A Radical Revision', *Social Science History*, vii (1983), 3–30; Don R. Leet and John A. Shaw, 'French Economic Stagnation: Old Economic History Revisited', *Journal of Interdisciplinary History*, viii (1978), 531–44; and note 32 above.

[49] Francois Caron, 'Dynamisme et freinages de la croissance industrielle', in Braudel and Labrousse, iv. 278 [Transl. S.P.]; Bergeron, *Capitalistes*, 125–33; Palmade, *Zeitalter*,

Less time need, perhaps, be spent on the rest of the continent. There were few even among the severest critics of the British entrepreneur who considered him inferior to his counterparts in Central, Eastern or Southern Europe.

Of Austria it has been said that 'entrepreneurs, properly speaking, never emerged there at all, at any rate, they were so exceptional as to be insignificant'. The slow growth of the Austrian economy in the nineteenth century has more than once been put down to her poor entrepreneurship.[50]

Socially, the entrepreneurs'

> desired status symbols were: landed property, gentry titles, large villas with parks in the suburbs, . . . in general a life style after the pattern of the nobility . . .
>
> They began to esteem highly the life in the country, hunting, keeping horses, they were even occasionally prepared to fight duels, to value foreign languages and smooth manners, and they showed an interest in genealogy and the arts . . .
>
> The feudalization of the entrepreneurs was more rapid and went deeper in the Habsburg monarchy than in the other countries in the process of industrialization.[51]

Of course, their political power and influence were negligible.[52]

The Hungarian bourgeoisie was even less in a position to challenge the agrarian semi-feudal order than the Austrian. The most successful of them became 'feudalized' or ennobled, eager to ape the manners of their betters. Curiously, some thought that this was a peculiarly Hungarian trait. As one loving daughter wrote of her recently ennobled Jewish father: he had become 'a spendthrift, altruistic, conceited landlord, addicted to horse racing and mistresses, typically "gentry" (to use a Magyar expression)'.[53]

---

172 [Transl. S.P.]. Also see Kurt Weidenfeld, 'Das Persönliche im modernen Unternehmertum', *Jahrbuch für Gesetzgebung, Verwaltung und Volkswirtschaft*, Neue Folge, xxxiv (1910), I. 230–1.

[50] Cited in Herbert Matis, 'Der österreichische Unternehmer', in: Karl-Heinz Manegold, ed., *Wissenschaft, Wirtschaft und Technik*, (Munich, 1969), 286 [Transl. S.P.]; K. H. Kaufhold, 'Handwerk und Industrie', in: Hermann Aubin und Wolfgang Zorn, eds., *Handbuch der Deutschen Wirtschafts- und Sozialgeschichte* (2 vols., Stuttgart, 1976), ii. 362.

[51] Josef Mentschl, 'Das österreichische Unternehmertum', in: Alois Busatti, ed., *Die Habsburgermonarchie 1848–1918, vol. 1. Die wirtschaftliche Entwicklung* (Vienna, 1973), 264–5, 276. [Transl. S.P.].

[52] Matis, 298; Ferdinand Tremel, ed., *Steirische Unternehmer des 19, und 20, Jahrhunderts*, (Graz, 1965), 106; Ernst Bruckmüller and Hannes Stekl, 'Zur Geschichte des Bürgertums in Oesterreich', in: Kocka, *Bürgertum*, i. 172–3, but see also 175–6.

[53] Cited in W. O. McCragg, Jr., 'Hungary's 'Feudalized' Bourgeoisie'. *Journal of Modern History*, xliv (1972), 75. Also Peter Hánák, 'Probleme der Entstehung des Unternehmerbürgertums in Ungarn' (unpubl. cyclost., Bielefeld, 1989); György Ránki,

In Prague, we are told, even the first generation of rich entrepreneurs had a tendency to seek titles and to acquire country mansions and landed estates. In Poland, especially in the 'Kingdom' of Poland belonging to the Russian Empire, the middle classes were politically and culturally weak, and in the cities, the 'supremacy of a capitalist merchant over a factory owner' was evident.[54]

Further East, in Russia, the position of the industrial entrepreneur was obviously even less highly regarded, though there was a tradition, going back to the years of serfdom, of noble mines, ironworks and even factories. Against this, other factories were owned by serfs,[55] which did not contribute much to the social status of factory owners. There is a fair degree of unanimity that 'Russia lacked adequate entrepreneurship as well as capital and technology on the eve of rapid industrialization'.[56] A society of nobles and recently emancipated serfs, together with a thin layer of urban merchants and a powerful ultraconservative bureaucracy was not an ideal social matrix out of which to develop entrepreneurial talent. When opportunities for rapid growth, and for making quick fortunes in industry and commerce, appeared in the 1880s, they were frequently seized by foreign entrepreneurs, particularly in the Ukraine and in St Petersburg: the Moscow region, it appeared, had enough native talent. There was also 'a spontaneous entrepreneurial explosion in the ghettos of Russia ... (which) followed Alexander's (II) reforms'.[57] This raises, incidentally, the more general issue of entrepreneurship supplied by minorities of low social status, which cannot be pursued here.

There would probably be little point in heaping further examples upon examples from Europe's periphery, such as 'the native entre-

---

'Die Entwicklung des ungarischen Bürgertums vom späten 18. zum frühen 20. Jahrhundert', in: Kocka, *Bürgertum*, i. 247–65.

[54] Jan Havránek, 'Prag in der Zeit der Industrialisierung', in: Monika Glettler et al., eds., *Zentrale Städte und ihr Umland* (St Katharinen, 1985) 102–2; Ryszard Kolodziejczyk, 'The Bourgeoisie in Poland in the 19th and 20th Century against the European Background', *Studia Historiae Oeconomicae*, v (1970), 225; also Waclaw Dlugoborski, 'Das polnische Bürgertum vor 1918 in vergleichender Perspektive', in: Kocka, *Bürgertum*, i. 266–99.

[55] Alexander Gerschenkron, *Economic Backwardness in Historical Perspective*, (Cambridge, Mass., 1962), 60–3; Josef Kulischer, 'Die kapitalistischen Unternehmer in Rußland (insbesondere die Bauern als Unternehmer) in den Anfangsstadien des Kapitalismus', *Archiv für Sozialwissenschaft und Sozialpolitik*, lxv (1931), 309–55; Kurt Weidenfeld, 'Die Herkunft der Unternehmer und Kapitalisten im Aufbau der kapitalistischen Zeit', *Weltwirtschaftliches Archiv*, lxxii (1954), 268–9.

[56] John P. McKay, *Pioneers for Profit, Foreign Entrepreneurship and Russian Industrialization 1885–1913* (Chicago, 1970), 383.

[57] Kurt Grunwald, *Europe's Railways and Jewish Enterprise* (1967), 187. Also James D. White, 'Moscow, Petersburg and the Russian Industrialists', *Soviet Studies*, xxiv (1972–3), 414–20; McKay, *Pioneers*.

preneurs [of the later Yugoslav regions], whose prestige was even lower in the social structure of their country than that of the Central European entrepreneurs in theirs', in part because they belonged to despised foreign nations, as Jews or Germans and where 'the shortage of entrepreneurial initiative was by all accounts a major handicap for Serbian industry';[58] or Italy, where 'the industrialists assumed that, owing to the backwardness of their society, and thanks to the protection by the State, they could look forward to gaining benefits without having to run large entrepreneurial risks'; or Spain, where there was an 'absence of an entrepreneurial spirit and of motivation for industrial progress'.[59] These regions provided an environment which bore little resemblance to the position in Britain.

In principle, circumstances could be imagined that are so adverse, that potential markets will not be supplied, and potentially available new techniques will not be used, because of missing entrepreneurship. This possibility has forced itself upon some European and American historians partly as a result of their experience with third-world countries.

> In the last analysis the scope of ... entrepreneurial activities is shaped by a whole complex of outside factors: geography and resources, population movement, law and government, and, above all, the body of social tradition and mores, which create in large measure some of the others ... The capacity of the innovator to create change is strictly limited by his geographic and social environment.[60]

Socio-religious or caste systems, inherited monopolies, and value systems and ideals[61] have been variously held responsible for these inhibitions. In an extreme form this may be expressed as 'growth or change is a cultural process in which it is difficult to segregate the

[58] Wolfgang Zorn and Sibylle Schneider, 'Das Unternehmertum im Gebiet der heutigen föderativen Volksrepublik Jugoslawien im 19. Jahrhundert', *Tradition*, xvi (1971), 15; Ivan T. Berend, 'Investment Strategy in East-Central Europe', in Daems and van der Wee, 170–96; John R. Lampe, 'Serbia 1878–1912', in: Rondo Cameron, ed., *Banking and Economic Development* (New York, 1972), 134.

[59] Marco Meriggi, 'Italienisches und deutsches Bürgertum im Vergleich', in: Kocka, *Bürgertum*, 154 [Transl. S.P.]; Juergen B. Donges, *La Industrialización en España, Politicas, Logros, Perspectivas* (Barcelona, 1976), 26 [Transl. S.P.].

[60] David S. Landes, 'A Note on Cultural Factors in Entrepreneurship', *Explorations in Entrepreneurial History*, i (Jan. 1949). 8, 9. Also see Cole, 'Approach'.

[61] Rudolf Braun, 'Zur Einwirkung sozio-kultureller Umweltbedingungen auf das Unternehmerpotential und das Unternehmerverhalten', in: Wolfram Fischer, ed., *Wirtschafts- und Sozialgeschichtliche Probleme der frühen Industrialisierung* (Berlin, 1968), 249–54.

economic factors'.[62] On a different view, some less developed societies have been held to have lacked the 'investment ability',[63] that is the ability to direct funds into productive investments, even when these funds were available, and examples for this could be found in parts of Europe right up to the end of the nineteenth century.

However, all these expressions of pessimism leave us with a problem: how could change ever have come about in such a rigidly traditionalist and unchanging environment to being forth the present-day advanced countries? If the social environment inhibits entrepreneurship, how does it itself become transmuted?[64]

One answer would be the action of someone like the Schumpeterian entrepreneur: He may have

> the ability to inspire others to follow new cultural paths. The entrepreneur is also able to work with the cultural system while consciously upsetting its state of equilibrium to his advantage. If successful, entrepreneurs may change the economy of a region ... In many ways, the entrepreneurs are the movers and shakers of society.[65]

In that case, 'the historian's interest in the entrepreneur centers in explaining how societies have produced the clever vigorous, rational, profit-minded individuals the economist orders'.[66]

Alternatively, perhaps, no truly enterprising individual is ever put down if the slightest realistic chance exists for him. In traditional Tokugawa Japan, for example, merchants had the lowest status, below even peasants and craftsmen. Yet even while they were despised, they might manage to become rich, and then they were not without influence. When their real chance came after the Meiji Restoration, they were among those whose made up the 'ruthless group of successful business men of a new type'[67] who carried through the first stages of the Japanese economic miracle. Others had came from the equally unlikely origins of the knightly Samurai class.

All this has taken us rather a long way from the British entrepreneur

[62] Thomas C. Cochran, 'Cultural Factors in Economic Growth', in: Aitken, *Explorations*, 123.

[63] A. O. Hirschman, *Strategy of Economic Development* (New Haven, 1958), 35–9.

[64] Gerschenkron, *Backwardness*, 58 f.

[65] Greenfield et al, introduction, vii.

[66] Parker, 'Entrepreneurship', 381.

[67] Johannes Hirschmeier, *The Origins of Entrepreneurship in Meiji Japan* (Cambridge, Mass., 1968), 288; also T. C. Smith, 'Pre-Modern Economic Growth: Japan and the West', *Past and Present*, 60 (1973), 151–3; Yoshihara Kunio, *Japanese Economic Development* (Oxford, 1979), 88. But see Kozo Yamamura, 'A Re-examination of Entrepreneurship in Meiji Japan', in: Peter Kilby, ed., *Entrepreneurship and Economic Development* (New York, 1971), 267–86.

in late Victorian and Edwardian times. But it has helped to establish that, if he had his faults, if he hankered after titles and estates, after unspoilt nature and contemplative leisure, if he could not wait, as soon as he had made his pile, to leave his business for more noble pursuits and preferably take his sons with him, he was not alone in this. The Old Regime, in Arno Mayer's phrase,[68] persisted everywhere in Europe, and only the Americans, the Japanese and possibly the Swiss were without sin.

But of course, if would be absurd to put the British entrepreneur on the same level with most of the others mentioned. Even as compared with his nearest rival, the German, he had achieved, in 1910, a average national product per head some 36% above the German, and in 1913, GDP per man-hour 42% higher and GNP per capita 30% higher. Exports were growing at the very comfortable rate of 4.2% a year by volume and by 6.1% by value in the last peacetime years 1900–13.[69] In shipping, finance, insurance, the British entrepreneur was without doubt the envy of the world.

Yet there is no smoke without fire. We must return to the critics of the British entrepreneur in our concluding remarks.

V

If we are to make the British entrepreneur responsible for the unnecessary retardation of the British economy before 1914 (assuming such retardation to have taken place), and if we exclude a hostile environment such as might be found in hidebound non-capitalist societies as wholly inapplicable, we are left with four possible ways, and those not independent of each other, in which the entrepreneurs could have been guilty. Time forbids more than a cursory examination of each.

It could be that entrepreneurs were stupid, ignorant or irrational; that they were trying to do the right thing, but were unable to find the right way to achieve it. Very few critics have actually alleged this kind of failing, and it obviously did not apply to very large sectors of the economy. While it might well have been the case in one or other boardroom that total incompetents were in charge, a development in

[68] Arno Mayer, *The Persistence of the Old Regime* (New York, 1981). Also see Reinhard Bendix, *Work and Authority in Industry* (New York, 1956), 20–21; Gustav Stein (ed.), *Unternehmer in der Politik* (Düsseldorf, 1954), 46–51; Michels, *Umschichtungen*, 44–6; J.-F. Bergier, 'The Industrial Bourgeoisie and the Rise of the Working Class 1700–1914', in: Carlo Cipolla, ed., *Fontana Economic History of Europe* (1973–6), iii. 410–16; Werner Mosse, 'Adel und Bürgertum im Europa des 19. Jahrhunderts. Eine vergleichende Betrachtung', in: Kocka, *Bürgertum*, ii. 277–314.

[69] Details in Pollard, *Britain's Prime*, 6–7.

which these dominate in certain industries but are not found at all in others is surely highly unlikely.

Secondly, and more subtly, there may have been a failure to overcome tradition, or an unwillingness to do so.[70] Possibly under the same heading might come the wish for a quiet life, that is to say, a preference for aims other than the firm's growth and success in return for a lesser expenditure of effort. This was, no doubt, more common and individual examples may be found; but it should in the normal course of events have led to a growth of other British firms at the laggards' expense rather than a national slowing-down.

There might, thirdly, have been a general failure of technical innovation, of new industries to emerge while the older ones were reaching the limits of their expansion.[71] This would ultimately affect all countries, but hit Britain then, because she alone was at the technological frontier. The problem here is that this limitation does not seem to have inhibited American growth well beyond the British per capita level.

Fourthly, and most insidiously, there might have been 'wrong' signals from the market. British entrepreneurs may have acted 'correctly' from their current point of view but, in ways which could not have been foreseen, they turned out to be 'wrong' in the long term. This is the theme of some of the foreign apologists. It may, however, hide the distinct fault, ascribed to British entrepreneurs in several branches of industry, of taking a short-term view only, while foreign business leaders thought further ahead. That, in turn, may however have been caused by the much slower growth of the sated British home market, while foreign markets were closed to the British by the tariff barriers abroad. Alternatively, this short-term vision may be held to account for the failure to appoint trained technologists and scientists in adequate numbers, the failure to see the need for them, or the lack of training on the part of the entrepreneurs themselves which induced that blindness.[72]

All this kind of argumentation leaves a nagging feeling of inadequacy. Set against the background of European backwardness, not least in entrepreneurship, can it really be that it was none but the British entrepreneurs who let the side down? Is there not anything else which is specifically British and which might explain the failure?

[70] Something of this kind is suggested by Jürgen Kocka and Hannes Siegrist, 'Die hundert größten deutschen Industrieunternehmen in späten 19. und frühen 20. Jahrhundert', in: Norbert Horn and Jürgen Kocka, eds., *Law and the Formation of the Big Enterprises in the 19th and 20th Centuries* (Göttingen, 1979), 89–95.

[71] Simon Kuznets, 'Retardation of Industrial Growth', *Journal of Economic and Business History*, i (1928–9), 534–60.

[72] See the general discussion in Coleman, 'Gentlemen'.

One specific British feature has been mentioned briefly: the lack of access by British industrial firms to economic power and to London capital.[73] It may be that the City's predilection for financing foreign railways and colonial governments, and its total disinterest in British manufacturing, may have held back British industrial growth, especially by comparison with Germany, where the large banks were fully engaged in supporting the expansion especially of the key industries in iron and steel, coal, chemicals and other successful sectors.[74] But the argument that British firms failed to grow because of lack of capital, which has been made in individual cases, is difficult to sustain on a large or general basis.

Another peculiarity of the British was their free-trade policy. This is a huge subject, into which we cannot enter at this stage. Certainly, arguments can be developed to show that the lack of tariff protection retarded the British growth rate in comparison with others;[75] but the widespread contrary opinion, not least by contemporaries, may, I think, be taken as proof that that factor, if it had an influence, could not have been a major one.

We are left, then, with a number of doubts. It is doubtful if there was a true secular retardation in Britain, other than part of an irregular growth cycle in which the incipient acceleration visible just before 1913 was cut off by the War. There is doubt, if a cause has indeed to be sought for failure, that the entrepreneurs have to take the sole, or even the major part of the blame. There is more doubt, amounting almost to certainty of the contrary, whether the British entrepreneur of that age was inferior to any other in Europe, and whether British culture was more harmful to industrial entrepreneurship than that of contemporary Europe.

It is, to be sure, convenient for those who may think themselves in part responsible for the failures of the British economy in more recent years to place the beginning of the decline well out of reach, into the later Victorian and Edwardian ages. The historian is not in a position to support that alibi.

[73] Literature in note 4 above.

[74] There is a large literature. For an introduction, see Jürgen Kocka, *Unternehmer*, 102 ff.

[75] Paul Bairoch, *Commerce extérieur et développement économique de l'Europe au XIXe siècle* (Paris, 1976); Donald N. McCloskey, 'Magnanimous Albion: Free Trade and British National Income, 1841–1881', in his *Enterprise and Trade*, 155–72.

ENTERPRISE AND WELFARE STATES: A COMPARATIVE PERSPECTIVE

by Jose Harris

READ 23 SEPTEMBER 1989

DO 'welfare states' enhance or subvert economic enterprise, civic virtue, private moral character, the integrity of social life? Though these questions have a piquantly contemporary ring in modern British politics, they are nevertheless old quandaries in the history of social policy. Since the seventeenth century, if not earlier, practitioners, theorists and critics of public welfare schemes have argued for and against such schemes in contradictory and adversarial terms; claiming on the one hand that social welfare schemes would supply a humanitarian corrective to the rigours of a market economy; and on the other hand that they would support and streamline market forces by enhancing individual and collective efficiency. Similarly, for several hundred years models of civic morality which emphasize independence and self-sufficiency have jostled with alternative models which emphasize paternalism, altruism and organic solidarity.[1] Few phases of social policy in Britain and elsewhere have not contained elements of more than one approach. Even the New Poor Law, notorious for its subordination to market pressures, nevertheless harboured certain residual anti-market principles and often lapsed into practices that were suspiciously communitarian;[2] whilst Edwardian New Liberalism, famous for its philosophy of organic solidarism, in practice tempered social justice with the quest for 'national efficiency'.[3] These varying emphases have all been reflected in the fashions and

[1] On the evolution of such dichotomies, see Istvan Hont and Michael Ignatieff (eds.), *Wealth and Virtue. The Shaping of Political Economy in the Scottish Enlightenment* (Cambridge, 1983), ch. 1; Gertrude Himmelfarb, *The Idea of Poverty: England in the Early Industrial Age* (1984), chs. 1 and 2; E. P. Thompson, 'The Moral Economy of the English Crowd in the Eighteenth Century', *Past and Present*, 50 (1971), 76–136; A. W. Coats, 'Contrary Moralities: Plebs, Paternalists and Political Economists', *Past and Present*, 54 (1972), 130–33.

[2] M. A. Crowther, *The Workhouse System, 1834–1929. The history of an English social Institution* (1981), esp. ch. 9; David Thomson, 'Welfare and the Historians', in Lloyd Bonfield, Richard M. Smith and Keith Wrightson, *The World We Have Gained. Histories of Population and Social Structure* (Oxford, 1986), 355–78.

[3] Michael Freeden, *The New Liberalism. An Ideology of Social Reform* (Oxford, 1978); Geoffrey Searle, *The Quest for National Efficiency. A study in British Politics and British Political Thought 1899–1914* (Oxford, 1971), esp. 171–204.

phases of welfare state historiography—fashions and phases that appear to have been at least partly determined by the vagaries of prevailing political climate. Thus, in the aftermath of the Second World War, historians tended to portray the history of social policy as a series of governmental battles against private vested interests—battles in which the mantle of civic virtue was worn by an altruistic administrative elite, while civic vice was embodied in the motley crew of doctors, landlords, employers and insurance companies who viewed social welfare as a commodity in the market.[4] A slightly later generation of historians, heavily influenced by nineteen sixties-style Marxism and French structuralism, then shifted towards a different stance—emphasising not the conflict but the symbiosis between welfare and private enterprise. Social policy appeared increasingly not as the brake but as the tool of industrial capitalism, transmitting into the social democratic era the self-help maxims of the age of Cobden and Smiles; and social policy-makers and public administrators were recast not as Davids of social reform but as Goliaths of the capitalist state.[5] Fashion is fickle, however, and the 1980s have brought to the fore a third vein in writing about the history of social welfare; a vein in which administrators and reformers once again appear as villains, but guilty now not of regulating the proletariat but of sapping and subverting that very same entrepreneurial capitalism which only a few years ago they were accused of reinforcing. This argument has lurked for several decades in the writings of the Institute of Economic Affairs,[6] and for long was treated somewhat disdainfully by the academic establishment; but it has been brought to the forefront of historical debate by Correlli Barnett's *The Audit of War*, published in 1986, which portrayed the welfare state as one of the major links in the chain of Britain's post-Second World War national decline.[7]

Correlli Barnett's thesis seems to me an important one, less easily dismissable in many respects than some of its critics have supposed; and its message is doubly important in that, regardless of the accuracy

[4] M. Ginsberg (ed.), *Law and Opinion in England in the Twentieth Century* (1959); S. Finer, *The Life and Times of Sir Edwin Chadwick* (1952); Royston Lambert, *Sir John Simon 1818–1904 and English Social Administration* (1963).

[5] Gareth Stedman Jones, *Outcast London. A Study in Relations between the Classes* (Oxford, 1971); J. R. Hay, 'Employers' Attitudes to Social Policy and the Concept of Social Control, 1900–1920', in P. M. Thane (ed.) *The Origins of British Social Policy* (1978), 107–125; Roger Davidson, *Whitehall and the Labour Problem in late-Victorian and Edwardian Britain* (1985).

[6] Arthur Seldon, *Taxation and Welfare. A Report on Private Opinion and Public Policy* (1969); Hermione Parker, *The Moral Hazard of Social Benefits. A study of the Impact of Social Benefits and Income Tax on Incentives to Work* (1982).

[7] Correlli Barnett, *The Audit of War. The Illusion and Reality of Britain as a Great Nation* (1986).

of its acount of the more distant past, it has undoubtedly been helping to *make* history over the recent decade—in that no less a person than Mr Nigel Lawson has cited 'Correlli's book' as a major source of authority for his fiscal and social policies as Chancellor of the Exchequer.[8] In this paper I propose to review the interpretation of the history of the welfare state set out by Barnett, and to assess its strengths and weaknesses; and then to identify some important unresolved questions which it raises about the historical significance of welfare states and their influence upon social structure, economic performance and entrepreneurial skills.

What then is the connection between the rise of the welfare state and the secular decline of Britain as set out in Barnett's *Audit of War?* Barnett catalogues the substance of this decline in fairly familiar and unremarkable terms; loss of empire, loss of world power status, slippage from being the 'workshop of the world' to being fourteenth in the league table of world industrial nations, with a massive adverse trade balance, high unemployment, low domestic investment, weak entrepreneurship and low factor productivity, and a per capita output of little more than one third of that of West Germany—once Britain's main industrial rival.[9] And what was the cause of this decline? Barnett's answer is a very simple one: Britain threw away the historic moment of reconstruction and recovery at the end of the Second World War, and instead of investing in the modernization of industry and technology, frittered away her dwindling resources on building a comprehensive system of state welfare, which turned the mass of the British people into a 'segregated, subliterate, unskilled, unhealthy and institutionalised proletariat hanging on the nipple of state maternalism.[10] And at the same time the famous Education Act of 1944, which purported to be bringing about secondary education for all, merely replicated the traditional faults of the British education system by ignoring science, technology and productive skills and by shoring up the cultural hegemony of an arts-and-classics trained gentlemanly elite.[11] And who or what brought about this state of affairs? Here Barnett's analysis is slightly more ambivalent. The main thrust of his attack is upon a wartime conspiracy of evangelical, nonconformist and humanitarian Christians—headed by William Beveridge, Clement Attlee, Hugh Dalton, Harold Laski, William Temple and indeed virtually the whole of the British Labour and Liberal parties—whom he portrays as corrupting the people with promises of a social New Jerusalem when they should have been facing up to the chill realities

[8] B.B.C., Radio Four, 'Any Questions' programme, March 1987.
[9] Barnett, *op. cit.*, 304.
[10] *Ibid.*
[11] *Ibid.*, 278–91.

of economic bankruptcy and industrial reconstruction.[12] And behind this wartime conspiracy lay another more long-term and deep-seated factor. Ever since the early nineteenth century, a romantic-cum-Christian evangelical and 'Victorian' inheritance had weaned the British people away from productive and entrepreneurial values and substituted instead an ethic of humane learning, gentlemanly personal behaviour, pacific internationalism and disdain for materialism; an ethic mediated among the working classes by nonconformist chapels, and among the upper and middle classes by the public schools.[13] The all-pervasiveness of this ethic meant that over the previous hundred and fifty years Britain had *never* been well-adapted to the highly competitive, disciplined and organised framework of advanced industrial capitalism. Even Britain's much-vaunted technological miracles of the Second World War had been propped up by the American lend-lease programme; and British per capita wartime productivity had been considerably lower not merely than that of German workers but than that of 'the hundreds of thousands of foreign workers recruited onto German soil' (in other words, of workers conscripted by the S.S. into slave labour camps). This point introduces one of the main underlying subsidiary themes of Barnett's thesis; namely, the long-drawn out structural and cultural superiority of Germany at all stages of nineteenth- and twentieth-century British history. Even in the nineteen thirties and early forties, Barnett argues, Germany had a basically strong and well-functioning social, political and economic system which had been temporarily hijacked by a handful of lunatic gangsters whom he sees as wholly extraneous to Germany's wider history. Nazism had only to be got rid of for healthy normality to be restored;[14] whereas Britain had a much more congenital and engrained problem of stagnation, sentimentalism, misplaced egalitarianism and deep-seated hostility to industrial and technological modes of thought and life.

In this paper I want to leave on one side the wider issue of Britain's loss of world power status, and to concentrate particularly on the equation between national economic decline and the setting up of a welfare state. I want also to get beyond the rather generalised criticisms that have been put forward by historians of the general plausibility of Correlli Barnett's thesis, and to look instead at the factual and archival evidence with which he supports his case. In particular, I want to focus upon the evidence for three cardinal points. Firstly,

[12] *Ibid.*, 13–19, 36–7, 279–304.
[13] *Ibid.*, 12–15, 213–33.
[14] *Ibid.*, 62, 93, 145–51.

was the British economy burdened from the mid-1940's onwards by excessively high welfare state expenditure which sapped investment and enabled Britain to be rapidly outstripped by more realistic commercial rivals? Secondly, can the faults in Britain's welfare and education systems be ascribed to the extravagant idealism and disdain for entrepreneurship of the Second World War reconstruction movement? And thirdly, what evidence is there to suggest that (in a ghostly echo of Gibbon's account of the Roman empire) it was the debilitating influence of Christianity that was the secret cause of Britain's decline and fall?

Firstly, then, the volume and impact of welfare state expenditure. As several of Barnett's critics have pointed out, Britain was by no means unique in introducing new and comprehensive social security plans in the late 1940s; and something which can loosely be described as a 'welfare state' emerged in nearly all western industrial countries in the decade after the Second World War. Is there nevertheless a case for saying that Britain, widely regarded at the time as the *locus classicus* of welfare statism, was crippling her economy with a disproportionately large amount of welfare expenditure which ate into the national dividend and national wealth creation in a way that did not happen elsewhere? What are the facts? Data relating to all European social welfare systems is readily available in many forms: in EEC and OECD reports on public expenditure, in the comparative studies of social policy carried out by Gaston Rimlinger, Peter Caim Kaudle and others; in the digests of European historical statistics published by Brian Mitchell; and most spectacularly in the massive volumes of data on European welfare states published since 1983 by an international team at the European University in Florence under the direction of Professor Peter Flora.[15] None of these very obvious sources was cited by Barrett, and indeed detailed evidence about the social welfare systems of other countries is conspicuous by its absence from his whole account. What support does such evidence lend to the view that Britain's poor economic performance since the Second World War has been peculiarly linked to the crippling fiscal and demoralising moral impact of its welfare state system?

[15] OECD Social Policy Studies, *Social Expenditure 1960–1990. Problems of Growth and Control* (Paris 1985); Gaston Rimlinger, *Welfare Policy and Industrialization in Europe, America and Russia* (New York, 1971); P. R. Kaim-Caudle, *Comparative Social Policy and Social Security. A Ten Country Study* (1973); B. R. Mitchell, *European Historical Statistics 1750–1975* (second revised edition, 1981); Peter Flora et al., *State, Economy and Society in Western Europe, 1815–1975*. Vol. 1, *The Growth of Mass Democracies and Welfare States*. Vol. II, *The Growth of Industrial Societies and Capitalist Economies* (Frankfurt and London, 1983 and 1987); Peter Flora (ed.), *Growth to Limits. The Western European Welfare States since world War Two*, Vols. I, II and IV (New York and Berlin, 1987–8).

Some at least of the facts are as follows. Britain's new social security and national health legislation came into operation in 1948, and comparative data is available for social services expenditure in nearly all European countries from 1949 or 1950 onwards. Even in 1950, in a year when much of western Europe had only recently been rescued from economic collapse by the first instalments of the Marshall Plan, Britain's spending on social security as a percentage of gross domestic product was lower than that of West Germany, Austria and Belgium. By 1952 her social security expenditure was also lower than that of France and Denmark, in 1954 it was outstripped by that of Italy, in 1955 by Sweden, in 1957 by the Netherlands, and in 1970 by Norway and Finland. From that time onwards until the early 1980s (the last point in time for which full comparative data are available) Britain consistently devoted a lower proportion of national income to social security purposes than any other European country, with the sole exception of Switzerland.[16] But what about the national health service—that institution which in Correlli Barnett's eyes more clearly than any other symbolised the subordination of competitive economic values to social, egalitarian and solidaristic goals? Here again we have detailed and reliable sources of comparative data although they are not cited by Barnett. Studies of the 1950s and early 1960s showed that although the per capita health spending channeled through central government was *higher* in Great Britain than in other European countries, the aggregate volume of per capita health expenditure through central, local and private agencies was *lower* in Britain than anywhere else in Europe except Italy and Ireland. In other words the volume of investment being putatively siphoned away from wealth creation by expenditure on health care was considerably lower than elsewhere; and a committee appointed by a Conservative health minister in 1956 to investigate the problem of rising health costs concluded that by comparison with possible alternatives the National Health Service was both cheap and cost effective.[17] Moreover, even if we confine our discussion solely to *public* sector health expenditure, Britain's lead under this head did not last very long. West Germany's combined public expenditure on social insurance and health care was already proportionately greater than that of the United Kingdom in 1949, and by the early 1950s Britain was overtaken in these spheres by Austria, Belgium, Denmark and Sweden. By the early 1970s Britain's

[16] Flora, *State, Economy and Society*, Vol. I, 456; Edward James and Andre Laurent, 'Social Security: the European Experiment', *Social Trends*, 5, 1974, 26–34.

[17] Brian Abel-Smith, *An International Study of Health Expenditure*, WHO Public Paper No. 32 (Geneva, 1967); *Report of the Committee of Enquiry into the Cost of the National Health Service* (Cmnd. 9663, 1956), 286–9.

expenditure on health care and health benefits was lower than that of all west European countries except Austria and Switzerland, and her joint expenditure on health care and pensions lower than that of any other European country with no exceptions.[18]

These findings are corroborated by many other studies. A comparative study of international patterns of public expenditure by Dr Jurgen Kohl found that throughout the period Britain devoted a lower proportion of her gross national product to social transfer incomes of all kinds (pensions, insurance, public assistance, benefits in kind) than all the large western European countries and most of the smaller ones.[19] European Economic Community data shows that throughout the 1970s Britain's social expenditure as a proportion both of national income and of gross domestic product was lower than that of any other community member except Ireland; and also that the rate of growth of her social expenditure was lower than that of any other EEC country.[20] Even more germane to the debate about the impact of welfare on enterprise, data published by the OECD in 1985 showed that over the period 1960–81 Britain's annual growth in gross domestic product had been lower than that of all other OECD countries; and that at the same time the rate of growth of Britain's expenditure on social services had *also* been consistently lower than that of the other eighteen OECD members.[21] As Harold Wilensky observed in an OECD conference paper of 1980 the 'big spenders' on social welfare such as Germany, the Netherlands, Norway and Belgium were all near the top of the international league table for economic growth rates; whereas what he called the 'lean-spending democracies' such as Britain, the USA, Canada, Australia and New Zealand were all somewhere near the bottom.[22]

The generalised case for the existence of a parasitic welfare state, which since the 1940s has crippled the economy of Britain but not that of her economic rivals, therefore looks weak. Like other forms of

[18] Flora, *State, Economy and Society*, Vol. I, 456–7; Brian Abel-Smith and Alan Maynard, *The Organization, Financing and Cost of Health Care in the European Community* (Commission of the European Communities, Social Policy Series, No. 36, Brussels, 1978), esp. pp. 108–12.

[19] Jurgen Kohl, 'Trends and Problems in Postwar Public Expenditure Development in Western Europe and North America', in Peter Flora and Arnold J. Heidenheimer (eds.) *The Development of Welfare States in Europe and America* (1981), 307–44, esp. Table 9.4 on p. 317.

[20] Statistical Office of the European Communities (Eurostat), *Social Indicators for the European Community 1960–1975* (Brussels, 1977), Table V/1, 184–5, and Table V/4, 190–1.

[21] OECD, *Social Expenditure 1960–1990*, 21. See also Jurgen Kohl, *loc. cit.*, 319.

[22] Harold L. Wilensky, 'Democratic Corporatism, Consensus, and Social Policy', in *The Welfare State in Crisis. An account of the Conference on Social Policies in the 1980s*, 20–23 October 1980, 191–2 (OECD, Paris, 1981).

taxation, however, the fiscal burden of welfare spending can fall in many ways, and although Correlli Barnett is clearly *wrong* in suggesting that the global volume of British welfare state expenditure from the 1940s onwards was disproportionately high, nevertheless he *might* have a case if he argued that British welfare funding was either levied in such a way or spent in such a manner as to do more economic damage than similar funds levied elsewhere. Correlli Barnett at no point even considers any argument as relatively complex and historically specific as this, but in order to get at the historical truth of the matter, I shall do so on his behalf. Is there any evidence to suggest that Britain's relatively small welfare state was more economically burdensome than the relatively large welfare states of her continental neighbours?

One fact that very clearly emerges from the data compiled by the Peter Flora study is that far more of the cost of welfare expenditure in Britain fell upon the direct taxpayer and far less on employers and workers than in nearly all other European countries throughout the period 1948 to 1982.[23] In other words it seems probable that the British social security system ws at least marginally more redistributive than that of most other European countries. And another point that appears to emerge is that a comparatively *low* percentage of Britain's welfare budget was channelled through contributory social insurance; while a much higher proportion than in most European countries was channelled through means-tested public assistance. This meant that a lower proportion of Britain's social security expenditure was allocated to active workers temporarily sick and unemployed (that is to say, to servicing the efficient working of the productive sector of the economy) and a higher proportion to support of those who were marginal to or wholly outside the labour market. Moreover, this disparity grew over time. Whilst in Britain the share of social security spending absorbed by public assistance doubled between the late 1940s and the mid-1970s, in Germany, Austria and Italy it fell dramatically over the same period.[24] In France centralised public assistance was wholly abolished in 1966, leaving the long-term poor to a localised system of *aide sociale* far more marginal and limited in scope than the British system of 'supplementary benefit'. In fact, paradoxically, though Britain was believed to be the homeland of a 'Beveridge'-based universal insurance system, almost the opposite was really

[23] Flora, *State, Economy and Society,* Vol. I, 459, 462–551; Edward James and Andre Laurent, *loc. cit.*, 27–8.

[24] Flora, *op. cit.*, 462–3, 476–7, 483–4, 490–1, 504–5, 518–19, 525–6, 532–3, 539–40, 546–7. One major cause of the growth of Britain's public assistance sector was that her social insurance benefits were so much lower than in most other western European countries; hence, the phenomenon of 'supplementary benefit'.

the case. It was the European countries, most notably France and Germany, which most wholeheartedly adopted a comprehensive, contributory social insurance system (albeit differing from the Beveridge scheme in many important respects); whereas Britain, for all her much vaunted abolition of the Poor Law, retained in addition to social insurance a substantial means-tested, tax-financed welfare system, directly inherited from the Poor Law, but shorn of much of the Poor Law's aura of deterrence and stigma, and shorn also of its local democratic and communitarian controls.[25] This latter system, in marked contrast to the contributory national insurance system, was primarily concerned with relief of poverty and was almost entirely divorced from market or actuarial constraints (except insofar as these were mediated through political pressures). The same emphasis on relief of poverty as the prime aim of social policy can perhaps be seen in the policy of support for families: whereas most other European countries in the post-war era paid substantial child allowances and other forms of family grant, Britain until the late 1970s paid very small 'universal' family allowances (excluding first and only children) and channelled the bulk of her family support services through means-tested public assistance.[26] In the National Health Service priorities were different, in that the old Poor Law principle of concentrating public services upon the poor was abandoned in favour of equal access for all citizens. But again the financial structure of Britain's health service was very different from that of her continental neighbours, and Britain alone among the major European countries had a national health system offering total coverage and funded primarily by taxation rather than contractual social insurance.[27]

To this extent Barnett's critique of the welfare state as a hidden cause of Britain's poor economic performance may have some foundation. Though it is *not* true that Britain's global social security expenditure was larger than anyone else's, it appears to be the case that both the financial structure and the substantive priorities of Britain's welfare state *were* different: that the non-economic goals of unconditional relief of poverty and, particularly in the case of the health service, of equality of access for all citizens, were more strongly built into the British welfare system than those of most other European

[25] The story of the gradual dismantling and transformation of the Poor Law remains to be told. For analysis of some of the later stages of that process, see Alan Deacon, 'An End to the Means Test? Social Security and the Attlee Government', *Journal of Social Policy,* xi (1982), 289–306; and Phoebe Hall, Hilary Land, Roy Parker and Adrian Webb, *Change, Choice and Conflict in Social Policy* (1975), 410–71.

[26] Edward James and Andre Laurent, *loc. cit,* 31–2

[27] Apart from Britain, only Denmark had a tax-financed health service with 100% coverage (Abel-Smith and Maynard, op. cit., pp. 9–102, and Table 4 on p. 116).

countries; while the welfare systems of many European states and particularly of France and Germany were much more directly concerned with contractual entitlement and promotion of industrial efficiency. In other words, contrary to what most academic commentators and popular folk-lore have believed,[28] it was not contributory social insurance, but 'free' services financed out of direct taxation that was the most marked characteristic of Britain's welfare state system in the thirty years after the Second World War.

If one adjusts and amplifies Correlli Barnett's argument in this way, however, one automatically torpedoes the *second* major plank in his case against the British welfare state, which is that the sentimental, egalitarian rot set in with the wartime social reconstruction movement—because that reconstruction movement was overwhelmingly devoted to promoting a Beveridge-based contractual social insurance system and to abolishing the centuries-old system of relief of need through the Poor Law. This brings me to my second major objection to Correlli Barnett's thesis, which is that he largely misrepresents the content of the wartime social reconstruction movement and particularly that part of it articulated through the ideas of William Beveridge and the famous Beveridge Plan of 1942.

Barnett portrays Beveridge throughout his book as the veritable incarnation of that 'Victorian', sentimental, Christian, pacifistic, classical, public school, Oxbridge culture, which he believes to have been the Achilles heel of British public life over the previous century; and he portrays Beveridge's plan of 1942 as the high peak of the hysterical surge of popular wartime feeling that demanded the instant sunshine of Brave New World and ignored the cold reality of national bankruptcy.[29] The papers of Beveridge's Social Insurance committee reveal, so Barnett claimed in *a* resumé of his thesis published in the *Telegraph* in 1987, that Beveridge deliberatly set out to create 'the most lavish welfare state in the world', regardless of national resources and market criteria.[30] Beveridge's proposals were instantly taken up by that sentimental Christian pacifist sector of public opinion which thought that the Second World War needed some other purpose than mere military victory: the very *same* people, Barnett states, who only a few years earlier had been to the forefront of appeasement of dictators.[31] Beveridge's orchestration of public opinion ultimately

[28] The Guillebaud committee in 1956, for example, found that most NHS patients firmly believed that they had paid for their treatment through contributory national insurance.

[29] Barnett, *op. cit.*, 26–31, 45–9.

[30] Correlli Barnett, 'Decline and Fall of Beveridge's New Jerusalem', *Daily Telegraph*, 1 Dec. 1986.

[31] Barnett, *Audit of War*, 19, 25.

forced a weak-kneed coalition government, deeply penetrated by sentimentalist Christian Labour elements, into acceptance of social welfare commitments which it knew to mean economic ruin.[32] Much the same forces were at work, Barnett suggests, in the planning of the 1944 Education Act—where scientific and technological imperatives were wholly ignored, and an Act whose main ingredients were the retention of compulsory religious education in schools and the continued entrenchment of sectarianism within the national education system.[33] This whole dismal story, Barnett claims, is enshrined in the public archives of the Second World War, sheltering behind all the rhetoric of patriotism and digging for victory.

It is impossible in a brief article to cite every instance in which the documentary evidence is open to a wholly or partially different interpretation from that which Barnett suggests, but I will confine myself to a few key examples. First of all, the person of Sir William Beveridge. Contrary to the account given by Barnett, Beveridge was not at any time in his life a Christian, nor had he been brought up as a Christian, which was unusual for an upper-middle class person born in the late nineteenth century. His only formal religious affiliation, abandoned after early childhood, was with the Unitarians, a sect notable in British welfare history for producing a long line of social theorists and reformers strongly committed to 'state sternness' in the treatment of the poor and to gearing social policy to industrial efficiency.[34] Beveridge was also never at any stage a pacifist, and throughout the 1930s he had been a powerful critic of appeasement. It is true that he had a first-class degree in classics (that alleged litmus test of inept idealism), but he also had a first in mathematics which Barnett does not mention; and throughout his eighteen years as director of the London School of Economics he had been a powerful advocate of the kind of business, vocational and practical studies that Barnett sees as having been at such a discount in British education.[35] Beveridge was of course a 'Victorian', in the sense that he was born during the reign of Queen Victoria; but since Victoria died only thirty eight years before the Second World War broke out this was necessarily true of all middle-aged leaders of public opinion during

[32] *Ibid.*, 30–32.

[33] *Ibid.*, 276–91.

[34] Harriet Martineau, Joseph Chamberlain, Charles Booth and Helen Bosanquet spring to mind as prominent examples. The phrase 'state sternness' comes from a famous letter written by Joseph Chamberlain to Beatrice Webb, in which he stressed the need to legitimise the state's 'power of being very strict with the loafer and the confirmed pauper' [quoted in Peter Fraser, *Joseph Chamberlain: Radicalism and Empire* (1966), 125].

[35] Jose Harris, *William Beveridge. A Biography* (Oxford, 1977), 271–2.

this period. More immediately relevant to this paper, Beveridge throughout his life had been a protagonist of the disciplined and highly organised 'Prussian' model of government so much admired by Barnett.[36] As a civil servant in the Board of Trade during the First World War period Beveridge had been one of the earliest, if not the earliest, advocate of the view that large-scale modern public administration needed not classicists and philosophers but technocrats and business managers.[37] And throughout his life he had been a strong defender of the maintenance of rational incentives and market criteria in state systems of social security.[38] Not perhaps unreasonably in the context of the Second World War, he came to the conclusion in the early 1940s that at the level of macro-economic management a pure free market had irretrievably broken down and that both national and international economies in the future would need much more governmental direction;[39] but there is no suggestion in the Beveridge Report that market criteria were to be ignored at the level of paying benefits to the individual citizen. In fact, quite the contrary is true. The definition of subsistence on which Beveridge's estimates of welfare benefits were based was deliberately kept to a very basic spartan minimum, both to encourage private saving and to maintain the traditional Poor Law principle of a substantial incentive gap between wages and benefits—the so-called 'principle of less eligibility'.[40]

The same is true of Beveridge's whole construction of a total social security budget. The only glimmer of support for Barnett's (inherently unlikely) claim that Beveridge deliberately set out to devise the most expensive welfare system ever known lay in the fact that early on in his enquiry he made a notional calculation of what a national social welfare system *would* cost if all forms of want were to be universally covered by a subsistence minimum.[41] Having made this calculation he used it as a benchmark of what was socially desirable, but then proceeded with the help of advisers from the Treasury and the Economic Section of the War Cabinet to prune it down to what was

[36] Barnett, *op. cit.*, 228–30. On Beveridge's early admiration for Bismarckian welfare institutions, an admiration that inspired his whole subsequent career as a social reformer, see the series of articles on 'Social Reform: How Germany deals with it', *Morning Post*, Sept. 1907.

[37] Harris, *op. cit.*, 156–7, 166.

[38] *Ibid.*, 99–100, 171–6, 323, 353, 355–6.

[39] Beveridge Papers, VIII 45, Advisory Panel on Home Affairs, minutes, 9 July 1942.

[40] Harris, *op. cit.*, 396–9; John McNicol, *The Movement for Family Allowances 1918–45. A Study in Social Policy Development* (1980), 185–7.

[41] Beveridge Papers, IXa, 37(2), 'Social Insurance—General Considerations', by W. H. Beveridge, July 1941; PRO,CAB 87/76, 'Basic Problems of Social Security with Heads of a Scheme', by W. H. Beveridge, 11 Dec. 1941; and PRO,CAB 87/76, 'Finance of Social Insurance. Some Statistical Short Cuts', by W. H. Beveridge, 19 Dec. 1941.

economically and fiscally viable.[42] Barnett portrays this process of amendment as mere reluctant cosmetic tinkering on Beveridge's part; a view scarcely borne out by the fact that it involved the jettisoning of such items as subsistence-level pensions, state insurance for industrial injuries, family allowances for first children, insurance for housewives, and benefits for persons unable to work because they were caring for sick or aged relatives. The result was that the 'social security budget' eventually included in the Beveridge Plan amounted to less than one-fifth of the initial 'utopian' calculation. Moreover, the vast bulk of the Beveridge committee papers in the British Library of Political Science and the Public Record Office are devoted to discussions with the Treasury, the Government Actuary and the Whitehall social policy departments about methods of keeping costs down, and to statistical and nutritional inquiries about how to define the lowest possible level of provision for basic human need compatible with both healthy existence and budgetary reality.[43] A major consequence of this pruning process was that in place of subsistence-level pensions the Beveridge Plan scheme allowed for a gradual increase in pension rates over a period of twenty years, to allow for the accrual of appropriate insurance contributions—scarcely a proposal of wild imprudence or fiscal impetuosity.[44] Beveridge doubtless personally regretted the need for such economies. But regret is one thing, obtuse refusal to bow to facts quite another; and the final text of the Beveridge Plan firmly stressed the need to make the burden of social security 'as light as possible' in the aftermath of war, 'in accord with the probable economic and political requirements'.[45]

Moreover, central to Beveridge's whole philosophy of social welfare was the principle that the non-contributory Poor Law—with its means-tested benefits paid for out of general taxation and consequent

[42] Harris, *op. cit.*, 407–12. Beveridge agreed with the Treasury to keep the proposed public costs of his scheme to within £100 million p.a. during the first five years of its operation. The total sum expended by public authorities on all social services (not just social insurance) in 1938 was £596.3 million.

[43] Beveridge Papers VIII, files 28 and 37. The whole question of the benefit levels envisaged in the Beveridge Report has recently been analysed in detail by Professor John Veit-Wilson, who concludes that, beneath Beveridge's somewhat ambiguous utterances on this issue, there was no intention on Beveridge's part to accept the more broadly-based and relativistic definition of need currently being propounded by Seebohm Rowntree (John Veit-Wilson, 'Genesis of confusion: the Beveridge Committee's Poverty Line for Social Security', paper for the seminar at the Suntory Toyota International Centre for Economics and Related Disciplines, London School of Economics, 1 Nov. 1989). I am grateful to Professor Veit-Wilson for letting me see his paper.

[44] *Social Insurance and Allied Services*, Cmd. 6404, 1942, 92–5.

[45] *Ibid.*, para. 292.

penalisation of effort and thrift—was servile and quasi-feudal and wholly unsuited to an advanced industrial economy. Instead, in Beveridge's view, people should pay for, and indeed wanted to pay for, their own welfare benefits. In the course of cross-examination of witnesses before the Social Insurance committee, he scathingly invoked the image of 'the Santa Claus state' as the epitome of the kind of welfare system that he was determined to avoid (an ironic commentary upon the 'Father Christmas system' foisted upon him by Correlli Barnett).[46] 'Benefits in return for contributions, rather than free allowances from the State is what the people of Britain desire', was perhaps the key sentiment in the whole of the Beveridge report and the one most often quoted by contemporary commentators.[47] 'Contract' not 'status' was the fundamental theoretical basis of Beveridge's conception of state social policy.[48] And, in addition, Beveridge envisaged that people who attempted to exploit the social security system were to be subject to a stringent labour test, 'conditions as to behaviour', and programmes of compulsory industrial retraining of the kind envisaged in an earlier generation by Sidney and Beatrice Webb.[49] ('No man should be subject to criminal penalties in peace for refusing work however unreasonably. But he should not be assisted to be unreasonable by provision of an insurance income.') The serious enforcement of such personal controls was to be never politically acceptable in post-war Britain, but Beveridge's advocacy of such controls could scarcely be more remote from the tender-hearted sentimentalism with which Barnett endows him. Moreover, though Barnett quotes extensively from Whitehall authorities who feared the costs of the Beveridge scheme, he makes no reference at all to the many expressions of the contrary view; to the economists and administrators in Whitehall and elsewhere who pointed out that the Beveridge subsistence-level benefits were actually in many cases lower than those currently payable under the Poor Law, who thought that the Beveridge system in sum would cost no more than all the fragmentary and overlapping services of the 1930s, and who believed that comprehensive insurance would help rather than hinder industrial recovery.[50] 'On balance the scheme should improve rather than worsen our

[46] PRO, CAB 87/78, Social Insurance Committee minutes, 17 June 1942, QQ. 4720, 4726; Barnett, *op. cit.*, 30.

[47] *Social Insurance and Allied Services*, 11.

[48] W. H. Beveridge, *Unemployment: a Problem of Industry* (1930 ed.), 288–94.

[49] *Social Insurance and Allied Services*, paras. 369, 440; *W. H. Beveridge, Full Employment in a Free Society* (1944), 173.

[50] Hubert Henderson Papers, memorandum on 'The Beveridge Proposals', by J. M. Keynes, 20 July 1942; Norman Chester Papers, 'Finance of the Proposals in the Beveridge Report', by D. N. Chester, 18 Nov. 1942.

economic conditions', wrote one such adviser to Lord Cherwell in 1943. '... the Beveridge scheme should not, therefore, be regarded as something desirable on altruistic grounds but perhaps too expensive in practice, for its cost, so far as one can see, will be less than nothing'.[51]

The historic cost of the welfare state is a subject that could be pursued in far greater detail than there is space for here. There is, however, very little evidence to suggest that welfare state spending in Britain got out of control before the mid-1960s; and, if it did so then, this was by no means a peculiarly British problem, but a European-wide and even global phenomenon. In many advanced countries between 1950 and 1970 social security payments soared ahead of economic growth and the margin between wages and benefits substantially narrowed;[52] but whilst it is not hard to imagine that this may have had an adverse effect on both savings and work incentives, it can scarcely be invoked as an explanation of the peculiar difficulties of Britain. In nearly every country, one of the most powerful pressures upon the upward spiral of welfare expenditure was demographic: the wholly unprecedented and at least partially unexpected burden of old age. But, insofar as social policies were influenced by cultural factors, it may be argued that the welfare state explosion stemmed not from the utopian visions of the 1940s, but from precisely the opposite source. The stern, sober and somewhat spartan limits to state welfare imposed by planners in the 1940s began to be challenged in the 1960s by utopian thinking of an entirely different order: by academics and pressure groups and social policy activists who wanted to make welfare rather than wages or investment a first charge upon national income and who looked with moral disdain upon the efforts of earlier reformers to harness social policy to economic and entrepreneurial goals. That epoch of the late 1960s fits the cap woven by Barnett far more closely than the austere and cautious 1940s. In other words, as T. H. Marshall argued long ago, the Beveridge-based welfare state was the 'child of austerity', and it broke down not because of its extravagance, but because its spartan, minimalist, safety-net character increasingly clashed with the values and aspirations of a more affluent and millenarian age.[53]

I want to conclude this discussion of Correlli Barnett's ideas by

[51] Cherwell papers, H256, memorandum by an unnamed economist to Lord Cherwell, 22 Jan. 1943. I am most grateful to Dr Derek Fraser, who has been working for some years on the making and impact of the Beveridge report, for drawing my attention to this paper.

[52] Brian Abel-Smith, 'Public Expenditure on the Social Services', *Social Trends*, 1, 1970, 19; Edward James and Andre Laurent, *loc. cit.*, 26–34; Jurgen Kohl, *loc. cit.*, 307–44.

[53] T. H. Marshall, *Sociology at the Crossroads and other Essays* (1953), 267–308.

commenting briefly on the third aspect of his welfare state thesis; namely, his claim that it was the all-pervasive influence of Christianity that led to the setting-up of a comprehensive welfare system and to the consequent enervation of the British economy and corruption of the British state. That there is some kind of underlying connection between Christianity and welfare states is not quite so fanciful a thesis as many of Barnett's critics have supposed, since one of the major findings of the international survey carried out by Peter Flora and others was that throughout Europe confessional parties and particularly Catholic parties have been the most ambitious and open-handed social welfare spenders—far more markedly so than parties of the secularist left.[54] But Britain of course has no confessional parties and little tradition of social catholicism, and the interaction of her politics with religious opinion has always been more varying and nebulous than elsewhere. Nevertheless, is there any evidence to sustain the view that in Britain, as elsewhere, there has been some direct causal connection between Christian conviction and the growth of a welfare state and that, as Barnett claims, Christianity seduced the nation away from the struggle for economic survival? Whether he means all forms of Christianity or just some of them is not quite clear, as he frequently qualifies the noun Christian with pejorative adjectives; the terms 'Evangelical', 'nonconformist', 'Christian socialist', 'humanitarian' and 'godly notable' are used throughout his book apparently interchangeably. As exemplars of the Christian ethic he cites specifically Beveridge, Keynes, Hugh Dalton ('wearing his shovel hat as a Christian and a Socialist'), Clement Attlee and Archbishop William Temple, and at times suggests that the whole Liberal and Labour movements were embodiments of a particularly crass and worm-like Christianity—a Christianity that he also holds responsible for the 1930s policies of appeasement of dictators.[55] Just occasionally there is some slight suggestion that he is aware of something amiss with this thesis; as, for instance, when he aims a passing blow at Stanley Baldwin and Neville Chamberlain (both of whom he explains were 'liberals at heart' and had a 'family connection' with nonconformity).[56] But that there is something far *more* wrong with his thesis than that must be obvious to anyone who has the slightest familiarity with the *dramatic personae* of British history in this period—namely, that many of the people whom Barnett cites as leaders of the

[54] Harold L. Wilensky, 'Leftism, Catholicism and Democratic Corporatism: the Role of Political Parties in Recent Welfare State Development', in Peter Flora and Arnold Heidenheimer, *op. cit.*, 345–82, and esp. 356–62.

[55] Barnett, *op. cit.*, 13–18, 25, 243, 250.

[56] *Ibid.*, 14–15.

social reconstruction movement were not in fact Christians at all, let alone nonconformists, Christian Socialists or evangelicals. I have already mentioned the non-Christianity of Beveridge; but the same is true of nearly all the rest. Clement Attlee was an agnostic, J. M. Keynes a self-confessed 'immoralist', while Hugh Dalton's only adult connection with Christianity was the fact that his father had been an Anglican dean.[57] Barnett acknowledges Harold Laski to have been a Jew, but persists in treating him as a kind of honorary Christian gentleman. Of the major villains cited by Barnett the only one who was self-evidently a Christian was William Temple, and he could scarcely avoid being one as he was Archbishop of Canterbury; but the evidence of Temple's substantive influence on the planning of the British welfare state is minimal (other than the fact that he appears to have been responsible for popularising the term). Of the post-war Labour front bench the most prominent practising Christian was Sir Stafford Cripps: but Barnett explicitly exempts Cripps from his diatribe against the rest, on the grounds that Cripps was 'oddly realist'.[58]

That there *were* individual Christians and groups of Christians in the social reconstruction movement is undeniable (indeed it would be odd if there had not been in a country in which about one-tenth of the population were still active churchgoers and the vast majority still claimed to subscribe to the Christian ethic). And undoubtedly some Christians were tender-minded, leftist-inclined, enterprise-despising, libertarian utopians of the kind that Barnett finds most abhorrent. But the involvement of at least some of these reformist Christian groups was of a character quite opposite to that which Barnett suggests. One of the most vocal and organised Christian groups within the reconstruction movement was that which advised the Secretary of State for Education, R. A. Butler, on the reconstruction of the post-war secondary education system. Headed by the publisher and historian, Geoffrey Faber, this group included the high master of St Paul's school, Walter Oakeshott, and a number of prominent conservative business men and manufacturers. Whether by accident or design nearly all the members of this group were active Christians or Unitarians, and their reconstruction proposals were strongly imbued with the goal of rebuilding a Christian commonwealth. The group drew much of its social theory and many of its practical ideas from the refugee Hungarian sociologist, Karl Mannheim; and it was strongly influenced by Mannheim's view that the libertarian chaos of Britain's

[57] Dalton, an atheist, had 'abandoned Christianity on the playing fields of Eton', Ben Pimlott, *Hugh Dalton* (1985), 35.

[58] Barnett, *op. cit.*, 15, 253.

past history had got to be replaced by a morally-integrated organic state, functionally adapted to the technological and organizational needs of modern industrial society.[59] This group set out a programme for the reform of the post-war education system, based on state take-over of the public schools, compulsory technical and vocational training for all 14–18 year olds, conscription of youth into organised youth movements, the replacement of classics by a national curriculum of science and technology, and the inculcation of public spirit through the teaching of Christian doctrine. Such a programme, it was argued, would equip Britain to meet the challenges of international competition and advanced modernity at the end of the war. With the sole exception of the emphasis on Christian doctrine, this programme was an almost exact replica of the kind of policies that Correlli Barnett appears to think *should* have been adopted by Britain's wartime planners. The programme was submitted to the Conservative Party's Central Council in September 1942 and rejected root and branch by the Conservative party faithful as an obnoxious form of 'Christian Fascism', 'stark totalitarianism', Bismarck-inspired 'new liberalism' and the 'importation of the Hitler Youth'. It would mean a 'brass-bound sausage machine' designed to 'turn out thousands upon thousands of loathesome young prigs' and would deprive the nation's youth of their freedom, leisure and pleasure.[60] It was the total defeat of this technological programme by the rank and file of the Conservative party that shifted R. A. Butler's educational thinking and planning towards the more bland compromise of the 1944 Education Act. This whole sequence of events within the wartime reconstruction movement is totally ignored by Barnett, and indeed like most abortive policy proposals has been largely ignored by historians in general. Yet it shows very clearly that cultural resistance to technological and organisational change had no necessary connection with support for Christianity, and that defence of traditional libertarian values was by no means confined to nonconformist chapels.

What if anything is to be learned from this discussion about the modern history of the welfare state and its impact on national culture and economic decline? Although I have been critical of many specific points of Correlli Barnett's thesis, I see the overall significance of his

[59] Conservative Party archives, CRD 600/02, Geoffrey Faber to Walter Oakeshott, 27 Aug. 1942; and CRD 600/05, 'The Ultimate Religious Field and the State', n.d.; CRD 058, 'Planning for Freedom: Some Remarks on the Necessity for Creating a Body which could Co-ordinate Theory and Practice in our Future Policy', by Karl Mannheim. On the curious vogue for Mannheim's ideas among certain sections of the Conservative intelligentsia in this period, see Colin Loader, *The Intellectual Development of Karl Mannheim, Culture, Politics and Planning* (Cambridge, 1985), 149–77.

[60] CRD, 600/05, press cuttings, 1942.

study as being far from wholly negative. He is surely correct in suggesting that historians should investigate the welfare state, not simply as a series of episodes in high politics but as a complex of institutions and values that interact with the lives of citizens at many levels, on a par with churches or property-ownership in earlier epochs. If, for good or ill, particular welfare policies do encourage particular types of economic, moral or civic behaviour, then historians should not be too squeamish to acknowledge and inquire into this fact (a view that the Victorians whom Barnett so much despises would have fervently endorsed). Where Barnett goes astray, however, is in implying that all welfare policies have an identical and undifferentiated character, and in his curiously insular assumption that the welfare state stops at the English Channel. These perspectives underscore the need for historians who write about social welfare to define their terms and categories much more clearly. When we talk about the welfare state, do we mean by it a Beveridge-based system of contractual social insurance? or do we mean the modern residue of a much older system rooted in economic status and citizen rights? or do we mean the whole complex of social and educational policies and institutions which in modern societies bear upon individual and collective socio-economic needs? Do we mean something peculiar to Britain, or do we see some form of welfare state system as well-nigh universal throughout the developed world? Although there is still a residual tendency among British writers to refer to the welfare state as quintessentially British, European and north American historians have long ago moved away from the view that the pure form of the welfare state, rather like constitutional monarchy, is to be found only in Britain. It is ironic, in view of Barnett's sustained admiration for all things German, to recall that the term 'welfare state' was originally coined, not by English social reformers, but by the old Prussian right in the dying embers of Weimar Germany who (in terms very resonant of *The Audit of War*) blamed their country's moral and economic ills on *der Wohlfahrstaat*, and sought to cure them by a mixture of retrenchment, deflation and authoritarian rule.[61]

In the British context popular parlance often equates the welfare state with the proposals of Beveridge. Yet a comparative perspective suggests that in many respects this is a mistake, and that the peculiarity of the English in the context of state welfare lies not in Beveridge but in the Poor Law; that it is the continuing institutional inheritance of an absolute statutory right to non-contributory public relief, rather than the national insurance system, that has most markedly distinguished Britain's welfare state from that of most other parts of

[61] Peter Flora and Arnold Heidenheimer, *op. cit.*, 19.

Western Europe.[62] Progressive historians, following faithfully in the footsteps of the Webbs, have been inclined to treat the residue of the Poor Law as a mere pathological anachronism in twentieth-century British social policy. I would like to suggest that this view needs reconsideration: that on the contrary the underlying continuity between the Poor Law and the British version of the welfare state is much more tenacious and much more functionally and ideologically complex than is often supposed. And conversely, if we are looking for a structural embodiment of Beveridgean principles, we may find at least some of those principles embodied in the schemes of continental reformers such as Pierre Laroque and Dr Erhard as strongly as in the welfare institutions of post-war Britain. The whole question of the similarities and differences—economic, fiscal, political and philosophical—between the welfare policies of different countries seems to need more detailed and discriminating exploration than it has so far received. And only when this has been done will wider claims about the impact of such policies upon enterprise, incentives and economic efficiency be either refuted or sustained.

Finally, I would like to suggest that the intellectual and ethical roots of mid-twentieth century social policies need more rigorous scrutiny from historians than they have so far received, in order to liberate the subject from naive assumptions about the goals and character of practitioners of 'social reform'. The archives of the Second World War and studies of wartime reconstruction thought make it abundantly clear that the welfare state was not the creature of any one particular group in British society, but something in which many diverse groups and ideological traditions had shaping hands; groups which included business men, accountants and enthusiasts for Prussian-style state corporatism, as well as the more obvious advocates of brotherly love, community, progressivism and democratic socialism.[63] Social policies may be about helping people but they are also about power, and there is a case for arguing that social welfare in the

[62] My point applies to the financing of social security rather than to its organisation. One respect in which the British system is indubitably 'Beveridgean' (or at least stems from the tradition of administrative reform of which Beveridge was an exemplar) is that it is nationally uniform, centralised and bureaucratic, whereas most continental systems allow much more scope for pluralism, localism and democratic self-government. An observor writing a century ago would surely have predicted the exact opposite. The role played by social policy in bringing about this kind of transformation of political culture in Britain and elsewhere deserves further analysis.

[63] See e.g. Harold L. Smith (ed.), *War and Social Change, British Society in the Second World War* (Manchester, 1986); H. Kopsch, 'The Approach of the Conservative Party to Social Policy during World War Two', London Ph.D. thesis, 1970; Kevin Jeffreys, 'British Politics and Social Policy during the Second World War, *H.J.*, XXX (1987), 123–44.

twentieth century has joined the traditional spheres of defence, public order and protection of property as one of the quintessential and definitive purposes of the state—as one of the 'ends' which potentially reconcile citizens to the fact of state dominion. If that is so, then historians must move beyond the kind of blanket perceptions of 'social welfare' that I noted in my introduction, as a guaranteed repository of either vice or virtue. As with foreign policy, the relevant question for historians to ask is not, did a particular state *have* social welfare policies? (one can be sure that it did in some form or another). Nor is it, is the existence of such policies a good or bad thing? (there is no sensible answer to that question). Instead, one should ask: what sort of policies were they, what was their specific rationale and purpose, how were they related to economic behaviour, political philosophy, culture and social structure? The answers to such questions will not be found in knee-jerk condemnation or exaltation of welfare states, but will vary according to content and context. Like the struggles over the emergence of the state itself in the sixteenth and seventeenth centuries, the welfare state should be analysed by historians, not as the marginal territory of a minority of high-minded do-gooders, but as part of the continuing contest over the structure, character and distribution of power and resources in the modern world.

DOCTORS, PUBLIC SERVICE AND PROFIT: GENERAL PRACTITIONERS AND THE NATIONAL HEALTH SERVICE

by Charles Webster

READ 23 SEPTEMBER 1989

GENERAL medical practitioners are a dominant element within the medical workforce. They are the largest specialism, currently accounting for about two-thirds of the senior medical personnel employed by the National Health Service (NHS).[1] They exert a strong political influence by virtue of their importance in the British Medical Association (BMA) and its complicated representative and negotiating machinery.

The assessment of primary health care in Britain admits two contrasting perspectives, each of which possesses a strong degree of legitimacy. On the positive side, the local doctor has consistently maintained esteem within the local community, while expert observers from abroad regard primary health care as one of the most conspicuous successes of the NHS. General practice has gradually emerged as the most favoured career option of medical graduates. Building on the deep-rooted tradition of the family doctor, the NHS from its outset encouraged the development of primary care teams headed by general practitioners. This system of primary health care has proved to be economical, humane and versatile. One of its most conspicuous merits is relief of pressure on expensive hospital services. Extensive development of the general medical service has thus contributed to Britain's overall low spending on health care. Ministerial addresses have therefore understandably tended to describe general medical practice as the 'key' or 'pivot' of the NHS.[2]

From a more critical angle, general practitioners emerge as a backward-looking and commercially-minded residuum of the medical pro-

[1] In 1939 there were about 18,000 general practitioners giving service under National Health Insurance, compared with 6,000 consultants and specialists, A. Bradford Hill, 'The Doctor's pay and day', *Journal of the Royal Statistical Society*, civ (1951), 1–34. The numbers had not changed appreciably in 1949. In 1988 there were about 26,000 general practitioners registered with the NHS, and 13,500 consultants employed by health authorities.

[2] *Address of I. Macleod to the Fifth Annual Conference of the Executive Councils Association*, October 1952, 2. *Address of R.H. Turton to the Ninth Annual Conference of the Executive Councils Association*, October 1956, 6.

fession, who have repeatedly used their monopolistic position and strength in industrial organisation to secure artificially advantageous conditions and living standards, heedless of the damage to the health service occasioned by their actions. Through the BMA they have held elected governments to ransom, and have unscrupulously exploited their power over patients and inferior members of the primary health care team. By virtue of its low expectations, the public has accepted with gratitude an inferior quality of service, delivered by practitioners of limited professional competence, whose deficiencies are disguised by the availability of hospital referral. The general practitioner has traditionally faced the accusation of lax certification and irresponsible prescribing, the latter being the more important, since it has contributed to the soaring cost of pharmaceutical services under the NHS.

General practitioners therefore present a paradox. On the one hand, among the higher professions they possess the best reputation for altruism. Thus in 1946 at the height of the controversy over the new health service, Sir Will Spens advocated a generous wage settlement for doctors because 'the medical profession was still the least commercially-minded amongst the professions generally'.[3] On the other hand, general practitioners have periodically engaged in acts of ruthless self-interest. Offering a different perspective on the events of 1946, doctors were censured for their lack of sensitivity to their social obligations: 'For any profession to claim that remuneration should be increased to the full extent of the increase in the cost of living would in effect be to claim that their share of the sacrifices involved by the war should be borne on other shoulders'.[4]

There is an accumulating literature on the BMA, especially on its part in the momentous negotiations leading up to the establishment of the NHS.[5] We now possess ample narrative, but still insufficient insight into the deeper motives underlying the superficial conflict. The present essay emphasises the economic preoccupations underlying the political activities of the BMA, with the aim of attaining a fuller understanding of the tensions which prevented the medical profession participating with confidence in the new health service created after

[3] Spens to Sir E. Fass, 15 February 1946, Public Record Office, MH 77/176.

[4] Note by official on meeting with Insurance Acts Committee, 13 November 1946, PRO, MH 77/177.

[5] H. Eckstein, *The English Health Service, its Origins, Structure and Achievements* (Cambridge, Mass., 1958); *idem*, *Pressure Group Politics, the Case of the British Medical Association* (1960); F. Honigsbaum, *The Division in British Medicine: A History of the Separation of General Practice from Hospital Care, 1911–1968* (1979); *idem*, *Health, Happiness, and Security, The Creation of the National Health Service* (1989); J. Pater, *The Making of the National Health Service* (1981); R. Stevens, *Medical Practice in Modern England. The Impact of Specialization and State Medicine* (New Haven, 1966); C. Webster, *Problems of Health Care: the National Health Service before 1957* (1988).

the Second World War. Of the more important writings on the early NHS, only Eckstein's influential *Pressure Group Politics* discusses the remuneration question in detail, and his account is open to criticism on points of detail and interpretation.

Three distinct impressions spring from any acquaintance with the voluminous records relating to medical practitioners and the early NHS. First, the practitioners were animated by a strong sense of grievance. Secondly, their anxieties were historically deep-seated. Thirdly, the concern related to remuneration more than to any other factor. In the course of negotiation few issues of substance were divorced from the issue of pay.

General practitioners were the leading politicians of the medical profession. They dominated the Representative Committee and its successor, the Negotiating Committee, which represented the profession in the NHS negotiations. These committees, as well as the Insurance Acts Committee representing practitioners involved in National Health Insurance, regarded the NHS negotiations as their supreme opportunity to right past wrongs. Retribution was demanded from the government for disappointments extending back at least to the introduction of National Health Insurance. The herd memory was long and retentive. On both the civil service and professional sides the negotiators were experienced. But the profession possessed the advantage in numbers and its leadership was by the War prepared for an uncompromising struggle. In 1946 the Labour government was exposed to the full blast of a campaign which had been gathering momentum since 1911.

Although National Health Insurance (NHI) was introduced in the face of BMA opposition, the great majority of general practitioners soon joined panel practice and NHI capitation became a useful basis for their income. There is a tendency to regard the income derived from health insurance medical practice as the key to the rising status and relative economic prosperity of general practitioners during the inter-war period. The growth of earnings from panel practice is thought to compensate for decline in earnings from private practice.[6] This interpretation has been undermined by the findings of Digby and Bosanquet.[7] They point out that general practitioners fared better than other comparable professions and enjoyed a substantial real improvement in income during the inter-war period. However, the

[6] R. M. Titmuss, *Essays on 'The Welfare State'* (2nd edn., 1963), 160: 'private practice was much less remunerative in the 1930s than most people were aware then or imagine today'.

[7] A. Digby and N. Bosanquet, 'Doctors and patients in an era of national health insurance and private practice, 1913–1938', *Ec.H.R.*, 2nd ser., xli (1988), 74–94.

rise in income is not attributable to receipts from panel practice. Between 1922 and 1938 there was an 8 per cent decline in NHI income, compared with a 79 per cent increase in 'private income'. These conclusions are slightly surprising considering the constriction of incomes experienced by many social groups, the growth of local authority clinics taking care of such categories as mothers, infants and children, or hospital savings schemes which in some areas competed with services of general practitioners. General practitioners faced these problems with resilience. They worked for 'clubs', established 'public medical services', and they obtained fees for services to collieries, industrial companies, or insurance firms. Especially important were the growing opportunities to provide services for public bodies.[8] For instance, a witness to the Spens Committee reported that he was a medical referee for the Ministry of Labour, police surgeon, public vaccinator, Post Office medical officer, Public Assistance medical officer, and medical officer for the Forestry Commission.[9] In some areas general practitioners assisted in the Maternity and Child Welfare Clinics of local authorities. The latter paid a variety of fees for special services performed by general practitioners under their expanding public health and welfare programmes.[10] Consequently, payments from public bodies must have constituted a significant element in the expanding 'private income' of general practitioners described by Digby and Bosanquet. Generosity of fees received for public service work reinforced the impression that NHI capitation was unrealistically low.

By 1939 doctors were accommodated to reliance on income from public sources, but they came no nearer to relinquishing their status as independent contractors. There was no diminution in their antipathy to the local Medical Officer of Health, whom they regarded as an inflated bureaucrat.

Although it became common to regard general practice as one of the select group of occupations offering prospects of £1,000 net salary to persons in their mid-thirties, the burgeoning of medical incomes should not be exaggerated.[11] The salary investigation upon which we rely stressed that averages are misleading owing to the wide scatter of medical incomes. While a substantial number of well-organised practices, employing assistants, were generating high profits, 42 per

[8] Political and Economic Planning, *Report on the British Health Services* (1937), 149–54.

[9] Dr G. L. Pierce, Abercynon, Glamorgan, 13 July 1945, PRO, MH 177/173.

[10] The fees included: 3 gn for obstetric service under the Midwives Acts 1902–36, 2 gn for examination and certification of persons of unsound mind or those judged mental defective, and £1 5s for examinations conducted for superannuation purposes.

[11] Sources for the £1,000 idea, see Digby and Bosanquet, 77, also T. Lister, Spens Committee, 11 January 1946, PRO, MH 77/173.

cent of net incomes fell below £1,000. In the 45–64 peak-earning age group 44 per cent of net incomes were below £1,000. For this age group in urban practices, 46 per cent fell below £1,000 net income.[12] An Inland Revenue sample from 1938 found that 55 per cent of urban practitioners fell below a £1,000 net income.[13] With respect to 1942 the Ministry of Health conceded an average net income for panel practitioners of £900.[14] General practitioners working in depressed regions faced genuine economic hardship and even the prospect of bankruptcy.[15] Such doctors might be driven to work long after the normal retirement age, while in exceptional cases their widows fell into dependency on charity. Whether poor or prosperous the general practitioner's NHI income was hard-earned. Routine in single-handed practice in an industrial area might well involve responsibility for 4,000 persons, half of them on the panel, the rest paying minimal fees, or none at all in cases of exceptional poverty. During winter days the surgery might be visited by 80 patients, and 50 domiciliary visits each week might be made. The doctor might well toil into the evening, take one half-day off in midweek and finish for the week at lunch-time on Sunday.

At the outbreak of the Second World War general practitioners were despondent about their future. Some financial gains had been made, but repeated attempts to extend the scope of NHI medical benefit, or to improve rates of remuneration for panel practice, had resulted in failure. The Dawson Report, the official blueprint for the development of the inter-war health services, which envisaged the establishment of a system of primary health centres staffed by general practitioners, met with a negative response in official circles. Expansion in the volume of health services occurred predominantly in the local authority sector. This provided attractive opportunities for secure and adequately remunerated salaried employment, reminding general practitioners of their vulnerability and strengthening resentment concerning their NHI remuneration. Local authority clinics attracted patients away from general practitioners. By 1936 these specialised clinics were sufficiently extensive for the Ministry of Health to regard them as the basis for a comprehensive national health service. Officials dismissed the panel system as an obsolete relic, unsuitable for further development. Adding to the indignity faced by general practitioners, Medical Officers of Health increasingly christened their

[12] Calculated from Spens Report (see n. 30 below), Table 4, p. 22, and Hill, Table 13, p. 22. Titmuss, *Essays*, 159, is sceptical about Hill's findings.

[13] PRO, MH 77/172.

[14] NHS 9, 1943, PRO, MH 77/26.

[15] Pierce to Spens Committee, PRO, MH 77/173.

new clinics and administrative buildings 'health centres'. The Dawson plan had thus been snatched from the general practitioners and appropriated by the local authorities.[16]

Although the medical profession, along with other professional groups, was drawn into preparations for post-war reconstruction, its appetite for participation in bold social experiments soon evaporated. The BMA studiously avoided the Beveridge Committee, and the Beveridge Report responded by pronouncing firmly against an insurance basis for the comprehensive health and rehabilitation service.[17] Plans for implementing the Beveridge proposals predictably opted for the local government model. It was assumed that general practitioners would revert from being independent contractors to become full-time salaried officers of local authorities, working collaboratively in health centres, in company with district nurses, health visitors, midwives and other local authority personnel. General practitioners would therefore fall within the empire of the feared and hated Medical Officer of Health.[18] Recognising the contentiousness of this prospect, Sir John Maude, Permanent Secretary to the Ministry of Health, predicted: 'I do not doubt that the opposition to a universal and compulsory system of salaries will be bitter and sustained'.[19] As the intentions of the government gradually became clear in the course of 1942 and 1943 the BMA responded by retreating into a defence of its traditional policies based on the correction and extension of the existing NHI scheme. It was especially important to establish definitively that NHI practice was under-rewarded. Otherwise there was a risk that the medical profession would suffer a quantum fall in its status in the extended public service planned for the future. With these problems in mind the medical profession became locked into a pay battle with the coalition government. Attention was fastened on past grievances and BMA negotiators were unwilling to countenance significant change in the pattern of health care in the future.[20] Among general practitioners there was little sign of the idealistic 'revision of ideas and rearrangement in values' which Richard Titmuss regarded as the basis for acceptance of 'great extensions and additions to the social services'.[21]

The tangled negotiations between the government and the medical

[16] Webster, 5–9.

[17] Webster, 34–9; J. Harris, *William Beveridge: A Biography* (Oxford, 1977), 378–418.

[18] Webster, 44–50; Honigsbaum, *Health, Happiness*, 33–51. J. Lewis, *What Price Community Medicine? The Philosophy, Practice and Politics of Public Health Since 1919* (Brighton, 1986).

[19] Maude, 23 June 1943, PRO, MH 80/26.

[20] Honigsbaum, *Health, Happiness*, 51–94.

[21] R. M. Titmuss, *Problems of Social Policy* (1950), 517; *idem*, *Essays*, 75–87.

profession, conducted almost without interruption between 1943 and 1948, revealed a chasm between the two sides.[22] Although the new health service was introduced as planned in 1948, the full confidence of the profession was not gained. After the briefest respite at the beginning of the Second World War, the profession resumed its thirty-year-old campaign over NHI capitation. Maude complained that the BMA and the *BMJ* were exercising a 'powerful influence' among general practitioners by 'stoking up the controversies of 1912'.[23] The Insurance Acts Committee had forgotten none of the prehistory. Indeed, the leading members of this committee possessed experience of BMA affairs reaching back almost to the introduction of National Health Insurance.[24] The BMA was still smarting about the Plender Report of 1911, in which Sir William Plender suggested a capitation of 4s 5d on the basis that general practitioners in selected industrial towns performed 1.7 services each year per patient.[25] Since that moment everything seemed to go against the profession. When the NHI scheme was introduced in 1913 the capitation fee of 7s 3d (or 9s including drugs) was not arrived at by precise evaluation or by negotiation. Against the advice of the BMA, general practitioners overwhelmingly agreed to participate. The BMA also failed at the next hurdle, when in 1920 an arbitration award granted a fee of 11s, against the doctors' claim of 13s 6d. Cuts in the capitation fee were accepted during the depression. Between 1922 and the Second World War the fee stood at around 9s. The BMA made a vigorous attempt at restitution to 12s 6d at a Court of Inquiry appointed in 1937, whereas the Ministry of Health argued that 9s was overgenerous. The recommendation of the Court that the fee should remain at 9s was taken badly by the BMA and relations with the Ministry were noticeably soured. The BMA complained to the Spens Committee that this decision was 'grossly unfair'.[26] A further Court of Inquiry investigation was postponed because of the wartime emergency. But the matter was not allowed to rest. The government's decision to include workers within the £250–£420 wage range in the insurance scheme led to further negotiation. A capitation increase from 9s to 9s 9d was accepted by the BMA under protest. An increase of 6d was granted owing to an increase in practice expenses, and 3d for the loss of private

[22] See sources cited in n. 5 above.

[23] Maude, 23 June 1943, PRO, MH 80/26.

[24] The chief veterans were: H. G. Dain (born 1870), E. A. Gregg (born 1881), and S. Wand (born 1899). They were advised from the sidelines by such figures as Alfred Cox (1866–1954), who was Medical Secretary of the BMA from 1912 to 1932.

[25] BMA, evidence to Spens Committee, 28 November 1945, PRO, MH 77/173. See also B. B. Gilbert, *The Evolution of National Insurance in Great Britain* (1966), 408–9.

[26] BMA, memorandum to Spens Committee, 1945, PRO, MH 77/172.

practice earnings due to the wider scope of the scheme. When in 1943 it became evident that the BMA was exploiting the remuneration argument to block discussion over the new health service, the government offered a war-time bonus, taking the capitation fee to 10s 6d.[27] The BMA accepted, but only on condition of 'the Minister's re-affirmation of the assurance that the whole question of the basic capitation fee will be re-opened after the war'.[28] This promise to allow the investigation of capitation 'from the ground up' was accepted by the BMA as the condition for cooperating in an independent assessment of salaries appropriate to doctors working in a public service. Even then, the BMA participated reluctantly and only after being satisfied that the membership of the committee and its terms of reference were thoroughly acceptable to the profession.[29] It was more than a year before the BMA finally agreed to the independent inquiry. The Committee chaired by Sir Will Spens, Master of Corpus Christi College, Cambridge, began work only in February 1945, and reported in April 1946. The Spens Report was published in May 1946.[30]

On this occasion the profession benefited from the atmosphere of appeasement prevalent during H. U. Willink's short term of office as Minister of Health. The Spens Committee was seen as a necessary means to restore the confidence of an increasingly embattled profession. The government seems to have given little regard to the consequences of this action. Key decisions affecting the future of general medical practice were in effect handed over to a weak committee having little capacity to withstand pressure from the BMA. Even on questions of remuneration dangerous precedents were likely to be set which would tie the hands of government in its dealing with general practitioners, and have repercussions, first among other medical personnel in the NHS, and then throughout the entire public sector. Therefore the Spens recommendations constituted a major hazard to a succession of post-war governments faced with a problem of inflation and escalating wages.

The Spens Committee was asked to recommend a range of pro-

[27] More detailed consideration of inter-war controversies surrounding the NHI capitation fee is contained in N. R. Eder, *National Health Insurance and the Medical Profession in Britain, 1913–39* (New York, 1982); Gilbert, *National Insurance*; *idem*, *British Social Policy, 1914–1939* (1970), 267–76.

[28] *British Medical Journal*, 1944, i, Supplement, 6–7.

[29] Maude to Charles Hill (the newly appointed Secretary of BMA), 17 May and 10 July 1944, PRO, MH 77/172.

[30] Ministry of Health and Department of Health for Scotland, *Report of the Inter-Departmental Committee on the Remuneration of General Practitioners*, Cmd. 6810 (1946), Spens Report.

fessional income suitable for a publicly-organised medical service, and it was allowed to consider this problem in the light of legitimate financial expectations in the past, and with regard to maintaining the future social and economic status of general medical practice, including its power to attract the right calibre of recruit. The Committee was overwhelmingly sympathetic towards general practitioners. Four of the eight members were general practitioners nominated by the BMA. Its work was dominated by the BMA and the evidence upon which the Committee relied was provided by a statistician retained by the BMA.

The statistical inquiry conducted by A. Bradford Hill was meticulous and impartial. It provided both the Committee and subsequent scholars with the most reliable data we possess on the work and pay of general practitioners between 1936 and 1938.[31] On long-standing questions of dispute between the Ministry and the profession Hill's findings pointed to the correctness of claims made by the BMA at the 1937 Court of Inquiry. Hill's findings on the question of services rendered to patients based on investigation into the year 1938–9 are indicated in Table 1.[32]

Table 1

Services Rendered per Insured Person *per annum*

	Surgery Attendances	Domiciliary Visits	Total Services Rendered
Court of Inquiry 1937			
Ministry of Health	2.90	0.76	3.66
British Medical Association	3.80	1.33	5.13
A. Bradford Hill			
Method (a)	3.69	1.12	4.81
Method (b)	4.13	1.26	5.39
Average of (a) and (b)	3.91	1.19	5.10

Hill's investigation into incomes for the years 1936–8 was the foundation stone of the BMA's evidence to the Spens Committee. These findings have already been mentioned. An important aspect of this exercise was determination of the practice expenses incurred by doctors. In 1937 the BMA had claimed 35 per cent practice expenses, while the Ministry of Health insisted on 25 per cent, a figure deriving from the BMA at the 1924 Court of Inquiry. The Ministry's view was

[31] BMA, memorandum to Spens Committee, 1945, PRO, MH 77/172.
[32] Hill, 1–18. This and other evidence is considered by Titmuss, *Essays*, 206–7.

accepted by the 1937 Court of Inquiry, but Hill discovered that the mean level for expenses was at that time 37.4 per cent.[33]

The Spens Committee concluded that medical practitioners had not been credited adequately under NHI for their expenses or increasing level of service. The Committee was divided over its response to the voluminous statistical and impressionistic evidence with which it was confronted. One member was inclined to adopt the BMA's recommendation of £2,000 as the average net income for full-time public service.[34] Another believed that the pre-war mean net income of £938 revealed in Hill's survey was adequate to sustain the profession.[35] Finally the Report recommended a scale which implied a modest rise in the average net income to £1,111, an increase of £173 above the pre-war estimate. The scales of pay included in the Spens Report were designed particularly to improve the position of less well-off doctors working largely in the public service. Also, as a concession to the BMA, the prospect of substantial rewards was offered to doctors at the top of their profession, on the assumption that few would reach this level.

It was expected that the Spens inquiry, by clearing up the controversy over remuneration, would guarantee a smooth reception for the new health service. In practice disagreements over implementation of the Spens Report made a troubled situation worse. It is generally stated that the Spens Report was publicly accepted by the Government. Indeed, Eckstein claims that the Spens recommendations were 'accepted with some enthusiasm on both sides'.[36] The Spens recommendations were indeed immediately welcomed by the profession, but the government was reticent and evasive. There seems to have been no public acceptance of the Report. Initially the profession was told that the Spens Report had no application beyond its date. Eventually on 22 July 1946 a more forthcoming statement was extracted from the Ministry of Health, which was the nearest the BMA came to obtaining an acceptance:

> The Minister desires to make his attitude to the Spens Report quite clear. He fully accepts the substance of the recommendations upon the general scope and range of remuneration which general practitioners should enjoy in a public service.[37]

[33] Hill, 24–6.

[34] BMA evidence to Spens Committee, 28 November 1945, PRO, MH 77/173.

[35] Meeting of Spens Committee, 11 January 1946, PRO, MH 77/173.

[36] Eckstein, *Pressure Group Politics*, 127.

[37] Douglas to Hill, 22 July 1946, PRO, MH 77/177. Sir James Douglas succeeded Maude as Permanent Secretary in the autumn of 1945.

However, the same letter insisted that implementation of the Spens recommendations with respect to current and future remuneration was a complex issue, which could only be settled by negotiation. Subsequent exchanges revealed that the two sides were far apart in their perception of the Spens recommendations.

In the eyes of the profession the Spens Report represented a belated but definitive vindication of its case. Spens set the record straight on NHI remuneration and it established a superior baseline for payment under the new health service, containing a guarantee against inflation by indexation. From the perspective of the government the Spens Report was a liability, a potential blank cheque for the medical profession, with dangerous implications for the NHS and the whole economy. The government was therefore committed to minimising adjustment of NHI capitation, and evolving the most economical formula for meeting its Spens obligations under the new health service, without conceding a case for future adjustments.

In fact the Spens recommendations constituted an equation incapable of solution. Introduction of payment largely by salary offered the best prospects for realisation of the Spens formula, and the Labour Government was committed to this approach. However, although the remit of the Spens Committee was confined to levels of remuneration, its report urged that 'capitation affords the method of differentiation which is acceptable to the majority of the profession' and it advocated a method of payment relating to responsibility rather than a scale relating to age.[38] Unfortunately, the capitation system of remuneration recommended by the Spens Committee and demanded by the profession was inherently unlikely to yield the income distribution recommended in the Spens Report. Therefore, by complying with the capitation principle recommended in the Spens Report, the government embarked on a course destined to place it at variance with the Spens distribution scheme. Income distribution was also affected by such variables as the limits set for NHS lists, mileage payments, or maternity fees, all of which created idiosyncrasies in income distribution.

Application of the Spens recommendations also required agreement over such issues as compensation for practice expenses, levels of additional sources of income, and on betterment of fees with respect to changing workload, professional relativities, or changes in the value of money. Most of these issues had been under discussion since 1911 and it was by 1946 clear that such problems defied equitable resolution. Consequently, as a result of the Spens Report, general medical

[38] Spens Report, para. 13.

practitioners became further tied into a system of remuneration guaranteed to generate tension and dissatisfaction.

The profession was determined not to be trapped into discussion of the new service until scores were settled on NHI remuneration. The BMA demanded a capitation of 15s for the interim period until the start of the NHS, but this was unacceptable to the Ministry on the grounds that insurance funds should not bear the whole of the remuneration increase for a profession deriving only 40 per cent of its income from NHI. In July 1946 the profession was formally offered a capitation of 12s 6d from 1 January 1946.[39] After further negotiation, in October 1946 the profession was offered and accepted a capitation of 15s 6d on the understanding that the 22 per cent 'betterment' on net income included was accepted for the estimation of salaries under the NHS.[40] The Ministry was adamant that this betterment factor was introduced to maintain parity with other professional incomes, not as compensation for a rise in the cost of living.

The Ministry's strictures were of little avail because the BMA promptly entered a claim for a capitation of 20s for service under the NHS, including a betterment factor of 55 per cent, most of which related to the rise in the cost of living.[41] By this stage the government was alerted to the inflationary implications of the pay awards to doctors. The increase received by most comparable professions since 1939 was about 10 per cent. Recognised as a special case, university and school teachers had received between 20 and 30 per cent. Doctors had already reached this level if the 12s 6d capitation fee had been adopted. On the basis of a 20s capitation fee their increase would amount to more than 100 per cent.

Breakdown in relations between the government and the medical profession slowed down negotiations over the capitation fee to be applied in the new health service. Behind the scenes the Treasury regarded 17s as the maximum legitimate offer. Bevan was accused of impatience and unwarrantable generosity in favouring a final and non-negotiable offer of 18s. Against his officials' advice Cripps supported Bevan.[42]

An 18s capitation fee was reached on the basis that in 1939 17,900 general practitioners participated in the scheme. To their calculated total gross income was added the £3 million recommended by Spens in compensation for underpayment. A betterment factor of 20 per

[39] Douglas to Hill, 22 July 1946, PRO, MH 77/177.

[40] PRO, MH 77/177.

[41] The BMA regarded a capitation fee of 20s as the basis for an average net salary of £2,000; evidence to Spens Committee, 28 November 1945, PRO, MH 77/173.

[42] Sir B. Gilbert to B. F. St. J. Trend, 28 November 1947, and note by Cripps, 29 November 1947, Treasury, SS 5/150/01A.

cent net was applied primarily to account for comparabilities with other professions. Practice expenses were assessed at 55 per cent above the pre-war level. Three per cent was added for growth in population. Finally, five per cent of the total was deducted because it was expected that only 95 per cent of the population would avail themselves of the new service. The total sum remaining constituted a Central Pool, which was divided among practitioners contracted with Executive Councils, after the removal as a prior claim on the Pool of certain agreed fees which were paid separately.[43]

The 18s capitation was accepted by the profession, but only late in May 1948, a few weeks before the inception of the NHS, and then provisionally and without enthusiasm. Eckstein is therefore again in error in concluding that 'the Spens details were negotiated and agreed upon through the usual channels, with apparent satisfaction to both sides'.[44]

In practice the BMA never accepted the government's calculation of the Central Pool. Of the variables affecting the size of the Pool the negotiators continued to argue for higher allowances for practice expenses, a substantial improvement in the betterment factor, and an estimate of the population at risk above the 95 per cent adopted.[45]

Although the launch of the NHS on 5 July 1948 was accompanied by ritual expressions of goodwill on all sides, signs of strained relations with the general practitioners resurfaced, and the familiar acrimonious negotiations were soon resumed. On this occasion the BMA leadership became enmeshed in problems of its own making. Having imposed a minor variant of the panel system of remuneration the BMA negotiators should not have been surprised when it emerged that the NHS replicated the shortcomings of the old system, especially by generating low earnings for doctors who had traditionally fared badly. The victims were practitioners working in remote rural areas, or in situations of social deprivation, or young doctors attempting to gain a foothold in the profession, and especially women. The sense of grievance among the underpaid was exacerbated by evidence of the comfortable circumstances of large-list doctors in established practices, precisely the group which dominated the BMA. The BMA leadership was blamed for protecting this inequality, while its policies of opposing the basic salary, health centres, or restrictions on the availability of fixed annual payments, had evidently increased the disadvantages of the low paid. The BMA negotiators had therefore unwittingly

[43] For further detail, see Ministry of Health, *Handbook for General Medical Practitioners* (1955), 36–53.

[44] Eckstein, *Pressure Group Politics*, 127.

[45] Department of Health (DH), 94256/5/2, 94256/6/75.

thwarted the efforts of the Spens Committee to raise living standards of the less-well-paid doctors active in public service.

Immediately the deficiencies of the new distribution system became evident, the BMA leadership came under siege from the underprivileged classes of its membership. Having mounted an intransigent defence of the capitation system it was scarcely open to the leadership to reverse the policy. Also capitation was sanctioned by the Spens Committee, while deviation from this principle was politically unacceptable because capitation served the interests of the politically dominant element in the BMA.

The BMA negotiators decided that the best means to assuage the poor without offending the rich was to press for a general increase in remuneration based on the argument that the profession had never acceded to the government's formula for estimating the Central Pool. The BMA insisted that the Spens 'settlement' was imposed rather than agreed. From the vantage point of 1951 the BMA urged that the

> aggregate amount which has in fact been provided for each year up to now in respect of the total remuneration of the general practitioners in the service has been fixed by the Ministers themselves, and in the face of protests by the practitioners that such aggregate sum was inadequate and did not properly give effect to the Spens basis.[46]

Driven on by mounting indignation among the rank and file, early in 1949 the BMA embarked on a campaign for a reformulation of the Central Pool. The question was resolved only in March 1952 with the Danckwerts Award.[47] The contest was marked by the features characteristic of earlier and later exchanges between the BMA and the government: complicated manoeuvring between the various committees and representative meetings which gave vent to the democratic voice of the BMA; a cumbersome negotiation process involving periodic breakdowns in communication; frequent misunderstandings, provoking mutual recrimination and accusations that the government was acting in bad faith, and leading ultimately to the threat of resignation from the NHS.

The government seriously misjudged the situation. In particular it underestimated the strength of the opposition. Old hands at the Ministry of Health complacently believed that they could continue to

[46] General Medical Services Committee, Statement of Case, Danckwerts Adjudication, 1952, Treasury, SS5/150/OIC.

[47] Eckstein, *Pressure Group Politics*, 126–50, an excellent condensation, but faulty on many points of detail, including dates.

trounce the BMA as readily as during the depression. The formula adopted for implementing the Spens recommendations was regarded by officials as an overgenerous deal, adequate to satisfy the aspirations of general practitioners for the foreseeable future. At first the Ministry was dismissive towards the doctors' supplications. Next it offered unrealistic concessions. Finally, the Ministry allowed itself to be manoeuvred into arbitration, thus allowing the profession to use its superior forces to the same effect as in the Spens inquiry. The resultant Danckwerts adjudication represented the worst humiliation for the government ever experienced in negotiations with the medical profession. Originally the BMA entered a demand for £15m, but as late as May 1951 the doctors might have settled for as little as £6m. During Bevan's tenure as Minister the Treasury resisted any concession to the doctors, but in a gesture of support for Marquand, Gaitskell, who took a personal interest in the negotiations, allowed £2m additional for the Central Pool. This was offered to the negotiators, but on condition that the doctors participated in a campaign of economy in prescribing.[48] Unsurprisingly this self-financing formula was rejected with indignation by the doctors, who were further alienated by the establishment in February 1951 of a committee to investigate general practice. Although this committee under Sir Henry Cohen was formally an initiative of the independent Central Health Services Council, the timing and frame of reference led the BMA to suspect sinister intentions. The files give some justification for the fears of the BMA. The committee was in fact set up at the initiative of the Minister and it was expected to generate findings helpful to the Ministry's approach to the remuneration issue.[49] However, Cohen's Committee proved to be a blunt instrument. Like most other CHSC ventures the inquiry dragged on inconsequentially, while the Cohen report produced in 1954 offered little tangible support for the government line.[50]

By the summer of 1951 the government's campaign of delay and obstruction had run out of steam. In July 1951, the Special Conference of Local Medical Committees demanded arbitration, and this was conceded by Marquand in August 1951. In 1946 the Labour Minister had picked up the bill for his Conservative predecessor. In 1952 Churchill's Conservative administration faced the consequences of Labour's collapse in resistance. The Danckwerts adjudication was a

[48] Meeting between GMSC representatives and Ministers, lasting 6 hours, 9 May 1951, Treasury SS5/150/O1B.

[49] DH, 94157/1/1.

[50] *Report of the Committee on General Practice within the National Health Service* (1954), Cohen Report.

contrast with Spens in method, but the outcome was similar. After a hearing lasting only a few days, Mr Justice Harold Danckwerts expressed his decision in the briefest terms. The BMA influenced the single adjudicator just as effectively as it had dominated the Spens Committee. The Danckwerts adjudication announced on 24 March 1952 contained recommendations which amounted to an award of nearly £40m.[51] The adjudication almost totally conceded the doctors' case. On the crucial issue of the betterment factor, left for later settlement by the Spens Committee, Danckwerts granted 100 per cent above 1939 incomes, with 85 per cent applying to 1948. This almost totally indemnified the profession for the rise in the cost of living. Furthermore, Danckwerts ominously stated that 'this determination may be applied to other years', which was taken by the profession as a commitment for the future, and was difficult to interpret in any other way. On subsidiary questions Danckwerts also accepted the profession's argument. On practice expenses the Ministry refused to concede more than 36.5 per cent, whereas the BMA originally insisted on 37.5 per cent. This was raised to 38.7 per cent in the evidence to Danckwerts and this latter figure was accepted in the award.

Danckwerts also refuted the Ministry's contention that the Central Pool should be adjusted according to the population at risk rather than the number of doctors in the scheme. The formula adopted for implementing Spens had already added 3 per cent for the rise in population. Danckwerts insisted that the Central Pool should also be adjusted to allow for a 7.4 per cent rise in principals participating (17,900 in 1939; 19,227 in March 1951). The Spens recommended average net salary of £1,111 in 1939 terms, was translated into £2,222 with effect from 1 April 1951, and £1,849 for 1948. The BMA was therefore not far short of its target for an average net salary of £2,000 for the new health service.

The only consolation for the government from the dismal experience of the Danckwerts adjudication emerged from the recommendations of the working party which advised on the distribution of the enhanced Central Pool.[52] The most important proposal of the working party was the introduction of an extra 10s 'loading' for every patient between 501 and 1,500 on a doctor's list, which was added to the new capitation fee fixed at 17s. Maximum permitted lists were adjusted downwards, minor incentives being given to doctors in partnership. The maximum list for single-handed practitioners was reduced from 4,000 to 3,500.

[51] The essential sections of the Danckwerts adjudication are given in J. S. Ross, *The National Health Service in Great Britain* (1952), 387 and *Report of the Ministry of Health 1952* (1953), 37–8.

[52] *Distribution of Remuneration among General Practitioners* (1952).

As a minor expedient to ease the position of practitioners in underdeveloped areas a new 'initial practice allowance' was introduced to replace the 'fixed annual payment', which had been stigmatised as a relic of the basic salary and had been effectively blocked by the opposition of Local Medical Committees. Finally, it was agreed to set aside £100,000 annually from the Central Pool to provide loans for improvement of practice premises. This fund was limited to group practices.

The distribution working party represented an amicable interlude in a tense drama. Having gained handsomely from the Danckwerts award and obtained positive benefits for the less favoured practitioners the BMA was able to sanction reduction in the premium on large lists and accept minor inducements towards group practice.

The working party exercise demonstrates how the system of remuneration could be employed as a minor instrument of social engineering in the general medical service. But this method was indirect in its operation and it was incapable of generating anything like the degree of change required for the maximisation of the potential of primary health care under the new health service. The new rules for maximum lists constituted reversion to the limits current under the panel system. In the 1950s progressive opinion favoured adoption of a 2,000 maximum. Availability of loans for improvement of practice premises was offset by inducements in the system to reduce practice expenses to a minimum. Minor advantages given to group practice were no substitute for the health centre programme, which was designed as a key feature of the new service, but was scrapped even before the NHS commenced. The general medical service lacked leadership and its Executive Councils (replacements for the former Insurance Committees) were not effective planning agencies. As a professional group general practitioners sank to the level of a subspecialism. Ideas about the development of multidisciplinary primary care teams and integration between the branches of the NHS remained the preserve of ministerial speeches and of a literature which was unknown to the majority of practitioners. Pious ministerial rhetoric fails to disguise the neglect of general medical practice. The Executive Council services in general became a neglected backwater of the NHS. Learning from painful experience Ministers developed an aversion to dealing with them. There was always the risk that any initiative for change would become translated into a claim for higher remuneration.

Improvement was accordingly sacrificed for the sake of economy. Even with the changes introduced in the wake of the Danckwerts award, general medical service under the NHS retained the characteristics of the old panel system. Essentially the spirit of panel practice extended over the whole population. The long years of negotiation had removed fears of salaried employment and the threat of assimilation into the empire of the Medical Officer of Health. Above all general practitioners retained their congenial system of remuneration by capitation, but at an enhanced level and without the injustices contained under the flat rate method. General practitioners had therefore not sacrificed their traditional freedoms in the transition to the NHS, but the price for the retention of the capitation system was ossification of the less desirable features of insurance medical practice.

The NHS failed to improve the general medical service available to the bulk of the population. The middle classes benefited to some extent, but the lower classes continued to experience a humiliating standard of care.[53] The middle classes were liberated from doctors' fees and they enjoyed the services of the better practitioners, while the lower classes, especially after the imposition of the prescription charge in 1952, continued to receive an inferior service, but for a higher level of payment through taxes and direct charges. The shortcomings of primary care were only slowly corrected and they were not widely publicised. Nevertheless, adverse evidence accumulated, and strikingly effective critiques were produced by two observers from abroad in 1950 and 1953. Their descriptions of general practice in industrial areas showed that the NHS had not brought about essential improvements. In 'Factory Town' the eight doctors averaged 3,500 patients per practitioner. During the winter the average surgery attendance was 64 each day. At this time of the year the doctor made home visits to an average of 20 patients each day. The doctors were not quite as hard-worked as their insurance predecessors, but they nevertheless worked long hours and felt under pressure, which was thought to account for their unpleasantness to patients.[54]

In a more wide-ranging survey Collings blamed the capitation system for giving incentives to practitioners in under-doctored areas to build up inflated lists. These doctors he called 'mercenaries'. Doctors in such places were providing 'at the best a very unsatisfactory medicine service and at the worst a positive source of public danger'. He concluded that 'the over-all state of general practice is bad and still deteriorating'. Collings believed that Abraham Flexner's characterisation of medical practice in the slums before 1900 was 'almost a perfect word-picture of general practice as I found it in the industrial areas of England in 1949'.[55] The critics may have erred on the side of

[53] Titmuss, *Essays*, 208–9.

[54] R. Ross, 'The Family Doctor in Factory Town', CHSC (GP)(53)E87, DH 94157/4/4.

[55] J. S. Collings, 'General Practice in England Today, A Reconnaissance', *The Lancet*, 1950, i, 555–85, 558, 568.

pessimism, but even a cautious observer concluded that 'there seems to be little disagreement that general practice is not as good as it should or could be'.[56]

It is therefore open to doubt whether the more costly general medical service introduced under the NHS brought about a proportionate improvement in standards of care. In 1938 the fees paid to NHI practitioners amounted to £8.4m and to chemists £2.4m. The 1944 White Paper estimated the cost of a complete general medical and pharmaceutical service as £30m. The fees paid to doctors and pharmacists in 1945 amounted to £13.6m. The rate of spending during the last six months of the insurance medical service was £24m per annum. Expenditure on the general medical service of the NHS was about £48m during each of the first three full years of operation of the service, and this escalated to £85m in 1952–3. Between 1949 and 1953 the cost of the pharmaceutical service rose from £35m to £53m. Consequently a front line medical service projected to cost £30m turned out in 1952–3 to cost £138m.[57] This trend in costs was greeted with dismay in government circles, and prevention of further steep rises in spending on the general practitioner and pharmaceutical services assumed a high priority throughout the 1950s. Initially it was hoped that the secular increase in costs resulting from the Danckwerts award would break the impasse over remuneration and usher in a new age of progress. The Ministry of Health Report for 1952 opened with the proclamation that 'the year 1952 undoubtedly constituted a significant milestone in the progress of general practice within the framework of the National Health Service'.[58] Such prognostications proved to be wildly optimistic. Modernisation within general practice proceeded at snail's pace, while soon the profession became caught up in a further frenzy over remuneration. In 1956 the BMA entered a pay claim of 24 per cent. On this occasion the government devised a Royal Commission to break out of the deadlock. The result was an award of 15 per cent, with the grant of a Standing Review Body, to report annually on professional remuneration. Commitment to annual reassessment represented a further significant milestone in the campaigns of the BMA. This system broke down in 1965 and preparations were made yet again for mass resignation from the NHS. The deadlock was broken by yet a different device, the introduction of a new formula for the remuneration of doctors based on the 'Family Doctor's Charter'

[56] O. L. Peterson, *A Study of the National Health Service of Great Britain*, Typescript, Rockefeller Foundation, New York, November 1951, 54.

[57] *A National Health Service*, Cmd. 6502 (1944), 83–4; *Royal Commission on the National Health Service Report*, Cmnd. 7615 (1979), Table E9.

[58] *Report of the Ministry of Health, 1952*, 37.

devised by the BMA. This gave a new lease of life to the Standing Review Body, but the accord dissolved in 1970, when the Wilson government refused to accept the recommended award. Once again the profession rose up in indignation and mass resignation was threatened. By this stage a pattern of periodic confrontations was established which it seemed would never be broken. Throughout the 1970s and early 1980s the problem of remuneration was rarely out of the headlines. The annual contests over pay absorbed all the energy and acted as a surrogate for planning in the field of primary care. The first concern of the profession remained the level of remuneration, but also from 1966 onwards there was a steady shift away from capitation, which by 1985 accounted for only one-third of an average practitioner's income, while an equivalent of basic salary accounted for a further one-third. Consequently the profession gradually sacrificed the principles upon which it had fought with such determination before 1948. Attrition of capitation and introduction of the equivalent of a basic salary led the profession after decades of negotiation to accept a system of remuneration similar to that proposed by the government in 1946.

The process of evolving a stable contractual arrangement for general medical practice under the NHS has been slow and arduous. It took nearly twenty years before the profession could escape from preoccupations associated with panel practice. Even in the more constructive atmosphere existing after 1966 the new equilibrium was delicate and complex, and its disturbance constitutes a perilous operation for any government unwilling to learn lessons from the history of past negotiations. Any administration insensitive to the role of this past history in determining the collective mentality of general practitioners will discover it has stepped into a dangerous minefield from which there might be no escape.

TWO ABBOTS IN POLITICS: WALA OF CORBIE AND BERNARD OF CLAIRVAUX

By Henry Mayr-Harting

READ 13 OCTOBER 1989

ABBOTS in politics were surely a medieval commonplace, one might be tempted to say: what have these two egregious examples, Wala of Corbie (826–34, ob. 836) and Bernard of Clairvaux (1115–53), to say to us which countless others could not also say? If my two were not unique, however, they were comparative rarities, in that they became involved in politics (if that is the right word), not because of their feudal obligations, nor because they sought to propagate monastic reform on the basis of the observance of their own monastery, nor again because they associated the glory of their own house with a particular cause or royal line,[1] but avowedly for the sake of moral principle, incurring enmities in the process, and, cloistered monks as they were, acting to some extent against the interests and wishes of their own flocks. The monk-bishop was a common enough figure, and the greatest men of this type, pre-eminently Augustine of Hippo and Pope Gregory the Great, have given us profound thoughts about how contemplation could and should be kept alive amidst the cares of the active and pastoral life.[2] But neither Wala nor Bernard became a bishop, and paradoxically the latter's widespread and non-institutionalised influence might have been diminished had he done so. As one of Bernard's biographers felicitously but ingenuously put it in recounting that the saint had actually refused many bishoprics, 'from under the bushel of his humility he gave a greater light to the church than others raised to the chandeliers'.[3] Some will remember Beryl

[1] E.g. for Odilo of Cluny and the propagation of Cluniac observance, see J. Hourlier, *Saint Odilon Abbé de Cluny* (Louvain, 1964), esp. 61–72; for Suger of St Denis and the glory of his own house in relation to the Capetians, see E. Panofsky, *Abbot Suger on the Abbey Church of St Denis* (Princeton, 1946), esp. 2–3, 31–37. Wibald of Stavelot and Corvey might have some likeness to Wala and Bernard; see Colin Morris, *The Papal Monarchy: The Western Church from 1050 to 1250* (Oxford, 1989), 187, 189, 230; but neither did he brave hostility and opposition in the way they did, nor were Stavelot and Corvey left unrequited for his efforts, DDFI, no. 44 (1153) for Stavelot, and nos. 21 (1152), 155 (1156–57) for Corey.

[2] Cuthbert Butler, *Western Mysticism* (1922), esp. part II.

[3] Et lucens amplius illustraret ecclesiam velut de sub modio humilitatis suae, quam ceteri super candelabra constituti: Geoffrey of Auxerre, *Vita Prima*, iii, 8, PL 185, col. 307D. *Vita Prima* = Vita Prima S. Bernardi, consisting of works by William of

Smalley's characteristic observation that had Bernard unwisely accepted a bishopric he would have had a diocese, and his diocese would have had boundaries.[4] That consummate ecclesiastical politician of our own times, Cardinal Heenan, grasped this point well enough in his dealing with Christopher Butler. As Abbot of Downside, Butler had emerged to be the most powerful force amongst the English prelates at the Second Vatican Council; whereupon Heenan, perhaps thinking of Manning's mistake in leaving the charismatic Newman at large, appointed him Auxiliary Bishop of Westminster with special responsibility for Hertfordshire. After that Butler was scarcely heard of again—outside Hertfordshire. Wala, a Carolingian by birth and a cousin of Charlemagne, was in every sense a great man of his age; Bernard, a minor Burgundian nobleman, dominated his. We should not try to set up too close a comparison, too strained a conversation, between these men so widely separated in time. When set against their respective cultural surroundings, however, and lightly compared with each other, they can perhaps tell us something about the difference between what historians call the Carolingian Renaissance and the Renaissance of the Twelfth Century.

Wala, whose father was Count Bernard the brother of Pepin III and whose mother was a Saxon, had been a high administrator under Charlemagne, became a monk of Corbic in 814 when Louis the Pious cleared his father's counsellors out of the court, was reinstated in Louis's favour in 821, and soon went as Lothar I's chief adviser and intermediary with the pope to Italy, becoming abbot of Corbie in 826 in succession to his half-brother Adalard not long after his return.[5] He was vocal in his opposition to what he saw as the hijacking of

St Thierry, Arnold of Bonneval and Geoffrey of Auxerre, edited as a collection in the 1160s by Geoffrey to support St Bernard's canonization (1174), as well as for pastoral edification. It has not, therefore, got the kind of specific purpose which the *Epitaphium Arsenii* has, see A. H. Bredero, *Études sur la 'Vita Prima' de Saint Bernard* (Rome, 1960), 2–4, 147–61. And of course the writings of St Bernard, his own self-explanation, are much more important for our purposes than hagiographical writing, a genre on which we depend almost entirely in the case of Wala.

[4] At an Oxford seminar on St Bernard in the Hilary Term of 1957; for the general run of those Cistercians who *did* become bishops, however, the illuminating discussion about Carthusians and bishoprics in Henrietta Leyser, 'Hugh the Carthusian', *Saint Hugh of Lincoln*, ed. Henry Mayr Harting (Oxford, 1987), at 13–17, has doubtless no little applicability. See also, from another interesting point of view on the same theme, H. E. J. Cowdrey, 'Hugh of Avalon, Carthusian and Bishop', *De Cella in Saeculum*, ed. D. S. Brewer (1988).

[5] Dümmler = *Radbert's Epitaphium Arsenii*, ed. E. Dümmler, *Abhandlungen der königlichen Akademie der Wissenschaften zu Berlin*, Phil-Hist Kl. 2 (1900), 1–98, 13, 16; Lorenz Weinrich, *Wala: Graf, Mönch und Rebell: Die Biographie eines Karolingers* (Lübeck & Hamburg, 1963), pp. 18–58. The translation of the *Epitaphium* by A. Cabaniss, *Charlemagne's Cousins: Contemporary Lives of Adalhard and Wala* (1967), should be used with caution.

Louis's government and the exercise of patronage by the unholy alliance of the Empress Judith and Bernard of Septimania, with its disastrous consequences for the unity of the empire and thus for the well-being of the church. He was a persistent opponent of anything which looked like the partition of the empire amongst Louis's sons; he adhered through thick and thin to the *Ordinatio Imperii* of 817 which had bestowed with solemn oaths the succession to a unified empire on Lothar, Louis's eldest son;[6] and he joind both Lothar's rebellions of 830 and 833, on each occasion to his cost and subsequent exile. Our principle knowledge of him comes from his *Life*, the *Epitaphium Arsenii*, written by Pascasius Radbertus, Wala's learned successor as abbot of Corbie. In a culture which loved nicknames, Arsenius, the name of a saint who had been the Emperor Theodosius's court steward before embracing a life of solitude, was the nickname of Wala.[7] We do not depend only on Pascasius's hero-worship, however, to mark the genuine prominence of Wala in the rearguard action of 828–34 against the break-up of Charlemagne's empire; other sources attest it too.[8]

Dümmler, who edited the *Epitaphium* with fine learning in 1900, declared that it was difficult to measure so subjective a writer as Pascasius against the yardstick of historical trustworthiness;[9] but that did not stop him from trying. Treated as a quarry of information, however, it is a rhetorical work, lacking in every factual precision, and altogether exasperating. So perhaps one should take the line of least resistance and ask rather why and for whom it was written. And why an *Epitaphium*, a funeral oration, in form? The *Epitaphium* was a well known form in the early Middle Ages and served the purpose of rhetorical protestation and championship of the subject.[10] It is not chronicle, annals or hagiography in the ordinary sense of unfolding a life. Here we must distinguish between the two books of the *Epitaphium Arsenii*, the first composed soon after Wala's death, around 838, and the second only some fifteen years later, after Pascasius had ceased to be abbot of Corbie, i.e. not before 852.[11] The two books are in various ways woven into a connected work, for instance by sharing the

[6] See F. Ganshof, 'Some observations on the Ordinatio Imperii of 817', in his *The Carolingians and the Frankish Monarchy*, trans. Janet Sondheimer (1971), 273–88, esp. pp. 278–80.

[7] Dümmler, 5–7.

[8] E.g. Agobard of Lyon as cited by Dümmler, 10, note 1.

[9] Dümmler, 9.

[10] L. Bornscheuer, *Miseriae Regum* (Berlin, 1968), 41–59; F. Lotter, 'Zur literarischen Form und Intention der Vita Heinrici IV', *Festschrift H. Beumann*, ed. K. U. Jäschke & R. Wenskus (Sigmaringen, 1977), 293–303; Patrick Corbet, *Les Saints Ottoniens* (Sigmaringen, 1986), p. 83.

[11] Dümmler, 11.

character of a funeral lament, but the purpose of each stares one in the face, and it is not identical with the other.

The first book sets out its purpose clearly from the start. Wala had the *officium* of a Jeremiah but the *persona* of St Benedict.[12] The tears and lamentations about the state of the empire have made their impression on historians alright, but the depth to which Wala's image is presented according to the Rule of St Benedict (RB) has not been so firmly appreciated, although Weinrich in his monograph on Wala of course recognised that Wala based his abbatial rule on RB, as the *Epitaphium* is explicit to say.[13] Let me mention some of the more obvious Benedictine strokes in Pascasius's picture.

The *Epitaphium* is cast in the form of a conversation between Pascasius and various Corbie monks, one of whom at least is otherwise identifiable. This could have had either classical or Christian models.[14] In Chapter I, Adeodatus asks how Wala could have been 'a man of strife and discord', like Jeremiah, if he was loved by all as Pascasius said. Pascasius's reply is that he sought to form friendships with noblemen and others, rather than to be a Jeremiah deploring their sins and troubles (*plus ... amicitias studebat, quam, secundum Hieremiam, peccata ... deplorare*).[15] This surely is a reminiscence of RB64 on the abbot, that he should strive to be loved rather than feared (*studeat plus amari quam timeri*)?[16]

Chapter 9 refers to Wala as a novice at Corbie. The present abbot and monks are witness, says Pascasius with solemnity, that as a novice

[12] Dümmler, 20 (Epitaph. Ars. i, intro.).

[13] Weinrich, 53, 59; cf. Dümmler, 50 (Epitaph., i, 21).

[14] See M. Manitius, *Geschichte der lateinischen Literatur des Mittelalters*, i (Munich, 1911), 405–6.

[15] Dümmler, 22 (Epitaph. i, 1). One may note the somewhat different line of Hildemar of Corbie (after 833) in his commentary on RB at this point. He stresses the abbot's need to correct his monks prudently and with charity, Mittermüller = *Expositio Regulae ab Hildemaro Tradita*, ed. R. Mittermüller (Regensburg, New York and Cincinnati, 1880), 594. David Ganz wisely urged on me the desirability of studying this work. It shows how independent and distinctive was Pascasius in his approach to RB. Not only does Hildemar (and Warnefrid before him) generally take a different line or emphasis in commenting on the spiritual meaning of RB, but he also is much more concerned with its practical implications for ordinary monks than Pascasius is in the *Epitaphium* (not unnaturally), e.g. note 27 below. The commentaries, therefore, are much closer to the world of Benedict of Aniane's *consuetudines*, and to Adalhard of Corbie's statutes, see A. E. Verhulst & J. Semmler, 'Les Statuts d'Adalhard de Corbie de l'an 822', *Le Môyen Age*, lxviii (1962), esp. 253–9, than they are to the *Epitaphium*, which creates its image of Wala out of RB's idealism. For the Aniane legislation, see below, note 49.

[16] The standard edition of and commentary on the Rule of St Benedict is A. de Vogüé (ed), *La Règle de Saint Benoit* (Cerf, Sources Chretiennes, 181–6, 1971–72. For Latin text and good English translation, see Justin McCann (ed.), *The Rule of Saint Benedict* (1952).

Wala was tested as gold in the furnace, quoting RB1 (or rather quoting the Book of Wisdom with RB) on the detestable kind of monks called Sarabaites who had not been so tested and were as soft and yielding as lead. Pascasius continues that this was amidst harsh and sharp rebukes (*inter omnia increpationum dura et aspera*), thus quoting the famous phrase *dura et aspera* from RB58, where it says that a newly admitted monk must be told all the hardships and trials through which we travel to God.[17]

In the following chapter one comes to the one citation of RB noted by Dümmler in this book. Wala is said to have rejoiced to be subject rather than ruler (*magisque subesse gaudens, quam praeesse*: *prodesse tam sub iugo magistri, quam prelatus postea curavit*), alluding to RB64 on the abbot again: 'Let him know that it is his duty rather to profit his brethren than to preside over them' (*prodesse magis quam praeesse*). Pascasius adds pessimistically that few were like this in his day, otherwise there would not have been such a penury of perfect prelates. In the same chapter we have a rather high-blown account of Wala as guest-master, his washing the wounds of the poor and their fetid clothes as if they were aromatic, exemplifying RB53 on the reception of guests, that poor men should be shown especial attention 'because in them Christ is more truly welcomed'.[18]

The relation of the two brothers, Adalard and Wala, is touched upon in chapter 16: each pre-eminent in worldly dignity (*seculi dignitatem eximius*), they nonetheless vied with each other in humility. Here the echo is of RB2, that the abbot must not prefer one person to another on grounds of social background, for 'we are only distinguished in his sight if we are found better than others in good works and humility'. Then Pascasius launches into pure RB55 on Wala's clothes. He was content with the ordinary clothes and shoes of the region, and so had a sort of shoes known as *ruhilingos* made for himself (thus giving us an otherwise unknown Germanic word for shoes); he considered it unworthy that a monk should dress more smartly than the *conprovintiales* amongst whom he lived.[19] Monks, says RB55, must

[17] Dümmler, 35. Hildemar (Mittermüller, 536) comments mainly on the duties of the novice-master when dealing with RB 58.

[18] Dümmler, 37.

[19] Dümmler, 46. The principal point of Warnefrid (and Hildemar), also derived from RB, in connection with clothes was that they should be neither too cheap nor too expensive, and this was taken over in the legislation of Benedict of Aniane, see A. M. Schroll, *Benedictine Monasticism as reflected in the Warnefrid-Hildemar Commentaries on the Rule* (Columbia, NY, 1941), 46, and the Capitulary of 816, in *Corpus Consuetud. Monast.* (as in note 49 below), 436. There is nothing in Hildemar on the contest of humility (Mittermüller, 99–107).

be content with such clothes as can be found in the *provincia* in which they live.

There is in chapter 23 one of several passages corresponding closely to RB27 on the abbot's solicitude towards excommunicates and delinquents: 'for the abbot is bound to use the greatest solicitude, and to exercise all sagacity and diligence (*industria*) lest he lose any of the sheep entrusted to him'. With all *industria* and *sagacitate*, says Pascasius, Wala cared for each lest he should lose anyone through the devil's cunning, and then he goes on to describe in terms very similar to RB2 his varied methods of dealing with his monks: threats, rewards, persuasion.[20] In fact Book I as a whole is deeply impregnated with the vocabulary of RB: *abstinentia, moderatio, lenitas, ratio aequitatis, gravitas*, and *taciturnitas* (as a virtue), to give some examples.[21]

Amidst all the reforming statutes and ordinances of Benedict of Aniane and Adalard and others, and the commentaries such as those of Smaragdus of Verdun and Hildemar,[22] it is not easy to find another Carolingian text which so well expresses how that age was stirred by the eloquence and nobility of RB. Given the lack of such precise detail in Book I on any other subject, even Wala's involvements in Carolingian justice,[23] we may conclude that Pascasius's primary purpose in this book was to present Wala as an outstanding model of the monastic rule which he followed. Of course this is not surprising (though historians have not given themselves much chance to be unsurprised by it), considering the hold which RB had taken in Carolingian society. I doubt, however, if it would be found to have been common in Carolingian hagiographical writings. Eigil's *Life of Sturm*, for instance, while explicit that Sturm based Fulda observance on RB, otherwise refers to it hardly at all.[24] Pascasius also, in his *Life of Adalard*, Wala's brother and predecessor at Corbie, while mentioning RB here and there, follows a completely different pattern. He tells us himslf that he has resorted to 'the rhetoricians' (meaning something like Alcuin's *De Rhetorica* or Cicero's *De Inventione* which Alcuin plagiarised) to describe the qualities of a perfect man; no wonder, then, that he compares Adalard, Wala, their sister Gundrada,

[20] Dümmler, 53–4.

[21] E.g. in Dümmler, abstinentia, 26, l.12; lenitas, 53, l.25; aequalitas vitae, 34, l.17; gravitas, 36, l.16, 49, l.27, 54, l.28; taciturnitas (in effect), 34–5; modestia vitae, 54, l.8.

[22] For Hildemar, see Mittermüller and Schroll, as in notes 15 and 19 above; for Smaragdus's commentary, PL 102, cols. 689–932.

[23] For this subject, see H. Fichtenau, *The Carolingian Empire*, trans. Peter Munz (Oxford, 1957), 116–18, using the *Epitaphium Arsenii*, i, 26.

[24] *Eigilis Vita Sancti Sturmi*, c. 14, MGH SS II, 371, l.34, 372, l.6. This work is translated into English by C. H. Talbot, *The Anglo-Saxon Missionaries in Germany* (1954), 181–202.

and two others, to a Greek diapason![25] Nor is the RB element in Book I unimportant in explaining the problem of Wala in politics, which is what Book II of the *Epitaphium Arsenii* is about. For the student of Carolingian politics, above all in the crucial years 828–34, Book II, shorter than Book I, is vastly the more important, though bombast frustratingly takes precedence over fact.

By the early 850s, when Pascasius wrote Book II, his mind had been focussed, presumably by talk at Corbie in the intervening years, on a somewhat different issue concerning Wala from that treated in Book I, though connected. This was not at all the role which he had played in politics as such: on this he is adamant but very generalised. He runs through Wala's aims in chapter 10: the liberation of the emperor from death and his sons from perdition, the driving of abominations out of the imperial palace, the watch against the division of the Empire into parts, the ensuring that oaths taken to Lothar I (i.e. to the *Ordinatio Imperii* of 817) were kept, the preservation of the unity and dignity of the empire for the sake of the defence of the *patria* and the liberty and possessions of churches (one should remember that Corbie itself, in the western part of the empire, had recently founded an important daughter-house, Corvey, as a missionary base in the East).[26] These were all important issues, and Wala was playing for high stakes; nobody foresaw what would be put in the place of Charlemagne's empire; Wala could not have known that he was holding up the origins of France and Germany. All this, however, was the surrounding of Pascasius's real target.

The pivotal passage of Book II comes in chapter 15, when Adeodatus, the one survivor from Book I amongst the conversationalists in Book II, apart from Pascasius himself, puts a very pertinent question. 'Many people charge him (Wala) with this', he says, 'that it did not behove him to worry so much about these things, nor to get mixed up in such business. There was no prescription of the Holy Spirit for it, nor authority in the Rule, ... for one reads in the Rule (i.e. RB4) that monasteries are *enclosures* of virtues (*claustra virtutum*) and instruments of good works where everything can be diligently and regularly accomplished'.[27] It is generally assumed that Pascasius's interlocutors, with their nicknames and disguises, were all monks of

[25] *Vita Sancti Adalhardi*, cc. 32–34, PL 120, cols. 1525–27, esp. col. 1527A.

[26] Dümmler, 76. For the relations of Corbie and Corvey, see *Epitaphium*, i, 12, Dümmler, 41, and Weinrich, 39–43.

[27] Dümmler, 81–2. This is a perfect example of the different purposes and thus approach of Pascasius and Hildemar (see note 15 above). Apart from etymology and stressing the occasions of sin outside the enclosure, Hildemar has nothing to say on involvement in affairs but concentrates on the practical question of how large the enclosure should ideally be, Mittermüller, 183.

Corbie, and Dümmler pointed out that this work cannot have been written for a wide circle of readers, with its outspokenness about Charles the Bald's mother, Judith, and other associates of his.[28] My supposition would be that it was written for internal Corbie consumption, and what the monks of Corbie wanted to know about Wala was not a blow by blow account of his actions in politics, but one good reason why this luminary of Benedictine observance was in politics in the first place. After all, he could be of little benefit to them as abbot, in their cloister of virtues, while exiled on an Atlantic island for his pains, 'contemplating the tides and musing on the wheels and revolutions by which the world was turned'.[29] That Wala's place was at Corbie, and not gallivanting around the public synods, was an objection to his behaviour which had also occurred to others. After the meeting at Nijmegen, where Louis reasserted himself in October 830, the Metz chronicler called the Astronomer tells us that Wala was ordered 'to retire to the monastery of Corbie and there live as one bound by the Rule'.[30]

Chapter 15 is not the only place in Book II where the issue of an abbot in politics is raised; it runs like a *Leitmotif* through the whole book. If he was so humble and none was more dead to the world, asks Adeodatus elsewhere, why was it Wala who had constantly to speak amongst the highest ecclesiastics and 'senators'? Teofrastus wonders, and so do many others, why in such a great empire there were never many bishops or 'senators' who dared to put their own safety at risk for the common safety. Given the bad times, should one not think of oneself rather than the *respublica*? Again Teofrastus returns to the charge, not this time to criticise Wala's involvement in politics as such, but still his neglect of Corbie, when for the last two years of his life (834–36) he took the abbacy of Bobbio in Italy.[31] Why was it always Wala who had to speak? Did he have to neglect and endanger Corbie? Was it not more than possible that he had passed over to secularity and the very pomps of the world which he had renounced? These are the questions, not totally absent from Book I, which are put insistently to Pascasius in Book II. Obviously, therefore, detailed political analysis by himself would only have compounded the evil; it might have suggested that Pascasius too was obsessed by pomps and secularities. Once we see aright the problem which faced Pascasius, it becomes apparent why rhetorical innuendo was a far more effective solution to

[28] Dümmler, 7, 11.

[29] Dümmler, 79: considerabat rotas et volubilitates quibus vertitur saeculum.

[30] *Vita Hludowici Imperatoris*, c. 45, MGH SS II, 633: Walach abbas iussus est ad monasterium redire Corbeiae, ibique regulariter observari.

[31] Dümmler, 92.

it than getting bogged down in the political mire which he professed to abhor; and an *Epitaphium* became the perfect medium for the sort of indeterminate rhetoric whose aim was to vindicate the dead.

The reason why I have called the intervention of Adeodatus in chapter 15 the pivotal passage of the Book, perhaps of the whole two Books, is that the objection to Wala's political involvements is there brought squarely out of RB, and has the full force of Book I and the image of Wala as a model Benedictine behind it. I would suggest also that Pascasius has the full force of Book I behind *him* when trying to meet it. We have already noted various links between Books I and II, not least the genre of *Epitaphium* itself; despite the years which separate them, Pascasius seems to have been conscious of completing a unified work. Therefore Book I carries a large implication against any suggestion that Wala's politics was a breach of RB: how could such a profound and exemplary follower of RB have been guilty of throwing it to the winds in any point? Surely, Pascasius seems to say, one must rather give him credit for being drawn out of his monastery by what he judged to be extreme necessity. Let me give, however, Pascasius's own answer to Adeodatus:

> Many say this (i.e. that Wala should not have been mixed up in politics), but they are people who have not taken due notice of his *dignitas* and *ordo*. After being elected a pastor by all, he was called by God, as we believe, to be a counsellor of the whole Empire. Even before he was elected he was revered for his intelligence and nobility by all. Therefore, once he was a prelate and one of the pastors of churches, he was constituted a senator together with other members of the palace and senators of the kingdom, so that, as it seems to me, he could not *fail* to give counsel about all matters without danger to his soul.[32]

To draw a conclusion in such a way as to facilitate the comparison with Bernard later: Pascasius puts the problem of Wala in politics directly from the Rule of St Benedict, and he attempts to answer it in quasi-classical, institutional terms. Once an abbot, Wala was a *senator* and participated in the shared responsibility for the *respublica*; if he stood nearly alone amidst the crises, that was not because he was at fault but because others were too faint-hearted to do their duty. We have to be careful in giving institutional content to Pascasius's thinking, for Johannes Fried has argued powerfully that the Carolingians gave no abstract idea of institution or order whatsoever to the *respublica*; that they used the language of Cicero, but with the understanding of Isidore of Seville which amounted to little; that

[32] Dümmler, 82.

every effort to express the ordered totality of the people led not to *Staats*—but to *Kirchendenken*, and the institutional strain even in church-thinking was liable to evaporate into ideas of the church as the mystical body of Christ.[33] One hesitates to suggest even a minor shift of emphasis in the case of an article so majestic in its learning and coherence, and it is true that without the church or the churches Pascasius's *respublica* would be an empty shell indeed. But precisely because Pascasius was confronted with a difficult problem, and was a highly intelligent member of a sharp-witted community, with an exceptional capacity for abstract thinking, the very challenge of explaining Wala in politics perhaps stimulated him more than it did most Carolingians to conceiving of the *respublica* as an ordered unity.

It is part of Pascasius's rhetoric to keep the discussion of Wala's actions on the level of high principle, but there is another aspect of his interventions in politics which I have held back until now, because it seemed desirable first to establish what the question was which Pascasius sought to answer, what terms of reference he used for this question and answer, i.e. in no small part Benedictine, and what principles of justification for Wala he considered most relevant. The other aspect to which I refer is there to be read in the *Epitaphium Arsenii*, though rather between the lines, namely the defence of the material possessions of bishoprics and abbeys, including Corbie. It is obvious that most great churches had a material interest in the unity of the empire. One has only to think how Lupus of Ferrières found it increasingly difficult to administer his abbey lands without his monks knowing German; how, at about the time that Agobard of Lyon was advocating uniform laws for the whole empire, Hrabanus Maurus at Fulda found his holding of Gottschalk's endowment challenged by the relatives of the latter on the basis of Saxon law; how, as we have mentioned, Corbie itself had a daughter house, Korvey, in the German part of the empire.[34] Here we must take issue with Wolfgang Wehlen in his very interesting and stimulating work on Wala. While rightly emphasising the connection between imperial unity and the hold of churches on their lands and possessions, their *integritas rerum*, Wehlen keeps wanting to talk about the church in the singular, as if Wala's cause was some over-arching, universalist concept of the imperial church; whereas Pascasius practically always talks about the churches

[33] Johannes Fried, 'Der karolingische Herrschaftsverband im 9 Jahrhundert zwischen Kirche und Königshaus', *Historische Zeitschrift*, ccxxxv (1982), 1–43

[34] *Loup de Ferrières, Correspondance*, ed. L. Levillain (Paris, 1964), ii, 6, no. 70; Agobard's *Adversus Legem Gundobadi Ad Ludovicum* in *Agobardi Lugdunensis Opera Omnia*, ed. L. Van Acker, *Corpus Christianorum* 52, 19–28, and for the date of 817–22, xxxix; *Die Klostergemeinschaft von Fulda im früheren Mittelalter*, ed. K. Schmidt et al (Munich, 1978), vol. 2/3 (Eckhard Freise), 1017–29; *Epitaphium Arsenii*, as in note 32 above.

in the plural, as if to imply that Wala championed the rights of individual churches including his own of Corbie.[35] The Carolingians of course fully grasped the concept of the universal church, but they also knew well how to make the distinction between the *generalis ecclesia* and *speciales ecclesiae* like Corbie or Fulda or Volturno, to use the terminology of Ambrosius Autpertus.[36] There is a streak in Wala, after all, which relates him to those many medieval abbots who engaged in politics as the protagonists of the rights of their monasteries.

This is not something which could be said of St Bernard. At one time there seemed to me force in the argument that as a public figure between 1130 and his death in 1153, Bernard's actions were strongly motivated by the political interests, not perhaps of Clairvaux alone, but of the whole Cistercian order. The party of Innocent II which Bernard supported in the papal schism during the 1130s has been shown to have had close links with the new orders, while the opposing party of Anacletus II was associated with Cluniac monasticism;[37] Bernard intervened with a high profile and strong language in several episcopal elections, almost invariably to press the claims of a Cistercian candidate or one favourable to the Cistercians;[38] his preaching tours were said to have won many recruits for the Cistercian order;[39] and even his attacks upon famous scholars like Abelard and Gilbert of Poitiers could be seen as an attempt to force a Cistercian attitude to learning on the schools where Bernard already had close personal connections.[40] This argument, however, I now find superficial, largely because it completely mistakes Bernard's sights, since his whole political interest seems swept up in the staggeringly optimistic aim of stamping Cistercian idealism on the whole world.

[35] Wolfgang Wehlen, *Geschichtsschreibung und Staatsauffassung im Zeitalter Ludwigs des Frommen* (Lübeck & Hamburg, 1970), 107–22; and see Dümmler, e.g., 65, 76, 81, 82, esp. at p. 76, where stress is laid on this: ob ecclesiarum liberationem ... et dispensationem facultatum ecclesiarum.

[36] *Ambrosius Autpertus in Apocalypsim Libri Decem*, in *Maxima Bibliotheca Veterum Patrum* 13 (Lyon, 1677), e.g. 422F–H. For evidence that this work was known amongst the Carolingians, Bernhard Bischoff, 'Italienische Handschriften des neunten bis elften Jahrhunderts im frümittelalterlichen Bibliotheken ausserhalb Italiens', in *Il Libro e il Testo 1982: Atti del Convegno Internazionale* (Urbino, 1984), 186.

[37] H-W Klewitz, 'Das Ende des Reformpapsttums', *Deutsches Archiv*, iii (1939), 372–412.

[38] E.g. David Knowles, 'The case of St William of York', in his *Historian and Character* (Cambridge, 1963), 76–97; Giles Constable, 'The disputed election at Langres in 1138', *Traditio*, xiii (1957), 119–52; P. Imbart de la Tour, *Les Elections Episcopales dans l'Eglise de France du IXe au XIIe Siècle* (Paris, 1890).

[39] *Vita Prima*, i, 61, PL 185, col. 260; ibid., vi, col. 401D.

[40] E.g. Beryl Smalley, *The Study of the Bible in the Middle Ages* (Oxford, 1952), 173. For St Bernard's connections with Parisian masters, E. Vacandard, *Vie de St Bernard* (Paris, 1920), ii, 112–18.

One sees an example of this aim in his preaching of the Second Crusade in 1146. If a man were interested to go to Jerusalem, the best Jerusalem to which he could go was not 'the earthly Jerusalem to which Mount Sinai in Arabia is joined' (writes Bernard with dubious geography though clear purport), 'but that free Jerusalem which is above and the mother of us all,' namely Clairvaux: 'she is the Jerusalem united to the one in heaven by whole-hearted devotion, by conformity of life, and by spiritual affinity.'[41] Bernard was here writing to Bishop Alexander of Lincoln explaining to him why a protegé of his called Philip, who had set out on a pilgrimage to the earthly Jerusalem (before the time of the Second Crusade), would not be returning to Lincoln, because he had on the way become an 'enrolled citizen' of the said heavenly Jerusalem. Not quite everyone in the world, however, could be persuaded to become a Cistercian monk, and for the resistant residue, the Second Crusade offered an opportunity to do something very similar at a lower level; instead of repenting of their sins and joining the heavenly Jerusalem at Clairvaux, they could repent of their sins and journey to the earthly Jerusalem. Sir Steven Runciman has severely criticized Bernard for his preaching of the Second Crusade, maintaining that by preaching it to the Germans he defeated the original object of Pope Eugenius III to raise a small skilled force of French knights who would be effective in the East; a large German army arrived before anyone else at Constantinople in 1147, ate everything, and thus created the logistical and supply problems which contributed in great measure to the failure of the crusade.[42] No doubt similar criticisms were voiced against Bernard by his contemporaries, for criticised he certainly was.[43] To him, however, every practical consideration was totally irrelevant. If the freeing of the holy places was all that was in question, who could doubt that God had twelve legions of angels with which to free them; indeed he had but to say the word. No, God had other purposes, to which Bernard was privy. He had taken pity on his people, and by an exquisite act of courtesy he had given every murderer, thief, adulterer, perjurer, 'and such like persons', an opportunity to repent and be pardoned of their sins.[44] This was no ordinary way to advance a political reputation or interest.

[41] Ep. 64, Opera = *Sancti Bernardi Opera*, ed. J. Leclercq, C. H. Talbot, H. M. Rochais, (Rome, 1957–77), vii, 157–8, BSJ = *The Letters of St Bernard of Clairvaux*, trans. Bruno Scott James (1953), a good translation, BSJ 67.

[42] Steven Runciman, *A History of the Crusades*, ii (1952), 247–88, esp. 263.

[43] Otto of Freising and the *Vita Prima* are the principal sources which show this, and see Bernard's self-defence in his *De Consideratione*, ii, cc 1–2, *Opera*, iii, 410–12.

[44] *Opera*, viii, 313–14, letter to the archbishops of East Francia and Bavaria; BSJ, no. 391, as Letter to the English People.

Like Wala, in Pascasius's account of him, Bernard knew that as a monk who was not a bishop he was open to criticism for his involvements in public life. 'I am forced to move in affairs that trouble the peace of my soul, and are not perhaps very compatible with my vocation', he wrote to the monks of Clairvaux while he was engaged in the papal schism;[45] and in another letter in which he protested his misery at being absent from them, he proffered the following Ciceronian gem: 'I should like to tell you, for your consolation, how necessary my presence here was, were it not that it would savour of boasting'.[46] To a Carthusian prior he wrote: 'May my monstrous life, my bitter conscience, move you to pity. I am a sort of modern chimera, neither cleric nor layman. I have kept the habit of a monk, but I have long ago abandoned the life.'[47] That Bernard felt answerable to the monks of Clairvaux in particular for his absences is readily intelligible when one reads of how opposed they were to his taking a bishopric for fear of losing him.[48] Yet in all this, in contrast to Pascasius, there is not a word about the Rule of St Benedict, all the more noteworthy considering the emphasis on accurate and uniform texts of RB amongst the Cistercians.

The reason is that Pascasius and Bernard had completely different starting-points in their attitudes to RB and in how they thought to discuss it. The Carolingians regarded RB as a body of spiritual teaching, indeed, but also as a body of precepts which had legal force, as if it were a great monastic capitulary. All the capitularies surrounding Benedict of Aniane's monastic reforms under Louis the Pious assumed this position for it; in fact they secured it. Josef Semmler has said that Benedict of Aniane ensured that RB would become the exclusive and basic law of western monasticism, and that he produced his uniform customs to be followed by all monasteries in the empire, 'in order to fill out the Benedictine framework of law, i.e. the Rule of St Benedict'.[49]

[45] Ep. 143 (BSJ 144), *Opera*, vii, 342.
[46] Ep. 144 (BSJ 146), *Opera*, vii, 345–6.
[47] Cited by Morris, 259.
[48] *Vita Prima*, ii, 27, Pl 185, col. 283.
[49] J. Semmler, 'Benedictus II: una regula una consuetudo, in *Benedictine Culture, 750–1050*, ed. W. Lourdaux & D. Verhulst (Leuven, 1983), 1–49, citation at p. 48. Similarly, J. Semmler, 'Zur Überlieferung der monastischen Gesetzgebung Ludwigs des Frommens', *Deutsches Archiv*, xvi (1960), 309–88. The principal Aniane material is edited by Semmler in *Corpus Consuetudinum Monasticarum*, i (Siegburg, 1963), 425–582. For a useful survey of the manuscript transmission of RB amongst the Carolingians, see Rosamond McKitterick, *The Frankish Kingdoms under the Carolingians, 751–987* (1983), 119–21. T. FX. Noble, 'The monastic ideal as a model for Empire: the case of Louis the Pious', *Rév. Bén.* 86 (1976), 235–50, is of value but relates Louis to RB only in a much more general way (and principally to the abbot) than I have shown that Wala can be related in the *Epitaphium*.

Bernard, on the other hand, gave us his views in his treatise on RB, *De Praecepto et Dispensatione* (pre 1143–44), about which there is a great deal more dispensation than precept. Subject monks, he agrees, must treat the rule as precept and necessary. But prelates, though they must treat matters of divine institution such as charity and humility as precept and necessary, can regard human observances as voluntary and dispensable.[50] There is a difference between matters *de necessario stabili*, which should not be changed if they conduce to charity, but can be omitted, suspended or changed for the sake of charity; and matters *de necessario incommutabili* (Bernard shows himself a true schoolman in his love of scholastic distinctions), such as the whole Sermon on the Mount and virtues like humility and *mansuetudo*, which can never be changed. The abbot cannot leave off what is *de spiritualibus* in the Rule, but only what is *de corporalibus observantiis*, where charity is all important.[51] It is an attitude which surely owes something to Augustine's *De Doctrina Christiana* and the idea that every allegorical interpretation of scripture had value if it conduced to the reign of charity.[52] In Bernard's treatise there is a lengthy passage on the *stabilitas loci*, i.e. that monks should stay in their monasteries, the very issue which had most exercised Pascasius in his discussion of Wala. It is all about the pros and cons of monks moving from one monastery to another, not a word about external involvements and cloisters of virtue.[53]

Thus, although of course both Bernard and Pascasius hold that 'necessity' may justify a breach of the precepts of RB, their perceptions of the whole problem of abbots or monks in politics differ greatly from each other. Pascasius grapples with it in essentially institutional terms congruent with the whole effort to fit monasticism and RB into the Carolingian Empire, while Bernard takes a much more free-ranging humanistic view in which legalism or institutionalism and love seem often to be opposed in antithesis. To Bernard, whatever enlarged the prevalence of love in human affairs must be for the best. 'Charity sets me free', wrote the Holy Man in almost threatening vein, and there were certainly those whose knees quaked at the thought of it. When the abbots of Rievaulx and Fountains received a letter saying, 'I am obliged by the rule of our order to go out of my house on visitations, but charity spurs me to attempt something greater than this', they could have experienced an anxious moment, until reading on they found that it was the excuse for Bernard's not coming at all.[54]

[50] *Opera*, iii, 255–6.
[51] *Ibid.*, 257–9.
[52] Corpus Christianorum, Ser. Lat, 32 (Turnhout, 1962), iii, 15, p. 91.
[53] *Opera*, iii, 283–91.
[54] Ep. 143 (BSJ 144), *Opera*, vii, 343, line 17; Ep. 535 (BSJ 201), *Opera*, viii, 500–1.

It is obviously an enormous difference between Wala and Bernard that the latter offers his own mind and soul in a wonderfully rich and self-expressive corpus of writings. If we wish to understand the positive drive which took Bernard out of his cloister and into the astonishing venture of turning the whole world into a Cistercian cloister, it is worth looking a little more closely at the key concept of love in his thought.[55] *Caritas* is a word that figures in the title of the earliest Cistercian constitutional document, the *Carta Caritatis*, and very paradoxically. What can all these stipulations about accurate texts, general chapters, visitations, procedures for resolving disputes, have to do with love? The answer is clear. *Caritas* was not only 'the sacrament of endless union with God',[56] which was the ultimate goal of all Cistercian monastic life, the final concurrence of wills between man and God;[57] it was also the whole system of external and internal discipline which led to this union. No wonder that apart from the majestic analysis of the ascent to God through the stages of love in the *De Diligendo Deo*, Bernard chose to say so much about the system by which the union with God could be achieved through the medium of his incomparable sermons on the Song of Songs. That he should not have eschewed the allegory of eroticism and its preparation for physical union speaks volumes for his confidence that human beings, involved with body and soul, could work their way towards God systematically.[58] 'Only the mind disciplined by persevering study', he wrote, 'is truly prepared for nuptial union with the divine partner.' This is why his friend William of St Thierry, taking his cue from RB's observation that a monastery was a 'school of the Lord's service', could hail a Cistercian monastery as a *schola caritatis*.[59]

St Bernard's idea of love must be set in the context of his optimism about human potentiality.[60] The Carolingian theologians dreaded Pelagianism, the heresy which taught that man could achieve salvation by his own free will and innate goodness without the anterior

[55] On the distinction between the words *amor* and *caritas*, see Morris, 369. For lower kinds of love St Bernard would not use the word *caritas*, but for divine love he appears to use the words *amor* and *caritas* almost interchangeably, see, for instance, E. Gilson, *The Mystical Theology of St Bernard*, trans. A. H. C. Downes (1940), 245.

[56] *Cant* = *Sancti Bernardi Sermones super Cantica Canticorum, Opera* i, ii. *Cant*, Sermo 1, 8, *Opera*, i, 6, line 14: aeterni connubii ... sacramenta. Here the word *amor* is used, but *caritas* is associated with the same idea in *Cant*, 71, 8–9, *Opera*, ii, 219, esp. lines 6–10. St Bernard's Sermons on the Song of Songs have been translated into English by Kilian Walsh and Irene Edmonds in the *Cistercian Father Series*, vols. 4, 7, 31, 40 (1971–80).

[57] *Cant*, Sermo 71, 8–10, *Opera*, ii, 220–21.

[58] *Cant*, Sermo 9, *Opera*, i, 46.

[59] Gilson, chapter 3, and p. 67.

[60] My debt to the influential title paper in R. W. Southern, *Medieval Humanism and other Studies* (Oxford, 1970), 29–60, will be clear.

workings of God's grace. Bernard was no Pelagian; in his early treatise *De Gratia et Libero Arbitrio* he could not have been more explicit on the subject of man's total helplessness without grace.[61] Anyone familiar with Carolingian writings on this subject and on predestination, however, will mark the great difference of atmosphere. In Bernard, the promise of salvation, the charting of the course which grace and free will take together, the gaining of 'the crown of righteousness',[62] these dominate the tone of the work, not the punishment prepared for sinners as in the Carolingian works on predestination. The latter emanate from 'a society all too aware of its sins, all too uncertain of their forgiveness', as David Ganz has finely said.[63] Bernard's view was as follows: 'every soul standing under condemnation has the power to turn and find that it can not only breathe the fresh air of hope and pardon, but also aspire to the nuptials of the Word, alliance with God, and the bearing of the sweet yoke of love with the king of angels'. Fear in religion was anathema to him; love was all. One of the most moving passages in the whole of the Sermons on the Song of Songs is on this theme:

> Love is the only one of the motions of the soul, of its senses and affections, in which the creature can respond to its Creator, even if not as an equal, and repay his favour in some similar way. For example if God is angry with me, am I to be angry in return? No, indeed, but I shall tremble with fear and ask pardon. So also if he accuses me, I shall not accuse him in return, but rather justify him. Nor, if he judges me, shall I judge him, but I shall adore him. . . . Now you see how different love is, for when God loves, he desires nothing but to be loved, since he loves us for no other reason than to be loved, knowing that those who love him are blessed in their very love.[64]

Bernard was confident in the power of the human mind to analyse and master itself, as well as to master the souls of others. It is noticeable in the miracles recounted by his biographers that he himself by no means recoiled from the exercise of a mental and psychological ascendancy over his monks at Clairvaux. He cured one brother who took communion in sin and could not swallow the host; for another

[61] Esp. c. 6, *Opera*, iii, 178.

[62] Esp., c. 14, *Opera*, iii, 199–200; corona iustitiae, c. 14; *ibid.*, 203, ll.3–4.

[63] David Ganz, 'The debate on predestination', in *Charles the Bald: Court and Kingdom*, ed. Margaret Gibson and Janet Nelson, *British Archaeol. Reports, International Series* 101 (1981), 353–73, the citation at p. 366.

[64] *Cant*, Sermo 83, *Opera*, ii, 298, ll.19–23, and 300–1. Against what one might expect (see Morris, 374), Bernard seems to have denied the rights of the devil in human affairs, e.g. *Cant*, Sermo 85, cc. 3–4, *Opera*, ii, 309–10.

he obtained the gift of tears; he was able to perceive the needs and errors of monks in other houses; he had premonitions of the 'wicked spirit' which led Master Stephen of Vitry to his monastery.[65] He also believed that external behaviour and the inner workings of the soul interacted on each other, and was confident that a system of external discipline could help lead the soul to God. He held strong views that clothes were a reflection of the soul, and he was an ardent opponent of laughter.[66] The custody of the eyes, a prime tenet in the whole Cistercian religious culture, amounted with him almost to an obsession, perhaps for the very reason that he was a man sensitive to nature, acutely observant of art,[67] and susceptible to good looks in people.[68] It was said that he once spent the whole day travelling along the shore of Lake Geneva, but was unaware of any lake when his company referred to it in the evening.[69] After a year at Citeaux as a novice, he was ignorant of the configuration of windows and vault in the church, and here William of St Thierry shows us exactly how this particular discipline was related to the soul's journey to God, for he adds that St Bernard, 'mortified not only the desires of the flesh experienced through the senses, but the senses themselves, and so he achieved an *inner* sense of love and illumination'.[70] Of Bernard's belief in the interaction of bodily discipline and spiritual advance, there is an excellent example in the sermons on the Song of Songs, when he draws attention to the appearance of the novices at Clairvaux, and their blossoming in their new way of life: 'Do you see these novices? . . . They have assumed a disciplined appearance, a proper deportment in their whole body. What can be seen of them is pleasing; one notices less attention to painstaking care of the body and dress; they speak less, their faces are more cheerful, their looks more modest, their movements more correct'.[71] In general, moral and material improvement went hand in hand in the Cistercian ethic, with its social dynamism. While the Cluniac Bernard of Morlaas was writing his poem *De Contemptu Mundi*,[72] Cistercian engineers were constructing superb stone mill races and vaulted drains.[73] This was Cistercian humanism.

[65] *Vita Prima*, i, cc. 51, 61. 65. 68. PL 185, cols. 256, 260, 263, 264.

[66] *Vita Prima*, iii, c. 5, PL 185, col. 306.

[67] As the famous, or notorious, passage on Cluniac art, *Apologia ad Guillelmum*, c. 29, shows, *Opera*, iii, 106, see Panofsky 25.

[68] E.g. saying how dark hair on fair-skinned faces enhances their beauty and grace: et nigri capilli candidis vultibus etiam decorem augent et gratiam, *Cant*, Sermo 25, *Opera*, i, 164, ll.16–17.

[69] *Vita Prima*, iii, 4, PL 185, col. 306A.

[70] *Vita Prima*, i, 20, PL 185, col. 238. My translation is something of a paraphrase here.

[71] *Cant*, Sermo 63, *Opera*, ii, 165.

[72] Joan Evans, *Monastic Life at Cluny* (Oxford, 1931), 112–14.

[73] As at Fountains and Rievaulx (Yorks.) respectively.

Caritas in St Bernard's mind, therefore, was a concept which virtually demanded action beyond the confines of a small monastic circle, because it could be achieved by teaching and learning, by analysis and discipline, in theory open to any human being. It imposed a duty even on contemplatives to face the needs of others in the active life. Bernard has a compelling passage in Sermon 50 on the Song of Songs, which is a mixture of patristic learning and psychological self-awareness, on how *caritas* actually draws a man from contemplation to action. He is speaking to the words, 'the king led me into the wine cellar; he set in order love within me':

> For actual charity puts the lower things first, affectual the higher. There is no doubt in the rightly disposed mind that the love of God comes before the love of man, as the more perfect things in men themselves come before the less perfect, and heaven before earth, eternity before time, soul before flesh. Nonetheless, in well ordered action the order is found often, or even always, to be reversed. For we are galvanized by concern for our neighbour and become more and more taken up with this; we take pains to help our weaker brethren; we pay more attention, on account of the rights and needs of men, to peace on earth than to the glory of heaven; and in our anxiety for temporal cares, we are hardly allowed to feel those of eternity; and having put aside the cultivation of our own soul we look almost continuously to the tiredness of our body; and then at last we achieve in our very tiredness more abundant honour, according to the saying of the Apostle: 'the last shall be first and the first last'.[74]

The tables are turned and action is suddenly felt to be the higher vocation. It is not difficult to divine whence the ideas in this passage derive; they are a subtle blend of Augustine and Gregory. Augustine in the *City of God* has a distinction between *caritas veritatis* which seeks holy leisure and *necessitas caritatis* which accepts just business, similar to Bernard's between *affectualis* and *actualis caritas*;[75] while Gregory in the *Moralia in Job* would have those with spiritual gifts lend themselves with the condescension of charity to the earthly necessity of others and bend their minds to manage the least concerns.[76] But like Abelard, Bernard always made his sources his own (in the case of the Bible his biographers commented on his free use of it),[77] and notwithstanding

[74] *Opera*, ii, 80–81.

[75] *De Civitate Dei*, xix, 9, *Corpus Christianorum* 48, 686, cited G. B. Ladner, *The Idea of Reform* (Cambridge, Mass., 1959), 337–9.

[76] *Moralia in Job*, xix, c. 45, PL 76, col. 126B.

[77] *Vita Prima*, i, 24, and iii, 7, PL 185, cols. 241 and 307B–C.

his prodigious patristic learning,[78] one cannot fail to sense in the passage just quoted that he is speaking of problems, feelings, and tirednesses, which he had himself experienced.

Perhaps the most breath-taking fact of all about St Bernard's public life was that he rated himself peculiarly well qualified to teach *caritas* to the world at large and in effect to be the moral arbiter, or Rousseauesque *législateur*, of Europe;[79] and moreover, that so many people accepted his credentials. John of Salisbury expressed it to perfection in a celebrated back-handed compliment: 'he was a man powerful in the sight of God as some believe, and in the sight of men as we all know'.[80] Bernard held to the conviction, in considerable measure self-fulfilling, that life and politics could be moulded by prayer. His *De Consideratione* (after 1148), written for the Cistercian Pope Eugenius III, was a plea for self-knowledge and reflection, or *consideratio*, rather than the bustle of justice and administration. Its mightiest passage on the plenitude of paper power is followed by the words, 'En quis es?' (And who are you?). You are nothing without prayer and self-knowledge.[81] Bernard was not a high churchman, a late Hildebrandine, with a theory of papal supremacy, as has sometimes been supposed;[82] rather his point, following Pope Gregory the Great, was that the higher a person's position, the greater was the need for a sense of moral responsibility and inner contemplation. He believed himself to be directly inspired by prayer in his own political actions, as well as in his interpretation of scripture, apparently sinking into meditation at council meetings and comparing himself to Moses in his preaching of the Second Crusade.[83]

The sermons on the Song of Songs, with all the white heat of their spirituality, read at one level like a gigantic and highly self-aware testimonial of Bernard's own qualifications to intervene in public life. The first twenty or so sermons are less like a commentary on the text than a stupendous fugue on the single theme, 'Thy name is as ointment poured forth'. Who, after all, was the great pourer forth of this ointment? If along with one's endowment of inner virtues, Bernard

[78] Gillian Evans, *The Mind of St Bernard* (Oxford, 1983), 74, 81.

[79] Gilson, 72, distinguishes between the 'proper will' and the 'common will', the latter being, 'the will common to man and God'. This is a concept very close to, if not exactly the same as, Rousseau's General Will.

[80] *Ioannis Saresberiensis Historia Pontificalis*, ed. with trans. Marjorie Chibnall (1956), 20.

[81] *De Consideratione*, ii, cc. 16–17, *Opera*, iii, 424–5.

[82] E.g. by Bernard Jacqueline, *Episcopat et Papauté chez Saint Bernard de Clairvaux* (Saint-Lo, 1975), 205–7.

[83] *Vita Prima*, iii, 2, PL 185, cols. 304–5 (there is no reason to doubt this merely because it is an hagiographical *topos*, which can be found in C10 Ruotger's *Vita Brunonis*, c. 29, for instance); *De Consideratione*, ii, cc. 1–2, Opera, iii, 410–12.

argued, one is adorned with external gifts of knowledge and eloquence, it is wrong through sloth or ill-judged humility to hoard them for oneself and withhold them from one's neighbour. They should not indeed be poured out in the manner of a water-channel, which simultaneously receives and pours out what it receives, but like a reservoir, which retains its water until it is full and then discharges the overflow without loss to itself. 'Today there are many in the Church who act like channels', he opines, 'whereas the reservoirs are far too rare'.[84] By the time he wrote this, Bernard could have reflected that it was the rhetorical masterpiece of his *Apologia ad Guillelmum* which had first brought him into public prominence, while the wit and eloquence of his letters, with their deep knowledge and clever use of the Bible, had made an impact on the events of the papal schism in the 1130s.[85] There was no ill-judged humility (or any apparent humility at all) in his exhortation to Archbishop Hildebert of Tours, 'and so my father, we all expect your support, late though it may be, to fall upon us like due upon the fleece'; nor reticence in his observation that the Archbishop of Bordeaux had deserted Innocent II, in order, 'to cleave unto his schismatic, so that they became two in one vanity'.[86] But Bernard had not poured himself out too early. He had been Abbot of Clairvaux for some ten years when he wrote the *Apologia ad Guillelmum*, and he did not take the political limelight until he was in his forties and had had a long career as a contemplative monk. On his own showing, he was very much a reservoir; people like Abelard, and the Cistercian monk Ralph who later stirred up crusading fervour in the Rhineland independently of Bernard's own preaching,[87] might be considered channels.

Here we seem to be at the heart of the difference between Wala and Bernard, if they do not now look so distant from each other as to make comparison meaningless. Wala's justification was made for him; Bernard was unabashed to justify himself. Pascasius discussed Wala's public life in institutional terms: how it accorded with the Rule of St Benedict, how it met the needs of the *respublica*, how it protected church property. Bernard launched himself on the high seas of a humanism, in which God-given human and spiritual gifts, hard soul-searching, and the achievement of a direct relationship with God, were everything, while institution and earthly position (even the

[84] *Cant*, Sermo 18, *Opera*, i, 104.

[85] For the date of the Sermons on the Song of Songs, *Opera*, i, xv–xvi.

[86] Ep. 124 (BSJ 127): Et quod sane et vestra, Pater, exspectatur sicut pluvia in vellus, vel sera sententia; and Ep. 126 (BSJ 129), *Opera*, vii, 307, 310, l. 23.

[87] Otto of Freising, *Gesta Friderici I Imperatoris*, ed. G. Waitz (MGH Script. rer. Ger. in usum scholarum, Hannover & Leipzig, 1912), i, c. 40, 59.

papacy) were nothing.[88] Wala was drawn into politics by the sense of catastrophe in which all hands were needed on deck, and it was the duty of every churchman and aristocrat to speak out, however many in fact lacked the courage to do so; no other qualification was required than being a prelate or a *senator*, *any* prelate or *senator*, with courage. Bernard, though he faced troubles indeed, was drawn in by the positive idealism of *caritas*, by the belief that the journey of every human soul to God could be charted and the destination gained, and by his conviction that he himself was professionally qualified to be cartographer and guide in this enterprise. The *Epitaphium Arsenii* is all lamentations; indeed the saintly Arsenius himself, who gave Wala his nickname, wept so constantly and profusely, even amidst the hagiographical *topoi* of tears, that he had to carry a handkerchief with him wherever he went.[89] With Bernard for all his sternness, tears and asceticism, we are really amidst the festivities of the king's chambers where the bride avers, 'we will be glad and rejoice in thee, we will remember thy love more than wine' (Song of Songs, i, 4).

[88] Although the analogy should not be pressed too far, Peter Brown has made a distinction, a propos of Late Antiquity, between *articulate* power, the normally vested and agreed authority in a society, exercised by its holders through well-defined articulate channels, and *inarticulate* or *achieved* power, whose holders have an ill-defined status, acquired largely through their personal skills, a distinction which helps to express the phenomenon of St Bernard: Peter Brown, 'Sorcery, Demons, and the Rise of Christianity: from Late Antiquity into the Middle Ages', reprinted in his book, *Religion and Society in the Age of Saint Augustine* (1972), 119–46, esp. 123–9.

[89] See Dümmler, 5–6.

CONSTRUCTING MAU MAU[1]

by John Lonsdale

READ 8 DECEMBER 1989

WHY was the Mau Mau movement in colonial Kenya believed to be so evil?[2] It was the horror story of Britain's empire in the 1950s. Less of a military or strategic threat, it was thought to be more atrocious than either the Communists in Malaya or the Cypriot EOKA. It has lived in British memory as a symbol of African savagery, and modern Kenyans are divided by its images, militant nationalism or tribalist thuggery. This essay explores some of these constructions of Mau Mau.

Narrative

The Mau Mau secret society first emerged in 1948, among Kikuyu labour tenants on white settler farms. 250,000 of these squatters lived on the 'White Highlands', a quarter of the Kikuyu people. The movement was banned in 1950. In 1952 violence flared on the farms,[3] in the slums of Nairobi and in the Kikuyu reserve. A new governor, Evelyn Baring, declared an emergency in October. Jomo Kenyatta, alleged to be the movement's manager, was arrested with 180 others. Mau Mau did not, as expected, collapse; it became a formidable guerrilla force. The British did not win the military initiative until early 1954. The army was then a full infantry division; the police had multiplied threefold; and the Kikuyu 'resistance' had become a patchwork militia, the Kikuyu Guard, over 20,000 strong. The army left in 1956, after a four-year war.[4]

The relationship between the containment of Mau Mau and the concession of majority rule has yet to be unravelled, but its intimacy can be suggested by citing three coincidences. Over white protest, the

[1] Much of my material is derived from a research project on 'Explaining Mau Mau' shared with Bruce Berman of Queen's University, Ontario. Some of my ideas are also his, but I have been unable to test on him this particular approach, which is preliminary to our larger work.

[2] I was unable to give a satisfactory answer when John Dunn put this question at a Cambridge University African Studies Centre seminar; this essay is a second attempt. But I end with the same question, put to me in 1988 by Justus Ndung'u Thiong'o.

[3] Frank Furedi, *The Mau Mau war in perspective* (1989), chapters 3 and 4.

[4] Anthony Clayton, *Counter-insurgency in Kenya 1952–60* (Nairobi, 1976). My research student Mr Randall W. Heather, working on the intelligence war, has been generous with material and ideas.

first African was appointed minister in 1954, in a reform of government designed to quicken the war; two months later the army cleared Mau Mau and thousands of Kikuyu from Nairobi. Then the first African general election was held in 1957, barely a month after Mau Mau's forest leader, Field-Marshal Sir Dedan Kimathi as he entitled himself, was hanged. Finally, the emergency ended in 1960 as delegates went to London for a conference which promised African rule. The right-wing settler leader, Group-Captain Briggs, called this remaking of Kenya 'a victory for Mau Mau'.[5] His supporters felt overcome by the evil out of which they had imaginatively made the rising. One of them threw thirty pieces of silver at the feet of Michael Blundell, whose liberalism they believed had destroyed white supremacy.[6]

Argument

This essay explains neither Mau Mau nor its connexions with decolonisation. It addresses the prior question of how to read the evidence. We must know how Mau Mau was intellectually constructed before we can decide what it was and how it may have changed history. Behind the solidarities of war, myths of Mau Mau were more disputed than has been thought, with Africans as divided as whites.[7] For the future of Kenya was more anxiously contested after the Second World War than ever before; and all contenders were ignorant of their situation. Mau Mau was an almost entirely Kikuyu movement, and whites knew little of Kikuyu society. They knew 'what everybody knew', that the Kikuyu were a 'tribe', but an unusual and unsettling one. Mau Mau challenged the imaginative structures of race and tribe which underwrote the colonial order. It forced whites to decide between punishing a tribe and dissolving race as strategies of survival.

Kikuyu were just as ignorant and uncertain. Always a fragmented

[5] George Bennett and Carl Rosberg, *The Kenyatta election: Kenya 1960–1961* (1961) 22.

[6] Sir Michael Blundell, *So rough a wind* (1964), 283.

[7] The classic study of the Kenya whites' imaginative construction of Mau Mau is Carl G. Rosberg and John Nottingham, *The myth of 'Mau Mau': nationalism in Kenya* (1966); this essay is part of the revision to which this work is now subject with the availability of archival material. Four other colleagues have helped my understanding of the European construction of Mau Mau: Frederick Cooper, 'Mau Mau and the discourses of decolonization', *Journal of African History*, xxix (1988), 313–20; Dane Kennedy, 'The political mythology of Mau Mau', paper presented to the American Historical Association, December 1989; David W. Throup, *Economic and social origins of Mau Mau* (1987); Luise White, 'Separating the men from the boys: colonial constructions of gender, sexuality and terrorism in central Kenya, 1939–1959', University of Minnesota seminar paper, 1989. I also revise the 'Euro-African myth' presented in Robert Buijtenhuijs, *Mau Mau twenty years after: the myth and the survivors* (The Hague, 1973), 49–62, which has no consideration of Kikuyu political thought. For this I lean heavily on the unpublished work of Greet Kershaw and on Tabitha Kanogo, *Squatters and the roots of Mau Mau* (1987).

set of parochial societies, they had become a divided people. Their oaths of allegiance reflected both parts of their history. They had been rituals of initiation which imposed on aspirants the costs of civic accountability in a small community. They now demanded a hidden, factional loyalty to persons often unknown, on pain of death. For Mau Mau emerged as the militant wing in a struggle for political allegiance within Kikuyu society. Apprehensive ignorance ruled. Lies and intrigue flourished.

Once battle was joined, ignorance and imagination were poor guides to action. As the enemy had to be better known, allies courted and decisions faced, so four mutually incompatible meanings of Mau Mau occupied white minds, conservative, liberal, revivalist and military. Whites preserved a united front by damning Mau Mau's savagery which, all agreed, had to be destroyed. But they divided over its civil remedies, which governed their view of its causes.

While whites negotiated unity, it seems that Kikuyu were forced into it by the first fury of repression. An official enquiry secretly admitted as much. Mau Mau members generally had one set of enemies. Their opponents often had two, 'Mau Mau on the one hand and the forces of law and order on the other.' Many Kikuyu, who had welcomed the emergency as a defence against terror, 'became disillusioned' when all Kikuyu were treated as rebels.[8] This was part of the liberal construction of the movement; it was a product of its environment. But many settlers believed that up to eighty per cent of Kikuyu had taken the first oath of initiation by October 1952, in agreement with or from fear of their fellows, not from fear of whites.[9] This reflected the conservative view, that terror was inherent in Kikuyu society. Estimates of the movement's growth were political claims on the future. The more initiates there were before the emergency, the more the entire tribe was a criminal gang which had forfeited all prospective liberties. The very limited data available from the screening teams, which certified people's loyalties, support the liberal view. They suggest that the number of Mau Mau members, at least in the Kiambu district of the reserve, more than doubled in the first five months of the emergency.[10] If one were treated as Mau Mau by the police, it looks as if it seemed prudent to become one.

These blurred distinctions on both sides, in which the divided

[8] 'Report on the sociological causes underlying Mau Mau with some proposals on the means of ending it' (mimeograph, 21 April 1954, seen by courtesy of Greet Kershaw), paras 2 and 34.

[9] Rob Buijtenhuijs, *Essays on Mau Mau* (Leiden, 1982), 35–6, discusses Mau Mau recruitment rates.

[10] Figures seen by courtesy of Greet Kershaw; full discussion must await her own publication.

opinions of peace were compromised by the tactical agreements of war, have been insufficiently recognised. The evidence has to be read with these tensions in mind. The white conventional wisdoms of the day glossed over them, skimming with care the fragile surface of racial solidarity. They only begin to address the question of evil. But one has to start with them before one can follow the divisions, white and black, which lead one down to the roots of social dread.

Common knowledge and private doubt

At the time whites thought Mau Mau uniquely depraved, even by the standards of modern terror and partisan war. It stood condemned on three grounds, its leader's treachery, the bestiality of its ritual, and its savage killings. Kenyatta, who had enjoyed the best that Britain offered, a course of study at the London School of Economics (LSE) and the love of an English wife, was the most likely artificer of the oaths.[11] British propaganda found it easy to present these as obscene and degrading. Mau Mau oaths produced Mau Mau murders. The murder and magic will be considered first, leaving the making of the manager till later.

The American journalist John Gunther remarked that Mau Mau killings were, 'as everybody knows, peculiarly atrocious'. Victims were 'chopped to bits', partly for security's sake; all gang members had to join in and share the guilt. They might also remove a corpse's accusing eyes, for Kikuyu were 'profoundly superstitious'.[12] Perhaps some reporters were too superstitious of what 'everybody knew'; for one of them, Graham Greene, thought that a Bren gun wounded just as savagely as a *panga*, the heavy farm knife used by Mau Mau, as the British demonstrated to passers-by in exposing guerrilla corpses.[13] The one systematic survey of Mau Mau victims suggested that chopping up was in fact rare. Dr Wilkinson examined 210 dead. Yes, many had multiple wounds. But these were generally superficial. The fatal ones were often six blows to the head, almost as if insurgents had been taught to ensure 'a quick and certain death for their victims'.[14]

As to the oaths, they made sensational reading. It was reliably reported that initiates swore allegiance while swallowing a stew of mutton or goat, vegetables and cereals, sprinkled with soil, marinated in goat's blood, watched by uprooted sheep's eyes transfixed on thorns.

[11] To use the language of Bishop L. J. Beecher, 'Christian counter-revolution to Mau Mau', in F. S. Joelson (ed.), *Rhodesia and East Africa* (1958), 82.

[12] John Gunther, *Inside Africa* (New York, 1953, 1954, 1955), 361.

[13] Graham Greene to editor, *The Times*, 1 December 1953, under the heading 'A nation's conscience'.

[14] J. Wilkinson, 'The Mau Mau Movement: some general and medical aspects', *East Africa Medical Jl*, 31, 7 (1954), 309–10.

All this was cruel, not bestial.[15] But that was just the beginning of horror. For it was reported, possibly less reliably in some respects, that oaths became more ghastly as the war dragged on and insurgents despaired. Many writers left the details unsaid and readers' imaginations free to range in fascinated self-disgust. Others adopted a formula which withheld 'the full details' but then gave specifics which one could scarcely bear to think of as less than complete. If it was enough to say, with Blundell, that they included 'masturbation in public, the drinking of menstrual blood, unnatural acts with animals, and even the penis of dead men' then even a dirty mind must shrink from exploring further.[16] Yet many whites continued to employ Kikuyu. They badgered officials to waive emergency rules in respect of their employees.[17] Whatever they said in public, whites acted in private as if cross-racial trust and the wage relation were stronger than any oath, however bestial.[18]

Social order and moral confusion

After this public horror it is instructive to remember that the principal white authority on Mau Mau, Louis Leakey, said nothing about their ritual in his first account of the oaths. Initiates' deeds did not offend custom; in any culture legal oaths were strong meat. It was the sociology of oathing which, he thought, subverted Kikuyu values. Customary oaths-at-law were voluntary acts of responsible adults, taken in the open, before witnesses and by agreement with close relatives who risked magical harm in the event of a litigant's perjury.

[15] All this is to be found not only in white narratives and Mau Mau memoirs but also in a scholarly Kikuyu account: R. M. Githige, 'The religious factor in Mau Mau with particular reference to Mau Mau oaths' (University of Nairobi MA thesis, 1978). The white attitude to the oaths can most conveniently be found in Colonial Office, *Historical survey of the origins and growth of Mau Mau* (Cmnd. 1030, 1960), 163–70 (cited henceforth as *Corfield report*).

[16] Blundell, *Wind*, 168; one must be thankful that the British popular press did not then include the *Sun*.

[17] R. D. F. Ryland (Officer-in-charge Nairobi extra-provincial district) to R. G. Turnbull (Minister for African affairs), 23 December 1954: Kenya National Archives, Nairobi (KNA), MAA. 9/930.

[18] KNA, Rift Valley Province annual report (1953), 2, 16, reporting the systematic screening of the remaining Kikuyu farmworkers after large-scale repatriation to the reserve in early 1953: while 95 per cent were shown to have been oathed, no less than 80 per cent were allowed to remain at work. Much evidence could be cited which casts doubt on the factual details of the 'advanced' oaths other than in the minds of some interrogators. But there is no reason to doubt the public masturbation (mentioned also by Frank Kitson, below). See, L. S. B. Leakey, *The southern Kikuyu before 1903* (1977), i, 24, ii, 691–2; and H. E. Lambert, *Kikuyu social and political institutions* (1956), 53–4, for the ceremonial group rape-cum-masturbation performed by circumcision initiates in the past, to symbolise the ending of adolescent restrictions. Leakey's material was collected in 1937, Lambert's in the 1930s and '40s.

Mau Mau oaths were often taken under duress, at night, in unlit huts, in the presence of persons unknown, without the knowledge of kin.[19] While Leakey did briefly mention the Mau Mau cocktail in a later book, he again stressed something different, the morally liminal status of initiates. These had to undergo for a second, customarily unthinkable, time the passage between careless youth and tested adulthood, by crawling through a ceremonial circumcision arch before taking the oath. Leakey believed that enforced re-entry into this fluid state must cause intense shock.[20] Blundell thought that oathing sowed a 'mind-destroying disease'.[21]

Leakey was no disinterested expert; he regarded himself as both Kikuyu elder and white settler. From his accounts one can infer an explanation of evil deeper than any drinking of a devil's brew, and one to which many Kikuyu subscribed.[22] What disturbed him was the mixing of moral and social categories which Kikuyu culture separated in creating order. Mau Mau's offence lay in its confusion between persons of hitherto distinct legal status, gender and generation; its subversion of morally responsible legal tests, which resolved disputes, into coerced submission to unknown wills; and its inversion of actions proper to the day, social time, into the deeds of anti-social time, of darkness visible and spiritual.

Disease enters society, body and mind by subverting order or infiltrating boundaries, natural or socially invented. This was the internal Kikuyu evil of which Leakey warned, with the elders. But Mau Mau also presented whites with a violent concentration of all the dangers to which their own Kenya was exposed. The essence of treason was social dissolution, twice over. If tribes were tottering, one had to ask if white supremacy could survive.

Before the Second World War the colonial world had rested on a mental construction of social separation. Rulers and ruled were distinguished, and differentially valued, by their race. Subjects, otherwise anonymous, were recognised by tribe. Tribal character was inherited in cultural isolation. Colonial rule, cash and Christianity were then a whirlwind of change which uprooted communal fences, especially around the fields of labour and learning. Here Africans invaded the white world[23] and injured their own. 'Detribalised' and

[19] L. S. B. Leakey, *Mau Mau and the Kikuyu* (1952), 98–100.

[20] L. S. B. Leakey, *Defeating Mau Mau* (1954), 77–81.

[21] Blundell, *Wind*, 171.

[22] See Ngugi wa Thiong'o, *Weep not child* (1964), 83f., where the elderly Nogotho saw no harm in Mau Mau oaths but was shocked that they were administered by his son. Also, B. A. Ogot, 'Revolt of the elders', chapter 7 in Ogot (ed.), *Hadith 4: Politics and nationalism in colonial Kenya* (Nairobi, 1972).

[23] The metaphor is Gunther's: *Inside Africa*, 9.

'semi-educated', they were failures in themselves and a threat to whites. On entering Kenya, therefore, settlers also entered a debate on how to construct political security on shifting social sands. It was never resolved. Some thought Africans inherently primitive, others that they were backward children who promised well as modern men. Some thought white control needed African adaptation, propping up tribal authorities against the gale in segregated but progressive local governments; others favoured assimilation, at least for the tiny minority of educated Africans. Some thought all African unrest must be repressed, others that cooptation was cheaper and safer in the end.[24] Africans were similarly divided. More tried to link the imported imperial and domestic household civilising missions within invented ethnic nationalisms than in a still more imaginary 'Kenya'.

After 1945 these border issues became ever more complex. The segmentary domains of political control were subject to trespass, as competing economic interests sought access to the high politics of Nairobi.[25] Conflict wracked all political levels. At the centre the watchword was 'multiracialism', but Africans were denied the political resources which might have won their cooperation. The local politics of African control engaged the collaboration only of very small elites while placing ever heavier burdens on peasants in the public works of soil conservation. In the deeper politics of labour, both paternalist white employers and anonymous black townsmen opposed the labour department's attempts to regulate their relations within registered trades unions.[26] The deepest politics of all opposed labour to land on the White Highlands. The Maasai had formerly grazed most of this area. Little more than one per cent—but the richest part—had been Kikuyu land. Settlers claimed sole right to the land by virtue of treaty and achievement; it was their one sure footing in uncertain times. Their squatters claimed a share, earned by two generations of labouring to tame the land.[27] But white farmers no

[24] For the debate in Kenya see, Robert G. Gregory, *Sidney Webb and East Africa* (Berkeley and Los Angeles, 1962); B. E. Kipkorir, 'The Alliance high school and the origins of the Kenya African elite' (Cambridge University Ph.D thesis, 1969); Kenneth J. King, *Pan-Africanism and education* (Oxford, 1961); Bruce Berman, *The dialectics of domination* (London, forthcoming, 1990); and in South Africa for the same period, Saul Dubow, *Racial segregation and the origins of apartheid in South Africa 1919–36* (Basingstoke, 1989).

[25] Throup, *Origins*; Berman, *Dialectics*.

[26] Anthony Clayton and Donald C. Savage, *Government and labour in Kenya 1895–1963* (1974), 265–346; Sharon B. Stichter, 'Workers, trade unions and the Mau Mau rebellion', *Canadian J. Afr. Studies*, ix (1975), 259–75; Frederick Cooper, *On the African Waterfront* (1987), 78–203.

[27] Something more than an old retainer's loyalty brought former headman Njombo back to Nellie Grant's farm to die in 1947; eighteen years later his heirs were among

longer wanted a tenantry and squatters had no wish to become mere labour; they called in the defensive resources of tribe. The conflict between settler and squatter, capital and labour, class and tribe, was the most bitterly complex border dispute in all the unfinished business of Kenya.[28]

Mau Mau blew indecision apart. It outraged tribal elders and household authority at the base of control. Its Kikuyu militance also fractured and then seemed to dominate the pan-ethnic urban elite, the only possible basis of African cooptation. Mau Mau thus destroyed past and blasted future images of social control. Policy could no longer wait on events. It had to be made. But a scapegoat had to be found for the crisis, an infiltrator-in-chief, Kenyatta.

Most whites feared and loathed Kenyatta, probably more for his English marriage than his trips to Moscow.[29] District officers resented the way his oratory had broken the politics of progress in Kikuyuland, when women downed hoes and refused to terrace their hills against soil erosion.[30] Missionaries, who may once have nursed him back to life, heard reports that he was attacking the faith which had saved him.[31] Settlers blamed him for stirring up squatters.[32] The rise of Mau Mau then proved Kenyatta, the enemy of tribal progress, to be a tribalist traitor to the African elite. Only he was clever enough to invent the oaths, perhaps at the LSE where, it was guessed, his anthropology had covered European witchcraft.[33] He also had charisma. His tours in early 1952 had everywhere been followed by, and

those who bought her out in a syndicate called Mataguri ('we have been here a long time') Farm: Huxley, *Nellie*, 165, 270.

[28] Kanogo, *Squatters*; Furedi, *Mau Mau war*; Throup, *Origins*, chapter 5.

[29] Kikuyu politicians must have distrusted Kenyatta as much as whites; before his departure for England they had sworn him against going with a white woman. Conversely, it seems that Kenyatta was more terrified by Moscow than inspired; see, Robin Cohen, editor's 'Introduction' to A. T. Nzula *et al.*, *Forced labour in colonial Africa* ([Moscow, 1933], London, 1979), 15. I owe this reference to David Throup.

[30] Throup, *Origins*, 152–64, shows how little the government understood Kenyatta's position in this 'terrace war'.

[31] Jeremy Murray-Brown, *Kenyatta* (1972), 45, reports how the young Kenyatta was nursed through pthisis by Scots missionaries in 1910; by 1951 pthisis had become 'some spine disease', an operation for which saved his life: see W. O. Tait, memorandum, May 1951, in press cutting file on Kenyatta with *The Standard*, Nairobi. M. G. Capon, 'Kikuyu 1948, a working answer', September 1948: KNA, DC/MUR.3/4/21.

[32] Throup, *Origins*, 129–30.

[33] Colony and Protectorate of Kenya (CPK), J. C. Carothers, *The Psychology of Mau Mau* (Nairobi, 1954), 16, is cautious on this point; Beecher, 'Christian counter-revolution', 82, much less so, comparing him with Marx and Engels in the British Museum. This accusation lingered long after it was understood that there was nothing exotic about the oaths, which merely reworked Kikuyu symbols of dangerous power: the strongest white attack on Kenyatta on this point was also the last; see, *Corfield Report*, 169–70.

must therefore have instigated, a spate of oaths and murders. He had got Kikuyu to boycott bottled beer. Yet his denunciations of Mau Mau, at government request, were ineffective; his heart cannot have been in them. This was the supporting evidence in Baring's request to call an emergency.[34] The presumed backwardness and conformity of tribes did not admit of any other than a sorcerous explanation for the cunning and internecine ferocity of Mau Mau.

To deconstruct the evil of Mau Mau is to reconstruct past boundaries of morally valid knowledge and power. It is to find not that Mau Mau was an official invention, as the British left thought, an alibi for suppressing legitimate African politics, but dreadful reality, a diseased image of the right social group relations which ought to order colonial life. In the several Mau Maus of their minds whites negotiated fresh African stereotypes, to bring new order out of confusion. In simpler times their model of black cultural transition had been a compensating process of loss and gain in which tribal identities were diluted into a larger, civilised one. Mau Mau smashed that innocent picture. Transition now looked like trauma. Loss of identity seemed to stir somnolent savagery. Education did not lead modern men out of the past; it allowed amoral men to awaken atavistic fears. Whites had to revise their ideas of social explanation.

Two ideas competed to control the conduct of war. Race was the most obvious boundary under threat, and was most simply defended by hardening the polemical frontier between white civilisation and black savagery. Conservatives thus demanded an end to the liberal imperial promises which had aroused primitive envy. But if that had been Mau Mau's only border outrage, it could never have been punished with such cost and brutality in a just war by the decolonising empire of the 1950s. Kwame Nkrumah was already the Queen's chief minister in the Gold Coast. The compelling construction of Mau Mau, which won the whites the right to fight the war, was of wider application. In this the unrest was within the African soul, on its psychic frontier between tradition and modernity, community and society, tribe and nation. Racial repression might have sharpened the conflict, but its cause was the trauma of transition. Mau Mau had to be destroyed, of course. But while diehards fought to keep the Kikuyu on the far bank of the river of transition, white liberals knew it had to be crossed. Peace would come only when Kikuyu society was on the modern side. The need for wartime allies, local Africans and the

[34] Baring, top secret telegram to Lyttelton, 10 Oct. 1952: PRO, CO.822/443, and reproduced in Charles Douglas-Home, *Evelyn Baring, the last proconsul* (1978), 227–8. See also, Kingsley Martin's reports in *New Statesman*, 22 November 1952, 'The case against Jomo Kenyatta'; and 6 December 1952, 'The African point of view'.

home government, nerved the liberal imagination to convert this conventional wisdom into government action. Whites thus failed to agree on a fresh African stereotype; they fought the war on different premises. Privately, many thought any means tolerable for punishing ancient Africa; publicly, government strove to force the modern transition.

This public, liberal construction of the issue did not, however, win the peace. Nor did its Christian subtext of spiritual conversion. Measures of modernity and loyalty were, it is true, used to ration out the franchise for the first African general elections in 1957. This was seen as essential for a future common electoral roll, in which white 'standards' would be safe. But this making of the future was blocked by African parliamentary boycotts and then killed by the deaths of eleven Mau Mau detainees at Hola camp in early 1959. At Lancaster House in 1960, the modernising mission gave way to political bargaining. The ideas which opened up, and then controlled, this longer future, were held by those who fought the war and were bound to outlast it, the British army and members of Kikuyu agrarian society. Generals were part of the British establishment; Tory politicians, their civil partners, finally accepted the army's view of the war. Mau Mau warriors were not privy to Kikuyu authority; they called themselves its *itungati*, its warrior servants. Their seniors, most of them 'loyalists', begrudged their service but enjoyed its rewards.

The conservative view

Mau Mau's horror united whites in demanding its forcible suppression. But the ambiguities of political security, based either on adapting African society or assimilating African individuals, divided them over the sort of power to which force must answer. Conservatives demanded a return to white supremacy and tribal discipline. Liberals thought that white control would be more surely preserved if Mau Mau were isolated in African opinion. This must mean some sharing of power between the races, as represented by their educated individuals. One cannot reduce their differences to class interest, between, say, liberal businessmen and hardline farmers. Theirs was too small a community for that, but the insecurity of farming on a mortgage was probably the closest Europeans came to living out a personal analogy of their community as a whole, an experience which put 'firmness' foremost in race relations.

The highland farm mocked white supremacy in its daily confusion of categories. A tribute to middle-class English effort, it was also the site of black peasant expansion. Whites had turned the transhumant pasture of Maasailand into field and meadow. They supported not only themselves but dozens of African farm families, immigrants from the cultivating peoples to whom Maasailand had previously been denied. Workers owed a reciprocal duty of loyal labour. But squatters were not a dependent class, tied by a moral economy of protection and service. They created their own tribal communities in hidden corners of white estates. They were part of white domestic life and yet unknowable. The tensions of the squatter relationship broke into conflict after the war. District councils enacted orders to restrict squatter rights to cultivation and pasture, and to require more labour. This reflected the settlers' new ability to farm intensively; wartime boom had liquidated debt. The political consolidation of civilisation was also urgent. The highland achievement must become unequivocally white. Squatters resisted the new contracts, talking of white 'sin' and 'hypocrisy'. Even white labour inspectors used the language of 'moral entitlement'.[35] Many settlers refused or failed to repudiate their squatters' rights. Nonetheless, squatter resistance had to be deprived of legitimacy. One district council counterattacked by infantilising 'the African', 'still a savage and a child', who responded to 'firmness' with a new 'respect' for whites who removed his freedoms.[36] It is difficult not to conclude that white guilt was assuaged by racial contempt. Africans ought not to make their masters behave so badly.

Most whites knew Mau Mau as the squatter armed. It was a stab in the back, 'a revolt of the domestic staff... It was as though Jeeves had taken to the jungle.'[37] The conservative response was the settler alarmed. It had six strands, entwined in a circular argument. The first related grievance and terror. Kikuyu had no grievance; white settlement had allowed them to colonise Maasailand. Since Mau Mau could not appeal against wrong, it had to impose by fear.[38] Then why had it emerged? Since 1945, in Kenya as elsewhere, 'the spineless policies of the rulers seemed to encourage the revolt of their subjects'.[39] Talk of democracy invited questions. Once privilege was queried, envy stirred. Thirdly, democracy was a 'fantastic idea'[40] for people whose recent history showed them unfitted to exercise it. Settlers were prepared to accept that Africans were potentially equal; but search their history and one found only alternating autocracy and anarchy. Mau Mau warned how thin was the modern veneer. Fourth, education had not improved Africans; Kenyatta's career suggested the

[35] Kanogo, *Squatters*, 45, 65, 72.

[36] Uasin Gishu district council resolution, April 1947, quoted in Furedi, *Mau Mau war*, 35–6.

[37] Graham Greene, *Ways of escape* (1980), 188; I owe this reference to David Throup.

[38] Most succinctly put by C. J. Wilson, *Kenya's warning* (Nairobi, 1954), 59.

[39] C. T. Stoneham, *Out of barbarism* (1955), 105.

[40] 'The voice of the settler', anonymous correspondent to *New Statesman* (4 October 1952), 378.

reverse. Fifthly, as for the squatters, so for Africans generally, firmness, even force, was the language they understood. Finally, the answer was plain. European dominance must be restored. In centuries to come, alien discipline might have shaped African potential. For the moment, they must respect whites more than they feared Mau Mau. If all this was too much for Whitehall, then settlers knew where to find friends, further south in Africa.[41]

For many whites the emergency offered, more simply, the prospect of revenge. That was why Baring had to reinforce its declaration with airlifted British troops. He feared that settlers would otherwise privately supply any violence the state appeared to lack.[42] From the start, he was determined not to fight a racial war. In the empire of 1952 that would in any case have been impossible.

Liberal pragmatism

Conservatives said what they meant. Liberals dissembled. This was partly because ignorance and panic made them share conservative views. It also preserved a united front. Lyttelton, colonial secretary, told the settlers that Mau Mau was not the child of economic pressure.[43] That was to calm them down; he himself knew better. Two months earlier his officials had considered with Baring, before he flew out, reforms which might meet 'any legitimate grievance of law-abiding Africans'. Baring called reform his 'second prong', to make the first, repression, look presentable. It was also an essential tactic of war. The government must stop driving moderate Africans into the arms of the extremists. Baring might well have to decide 'either to "bust" or "buy" Kenyatta'.[44] Events precluded that. London had to buy the settlers or they might bust the government. Some cried 'appeasement' when Baring revealed the second prong. If he was to keep the settlers at heel he would have to mind his tongue.[45] Official statements followed the conservative line.

Official action was different, and it remade Mau Mau in many official minds. Policy steered between two rocks of disaster. First, the settlers must be allowed no increase in power. They must not be stampeded into a ferment which could be calmed only by concession.

[41] This composite picture is drawn from *ibid.*; Stoneham, *Barbarism*; and Wilson, *Before the dawn* and *Kenya's warning*.

[42] Baring to Lyttelton, 9 October 1952: PRO, CO.822/443.

[43] Lyttelton, radio broadcast from Nairobi, 4 November 1952 (transcript in KNA, CD.5/173); and repeated in his statement to parliament: *House of Commons debates*, 5th series, vol. 507 (7 November 1952), col. 459.

[44] W. Gorell Barnes to Baring, 10 September 1952; note of a meeting with Baring, 23 September 1952: PRO, CO.822/544.

[45] I have adopted Kingsley Martin's reading of the situation: *New Statesman*, 8 November 1952.

Yet the state had to answer African grievance. For the second need was to prevent Mau Mau 'infecting' other African peoples; there was anxious evidence that it might.[46] The deputy head of the colonial office, Jeffries, squared the circle with some dog-eared official wisdom. 'The only sound line', he believed, was to 'build up a substantial "middle class" of *all* races to be the backbone of the country'.[47] This was by now the standard spell for conjuring new order out of colonial confusion. Race barriers must melt into class coalitions. Meanwhile a war had to be fought. Yet most of Kenya was at peace and must so remain. An awful war needed a beastly enemy. A solid peace needed radical reform. An ideology which joined the two in causal sequence emerged from the daily discourse of harassed men.

This liberal doctrine adopted a new stereotype, 'the African in transition'. It diagnosed Mau Mau as a disease which demanded as cure none other than the government's best intentions of the post-war years. It was codified by Dr Carothers, once a local medical officer who now practised psychiatry in England. He had been asked back to reassure the commissioner for community development, Askwith, that his approach to rehabilitating detainees was on the right lines.[48] He assumed that they were possessed by evil, and must be cleansed by customary public confession, paid labour, literacy classes, instruction in the beneficent colonial history of Kenya and, if they chose, by Christian witness.[49] It was a working theory of a guided transition. Carothers was asked to comment on the ideas of practical men; he did much more.

His contribution to constructing Mau Mau was to theorise the detention camps' commonsense concept of a crisis in modernisation, a war for the soul of transitional man. He had just published a liberal treatment of African psychiatry, which stressed the role of environment rather than heredity. The preliterate tribal personality, he had argued, was moulded from outside by the conformity of the community. Literate western man was inner-directed, disciplined by the competition of society. This general work neither mentioned Mau Mau nor forecast any unusual psychiatric problems for 'the African in transition'.[50] But when Carothers came to investigate, he found

[46] P. Rogers, minute to Gorell Barnes, 24 October 1952; Rogers, minute to Sir Charles Jeffries, 16 February 1953; Lyttelton to Baring, 5 March 1953: PRO, CO.822/440.

[47] Jeffries, minute to Lloyd, 17 February 1953 (original emphasis): CO.822/440.

[48] T. G. Askwith, typescript memoirs, chapter on 'Mau Mau', p. 8, seen by courtesy of the author.

[49] CPK, *Community development organization annual report 1953* (Nairobi, 1954), 2–3; CPK, *Annual report of the department of community development and rehabilitation 1954* (Nairobi, 1955), 21–33.

[50] J. C. Carothers, *The African mind in health and disease* (World Health Organization, Geneva, 1953), 54–5, 130–3.

that Mau Mau was, in part, a reaction to insecurity. Transitional men would have lost many cultural supports while still dreading the power of external, magical 'wills'. Their grievances would tell them that whites controlled a richer store of these than they did. Here lay the cunning of Mau Mau; its oaths promised redress of the magical balance.[51]

Carothers has been much misinterpreted, perhaps because he allowed his understanding to change as he wrote, without then revising earlier passages.[52] It is remembered that he thought the Kikuyu, allegedly secretive forest-dwellers with little of the music of social cohesion in their souls, very ill-fitted to the transition. It is forgotten that his report ended with a call for planned modernisation. If Mau Mau abused the bewilderment of transitional man, Africans must be given the reassurance of modernity. Confusion of category must cease, especially in the family. Disorder reigned where incomplete transition separated traditional woman from modern man.[53] New boundaries of order must be drawn around modern genders. Again, this was the view of practical men. Askwith believed that recovery from Mau Mau was complete only in regular employment and the companionship of family. Other officials had long called for a similar remedy for wider ills.

Post-war British colonial policy assumed that neither peasantry nor unskilled urban labour could sustain social order much longer, let alone provide for development and improved welfare. Neither side of African life was self-sufficient; each was debilitated by what connected them, the oscillation of male wage labour. As Carothers fitted Mau Mau into his concept of transition, officials did likewise. Their transitional man was the migrant worker. Mau Mau travelled home with him. The slum infected the countryside.[54] Two government plans and unprecedented sums of public finance were now devoted to separating them. The labour department pressed for improved wages and conditions, to create a new basis for society, the urban African family, where before Nairobi had accommodated labour units, bachelor

[51] Carothers, *Psychology*, 6–18.

[52] J. C. Carothers, 'The nature-nurture controversy', *Psychiatry: J. for the study of interpersonal processes*, xviii (1953), 303; this was in response to critics of his WHO monograph, but the same method was openly employed in his pamphlet on Mau Mau.

[53] Carothers, *Psychology*, 22–4; a message to which I have been alerted by the work of Luise White.

[54] The best summary statement of the district commissioner's view is in Margery Perham, 'Struggle against Mau Mau II: seeking the causes and the remedies', *The Times*, 23 April 1953; while reprinted in her *Colonial sequence 1949 to 1969* (1970), 112–15, it has been given the disastrously wrong date of 1955.

workers.[55] The department of agriculture embraced a freehold revolution in land tenure to produce the rural mirror image, the peasant family able to earn an increasing income on its own land by its own labour, neither subsidising nor being subsidised by its urban sons.[56] The disorders of customary tenures would give way to survey and straight lines. Both departments seized on the emergency to argue that the risks of pushing African communities through the transition to market society were as nothing to leaving them betwixt and between. Moreover, and this was vital, they could not be accused of appeasing Mau Mau; to the contrary, they were disciplining with individual obligations the collective disorders of transitional society. Each talked openly of class as the basis of order and power.

Missionaries had a not dissimilar idea of progress. While the two 'established' British missions, Anglican and Presbyterian, supported the government's multi-racial aim to 'evolve from components at present heterogeneous, a harmonious and organic society',[57] their private history taught them that their particular role in the war against Mau Mau was to transform individuals. They had reason to hate the movement. Congregations withered in mid-1952. Some Christians were martyred. The missionary sense of history almost welcomed the catastrophe. This was the second test for the young Kikuyu churches, purging them of nominal believers to leave the faithful remnant of rebirth. Presbyterians in particular had been persecuted in 1929, in the 'female circumcision crisis'. The Kikuyu Central Association had championed clitoridectomy and then spawned independent churches and schools which were thought to have inspired the new savagery of Mau Mau.[58] Their origin in backsliding defence of an 'old, cruel and degrading practice'[59] showed their dark potential. Moreover, just as the earlier opposition had followed an unprecedented period of church growth, so Mau Mau seemed to have been galvanised to defeat the challenge of Revival. This movement, potentially anti-clerical and schismatic, challenged

[55] CPK, *Report of the committee on African wages* (Nairobi, 1954).

[56] CPK, *A plan to intensify the development of African agriculture in Kenya* (Nairobi, 1954).

[57] For Mitchell's statement, see Church Missionary Society [CMS], *Mau Mau, what is it?* (1952), 8; and Church of Scotland Foreign Missions Committee [CSM], *Mau Mau and the church* (Edinburgh, 1953), 4, where 'organic' is rendered, in a splendidly illustrative slip, as 'organised'.

[58] The director of education investigated the schooling of the first detainees and found that it was statistically no different from other Kikuyu; there was thus no evidence for the general suspicion of the independent schools, another private doubt which did not sway the conventional wisdom: CPK, *Education department annual report 1953* (Nairobi, 1955), 39–40.

[59] CMS, *Mau Mau*, 5.

missionary authority with the priesthood of all 'saved' believers.[60] It took much missionary humility to avoid schism. Having demolished their own defences, missionaries saw Mau Mau as a counter revival, to rescue Kikuyu belief for nationalist ends and break racial comity once more.[61]

Missions willingly helped in the rehabilitation work of the detention camps, which in 1954 housed one-third of Kikuyu men and not a few women. Confession of sin and Christian teaching could restore dead souls. Thus far Christians agreed; like everybody else they then divided. Most thought that individual conversion was all they could pray for, but a few came close to a concept of structural sin. The first approach, to which fundamentalist belief attracted many missionaries, got more publicity. The best-known attempt to resolve political conflict by confession of racial brotherhood was the work of Moral Rearmament. The Christian Council of Kenya (CCK), which represented the Protestant missions, never approved; and the experiment was abandoned.[62] The CCK had humbler hopes of conversion. They understood Mau Mau to be a complex phenomenon, political, economic and social as well as spiritual. Individual conversion could thus be only an adjunct to political change, not a substitute. Moreover, the churches faced a particular disability, the nature of Revival. Hitherto it had produced men and women so convinced of the power of Christ that they chose martyrdom rather than to bear arms. District officers so distrusted their pacifism that they denied Revivalists the loyalty certificates which allowed free movement.[63] The churches also despaired of using such private conviction in social action.[64] Christianity could work its miracle of reconciliation only if justice had been created by other means. That, too, was conventional Christian wisdom, at least in the liberal theology of the CCK. Its separate members, the locally rooted mission churches, had little interest in a theology of power or, therefore, in political reform.[65] Neither fun-

[60] For two Kikuyu accounts, see E. N. Wanyoike, *An African pastor* (Nairobi, 1974), 151–68; Obadiah Kariuki, *A Bishop facing Mount Kenya* (Nairobi, 1985), 46–59, 78–9; Kariuki gives a glimpse of his relations with Kenyatta, his brother-in-law, *ibid.*, 79–81.

[61] CSM, *Mau Mau and the church*, 5. For Kikuyu comparisons between Revival and Mau Mau see, Wanyoike, *African pastor*, 175, 180–5, 195 f. By contrast, Githige, 'Religious factor', arguing from oral reminiscence, is doubtful of Christianity's influence on Mau Mau, whether as inspiration or antagonist.

[62] CPK, *Annual report of the department of community development 1954*, 26.

[63] The one notable exception to Christian pacifism was shown by the independent Africa Christian Church in Murang'a, whose headquarters at Kinyona was so bellicose that Mau Mau fighters christened it 'Berlin': 'A book of forest history' recovered by Willoughby Thompson in December 1953: RH.Mss.Afr.s.1534.

[64] T. F. C. Bewes, *Kikuyu conflict: Mau Mau and the Christian witness* (1953), 41–2, 68.

[65] As in all other aspects of this essay, there is a deeper history to be told; this analysis is derived principally from S. A. Morrison, 'What does rehabilitation mean?', 5 June

damentalists nor liberals exercised the influence which has been attributed to Christian rehabilitation as a whole.

Liberal beliefs, reinforced by pragmatic action, helped officials to fight a just war of transition, however frightful. But this construction of Mau Mau failed to provide a foundation for peace. Two men at the centre of the bid for liberal authority warned that it would not. The forgotten part of Carothers' report on Mau Mau psychology argued that it was futile to remake Kikuyu in the individualist English image unless they were given the chance to exercise responsibility, which meant power. Rehabilitation would be complete only with democracy.[66] Askwith conducted rehabilitation on the same assumption. The first was only an adviser, the second was sacked for not forcing the pace, when in 1957 the African elections demanded altogether more urgency, and the administration decided that persuasion must be stiffened with 'compelling force'.[67] The views of the army were quite a different matter. It trusted neither in force nor in reform.

Soldiers and Politicians

The army fought against Mau Mau's military confusions. These were very different from those which haunted the liberal myth of modernisation. General Erskine took a plain man's view of the oaths which so disturbed most observers. He recognised that Mau Mau had grievances and an aim, to eject Europeans. The connexion between strategic end and nauseating means was crisply rational. 'Secrecy was necessary, hence oaths were administered. Money was necessary, hence the oath had to be paid for. The whole tribe had to act as one, hence oaths were administered forcibly. Discipline was necessary, hence judges and stranglers became part of the organisation. It was perfectly clear from the nature of the oaths that violence was intended. Oaths became more and more binding and bestial.'[68] Cooling the mind the better to know the enemy was carried furthest by the soldier who had the best Mau Mau war, Captain Kitson. He found obsession with horror bad for intelligence. 'Looked at over one's shoulder the oath was a frightful business, suffused in evil.' If one looked at it

---

1954, seen by courtesy of Greet Kershaw who was employed by the CCK in the 1950s. For an indication of a wider approach see, John Lonsdale, with Stanley Booth-Clibborn and Andrew Hake, 'The emerging pattern of church and state co-operation in Kenya', in Edward Fashole-Luke *et al.* (ed.), *Christianity in independent Africa* (1978), 267–84. (My two co-authors had also been CCK employees in the 1950s.)

[66] Carothers, *Psychology*, 19–20, 28–9.

[67] T. G. Askwith, in conversation, 27 July 1989; Terence Gavaghan, in conversation over the years.

[68] General Sir George Erskine, despatch, 'The Kenya emergency June 1953–May 1955', 2 May 1955: PRO, WO.236/18 (seen by courtesy of Mr Heather).

straight, what was left? 'An arch of thorns with goat's eyes impaled on them: a silly scarecrow to frighten the feeble ... what next? The initiates are abusing themselves into a bowl of blood—prep school stuff ... The whole business ... is no more than the antics of naughty schoolboys.'[69] The colonial secretary, Lyttelton, saw a nobler likeness between Kikuyu and British. A veteran of the Great War, he respected men who had 'more than once pressed home attacks against wire, and in the face of hot fire, and heavy casualties'. He had asked no more of his Grenadiers. If Mau Mau gallantry was explained by 'dutch courage', had he not too, like others in his war, braced himself with rum before battle?[70]

Such recognition of equivalence, contrary to both the racialism which denied a common humanity and the liberalism which pitied dupes, was politically important. In London Blundell was shocked to hear that Churchill thought that Kikuyu 'fibre, ability and steel' deserved to be acknowledged by an offer of terms.[71] Erskine thought like Churchill. The settlers never trusted him after his statement that Mau Mau needed a political rather than military solution.[72] But that was a soldier's reaction to guerrilla war, the most difficult of all wars to fight. It blurs the border between military and civil and so too, more than other wars, between gallantry and crime.[73] Insurgents muddy the aims and reputation of security forces by denying them the clean tactical objective of a 'fair target' or 'fair fight'.[74] Erskine therefore determined that a political war must use political means. He angered whites most with his successive surrender offers to the forest fighters. These thwarted the lust for revenge. Negotiation also denied two elements of the conservative myth, that the obscenities of the oath turned men into beasts, and that Mau Mau lacked rational aims.[75] Even Kenyan-born white police found that Mau Mau commanded their respect. After sixty-eight hours of interrogating the captured 'General China', Superintendent Ian Henderson, the hero of the settlers' war, concluded that his prisoner was 'a complete fanatic'. Was he then mentally ill? Not at all. China had 'a good brain and a remarkable memory'. He knew why he was fighting; 'his sole

[69] Frank Kitson, *Gangs and counter-gangs* (London, 1960), 131.

[70] Lyttelton, secret and personal telegram to Prime Minister Churchill, 18 May 1953: PRO, CO.822/440; Oliver Lyttelton, *The Memoirs of Lord Chandos* (1962), 41, 59.

[71] Blundell, *Wind*, 184.

[72] James Cameron, 'Bombers? Kenya needs ideas', *News Chronicle*, 15 Nov. 1953.

[73] Michael Walzer, *Just and unjust wars* (Harmondsworth, 1980), chapter 11.

[74] The quoted phrases come from Erskine's despatch of 2 May 1955, para. 17: PRO, WO.236/18; and Kitson, *Gangs*, 46.

[75] For settler outrage see, Blundell, *Wind*, 189–92, but discussion of the surrender offers must await Mr Heather's findings.

wish was to expound his political testament before Legislative Council and then walk to the gallows without trial'.[76] When he too was captured, China's successor outlined Mau Mau's objective as 'the achievement of more land and power of self-determination. They do not consider this will be achieved by violence alone, but they firmly believe that those who are sympathetic to their cause can only succeed if Mau Mau continue to fight.'[77] The opposing generals understood each other. They could only exert the military pressure needed to force a political peace.

It took the tragedy of Hola, when eleven 'hard core' detainees were beaten to death in the name of modernisation, to bring the British government round to the military view. The liberal campaign for westernisation, as bridge of transition and condition of political rights, could no longer govern policy. Political change could not wait on repentance and the growth of a politically responsible (that is, guilt-conscious) middle class. Britain could not continue to remake Kenya by force when other European powers were abandoning attempts to remodel colonial rule for the moral high ground of informal empire.[78] A political war must be ended by political means. Civilisation had to be gambled on concession and agreement, not enforced by the tyranny of good intentions and warders' truncheons. Within months of Hola came Lancaster House and the prospect of majority rule.

Discipline and delinquency

The remaking of civilisation in Kenya, then, had to be a political creation, not a confessional crusade. But whose? The man who won the peace was the man found guilty of causing the war, Kenyatta. The government had charged him with imposing evil on the Kikuyu. But there were too many Mau Maus for that. They were the product of deep conflict within Kikuyu society. Their militants were inspired by Kenyatta, of that there is no doubt. But his exhortations were overtaken by their conclusions.[79]

On the surface, Mau Mau was an anti-colonial revolt to recover Kikuyu land, and to press the claim to much of the remainder of the White Highlands which had been lodged by two generations of squatter labour. But its inner meaning was given by its junior status in a

[76] 'Interrogation of Waruhiu s/o Itote, alias "General China"' (Kenya police special branch, Nairobi, 26 January 1954), para. 14; privately held.

[77] 'Flash Report No. 1—Interrogation of Kaleba', Special branch headquarters, 28 Oct. 1954, para. 37: KNA, DC/NYK.3/12/24 (by courtesy of Mr Heather).

[78] As argued by John Darwin, *Britain and Decolonisation: the Retreat from Empire in the post-war world* (1988), 244–69.

[79] As African leaders complained to Kingsley Martin: 'The case against Jomo Kenyatta', *New Statesman*, 22 November 1952.

long struggle for patriotic virtue within Kikuyuland. Kikuyu virtue lay in the labour of agrarian civilisation, directed by household heads. Honour lay in wealth, the fruit of burning back the forest and taming the wild, creating a cultivated space in which industrious dependants too might establish themselves in self-respecting independence.[80] But by the 1940s this myth of civic virtue began to mock the majority rather than inspire. Big men no longer welcomed dependants, they expropriated them. Wages fell behind the prices of land and marriage. Young men asked whether they would ever earn enough to marry and mature.[81] Those who had most cause to fight colonial rule had the least chance to merit responsibility. Those whose deeds might deliver power would have no right to enjoy it. That was the Kikuyu tragedy, a struggle about the moralities of class formation, not mental derangement.

The right to force political change was contested between men of authority like Kenyatta, who was the son-in-law of not one but two official chiefs, and the dispossessed, legal minors. The reputable, it began to appear, could not win power except at the appalling price of owing its achievement to men they despised. These latter, the hard men of Nairobi, took over the oath of respectable unity which Kenyatta knew, and pressed it, by force, deception and persuasion on those who hoped that desperate deeds, *ngero*, would earn them what they needed, the adulthood which entitled them to share the fruits of victory. These were the men and women whom Kikuyu knew as Mau Mau, not all those who had taken the oath of unity but the few who had taken the second, fighting oath.[82] But, however much Kikuyu may have denounced Mau Mau within, few were so careless of communal solidarity or their lives that they betrayed it without. Europeans mistook this fear and solidarity for tribal unity, a mystic force. The myth of tribal unity found Kenyatta guilty. If he was the tribal leader he was responsible for everything done in his name.

Throughout his career Kenyatta taught that authority was earned by self-discipline. In 1928 he had warned of the fate of native Australians, whom the British 'found were decreasing by reason of their sloth . . . and so they got pushed to the bad parts of the land'. Kikuyu ought to follow the Maori example. The British had found them 'to be a very diligent people. And now they are permitted to select four men

[80] What follows is a too brief sketch of Kikuyu political thought which I intend to develop elsewhere.

[81] See, Meja Mwangi's novel, *Kill me quick* (Nairobi, 1973).

[82] Rosberg and Nottingham, *Myth*, 234–76; M. Tamarkin, 'Mau Mau in Nakuru', *J. Afr. Hist.*, xvii (1976), 119–34; John Spencer, *KAU, the Kenya African Union* (1985), 202–49.

to represent them in the Big Council ...'[83] This simple contrast summed up his political thought. So he too made a meaning for Mau Mau. Before a huge crowd in July 1952 he compared it to theft and drunkenness. Henderson, the police observer, thought he equivocated. But he also reported Kenyatta as asking the crowd to 'join hands for freedom and freedom means abolishing criminality'.[84] That may not be an obvious point for a nationalist orator to make, but it is what one would expect of an elder. Freedom and criminality were at opposite poles in Kikuyu thought. Freedom was *wiathi*; this enjoined not only independence from others but also self-mastery. Criminality was *umaramari* or *ngero*. The former term derived adult delinquency from childhood disobedience; the latter conveyed the idea of failing a test.[85] Kenyatta was not alone in making a delinquent Mau Mau in the mind. Even the chairman of its central committee or *kiama kia wiathi*, Eliud Mutonyi, agreed with him. A self-made businessman himself, he regretted that in the Nairobi slums, from which Mau Mau recruited so many fighters, 'poverty knows no patriotism',[86] a modern rendering of the old dismissive proverb, 'poverty has no responsibilities'. The path of fecklessness, *umaramari*, could never lead to self-rule, *wiathi*.[87]

In the forests the struggle for respectability was as fierce as the fight for freedom. Guerrillas remembered in song Kenyatta's words, 'Vagrancy and laziness do not produce benefits for our country.'[88] And they anathematised ill-disciplined gangs as *komerera*, an appellation which pairs the concepts of idleness and concealment, mere thugs who practised anti-social violence and refused to cook for their leaders. They personified the nightmares not only of military discipline but also of civic virtue.[89]

But while Nairobi's hooligans crawled under the arch of Mau Mau

[83] Editor (Kenyatta), 'Conditions in other countries', *Muiguithania* i, 3 (July 1928), translation by A. R. Barlow of the CSM. KNA, DC/MKS.10B/13/1.

[84] *Corfield report*, 305.

[85] For these and other translations I depend on T. G. Benson (ed.), *Kikuyu–English dictionary* (Oxford, 1964), and on help from friends, especially John Karanja, Tabitha Kanogo, Mungai Mbayah, Godfrey Muriuki, Henry Muoria Mwaniki and George K. Waruhiu.

[86] Eliud Mutonyi, 'Mau Mau chairman', undated typescript, copy in author's possession.

[87] This Kikuyu political logic is strong ground for thinking that Kenyatta was sincere in his denunciations of Mau Mau; if he did equivocate, he had good reason to do so in the threats made on his life by the Nairobi militants: evidence of Fred Kubai for Granada Television's 'End of empire', screened 1 July 1985.

[88] D. L. Barnett and Karari Njama, *Mau Mau from within* (1966), 180.

[89] *Ibid.*, 213, 221, 293–5, 376, 390, 397, 479, 498; Waruhiu Itote (General China), *Mau Mau general* (Nairobi, 1967), 139–41.

circumcision in search of the responsible 'spirit of manhood',[90] and then fought to earn their right to land, they did not win. The remaking of Kenya and their place in it were decided by others. On emerging from forest or detention they were landless still, indeed more so than before in a rural world now realigned by land consolidation and freehold title. They remained debarred from the creation of order, outside its boundary fence. And on his release back to political life in 1961 Kenyatta took up his old refrain. His government would not be hooligan rule. He no doubt intended to calm white farmers and foreign investors. But he had a still more anxious audience to reassure, with nowhere else to go. Most Kenyans, certainly all household heads, were relieved to discover that Kenyatta was on the side of domestic order, after all. Their traditional civilising mission has now become a modern ruling ideology. By criminalising Mau Mau once more in the public mind, as he had tried a decade earlier, Kenyatta reasserted his authority to remake Kenya.[91]

There are therefore many answers to the question I was asked two years ago by a landless taxi-driver. As a schoolboy he had taken General Matenjagwo—General matted hair—his last bowl of beans before he met his death in action. His mother had lost her land rights to the senior wife during land-consolidation. 'Why,' he asked in some indignation, 'why did they call us *imaramari*?'

[90] Cf., Gakaara wa Wanjau's *The spirit of manhood and perseverance for Africans* (Nairobi, 1952), as translated in appendix to *idem, Mau Mau author in detention* (Nairobi, 1988), 227–43.

[91] Jomo Kenyatta, *Suffering without bitterness* (Nairobi, 1968), 124, 146, 147, 154, 159, 161, 163–8, 183, 189, 204. My view of Kenyatta's attitude to Mau Mau at this time is thus entirely different from Buijtenhuijs, *Mau Mau twenty years after*, 49–61, and is supported by the picture facing page 57 in this book, showing ex-Mau Mau in 1971 with the slogan 'Mau Mau is still alive: we don't want revolution in Kenya'.

THE ROYAL HISTORICAL SOCIETY

REPORT OF COUNCIL, SESSION 1989–1990

THE Council of the Royal Historical Society has the honour to present the following report to the Anniversary Meeting.

This year has been of particular importance for the future study of history in Britain, with the work of the National Curriculum History Working Group attracting much public interest. Council made very full responses to both the Interim and Final Reports, strongly supporting the general approach and recommendations of the Group, and worked hard to ensure that public discussion was not diverted from the essential issues. Naturally, Council continued to maintain very close contact with both the Historical Association and the History at the Universities Defence Group in their efforts to enhance the status and vitality of history teaching everywhere.

Council has pursued this same goal in a variety of other ways. In response to a request from the Advisory Board for the Research Councils, comments were submitted to its Working Group on Peer Review. Council continued to support financially the Historical Association's Young Historian Scheme, having been impressed with the success of the Scheme's first year of operation. Further encouragement was given to the organisers of the Cadbury-Schweppes Prize, who decided to invite entries for at least two more years from those involved in history degree teaching. Council has established a fund to support 'New Initiatives' in historical research and teaching; it has also continued to assist the work of the Association for History and Computing, has contributed to the V. H. Galbraith Memorial Fund at St. Hilda's College, Oxford, and has increased the value of the Society's own Alexander Prize. In recognition of the Dulwich Picture Gallery's outstanding educational achievements, further grants have been made from the Robinson Bequest to assist its exhibition programme; and assistance has been offered in response to the appeal from the National Library of Romania.

Significant developments have taken place in other aspects of the Society's own affairs. Having recognised the desirability of involving the whole Fellowship of the Society much more directly in the choice of Councillors, Council put forward a series of amendments to the By-Laws as the means of providing the Society with an open and liberal constitution suited to its large membership and to its role as the leading Society in the profession. These were adopted at the Anniversary Meeting in November 1989 and are being steadily introduced. Thanks to extremely generous grants from both the Leverhulme Foundation and the British Academy very substantial progress has been made in equipping and staffing the Society's major project for developing the *Bibliographies of British History*. For the time being, however, Council has decided to abandon plans for a parallel series of bibliographies of European history. It has also set in train a review of the progress and future development of the *Studies in History* monograph series. The decision has also been taken to begin a new series of the Society's *Transactions*. The first volume will include not only the papers read to ordinary meetings of the Society, but also those delivered at the annual one-day conference held in September 1990; in future the List of Fellows will be published separately.

Council was delighted to note the conferral of a knighthood on Professor J. C. Holt in the New Year Honours.

An evening party to mark the Centenary of the Society's Royal Charter was held for members and guests in the Upper Hall at University College London on Wednesday, 5 July 1989. 173 acceptances to invitations were received, and, despite the unhappy coincidence of another one-day rail strike, it was well-attended.

At the Anniversary Meeting on 17 November 1989, Dr J. A. Ramsden was elected to succeed Dr H. C. G. Matthew as Literary Director, and the remaining Officers of the Society were re-elected. The Society is, however, still without an Honorary Solicitor.

The representation of the Society upon various bodies was as follows: Professor G. W. S. Barrow, Mr M. Roper and Professor P. H. Sawyer on the Joint Committee of the Society and the British Academy established to prepare an edition of Anglo-Saxon charters; Professor H. R. Loyn on a committee to promote the publication of photographic records of the more significant collections of British Coins; Professor P. Lasko on the Advisory Council of the reviewing committee on the Export of Works of Art; Dr G. H. Martin on the Council of the British Records Association; Mr M. R. D. Foot on the Committee to advise the publishers of *The Annual Register*; Professor K. Cameron on the Trust for Lincolnshire Archaeology; Professor W. Doyle on the History at the Universities Defence Group; Dr A. I. Doyle on the Anthony Panizzi Foundation; Professor N. McCord on the Council of the British Association for Local History; and Dr Alice Prochaska on the National Council for Archives. Council received reports from its representatives.

Professor E. B. Fryde represents the Society on a committee to regulate British co-operation in the preparation of a new repertory of medieval sources to replace Potthast's *Bibliotheca Historica Medii Aevi*;

Professor Glanmor Williams on the Court of the University College of Swansea; Professor A. L. Brown on the University Conference of Stirling University; Professor W. Doyle on the Court of the University of Exeter; Professor C. N. L. Brooke on the British Sub-Commission of the Commission International d'Histoire Ecclésiastique Comparée; and Professor W. A. Speck at the Computers in Teaching Initiatives Centre for History. During the year, Professor A. G. Watson agreed to succeed Professor A. I. Doyle as the Society's representative on the Anthony Panizzi Foundation, and Miss Valerie Cromwell and Professor N. Hampson agreed to act on the Society's behalf on the British National Committee of the International Historical Congress. The Society also accepted an invitation to be included in the revised charter of the British School at Rome as a body nominating a member to the Schools' Council.

The Vice-Presidents retiring under By-law XVI were Professor R. B. Dobson and Professor G. S. Holmes. Mr. M. Roper and Professor C. S. R. Russell were elected to replace them. The members of Council retiring under By-law XIX were Dr C. T. Allmand, Professor K. Leyser, Professor B. S. Pullan and Professor C. S. R. Russell. Dr. Caroline Barron, Professor N. Hampson, Dr A. J. Pollard and Professor M. C. Prestwich were elected to fill the vacancies.

Messrs. Davies, Watson and Co., were appointed auditors for the year 1989–90 under By-law XXVIII.

Publications and Papers read

The Handbook of British Diplomatic Representatives, 1508–1688, ed. G. Bell, (Guides and Handbooks, No. 16), and *Transactions, Fifth Series,* Volume 40, and *The Diary of Sir J. Trelawny in the 1860s,* ed. T. A. Jenkins, (Camden, Fourth Series, Volume 40) went to press during the session and are due to be published in September and November 1990 respectively. The following works were published during the session: *Camden, Miscellany XXX*, (Camden, Fourth Series, Volume 39); and 5 volumes in the STUDIES IN HISTORY series: *Sir Robert Heath, 1574–1649: Window on an Age*, Paul E. Kopperman, (Volume 56); *Britain, the United States, and the end of the Palestine Mandate, 1942–1948,* Ritchie Ovendale, (Volume 57); *Protecting the Pub: Brewers and Publicans against Temperance,* David W. Gutzke, (Volume 58); *Parliamentary Army Chaplains, 1642–1651*, Anne Laurence, (Volume 59); and *Bertie of Thame: Edwardian Ambassador*, Keith Hamilton, (Volume 60).

At the ordinary meetings of the Society the following papers were read:

'Thomas Hobbes as a Theorist of Liberty', by Professor Quentin Skinner (5 July 1989: Prothero lecture).
'Two Abbots in Politics: Wala of Corbie and Bernard of Clairvaux', by Professor Henry Mayr-Harting (13 October 1989).
'The Construction of Mau Mau', by Dr John Lonsdale (8 December 1989).
'Social mentalities and the case of medieval scepticism' by Miss Susan M. G. Reynolds (26 January 1990).
'The Reputation of Robert Cecil' by Dr Pauline Croft (2 March 1990).
'The Decline and Fall of Slavery in Brazil, 1850–1888' by Professor L. M. Bethell (20 April 1990).

At the Anniversary Meeting on 17 November 1989, the President, Professor F. M. L. Thompson, delivered an address on 'English Landed Society in the Twentieth Century: I, Property, Collapse and Survival'.

A one-day conference entitled 'Elites, Enterprise and Industrial Society' was held in the British Local History Room at the Institute of Historical Research on 23 September 1989 at which the following papers were read:

'Reflections on Entrepreneurship and Culture in European Economies' by Professor Sidney Pollard;
'Enterprise and Welfare States' by Dr Jose F. Harris;
'The Professional Elite, Liberal Education and Economic Lag in Britain, 1850–1980' by Dr Adrian Wooldridge; and
'Doctors, Public Service and Profit: the Medical Profession and the National Health Service' by Dr Charles Webster.

The Whitfield Prize for 1989 was awarded to Dr Gervase Rosser for his book *Medieval Westminster, 1200–1540,* (Clarendon Press).

The Alexander Prize for 1990 was awarded to Ms. S. C. Lockwood, for her essay *Marsilius of Padua and the Case for the Royal Ecclesiastical Supremacy*, which was read to the Society on 18 May 1990.

Membership

Council records with regret the deaths of 21 Fellows, 2 Associates and 2 Corresponding Fellows. Among these Council would mention especially Professor J. R. Dinwiddy, a member of Council, and Corresponding Fellows, Mons M. Giusti and Professor J. Prawer.

The resignation of 6 Fellows, 2 Associates and 13 Subscribing Libraries were received. 75 Fellows and 3 Associates were elected and 4 Libraries were admitted. 38 Fellows transferred to the category of Retired Fellow. The membership of the Society on 30 June 1990 comprised 1811 Fellows (including 14 Life Fellows and 201 Retired Fellows), 37 Corresponding Fellows, 149 Associates and 682 Subscribing Libraries (1771, 39, 151 and 691 respectively on 30 June

1989). The Society exchanged publications with 14 Societies, British and foreign.

Finance

The Society's income has continued to show a sizeable increase in 1989/90 as in 1988/89, which reflects both the change in the level of subscriptions agreed by the Anniversary Meeting in November 1988, and the performance of the Society's investments. The higher income has been offset by an increase in expenditure, in particular upon publications, which has led to a fall in the excess of income over expenditure to £25,522 from £27,275 in the year 1988/89. The finances of the Society are still in a position to allow the active pursuit of its policy of new initiatives, which will be reflected in increased expenditure in the next financial year.

Benefactors of the Royal Historical Society:

Mr L. C. Alexander
The Reverend David Berry
Professor Andrew Browning
Mrs W. M. Frampton
Sir George Prothero
Professor T. G. Reddaway
Miss E. M. Robinson
Professor A. S. Whitfield

ROYAL HISTORICAL SOCIETY

Balance Sheet as at 30th June 1990

	Notes	1990 £	1990 £	1989 £	1989 £
Fixed Assets	2		1,993		2,700
Investments	3		730,897		666,210
Current Assets					
Stocks	1(c)	5,756		6,007	
Debtors	4	14,922		15,849	
Cash at Bank and in Hand	5	18,349		14,246	
		39,027		36,102	
Creditors: Amounts falling due within one year	6	45,430		45,284	
Net Current Liabilities			(6,403)		(9,182)
Net Total Assets			726,487		659,728
Represented by:					
General Fund			680,671		611,408
Miss E. M. Robinson Bequest			23,684		26,448
A.S. Whitfield Prize Fund			13,235		13,524
Studies in History			8,897		8,348
			726,487		659,728

ROYAL HISTORICAL SOCIETY

Income and Expenditure Account for the Year Ended 30th June 1990

GENERAL FUND

	Notes	1990 £	1990 £	1989 £	1989 £
INCOME					
Subscriptions	7		56,499		41,145
Investment income			77,907		64,548
Royalties and reproduction fees			2,638		441
Donations and sundry income			2,843		335
			139,887		106,469
EXPENDITURE					
Secretarial and Administrative					
Salaries, pensions and national insurance		16,357		14,927	
Printing and stationery		8,920		5,105	
Postage and telephone		1,658		2,064	
Bank charges		1,196		1,100	
Audit and accountancy		1,783		2,329	
Insurance		471		380	
Meetings and travel		4,697		3,584	
Repairs and renewals		552		276	
Depreciation	1(b)	1,316		1,164	
			36,950		30,929
Publications					
Literary directors' expenses		363		225	
Publishing costs for the year	8(a)	30,803		14,439	
Provisions for publications in progress	8(b)	31,000		29,000	
Other publication costs	8(c)	1,273		701	
Sales of publications		(463)		(5,616)	
			62,976		38,749
Library and Archives	1(d)				
Purchase of books and publications		305		1,257	
Binding		1,715		1,226	
			2,020		2,483
Other charges					
Centenary Fellowship		6,075	5,175		
Alexander prize		100		100	
Prothero lecture		286		258	
Grants		375		1,000	
Donations and sundry expenses		1,987		—	
A level prizes		500		500	
Young Historian		2,000		—	
British Bibliography		1,096	12,419	—	7,033
			114,365		79,194
Surplus for year			25,522		27,275
Surplus on sale of investments			43,741		20,012
			69,263		47,287
Balance brought forward at 1st July 1989			611,408		564,121
Balance carried forward at 30th June 1990			680,671		611,408

ROYAL HISTORICAL SOCIETY

Income and Expenditure Account for the Year Ended 30th June 1990

SPECIAL FUNDS

	1990		1989	
	£	£	£	£
MISS E. M. ROBINSON BEQUEST				
Income				
Investment income		963		909
Expenditure				
Grant to Dulwich Picture Gallery	1,000		1,000	
Other expenses	2,727	3,727	—	1,000
(Deficit) for the year		(2,764)		(91)
Balance brought forward at 1st July 1989		26,448		26,539
Balance carried forward at 30th June 1990		23,684		26,448
A. S. WHITFIELD PRIZE FUND				
Income				
Investment income		1,367		1,072
Expenditure				
Prize awarded	1,000		1,000	
Advertisement	309		—	
Other expenses	347		—	
		1,656		1,000
(Deficit)/Surplus for year		(289)		72
Balance brought forward at 1st July 1989		13,524		13,452
Balance carried forward at 30th June 1990		13,235		13,524
STUDIES IN HISTORY				
Income				
Royalties		3,843		2,064
Investment income		1,214		899
		5,057		2,963
Expenditure				
Honorarium	3,313		2,750	
Editor's expenses	791		716	
Ex gratia royalties and sundry expenses	404		—	
		4,508		3,466
Surplus/(Deficit) for year		549		(503)
Balance brought forward		8,348		8,851
Balance carried forward		8,897		8,348

ROYAL HISTORICAL SOCIETY

Statement of Source and Application of Funds for the Year Ended 30th June 1990

	1990 £	1990 £	1989 £	1989 £
SOURCE OF FUNDS				
Excess of income over expenditure for the year				
General fund		70,045		47,287
Miss E. M. Robinson Bequest		(2,764)		(91)
A. S. Whitfield prize fund		(1,071)		72
Studies in History fund		549		(503)
		66,759		46,765
Adjustment for items not involving the movement of funds				
Depreciation	1,316		1,164	
Surplus on sale of investments	(43,741)		(20,012)	
		(42,425)		(18,848)
Total generated from operations		24,334		27,917
Funds from other sources				
Sale of investments		166,779		51,744
		191,113		79,661
APPLICATION OF FUNDS				
Purchase of fixed assets	609		—	
Purchase of investments	185,871		101,744	
		186,480		101,744
		4,633		(22,083)
INCREASE/(DECREASE) IN WORKING CAPITAL				
Stock		(251)		2,894
Debtors		927		4.653
Creditors		(146)		(5,386)
Liquid funds		4,103		(24,244)
		4,633		(22,083)

ROYAL HISTORICAL SOCIETY

Notes to the Financial Statements for the Year Ended 30th June 1990

1. Accounting Policies
   (a) *Basis of accounting*
   These financial statements have been prepared under the historical cost convention.
   (b) *Depreciation*
   Depreciation is calculated by reference to the cost of fixed assets using a straight line basis at rates considered appropriate having regard to the expected lives of the fixed assets.
   The annual rates of depreciation in use are:

Furniture and equipment	10%
Computer equipment	25%

   Prior to 1st July 1987 the full cost of fixed assets was written off to General Fund in the year of purchase.
   (c) *Stocks*
   Stock is valued at the lower of cost and net realisable value.
   (d) *Library and archives*
   The cost of additions to the library and archives is written off in the year of purchase.

2. Fixed Assets

	Computer Equipment	Furniture and Equipment	Total
	£	£	£
Cost:			
At 1 July 1989	4,407	620	5,027
Additions during year	609	—	609
At 30th June 1990	5,016	620	5,636
Depreciation:			
As at 1st July 1989	2,203	124	2,327
Charge for year	1,254	62	1,316
At 30th June 1990	3,457	186	3,643
Net book value:			
At 30th June 1990	1,559	434	1,993
At 30th June 1989	2,204	496	2,700

The cost of additions to the library and archives is written off in the year of purchase.
Prior to 1st July 1987 the cost of furniture and equipment was written off in the year of purchase. Items acquired before that date are not reflected in the above figures.

3. Investments

	1990	*1989*
	£	£
Quoted securities at cost (market value £1,417,243; 1989 £1,247,352)	614,527	*576,628*
Money at call	116,370	*89,582*
	730,897	*666,210*

4. Debtors

	1990	*1989*
	£	£
Sundry debtors	12,276	*13,294*
Prepayments	2,646	*2,555*
	14,922	*15,849*

5. Cash at bank and in hand

	1990	*1989*
	£	£
Deposit accounts	15,242	*11,034*
Current accounts	3,058	*3,187*
Cash in hand	49	*25*
	18,349	*14,246*

6. CREDITORS

	1990 £	1989 £
Sundry creditors	2,420	2,616
Subscriptions received in advance	9,997	11,598
Accruals	2,013	2,070
Provision for publications	31,000	29,000
	45,430	45,284

7. SUBSCRIPTIONS

	1990 £	1989 £
Current subscriptions	53,569	38,761
Subscriptions arrears received	1,365	974
Income tax recovered on covenanted subscriptions	1,565	1,410
	56,499	41,145

8. PUBLICATIONS

		£	£
(a) Publishing costs for the year			
Transactions, fifth series	Vol. 39 (Vol. 38)	15,303	13,987
Camden, fourth series	Vol. 38 (Vol. 35)	15,439	20
	Vol. 39 (Vol. 36)	25,371	14,890
	— (Vol. 37)	—	9,542
Guides and Handbooks	No. 16	3,690	—
		59,803	38,439
Less: Provision brought forward		29,000	24,000
		30,803	14,439
(b) Provision for publications in progress			
Transactions, fifth series	Vol. 40 (Vol. 39)	13,000	14,000
Camden, fourth series	Vol. 40 (Vol. 38)	18,000	15,000
		31,000	29,000
(c) Other publication costs			
Annual bibliography		2,633	2,700
Less: Royalties received		(1,360)	(1,999)
		1,273	701

F. M. L. THOMPSON, *President*
M. J. DAUNTON, *Treasurer*

We have audited the financial statements on pages 7 to 12 in accordance with Auditing Standards.
In our opinion the financial statements give a true and fair view of the society's affairs at 30th June 1990 and of its surplus and source and application of funds for the year then ended.

118, SOUTH STREET, DORKING
14th September, 1990

DAVIES, WATSON & CO.
Chartered Accountants

THE DAVID BERRY ESSAY TRUST

Balance Sheet as at 30th June 1990

	Note	1990 £	1990 £	1989 £	1989 £
Investments					
1117.63(483.63) shares in the Charities Official Investment Fund	1		1,530		53
(Market value £5,746: 1989 £2,795)					
Current assets					
Cash at bank					
– deposit account		7,391		2,802	
		7,391		2,802	
Creditors: Amounts falling due within one year		3,842		372	
Net current assets			3,549		2,43
Net total assets			5,079		2,96
Represented by:					
Capital fund	1		1,000		—
Accumulated Income account			4,079		2,96
			5,079		2,96

1. In previous years the investments of David Berry Essay Trust have been shown as 483.63 units in th Charities Official Investment Fund relating to accumulated income only. An additional 634 units representin the capital fund of £1,000 had been excluded from the Balance Sheet. The total holding of 1117.63 units i now incorporated in the above figures.

Income and Expenditure Account for the Year Ended 30th June 1990

	1990 £	1990 £	1989 £	1989 £
Income				
Dividends		674		26
Interest		445		15
		1,119		41
Expenditure				
Prize	—		100	
Adjudicators' Fee	—		45	
		—		14
Excess of income over expenditure for the year		1,119		27
Balance brought forward		2,960		2,68
Balance carried forward		4,079		2,96

The late David Berry, by his Will dated 23 April 1926, left £1,000 to provide in every three years a gold med and prize money for the best essay on the Earl of Bothwell or, at the discretion of the Trustees, on Scottis History of the James Stuarts I to VI, in memory of his father the late Rev. David Berry.

The Trust is regulated by a scheme sanctioned by the Chancery Division of the High Court of Justice date 23 January 1930, and made in action 1927 A 1233 David Anderson Berry deceased, Hunter and Another Robertson and Another and since modified by an order of the Charity Commissioners made on 11 Januar 1978 removing the necessity to provide a medal.

The Royal Historical Society is now the Trustee. The investment consists of 1117.63 Charities Offici Investment Fund income shares (Market Value £5,746; 1989 £2,795).

The Trustee will in every second year of the three year period advertise, inviting essays.

We have audited the financial statements on pages 13 and 14 in accordance with Auditing Standards.

In our opinion the accounts give a true and fair view of the Trust's affairs at 30th June 1990 and of its surpl for the year then ended and comply with the provisions of the Trust deed.

118, South Street, Dorking
14th September, 1990

DAVIES, WATSON & C
Chartered Accountan

ALEXANDER PRIZE

The Alexander Prize was established in 1897 by L. C. Alexander, F.R.Hist.S. It consists of a silver medal and £250 awarded annually for an essay upon some historical subject. Candidates may select their own subject provided such subject has been previously submitted to and approved by the Literary Director. The essay must be a genuine work of original research, not hitherto published, and one which has not been awarded any other prize. It must not exceed 8,000 words, including footnotes, in length and must be sent in on or before 1 November of any year. The detailed regulations should be obtained in advance from the Secretary. Candidates must *either* be under the age of 35 *or* be registered for a higher degree *or* have been registered for a higher degree within the last three years.

LIST OF ALEXANDER PRIZE ESSAYISTS (1898–1990)[1]

1898. F. Hermia Durham ('The relations of the Crown to trade under James I').
1899. W. F. Lord, BA ('The development of political parties during the reign of Queen Anne').
1901. Laura M. Roberts ('The Peace of Lunéville').
1902. V. B. Redstone ('The social condition of England during the Wars of the Roses').
1903. Rose Graham ('The intellectual influence of English monasticism between the tenth and the twelfth centuries').
1904. Enid W. G. Routh ('The balance of power in the seventeenth century').
1905. W. A. P. Mason, MA ('The beginnings of the Cistercian Order').
1906. Rachel R. Reid, MA ('The Rebellion of the Earls, 1569').
1908. Kate Hotblack ('The Peace of Paris, 1763').
1909. Nellie Nield, MA ('The social and economic condition of the unfree classes in England in the twelfth and thirteenth centuries').
1912. H. G. Richardson ('The parish clergy of the thirteenth and fourteenth centuries').
1917. Isobel D. Thornely, BA ('The treason legislation of 1531–1534').
1918. T. F. T. Plucknett, BA ('The place of the Council in the fifteenth century').
1919. Edna F. White, MA ('The jurisdiction of the Privy Council under the Tudors').
1920. J. E. Neale, MA ('The Commons Journals of the Tudor Period').
1922. Eveline C. Martin ('The English establishments on the Gold Coast in the second half of the eighteenth century').
1923. E. W. Hensman, MA ('The Civil War of 1648 in the east midlands').
1924. Grace Stretton, BA ('Some aspects of mediæval travel').

[1] No award was made in 1900, 1907, 1910, 1911, 1913, 1914, 1921, 1946, 1948, 1956, 1969, 1975, 1977, and 1987. The Prize Essays for 1909 and 1919 were not published in the *Transactions*. No Essays were submitted in 1915, 1916 and 1943.

1925. F. A. Mace, MA ('Devonshire ports in the fourteenth and fifteenth centuries').
1926. Marian J. Tooley, MA ('The authorship of the *Defensor Pacis*').
1927. W. A. Pantin, BA ('Chapters of the English Black Monks, 1215–1540').
1928. Gladys A. Thornton, BA, PhD ('A study in the history of Clare, Suffolk, with special reference to its development as a borough').
1929. F. S. Rodkey, AM, PhD ('Lord Palmerston's policy for the rejuvenation of Turkey, 1839–47').
1930. A. A. Ettinger, DPhil ('The proposed Anglo-Franco-American Treaty of 1852 to guarantee Cuba to Spain').
1931. Kathleen A. Walpole, MA ('The humanitarian movement of the early nineteenth century to remedy abuses on emigrant vessels to America').
1932. Dorothy M. Brodie, BA ('Edmund Dudley, minister of Henry VII').
1933. R. W. Southern, BA ('Ranulf Flambard and early Anglo-Norman administration').
1934. S. B. Chrimes, MA, PhD ('Sir John Fortescue and his theory of dominion').
1935. S. T. Bindoff, MA ('The unreformed diplomatic service, 1812–60').
1936. Rosamund J. Mitchell, MA, BLitt ('English students at Padua, 1460–1475').
1937. C. H. Philips, BA ('The East India Company "Interest", and the English Government, 1783–4').
1938. H. E. I. Phillips, BA ('The last years of the Court of Star Chamber, 1630–41').
1939. Hilda P. Grieve, BA ('The deprived married clergy in Essex, 1553–61').
1940. R. Somerville, MA ('The Duchy of Lancaster Council and Court of Duchy Chamber').
1941. R. A. L. Smith, MA, PhD ('The *Regimen Scaccarii* in English monasteries').
1942. F. L. Carsten, DPhil ('Medieval democracy in the Brandenburg towns and its defeat in the fifteenth century').
1944. Rev. E. W. Kemp, BD ('Pope Alexander III and the canonization of saints').
1945. Helen Suggett, BLitt ('The use of French in England in the later middle ages').
1947. June Milne, BA ('The diplomacy of John Robinson at the court of Charles XII of Sweden, 1697–1709').
1949. Ethel Drus, MA ('The attitude of the Colonial Office to the annexation of Fiji').
1950. Doreen J. Milne, MA, PhD ('The results of the Rye House Plot, and their influence upon the Revolution of 1688').
1951. K. G. Davies, BA ('The origins of the commission system in the West India trade').
1952. G. W. S. Barrow, BLitt ('Scottish rulers and the religious orders, 1070–1153').
1953. W. E. Minchinton, BSc(Econ) ('Bristol—metropolis of the west in the eighteenth century').
1954. Rev. L. Boyle, OP ('The *Oculus Sacerdotis* and some other works of William of Pagula').
1955. G. F. E. Rudé, MA, PhD ('The Gordon riots: a study of the rioters and their victims').
1957. R. F. Hunnisett, MA, DPhil ('The origins of the office of Coroner').

1958. Thomas G. Barnes, AB, DPhil ('County politics and a puritan *cause célèbre*: Somerset churchales, 1633').
1959. Alan Harding, BLitt ('The origins and early history of the Keeper of the Peace').
1960. Gwyn A. Williams, MA, PhD ('London and Edward I').
1961. M. H. Keen, BA ('Treason trials under the law of arms').
1962. G. W. Monger, MA, PhD ('The end of isolation: Britain, Germany and Japan, 1900–1902').
1963. J. S. Moore, BA ('The Domesday teamland: a reconsideration').
1964. M. Kelly, PhD ('The submission of the clergy').
1965. J. J. N. Palmer, BLitt ('Anglo-French negotiations, 1390–1396').
1966. M. T. Clanchy, MA, PhD ('The Franchise of Return of Writs').
1967. R. Lovatt, MA, DPhil, PhD ('The *Imitation of Christ* in late medieval England').
1968. M. G. A. Vale, MA, DPhil ('The last years of English Gascony, 1451–1453').
1970. Mrs Margaret Bowker, MA, BLitt ('The Commons Supplication against the Ordinaries in the light of some Archidiaconal Acta').
1971. C. Thompson, MA ('The origins of the politics of the Parliamentary middle groups, 1625–1629').
1972. I. d'Alton, BA ('Southern Irish Unionism: A study of Cork City and County Unionists, 1884–1914').
1973. C. J. Kitching, BA, PhD ('The quest for concealed lands in the reign of Elizabeth I').
1974. H. Tomlinson, BA ('Place and Profit: an Examination of the Ordnance Office, 1660–1714').
1976. B. Bradshaw, MA, BD ('Cromwellian reform and the origins of the Kildare rebellion, 1533–34').
1978. C. J. Ford, BA ('Piracy or Policy: The Crisis in the Channel, 1400–1403').
1979. P. Dewey, BA, PhD ('Food Production and Policy in the United Kingdom, 1914–1918').
1980. Ann L. Hughes, BA, PhD ('Militancy and Localism: Warwickshire Politics and Westminster Politics, 1643–1647)'.
1981. C. J. Tyerman, MA ('Marino Sanudo Torsello and the Lost Crusade. Lobbying in the Fourteenth Century').
1982. E. Powell, BA, DPhil ('Arbitration and the Law in England in the Late Middle Ages').
1983. A. G. Rosser, MA ('The essence of medieval urban communities: the vill of Westminster 1200–1540').
1984. N. L. Ramsay, MA, LLB ('Retained Legal Counsel, c. 1275–1475').
1985. George S. Garnett, MA ('Coronation and Propaganda: Some Implications of the Norman Claim to the Throne of England in 1066').
1986. C. J. Given-Wilson ('The King and the Gentry in FourteenthCentury England').
1988. R. A. W. Rex, MA ('The English Campaign against Luther in the 1520s').
1989. J. S. A. Adamson, BA, PhD ('The Baronial Context of the English Civil War').
1990. S. C. Lockwood, BA ('Marsilius of Padua and the Case for the Royal Ecclesiastical Supremacy').

DAVID BERRY PRIZE

The David Berry Prize was established in 1929 by David Anderson-Berry in memory of his father, the Reverend David Berry. It consists of a money prize awarded every three years for Scottish history. Candidates may select any subject dealing with Scottish history within the reigns of James I to James VI inclusive, provided such subject has been previously submitted to and approved by the Council of the Royal Historical Society. The essay must be a genuine work of original research not hitherto published, and one which has not been awarded any other prize. The essay should be between 6,000 and 10,000 words, excluding footnotes and appendices. It must be sent in on or before 31 October 1991.

LIST OF DAVID BERRY PRIZE ESSAYISTS (1937–88)[1]

1937. G. Donaldson, MA ('The polity of the Scottish Reformed Church *c.* 1460–1580, and the rise of the Presbyterian movement').
1943. Rev. Prof. A. F. Scott Pearson, DTh, DLitt ('Anglo-Scottish religious relations, 1400–1600').
1949. T. Bedford Franklin, MA, FRSE ('Monastic agriculture in Scotland, 1440–1600').
1955. W. A. McNeill, MA ('"Estaytt" of the king's rents and pensions, 1621').
1958. Prof. Maurice Lee, PhD ('Maitland of Thirlestane and the foundation of the Stewart despotism in Scotland').
1964. M. H. Merriman ('Scottish collaborators with England during the Anglo-Scottish war, 1543–1550').
1967. Miss M. H. B. Sanderson ('Catholic recusancy in Scotland in the sixteenth century').
1970. Athol Murray, MA, LLB, PhD ('The Comptroller, 1425–1610').
1973. J. Kirk, MA, PhD ('Who were the Melvillians: A study in the Personnel and Background of the Presbyterian Movement in late Sixteenth-century Scotland').
1976. A. Grant, BA, DPhil ('The Development of the Scottish Peerage').
1985. Rev. G. Mark Dilworth ('The Commendator System in Scotland').
1988. J. Goodare ('Parliamentary Taxation in Scotland, 1560–1603').

[1] No essays were submitted in 1940 and 1979. No award was made in 1946, 1952, 1961 and 1982.

WHITFIELD PRIZE

The Whitfield Prize was established by Council in 1976 as a money prize of £400 out of the bequest of the late Professor Archibald Stenton Whitfield: in May 1981 Council increased the prize to £600. Until 1982 the prize was awarded annually to the STUDIES IN HISTORY series. From 1983 the prize, which was increased in 1988 to £1000, will be awarded annually to the best work of English or Welsh history by an author under 40 years of age, published in the United Kingdom. The award will be made by Council in the Spring of each year in respect of works published in the preceding calendar year. Authors or publishers should send three copies (non-returnable) of a book eligible for the competition to the Society to arrive not later than 31 December of the year of publication.

LIST OF WHITFIELD PRIZE WINNERS (1977–1989)

1977. K. D. Brown, MA, PhD (*John Burns*).
1978. Marie Axton, MA, PhD (*The Queen's Two Bodies: Drama and the Elizabethan Succession*).
1979. Patricia Crawford, MA, PhD (*Denzil Holles, 1598–1680: A study of his Political Career*).
1980. D. L. Rydz (*The Parliamentary Agents: A History*).
1981. Scott M. Harrison (*The Pilgrimage of Grace in the Lake Counties 1536–7*).
1982. Norman L. Jones (*Faith by Statute: Parliament and the Settlement of Religion 1559*).
1983. Peter Clark (*The English Alehouse: A social history 1200–1830*).
1984. David Hempton, BA, PhD (*Methodism and Politics in British Society 1750–1850*).
1985. K. D. M. Snell, MA, PhD (*Annals of the Labouring Poor*).
1986. Diarmaid MacCulloch, MA, PhD, FSA (*Suffolk and the Tudors: Politics and Religion in an English County 1500–1600*).
1987. Kevin M. Sharpe, MA, DPhil (*Criticism and Compliment: The politics of literature in the England of Charles I*).
1988. J. H. Davis, MA, DPhil (*Reforming London, the London Government Problem 1855–1900*).
1989. A. G. Rosser, MA, PhD (*Medieval Westminster, 1200–1540*).

The subject of this book is the small town which grew up around the royal abbey and palace of Westminster. As a royal capital, Westminster was unique, but in other respects it was characteristic of a large class of small medieval towns hitherto neglected by historians. It lacked incorporation by charter — its legal status and institutions were identical with those of agrarian villages — but its economic and social life was thoroughly urban. Study of its identity is rendered problematic by the continuous, unpredictable variation in both the size and the composition of the local community. The author asks how, given these vagaries, a tolerable degree of continuity could be maintained. Anarchy and social struggles were contained partly by the influence of a small elite of wealthy individuals, but principally by strategies of collective behaviour adopted by the population in local government, parochial life, and the activities of the guilds. These regular expressions of shared interest and common identity are found to have been essential to the survival of the town. The implications of Gervase Rosser's argument are confined neither to small towns nor to the Middle Ages.

THE ROYAL HISTORICAL SOCIETY

(INCORPORATED BY ROYAL CHARTER)

OFFICERS AND COUNCIL—1990

Patron

HER MAJESTY THE QUEEN

President

Professor F. M. L. THOMPSON, MA, DPhil, FSA

Honorary Vice-Presidents

G. E. Aylmer, MA, DPhil, FBA
Professor J. H. Burns, MA, PhD
Professor A. G. Dickens, CMG, MA, DLit, DLitt, LittD, FBA, FSA
Professor G. Donaldson MA, PhD, DLitt, DLitt, FRSE, FBA
Sir Geoffrey Elton, MA, PhD, LittD, DLitt, DLitt, DLit, FBA
Professor P. Grierson, MA, LittD, FBA, FSA
Sir John Habakkuk, MA, FBA
Professor D. Hay, MA, DLitt, FBA, FRSE, Dr h.c. Tours
Sir James Holt, MA, DPhil, DLitt, FBA, FSA
Professor R. A. Humphreys, OBE, MA, PhD, DLitt, LittD, DLitt, DUniv
Miss K. Major, MA, BLitt, LittD, FBA, FSA
Professor D. B. Quinn, MA, PhD, DLit, DLitt, DLitt, DLitt, LLD, DHL, Hon FBA
The Hon. Sir Steven Runciman, CH, MA, DPhil, LLD, LittD, DLitt, LitD, DD, DHL, FBA, FSA
Sir Richard Southern, MA, DLitt, LittD, DLitt, FBA
Professor C. H. Wilson, CBE, MA, LittD, DLitt, DLitt, DLitt, FBA

Vice-Presidents

Miss B. Harvey, MA, BLitt, FBA
Professor W. R. Ward, DPhil
Miss V. Cromwell, MA
Professor P. J. Marshall, MA, DPhil
Professor R. R. Davies, BA, DPhil, FBA
Professor W. A. Speck, MA, DPhil
M. Roper, MA
Professor C. S. R. Russell, MA

STANDING COMMITTEES 1988

Finance Committee

PROFESSOR OLIVE ANDERSON
PROFESSOR M. D. BIDDISS
P. J. C. FIRTH
Dr. G. H. MARTIN, CBE
Dr. P. MATHIAS, CBE, MA, DLitt, FBA
And the Officers

Publications Committee

C. R. ELRINGTON, MA, FSA
PROFESSOR R. A. GRIFFITHS
MISS B. HARVEY, FBA
PROFESSOR N. McCORD
PROFESSOR D. M. PALLISER
PROFESSOR M. C. PRESTWICH
PROFESSOR C. S. R. RUSSELL
Dr. GILLIAN SUTHERLAND
And the Officers

Library Committee

PROFESSOR OLIVE ANDERSON
PROFESSOR J. R. DINWIDDY
PROFESSOR P. J. MARSHALL
PROFESSOR C. S. R. RUSSELL
And the Officers

LIST OF FELLOWS OF THE ROYAL HISTORICAL SOCIETY

Names of Officers and Honorary Vice-Presidents are printed in capitals. Those marked have compounded for their annual subscriptions.*

Abels, Assoc. Professor R. P., PhD, 617 Edwards Road, Annapolis, Maryland 21401, U.S.A.

Abramsky, Professor Chimen A., MA, Dept of Hebrew and Jewish Studies, University College London, Gower Street, London WC1E 6BT.

Abulafia, D. S. H., MA, PhD, Gonville and Caius College, Cambridge CB2 1TA.

Acton, E. D. J., PhD, School of History, The University, P.O. Box 147, Liverpool L69 3BX.

Adam, Professor R. J., MA, Easter Wayside, Hepburn Gardens, St Andrews KY16 9LP.

Adams, Professor Ralph J. Q., PhD, Dept of History, Texas A & M University, College Station, Texas 77843–4236, U.S.A.

Adams, S. L., BA, MA, DPhil, 4 North East Circus Place, Edinburgh EH3 6SP.

Adamthwaite, Professor A.P., BA, PhD, 780 King Lane, Leeds LS17 7AU.

Addison, P., MA, DPhil, Dept of History, The University, William Robertson Building, George Square, Edinburgh EH8 9JY.

Ailes, A., MA, 24 Donnington Gardens, Reading, Berkshire RG1 5LY.

Akenson, D. H., BA, PhD, Dept of History, Queen's University, Kingston, Ontario, Canada, K7L 3N6.

Akrigg, Professor G. P. V., BA, PhD, FRSC, #8–2575 Tolmie Street, Vancouver, B.C., Canada, V6R 4M1.

Alcock, Professor L., MA, FSA, 29 Hamilton Drive, Glasgow G12 8DN.

Alder, G. J., BA, PhD, Dept of History, The University, Whiteknights, Reading RG6 2AA.

Alderman, G., MA, DPhil, 172 Colindeep Lane, London NW9 6EA.

Allan, D. G. C., MSc(Econ), PhD, c/o Royal Society of Arts, John Adam Street, London WC2N 6EZ.

Allen, D. F., BA, PhD, School of History, The University, P.O. Box 363, Birmingham B15 2TT.

Allen, D. H., BA, PhD, 105 Tuddenham Avenue, Ipswich, Suffolk IP4 2HG.

Allmand, C. T., MA, DPhil, FSA, 111 Menlove Avenue, Liverpool L18 3HP.

Alsop, J. D., BA, MA, PhD, Dept of History, McMaster University, 1280 Main Street West, Hamilton, Ontario, Canada L8S 4L9.

Altholz, Professor J., PhD, Dept of History, University of Minnesota, 614 Social Sciences Building, Minneapolis, Minn. 55455, U.S.A.

Altschul, Professor M., PhD, Case Western Reserve University, Cleveland, Ohio 44106, U.S.A.

Ambler, R. W., PhD, 37 Cumberland Avenue, Grimsby, South Humberside DN32 0BT.

Anderson, Professor M. S., MA, PhD, 45 Cholmeley Crescent, London N6 5EX.

Anderson, Professor Olive, MA, BLitt, Dept of History, Queen Mary and Westfield College, University of London, Kidderpore Avenue, Hampstead, London NW3 7ST.

Anderson, R. D., MA, DPhil, 7 North West Circus Place, Edinburgh EH3 6ST.

Anderson, Miss S. P., MA, BLitt, 17–19 Chilworth Street, London W2 3QU.

Andrew, C. M., MA, PhD, Corpus Christi College, Cambridge CB2 1RH.

Anglesey, The Most Hon., The Marquess of, FSA, FRSL, Plas-Newydd, Llanfairpwll, Anglesey LL61 6DZ.

Anglo, Professor S., BA, PhD, FSA, 59 Green Ridge, Withdean, Brighton BN1 5LU.

Angold, M. J., BA, DPhil, 17 Morningside Park, Edinburgh EH10 5HD.

Annan, Lord, OBE, MA, DLitt, DUniv, 16 St John's Wood Road, London NW8 8RE.

Annis, P. G. W., BA, 65 Longlands Road, Sidcup, Kent DA15 7LQ.

Appleby, J. S., Little Pitchbury, Brick Kiln Lane, Great Horkesley, Colchester, Essex CO6 4EU.

Armstrong, Miss A. M., BA, 7 Vale Court, Mallord Street, London SW3.

Armstrong, C. A. J., MA, FSA, Gayhurst, Lincombe Lane, Boars Hill, Oxford OX1 5DZ.

Armstrong, Professor F. H., PhD, Dept of History, University of Western Ontario, London, Ontario, Canada N6A 5C2.

Armstrong, J., BSc, MSc, 42 Inglis Road, Ealing, London W5 3RL.

Armstrong, W. A., BA, PhD, Eliot College, The University, Canterbury, Kent CT2 7NS.

Arnstein, Professor W. L., PhD, Dept of History, University of Illinois at Urbana-Champaign, 309 Gregory Hall, Urbana, Ill. 61801, U.S.A.

Artibise, Professor Alan F. J., PhD, Community and Regional Planning, University of British Columbia, 6333 Memorial Road, Vancouver, B.C., Canada, V6T 1W5.

Ashton, Professor R., PhD, The Manor House, Brundall, near Norwich NOR 86Z.

Ashworth, J., BA, MLitt, DPhil, School of English and American Studies, University of East Anglia, Norwich NR4 7TJ.

Ashworth, Professor W., BSc(Econ), PhD, 31 Calton Gardens, Bath, BA2 4QG.

Asquith, Ivon, BA, PhD, 19 Vicarage Lane, New Hinksey, Oxford OX1 4RQ.

Aston, Margaret E., MA, DPhil, Castle House, Chipping, Ongar, Essex CM5 9JT.

Austin, The Rev. Canon, M. R. BD, MA, PhD, 22 Marlock Close, Fiskerton, Nr Southwell, Notts. NG25 0UB.

Axelson, Professor E. V., DLitt, Box 15, Constantia, 7848, S. Africa.

*Aydelotte, Professor W. O., PhD, State University of Iowa, Iowa City, Iowa, U.S.A.

AYLMER, G. E., MA, DPhil, FBA, St Peter's College, Oxford OX1 2DL.

Ayres, P. J., PhD, Dept of English, Monash University, Clayton 3168, Victoria, Australia.

Azzopardi, F., OFMCAP, HisEcclLic, DiplArchiv., Capuchin Franciscan Friary, Floriana, Malta.

Bahlman, Professor Dudley W. R., MA, PhD, Dept of History, Williams College, Williamstown, Mass. 01267, U.S.A.

Bailie, The Rev. W. D., MA, BD, PhD, DD, 45 Morpra Drive, Saintfield, Co. Down, N. Ireland.
Bailyn, Professor B., MA, PhD, LittD, LHD, Widener J, Harvard University, Cambridge, Mass. 02138, U.S.A.
Baines, A. H. J., PhD, MA, LLB, FSA, FRSA, FSS, Finmere, 90 Eskdale Avenue, Chesham, Bucks. HP5 3AY.
Baker, D., BSc, PhD, MA, BLitt, 21 Valenciennes Road, Sittingbourne, Kent, ME10 1EN.
Baker, J. H., LLD, FBA, St Catharine's College, Cambridge CB2 1RL.
Baker, L. G. D., MA, BLitt, 5 Allendale, Southwater, Horsham, West Sussex RH13 7UE.
Baker, T. F. T., BA, Camden Lodge, 50 Hastings Road, Pembury, Kent.
Ball, A. W., BA, 71 Cassiobury Park Avenue, Watford, Herts. WD1 7LD.
Ballhatchet, Professor K. A., MA, PhD, 12 Park Lane, Richmond, Surrey TW9 2RA.
Banks, Professor J. A., MA, Caldecott House, Kilworth Road, Husbands Bosworth, Lutterworth, Leicestershire LE17 6JZ.
Barber, M. C., BA, PhD, Dept of History, The University, Whiteknights, Reading, Berks. RG6 2AA.
Barber, R. W., MA, PhD, FSA, Stangrove Hall, Alderton, near Woodbridge, Suffolk IP12 3BL.
Barker, A. J., BA, MA, PhD, Dept of History, University of Western Australia, Nedlands, Western Australia 6009.
Barker, Professor T. C., MA, PhD, Minsen Dane, Brogdale Road, Faversham, Kent.
Barkley, Professor The Rev. J. M., MA, DD, 2 College Park, Belfast, N. Ireland.
*Barlow, Professor F., CBE, FBA, FRSL, MA, DPhil, Hon DLitt, Middle Court Hall, Kenton, Exeter, EX6 8NA.
Barnard, T. C., MA, DPhil, Hertford College, Oxford OX1 3BW.
Barnes, Miss P. M., PhD, 6 Kings Yard, Kings Ride, Ascot, Berks. SL5 8AH.
Barnett, Correlli, MA, Catbridge House, Rast Carleton, Norwich, Norfolk.
Barratt, Miss D. M., DPhil, The Corner House, Hampton Poyle, Kidlington, Oxford.
Barratt, Professor G. R. de V., PhD, Dept of Russian, Paterson Hall, Carleton University, Ottawa, Canada K1S 5B6.
Barrett, The Rev. P. L. S., The Rectory, Kiln Lane, Otterbourne, Winchester SO21 2EJ.
Barron, Mrs C. M., MA, PhD, 9 Boundary Road, London NW8 0HE.
Barrow, Professor G. W. S., MA, BLitt, DLitt, FBA, FRSE, 12a Lauder Road, Edinburgh EH9 2EL.
Barrow, Julia S., MA, DPhil, Dept of History, Nottingham University, University Park, Nottingham NG7 2RD.
Bartlett, Professor C. J., PhD, Dept of Modern History, The University, Dundee DD1 4HN.
Bartlett, Professor R. J., MA, DPhil, Dept of History, University of Chicago, 1126 East 59th Street, Chicago, Illinois 60637, U.S.A.
Bates, D., PhD, School of History and Archaeology, University of Wales, P.O. Box 909, Cardiff CF1 3XU.
Batho, Professor G. R., MA, Fivestones, 3 Archery Rise, Durham DH1 4LA.
Baugh, Professor Daniel A., PhD, Dept of History, McGraw Hall, Cornell University, Ithaca, N.Y. 14853, U.S.A.
Baugh, G. C., MA, Glebe House, Vicarage Road, Meole Brace, Shrewsbury SY3 9EZ.

Baxter, Professor S. B., PhD, 608 Morgan Creek Road, Chapel Hill, N.C. 27514, U.S.A.

Baylen, Professor J. O., MA, PhD, 45 Saffron Court, Compton Place Road, Eastbourne, E. Sussex, BN21 1DY.

Beachey, Professor R. W., BA, PhD, 1 Rookwood, De La Warr Road, Milford-on-Sea, Hampshire.

Beales, Professor D. E. D., MA, PhD, LittD, Sidney Sussex College, Cambridge CB2 3HU.

Bealey, Professor F., BSc(Econ), Dept of Politics, The University, Taylor Building, Old Aberdeen AB9 2UB.

Bean, Professor J. M. W., MA, DPhil, 622 Fayerweather Hall, Columbia University, New York, N.Y. 10027, U.S.A.

Beardwood, Miss Alice, BA, BLitt, DPhil, 415 Miller's Lane, Wynnewood, Pa, U.S.A.

Beasley, Professor W. G., PhD, FBA, 172 Hampton Road, Twickenham, Middlesex TW2 5NJ.

Beattie, Professor J. M., PhD, Dept of History, University of Toronto, Toronto, Canada, M5S 1A1.

Beauroy, Dr Jacques M., 15 Avenue Marie-Amélie, Chantilly, France 60500.

Bebbington, D. W., MA, PhD, 5 Pullar Avenue, Bridge of Allan, Stirling FK9 4TB.

Beckerman, John S., PhD, 56 Burnet Street, Maplewood, New Jersey 07040, U.S.A.

Beckett, I. F. W., BA, PhD, Cottesloe House, The Dene, Hindon, Wiltshire SP3 6EE.

Beckett, Professor J. C., MA, 19 Wellington Park Terrace, Belfast 9, N. Ireland.

Beckett, J. V., BA, PhD, Dept of History, The University, Nottingham NG7 2RD.

Beddard, R. A., MA, DPhil, Oriel College, Oxford OX1 4EW.

*Beer, E. S. de, CBE, MA, DLitt, FBA, FSA, Stoke House, Stoke Hammond MK17 9BN.

Beer, Professor Samuel H., PhD, Faculty of Arts & Sciences, Harvard University, Littauer Center G-15, Cambridge, Mass. 02138, U.S.A.

Belchem, J. C., BA, DPhil, Dept of History, The University, 8 Abercromby Square, Liverpool L69 3BX.

Bell, P. M. H., BA, BLitt, School of History, The University, P.O. Box 147, Liverpool L69 3BX.

Bellenger, Dominic T. J. A., MA, PhD, Downside Abbey, Stratton-on-the-Fosse, Bath BA3 4RH.

Beloff, Lord, DLitt, FBA, Flat No. 9, 22 Lewes Crescent, Brighton BN2 1GB.

Benedikz, B. S., MA, PhD, Main Library, University of Birmingham, P.O. Box 363, Birmingham B15 2TT.

Bennett, M., MA, 48 Lye Copse Avenue, Farnborough, Hants. GU14 8DX.

Bennett, M. J., BA, PhD, History Dept, University of Tasmania, Box 252C, G.P.O., Hobart, Tasmania 7001, Australia.

Benson, Professor J., BA, MA, PhD, The Polytechnic, Wolverhampton, West Midlands, WV1 1LY.

Bentley, M., BA, PhD, Dept of History, The University, Sheffield S10 2TN.

Berghahn, Professor V. R., MA, PhD, Brown University, Providence, Rhode Island 02912, U.S.A.

Bergin, J., MA, PhD, Dept of History, The University, Manchester M13 9PL.

Bernard, G. W., MA, DPhil, 92 Bassett Green Village, Southampton.
Berridge, Virginia S., BA, PhD, AIDS Social History Unit, Dept of Public Health and Policy, London School of Hygiene and Tropical Medicine, Keppel Street, London WC1.
Bhila, Professor H. H. K., BA, MA, PhD, Parliament of Zimbabwe, Box 8055, Causeway, Harare, Zimbabwe.
Biddiss, Professor M. D., MA, PhD, Dept of History, The University, Whiteknights, Reading RG6 2AA.
Bidwell, Brigadier R. G. S., OBE, 8 Chapel Lane, Wickham Market, Woodbridge, Suffolk IP13 0SD.
Bill, E. G. W., MA, DLitt, Lambeth Palace Library, London SE1.
Biller, P. P. A., MA, DPhil, Dept of History, The University, Heslington, York YO1 5DD.
Binfield, J. C. G., MA, PhD, 22 Whiteley Wood Road, Sheffield S11 7FE.
Birch, A., MA, PhD, Dept of History, The University, Hong Kong.
Birke, Professor A. M., DPhil, DPhil-Habil, German Historical Institute, 17 Bloomsbury Square, London WC1A 2LP.
Bishop, A. S., BA, PhD, 44 North Acre, Banstead, Surrey SM7 2EG.
Bishop, T. A. M., MA, 16 Highbury Road, London SW19 7PR.
Bisson, Professor T. N., MA, PhD, 21 Hammond Street, Cambridge, MA 02138, U.S.A.
Black, Professor Eugene C., PhD, Dept of History, Brandeis University, Waltham, Mass. 02154-9110, U.S.A.
Black, J. M. PhD, 38 Elmfield Road, Gosforth, Newcastle, Tyne and Wear NE3 4BB.
Black, R. D., BA PhD, School of History, The University, Leeds LS2 9JT.
Blackbourn, D., MA, PhD, Dept of History, Birkbeck College, Malet Street, London WC1E 7HX.
Blackburn, M. A. S., MA, FSA, Faculty of History, University of Cambridge, West Road, Cambridge CB3 9EF.
Blackburn, R. W., BA, MSc, PhD, School of Law, King's College London, Strand, London WC2R 2LS.
Blackwood, B. G., BA, BLitt, DPhil, 4 Knights Close, Felixstowe, Suffolk IP11 9NU.
Blainey, G. N., MA, P.O. Box 257, East Melbourne, Victoria 3002, Australia.
Blake, E. O., MA, PhD, Roselands, Moorhill Road, Westend, Southampton SO3 3AW.
Blake, Lord, MA, FBA, Riverview House, Brundall, Norwich NR13 5LA.
Blakemore, H., PhD, 43 Fitzjohn Avenue, Barnet, Herts, EN5 2HN.
*Blakey, Professor R. G., PhD, c/o Mr Raymond Shove, Order Dept, Library, University of Minnesota, Minneapolis 14, Minn., U.S.A.
Blanning, T. W. C., MA, PhD, Sidney Sussex College, Cambridge CB2 3HU.
Blewett, Hon Dr N., BA, DipEd, MA, DPhil, 68 Barnard Street, North Adelaide, South Australia 5006.
Blinkhorn, RM., BA, AM, DPhil, Dept of History, The University, Bailrigg, Lancaster LA1 4YG.
Board, Mrs Beryl A., The Old School House, Stow Maries, Chelmsford, Essex CM3 6SL.
Bolton, Brenda, M., BA, Dept of History, Westfield College, Kidderpore Avenue, London NW3 7ST.
Bolton, Professor G. C., MA, DPhil, Dept of History, University of Queensland, St Lucia, Queensland 4067, Australia.
Bolton, J. L. BA, BLitt, Dept of History, Queen Mary College, Mile End Road, London E1 4NS.

Bond, Professor B. J., BA, MA, Dept of War Studies, King's College London, Strand, London WC2R 2LS.

Bonney, Professor R. J., MA, DPhil, Dept of History, The University, Leicester LE1 7RH.

Bonwick, C. C., MA, PhD, Dept of American Studies, The University, Keele, Staffs. ST5 5BG.

Booker, J. M. L., BA, MLitt, DPhil, Braxted Place, Little Braxted, Witham, Essex CM8 3LD.

Boon, G. C., BA, FSA, FRNS, 43 Westbourne Road, Penarth, S. Glamorgan CF6 2HA.

Borrie, M. A. F., BA, The British Library, Dept of Manuscripts, Great Russell Street, London WC1B 3DG.

Bossy, Professor J. A., MA, PhD, Dept of History, University of York, Heslington, York YO1 5DD.

Bottigheimer, Professor Karl S., Dept of History, State University of New York, Stony Brook, Long Island, N.Y., U.S.A.

Bourne, J. M., BA, PhD., 33 St. John's Road, Selly Park, Birmingham B29 7EP.

Bourne, Professor K., BA, PhD, FBA, London School of Economics, Houghton Street, Aldwych, London WC2A 2AE.

Bowker, Mrs M., MA, BLitt, 14 Bowers Croft, Cambridge CB1 4RP.

Bowyer, M. J. F., 32 Netherhall Way, Cambridge.

*Boxer, Professor C. R., DLitt, FBA, Ringshall End, Little Gaddesden, Berkhamsted, Herts.

Boyce, D. G., BA, PhD, Dept of Political Theory and Government, University College of Swansea, Swansea SA2 8PP.

Boyle, T., Cert.Ed, BA, MPhil, Jersey Cottage, Mark Beech, Edenbridge, Kent TN8 5NS.

Boynton, L. O. J., MA, DPhil, FSA, Dept of History, Westfield College, Kidderspore Avenue, London NW3 7ST.

Brading, D. A., MA, PhD, 28 Storey Way, Cambridge CB3 0DT.

Bradshaw, Rev. B., MA, BD, PhD, Queens' College, Cambridge CB3 9ET.

Brake, Rev. G. Thompson, 61 Westwood Gardens, Hadleigh, Benfleet, Essex SS7 2SH.

Brand, P. A., MA, DPhil, 155 Kennington Road, London SE11.

Brandon, P. F., BA, PhD, Greensleeves, 8 St Julian's Lane, Shoreham-by-Sea, Sussex BN4 6YS.

Breck, Professor A. D., MA, PhD, LHD, DLitt, University of Denver, Denver, Colorado 80208, U.S.A.

Breen, Professor T. H., PhD, Dept of History, North Western University, Evanston, Illinois 60208, U.S.A.

Brentano, Professor R., DPhil, University of California, Berkeley 4, Calif., U.S.A.

Brett, M., MA, DPhil, Robinson College, Cambridge CB3 9AN.

Breuilly, J. J., BA, DPhil, Dept of History, The University, Manchester M13 9PL.

Brewer, J., PhD, University of California—Los Angeles, Center for 17th and 18th Century Studies, 2221B Bunche Hall, Los Angeles, CA 90024-1404, U.S.A.

Bridge, C. R., BA, PhD, History Dept., University of New England, Armidale, N.S.W. 2350, Australia.

Bridge, F. R., PhD, The Poplars, Rodley Lane, Rodley, Leeds.

Bridges, R. C., BA, PhD, Dept of History, University of Aberdeen, King's College, Aberdeen AB9 2UB.

Brigden, Susan, BA, PhD, MA, Lincoln College Oxford, OX1 3DR.
Briggs, Lord, BSc(Econ), MA, DLitt, FBA, Worcester College, Oxford OX1 2HB.
Briggs, J. H. Y., MA, Dept of History, The University, Keele, Staffs. ST5 5BG.
Briggs, R., MA, All Souls College, Oxford OX1 4AL.
Britnell, R. H., MA, PhD, Dept of History, The University, 43–46 North Bailey, Durham, DH1 3EX.
Broad, J., BA, DPhil, Dept of History, Polytechnic of North London, Prince of Wales Road, London NW5 3LB.
Broadhead, P. J., BA, PhD, Dept of History, Goldsmiths' College, Lewisham Way, London SE14 6NW.
Brock, M. G., MA, St George's House, Windsor Castle, Berkshire SL4 1NJ.
Brock, Professor W. R., MA, PhD, 49 Barton Road, Cambridge CB3 9LG.
Brocklesby, R., BA, The Elms, North Eastern Road, Thorne, Doncaster, S. Yorks. DN8 4AS.
Brogan, D. H. V., MA, Dept of History, University of Essex, Wivenhoe Park, Colchester, Essex CO4 3SQ.
*Brooke, Professor C. N. L., MA, LittD, FBA, FSA, Faculty of History, West Road, Cambridge CB3 9EF.
Brooke, Mrs R. B., MA, PhD, c/o Faculty of History, West Road, Cambridge CB3 9EF.
Brooks, C. W., AB, DPhil, Dept of History, The University, 43 North Bailey, Durham, DH1 3EX.
Brooks, Professor N. P., MA, DPhil, Dept of Medieval History, The University, Birmingham B15 2TT.
Brown, Professor A. L., MA, DPhil, Dept of History, The University, Glasgow G12 8QQ.
Brown, The Rev. A. W. G., BA, BD, PhD, The Manse, 28 Quay Road, Ballycastle, Co. Antrim BT54 6BH, N. Ireland.
Brown, G. S., PhD, 1720 Hanover Road, Ann Arbor, Mich. 48103, U.S.A.
Brown, Judith M., MA, PhD, 8 The Downs, Cheadle, Cheshire SK8 1JL.
Brown, Professor K. D., BA, MA, PhD, Dept of Economic and Social History, The Queen's University, Belfast BT7 1NN, N. Ireland.
Brown, Professor M. J., MA, PhD, 350 South Candler Street, Decatur, Georgia 30030, U.S.A.
Brown, P. D., MA, 18 Davenant Road, Oxford OX2 8BX.
Brown, P. R. L., MA, FBA, Hillslope, Pullen's Lane, Oxford.
Brown, T. S., MA, PhD, Dept of History, The University, William Robertson Building, 50 George Square, Edinburgh, EH8 9JY.
Brown, Professor Wallace, PhD, Dept of History, University of New Brunswick, P.O. Box 4400, Fredericton, NB., Canada E3B 5AE.
Bruce, J. M., ISO, MA, FRAeS, 51 Chiltern Drive, Barton-on-Sea, New Milton, Hants. BH25 7JZ.
Brundage, Professor J. A., Dept of History, University of Wisconsin at Milwaukee, Milwaukee, Wisconsin, U.S.A.
Bryson, Professor W. Hamilton, School of Law, University of Richmond, Richmond, Va. 23173, U.S.A.
Buchanan, R. A., MA, PhD, School of Humanities and Social Sciences, The University, Claverton Down, Bath BA2 7AY.
Buckland, P. J. B., MA, PhD, 6 Rosefield Road, Liverpool L25 8TF.
Buisseret, Professor D. J., MA, PhD, The Newberry Library, 60 West Walton Street, Chicago, Ill. 60610, U.S.A.
Bullock, Lord, MA, DLitt, FBA, St Catherine's College, Oxford OX1 3UJ.

Bullough, Professor D. A., MA, FSA, Dept of Mediaeval History, The University, 71 South Street, St Andrews, Fife KY16 9AJ.
Bumsted, Professor J. M., PhD, St John's College, University of Manitoba, Winnipeg, Mb., Canada R3T 2M5.
Burgess, C. R., MA, DPhil, Dept of History, Royal Holloway and Bedford New College, Egham, Surrey TW20 0EX.
Burk, Kathleen M., BA, MA, DPhil, The Long Barn, Towns End, Harwell, Oxon. OX11 0DX.
Burke, U. P., MA, Emmanuel College, Cambridge CB2 3AP.
Burleigh, M., BA, PhD, Dept of International History, London School of Economics, Houghton Street, Aldwych, London WC2A 2AE.
BURNS, Professor J. H., MA, PhD, 6 Chiltern House, Hillcrest Road, London W5 1HL.
Burroughs, P., PhD, Dept of History, Dalhousie University, Halifax, Nova Scotia, Canada B3H 3J5.
Burrow, Professor J. W., MA., PhD, Sussex University, Falmer, Brighton BN1 9QX.
Burt, R., BSc, PhD, Dept of Economic History, Amory Building, University of Exeter, Devon.
Butler, R. D'O., CMG, MA, DLitt, All Souls College, Oxford OX1 4AL.
Byerly, Professor B. F., BA, MA, PhD, Dept of History, University of Northern Colorado, Greeley, Colorado 80631, U.S.A.
Bythell, D., MA, DPhil, Dept of History, University of Durham, 43/46 North Bailey, Durham DH1 3EX.

Cabaniss, Professor J. A., PhD, University of Mississippi, Box No. 253, University, Mississippi 38677, U.S.A.
Callahan, Professor Raymond, PhD, Dept of History, University of Delaware, Newark, Delaware 19716, U.S.A.
Callahan, Professor Thomas, Jr., PhD, Dept of History, Rider College, Lawrenceville, N.J. 08648, U.S.A.
Calvert, Brigadier J. M. (ret.), DSO, MA, MICE, 33a Mill Hill Close, Haywards Heath, Sussex.
Calvert, Professor P. A. R., MA, PhD, AM, Dept of Politics, University of Southampton, Highfield, Southampton SO9 5NH.
Cameron, A., BA, 6 Braid Crescent, Morningside, Edinburgh EH10 6AU.
Cameron, E. K., MA, DPhil, 35 Oaklands, Gosforth, Newcastle upon Tyne NE3 4YP.
Cameron, Professor J. K., MA, BD, PhD, St Mary's College, University of St Andrews, Fife KY16 9JU.
Cameron, Professor K., PhD, FBA, Dept of English, The University, Nottingham NG7 2RD.
Campbell, Professor A. E., MA, PhD, 3 Belbroughton Road, Oxford, OX2 6UZ.
Campbell, G. R., MA, DPhil, Dept of English, The University, Leicester LE1 7RH.
Campbell, J., MA, FBA, Worcester College, Oxford OX1 2HB.
*Campbell, Professor Mildred L., PhD, Vassar College, Poughkeepsie, N.Y., U.S.A.
Campbell, P. R., BA, PhD, School of European Studies, University of Sussex, Falmer, Brighton BN1 9QN.
Campbell, Professor R. H., MA, PhD, Craig, Glenluce, Newton Stewart, Wigtownshire DG8 0NR.

Cannadine, D. N., BA, MA, DPhil, Dept. of History, Fayerweather Hall, Columbia University, New York, NY 10027, USA.
Canning, J. P., MA, PhD, Dept of History, University College of North Wales, Bangor, Gwynedd LL57 2DG.
Cannon, Professor J. A., CBE, MA, PhD, Dept of History, The University, Newcastle upon Tyne NE1 7RU.
Canny, Professor N. P., MA, PhD, Dept of History, University College, Galway, Ireland.
Cant, R. G., MA, DLitt, 3 Kinburn Place, St Andrews, Fife KY16 9DT.
Cantor, Professor N. F., PhD, Dept of History, New York University, 19 University Place, 4th Floor, New York, NY 10003, U.S.A.
Capp, B. S., MA, DPhil, Dept of History, University of Warwick, Coventry, Warwickshire CV4 7AL.
Carey, P. B. R., DPhil, Trinity College, Oxford OX1 3BH.
*Carlson, Leland H., PhD, Huntington Library, San Marino, California 91108, U.S.A.
Carlton, Professor Charles, Dept of History, North Carolina State University, Raleigh, NC 27607, U.S.A.
Carman, W. Y., FSA, 94 Mulgrave Road, Sutton, Surrey.
Carpenter, D. A., MA, DPhil, Dept of History, King's College London, Strand, London WC2R 2LS.
Carpenter, M. Christine, MA, PhD, New Hall, Cambridge CB3 0DF.
Carr, A. D., MA, PhD, Dept of Welsh History, University College of North Wales, Bangor, Gwynedd LL57 2DG.
Carr, Sir Raymond, MA, FBA, Burch, North Molton, South Molton, EX36 3JU.
Carr, W., PhD, 22 Southbourne Road, Sheffield S10 2QN.
Carrington, Miss Dorothy, 3 Rue Emmanuel Arene, 20 Ajaccio, Corsica.
Carter, Jennifer J., BA, PhD, The Old Schoolhouse, Glenbuchat, Strathdon, Aberdeenshire AB3 8TT.
Carwardine, R. J., MA, DPhil, Dept of History, The University, Sheffield S10 2TN.
Casey, J., BA, PhD, School of Modern Languages and European History, University of East Anglia, University Plain, Norwich NR4 7TJ.
Cassels, Professor Alan, MA, PhD, Dept of History, McMaster University, Hamilton, Ontario, Canada L8S 4L9.
Cassis, Y., Docteur ès Lettres, 35 Hilltop, London NW11 6ED.
Catto, R. J. A. I., MA, Oriel College, Oxford OX1 4EW.
Cazel, Professor Fred A., Jr., Dept of History, University of Connecticut, Storrs, Conn. 06268, U.S.A.
Cell, Professor J. W., PhD, Dept of History, Duke University, Durham, NC 27706, U.S.A.
Cesarani, D., DPhil, 95 Greencroft Gardens, London NW6 3PG.
Chadwick, Professor W. O., OM, KBE, DD, DLitt, FBA, Selwyn Lodge, Cambridge CB3 9DQ.
Challis, C. E., MA, PhD, 14 Ashwood Villas, Headingley, Leeds 6.
Chalmers, C. D., Public Record Office, Ruskin Avenue, Kew, Richmond, Surrey TW9 4DU.
Chamberlain, Muriel E., MA. DPhil, Dept of History, University College of Swansea, Singleton Park, Swansea SA2 7BR.
Chambers, D. S., MA, DPhil, Warburg Institute, Woburn Square, London WC1H 0AB.
Chandaman, Professor C. D., BA, PhD, 23 Bellamy Close, Ickenham, Uxbridge UB10 8SJ.

Chandler, D. G., MA, Hindford, Monteagle Lane, Yateley, Camberley, Surrey.
Chaplais, P., PhD, FBA, FSA, Lew Lodge, Lew, Oxford OX8 2BE.
Chapman, Professor R.A., BA, MA, PhD, FBIM, Dept of Politics, The University, 48 Old Elvet, Durham, DH1 3LZ.
Charles-Edwards, T. M., DPhil, Corpus Christi College, Oxford OX1 4JF.
Charmley, J., MA, DPhil, School of English and American Studies, University of East Anglia, University Plain, Norwich NR4 7TJ.
Chartres, J. A., MA, DPhil, School of Economic Studies, The University, Leeds LS2 9JT.
Chaudhuri, Professor Kirti Narayan, BA, PhD, History Department, S.O.A.S., University of London, Malet Street, London WC1E 7HD.
Cheney, Mrs Mary, MA, 17 Westberry Court, Grange Road, Cambridge CB3 9BG.
Cherry, John, MA, 58 Lancaster Road, London N4.
Chibnall, Mrs Marjorie, MA, DPhil, FBA, 7 Croftgate, Fulbrooke Road, Cambridge CB3 9EG.
Child, C. J., OBE, MA, PhD, 94 Westhall Road, Warlingham, Surrey CR3 9HB.
Childs, J. C. R., BA, PhD, School of History, The University, Leeds LS2 9JT.
Childs, Wendy R., MA, PhD, School of History, The University, Leeds LS2 9JT.
Chitnis, Anand Chidamber, BA, MA, PhD, Principal, LSU College of Higher Education, The Avenue, Southampton SO9 5HB.
Christiansen, E., New College, Oxford OX1 3BN.
Christianson, Professor P. K., PhD, Dept of History, Queen's University, Kingston, Ontario, Canada K7L 3N6.
Christie, Professor I. R., MA, FBA, 10 Green Lane, Croxley Green, Herts. WD3 3HR.
Church, Professor R. A., BA, PhD, School of Social Studies, University of East Anglia, University Plain, Norwich NOR 88C.
Cirket, A. F., 71 Curlew Crescent, Bedford.
Clanchy, M. T., MA, PhD, FSA, 28 Hillfield Road, London NW6 1PZ.
Clapinson, Mrs Mary, MA, Dept of Western Manuscripts, Bodleian Library, Oxford OX1 3BG.
Clark, A. E., MA, 32 Durham Avenue, Thornton Cleveleys, Blackpool FY5 2DP.
Clark, D. S. T., BA, PhD, Dept of History, University College of Swansea, Swansea SA2 8PP.
Clark, J. C. D., MA, PhD, All Souls College, Oxford OX1 4AL.
Clark, P. A., MA, Dept of Economic and Social History, The University, University Road, Leicester LE1 7RH.
Clarke, Howard B., BA, PhD, Room K104, Arts-Commerce-Law Building, University College, Dublin 4, Ireland.
Clarke, P. F., MA, PhD, St John's College, Cambridge CB2 1TP.
Clementi, Miss D., MA, DPhil, Flat 7, 43 Rutland Gate, London SW7 1BP.
Clemoes, Professor P. A. M., BA, PhD, Emmanuel College, Cambridge CB2 3AP.
Cliffe, J. T., BA, PhD, 263 Staines Road, Twickenham, Middx. TW2 5AY.
Clifton, R., DPhil, 58 Mickleton Road, Coventry, West Midlands.
Clough, C. H., MA, DPhil, FSA, School of History, The University, P.O. Box 147, Liverpool L69 3BX.

Cobb, H. S., MA, FSA, 1 Child's Way, Hampstead Garden Suburb, London NW11.
Cobban, A. B., MA, PhD, School of History, The University, P.O. Box 147, Liverpool L69 3BX.
Cockburn, Professor J. S., LLB, LLM, PhD, History Dept, University of Maryland, College Park, Maryland 20742, U.S.A.
Cocks, E. J., MA, Middle Lodge, Ardingly, Haywards Heath, Sussex RH17 6TS.
Cohn, H. J., MA, DPhil, Dept of History, University of Warwick, Coventry CV4 7AL.
Cohn, Professor N. R. C., MA, DLitt, FBA, Orchard Cottage, Wood End, Ardeley, Herts. SG2 7AZ.
Coleby, A. M., BA, 24 Lumley Road, Newton Hall, Durham DH1 5NR.
Coleman, B. I., MA, PhD, Dept of History, The University, Exeter EX4 4QH.
Coleman, C. H. D., MA, Dept of History, University College London, Gower Street, London WC1E 6BT.
Coleman, Professor D. C., BSc(Econ.), PhD, LittD, FBA, Over Hall, Cavendish, Sudbury, Suffolk.
Colley, Professor Linda J., BA, MA, PhD, Dept of History, Yale University, PO Box 1504A Yale Station, New Haven, Connecticut 06520-7425, U.S.A.
Collier, W. O., MA, FSA, 34 Berwyn Road, Richmond, Surrey.
Collinge, J. M., BA, 36 Monks Road, Enfield, Middlesex EN2 8BH.
Collini, S. A., MA, PhD, Faculty of English, 9 West Road, Cambridge CB3 9DP.
Collins, B. W., MA, PhD, The Dean, School of Humanities, The University, Buckingham MK18 1EG.
Collins, Mrs I., MA, BLitt, School of History, The University, P.O. Box 147, Liverpool L69 3BX.
Collinson, Professor P., MA, PhD, DLitt, DUniv, FBA, FAHA, Trinity College, Cambridge, CB2 1TQ.
Colvin, H. M., CBE, MA, FBA, St John's College, Oxford OX1 3JP.
Colyer, R. J., BSc, PhD, Inst. of Rural Sciences, University College of Wales, Aberystwyth, Dyfed.
Connell-Smith, Professor G. E., PhD, 7 Braids Walk, Kirkella, Hull, Yorks. HU10 7PA.
Connolly, Sean J., BA, DPhil, Dept of History, University of Ulster, Coleraine, Northern Ireland BT52 1SA.
Constantine, S., BA, DPhil, Dept of History, The University, Bailrigg, Lancaster LA1 4YG.
Contamine, Professor P., DèsL., 12 Villa Croix Nivert, 75015 Paris, France.
Conway, Professor A. A., MA, University of Canterbury, Christchurch 1, New Zealand.
Conway, S. R., BA, PhD, The Bentham Project, Dept of History, University College London, Gower Street, London WC1E 6BT.
Cook, C. P., MA, DPhil, Dept of History, Philosophy and European Studies, The Polytechnic of North London, Prince of Wales Road, London NW5 3LB.
Cooke, Professor, J. J., PhD., Dept of History, University of Mississippi, College of Liberal Arts, University, Miss. 38677, U.S.A.
Coolidge, Professor R. T., MA, BLitt, P.O. Box 4070, Westmount, Quebec, Canada H3Z 2X3.

Cooper, Janet M., MA, PhD, 7 Stonepath Drive, Hatfield Peverel, Chelmsford CM3 2LG.

Cope, Professor Esther S., PhD, Dept of History, Univ. of Nebraska, Lincoln, Neb. 68508, U.S.A.

Copley, A. R. H., MA, MPhil, Rutherford College, The University, Canterbury, Kent CT2 7NX.

Corfield, Penelope J., MA, PhD, Dept of History, Royal Holloway and Bedford New College, Egham Hill, Egham, Surrey TW20 0EX.

Cornell, Professor Paul G., PhD, 202 Laurier Place, Waterloo, Ontario, Canada N2L 1K8.

Corner, D. J., BA, Dept of History, St Salvator's College, The University, St Andrews, Fife KY16 9AJ.

Cornford, Professor J. P., MA, The Brick House, Wicken Bonhunt, Saffron Walden, Essex CB11 3UG.

Cornwall, J. C. K., MA, 1 Orchard Close, Copford Green, Colchester, Essex.

Cosgrove, A. J., BA, PhD, Dept of Medieval History, University College, Dublin 4, Ireland.

Coss, P. R., BA, PhD, 20 Whitebridge Close, Whitebridge Grove, Gosforth, Newcastle upon Tyne NE3 2DN.

Costeloe, Professor M. P., BA, PhD, Dept of Hispanic and Latin American Studies, The University, 83 Woodland Road, Bristol BS8 1RJ.

Countryman, E. F., PhD, Dept of History, University of Warwick, Coventry CV4 7AL.

Cowan, A. F., BA, PhD, 18 Fern Avenue, Jesmond, Newcastle upon Tyne NE2 2QT.

Cowan, I. B., MA, PhD, Dept of History, University of Glasgow, Glasgow G12 8QQ.

Coward, B., BA, PhD, Dept of History, Birkbeck College, Malet Street, London WC1E 7HX.

Cowdrey, Rev. H. E. J., MA, St Edmund Hall, Oxford OX1 4AR.

Cowie, The Rev. L. W., MA, PhD, 38 Stratton Road, Merton Park, London SW19 3JG.

Cowley, F. G., PhD, 17 Brookvale Road, West Cross, Swansea, W. Glam.

Cox, D. C., BA, PhD, 12 Oakfield Road, Copthorne, Shrewsbury SY3 8AA.

Craig, R. S., BSc(Econ), The Anchorage, Bay Hill, St Margarets Bay, nr Dover, Kent CT15 6DU.

Cramp, Professor Rosemary, MA, BLitt, FSA, Department of Archaeology, 46 Saddler Street, Durham DH1 3NU.

Crampton, R. J., BA, PhD, Rutherford College, The University, Canterbury, Kent CT2 7NP.

Cranfield, L. R., Lot 9, Gregory Terrace, Spring Hill, Brisbane, Queensland 4006, Australia.

Craton, Professor M. J., BA, MA, PhD, Dept of History, University of Waterloo, Waterloo, Ontario, Canada N2L 3G1.

Crawford, Patricia M., BA, MA, PhD, Dept of History, University of Western Australia, Nedlands, Western Australia 6009.

*Crawley, C. W., MA, 93 Castelnau, London SW13 9EL.

Cremona, His Hon Chief Justice Professor J. J., KM, DLitt, PhD, LLD, DrJur, Villa Barbaro, Main Street, Attard, Malta.

Cressy, D. A., MA, PhD, 231 West Sixth Street, Claremont, Calif. 91711, U.S.A.

Crimmin, Patricia K., MPhil, BA, Dept of History, Royal Holloway and Bedford New College, Egham Hill, Egham, Surrey TW20 0EX.

Crisp, Professor Olga, BA, PhD, 'Zarya', 1 Milbrook, Arbrook Lane, Esher, Surrey.
Croft, J. Pauline, MA, DPhil, Dept of History, Royal Holloway and Bedford New College, Egham Hill, Egham, Surrey TW20 0EX.
Crombie, A. C., BSc, MA, PhD, Trinity College, Oxford OX1 3BH.
Cromwell, Miss V., MA, Arts Building, University of Sussex, Brighton, Sussex BN1 9QN.
Crook, D., MA, PhD, Public Record Office, Chancery Lane, London WC2A 1LR.
Crosby, Professor T. L., Dept of History, Wheaton College, Norton, Mass., 02766 USA.
Cross, Professor M. Claire, MA, PhD, Dept of History, The University, York YO1 5DD.
Crossick, G. J., MA, PhD, Dept of History, University of Essex, Wivenhoe Park, Colchester CO4 3SQ.
Crouch, D. B., PhD, 17c St Johns Grove, Archway, London N19 5RW.
Crowder, Professor Emeritus C. M. D., MA, DPhil, Dept of History, Queen's University, Kingston, Ontario, Canada K7L 3N6.
Crowe, Miss S. E., MA, PhD, 112 Staunton Road, Headington, Oxford.
Crozier, A. J., BA, MA, PhD, 49 Strongbow Crescent, Eltham, London SE9 1DN.
Cruickshanks, Eveline G., PhD, 46 Goodwood Court, Devonshire Street, London W1N 1SL.
Cueto, R., MA, Dr Fil Y Let, 32 Parkside, Horsforth, Leeds.
Cumming, Professor A., MA, DipMA, PGCE, PhD, Carseldine Campus of the Brisbane College of Advanced Education, P.O. Box 284, Zillmere, Queensland 4034, Australia.
Cumming, I., MEd, PhD, 7 Kirkfell Court, Benwick, Victoria 3806, Australia.
Cummins, Professor J. S., PhD, University College London, Gower Street, London WC1E 6BT.
Cunliffe, Professor M. F., MA, BLitt, DHL, Room 102, T Building, George Washington University, 2110 G. Street N.W., Washington, D.C., 20052, U.S.A.
Currie, C. R. J., MA, DPhil, V.C.H., Institute of Historical Research, Senate House, Malet Street, London WC1E 7HU.
Currie, R., MA, DPhil, Wadham College, Oxford OX1 3PN.
Curry, Anne E., BA, MA, PhD, 5 Melrose Avenue, Reading, Berkshire RG6 2BN.
Curtis, Professor L. Perry, Jr, PhD, Dept of History, Brown University, Providence, R.I. 02912, U.S.A.
*Cuttino, G. P., DPhil, FBA, FSA, 1270 University Dr. N. E., Atlanta, Ga. 30306, U.S.A.
Cuttler, S. H., BPhil, DPhil, 5051 Clanranald →302, Montreal, Quebec, Canada H3X 2S3.

*Dacre, Lord, MA, FBA, Peterhouse, Cambridge CB2 1RD.
Dakin, Professor D., MA, PhD, 20 School Road, Apperley, Gloucester GL19 4DJ.
Dales, Rev. D. J., MA, Hillside, Bath Road, Marlborough, Wiltshire SN8 1NN.
Danchev, A., MA, PGCE, PhD, Dept of International Relations, University of Keele, Keele, Staffs. ST5 5BG.

Das Gupta, Professor A., MA, PhD, National Library, Belvedere, Calcutta, India 700027.
DAUNTON, Professor M. J., BA, PhD (*Hon. Treasurer*), Dept of History, University College London, Gower Street, London WC1E 6BT.
Davenport, Professor T. R. H., MA, PhD, 78c Palmyra Road, Newlands 7700, South Africa.
Davenport-Hines, R. P. T., PhD, BA, 51 Elsham Road, Holland Park, London W14 8HD.
Davidson, R., MA, PhD, Dept of Economic and Social History, The University, 50 George Square, Edinburgh EH8 9JY.
Davies, C. S. L., MA, DPhil, Wadham College, Oxford OX1 3PN.
Davies, I. N. R., MA, DPhil, 22 Rowland Close, Wolvercote, Oxford.
Davies, P. N., MA, PhD, Cmar, Croft Drive, Caldy, Wirral, Merseyside.
Davies, R. G., MA, PhD, Dept of History, The Victoria University of Manchester, Oxford Road, Manchester M13 9PL.
Davies, Professor R. R., BA, DPhil, University College of Wales, Dept of History, Hugh Owen Building, Aberystwyth SY23 3DY.
Davies, Professor Wendy, BA, PhD, Dept of History, University College London, Gower Street, London WC1E 6BT.
*Davis, G. R. C., CBE, MA, DPhil, FSA, 214 Somerset Road, London SW19 5JE.
Davis, J. A., MA, DPhil, Dept of History, University of Warwick, Coventry CV4 7AL.
Davis, Professor J. C., Dept of History, Massey University, Palmerston North, New Zealand.
Davis, J. H., BA, DPhil, The Queen's College, Oxford OX1 4AW.
Davis, Professor R. H. C., MA, FBA, FSA, 349 Banbury Road, Oxford OX2 7PL.
Davis, Professor Richard W., Dept of History, Washington University, St Louis, Missouri 63130, U.S.A.
*Dawe, D. A., 46 Green Lane, Purley, Surrey.
Day. A. F., PhD, Dept of History, The University, Wm. Robertson Building, George Street, Edinburgh EH8 9JY.
Deane, Professor Phyllis M., MA, 4 Stukeley Close, Cambridge CB3 9LT.
de Hamel, C. F. R., BA, DPhil, FSA, Chase House, Perry's Chase, Greenstead Road, Ongar, Essex CM5 9LA.
de la Mare, Miss A. C., MA, PhD, King's College London, Strand, London WC2R 2LS.
Denham, E. W., MA, 4 The Ridge, 89 Green Lane, Northwood, Middx. HA6 1AE.
Denley, P. R., Dept of History, Queen Mary & Westfield College, University of London, Hampstead Campus, Kidderpore Avenue, London NW3 7ST.
Dennis, Professor P. J., MA, PhD, Dept of History, University College, University of New South Wales, Australian Defence Force Academy, Campbell, A.C.T. 2600, Australia.
Denton, Barry, 10 Melrose Avenue, off Bants Lane, Northampton, NN5 5PB.
Denton, J. H., BA, PhD, Dept of History, The University, Manchester M13 9PL.
Derry, J. W., MA, PhD, Dept of History, The University, Newcastle upon Tyne NE1 7RU.
Devine, T. M., BA, Viewfield Cottage, 55 Burnbank Road, Hamilton, Strathclyde Region.

Dewey, P. E., BA, PhD, Dept of History, Royal Holloway and Bedford New College, Egham Hill, Egham, Surrey TW20 0EX.

DICKENS, Professor A. G., CMG, MA, DLit, DLitt, LittD, FBA, FSA, Institute of Historical Research, University of London, Senate House, London WC1E 7HU.

Dickinson, Professor H. T., BA, MA, PhD, DLitt, Dept of Modern History, The University, Edinburgh EH8 9YL.

Dickinson, Rev. J. C., MA, DLitt, FSA, Yew Tree Cottage, Barngarth, Cartmel, South Cumbria.

Dickson, M. G., AB, MA, PhD, 25A Abercorn Terrace, Edinburgh EH15 2DF.

Dickson, Professor P. G. M., MA, DPhil, FBA, St Catherine's College, Oxford, OX1 3UJ.

Dilks, Professor D. N., BA, Dept of International History, The University, Leeds LS2 9JT.

Dilworth, Rev. G. M., OSB, MA, PhD, Scottish Catholic Archives, Columba House, 16 Drummond Place, Edinburgh EH3 6PL.

Ditchfield, G. McC, BA, PhD, Darwin College, University of Kent, Canterbury, Kent CT2 7NY.

Dobson, Professor R. B., MA, DPhil, Professor of Medieval History, Christ's College, Cambridge CB2 3BU.

Dockrill, M. L., MA, BSc(Econ), PhD, Dept of History, King's College London, Strand, London WC2R 2LS.

*Dodwell, Miss B., MA, 30 Eaton Road, Norwich NR4 6PZ.

Don Peter, The Rt Revd Monsignor W. L. A., MA, PhD, St. John Vianney Seminary, Tudella, Ja-ela, Sri Lanka.

Donahue, Professor Charles, Jr, AB, LLB, Dept of Law, Harvard University, Cambridge, Mass. 02138, U.S.A.

*DONALDSON, Professor G., CBE, MA, PhD, DLitt, DLitt, DUniv, FRSE, FBA, 6 Pan Ha', Dysart, Fife KY1 2TL.

Donaldson, Professor P. S., MA, PhD, Dept of Humanities, 14N-422, Massachusetts Institute of Technology, Cambridge, Mass. 02139, U.S.A.

*Donaldson-Hudson, Miss R., BA, (address unknown).

Donoughue, Lord, MA, DPhil, 1 Sloane Square, London SW1W 8EE.

Doran, Susan M., BA, PhD, Downgate House, 25 Wharf Road, Shillingford, Oxfordshire OX9 8EW.

Dore, R. N., MA, Holmrook, 19 Chapel Lane, Hale Barns, Altrincham, Cheshire WA15 0AB.

Dow, Frances D., MA, DPhil, Dept of History, University of Edinburgh, George Square, Edinburgh EH8 9JY.

Dowling, Maria J. C., BA, PhD, c/o Institute of Historical Research, Senate House, Malet Street, London WC1E 7HU.

Downer, L. J., MA, BA, LLB, 29 Roebuck Street, Red Hill, Canberra 2603, Australia.

Doyle, A. I., MA, PhD, University College, The Castle, Durham.

Doyle, Professor W., MA, DPhil, DrHC, Dept of History, The University, 13–15 Woodland Road, Bristol BS8 1TB.

Driver, J. T., MA, BLitt, PhD, 25 Abbot's Grange, Chester CH2 1AJ.

*Drus, Miss E., MA, 18 Brampton Tower, Bassett Avenue, Southampton SO1 7FB.

Duckham, Professor B. F., MA, Bronllan, Betws Bledrws, near Lampeter, Dyfed SA48 8NY.

Duffy, Michael, MA, DPhil, Dept of History and Archaeology, The University, Queen's Drive, Exeter EX4 4QH.

Duggan, Anne J., BA, PhD, Dept of History, King's College London, Strand, London WC2R 2LS.

Duggan, C., PhD, Dept of History, King's College London, Strand, London WC2R 2LS.

Dugmore, The Rev. Professor C. W., DD, Thame Cottage, The Street, Puttenham, Guildford, Surrey GU3 1AT.

Duke, A. C., MA, Dept of History, The University, Southampton SO9 5NH.

Dumville, D. N., MA, PhD, Dept of Anglo-Saxon, Norse and Celtic, University of Cambridge, 9 West Road, Cambridge CB3 9DP.

Dunbabin, Jean H., MA, DPhil, St Anne's College, Oxford OX2 6HS.

Dunbabin, J. P. D., MA, St Edmund Hall, Oxford OX1 4AR.

Duncan, Professor A. A. M., MA, Dept of History, The University, 9 University Gardens, Glasgow G12 8QQ.

Dunn, Professor R. S., PhD, Dept of History, The College, University of Pennsylvania, Philadelphia, 19104, Pa., U.S.A.

Dunning, R. W., BA, PhD, FSA, Musgrove Manor East, Barton Close, Taunton TA1 4RU.

Dunthorne, H. L. A., MA, PhD, Dept of History, University College, Swansea, SA2 8PP.

Durack, Mrs I. A., MA, PhD, 34 Melvista Aveue, Claremont, Western Australia 6010.

Durey, M. J., BA, DPhil, School of Social Inquiry, Murdoch University, Perth, Western Australia 6150.

Durie, A. J., MA, PhD, Dept of Economic History, Edward Wright Building, The University, Aberdeen AB9 2TY.

Durkan, J., MA, PhD, DLitt, Dept of Scottish History, The University, Glasgow G12 8QH.

Durston, C. G., MA, PhD, 42 Hawthorn Avenue, Headington, Oxford OX3 9JG.

Dusinberre, W. W., PhD, Dept of History, University of Warwick, Coventry CV4 7AL.

Dutton, D. J., BA, PhD, School of History, The University, P.O. Box 147, Liverpool L69 3BX.

Dyer, C. C., BA, PhD, School of History, The University, P.O. Box 363, Birmingham B15 2TT.

Dykes, D. W., MA, Cherry Grove, Welsh St Donats, nr Cowbridge, Glam. CF7 7SS.

Dymond, D. P., MA, FSA, 4 Honey Hill, Bury St. Edmonds, Suffolk IP33 1RT.

Dyson, Professor K. H. F., BSc(Econ), MSc(Econ), PhD, Undergraduate School of European Studies, The University, Bradford, West Yorkshire BD7 1DP.

Earle, P., BSc(Econ), PhD, Dept of Economic History, London School of Economics, Houghton Street, London WC2A 2AE.

Eastwood, Rev. C. C., PhD, Heathview, Monks Lane, Audlem, Cheshire SW3 0HP.

Eckles, Professor R. B., PhD, P.O. Box 6558. San Antonio, Texas 78209, U.S.A.

Edbury, P. W., MA, PhD, School of History and Archaeology, University of Wales College of Cardiff, P.O. Box 909, Cardiff CF1 3XU.

Eddy, Rev. J. J., BA, DPhil, History Dept, The Research School of Social Sciences, The Australian National University, GPO Box 4, Canberra, A.C.T. 2601, Australia.

Ede, J. R., CB, MA, Palfreys, East Street, Drayton, Langport, Somerset TA10 0JZ.
Edmonds, Professor E. L., MA, PhD, University of Prince Edward Island, Charlottetown, Prince Edward Island, Canada.
Edwards, Rev. F. O., SJ, BA, FSA, 114 Mount Street, London W1Y 6AH.
Edwards, J. H., MA, DPhil, School of History, The University, P.O. Box 363, Birmingham B15 2TT.
Edwards, O. D., BA, Dept of History, William Robertson Building, The University, George Square, Edinburgh EH8 9YL.
Ehrman, J. P. W., MA, FBA, FSA, The Mead Barns, Taynton, Nr Burford, Oxfordshire OX8 5UH.
Eisenstein, Professor Elizabeth L., PhD, 82 Kalorama Circle N.W., Washington D.C. 20008, U.S.A.
Eldridge, C. C., PhD, Dept of History, Saint David's University College, Lampeter, Dyfed SA48 7ED.
Eley, G. H., BA, DPhil, MA, MA, Dept of History, University of Michigan, Ann Arbor, Michigan 48109, U.S.A.
Elliott, Professor J. H., MA, PhD, FBA, The Institute for Advanced Studies, Princeton, New Jersey 08540, U.S.A.
Elliott, Professor J. R., Jr., PhD, Syracuse University, Syracuse, NY13244-1170, U.S.A.
Elliott, Marianne, BA, DPhil, Dept of History, The University, P.O. Box 147, Liverpool L69 3BX.
Ellis, G. J., MA, DPhil, Hertford College, Oxford OX1 3BW.
Ellis, R. H., MA, FSA, Cloth Hill, 6 The Mount, London NW3.
Ellis, S. G., BA, MA, PhD, Dept of History, University College, Galway, Ireland.
Ellsworth, Professor Edward W., AB, AM, PhD, 27 Englewood Avenue, Brookline, Mass. 02146, U.S.A.
Ellul, M., BArch, DipArch, 'Pauline', 55 Old Railway Road, Birkirkara, Malta.
Elrington, C. R., MA, FSA, Institute of Historical Research, Senate House, Malet Street, London WC1E 7HU.
ELTON, Professor Sir Geoffrey, MA, PhD, LittD, DLitt, DLitt, DLit, FBA, 30 Millington Road, Cambridge CB3 9HP.
Elvin, L., FSA, FRSA, 10 Almond Avenue, Swanpool, Lincoln LN6 0HB.
*Emmison, F. G., MBE, PhD, DUniv, FSA, 8 Coppins Close, Chelmsford, Essex CM2 6AY.
Emsley, C., BA, MLitt, Arts Faculty, The Open University, Walton Hall, Milton Keynes MK7 6AA.
Emsley, K., MA, LlM, 34 Nab Wood Drive, Shipley, West Yorkshire BD18 4EL.
Emy, Professor H. V., PhD, Dept of Politics, Monash University, Wellington Road, Clayton, Melbourne 3146, Australia.
English, Barbara A., MA, PhD, FSA, Centre of Regional and Local History, Loten Building, The University, Hull, HU6 7RX.
Erickson, Charlotte, J., PhD, 8 High Street, Chesterton, Cambridge CB4 1NG.
*Erith, E. J., Holyport Lodge, The Green, Holyport, Maidenhead, Berkshire SL6 2JA.
Erskine, Mrs A. M., MA, BLitt, FSA, 44 Birchy Barton Hill, Exeter EX1 3EX.
Etherington, N. A., PhD, BA, Dept of History, University of Western Australia, Nedlands, Western Australia 6009.

Evans, Mrs A. K. B., PhD, FSA, White Lodge, 25 Knighton Grange Road, Leicester LE2 2LF.
Evans, E. J., MA, PhD, Dept of History, Furness College, University of Lancaster, Bailrigg, Lancaster LA1 4YG.
Evans, Gillian R., PhD, Fitzwilliam College, Cambridge CB2 3HU.
Evans, R. J., MA, DPhil, School of European Studies, University of East Anglia, Norwich NR4 7TJ.
Evans, R. J. W., MA, PhD, FBA, Brasenose College, Oxford OX1 4AJ.
Everitt, Professor A. M., MA, PhD, FBA, Fieldedge, Poultney Lane, Kimcote, nr Lutterworth, Leicestershire LE17 5RX.
Eyck, Professor U. F. J., MA, BLitt, Dept of History, University of Calgary, 2500 University Drive NW, Calgary, Alberta, Canada T2N IN4.

Fage, Professor J. D., MA, PhD, Hafod Awel, Pennal, Machynlleth, Powis SY20 9DP.
Fairs, G. L., MA, Thornton House, Bear Street, Hay-on-Wye, Hereford HR3 5AN.
Falkus, M. E., BSc(Econ), Dept of History, London School of Economics, Houghton Street, London WC2A 2AE.
Farmer, D. F. H., BLitt, FSA, 26 Swanston Field, Whitchurch, Pangbourne, Berks. RG8 7HP.
Farmer, Professor D. L., 411 Quance Avenue, Saskatoon, Sask., Canada S7H 3B5.
Farr, M. W., MA, FSA, 12 Emscote Road, Warwick.
Fell, Professor C. E., MA, Dept of English, The University, Nottingham NG7 2RD.
Fellows-Jensen, Gillian M., BA, PhD, Københavns Universitets, Institut For Navneforskning, Njalsgade 80, DK-2300 København S, Denmark.
Fenlon, Rev. D. B., BA, PhD, The Oratory, 141 Hagley Road, Birmingham B16 8UE.
Fenn, Rev. R. W. D., ThD, MA, BD, FSA, FSAScot, The Ditch, Bradnor View, Kington, Herefordshire.
Fennell, Professor J., MA, PhD, 8 Canterbury Road, Oxford OX2 6LU.
Fernandez-Armesto, F. F. R., DPhil, River View, Headington Hill, Oxford.
Feuchtwanger, E. J., MA, PhD, Highfield House, Dean Sparsholt, nr Winchester, Hants.
Fieldhouse, Professor D. K., MA, Jesus College, Cambridge CB5 8BL.
Finer, Professor S. E., MA, All Souls College, Oxford OX1 4AL.
Fines, J., MA, PhD, 119 Parklands Road, Chichester.
Finlayson, G. B. A. M., MA, BLitt, 11 Burnhead Road, Glasgow G43 2SU.
Fisher, Professor Alan W., PhD, Dept of History, Michigan State University, East Lansing, Michigan 48824, U.S.A.
Fisher, D. J. V., MA, Jesus College, Cambridge CB3 9AD.
Fisher, H. E. Stephen, BSc, PhD, Dept of History, The University, Amory Building, Rennes Drive, Exeter EX4 4RJ.
Fisher, J. R., BA, MPhil, PhD, School of History, The University, P.O. Box 147, Liverpool L69 3BX.
Fisher, R. M., MA, PhD, Dept of History, University of Queensland, St Lucia, Queensland, Australia 4067.
Fishwick, Professor D., BA, MA, DLitt, Dept of Classics, Humanities Centre, University of Alberta, Edmonton, Alberta, Canada T6G 2E6.
Fitch, Dr M. F. B., CBE, HonFBA, FSA, 22 Ave de Budé, 1202 Geneva, Switzerland.

Fitzpatrick, M. H., PhD, 'Garreg-Wen', Bronant, Aberystwyth, Dyfed SY23 4TQ.
Fletcher, Professor A. J., MA, Dept of History, University of Durham, 43/46 North Bailey, Durham, DH1 3EX.
*Fletcher, The Rt Hon. The Lord, PC, BA, LLD, FSA, 51 Charlbury Road, North Oxford OX2 6UX.
Fletcher, R. A., MA, Dept of History, The University, Heslington, York YO1 5DD.
Flint, Professor J. E., MA, PhD, Dalhousie University, Halifax, Nova Scotia, Canada B3H 3J5.
Flint, Valerie I. J., MA, DPhil, Dept of History, The University, Private Bag, Auckland, New Zealand.
Floud, Professor R. C., MA, DPhil, City of London Polytechnic, 117–119 Houndsditch, London EC3A 7BU.
Fogel, Professor Robert W., PhD, Center for Population Economics, University of Chicago, 1101 East 58th Street, Chicago, Illinois 60637, U.S.A.
Foot, M. R. D., MA, BLitt, 45 Countess Road, London NW5 2XH.
Forbes, D., MA, 18 Thornton Close, Girton, Cambridge CB3 0NQ.
Ford, W. K., BA, 48 Harlands Road, Haywards Heath, West Sussex RH16 1LS.
Forster, G. C. F., BA, FSA, School of History, The University, Leeds LS2 9JT.
Foster, Professor Elizabeth R., AM, PhD, 205 Strafford Avenue, Wayne, Pa. 19087, U.S.A.
Foster, R. F., MA, PhD, Dept of History, Birkbeck College, Malet Street, London WC1E 7HX.
Fowler, Professor K. A., BA, PhD, 2 Nelson Street, Edinburgh 3.
Fowler, Professer P. J., MA, PhD, Dept of Archaeology, The University, Newcastle upon Tyne NE1 7RU.
Fox, J. P., BSc(Econ), MSc(Econ), PhD, 98 Baring Road, London SE12 0PT.
Fox, L., OBE, DL, LHD, MA, FSA, FRSL, Silver Birches, 27 Welcombe Road, Stratford-upon-Avon, Warwickshire.
Fox, R., MA, DPhil, Modern History Faculty, The University, Broad Street, Oxford OX1 3BD.
Frame, R. F., MA, PhD, Dept of History, The University, 43 North Bailey, Durham DH1 3HP.
France, J., BA, PhD, 10 Brynfield Road, Langland, Swansea SA3 4SX.
Franklin, M. J., MA, PhD, Wolfson College, Cambridge CB3 9BB.
Franklin, R. M., The Corner House, Eton College, Windsor, Berkshire SL4 6DB.
Fraser, Lady Antonia, 52 Campden Hill Square, London W8.
*Fraser, Miss C. M., PhD, 39 King Edward Road, Tynemouth, Tyne and Wear NE30 2RW.
Fraser, D., BA, MA, PhD, 117 Alwoodley Lane, Leeds, LS17 7PN.
Freeden, M. S., DPhil, Mansfield College, Oxford OX1 3TF.
French, D. W., BA, PhD, Dept of History, University College London, Gower Street, London WC1E 6BT.
Frend, Professor W. H. C., MA, DPhil, DD, FRSE, FBA, FSA, The Rectory, Barnwell, nr Peterborough, Northants. PE8 5PG.
Fritz, Professor Paul S., BA, MA, PhD, Dept of History, McMaster University, Hamilton, Ontario, Canada.
Frost, A. J., BA, MA, MA, PhD, Dept of History, La Trobe University, Bundoora, Victoria 3083, Australia.

Fryde, Professor E. B., DPhil, Preswylfa, Trinity Road, Aberystwyth, Dyfed SY23 1LU.
Fryde, Natalie M., BA, DrPhil, Schloss Grünsberg, D-8503 Altdorf, Germany.
*Fryer, Professor C. E., MA, PhD (address unknown).
Fryer, Professor W. R., BLitt, MA, 68 Grove Avenue, Chilwell, Beeston, Nottingham NG9 4DX.
Frykenberg, Professor R. E., MA, PhD, 1840 Chadbourne Avenue, Madison, Wis. 53705, U.S.A.
Fuidge, Miss N. M., Flat 3, 17 Cleve Road, London NW6 3RR.
Fulbrook, Mary J. A., MA, AM, PhD, Dept of German, University College London, Gower Street, London WC1E 6BT.
*Furber, Professor H., MA, PhD, c/o History Department, University of Pennsylvania, Philadelphia 4, Pa., U.S.A.
Fyrth, H. J., BSc(Econ), 72 College Road, Dulwich, London SE21 7LY.

Gabriel, Professor A. L., PhD, FMAA, CFIF, CFBA, P.O. Box 578, University of Notre Dame, Notre Dame, Indiana 46556, U.S.A.
*Galbraith, Professor J. S., BS, MA, PhD, Dept of History C–004, University of California, San Diego, La Jolla, Calif. 92093, U.S.A.
Gale, W. K. V., 19 Ednam Road, Goldthorn Park, Wolverhampton WV4 5BL.
Gann, L. H., MA, BLitt, DPhil, Hoover Institution, Stanford University, Stanford, Calif. 94305, U.S.A.
Garnett, G., MA, St John's College, Cambridge CB2 1TP.
Gash, Professor N., CBE, MA, BLitt, FBA, Old Gatehouse, Portway, Langport, Somerset TA10 0NQ.
Gaskell, S. M., MA, PhD, Director, Nene House, Nene College, Moulton Park, Northampton, NN2 7AL.
Gates, D. E., MA, DPhil, Dept of History, The University, Aberdeen AB9 2TY.
Geggus, D. P., MA, DPhil, Dept of History, University of Florida, Gainesville, Florida 32611, U.S.A.
Genet, J.-Ph., Agrégé d'Histoire, 147 Avenue Parmentier, Paris 75010, France.
Gentles, Professor I., BA, MA, PhD, Dept of History, Glendon College, 2275 Bayview Avenue, Toronto, Canada M4N 3M6.
Gerlach, Professor D. R., MA, PhD, University of Akron, Akron, Ohio 44325, U.S.A.
Gibbs, G. C., MA, Dept of History, Birkbeck College, Malet Street, London WC1E 7HX.
Gibson, J. S. W., FSA, Harts Cottage, Church Hanborough, Oxford OX7 2AB.
Gibson, Margaret T., MA, DPhil, School of History, The University, P.O. Box 147, Liverpool L69 3 BX.
Gilbert, Professor Bentley B., PhD, Dept of History, University of Illinois at Chicago Circle, Box 4348, Chicago, Ill. 60680, U.S.A.
Gildea, R. N., MA, DPhil, Merton College, Oxford OX1 4JD.
Gilkes, R. K., MA, 75 Fouracre Road, Downend, Bristol.
Gillespie, J. L., AB, MA, PhD, Dept of History, Notre Dame College of Ohio, 4545 College Road, Cleveland, Ohio 44121, U.S.A.
Gilley, S. W., BA, DPhil, Dept of Theology, University of Durham, Abbey House, Palace Green, Durham DH1 3RS.

Gillingham, J. B., MA, London School of Economics, Houghton Street, Aldwych, London WC2A 2AE.
Ginter, Professor D. E., AM, PhD, Dept of History, Concordia University, 1455 De Maisonneuve Blvd. W., Montreal, Quebec, Canada H3G 1M8.
de Giorgi, Roger, Development House, Floriana, Malta.
Girtin, T., MA, Butter Field House, Church Street, Old Isleworth, Middx.
Giry-Deloison, C., Agrégé de l'Université, DrHist, 46 Thornton Avenue, Chiswick, London W4 1QG.
Glassey, L. K. J., MA, DPhil, Dept of Modern History, The University, Glasgow G12 8QQ.
Gleave, Group Capt. T. P., CBE, RAF (ret.), Willow Bank, River Gardens. Bray-on-Thames, Berks. SL6 2BJ.
*Glover, Professor R. G., MA, PhD, 2937 Tudor Avenue, Victoria, B.C. Canada V8N IM2.
*Godber, Miss A. J., MA, FSA, Charterhouse, Kimbolton, Bedford.
*Godfrey, Professor J. L., MA, PhD, Carolina Meadows, Villa 253, Chapel Hill, NC 27514 U.S.A.
Goldie, Mark, MA, PhD, Churchill College, Cambridge CB3 0DS.
Golding, B. J., MA, DPhil, Dept of History, The University, Highfield, Southampton SO9 5NH.
Goldsmith, Professor M. M., PhD, Dept of Politics, Victoria University, Wellington, New Zealand.
Goldsworthy, D. J. BA, BPhil, DPhil, Dept of Politics, Monash University, Clayton, Victoria 3168, Australia.
Gollin, Professor A., DLitt, Dept of History, University of California, Santa Barbara, Calif. 93106, U.S.A.
Gooch, John, BA, PhD, Dept of History, The University, Bailrigg, Lancaster LA1 4YG.
Goodman, A. E., MA, BLitt, Dept of Medieval History, The University, Edinburgh EH8 9YL.
Goodspeed, Professor D. J., BA, 164 Victoria Street, Niagara-on-the-Lake, Ontario, Canada.
*Gopal, Professor S., MA, DPhil, 30 Edward Elliot Road, Mylapore, Madras, India.
Gordon, G. A. H., PhD, 71A Waldemar Avenue, London SW6 5LS.
Gordon, Professor P., BSc(Econ), MSc(Econ), PhD, 58 Waxwell Lane, Pinner, Middlesex HA5 3EN.
Goring, J. J., MA, PhD, 31 Houndean Rise, Lewes, East Sussex BN7 1EQ.
Gorton, L. J., MA, 41 West Hill Avenue, Epsom, Surrey.
Gosden, Professor P. H. J. H. MA, PhD, School of Education, The University, Leeds LS2 9JT.
Gough, Professor A. G., BA, DPhil, Dept of History, University of Adelaide, GPO Box 498, Adelaide, South Australia 5001.
Gough, Professor Barry M., PhD, History Dept, Wilfrid Laurier University, Waterloo, Ontario, Canada N2L 3C5.
Gowing, Professor Margaret, CBE, MA, DLitt, BSc(Econ), FBA, Linacre College, Oxford OX1 1SY.
Graham-Campbell, J. A., MA, PhD, FSA, Dept of History, University College London, Gower Street, London WC1E 6BT.
Gransden, Antonia, MA, PhD, DLitt, FSA, 10 Halifax Road, Cambridge CB4 3PX.
Grant, A., BA, DPhil, Dept of History, The University, Bailrigg, Lancaster LA1 4YG.
Grattan-Kane, Peter, 12 St John's Close, Helston, Cornwall.

Graves, Professor Edgar B., PhD, LLD, LHD, 318 College Hill Road, Clinton, New York 13323, USA.
Gray, Canon D. C., PhD, MPhil, 1 Little Cloister, Westminster Abbey, London SW1P 3PL.
Gray, Professor J. R., MA, PhD, School of Oriental and African Studies, University of London, London WC1E 7HP.
Gray, J. W., MA, Dept of Modern History, The Queen's University, Belfast BT7 1NN, N. Ireland.
Gray, Miss M., MA, BLitt, 68 Dorchester Road, Garstang, Preston PR3 1HH.
Greatrex, Professor Joan G., MA, PhD, The Highlands, Great Doward, Symonds Yat, Herefordshire, HR9 6DY.
Greaves, Professor Richard L., PhD, 910 Shadowlawn Drive, Tallahassee, Florida 32312, U.S.A.
Greaves, Mrs R. L., PhD, 1920 Hillview Road, Lawrence, Kansas 66044, U.S.A.
Green, I. M., MA, DPhil, Dept of Modern History, The Queen's University, Belfast BT7 1NN, N. Ireland.
Green, Judith A., BA, DPhil, Dept of Modern History, The Queen's University, Belfast BT7 1NN, N. Ireland.
Green, Professor Thomas A., BA, PhD, JD, Legal Research Building, University of Michigan Law School, Ann Arbor, Michigan 48109, U.S.A.
Green, Rev. V. H. H., MA, DD, Lincoln College, Oxford OX1 3DR.
Greene, Professor Jack P., Dept of History, The Johns Hopkins University, Baltimore, Md. 21218, U.S.A.
Greengrass, M., MA, DPhil, Dept of History, The University, Sheffield S10 2TN.
Greenhill, B. J., CB, CMG, DPh, FSA, West Boetheric Farmhouse, St Dominic, Saltash, Cornwall PL12 6SZ.
Greenslade, M. W., JP, MA, FSA, 20 Garth Road, Stafford ST17 9JD.
Greenway, D. E., MA, PhD, Institute of Historical Research, Senate House, Malet Street, London WC1E 7HU.
Gregg, E., MA, PhD, Dept of History, University of South Carolina, Columbia, S.C. 29208, U.S.A.
Grenville, Professor J. A. S., PhD, School of History, University of Birmingham, P.O. Box 363, Birmingham B15 2TT.
GRIERSON, Professor P., MA, LittD, FBA, FSA, Gonville and Caius College, Cambridge CB2 1TA.
Grieve, Miss H. E. P., BA, 153 New London Road, Chelmsford, Essex.
Griffiths, Professor R. A., PhD, University College, Singleton Park, Swansea SA2 8PP.
Grimble, I., MA, PhD, 14 Seaforth Lodge, Barnes High Street, London SW13 9LE.
Grisbrooke, W. J., MA, Jokers, Bailey Street, Castle Acre, King's Lynn, Norfolk PE32 2AG.
*Griscom, Rev. Acton, MA (address unknown).
Gruner, Professor Wolf D., DrPhil, DrPhil. Habil, Pralleweg 7, 2000 Hamburg 67 (Volksdorf), West Germany.
Gupta, Professor P. S., MA, DPhil, E-75 Masjid Moth, New Delhi, 110048, India.
Guth, Professor D. J., Faculty of Law, University of British Columbia, Vancouver, B.C., Canada V6T 1Y1.
Guy, A. J., BA, MA, DPhil, 145 Queens Road, Wimbledon, London SW19 8NS.

Guy, J. A., PhD, Dept of History, University of Rochester, Rochester, NY 14627, U.S.A.

HABAKKUK, Sir John (H.), MA, DLitt, FBA, Jesus College, Oxford OX1, 3DW.
Haber, Professor F. C., PhD, 3110 Wisconsin Avenue NW, #904, Washington, D.C. 20016, U.S.A.
Hackett, Rev. M. B., OSA, BA, PhD, St. Mary's Priory, Vivian Road, Harborne, Birmingham B17 0DN.
Hackmann, Willem D., DPhil, Museum of the History of Science, University of Oxford, Broad Street, Oxford OX1 3AZ.
Haddock, B. A., BA, DPhil, Dept of Political Theory and Government, The University, Singleton Park, Swansea, SA2 8PP.
Haffenden, P. S., PhD, 4 Upper Dukes Drive, Meads, Eastbourne, East Sussex BN20 7XT.
Haigh, C. A., MA, PhD, Christ Church, Oxford OX1 1DP.
Haight, Mrs M. Jackson, PhD, 3 Wolger Road, Mosman, N.S.W. 2088, Australia.
Haines, R. M., MA, MLitt, DPhil, FSA, 20 Luttrell Avenue, London SW15 6PF.
Hainsworth, D. R., MA, PhD, Dept of History, University of Adelaide, North Terrace, Adelaide, South Australia 5001.
Hair, Professor P. E. H., MA, DPhil, School of History, The University, P.O. Box 147, Liverpool L69 3BX.
Hale, Professor J. R., MA, FBA, FSA, Dept of History, University College London, Gower Street, London WC1E 6BT.
Haley, Professor K. H. D., MA, BLitt, 15 Haugh Lane, Sheffield S11 9SA.
Hall, Professor Emeritus A. R., MA, PhD, DLitt, FBA, 14 Ball Lane, Tackley, Oxford OX5 3AG.
Hall, B., MA, PhD, FSA, DD (Hon.), 2 Newton House, Newton St Cyres, Devon EX5 5BL.
Hallam, Elizabeth M., BA, PhD, Public Record Office, Chancery Lane, London WC2A 1LR.
Hallam, Professor H. E., MA, PhD, 2 Pool Street, York, Western Australia 6302.
Hamer, Professor D. A., MA, DPhil, History Dept, Victoria University of Wellington, P.O. Box 600, Wellington, New Zealand.
Hamilton, B., BA, PhD, Dept of History, The University, Nottingham NG7 2RD.
Hamilton, Associate Professor J. S., 1912 Sulgrave Avenue, #1, Baltimore, MD 21209, U.S.A.
Hammersley, G. F., BA, PhD, 3 Gloucester Place, Edinburgh EH3 6EE.
Hamnett, B. R., BA, MA, PhD, Dept of History, University of Strathclyde, McLance Building, 16 Richmond Street, Glasgow G1 1XQ.
Hampson, Professor N., MA, Ddel'U, FBA, 305 Hull Road, York YO1 3LB.
Hand, Professor G. J., MA, DPhil, Faculty of Law, University of Birmingham, P.O. Box 363, Birmingham B15 2TT.
Handford, M. A., MA, MSc, 6 Spa Lane, Hinckley, Leicester LE10 1JB.
Hanham, H. J., MA, PhD, The Croft, Bailrigg Lane, Bailrigg, Lancaster LA1 4XP.
Harcourt, Freda, PhD, Dept of History, Queen Mary College, Mile End Road, London E1 4NS.
Harding, Professor A., MA, BLitt, School of History, The University, P.O. Box 147, Liverpool L69 3BX.

Harding, The Hon. Mr Justice H. W., BA, LLD, FSA, 39 Annunciation Street, Sliema, Malta.
Haren, M. J., DPhil, 5 Marley Lawn, Dublin 16, Ireland.
Harfield, Major A. G., BEM, Plum Tree Cottage, Royston Place, Barton-on-Sea, Hampshire BH25 7AJ.
Hargreaves, Professor J. D., MA, 'Balcluain', 22 Raemoir Road, Banchory, Kincardineshire AB3 3UJ.
Harkness, Professor D. W., MA, PhD, Dept of Irish History, The Queen's University, Belfast BT7 1NN, N. Ireland.
Harman, Rev. L. W., 72 Westmount Road, London SE9.
Harnetty, P., BA, AM, PhD, Dept of Asian Studies, University of British Columbia, 1873 East Mall, Vancouver, B.C., Canada V6T 1W5.
Harper Marjory-Ann D., MA, PhD, Silverdale, Disblair, Newmachar, Aberdeen AB5 0RN.
Harper-Bill, C., BA, PhD, 15 Cusack Close, Strawberry Hill, Twickenham, Middlesex TW1 4TB.
Harris, G. G., MA, 4 Lancaster Drive, London NW3.
Harris, Mrs J. F., BA, PhD, 30 Charlbury Road, Oxford OX1 3UJ.
Harris, Professor J. R., MA, PhD, Dept of History, The University, P.O. Box 363, Birmingham B15 2TT.
Harrison, B. H., MA, DPhil, Corpus Christi College, Oxford OX1 4JF.
Harrison, C. J., BA, PhD, Dept of History, The University, Keele, Staffs. ST5 5BG.
Harrison, Professor Royden J., MA, DPhil, 4 Wilton Place, Sheffield S10 2BT.
Harriss, G. L., MA, DPhil, FSA, Magdalen College, Oxford OX1 4AU.
Hart, C. J. R., MA, MB, DLitt, Goldthorns, Stilton, Cambs. PE7 3RH.
Hart, M. W., MA, DPhil, Exeter College, Oxford OX1 3DP.
Harte, N. B., BSc(Econ), Dept of History, University College London, Gower Street, London WC1E 6BT.
Hartley, T. E., BA, PhD, Dept of History, The University, Leicester LE1 7RH.
Harvey, Miss B. F., MA, BLitt, FBA, Somerville College, Oxford OX2 6HD.
Harvey, C. E., BSc, PhD, Dept of History, Royal Holloway and Bedford New College, University of London, Egham Hill, Egham, Surrey TW20 0EX.
Harvey, Margaret M., MA, DPhil, St Aidan's College, Durham DH1 3LJ.
Harvey, Professor P. D. A., MA, DPhil, FSA, Dept of History, The University, 43/46 North Bailey, Durham DH1 3EX.
Harvey, Sally P. J., MA, PhD, Swanborough Manor, Swanborough, Lewes, E. Sussex BN7 3PF.
Haskell, Professor F. J., MA, FBA, Trinity College, Oxford OX1 3BH.
Haskins, Professor G. L., AB, LLB, JD, MA, University of Pennsylvania, The Law School, 3400 Chestnut Street, Philadelphia, Pa. 19104 U.S.A.
Haslam, Group Captain E. B., MA, RAF (retd), 27 Denton Road, Wokingham, Berks. RG11 2DX.
Haslam, G., BA, MA, PhD, Fern Cottage, 83 Sharmsford Street, Chartham, Kent CT4 7RQ.
Haslam, Jonathan G., BSc(Econ), MLitt, PhD, King's College, Cambridge CB2 1ST.
Hasler, Peter W., BA, MA, History of Parliament Trust, Institute of Historical Research, 34 Tavistock Square, London WC1H 9EZ.
Hassall, W. O., MA, DPhil, FSA, The Manor House, 26 High Street, Wheatley, Oxon. OX9 1XX.

Hast, Adele, PhD, 210 Fourth Street, Wilmette, Illinois 60091, U.S.A.
Hastings, M. M., Guilsborough Lodge, Guilsborough, Northamptonshire NN6 8RB.
Hatcher, M. J., BSc(Econ), PhD, Corpus Christi College, Cambridge CB2 1RH.
Hatley, V. A., BA, ALA, 6 The Crescent, Northampton NN1 4SB.
Hattendorf, Professor J. B., BA, MA, DPhil, 28 John Street, Newport, Rhode Island 02840, U.S.A.
Hatton, Professor Ragnhild M., PhD, Cand.Mag(Oslo), Dr.h.c., 49 Campden Street, London W8.
Havighurst, Professor A. F., MA, PhD, 11 Blake Field, Amherst, Mass. 01002, U.S.A.
Havinden, M. A., MA, BLitt, Dept of Economic History, Amory Building, The University, Exeter EX4 4QH.
Havran, Professor M. J., MA, PhD, Corcoran Dept of History, Randall Hall, University of Virginia, Charlottesville, Va. 22903, U.S.A.
Hawke, Professor G. R., BA, BCom, DPhil, Dept of History, Victoria, University of Wellington, Private Bag, Wellington, New Zealand.
Hawkyard, A. D. K., BA, MA, 5 Bonny Street, London NW1 9PE.
HAY, Professor D., MA, DLitt, FBA, FRSE, Dr. h.c. Tours, 31 Fountainville Road, Edinburgh EH9 2LN.
Hayes, P. M., MA, DPhil, Keble College, Oxford OX1 3PG.
Hayter, A. J., BA, PhD, Chase House, Mursley, N. Bucks. MK17 0RT.
Hayton, D. W., BA, DPhil, 8 Baker Street, Ampthill, Bedford MK45 2QE.
Hazlehurst, Cameron, BA, DPhil, FRSL, 8 Hunter Street, Yarralumla, A.C.T. 2600, Australia.
Heal, Mrs Felicity, PhD, Jesus College, Oxford OX1 3DW.
Hearder, Professor H., BA, PhD, School of History and Archaeology, University of Wales College of Cardiff, P.O. Box 909, Cardiff CF1 1XU.
Heath, P., MA, Dept of History, The University, Hull HU6 7RX.
Heathcote, T. A., BA, PhD, Cheyne Cottage, Birch Drive, Hawley, Camberley, Surrey.
Heesom, A. J., MA, Dept of History, The University, 43 North Bailey, Durham DH1 3HP.
Hellmuth, Eckhart H., PhD, German Historical Institute, 17 Bloomsbury Square, London WC1A 2LP.
Helmholz, R. H., PhD, LLB, The Law School, University of Chicago, 1111 East 60th Street, Chicago, Ill. 60637, U.S.A.
Hembry, Mrs P. M., BA, PhD, Pleasant Cottage, Crockerton, Warminster, Wilts. BA12 8AJ.
Hempton, D. N., BA, PhD, Dept of Modern History, The Queen's University, Belfast, BT7 1NN, N. Ireland.
Hendy, M. F., MA, 29 Roberts Road, Cambridge, Mass. 02138, U.S.A.
Hennock, Professor E. P., MA, PhD, School of History, University of Liverpool, P.O. Box 147, Liverpool L69 3BX.
Henstock, A. J. M., BA, Nottinghamshire Record Office, County House, Nottingham NG1 1HR.
Heppell, Muriel, BA, MA, PhD, 97 Eton Place, Eton College Road, London NW3 2DB.
Herde, Professor Peter, PhD, Cranachstr. 7, D 8755 Alzenau, F.R. of Germany.
Herrup, Cynthia B., PhD, MA, BSJ, Dept of History, 6727 College Station, Duke University, Durham, N.C. 27708, U.S.A.

Hexter, Professor J. H., PhD, Dept of History, Washington University, Campus Box 1062, One Brookings Drive, St Louis, Missouri 63130-4899, U.S.A.
Hey, D. G., MA, PhD, Division of Continuing Education, The University, Sheffield S10 2TN.
Hicks, M. A., BA, MA, DPhil, Dept of History, King Alfred's College, Winchester Hampshire, SO22 4NR.
Higham, R. A., BA, PhD, Dept of History and Archaeology, University of Exeter, Queen's Building, Queen's Drive, Exeter, Devon.
Highfield, J. R. L., MA, DPhil, Merton College, Oxford OX1 4JD.
Higman, Professor B. W. C., PhD, Dept of History, University of the West Indies, Mona, Kingston 7, Jamaica.
Hilbert, Professor L. W., PhD, DES Etudes europeenes, DES Droit Compare, Seminar fur Zeitgeschichte Universitat Tubingen, D74 Tubingen, Wilhelm ST. 36, West Germany.
Hill, B. W., BA, PhD, School of English and American Studies, University of East Anglia, University Plain, Norwich NR4 7TJ.
Hill, J. E. C., MA, DLitt, FBA, Woodway House, Sibford Ferris, nr Banbury, Oxfordshire OX15 5RA.
Hill, Professor L. M., AB, MA, PhD, 5066 Berean Lane, Irvine, Calif. 92664, U.S.A.
*Hill, Miss M. C., MA, Crab End, Brevel Terrace, Charlton Kings, Cheltenham, Glos.
*Hill, Professor Rosalind M. T., MA, BLitt, FSA, Queen Mary and University of London, Westfield College, Kidderpore Avenue, Hampstead, London NW3 7ST.
Hilton A. J. Boyd, MA, DPhil, 1 Carlyle Road, Cambridge CB4 3DN.
Hilton, Professor R. H., DPhil, FBA, University of Birmingham, P.O. Box 363, Birmingham B15 2TT.
Himmelfarb, Professor Gertrude, PhD, The City University of New York, Graduate Center, 33 West 42 St, New York, NY 10036, U.S.A.
Hind, R. J., BA, PhD, Dept of History, University of Sydney, Sydney, N.S.W. 2006, Australia.
*Hinsley, Professor Sir (Francis) Harry, MA, OBE, FBA, St John's College, Cambridge CB2 1TP.
Hinton, J., BA, PhD, Dept of History, University of Warwick, Coventry CV4 7AL.
Hirst, Professor D. M., PhD, Dept of History, Washington University, Campus Box 1062, One Brookings Drive, St Louis, Missouri 63130-4899, U.S.A.
Hoak, Professor Dale E., PhD, Dept of History, College of William and Mary, Williamsburg, Virginia 23185, U.S.A.
*Hodgett, G. A. J., MA, FSA, 3 Grafton Mansions, Duke's Road, London WC1H 9AB.
Holderness, B. A., MA, PhD, School of Economic and Social Studies, University of East Anglia, Norwich NR4 7TJ.
Holdsworth, Professor C. J., MA, PhD, FSA, 5 Pennsylvania Park, Exeter EX4 6HD.
Hollis, Patricia, MA. DPhil, 30 Park Lane, Norwich NOR 4TF.
Hollister, Professor C. Warren, MA, PhD, University of California, Santa Barbara, Calif. 93106, U.S.A.
Holmes, Professor Clive A., MA, PhD, Dept of History, McGraw Hall, Cornell University, NY 14853, U.S.A.

Holmes, G. A., MA, PhD, Highmoor House, Weald, Bampton, Oxon. OX8 2HY.
Holmes, Professor G. S., MA, DLitt, FBA, Tatham House, Burton-in-Lonsdale, Carnforth, Lancs.
Holroyd, M. de C. F., 85 St Mark's Road, London W10.
HOLT, Professor Sir James C., MA, DPhil, DLitt, FBA, FSA, Fitzwilliam College, Cambridge CB3 0DG.
Holt, Professor P. M., MA, DLitt, FBA, Dryden Spinney, South End, Kirtlington, Oxford OX5 3HG.
Holt, The Rev. T. G., SJ, MA, FSA, 114 Mount Street, London W1Y 6AH.
Honey, Professor, J. R. de S., MA, DPhil, Faculty of Education, Kumamoto University, Kumamoto, 860 Japan.
Hopkin, D. R., BA, PhD, Maesgwyn, Llangawsai, Aberystwyth, Dyfed.
Hopkins, E., BA, MA, PhD, 77 Stevens Road, Stourbridge, West Midlands DY9 0XW.
Hoppen, K. T., MA, PhD, Dept of History, The University, Hull HU6 7RX.
Hoppit, J., MA, PhD, Dept of History, University College London, Gower Street, London WC1E 6BT.
Horrox, Rosemary E., MA, PhD, 61–3 High Street, Cottenham, Cambridge CB4 4SA.
Horton, A.V.M., BA, MA, PhD, 180 Hither Green Lane, Bordesley, Worcs. B98 9AZ.
Horwitz, Professor H. G., BA, DPhil, Dept of History, University of Iowa, Iowa City, Iowa 52242, U.S.A.
Houlbrooke, R. A., MA, DPhil, Faculty of Letters and Social Sciences, The University, Whiteknights, Reading RG6 2AH.
Housley, N. J., MA, PhD, Dept of History, The University, Leicester, LE1 7RH.
Houston, R. A., MA, PhD, Dept of Modern History, The University, St Andrews KY16 9AL.
*Howard, C. H. D., MA, 15 Sunnydale Gardens, Mill Hill, London NW7 3PD.
*Howard, Sir Michael, CBE, MC, DLitt, FBA, Apt. B6, 309 St. Ronan Street, New Haven, Connecticut 06511, U.S.A.
Howarth, Mrs J. H., MA, St Hilda's College, Oxford OX4 1DY.
Howat, G. M. D., MA, MLitt, PhD, Old School House, North Moreton, Didcot, Oxfordshire OX11 9BA.
Howell, Miss M. E., MA, PhD, 10 Blenheim Drive, Oxford OX2 8DG.
Howell, P. A., MA., PhD, School of Social Sciences, The Flinders University of South Australia, Bedford Park, South Australia 5042.
Howells, B. E., MA, Whitehill, Cwm Ann, Lampeter, Dyfed.
Hoyle, R. W., BA, DPhil, 13 Parker St., Oxford OX4 1TD.
Hudson, Miss A. M., MA, DPhil, Lady Margaret Hall, Oxford OX2 6QA.
Hudson, T. P., MA, PhD, 23 Glenwood Avenue, Bognor Regis, West Sussex, PO22 8BT.
Hufton, Professor Olwen H., BA, PhD, Center for European Studies, Harvard University, 5 Bryant St, Cambridge, Mass. 02138, U.S.A.
Hughes, Ann L., BA, PhD, Dept of History, The University, Manchester M13 9PL.
Hughes, J. Q., MC, MA, BArch, PhD, Dip. Civic Design, 10a Fulwood Park, Liverpool L17 5AH.
Hull, F., BA, PhD, 135 Ashford Road, Bearsted, Maidstone ME14 4BT.
HUMPHREYS, Professor R. A., OBE, MA, PhD, DLitt, LittD, DLitt, DUniv, 5 St James's Close, Prince Albert Road, London NW8 7LG.

Hunnisett, R. F., MA, DPhil, 23 Byron Gardens, Sutton, Surrey SM1 3QG.
Hunt, K. S., PhD, MA, Rhodes University Grahamstown 6140, South Africa.
Hurst, M. C., MA, St John's College, Oxford OX1 3JP.
Hurt, J. S., BA, BSc(Econ), PhD, Sutton House, Madeira Lane, Freshwater, Isle of Wight PO40 9SP.
*Hussey, Professor Joan M., MA, BLitt, PhD, FSA, Royal Holloway and Bedford New College, Egham Hill, Egham, Surrey TW20 0EX.
Hutchinson, J. H., 182 Burton Stone Lane, York YO3 6DF.
Hutton, R. E., BA, DPhil, Dept of History, The University, 13–15 Woodland Road, Bristol BS8 1TB.
Hyams, P. R., MA, DPhil, Pembroke College, Oxford OX1 1DW.

Ingham, Professor K., OBE, MA, MA, DPhil, The Woodlands, 94 West Town Lane, Bristol BS4 5DZ.
Ingram Ellis, Professor E. R., MA, PhD, Dept of History, Simon Fraser University, Burnaby, B.C., Canada V5A IS6.
Inkster, Ian, PhD, Dept of Economic History, University of New South Wales, P.O. Box 1, Kensington, N.S.W. 2033, Australia.
Israel, Professor J. I., MA, DPhil, Dept of History, University College London, Gower Street, London WC1E 6BT.
Ives, E. W., PhD, 214 Myton Road, Warwick CV34 6PS.

Jack, Professor R. I., MA, PhD, University of Sydney, Sydney, N.S.W., Australia.
Jack, Mrs S. M., MA, BLitt, Dept of Economic History, University of Sydney, Sydney, N.S.W., Australia.
Jackman, Professor S. W., PhD, FSA, 1065 Deal Street, Victoria, British Columbia, Canada.
Jackson, J. T., PhD, Dept of History, University College of Swansea, Singleton Park, Swansea SA2 7BR.
Jackson, P., MA, PhD, Dept of History, The University, Keele, Staffs. ST5 5BG.
Jackson, T. A., MA, DPhil, Dept of Modern History, University College, Belfield, Dublin 4, Republic of Ireland.
Jacob, Professor Margaret C., Office of the Dean, Lang College, New School for Social Research, 66 West 12th Street, New York, NY 10071, U.S.A.
Jagger, Rev. P. J., MA, MPhil, PhD, St Deiniol's Library, Hawarden, Deeside, Clwyd CH5 3DF.
Jalland, Patricia, PhD, MA, BA, School of Social Inquiry, Murdoch University, Murdoch, Western Australia 6150.
James, Edward, MA, DPhil, FSA, Dept of History, The University, Heslington, York YO1 5DD.
James, M. E., MA, DLitt, FSA, Middlecote, Stonesfield, Oxon. OX7 2PU.
James, R. Rhodes, MP, MA, FRSL, The Stone House, Great Gransden, nr Sandy, Beds.
James, Thomas B., MA, PhD, 35 Alresford Road, Winchester SO23 8HG.
Jankowski, P. F., DPhil, Dept of History, Stanford University, Stanford, CA 94305-2029, U.S.A.
Jansson, Maija, BA, MA, PhD, 117 Glen Parkway, Hamden, Conn. 06517, U.S.A.
Jarrett, J. D., Withiel House, Withiel, nr Bodmin, Cornwall PL30 5NN.
Jeffery, K. J., MA, PhD, Dept of History, University of Ulster, Shore Road, Newtownabbey, Co. Antrim, N. Ireland BT37 0QB.

Jeffreys-Jones, R., BA, PhD, Dept of History, University of Edinburgh, Wm. Robertson Building, George Square, Edinburgh, EH8 9YL.
Jenkins, Professor B. A., PhD, 133 Lorne, Lennoxville, Quebec, Canada.
Jenkins, Professor D., MA, LLM, LittD, Dept of Law, University College of Wales, Adeilad Hugh Owen, Penglais, Aberystwyth SY23 3DY.
Jenkins, T. A., PhD, 50 Harvey Goodwin Gardens, Cambridge CB4 3EZ.
Jennings, J. R., MA, DPhil, Dept of Political Theory and Government, University College of Swansea, Singleton Park, Swansea SA2 8PP.
Jeremy, D. J., BA, MLitt, PhD, Heatherbank, 2 Old Hall Drive, Whaley Bridge, nr. Stockport, Cheshire SK12 7HF.
Jewell, Miss H. M., MA, PhD, School of History, The University, P.O. Box 147, Liverpool L69 3BX.
Johnson, D. J., BA, 41 Cranes Park Avenue, Surbiton, Surrey.
Johnson, Professor D. W. J., BA, BLitt, Dept of History, University College London, Gower Street, London WC1E 6BT.
Johnson, P. A., MA, DPhil, Dept of Economic History, London School of Economics, Houghton Street, London WC2A 2AE.
Johnston, Professor Edith M., MA, PhD, Dept of History, Macquarie Univ., North Ryde, NSW 2113, Australia.
Johnston, Professor S. H. F., MA, Pantyrhos, Waunfawr, Aberystwyth, Dyfed.
Jones, A. T., MA, PhD, Institut für Historishe Ethnologie, J. W. Goethe-Universitat, Liebigstr. 41, D-6000 Frankfurt am Main, West Germany.
Jones, C. D. H., BA, DPhil, Dept of History and Archaeology, The University, The Queen's Drive, Exeter EX4 4QH.
Jones, Clyve, MA, MLitt, 41 St Catherines Court, London W4 1LB.
Jones, D. J. V., BA, PhD, Dept of History, University College of Swansea, Singleton Park, Swansea SA2 8PP.
Jones, Dwyryd W., MA, DPhil, Dept of History, The University, Heslington, York YO1 5DD.
Jones, Revd F., BA, MSc, PhD, Casa Renate, Carrer des Pinsas 86, Port de Pollença, Mallorca, Spain.
Jones, G. A., MA, PhD, Monks Court, Deddington, Oxford OX5 4TE.
Jones, G. E., MA, PhD, MEd, 130 Pennard Drive, Pennard, Gower, West Glamorgan.
Jones, Professor G. Hilton, PhD, Dept of History, Eastern Illinois University, Charleston, Ill. 61920, U.S.A.
Jones, Greta J., BA, DipHE, PhD, Dept of History, University of Ulster at Jordanstown, Shore Road, Newtownabbey, Co. Antrim BT37 0QB.
Jones, Professor G. W., BA, MA, DPhil, Dept of Government, London School of Economics, Houghton Street, London WC2A 2AE.
Jones, H. E., MA, DPhil, Flat 3, 115–117 Highlever Road, London W10 6PW.
Jones, Professor I.G., MA, DLitt, 12 Laura Place, Aberystwyth, Dyfed SY23 2AU.
Jones, J. D., MA, PhD, Woodlands Cottage, Marvel Lane, Newport, Isle of Wight PO30 3DT.
Jones, Professor J. R., MA, PhD, School of English and American Studies, University of East Anglia, Norwich NOR 30A.
Jones, Professor M. A., MA, DPhil, Dept of History, University College London, Gower Street, London WC1E 6BT.
Jones, Mrs Marian H., MA, Glwysgoed, Caradog Road, Aberystwyth, Dyfed.
Jones, M. C. E., MA, DPhil, FSA, Dept of History, The University, Nottingham NG7 2 RD.

Jones, The Venerable O. W., MA, 10 Golden Cross, West Cross, Swansea SA3 5PE.
Jones, P. J., DPhil, FBA, Brasenose College, Oxford OX1 4AJ.
Jones, Professor W. J., PhD, DLitt, FRSC, Dept of History, The University of Alberta, Edmonton, Canada T6G 2H4.
Jones-Parry, Sir Ernest, MA, PhD, Flat 3, 34 Sussex Square, Brighton, Sussex BN2 5AD.
Jordanova, Ludmilla J., MA, PhD, MA, Dept of History, University of Essex, Wivenhoe Park, Colchester CO4 3SQ.
Judd, Professor Denis, BA, PhD, Dept of History, Polytechnic of North London, Prince of Wales Road, London NW5 3LB.
Judson, Professor Margaret A., PhD, 8 Redcliffe Avenue, Highland Park, NJ 08904, U.S.A.
Judt, T. R., 37 Washington Square W. 12D., New York, NY 10011, U.S.A.
Jupp, P. J., BA, PhD, 42 Osborne Park, Belfast, N. Ireland BT9 6JN.

Kaeuper, Professor R. W., MA, PhD, 151 Village Lane, Rochester, New York 14610, U.S.A.
Kamen, H. A. F., MA, DPhil, Dept of History, The University of Warwick, Coventry CV4 7AL.
Kanya-Forstner, A. S., PhD, Dept of History, York University, 4700 Keele Street, Downsview, Ontario, Canada M3J 1P3.
Kapelle, Asst. Professor, William E., PhD, History Department, Brandeis University, Waltham, Mass. 00254-9110, U.S.A.
Kealey, Professor Gregory S., PhD, Dept of History, Memorial University of Newfoundland, St John's, Newfoundland. Canada A1C 5S7.
Kedward, H. R., MA, MPhil, 137 Waldegrave Road, Brighton BN1 6GJ.
Keefe, Professor Thomas K., BA, PhD, Dept of History, Appalachian State University, Boone, N.C. 28608, U.S.A.
Keegan, J. D. P., MA, The Manor House, Kilmington, nr. Warminster, Wilts. BA12 6RD.
Keeler, Mrs Mary F., PhD, 302 West 12th Street, Frederick, Maryland 21701, U.S.A.
Keen, L. J., MPhil, Dip Archaeol, FSA, 7 Church Street, Dorchester, Dorset.
Keen, M. H. MA, DPhil, Balliol College, Oxford OX1 3BJ.
Keene, D. J., MA, DPhil, 162 Erlanger Road, Telegraph Hill, London SE14 5TJ.
Kellas, J. G., MA, PhD, Dept of Politics, Glasgow University, Adam Smith Building, Glasgow G12 8RT.
Kellaway, C. W., MA, FSA, 18 Canonbury Square, London N1.
Kelly, Professor T., MA, PhD, FLA, Oak Leaf House, Ambleside Road, Keswick, Cumbria CA12 4DL.
Kemp, Miss B., MA, FSA, St Hugh's College, Oxford OX2 6LE.
Kemp, B. R., BA, PhD, 12 Redhatch Drive, Earley, Reading, Berks.
Kemp, The Right Rev. E. W., DD, The Lord Bishop of Chichester, The Palace, Chichester, Sussex PO19 1PY.
Kemp, Lt-Commander P. K., RN, Malcolm's, 51 Market Hill, Maldon, Essex.
Kendle, Professor J. E., PhD, St John's College, University of Manitoba, Winnipeg, Manitoba, Canada R3T 2M5.
Kennedy, J., MA, 14 Poolfield Avenue, Newcastle-under-Lyme, Staffs. ST5 2NL.
Kennedy, Professor P. M., BA, DPhil, Dept of History, Yale University, 237 Hall of Graduate Studies, New Haven, Conn. 06520, U.S.A.

Kent, Professor C. A., DPhil, Dept of History, University of Saskatchewan, Saskatoon, Sask. Canada S7N 0W0.

Kent, Professor J. H. S., MA, PhD, Dept of Theology, University of Bristol, 3–5 Woodland Road, Bristol BS8 1TB.

Kent, Miss M. R., PhD, BA, BA, School of Social Sciences, Deakin University, Geelong, Victoria, Australia 3217.

Kenyon, Professor J. P., PhD, Dept of History, University of Kansas, 3001, Wescoe Hall, Lawrence, Kansas 66045–2130, U.S.A.

Kenyon, J. R., BA, ALA, FSA, The Library, National Museum of Wales, Cardiff CF1 3NP.

Kerridge, Professor E. W. J., PhD, 2 Bishops Court, off Church Road, Broughton, Chester CH4 0QZ.

Kettle, Miss A. J., MA, FSA, Dept of Mediaeval History, The University, 71 South Street, St Andrews, Fife KY16 9AL.

Keynes, S. D., MA, PhD, Trinity College, Cambridge CB2 1TQ.

Kido, Takeshi, MA, PhD, Dept of European History, Faculty of Letters, The University, Hongo, Bunkyo-Ku, Tokyo 113, Japan.

Kiernan, Professor V. G., MA, 'Woodcroft', Lauder Road, Stow, Galashiels, Scotland TD1 2QW.

Killingray, D., BSc, PhD, 72 Bradbourne Road, Sevenoaks, Kent TN13 3QA.

King, Professor E. B., PhD, Dept of History, The University of the South, Box 1234, Sewanee, Tennessee 37375, U.S.A.

King, Professor E. J., MA, PhD, Dept of History, The University, Sheffield S10 2TN.

King, P. D., BA, PhD, Dept of History, Furness College, The University, Bailrigg, Lancaster LA1 4YG.

Kinnear, M. S. R., DPhil, History Dept, University College, University of Manitoba, Winnipeg, Manitoba, Canada R3T 2M8.

Kirby, D. P., MA, PhD, Manoraven, Llanon, Dyfed.

Kirby, J. L., MA, FSA, 209 Covington Way, Streatham, London SW16 3BY.

Kirby, M. W., BA, PhD, Dept of Economics, Gillow House, The University, Lancaster LA1 4YX.

Kirk, J., MA, PhD, DLitt, Dept of Scottish History, University of Glasgow, Glasgow G12 8QQ.

Kirk, Linda M., MA, PhD, Dept of History, The University, Sheffield S10 2TN.

Kirk-Greene, A. H. M., MBE, MA, St Antony's College, Oxford OX2 6JF.

Kishlansky, Professor Mark, Dept of History, University of Chicago, 1126 East 59th Street, Chicago, Illinois 60637, U.S.A.

Kitchen, Professor J. Martin, BA, PhD, Dept of History, Simon Fraser University, Burnaby, B.C., Canada V5A 1S6.

Kitching, C. J., BA, PhD, FSA, 11 Creighton Road, London NW6 6EE.

Klibansky, Professor R., MA, PhD, DPhil, FRSC, 608 Leacock Building, McGill University, P.O. Box 6070, Station A, Montreal, Quebec, Canada H3C 3G1.

Knafla, Professor L. A., MA, PhD, Dept of History, The University of Calgary, 2500 University Drive N.W., Calgary, Alberta, Canada T2N 1N4.

Knecht, Professor R. J., MA, DLitt, 79 Reddings Road, Moseley, Birmingham B13 8LP.

Knight R. J. B., MA, PhD, 133 Coleraine Road, London SE3 7NT.

Knowles, C. H., PhD, School of History and Archaeology, University of Wales College of Cardiff, P.O. Box 909, Cardiff CF1 1XU.

Knox, B. A., BA, BPhil, Dept of History, Monash University, Clayton, Victoria, 3168, Australia.

Koch, Hannsjoachim W., BA, DPhil, Dept of History, The University, Heslington, York YO1 5DD.

Kochan, L. E., MA, PhD, 237 Woodstock Road, Oxford OX2 7AD.

Koenigsberger, Dorothy M. M., BA, PhD, 41a Lancaster Grove, London NW3.

Koenigsberger, Professor H. G., MA, PhD, 41a Lancaster Grove, London NW3.

Kohl, Professor Benjamin G., AB, MA, PhD, Dept of History, Vassar College, Poughkeepsie, New York, 12601, U.S.A.

Kollar, Professor Rene M., BA, MDiv, MA, PhD, St Vincent Archabbey, Latrobe, Pa. 15650, U.S.A.

Kondo, Assoc. Professor K., BA, MA, Faculty of Letters, University of Tokyo, Hongo, Tokyo 113, Japan.

Korr, Charles P., MA, PhD, College of Arts and Sciences, Dept of History, University of Missouri, 8001 Natural Bridge Road, St Louis, Missouri 63121, U.S.A.

Kossmann, Professor E. H., DLitt, Rijksuniversiteit te Groningen, Groningen, The Netherlands.

Kouri, Professor E. I., PhD, Institute of History, University of Helsinki, Hallituskatu 15, 00100 Helsinki, Finland.

Kramnick, Professor I., PhD, Dean's Office, 201 Lincoln Hall, Cornell University, Ithaca, NY 14853, U.S.A.

Kubicek, Professor R. V., BEd, MA, PhD, Dept of History, University of British Columbia, Vancouver, B.C., Canada V6T 1W5.

Kybett, Mrs Susan, McL, 751 West Morrell Street, Jackson, Michigan 49203, U.S.A.

Lake, P., BA, PhD, Dept of History, Royal Holloway and Bedford New College, Egham Hill, Egham, Surrey TW20 0EX.

Lambert, The Hon. Margaret, CMG, PhD. 39 Thornhill Road, Barnsbury Square, London N1 1JS.

Lambert, W. R., BA, PhD, 47 Llandennis Avenue, Cyncoed, Cardiff CF2 6JF.

Lamont, W. M., PhD, Manor House, Keighton Road, Denton, Newhaven, Sussex BN9 0AB.

Lander, J. R., MA, MLitt, FRSC, 5 Withrington Road, London N5 1PN.

Landes, Professor D. S., PhD, Widener U, Harvard University, Cambridge, Mass. 02138, U.S.A.

Landon, Professor M. de L., MA, PhD, Dept of History, The University of Mississippi, University, Mississippi 38677, U.S.A.

Langford, P., MA, DPhil, Lincoln College, Oxford OX1 3DR.

Langhorne, R. T. B., MA, 15 Madingley Road, Cambridge.

Lannon, Frances, MA, DPhil, Lady Margaret Hall, Oxford OX2 6QA.

Lapidge, M., BA, MA, PhD, Dept of Anglo-Saxon, Norse and Celtic, University of Cambridge, 9 West Road, Cambridge CB3 9DP.

Larkin, Professor M. J. M., MA, PhD, Dept of History, The University, George Square, Edinburgh EH8 9JY.

Larner, J. P., MA, Dept of History, The University, Glasgow G12 8QQ.

Lasko, Professor P. E., BA, FSA, 53 Montagu Square, London W1H 1TH.

Latham, R. C., CBE, MA, FBA, Magdalene College, Cambridge CB3 0AG.

Law, J. E., MA, DPhil, Dept of History, University College of Swansea, Swansea SA2 8PP.

Lawrence, Professor C. H., MA, DPhil, Royal Holloway and Bedford New College, Egham Hill, Egham, Surrey TW20 0EX.

Laws, Captain W. F., BA, MLitt, 23 Marlborough Road, St Leonard's, Exeter EX2 4TJ.

Lead, P., MA, 11 Morland Close, Stone, Staffs. ST15 0DA.

Le Cordeur, Professor Basil A., MA, PhD, Dept of History, University of Cape Town, Rondebosch 7700, Republic of South Africa.

Leddy, J. F., MA, BLitt, DPhil, The Leddy Library, University of Windsor, Windsor, Ontario, Canada N9B 3P4.

Lee, Professor J. M., MA, BLitt, Dept of Politics, The University, 12 Priory Road, Bristol BS8 1TU.

Lehmann, Professor H., DPhil, c/o German Historical Institute, 1759 R.St.N.W., Washington D.C., 20009, U.S.A.

Lehmann, Professor J. H., PhD, De Paul University, 25E Jackson Blvd., Chicago, Illinois 60604, U.S.A.

Lehmberg, Professor S. E., PhD, Dept of History, University of Minnesota, 614 Social Sciences, 267 19th Avenue South, Minneapolis, Minn. 55455, U.S.A.

Leinster-Mackay, D. P., MA, MEd, PhD, Dept of Education, University of Western Australia, Nedlands, Western Australia 6009.

Le May, G. H. L., MA, 6 Dale Close, St. Ebbe's, Oxford OX1 1TU.

Lenman, B. P., MA, LittD, Dept of Modern History, University of St Andrews, St Andrews, Fife KY16 9AL.

Lentin, A., MA, PhD, 57 Maids Causeway, Cambridge CB5 8DE.

Leslie, Professor R. F., BA, PhD, Market House, Church Street, Charlbury, Oxford OX7 3PP.

Lester, Professor M., PhD, Dept of History, Davidson College, Davidson, NC 28036, U.S.A.

Leventhal, Professor F. M., PhD, 18 Hollis Street, Newton, Massachusetts 02158, U.S.A.

Levine, Professor Joseph M., Dept of History, Syracuse University, Syracuse, New York 13210, U.S.A.

Levine, Professor Mortimer, PhD, 529 Woodhaven Drive, Morgantown, West Va. 26505, U.S.A.

Levy, Professor F. J., PhD, University of Washington, Seattle, Wash. 98195, U.S.A.

Lewis, Professor A. R., MA, PhD, History Dept, University of Massachusetts, Amherst, Mass. 01003, U.S.A.

Lewis, Professor B., PhD, FBA, Near Eastern Studies Dept, Jones Hall, The University, Princeton, N.J. 08540, U.S.A.

Lewis, C. W., BA, FSA, University College, P.O. Box 78, Cardiff CF1 1XL.

Lewis, Professor G., MA, DPhil, Dept of History, University of Warwick, Coventry CV4 7AL.

Lewis, P. S., MA, All Souls College, Oxford OX1 4AL.

Lewis, R. A., PhD, Y Berth Glyd, Siliwen Road, Bangor, Gwynedd LL57 2BS.

Lewis, R. Gillian, St Annes College, Oxford OX2 6HS.

Leyser, Professor K., TD, MA, FBA, FSA, All Souls College, Oxford OX1 4AL.

Liddell, W. H., BA, MA, Dept of Extra-Mural Studies, University of London, 26 Russell Square London WC1B 5DG.

Liddle, Peter H., BA, MLitt, Dipity House, 282 Pudsey Road, Bramley, Leeds LS13 4HX.

Lieu, Samuel N. C., MA, DPhil, FSA. 2a Dickinson Square, Croxley Green, Rickmansworth, Herts. WD3 3EZ.

Lindley, K. J., BA, MA, PhD, Dept of History, New University of Ulster, Coleraine, N. Ireland BT52 1SA.

*Lindsay, Mrs H., MA, PhD, 3 Ann Street, Edinburgh EH4 1PL.

Lindsay, Colonel Oliver J. M., MBIM, Brookwood House, Brookwood, nr Woking, Surrey.

Linehan, P. A., MA, PhD, St John's College, Cambridge CB2 1TP.

Livermore, Professor H. V., MA, Sandycombe Lodge, Sandycombe Road, St Margarets, Twickenham, Middx.

Lloyd, Professor H. A., BA, DPhil, Dept of History, The University, Cottingham Road, Hull HU6 7RX.

Lloyd, Simon D., BA, DPhil, Dept of History, The University, Newcastle upon Tyne NE1 7RU.

Lloyd, Professor T. O., MA, DPhil, Dept of History, The University, Toronto, Canada, M5S 1A1.

Lloyd-Jukes, Rev. H. A. MA, STh, St Catherines, 1 St Mary's Court, Ely, Cambs. CB7 4HQ.

Loach, Mrs J., MA, Somerville College, Oxford OX2 6HD.

Loades, Professor D. M., MA, PhD, Dept of History, University College of North Wales, Bangor, Gwynedd LL57 2DG.

Lobel, Mrs M. D., BA, FSA, Flat 2, Emden House, Barton Lane, Headington, Oxford, Oxon.

Lockie, D. McN., MA, 25 Chemin de la Panouche, Saint-Anne, 06130 Grasse, France.

Lockyer, R. W., MA, 63 Balcombe Street, London NW1 6HD.

Logan, F. D., MA, MSD, Emmanuel College, 400 The Fenway, Boston, Mass. 02115, U.S.A.

Logan, O. M. T., MA, PhD, 18 Clarendon Road, Norwich NR2 2PW.

London, Miss Vera C. M., MA, 55 Churchill Road, Church Stretton, Shropshire SY6 6EP.

Longley, D. A., MA, PhD, Dept of History, Taylor Building, King's College, The University, Old Aberdeen AB9 2UB.

Longmate, N. R., MA, 30 Clydesdale Gardens, Richmond, Surrey.

Loomie, Rev. A. J., SJ, MA, PhD, Fordham University, New York, NY 10458-5159, U.S.A.

Lottes, Professor G., MA, DPhil, DPhil–Habil, Kreidenweg 7, 8420 Kelheim-Hernsaal, FRG.

Loud, G. A., MA, DPhil, School of History, The University, Leeds LS2 9JT.

Louis, Professor William R., BA, MA, DPhil, Dept of History, University of Texas, Austin, Texas 78712, U.S.A.

Lourie, Elena, MA, DPhil, Dept of History, Ben Gurion University of The Negev, P.O. Box 653, Beer Sheva 84 105, Israel.

Lovatt, R. W., MA, DPhil, Peterhouse, Cambridge CB2 1RD.

Lovegrove, D. W., MA, BD, PhD, Dept of Ecclesiastical History, St Mary's College, The University, St Andrews, Fife KY16 9JU.

Lovell, J. C., BA, PhD, Eliot College, University of Kent, Canterbury CT2 7NS.

Lovett, A. W., MA, PhD, 26 Coney Hill Road, West Wickham, Kent BR4 9BX.

Low, Professor D. A., DPhil, PhD, FAHA, FASSA, Clare Hall, Cambridge CB3 9AL.

Lowe, P. C., BA, PhD, The University, Manchester M13 9PL.

Lowe, R., BA, PhD, Dept of Economic and Social History, The University, 13–15 Woodland Road, Bristol BS8 1TB.

Lowerson, J. R., BA, MA, Centre for Continuing Education, University of Sussex, Brighton.
Lowry, M. J. C., BA, MA, PhD, Dept of History, University of Warwick, Coventry CV4 7AL.
Loyn, Professor H. R., MA, FBA, FSA, Dept of History, Queen Mary and Westfield College, University of London, Kidderpore Avenue, Hampstead, London NW3 7ST.
Lucas, C. R., MA, DPhil, Balliol College, Oxford OX1 3BJ.
Lucas, P. J., MA, PhD, Dept of English, University College, Belfield, Dublin 4, Ireland.
*Lumb, Miss S. V., MA, Torr-Colin House, 106 Ridgway, Wimbledon, London SW19.
Lunn, D. C. J., STL, MA, PhD, 25 Cornwallis Avenue, Clifton, Bristol BS8 4PP.
Lunt, Major-General J. D., MA, Hilltop House, Little Milton, Oxfordshire OX9 7PU.
Luscombe, Professor D. E., MA, PhD, LittD, FBA, FSA, 4 Caxton Road, Broomhill, Sheffield S10 3DE.
Luttrell, A. T., MA, DPhil, 14 Perfect View, Bath BA1 5JY.
Lyman, Professor Richard W., PhD, 101 Alma Street, Apt. 107–8, Palo Alto, CA 94301, U.S.A.
Lynch, Professor J., MA, PhD, Inst. of Latin American Studies, University of London, 31 Tavistock Square, London WC1H 9HA.
Lynch, M., MA, PhD, Dept of Scottish History, The University, William Robertson Building, 50 George Square, Edinburgh EH8 9YW.
Lyttelton, The Hon. N. A. O., BA, 30 Paulton's Square, London SW3.

Mabbs, A. W., 32 The Street, Wallington, Herts. SG7 6SW.
Macaulay, J. H., MA, PhD, 11 Kirklee Circus, Glasgow G12 0TW.
McBriar, Professor A. M., BA, DPhil, FASSA, Dept of History, Monash University, Clayton, Victoria 3168, Australia.
McCaffrey, J. F., MA, PhD, Dept of Scottish History, The University, Glasgow G12 8QH.
MacCaffrey, Professor W. T., PhD, 745 Hollyoke Center, Harvard University, Cambridge, Mass. 02138, U.S.A.
McCann, W. P., BA, PhD, 41 Stanhope Gardens, Highgate, London N6.
McConica, Professor J. K., CSB, MA, DPhil, All Souls College, Oxford, OX1 4AL.
McCord, Professor N., BA, PhD, 7 Hatherton Avenue, Cullercoats, North Shields, Tyne and Wear NE30 3LG.
McCracken, Professor J. L., MA, PhD, 196 Tenth Street, Morningside, Durban 4001, South Africa.
MacCulloch, The Rev. D. N. J., MA, PhD, FSA, 28 William Street, Totterdown, Bristol BS3 4TT.
MacCurtain, Margaret B., MA, PhD, Dept of History, University College, Belfield, Dublin 4, Ireland.
McCusker, J. J., MA, PhD, Dept of History, University of Maryland, College Park, Maryland 20742, U.S.A.
MacDonagh, Professor O., MA, PhD, Research School of Social Sciences, Institute of Advanced Studies, Australian National University, P.O. Box 4, Canberra, A.C.T. 2601, Australia.
MacDonald, C. A., MA, DPhil, Dept of History, University of Warwick, Coventry CV4 7AL.
McDowell, Professor R. B., PhD, LittD, Trinity College, Dublin, Ireland.

Macfarlane, A. D. J., MA, DPhil, PhD, King's College, Cambridge CB2 1ST.
Macfarlane, L. J., PhD, DLitt, DLitt, LLD, FSA, 43 The Spital, Old Aberdeen AB2 3HX.
McGrath, Professor P. V., MA, Dept of History, University of Bristol, 13–15 Woodland Road, Bristol BS8 1TB.
MacGregor, D. R., MA, ARIBA, FSA, 99 Lonsdale Road, London SW13 9DA.
McGregor, J. F., BA, BLitt, Dept of History, University of Adelaide, SA 5001, Australia.
McGurk, J. J. N., BA, MPhil, PhD, Flat 2, 43 Lulworth Road, Birkdale, Southport, Merseyside, Lancs PR8 2JN.
McGurk, P. M., PhD, 11 Ashdon Close, Woodford Green, Essex IG8 0EF.
McHardy, Alison K., MA, DPhil, Dept of History, University of Nottingham, University Road, Nottingham NG7 2RD.
Machin, Professor G. I. T., MA, DPhil, Dept of Modern History, University of Dundee, Dundee DD1 4HN.
MacIntyre, A. D., MA, DPhil, Magdalen College, Oxford OX1 4AU.
MacKay, A. I. K., MA, PhD, Dept of History, The University, Edinburgh EH8 9YL.
McKay, D., BA, PhD, Dept of International History, London School of Economics, Houghton Street, London WC2A 2AE.
McKendrick, N., MA, Gonville and Caius College, Cambridge CB2 1TA.
McKenna, Professor J. W., MA, PhD, Orchard Hill Farm, Sandown Road, P.O. Box 343, N. Danville, N.H. 03819, U.S.A.
MacKenney, R. S., MA, PhD, Dept of History, University of Edinburgh, William Robertson Building, George Square, Edinburgh EH8 9JY.
MacKenzie, J. MacD., MA, PhD, Dept of History, The University, Bailrigg, Lancaster LA1 4YG.
Mackesy, P. G., MA, DPhil, DLitt, FBA, Leochel Cushnie House, Cushnie, Alford, Aberdeenshire AB3 8LJ.
McKibbin, R. I., MA, DPhil, St John's College, Oxford OX1 3JP.
McKinley, R. A., MA, 42 Boyers Walk, Leicester Forest East, Leicester LE3 3LN.
McKitterick, D. J., MA, Trinity College Library, Cambridge CB2 1TQ.
McKitterick, Rosamond D., MA, PhD, Newnham College, Cambridge CB3 9DF.
Maclagan, M., MA, FSA, Trinity College, Oxford OX1 3BH.
MacLane,, Assoc. Professor B. W., PhD P.O. Box 925 Hanover, New Hampshire 03755, U.S.A.
MacLean I. W. F., MA, DPhil, The Queen's College, Oxford OX1 4AW.
McLean, D. A., BA, MA, PhD, Dept of History, King's College London, Strand, London WC2R 2LS.
MacLeod, Professor R. M., AB, PhD, Dept of History, The University of Sydney, Sydney, N.S.W. 2006, Australia.
McLynn, F. J., MA, MA, PhD, 46 Grange Avenue, Twickenham, Middlesex TW2 5TW.
*McManners, Rev. Professor J., MA, DLitt, FBA, All Souls College, Oxford OX1 4AL.
McMillan, J. F., MA, DPhil, Dept of History, The University, Heslington, York YO1 5DD.
MacNiocaill, Professor G., PhD, DLitt, Dept of History, University College, Galway, Ireland.
McNulty, Miss P. A., BA, 84b Eastern Avenue, Reading RG1 5SF.

Madariaga, Professor Isabel de, PhD, 25 Southwood Lawn Road, London N6.

Madden, A. F., McC, DPhil, Nuffield College, Oxford OX1 1NF.

Maddicott, J. R., MA, DPhil, Exeter College, Oxford OX1 3DP.

Maehl, Professor W. H., PhD, The Fielding Institute, 2112 Santa Barbara Street, Santa Barbara, CA 93105, U.S.A.

Maffei, Professor Domenico, MLL, DrJur, Via delle Cerchia 19, 53100 Siena, Italy.

Maguire, W. A., MA, PhD, 18 Harberton Park, Belfast, N. Ireland BT9 6TS.

Mahoney, Professor T. H. D., AM, PhD, DPA, 130 Mt. Auburn Street, #410, Cambridge, Mass. 02138, U.S.A.

*MAJOR, Miss K., MA, BLitt, LittD, FBA, FSA, 21 Queensway, Lincoln LN2 4AJ.

Malcolm, Dr Joyce L., 1264 Beacon Street, Brookline, Mass. 02146, U.S.A.

Mallett, Professor M. E., MA, DPhil, Dept of History, University of Warwick, Coventry CV4 7AL.

Mallia-Milanes, V., BA, MA, PhD, 135 Zabbar Road, Paola, Malta.

Mangan, James A., BA, PhD, PGCE, ACSE, DLC, 39 Abercorn Drive, Hamilton, Scotland.

Manning, Professor A. F., Bosweg 27, Berg en Dal, The Netherlands.

Manning, Professor B. S., MA, DPhil, Dept of History, New University of Ulster, Coleraine, Co. Londonderry, Northern Ireland BT52 1SA.

Manning, Professor R. B., PhD, 2848 Coleridge Road, Cleveland Heights, Ohio 44118, U.S.A.

Mansergh, Professor P. N. S., OBE, MA, DPhil, DLitt, LittD, FBA, St John's College, Cambridge CB2 1TP.

Maprayil, C., BD, LD, DD, MA, PhD, c/o Institute of Historical Research, Senate House, London WC1E 7HU.

Marchant, The Rev. Canon R. A., PhD, BD, Laxfield Vicarage, Woodbridge, Suffolk IP13 8DT.

Marett, W. P., BA, MA, PhD, BSc(Econ), BCom, 20 Barrington Road, Stoneygate, Leicester LE2 2RA.

Margetts, J., MA, DipEd, DrPhil, 5 Glenluce Road, Liverpool L19 3BX.

Markus, Professor Emeritus R. A., MA, PhD, 100 Park Road, Chilwell, Beeston, Nottingham NG9 4DE.

Marquand, Professor D., MA, Dept of Politics and Contemporary History, The University, Salford M5 4WT.

Marriner, Sheila, MA, PhD, Dept of Economic History, University of Liverpool, Eleanor Rathbone Building, Myrtle Street, P.O. Box 147, Liverpool L69 3BX.

Marsh, Professor Peter T., PhD, Dept of History, Syracuse University, Syracuse, New York 13210, U.S.A.

Marshall, J. D., PhD, Brynthwaite, Charney Road, Grange-over-Sands, Cumbria LA11 6BP.

Marshall, Professor P. J., MA, DPhil, King's College London, Strand, London WC2R 2LS.

Martin, A. Lynn, MA, PhD, Dept of History, The University of Adelaide, Box 498, GPO, Adelaide, South Australia 5001.

Martin, E. W., Crossways, Editha Cottage, Black Torrington, Beaworthy, Devon EX21 5QF.

Martin, G. H., CBE, MA, DPhil, Flat 27, Woodside House, Woodside, Wimbledon, London SW19 7QN.

Martin, Professor Miguel, P.O. Box 1696, Zone 1, Panama 1, Republic of Panama.

Martindale, Jane P., MA, DPhil, School of English and American Studies, University of East Anglia, University Plain, Norwich NR4 7TJ.

Marwick, Professor A. J. B., MA, BLitt, Dept of History, The Open University, Walton Hall, Milton Keynes, Bucks MK7 6AA.

Mason, A., BA, PhD, 1 Siddeley Avenue, Kenilworth, Warwickshire CV8 1EW.

Mason, E. Emma, BA, PhD, Dept of History, Birkbeck College, Malet Street, London WC1E 7HX.

Mason, F. K., Beechwood, Watton, Norfolk IP25 6AB.

Mason, J. F. A., MA, DPhil, FSA, Christ Church, Oxford OX1 1DP.

Mate, Professor Mavis E, MA, PhD, Dept of History, University of Oregon, Eugene, OR 97405, U.S.A.

Mather, Professor Emeritus F. C., MA, 69 Ethelburt Avenue, Swaythling, Southampton SO2 3DF.

Mathew, W. M., MA, PhD, School of English and American Studies, University of East Anglia, University Plain, Norwich NR4 7TJ.

Mathias, P., CBE, MA, DLitt, FBA, Downing College, Cambridge, CB2 1DQ.

*Mathur-Sherry, Tikait Narain, BA, LLB, 3/193–4 Prem-Nagar, Dayalbagh, Agra-282005 (U.P.), India.

Matthew, Professor D. J. A., MA, DPhil, Dept of History, The University, Reading RG6 2AA.

Matthew, H. C. G., MA, DPhil, St Hugh's College, Oxford OX2 6LE.

Matthews, J. F., MA, DPhil, Queen's College, Oxford OX1 4AW.

Mattingly, Professor H. B., MA, 40 Grantchester Road, Cambridge CB3 9ED.

Mayer, Professor T. F., PhD, Dept of History, Augustana College, Rock Island, IL 61201, U.S.A.

Mayhew, G. J., BA, DPhil, 29 West Street, Lewes, East Sussex BN7 2NZ.

Mayhew, N. J. MA, 101 Marlborough Road, Oxford OX1 4LX.

Mayr-Harting, H. M. R. E., MA, DPhil, St Peter's College, Oxford OX1 2DL.

Mbaeyi, P. M., BA, DPhil, PO Box 6175, Aladinma Post Office, Owerri, Imo State, Nigeria.

Meek, Christine E., MA, DPhil, 3145 Arts Building, Trinity College, Dublin 2, Ireland.

Meek, D. E., MA, BA, Dept of Celtic, University of Edinburgh, David Hume Tower, George Square, Edinburgh EH8 9JX.

Meller, Miss Helen E., BA, PhD, 2 Copenhagen Court, Denmark Grove, Alexandra Park, Nottingham NG3 4LF.

Melton, Professor F. T., BA, MA, PhD, Dept of History, University of North Carolina at Greensboro, 214 McIver Building, Greensboro, NC 27411-5001, U.S.A.

Merson, A. L., MA, Flat 12, Northerwood House, Swan Green, Lyndhurst, Southampton SO4 17DT.

Metcalf, Professor M, History Dept, 614 Social Sciences, 267 19th Avenue South, Minneapolis, Minn 55455, U.S.A.

Mettam, R. C., BA, MA, PhD, Dept of History, Queen Mary College, Mile End Road, London E1 4NS.

Mews, Stuart, PhD, Dept of Religious Studies, Cartmel College, Bailrigg, Lancaster.

Micklewright, F. H. A., PhD, 4 Lansdowne Court, 1 Lansdowne Road, Ridgway, Wimbledon, London SW20.

Middlebrook, Martin, 48 Linden Way, Boston, Lincs. PE21 9DS.

Middleton, Professor C. R., AB, MA, PhD, Office of the Dean, College of Arts and Sciences, 43 Main, Campus Box 275, University of Colorado, Boulder, CO 80309-0234, U.S.A.
Middleton, R., BA, PhD, Dept of Economic and Social History, University of Bristol, 13–15 Woodland Road, Bristol BS8 1TB.
Midgley, Miss L. M., MA, 84 Wolverhampton Road, Stafford ST17 4AW.
Miller, Professor A., BA, MA, PhD, Dept of History, University of Houston, Houston, Texas, U.S.A.
Miller, E., MA, LittD, 36 Almoners Avenue, Cambridge CB1 4PA.
Miller, Miss H., MA, Top Meadow, Woodchurch Road, Tenterden, Kent, TN30 7AD.
Miller, J., MA, PhD, Dept of History, Queen Mary and Westfield College, Mile End Road, London E1 4NS.
Milne, A. T., MA, 9 Frank Dixon Close, London SE21 7BD.
Milne, Miss D. J., MA, PhD, King's College, Aberdeen, AB9 1FX.
Milsom, Professor S. F. C., MA, FBA, 113 Grantchester Meadows, Cambridge CB3 9JN.
Minchinton, Professor W. E., BSc(Econ), 53 Homefield Road, Exeter, Devon, EX1 2QX.
Mingay, Professor G. E., PhD, Mill Field House, Selling Court, Selling, nr Faversham, Kent ME13 9RJ.
Mitchell, C., MA, BLitt, LittD, Sundial House, 21 Cowley Road, Littlemore, Oxford, OX4 4LE.
Mitchell, L. G., MA, DPhil, University College, Oxford OX1 4BH.
Mitchison, Professor Rosalind, MA, Great Yew, Ormiston, East Lothian EH35 5NJ.
Miyoshi, Professor Yoko, 1–29–2 Okayama, Meguro, Tokyo 152, Japan.
Moloney, Thomas M., PhD, 9 Treetops, Sydney Road, Woodford Green, Essex IG8 0SY.
Mommsen, Professor Dr W. J., Leuchtenberger Kirchweg 43, 4000 Dusseldorf-Kaiserswerth, West Germany.
Mondey, D. C., 175 Raeburn Avenue, Surbiton, Surrey KT5 9DE.
Money, Professor J., PhD, 912 St Patrick Street, Victoria, B.C., Canada V8S 4X5.
Moody, Professor Michael E., PhD, 2713 Third Street, La Verne, Calif. 91750, U.S.A.
Moore, B. J. S., BA, Dept of Economic and Social History, University of Bristol, 13–15 Woodland Road, Bristol BS8 1TB.
Moore, Professor D. Cresap, 1 Richdale Avenue, #15, Cambridge, Mass. 02140, U.S.A.
Moore, M. J., Dept of History, Appalachian State University, Boone, NC 28608, U.S.A.
Moore, R. I., MA, Dept of History, The University, Sheffield S10 2TN.
Moore, Professor R. J., DLit, PhD, BA, MA, School of Social Sciences, Flinders University of South Australia, Bedford Park, South Australia 5042, Australia.
Morgan, B. G., BArch, PhD, Tan-y-Fron, 43 Church Walks, Llandudno, Gwynedd.
Morgan, D. A. L., Dept of History, University College London, Gower Street, London WC1E 6BT.
Morgan, David R., MA, PhD, Dept of Politics, Roxby Building, The University, P.O. Box 147, Liverpool L69 3BX.
Morgan, K. O., MA, DPhil, FBA, The Queen's College, Oxford OX1 4AW.

Morgan, N. J., BA, PhD, Dept of Scottish History, University of Glasgow, 9 University Gardens, Glasgow G12 8QQ.
Morgan, Miss P. E., 6 The Cloisters, Hereford HR1 2NG.
Morgan, P. T. J., MA, DPhil, Dept of History, University College of Swansea, Singleton Park, Swansea SA2 7BR.
Morgan, Victor F. G., BA, School of English and American Studies, University of East Anglia, Norwick NR4 7TJ.
Morioka, Professor K., BA, 3–12 Sanno 4 Chome, Ota-Ku, Tokyo 143, Japan.
Morrell, J. B., BSc., MA, Dept of European Studies, The University, Bradford, West Yorkshire BD7 1DP.
Morrill, J. S., MA, DPhil, Selwyn College, Cambridge CB3 9DQ.
Morris, The Rev. Professor C., MA, 53 Cobbett Road, Bitterne Park, Southampton SO2 4HJ.
Morris, G. C., MA, King's College, Cambridge CB2 1ST.
Morris, R. J., BA, DPhil, 41 Kirkhill Road, Edinburgh EH16 5DE.
Mortimer, R., PhD, 10 Orchard Avenue, Cambridge CB2 4AH.
Mosse, Professor W. E. E., MA, PhD, Dawn Cottage, Ashwellthorpe, Norwich, Norfolk.
Mullins, E. L. C., OBE, MA, Institute of Historical Research, University of London, Senate House, London WC1E 7HU.
Munro, D. J., MA, 65 Meadowcroft, St Albans, Herts. AL1 1UF.
Murdoch, D. H., MA, School of History, The University, Leeds LS2 9JT.
Murfett, Professor M. H., BA, DPhil, Dept of History, York University, 4700 Keele Street, North York, Ontario, Canada M3J 1P3.
Murray, A., MA, BA, BPhil, University College, Oxford OX1 4BH.
Murray, Athol L., MA, LLB, PhD, 33 Inverleith Gardens, Edinburgh EH3 5PR.
Murray, Professor B. K., PhD, BA, History Department, University of Witwatersrand, Johannesburg, South Africa.
Myatt-Price, Miss E. M., BA, MA, 20 Highfield Drive, Epsom, Surrey KT19 0AS.
Myerscough, J., MA, 39 Campden Street, London W8 7ET.

Nelson, Janet L., BA, PhD, Dept of History, King's College London, Strand, London WC2R 2LS.
Newbould, Professor I. D. C., BA, MA, PdD, 1815–20 Avenue South, Lethbridge, Alberta, Canada T1K 1G3.
Neveu, Dr Bruno, 30 rue Jacob, Paris VIe, France.
New, Professor J. F. H., Dept of History, Waterloo University, Waterloo, Ontario, Canada.
Newbury, C. W., MA, PhD, Linacre College, Oxford OX1 3JA.
Newitt, M. D. D., BA, PhD, Queen's Building, University of Exeter, Exeter, Devon EX4 4QH.
Newman, Professor A. N., MA, DPhil, 33 Stanley Road, Leicester LE2 1RF.
Newman, P. R., BA, DPhil, 1 Ainsty Farm Cottage, Bilton in Ainsty, York YO5 8NN.
Newman, R. K., BA, MA, DPhil, Dept of History, University College, Swansea SA2 8PP.
Newsome, D. H., MA, LittD, Master's Lodge, Wellington College, Crowthorne, Berks. RG11 7PU.
Nicholas, Professor David, PhD, Dept of History, Clemson University, Clemson, South Carolina 29634–1507, U.S.A.
Nicholas, Professor H. G., MA, FBA, New College, Oxford OX1 3BN.

Nicholls, A. J., MA, BPhil, St Antony's College, Oxford OX2 6JF.
Nicol, Mrs A., MA, BLitt, Public Record Office, Chancery Lane, London WC2A 1LR.
Nicol, Professor D. M., MA, PhD, 16 Courtyards, Little Shelford, Cambridge CB2 5ER.
Nightingale, Pamela, MA, PhD, 20 Beaumont Buildings, Oxford OX1 2LL.
Noakes, J. D., BA, MA, DPhil, Dept of History, The University, Queen's Bldg, Queen's Drive, Exeter EX4 4QH.
Norman, E. R., MA, PhD, Christ Church College, Canterbury, Kent CT1 1QU.

Obolensky, Professor Sir Dimitri, MA, PhD, DLitt, FBA, FSA, Christ Church, Oxford OX1 1DP.
O'Brien, M. G. R., BA, MA, PhD, Magee College, University of Ulster, Northlands Road, Londonderry, Northern Ireland.
O'Brien, P. K., MA, DPhil, BSc(Econ), St Antony's College, Oxford OX2 6JF.
O'Connor, Professor J. E., PhD, Dept of Humanities, New Jersey, Institute of Technology, Newark, NJ 07102, U.S.A.
O'Day, A., BA, MA, PhD, Polytechnic of North London, Prince of Wales Road, London NW5.
O'Day, M. R. (Mrs Englander), BA, PhD, 14 Marshworth, Tinkers Bridge, Milton Keynes MK6 3DA.
*Offler, Professor H. S., MA, 28 Old Elvet, Durham DH1 3HN.
O'Gorman, F., BA, PhD, The University, Manchester M13 9PL.
Okey, R. F. C., MA, DPhil, 10 Bertie Road, Kenilworth, Warwickshire CV8 1JP.
Olney, R. J., MA, DPhil, Historical Manuscripts Commission, Quality House, Quality Court, Chancery Lane, London WC2A 1HP.
O'Neill, Professor R. J., MA, DPhil, All Souls College, Oxford, OX1 4AL.
Orde, Miss A. W., MA, PhD, Dept of History, University of Durham, 43 North Bailey, Durham DH1 3EX.
Oresko, R. C. J., BA, MA, PhD, 53 Bedford Gardens, London W8 7EF.
Orme, Professor N. I., MA, DPhil, DLitt, FSA, Dept. of History and Archaeology, University of Exeter, Exeter, EX4 4QH.
Ó Tuathaigh, M. A. G., MA, Dept of History, University College, Galway, Ireland.
Outhwaite, R. B., MA, PhD, Gonville and Caius College, Cambridge CB2 1TA.
Ovendale, R., MA, DPhil, Dept of International Politics, University College of Wales, Aberystwyth SY23 3DY.
Owen, A. E. B., MA, 35 Whitwell Way, Coton, Cambridge CB3 7PW.
Owen, Mrs D. M., MA, LittD, FSA, 35 Whitwell Way, Coton, Cambridge CB3 7PW.
Owen, G. D., MA, PhD, 21 Clifton Terrace, Brighton, Sussex BN1 3HA.
Owen, J. B., BSc, MA, DPhil, 24 Hurdeswell, Long Hanborough, Oxford OX7 2DH.

Pagden, A. R. D., MA, DPhil, King's College, Cambridge CB2 1ST.
Palgrave, D. A., MA, CChem, FRSC, FSG, Crossfield House, Dale Road, Stanton, Bury St. Edmunds, Suffolk IP31 2DY.
Palliser, Professor D. M., MA, DPhil, FSA, Dept of History, The University, Hull HU6 7RX.

Palmer, J. G., MA, MSc(Econ), MPhil, 78 Norroy Road, London SW15 1PG.
Palmer, J. J. N., BA, BLitt, PhD, 59 Marlborough Avenue, Hull HU5 3JR.
Palmer, Professor R. C., PhD, Dept of History, The University, Houston, Texas 77204, U.S.A.
Palmer, Sarah, PhD, MA, MA, Dept of History, Queen Mary College, Mile End Road, London E1 4NS.
Paret, Professor P., Inst. for Advanced Study, School of Historical Studies, Princeton, NJ 08540, U.S.A.
Parish, Professor P. J., BA, Institute of U.S. Studies, 31 Tavistock Square, London WC1H 9EZ.
Parker, Professor N. G., MA, PhD, LittD, FBA, Dept of History, University of Illinois, 309 Gregory Hall, 810 South Wright Street, Urbana, Ill. 61801, U.S.A.
Parker, R. A. C., MA, DPhil, The Queen's College, Oxford OX1 4AW.
Parkes, M. B., BLitt, MA, FSA, Keble College, Oxford OX1 3PG.
*Parkinson, Professor C. N., MA, PhD, Delancey, 36 Harbour Drive, Canterbury, Kent.
Parris, H. W., MA, PhD, Warwick House, 47 Guildhall Street, Bury St Edmunds, Suffolk IP33 1QF.
Parrott, D. A., MA, DPhil, Dept of History, University of York, Heslington, York YO1 5DD.
Parry, G. J. R., MA, PhD, History Dept, Victoria University of Wellington, PO Box 600, Wellington, New Zealand.
Parry, J. P., PhD, Peterhouse, Cambridge CB2 1RD.
Patrick, Rev. J. G., MA, PhD, DLitt, 8 North Street, Braunton, N. Devon EX33 1AJ.
Partridge, M. S., BA, PhD, 15 Pearman Street, Lambeth, London SE1 7RB.
Pavlowitch, Stevan K., MA, LEsL, Dept of History, The University, Southampton SO9 5NH.
Payne, Mrs. Ann, BA, 138 Culford Road, London N1 4HU.
Payne, Professor Peter L., BA, PhD, 68 Hamilton Place, Aberdeen AB2 4BA.
Payton, P. J., BSc, PhD, PhD, 5 Trecarne View, St Cleer, Liskeard, Cornwall.
Paz, Denis G., PhD, Dept of History, Clemson University, Clemson, South Carolina 29634–1507, U.S.A.
Peake, Rev. F. A., DD, DSLitt, 310 Dalehurst Drive, Nepean, Ontario, Canada K2G 4E4.
Pearce, R. D., BA, DPhil, Dept of History, St Martin's College, Lancaster LA1 3JD.
Pearl, Mrs Valerie L., MA, DPhil, FSA, New Hall, Cambridge CB3 0DF.
Peck, Professor Linda L., PhD, Dept of History, Purdue University, University Hall, West Lafayette, Indiana 47907, U.S.A.
Peden, G. C., MA, DPhil, Dept of History, University of Stirling, Stirling FK9 4LA.
Peek, Miss H. E., MA, FSA, FSAScot, Taintona, Moretonhampstead, Newton Abbot, Devon TQ13 8LG.
Peel, Lynnette J., BAgrSc, MAgrSc, PhD, 49 Oaklands, Hamilton Road, Reading RG1 5RN.
Peele, Miss Gillian R., BA, BPhil, Lady Margaret Hall, Oxford OX2 6QA.
Pelling, Margaret, BA, MLitt, Wellcome Unit for the History of Medicine, University of Oxford, 45–47 Banbury Road, Oxford OX2 6PE.
Pennington, D. H., MA, Rose Cottage, Linton Hill, near Ross-on-Wye HR9 7RT.

Perkin, Professor H. J., MA, Dept of History, Northwestern University, Evanston, Illinois 60208-2220, U.S.A.
Perry, C. R., PhD, Dept of History, The University of the South, Sewanee, Tennessee 37375, U.S.A.
Perry, Norma, BA, PhD, 2 Crossmead Villas, Dunsford Road, Exeter, Devon, EX2 9PU.
Peters, Professor E. M., PhD, Dept of History, University of Pennsylvania, Philadelphia 19174, U.S.A.
Pettegree, A. D. M., MA, DPhil, Dept. of Modern History, St Andrews University, St Andrews, Fife KY16 9AL.
Pfaff, Professor Richard W., MA, DPhil, Dept of History, Hamilton Hall 070A, University of North Carolina, Chapel Hill, NC 27514, U.S.A.
Phillips, Sir Henry (E. I.), CMG, MBE, MA, 34 Ross Court, Putney Hill, London SW15.
Phillips, Assoc. Professor John A., PhD, Dept of History, University of California, Riverside, Calif. 92521, U.S.A.
Phillips, J. R. S., BA, PhD, FSA, Dept of Medieval History, University College, Dublin 4, Ireland.
Phillips, P. T., PhD, Box 46, Dept of History, St Francis Xavier University, Antigonish, Nova Scotia, Canada B2G 1CO.
Phillipson, N.T., MA, PhD, Dept of History, The University George Square, Edinburgh EH8 9JY.
Phythian-Adams, C. V., MA, Dept of English Local History, The University, University Road, Leicester LE1 7RH.
Pierce, Professor G. O., MA, Dept of History of Wales, University College, P.O. Box 95, Cardiff CF1 1XA.
Piggin, F. S., BA, BD, DipEd, PhD, AKC, Dept of History, University of Wollongong, Wollongong, N.S.W. 2500, Australia.
Pitt, H. G., MA, Worcester College, Oxford OX1 2HB.
Platt, Professor C. P. S., MA, PhD, FSA, Dept of History, The University, Southampton SO9 5NH.
Plumb, Sir John, PhD, LittD, FBA, FSA, Christ's College, Cambridge CB2 3BU.
Pocock, Professor J. G. A., PhD, Dept of History, Johns Hopkins University, Baltimore, Md. 21218, U.S.A.
Pogge von Strandmann, H. J. O., MA, DPhil, University College, Oxford OX1 4BH.
Pole, Professor J. R., MA, PhD, St Catherine's College, Oxford OX1 3UJ.
Pollard, A. J., BA, PhD, 22 The Green, Hurworth-on-Tees, Darlington, Co. Durham DL2 2AA.
Pollard, Professor S., BSc(Econ), PhD (Corresponding), FBA, Abteilung Geschichte, Fakultät für Geschichtswissenschaft und Philosophie, Univer. Bielefeld, Postfach 8640, 4800 Bielefeld 1.
Polonsky, A. B., BA, DPhil, Dept of International History, London School of Economics, Houghton Street, London WC2A 2AE.
Port, Professor M. H., MA, BLitt, FSA, Dept of History, Queen Mary and Westfield College, Mile End Road, London E1 4NS.
PORTER, A. N., MA, PhD (*Hon. Secretary*), Dept of History, King's College London, Strand, London WC2R 2LS.
Porter, B. E., BSc(Econ), PhD, Merville, Allan Road, Seasalter, Whitstable, Kent CT5 4AH.
Porter, B. J., MA, PhD, Dept of History, The University, Hull HU6 7RX.
Porter, H. C., MA, PhD, Faculty of History, West Road, Cambridge CB3 9EF.

Porter, J. H., BA, PhD, Dept of Economic History, The University, Amory Buildings, Rennes Drive, Exeter EX4 4RJ.
Porter, S., BA, MLitt, PhD, Royal Commission on the Historical Monuments of England, Newlands House, 37–40 Berners Street, London W1P 4BP.
Post, J., MA, PhD, Public Record Office, Chancery Lane, London WC2A 1LR.
Postles, D. A., BA, PhD, c/o Dept of English Local History, Marc Fitch House, 3–5 Salisbury Road, Leicester LE1 7QR.
Potter, J., BA, MA(Econ), London School of Economics, Houghton Street, London WC2A 2AE.
Powell, E., MA, DPhil, 23 Mulberry Hill, Shenfield, Essex CM15 8JS.
Powell, Colonel G.S., 2 North End Terrace, Chipping Camden, Glos., GL55 6AE.
Powell, W. R., BLitt, MA, FSA, 2 Glanmead, Shenfield Road, Brentwood, Essex CM15 8ER.
Power, M. J., BA, PhD, School of History, The University, P.O. Box 147, Liverpool L69 3BX.
Powicke, Professor M. R., MA,. 67 Lee Avenue, Toronto, Ontario, Canada, M43 2P1.
Powis, J. K. MA, DPhil, Balliol College, Oxford OX1 3BJ.
Prall, Professor Stuart E., MA, PhD, PhD Program in History, Graduate School and University Center, C.U.N.Y., 33 West 42nd Street, New York, NY 10036, U.S.A.
Prentis, Malcolm D., BA, MA, PhD, 3 Marina Place, Belrose, New South Wales 2085, Australia.
Prest, W. R., MA, DPhil, Dept of History, University of Adelaide, North Terrace, Adelaide, S. Australia 5001.
Preston, Professor P., MA, DPhil, MA, Dept of History, Queen Mary and Westfield College, Mile End Road, London E1 4NS.
*Preston, Professor R. A., MA, PhD, Duke University, Durham, N.C., U.S.A.
Prestwich, J. O., MA, 18 Dunstan Road, Old Headington, Oxford OX3 9BY.
Prestwich, Mrs M., MA, St Hilda's College, Oxford OX4 1DY.
Prestwich, Professor M. C., MA, DPhil, Dept of History, The University, 43/46 North Bailey, Durham DH1 3EX.
Price, A. W., PhD, 19 Bayley Close, Uppingham, Leicestershire LE15 9TG.
Price, Rev. D. T. W., MA, St David's University College, Lampeter, Dyfed SA48 7ED.
Price, F. D., MA, BLitt, FSA, Lyndon, Wigginton, Banbury, Oxford OX15 4LD.
Price, Professor Jacob M., AM, PhD, University of Michigan, Ann Arbor, Michigan 48104, U.S.A.
Price, R. D., BA, DLitt, School of Modern Languages & European History, University of East Anglia, Norwich NR4 7TJ.
Prichard, Canon T. J., MA, PhD, Tros-Yr-Afon, Llangwnnadl, Pwllheli, Gwynedd LL53 8NS.
Priestley, E. J., MA, MPhil, 7 Inverleith Place, Edinburgh EH3 5QE.
Prins, G. I. T., MA, PhD, Emmanuel College, Cambridge CB2 3AP.
Pritchard, Professor D. G., PhD, 11 Coed Mor, Sketty, Swansea, W. Glam. SA2 8BQ.
Pritchard, R. J., PhD, 28 Star Hill, Rochester, Kent ME1 1XB.
Prochaska, Alice M. S., MA, DPhil, 9 Addison Bridge Place, London W14 8XP.
Prochaska, F. K., PhD, 9 Addison Bridge Place, London W14 8XP.

Pronay, N., BA, School of History, The University, Leeds LS2 9JT.
Prothero, I. J., BA, PhD, The University, Manchester M13 9PL.
Pugh, M. D., BA, PhD, Dept of History, The University, Newcastle upon Tyne NE1 7RU.
Pugh, T. B., MA, BLitt, 28 Bassett Wood Drive, Southampton SO2 3PS.
Pullan, Professor B. S., MA, PhD, FBA, Dept of History, The University, Manchester M13 9PL.
Pulman, M. B., MA, PhD, AB, History Dept, University of Denver, Colorado 80210, U.S.A.
Pulzer, Professor P. G. J., MA, PhD, All Souls College, Oxford OX1 4AL.

Quested, Rosemary K. I., MA, PhD, 30 Woodford Court, Birchington, Kent CT7 9DR.
Quinault, R. E., MA, DPhil, 21 Tytherton Road, London N19.
QUINN, Professor D. B., MA, PhD, DLit, DLitt, DLitt, DLitt, LLD, MRIA, DHL, Hon. FBA, 9 Knowsley Road, Liverpool L19 0PF.
Quintrell, B. W., MA, PhD, School of History, The University, P.O. Box 147, Liverpool L69 3BX.

Raban, Mrs S. G., MA, PhD, Trinity Hall, Cambridge CB2 1TJ.
Rabb, Professor T. K., MA, PhD, Princeton University, Princeton, N.J. 08540, U.S.A.
Radford, C. A. Ralegh, MA, DLitt, FBA, FSA, Culmcott, Uffculme, Cullompton, Devon EX15 3AT.
*Ramm, Miss A., MA, DLitt, Metton Road, Roughton, Norfolk NR11 8QT.
*Ramsay, G. D., MA, DPhil, 15 Charlbury Road, Oxford OX2 6UT.
RAMSDEN, J. A., MA, DPhil (*Literary Director*), Dept of History, Queen Mary and Westfield College, Mile End Road, London E1 4NS.
Ramsey, Professor P. H., MA, DPhil, Taylor Building, King's College, Old Aberdeen AB9 1FX.
Ranft, Professor B. McL., MA, DPhil, 32 Parkgate, Blackheath, London SE3 9XF.
Ransome, D. R., MA, PhD, 10 New Street, Woodbridge, Suffolk IP12 3DU.
Ratcliffe, D. J., MA, BPhil, PhD, Dept of History, The University, 43 North Bailey, Durham DH1 3EX.
Rawcliffe, Carole, BA, PhD, 24 Villiers Road, London NW2.
Rawley, Professor J. A., PhD, Dept of History, University of Nebraska Lincoln, 612 Oldfather Hall, Lincoln, Nebraska 68588-0327, U.S.A.
Ray, Professor R. D., BA, BD, PhD, Dept of History, University of Toledo, 2801 W. Bancroft Street, Toledo, Ohio 43606-3390, U.S.A.
Read, Professor D., BLitt, MA, PhD, Darwin College, University of Kent at Canterbury, Kent CT2 7NY.
Reader, W. J., BA, PhD, 46 Gough Way, Cambridge CB3 9LN.
Reay, B. G., BA, DPhil, Dept of History, University of Auckland, Private Bag, Auckland, New Zealand.
Reed, Michael A., MA, LLB, PhD, 1 Paddock Close, Quorn, Leicester LE12 8BJ.
Reeves, Professor A. C., MA, PhD, Dept of History, Ohio University, Athens, Ohio 45701, U.S.A.
Reeves, Miss M. E., MA, PhD, 38 Norham Road, Oxford OX2 6SQ.
Reid, B. H., MA, PhD, Dept of War Studies, Kings College London, Strand, London WC2R 2LS.
Reid, F., MA, DPhil, 24 Station Road, Kenilworth, Warwickshire CV8 1JJ.

Reid, Professor L. D., MA, PhD, 200 E. Brandon Road, Columbia, Mo. 65201, U.S.A.

Reid, Professor W. S., MA, PhD, University of Guelph, Guelph, Ontario, Canada N1G 2W1.

Rempel, Professor R. A., DPhil, Dept of History, McMaster University, 1280 Main Street West, Hamilton, Ontario, Canada L8S 4L9.

Renold, Miss P., MA, 51 Woodstock Close, Oxford OX2 8DD.

Renshaw, P. R. G., MA, Dept of History, The University, Sheffield S10 2TN.

Reuter, T. A., MA, DPhil, Monumenta Germaniae Historica, Ludwigstrasse 16, 8 München 34, West Germany.

Reynolds, D. J., MA, PhD, Christ's College, Cambridge CB2 3BU.

Reynolds, Miss S. M. G., MA, 26 Lennox Gardens, London SW1X 0DQ.

Richards, J. M., MA, Dept of History, The University, Bailrigg, Lancaster LA1 4YG.

Richards, Rev. J. M., MA, BLitt, STL, St Mary's, Cadogan Street, London SW3 2QR.

Richardson, P. G. L., BA, PhD, 16 Tanner Grove, Northcote, Victoria 3070, Australia.

Richardson, R. C., BA, PhD, Dept of History, King Alfred's College, Winchester.

Richter, Professor M., DrPhil.habil, Universität Konstanz, Postfach 5560, D–7750 Konstanz 1, Germany.

Riden, Philip J., MA, MLitt, Dept of Extramural Studies, University College, P.O. Box 78, Cardiff CF1 1XL.

Ridgard, J. M., PhD, Dennington Place, Dennington, Woodbridge, Suffolk IP13 8AN.

Riley, P. W. J., BA, PhD, 2 Cherry Tree Cottages, Meal Street, New Mills, Stockport SK12 5EB.

Riley-Smith, Professor J. S. C., MA, PhD, Royal Holloway and Bedford New College, Egham Hill, Egham, Surrey TW20 0EX.

Rimmer, Professor W. G., MA, PhD, University of N.S.W., P.O. Box 1, Kensington, N.S.W. 2033, Australia.

Ritcheson, Professor C. R., DPhil, Dept of History, University of Southern California, University Park, Los Angeles 90007, U.S.A.

Ritchie, J. D., BA, DipEd, PhD, FAHA, 74 Banambila Street, Aranda, ACT 2614, Australia.

Rizvi, S. A. G., MA, DPhil, 7 Portland Road, Summertown, Oxford.

Roach, Professor J. P. C., MA, PhD, 1 Park Crescent, Sheffield S10 2DY.

Robbins, Professor Caroline, PhD, 815 The Chetwynd, Rosemount, Pa. 19010, U.S.A.

Robbins, Professor K. G., MA, DPhil, DLitt, Dept of History, The University, Glasgow G12 8QQ.

Roberts, J. M., MA, DPhil, Merton College, Oxford OX1 4JD.

Roberts, Professor M., MA, DPhil, DLit, FilDr, FBA, 1 Allen Street, Grahamstown 6140, C.P., South Africa.

Roberts, P. R., MA, PhD, FSA, Keynes College, The University, Canterbury, Kent CT2 7NP.

Roberts, Professor R. C., PhD, 284 Blenheim Road, Columbus, Ohio 43214, U.S.A.

Roberts, Professor R. S., PhD, History Dept, University of Zimbabwe, P.O. Box MP 167, Harare, Zimbabwe.

Roberts, Stephen K., BA, PhD, East View, Iron Cross, Salford Priors, Evesham, Worcs. WR11 5SH.

Robertson, J. C., MA, DPhil, St Hugh's College, Oxford OX2 6LE.

Robinson, F. C. R., MA, PhD, Alderside, Egham Hill, Egham, Surrey TW20 0BD.
Robinson, K. E., CBE, MA, DLitt, LLD, The Old Rectory, Church Westcote, Kingham, Oxford OX7 6SF.
Robinson, R. A. H., BA, PhD, School of History, The University, Birmingham B15 2TT.
Robinton, Professor Madeline R., MA, PhD, 210 Columbia Heights, Brooklyn 1, New York, U.S.A.
Robson, Professor Ann P. W., PhD, 28 McMaster Avenue, Toronto, Ontario, Canada M4V 1A9.
Rodger, N. A. M., MA, DPhil, 40 Grafton Road, Acton, London W3.
*Rodkey, F. S., AM, PhD, 152 Bradley Drive, Santa Cruz, Calif., U.S.A.
Rodney, Professor Emeritus W., MA, PhD, 308 Denison Road, Victoria, B.C., Canada V8S 4K3.
Rodriguez-Salgado, Maria-Jose, BA, PhD, Dept of International History, London School of Economics, Houghton Street, London WC2A 2AE.
Roebuck, Peter, BA, PhD, Dept of History, New University of Ulster, Coleraine, N. Ireland BT48 7JL.
Rogers, Professor A., MA, PhD, FSA, Ulph Cottage, Church Plain, Burnham Market, Kings Lynn, Norfolk PE31 8EL.
Rogers, N. C. T., BA, PhD, Dept of History, York University, 4700 Keele Street, North York, Ontario, Canada M3J 1P3.
Rogister, J. M. J., MA, DPhil, 4 The Peth, Durham DH1 4PZ.
Rolo, Professor P. J. V., MA, The University, Keele, Staffordshire ST5 5BG.
Rompkey, R. G., MA, BEd, PhD, Dept of English, Memorial University, St John's, Newfoundland, Canada A1C 5S7.
Roots, Professor I. A., MA, FSA, Dept of History, University of Exeter, Queen's Building, The Queen's Drive, Exeter EX4 4QH.
Roper, M., MA, Public Record Office, Chancery Lane, London WC2A 1LR.
Rose, Margaret A., BA, PhD, c/o H.P.S. Faculty of Arts University of Melbourne, Parkville, Victoria 3052, Australia.
Rose, Professor P. L., MA, DenHist (Sorbonne), Dept of History, York University, North York, Toronto, Ontario, Canada.
Rosen, Professor F., BA, MA, PhD, Dept of History, University College London, Gower Street, London WC1E 6BT.
Rosenthal, Professor Joel T., PhD, Dept of History, State University, Stony Brook, New York 11794, U.S.A.
Roseveare, Professor H. G., PhD, King's College London, Strand, London WC2R 2LS.
Roskell, Professor J. S., MA, DPhil, FBA, The University, Manchester M13 9PL.
Rothblatt, Professor Sheldon, PhD, Dept of History, University of California, Berkeley, Calif. 94720, U.S.A.
Rothermund, Professor D., MA, PhD, DPhil Habil, Oberer Burggarten 2, 6915 Dossenheim, West Germany.
Rothney, Professor G. O., MA, PhD, LLD, St John's College, University of Manitoba, Winnipeg, Canada R3T 2M5.
Rothrock, Professor G. A., MA, PhD, Dept of History, University of Alberta, 2–28 Henry Marshall Tory Building, Edmonton, Alberta, Canada T6G 2H4.
Rothwell, V. H., BA, PhD, History Dept, The University, William Robertson Building, George Square, Edinburgh EH8 9JY.
Rousseau, P. H., MA, DPhil, Dept of History, University of Auckland, Private Bag, Auckland, New Zealand.

*Rowe, Miss B. J. H., MA, BLitt, St Anne's Cottage, Winkton, Christchurch, Hants.
Rowe, W. J., DPhil, Rock Mill, Par, Cornwall PL25 2SS.
Rowse, A. L., MA, DLitt, DCL, FBA, Trenarren House, St Austell, Cornwall.
Roy, I., MA, DPhil, FSA, Dept of History, King's College London, Strand, London WC2R 2LS.
Roy, Professor R. H., MA, PhD, 2841 Tudor Avenue, Victoria, B.C., Canada V8N 1L6.
Royle, E., MA, PhD, Dept of History, The University, Heslington, York YO1 5DD.
Rubens, A., FRICS, FSA, 16 Grosvenor Place, London SW1.
Rubini, D. A., DPhil, Temple University, Philadelphia 19122, Penn., U.S.A.
Rubinstein, Professor N., PhD, 16 Gardnor Mansions, Church Row, London NW3.
Rubinstein, Professor W. D., BA, PhD, School of Social Sciences, Deakin University, Victoria 3217, Australia.
Ruddock, Miss A. A., PhD, FSA, Wren Cottage, Heatherwood, Midhurst, W. Sussex GU29 9LH.
Rudé, Professor G. F. E., MA, PhD, 24 Cadborough Cliff, Rye, E. Sussex TN31 7EB.
Rule, Professor John C., MA, PhD, Dept of History, Ohio State University, 230 West 17th Avenue, Colombus, Ohio 43210-1367, U.S.A.
Rule, J. G., MA, PhD, Dept of History, The University, Southampton SO9 5NH.
Rumble, A. R., BA, PhD, Dip Arch Admin., Dept of Palaeography, University of Manchester, Oxford Road, Manchester M13 9PL.
*RUNCIMAN, The Hon. Sir Steven, CH, MA, DPhil, LLD, LittD, DLitt, LitD, DD, DHL, FBA, FSA, Elshieshields, Lockerbie, Dumfriesshire.
Runyan, Professor Timothy J., Dept of History, Cleveland State University, Cleveland, Ohio 44115, U.S.A.
Rupke, N. A., MA, PhD, History of Ideas Unit, Research School of Social Sciences, Australian National University, GPO Box 4, Canberra, ACT 2601, Australia.
Russell, Professor C. S. R., MA, Dept of History, King's College London, Strand, London WC2R 2LS.
Russell, Mrs J. G., MA, DPhil, St Hugh's College, Oxford OX2 6LE.
Russell, Professor P. E. L. R., MA, FBA, 23 Belsyre Court, Woodstock Road, Oxford OX2 6HU.
Ryan, A. N., MA, School of History, University of Liverpool, P.O. Box 147, Liverpool L69 3BX.
Ryan, Professor S., PhD, Dept of History, Memorial University, St John's Newfoundland, Canada A1C 5S7.
Rycraft, P., BA, Dept of History, The University, Heslington, York YO1 5DD.
Ryder, A. F. C., MA, DPhil, Dept of History, University of Bristol, 13–15 Woodland Road, Queen's Road, Bristol BS8 1TB.

Sachse, Professor W. L., PhD, 4066 Whitney Avenue, Mount Carmel. Connecticut 06518 U.S.A.
Sainty, Sir John, KCB, MA, 22 Kelso Place, London W8 5QG.
*Salmon, Professor E. T., MA, PhD, 36 Auchmar Road, Hamilton, Ontario, Canada LPC 1C5.
Salmon, Professor J. H. M., MA, MLitt, DLit, Bryn Mawr College, Bryn Mawr, Pa. 19101, U.S.A.

*Saltman, Professor A., MA., PhD, Bar Ilan University, Ramat Gan, Israel.
Salvadori, Max W., Dr Sc, LittD, 36 Ward Avenue, Northampton, Mass. 01060, U.S.A.
Samuel, E. R., BA, MPhil, Flat 4, Garden Court, 63 Holden Road, Woodside Park, London N12 7DG.
Sanderson, Professor G. N., MA, PhD, 2 Alder Close, Englefield Green, Surrey TW20 0LU.
Sar Desai, Professor Damodar R., MA, PhD, Dept of History, University of California, Los Angeles, Calif. 90024, U.S.A.
Saul, N. E., MA, DPhil, Dept of History, Royal Holloway and Bedford New College, Egham Hill, Egham, Surrey TW20 0EX.
Saunders, A. D., MA, FSA, 12 Ashburnham Grove, Greenwich, London SE10 8UH.
Saunders, D. B., MA, DPhil, 19 Albemarle Avenue, Newcastle upon Tyne NE2 3NQ.
Saville, Professor J., BSc(Econ), Dept of Economic and Social History, The University, Hull HU6 7RX.
Sawyer, Professor P. H., MA, Viktoriagatan 18, 441 33 Alingsas, Sweden.
Sayers, Miss J. E., MA, BLitt, PhD, FSA, University College London, Gower Street, London WC1E 6BT.
Scammell, G. V., MA, Pembroke College, Cambridge CB2 1RF.
Scammell, Mrs Jean, MA, Clare Hall, Cambridge.
Scarisbrick, Professor J. J., MA, PhD, 35 Kenilworth Road, Leamington Spa, Warwickshire.
Schofield, A. N. E. D., PhD, 57 West Way, Rickmansworth, Herts. WD3 2EH.
Schofield, R. S., MA, PhD, 27 Trumpington Street, Cambridge CB2 1QA.
Schreiber, Professor Roy E., PhD, Dept of History, Indiana University, P.O.B. 7111, South Bend, Indiana 46634, U.S.A.
Schreuder, Professor D. M., BA, DPhil, Dept of History, The University of Sydney, N.S.W. 2006, Australia.
Schroder, Professor H.-C., DPhil, Technische Hochschule Darmstadt, Institut fur Geschichte, Schloss, 6100 Darmstadt, West Germany.
Schurman, Professor D. McK., MA, MA, PhD, 191 King Street East, Kingston, Ontario, Canada K7L 3A3.
Schweizer, Karl W., MA, PhD, Dept of Humanities, New Jersey Institute of Technology, Newark, NJ 07102, U.S.A.
Schwoerer, Professor Lois G., PhD, 7213 Rollingwood Drive, Chevy Chase, Maryland 20015, U.S.A.
Scott, Dom Geoffrey, MA, PhD, Dip Theol, Douai Abbey, Upper Woolhampton, Reading RG7 5TH.
Scott, H. M., MA, PhD, Dept of Modern History, The University, St Salvator's College, St Andrews, Fife.
Scott, Tom, MA, PhD, School of History, The University, P.O. Box 147, Liverpool L69 3BX.
Scouloudi, Miss I., MSc(Econ), FSA, 82, 3 Whitehall Court, London SW1A 2EL.
Scribner, R. W., MA, PhD, Clare College, Cambridge CB2 1TL.
Seaborne, M. V. J., MA, Penylan, Cilcain Road, Pantymwyn, Mold, Clwyd CH7 5NJ.
Searle, A., BA, MPhil, Dept of Manuscripts, British Library, London WC1B 3DG.
Searle, Professor Eleanor, AB, PhD, 431 S. Parkwood Avenue, Pasadena, Calif. 91107, U.S.A.

Searle, G. R., MA, PhD, School of English and American Studies, University of East Anglia, University Plain, Norwich NR4 7TJ.
Seaver, Professor Paul S., MA, PhD, Dept of History, Stanford University, Stanford, Calif. 94305, U.S.A.
Seddon, P. R., BA, PhD, Dept of History, The University, Nottingham NG7 2RD.
Sell, Rev. Professor A. P. F., BA, BD, MA, PhD, Dept of Religious Studies, Faculty of Humanities, 2500 University Drive NW, Calgary, Alberta, Canada T2N 1N4.
Sellar, W. D. H., BA, LLB, 6 Eildon Street, Edinburgh EH3 5JU.
Semmell, Professor Bernard, PhD, Dept of History, State University of New York at Stony Brook, NY 11790, U.S.A.
Serjeant, W. R., BA, 51 Derwent Road, Ipswich, Suffolk IP3 0QR.
Seton-Watson, C. I. W., MC, MA, Oriel College, Oxford OX1 4EW.
Shannon, Professor R. T., MA, PhD, Dept of History, University College of Swansea, Swansea SA2 8PP.
Sharpe, J. A., MA, DPhil, Dept of History, The University, Heslington, York YO1 5DD.
Sharpe, K. M., MA, DPhil, Dept of History, University of Southampton, Highfield, Southampton SO9 5NH.
Sharpe, R., MA, PhD, 35 Norreys Avenue, Oxford OX1 4ST.
Shaw, I. P., MA, 3 Oaks Lane, Shirley, Croydon, Surrey CR0 5HP.
Shead, N. F., MA, BLitt, 8 Whittliemuir Avenue, Muirend, Glasgow G44 3HU.
Sheils, W. J., PhD, Goodricke Lodge, Heslington Lane, York YO1 5DD.
Sheldrake, J. S., MA, MPhil, 95 Blenheim Crescent, Leigh-on-Sea, Essex SS9 3DX.
Shennan, Professor J. H., PhD, Dept of History, University of Lancaster, Furness College, Bailrigg, Lancaster LA1 4YG.
Sheppard, F. H. W., MA, PhD, FSA, 10 Albion Place, West Street, Henley-on-Thames, Oxon RG9 2DT.
Sherborne, J. W., MA, 26 Hanbury Road, Bristol BS8 2EP.
Sheridan, Professor R. B., BS, MS, PhD, Dept of Economics, University of Kansas, Lawrence, Kansas 66045, U.S.A.
Sherwood, R. E., 22 Schole Road, Willingham, Cambridge CB4 5JD.
Short, K. R. MacD., BA, MA, BD, EdD, DPhil, School of Communication, 636 AH, University of Houston, 4800 Calhoun Road, Houston, Texas 77004, U.S.A.
Shukman, H., BA, DPhil, MA, St Antony's College, Oxford OX2 6JF.
Simpson, D. H., MA, 19 Waldegrave Gardens, Strawberry Hill, Twickenham, Middlesex.
Simpson, G. G., MA, PhD, FSA, Taylor Building, King's College, Old Aberdeen AB9 2UB.
Simpson, M. A., MA, MLitt, Dept of History, University College of Swansea, Singleton Park, Swansea SA2 8PP.
Sinar, Miss J. C., MA, 60 Wellington Street, Matlock, Derbyshire DE4 3GS.
Siney, Professor Marion C., MA, PhD, 1890 East 107th Street, Apt 534, Cleveland, Ohio 44106, U.S.A.
Singh, Professor B. S., PhD, 3732 Forsythe Way, Tallahassee, Florida 32308, U.S.A.
Sked, A., MA, DPhil, Flat 3, Aberdeen Court, 68 Aberdeen Park, London N5 2BH.
Skidelsky, Professor R. J. A., BA, PhD, Tilton House, Selmeston, Firle, Sussex.

Skinner, Professor Q. R. D., MA, FBA, Christ's College, Cambridge CB2 3BU.
Slack, P. A., MA, DPhil, Exeter College, Oxford OX1 3DP.
Slade, C. F., PhD, FSA, 28 Holmes Road, Reading, Berks.
Slater, A. W., MSc(Econ), 146 Castelnau, London SW13 9ET.
Slatter, Miss M. D., MA, 2 Tuscan Close, Tilehurst, Reading, Berks. RG3 6DF.
Slaven, Professor A, MA, BLitt, Dept of Economic History, University of Glasgow, Adam Smith Building, Glasgow G12 8RT.
Slavin, Professor A. J., PhD, College of Arts & Letters, University of Louisville, Louisville, Kentucky 40268, U.S.A.
Slee, P. R. H., PhD, BA, 10 Burghley Lane, Stamford, Lincolnshire.
Smith, A. G. R., MA, PhD, 5 Cargil Avenue, Kilmacolm, Renfrewshire PA13 4LS.
Smith, A. Hassell, BA, PhD, School of English and American Studies, University of East Anglia, Norwich NR4 7TJ.
Smith, B. S., MA, FSA, Historical Manuscripts Commission, Quality House, Quality Court, Chancery Lane, London WC2A 1HP.
Smith, D. M., MA, PhD, FSA, Borthwick Institute of Historical Research, St Anthony's Hall, York YO1 2PW.
Smith, E. A., MA, Dept of History, Faculty of Letters, The University, Whiteknights, Reading RG6 2AH.
Smith, F. B., MA, PhD, Research School of Social Sciences, Institute of Advanced Studies, Australian National University, G.P.O. Box 4, Canberra, A.C.T. 2601, Australia.
Smith, Professor Goldwin A., MA, PhD, DLitt, Wayne State University, Detroit, Michigan 48202, U.S.A.
Smith, I. R., MA, MA, DPhil, Dept of History, University of Warwick, Coventry CV4 7AL.
Smith, J. Beverley, MA, University College, Aberystwyth SY23 2AX.
Smith, Joseph, BA, PhD, Dept of History, The University, Exeter EX4 4QH.
Smith, Julia M. H., MA, DPhil, Dept of History, Trinity College, Hartford, Conn. 06106, U.S.A.
Smith, Professor L. Baldwin, PhD, Northwestern University, Evanston, Ill. 60201, U.S.A.
Smith, Professor P., MA, DPhil, Dept of History, The University, Southampton SO9 5NH.
Smith, Professor R. E. F., MA, 9 Serpentine Road, Selly Park, Birmingham 29.
Smith, Richard M., BA, PhD, All Souls College, Oxford OX1 4AL.
Smith, R. J., BSc, PhD, Dept of Surveying, Trent Polytechnic Nottingham, Burton Street, Nottingham NG1 4BU.
Smith, R. S., MA, BA, 7 Capel Lodge, 244 Kew Road, Kew, TW9 3JU.
Smith, S., BA, PhD, Les Haies, 40 Oatlands Road, Shinfield, Reading, Berks RG2 9DN.
Smith, Professor T. A., BSc(Econ), Queen Mary and Westfield College, Mile End Road, London E1 4NS.
Smith, W. H. C., BA, PhD, Erin Lodge, Symons Hill, Falmouth TR11 2SX.
Smith, W. J., MA, 5 Gravel Hill, Emmer Green, Reading, Berks. RG4 8QN.
Smyth, A. P., BA, MA, DPhil, FSA, Keynes College, The University, Canterbury CT2 7NP.
Smyth, Associate Professor D. P., BA, PhD, Dept of History, University of Toronto, Toronto, Canada M5S 1A1.

Snell, L. S., MA, FSA, FRSA, 27 Weoley Hill, Selly Oak, Birmingham B29 4AA.

Snooks, Professor G. D., MEC, PhD, Institute of Advanced Studies, The Australian National University, GPO Box 4, Cambera, Act 2601, Australia.

Snow, Professor V. F., MA, PhD, Dept of History, Syracuse University, 311 Maxwell Hall, Syracuse, New York 13244, U.S.A.

Snyder, Professor H. L., MA, PhD, 5577 Majestic Court, Riverside, Calif. 92506, U.S.A.

Soden, G. I., MA, DD, Buck Brigg, Hanworth, Norwich, Norfolk.

Soffer, Professor Reba N., PhD, 665 Bienveneda Avenue, Pacific Palisades, California 90272, U.S.A.

Soloway, R. A., PhD, Dept of History, Hamilton Hall, The University of North Carolina, Chapel Hill, NC 27515, U.S.A.

Somers, Rev. H. J., JCB, MA, PhD, St Francis Xavier University, Antigonish, Nova Scotia, Canada.

Somerville, Sir Robert, KCVO, MA, FSA, 3 Hunt's Close, Morden Road, London SE3 0AH.

Sommerville, Johann P., MA, PhD, Dept of History, University of Wisconsin-Madison. 3211 Humanities Building, 455 North Park Street, Madison, Wisconsin 53706, U.S.A.

SOUTHERN, Sir Richard (W.), MA, DLitt, LittD, DLitt, FBA, 40 St John Street, Oxford OX1 2LH.

Southgate, D. G., BA, DPhil, The Old Harriers, Bridford, nr Exeter, Devon EX6 7HS.

Spalding, Miss R., MA, 34 Reynards Road, Welwyn, Herts. AL6 9TP

Speck, Professor W. A., MA, DPhil, School of History, The University, Leeds LS2 9JT.

Spencer, B. W., BA, FSA, 6 Carpenters Wood Drive, Chorleywood, Herts. WD3 5RJ.

Spiers, E. M., MA, PhD, 170 Alwoodley Lane, Leeds, West Yorkshire LS17 7PF.

Spinks, Rev. B. D., BA, MTh, BD, DD, Churchill College, Cambridge CB3 0DS.

Spinner, Professor T. J. Jr, PhD, Dept of History, University of Vermont, 314 Wheeler House, Burlington, Vermont 05405, U.S.A.

Spooner, Professor F. C., MA, PhD, LittD, FSA, 31 Chatsworth Avenue, Bromley, Kent BR1 5DP.

Spring, Professor D., PhD, Dept of History, Johns Hopkins University, Baltimore, Md. 21218, U.S.A.

Spufford, Mrs H. M., MA, PhD, LittD, Newnham College, Cambridge CB3 9DF.

Spufford, P., MA, PhD, Queens' College, Cambridge CB3 9ET.

Squibb, G. D., QC, FSA, The Old House, Cerne Abbas, Dorset DT2 7JQ.

Stacey, Assistant Professor R. C., BA, MA, PhD, Dept of History, Yale University, New Haven, Connecticut 06520, U.S.A.

Stachura, P. D., MA, PhD, Dept of History, The University, Stirling FK9 4LA.

Stacpoole, Dom Alberic J., OSB, MC, MA, DPhil, Ampleforth Abbey, York YO6 4EN.

Stafford, Pauline A., BA, DPhil, Athill Lodge, St Helen's Lane, Adel, Leeds LS16 8BS.

Stanley, The Hon. G. F. G., MA, BLitt, DPhil, PO Box 790, Sackville, N.B., Canada E0A 3C0.

Stannage, Associate Professor C. T., PhD, Dept of History, University of Western Australia, Nedlands, Australia 6009.
Stansky, Professor Peter, PhD, Dept of History, Stanford University, Stanford, Calif. 94305-2024, U.S.A.
Stapleton, B., BSc, School of Economics, Portsmouth Polytechnic, Locksway Road, Milton, Southsea PO4 8JF.
Starkey, D. R., MA, PhD, 49 Hamilton Park West, London N5 1AE.
Steele, E. D., MA, PhD, School of History, The University, Leeds LS2 9JT.
Steinberg, J., MA, PhD, Trinity Hall, Cambridge CB2 1TJ.
Steiner, Mrs Zara S., MA, PhD, New Hall, Cambridge CB3 0DF.
Stephens, J. N., MA, DPhil, Dept of History, University of Edinburgh, William Robertson Building, George Square, Edinburgh EH8 9JY.
Stephens, W. B., MA, PhD, FSA, 37 Batcliffe Drive, Leeds 6.
Stephenson, Mrs Jill, MA, PhD, Dept of History, University of Edinburgh, William Robertson Building, George Square, Edinburgh EH8 9JY.
Steven, Miss M. J. E., PhD, 3 Bonwick Place, Garran, A.C.T. 2605, Australia.
Stevenson, David, MA, PhD, Dept of International History, London School of Economics, Houghton Street, Aldwych, London WC2A 2AE.
Stevenson, D., BA, PhD, Dept of History, Taylor Building, King's College, Old Aberdeen AB1 0EE.
Stevenson, Miss J. H., BA, c/o Institute of Historical Research, Senate House, Malet Street, London, WC1E 7HU.
Stevenson, J., MA, DPhil, Dept of History, The University, Sheffield S10 2TN.
Stewart, A. T. Q., MA, PhD, Dept of Modern History, The Queen's University, Belfast BT7 1NN.
Stitt, F. B., BA, BLitt, DLitt, 2 Ashtree Close, Little Haywood, Stafford ST18 0NL.
Stockwell, A. J., MA, PhD, Dept of History, Royal Holloway and Bedford New College, Egham Hill, Egham, Surrey TW20 0EX.
Stone, E., MA, DPhil, FSA, Keble College, Oxford OX1 3PG.
Stone, Professor L., MA, Princeton University, Princeton, NJ 08540, U.S.A.
Storey, Professor R. L., MA, PhD, 19 Elm Avenue, Beeston, Nottingham NG9 1BU.
Storry, J. G., The Eyot House, Sonning Eye, Reading RG4 0TN.
Story, Professor G. M., CM, BA, DPhil, FRSC, FSA, 335 Southside Road, St John's Newfoundland, Canada.
Stourzh, Professor G., DPhil, Brechergasse 14, A-1190 Vienna, Austria.
Stow, G. B., PhD, Dept of History, La Salle University, Philadelphia, Pennsylvania 19141, U.S.A.
*Stoye, J. W., MA, DPhil, Magdalen College, Oxford OX1 4AU.
Strachan, H. F. A., MA, PhD, Corpus Christi College, Cambridge CB2 1RH.
Street, J., MA, PhD, Badgers' Wood, Cleveley, Forton, Garstang, Preston PR3 1BY.
Stringer, K. J., BA, MA, PhD, Dept of History, Furness College, The University, Lancaster LA1 4YG.
Strong, Mrs F., MA, Traigh Gate, Arisaig, Inverness-shire PH39 4N1.
Stuart, C. H., MA, 9 Orchard Close, Combe, Oxford OX7 2NU.
Studd, J. R., PhD, Dept of History, The University, Keele, Staffs. ST5 5BG.
Sturdy, D. J., BA, PhD, Dept of History, New University of Ulster, Coleraine, N. Ireland BT52 1SA.
Supple, Professor B. E., BSc(Econ), PhD, MA, St Catharine's College, Cambridge CB2 1RL.

Sutcliffe, Professor A. R., MA, DU, Dept of Economic and Social History, The University, 21 Slayleigh Avenue, Sheffield S10 3RA.
Sutherland, Professor D. M. G., PhD, Dept of History, University of Maryland, College Park, MD 20742–7315, U.S.A.
Sutherland, Gillian, MA, DPhil, MA, PhD, Newnham College, Cambridge CB3 9DF.
Swanson, R. N., MA, PhD, School of History, The University, P.O. Box 363, Birmingham B15 2TT.
Swanton, Professor M. J., BA, PhD, FSA, Queen's Building, The University, The Queen's Drive, Exeter EX4 4QH.
Swart, Professor K. W., PhD, LittD, University College London, Gower Street, London WC1 6BT.
Sweet, D. W., MA, PhD, Dept of History, The University, 43 North Bailey, Durham DH1 3NP.
Sweetman, J., MA, PhD, 98 Kings Ride, Camberley, Surrey GU15 4LN.
Swenarton, M. C., BA, PhD, 10d Barnsbury Terrace, London N1 1JH.
Swift, R. E., PhD, MA, BA, 23 Deansway, Tarvin, nr Chester, Cheshire CH3 8LX.
Swinfen, D. B., MA, DPhil, 14 Cedar Road, Broughty Ferry, Dundee.
Sydenham, Professor Emeritus M. J., PhD, Dept of History, Carleton University, Ottawa, Canada K1S 5B6.
Sykes, A., BA, Dept of Modern History, University of St Andrews, St. Andrews, Fife KY16 9AL.
Syrett, Professor D., PhD, 329 Sylvan Avenue, Leonia, NJ 07605, U.S.A.
Szechi, D., BA, DPhil, History Dept, 7030 Haley Center, Auburn University, Alabama 36849-5207, U.S.A.

Taft, Barbara, PhD, 3101, 35th Street, Washington, D.C. 20016, U.S.A.
Talbot, C. H., PhD, BD, FSA, 47 Hazlewell Road, London SW15.
Tamse, Coenraad Arnold, DLitt, De Krom, 12 Potgieterlaan, 9752 Ex Haren (Groningen), The Netherlands.
Tanner, J. I., CBE, MA, PhD, DLitt, Flat One, 57 Drayton Gardens, London SW10 9RU.
Tanner, Rev. N. P., BTh, MA, DPhil, Campion Hall, Oxford OX1 1QS.
Tarling, Professor P. N., MA, PhD, LittD, University of Auckland, Private Bag, Auckland, New Zealand.
Tarn, Professor J. N., B.Arch, PhD, FRIBA, Dept of Architecture, The University, Leverhulme Building, Abercromby Square, P.O. Box 147, Liverpool L69 3BX.
Taylor, Arnold J., CBE, MA, DLitt, FBA, FSA, Rose Cottage, Lincoln's Hill, Chiddingfold, Surrey GU8 4UN.
Taylor, Professor Arthur J., MA, School of History, The University, Leeds LS2 9JT.
Taylor, Rev. Brian, MA, FSA, The Rectory, The Flower Walk, Guildford GU2 5EP.
Taylor, J., MA, School of History, The University, Leeds LS2 9JT.
Taylor, J. W. R., 36 Alexandra Drive, Surbiton, Surrey KT5 9AF.
Taylor, P. M., BA, PhD, School of History, The University, Leeds LS2 9JT.
Taylor, R. T., MA, PhD, Dept of Political Theory and Government, University College of Swansea, Swansea SA2 8PP.
Taylor, W., MA, PhD, FSAScot, 25 Bingham Terrace, Dundee.
Teichova, Professor Alice, BA, PhD, University of East Anglia, University Plain, Norwich NR4 7TJ.

Temperley, H., BA, MA, PhD, School of English and American Studies, University of East Anglia, University Plain, Norwich NR4 7TJ.
Temple, Nora C., BA, PhD, School of History and Archaeology, University of Wales College of Cardiff, P.O. Box 909, Cardiff CF1 1XU.
Terraine, J. A., 74 Kensington Park Road, London W11 2PL.
Thacker, A. T., MA, DPhil, Flat 1, 6 Liverpool Road, Chester, Cheshire.
Thackray, Professor Arnold W., PhD, E. F. Smith Hall D-6, University of Pennsylvania, Philadelphia 19104, PA, U.S.A.
Thane, Patricia M., BA, PhD, 5 Twisden Road, London NW5 1DL.
Thirsk, Mrs I. Joan, PhD, FBA, 1 Hadlow Castle, Hadlow, Tonbridge, Kent TN11 0EG.
Thistlethwaite, Professor F., CBE, DCL, LHD, 15 Park Parade, Cambridge CB5 8AL.
Thomas, Professor A. C., MA, DipArch, FSA, HonMRIA, Lambessow, St Clement, Truro, Cornwall.
Thomas, D. O., MA, PhD, Orlandon, 31 North Parade, Aberystwyth, Dyfed SY23 2JN.
Thomas, E. E., BA, The Shippen, Pilgrim's Way, Westhumble, Dorking, Surrey RH5 6AW.
Thomas of Swynnerton, Lord, MA, 29 Ladbroke Grove, London W11 3BB.
Thomas, J. H., BA, PhD, School of Social and Historical Studies, Portsmouth Polytechnic, Bellevue Terrace, Southsea, Portsmouth PO5 3AT.
Thomas, Sir Keith, MA, DLitt, FBA, Corpus Christi College, Oxford OX1 4JF.
Thomas, Professor P. D. G., MA, PhD, Dept of History, Hugh Owen Building, University College of Wales, Aberystwyth SY23 2AU.
Thomas, W. E. S., MA, Christ Church, Oxford OX1 1DP.
Thomis, Professor M. I., MA, PhD, University of Queensland, St Lucia, Brisbane 4067, Australia.
Thompson, A. F., MA, Wadham College, Oxford OX1 3PN.
Thompson, C. L. F., BA, Colne View, 69 Chaney Road, Wivenhoe, Essex.
Thompson, Mrs D. K. G., MA, Wick Episcopi, Upper Wick, Worcester WR2 5SY.
Thompson, D. M., MA, PhD, Fitzwilliam College, Cambridge CB3 0DG.
Thompson, E. P., MA, Wick Episcopi, Upper Wick, Worcester WR2 5SY.
THOMPSON, Professor F. M. L., MA, DPhil, FBA, (*President*) Institute of Historical Research, Senate House, London WC1E 7HU.
Thompson, I. A. A., MA, PhD, PhD, Dept of History, The University, Keele, Staffs. ST5 5BG.
Thompson, J. A., MA, PhD, St Catharine's College, Cambridge CB2 1RL.
Thompson, Rev. J., BA, BD, MTh, PhD, 27 Ravenhill Park, Belfast BT6 0DE.
Thompson, R. F., MA, School of English and American Studies, University of East Anglia, Norwich NR4 7TJ.
Thomson, J. A. F., MA, DPhil, The University, Glasgow G12 8QQ.
Thomson, R. M., MA, PhD, Dept of History, University of Tasmania, Box 252C, GPO, Hobart, Tasmania 7001, Australia.
Thorne, Professor C. G., MA, DLitt, FBA, School of European Studies, University of Sussex, Falmer, Brighton BN1 9QN.
Thornton, Professor A. P., MA, DPhil, University College, University of Toronto, Toronto, Canada, M5S 1A1.
Throup, D. W., MA, PhD, MSc, 232 Church Plantations, Keele, Staffordshire ST5 5AX.

*Thrupp, Professor S. L., MA, PhD, 57 Balsam Lane, Princeton, New Jersey 08540, U.S.A.
Thurlow, The Very Rev. A. G. G., MA, FSA, 2 East Pallant, Chichester, West Sussex PO19 1TR.
Tite, C. G. C., BA, MA, PhD, 12 Montagu Square, London W1H 1RB.
Todd, Associate Professor Margo, AB, MA, PhD, Dept of History, Vanderbilt University, Nashville, TN 37235, U.S.A.
Tomizawa, Professor Reigan, MA, DLitt, Dept of History, Kansai University, 3–10–12 Hiyoshidai, Taksukishi, Osaka 569, Japan.
Tomlinson, H. C., BA, DPhil, The Cathedral School, Old College, 29 Castle Street, Hereford HR1 2NN.
Tonkin, J. M., BA, BD, PhD, Dept of History, University of Western Australia, Nedlands, Western Australia 6009.
Townshend, C. J. N., MA, DPhil, Dept of Modern History, The University, Keele, Staffs. ST5 5BG.
Trainor, L., BA, PhD, History Dept, University of Canterbury, Private Bag, Christchurch, New Zealand.
Trainor, R. H., DPhil, Dept of Economic History, University of Glasgow, Adam Smith Building, Glasgow, G12 8RT.
Trebilcock, R. C., MA, Pembroke College, Cambridge CB2 1RF.
Tsitsonis, S. E., PhD, 31 Samara Street, Paleo Psyhico (15452), Athens, Greece.
Tuck, J. A., MA, PhD, Dept of History, The University, 13–15 Woodland Road, Bristol BS8 1TB.
Turnbull, Professor Constance M., BA, PhD, 36 Stoneleigh Avenue, Coventry, CV5 6BZ.
Turner, Mrs Barbara D. M. C., BA, 27 St Swithuns Street, Winchester, Hampshire.
Turner, G. L'E., FSA, DSc, The Old Barn, Mill Street, Islip, Oxford OX5 2SY.
Turner, J. A., MA, DPhil, 31 Devereux Road, London SW11 6JR.
Turner, Professor Ralph V., MA, PhD, History Department, Florida State University, Tallahassee, Florida 32306-2029, U.S.A.
Tyacke, N. R. N., MA, DPhil, 1a Spencer Rise, London NW5.
Tyerman, C. J., MA, DPhil, Exeter College, Oxford OX1 3DP.

Ugawa, Professor K., BA, MA, PhD, Minami-Ogikubo, 1-chome 25-15, Suginami-Ku, Tokyo 167, Japan.
Underdown, Professor David, MA, BLitt, DLitt, Dept of History, Yale University, P.O. Box 1504A, Yale Station, New Haven, Conn. 06520, U.S.A.
Upton, A. F., MA, 5 West Acres, St Andrews, Fife KY16 9UD.

Vaisey, D. G., MA, FSA, 12 Hernes Road, Oxford.
Vale, M. G. A., MA, DPhil, St John's College, Oxford OX1 3JP.
van Caenegem, Professor R. C., LLD, PhD, Veurestraat 47, B9821 Gent-Afsnee, Belgium.
Van Houts, Elisabeth, DLitt, The Old Vicarage, Thompson's Lane, Cambridge CB5 8AQ.
Van Roon, Professor Ger, Dept of Contemporary History, Vrije Universiteit, Amsterdam, Koningslaan 31–33, The Netherlands.
Vann, Professor Richard T., PhD, Dept of History, Wesleyan University, Middletown, Conn. 06457, U.S.A.
*Varley, Mrs J., MA, FSA, 164 Nettleham Road, Lincoln.

Vaughan, Sir (G) Edgar, KBE, MA, 9 The Glade, Sandy Lane, Cheam, Sutton, Surrey SM2 7NZ.
Veale, Elspeth M., BA, PhD, 31 St Mary's Road, Wimbledon, London SW19 7BP.
Véliz, Professor C., BSc, PhD, Dept. of Sociology, La Trobe University, Melbourne, Victoria 3083, Australia.
Vessey, D. W. T. C., MA, PhD, Dept of Classics, King's College London, Strand, London WC2R 2LS.
Vile, Professor M. J. C., Boston University, 43 Harrington Gardens, Kensington, London SW7 4JU.
Vincent, D. M., BA, PhD, Dept of History, The University, Keele, Staffs ST5 5BG.
Vincent, Professor J. R., MA, PhD, Dept of History, The University, 13 Woodland Road, Bristol BS8 1TB.
Virgoe, R., BA, PhD, School of English and American Studies, University of East Anglia, Norwich NR4 7TJ.

Waddell, Professor D. A. G., MA, DPhil, Dept of History, University of Stirling, Stirling FK9 4LA.
*Wagner, Sir Anthony (R.), KCVO, MA, DLitt, FSA, College of Arms, Queen Victoria Street, London EC4.
Waites, B. F., MA, FRGS, 6 Chater Road, Oakham, Leics. LE15 6RY.
Walford, A. J., MA, PhD, FLA, 45 Parkside Drive, Watford, Herts WD1 3AU.
Walker, Rev. Chancellor D. G., DPhil, FSA, University College of Swansea, Swansea SA2 8PP.
Walker, G., BA, PhD, Dept of English, University of Queensland, St Lucia, Brisbane, Queensland 4067, Australia.
Walker, Professor Sue S., MA, PhD, History Department, Northeastern Illinois University, Chicago, Illinois 60625, U.S.A.
Walkowitz, Professor Judith R., PhD, 133 W. 17th Street, Apt 5D, New York, NY 10011, U.S.A.
Wallace, Professor W. V., MA, Institute of Soviet and East European Studies, University of Glasgow, 9–11 Southpark Terrace, Glasgow G12 8LQ.
Waller, P. J., BA, MA, Merton College, Oxford OX1 4JD.
Wallis, Miss H. M., OBE, MA, DPhil, FSA, 96 Lord's View, St John's Wood Road, London NW8 7HG.
Wallis, P. J., MA, 43 Briarfield Road, Newcastle upon Tyne NE3 3UH.
Walne, P., MA, FSA, County Record Office, County Hall, Hertford.
Walsh, Margaret, MA, MA, PhD, Dept of Economic and Social History, University of Birmingham, PO Box 363, Birmingham B15 2TT.
Walton, J. K., BA, PhD, Dept of History, Furness College, The University, Lancaster LA1 4YG.
Walvin, J., BA, MA, DPhil, Dept of History, The University, Heslington, York YO1 5DD.
Wang, Professor Rongtang, BA, Dept of History, Liaoning University, Shenyang, People's Republic of China.
Wangermann, Professor E., MA, DPhil, Institut f. Geschichte, Universität Salzburg, A-5020 Salzburg, Mirabellplatz 1, Germany.
Wanklyn, M. D., BA, MA, PhD, Dept of Arts, The Polytechnic, Wulfruna Street, Wolverhampton, West Midlands.
Ward, Jennifer, C., MA, PhD, 51 Hartswood Road, Brentwood, Essex CM14 5AG.

Ward, Professor W. R., DPhil, 21 Grenehurst Way, The Village, Petersfield, Hampshire GU31 4AZ.

Warner, Professor G., MA, 11 Troutbeck, Peartree Bridge, Milton Keynes, MK6 3ED.

Warnicke, Professor Retha M., BA, MA, PhD, History Department, Arizona State University, Tempe, Arizona 85287–2501, U.S.A.

Warren, A. J., MA, DPhil, Vanbrugh Provost's House, 1 Bleachfield, Heslington, York YO1 5DD.

Warren, Professor W. L., MA, DPhil, FRSL, Dept of Modern History, The Queen's University, Belfast, N. Ireland BT7 1NN.

Washbrook, D. A., BA, MA, PhD, 29 Gretna Road, Green Lane, Coventry, West Midlands.

Wasserstein, Professor B. M. J., MA, DPhil, Dept of History, Brandeis University, Waltham, Mass. 02254, U.S.A.

Wasserstein, D. J., MA, DPhil, Dept of Semitic Languages, University College, Belfield, Dublin 4, Ireland.

*Waters, Lt-Commander D. W., RN, FSA, Jolyons, Bury, nr Pulborough, W. Sussex.

Wathey, A. B., MA, DPhil, Dept of Music, Royal Holloway and Bedford New College, Egham Hill, Egham, Surrey TW20 0EX.

Watkin, The Rt Rev. Abbot Aelred, OSB, MA, FSA, St Benet's, Beccles, Suffolk NR34 9NR.

WATSON, Professor A. G., MA, DLit, BLitt, FSA (*Hon Librarian*), University College London, Gower Street, London WC1E 6BT.

Watson, D. R., MA, BPhil, Dept of Modern History, The University, Dundee DD1 4HN.

Watt, Professor D. C., MA, London School of Economic, Houghton Street, London WC2A 2AE.

Watt, Professor D. E. R., MA, DPhil, St John's House, University of St Andrews, c/o 71 South Street, St Andrews KY16 9QW.

Watt, Professor J. A., BA, PhD, Dept of History, The University, Newcastle upon Tyne NE1 7RU.

Watts, D. G., MA, BLitt, 34 Greenbank Crescent, Bassett, Southampton SO1 7FQ.

Watts, M. R., BA, DPhil, Dept of History, The University, University Park, Nottingham NG7 2RD.

Webb, Professor Colin de B., BA, MA, University of Natal, PO Box 375, Pietermaritzburg 3200, S. Africa.

Webb, J. G., MA, 11 Blount Road, Pembroke Park, Old Portsmouth, Hampshire PO1 2TD.

Webb, Professor R. K., PhD, 3309 Highland Place NW, Washington, D.C. 20008, U.S.A.

Webster (A.) Bruce, MA, FSA, 5 The Terrace, St Stephens, Canterbury.

Webster, C., MA, DSc, FBA, Corpus Christi College, Oxford OX1 4JF.

Wedgwood, Dame (C.) Veronica, OM, DBE, MA, LittD, DLitt, LLD, Whitegate, Alciston, nr Polegate, Sussex.

Weinstock, Miss M. B., MA, 26 Way View Crescent, Broadway, Weymouth, Dorset.

Wellenreuther, H., PhD, 33 Merkel Str., 34 Gottingen, Germany.

Wells, R. A. E., BA, DPhil, Dept of Humanities, Brighton Polytechnic, Falmer, Brighton, Sussex.

Wende, Professor P. P., DPhil, Historisches Seminar der Johann Wolfgang Goethe-Universtat, Senckenberganlage 31, Postfach 11 19 32, D–6000 Frankfurt am Main 11, West Germany.

Wendt, Professor Bernd Jurgen, DrPhil, Beim Andreasbrunnen 8, 2 Hamburg 20, West Germany.
Wernham, Professor R. B., MA, Marine Cottage, 63 Hill Head Road, Hill Head, Fareham, Hants.
West, Professor F. J., PhD, Pro Vice Chancellor's Office, Deakin University, Victoria 3217, Australia.
Weston, Professor Corinne C., PhD, 200 Central Park South, New York, NY 10019, U.S.A.
Whaley, Joachim, MA, PhD, Gonville and Caius College, Cambridge CB2 1TA.
Whatley, C. A., BA, PhD, Dept of Modern History, The University, Dundee DD1 4HN.
White, Rev. B. R., MA DPhil, 55 St Giles', Regent's Park College, Oxford OX1 2LB.
White, G. J., MA, PhD, Chester College, Cheyney Road, Chester CH1 4BJ.
Whiteman, Miss E. A. O., MA, DPhil, FSA, Lady Margaret Hall, Oxford OX2 6QA.
Whiting, J. R. S., MA, DLitt, 15 Lansdown Parade, Cheltenham, Glos.
Whiting, R. C., MA, DPhil, School of History, The University, Leeds LS2 9JT.
Whittam, J. R., MA, BPhil, PhD, Dept of History, University of Bristol, 13–15 Woodland Road, Bristol BS8 1TB.
Wickham, C. J., MA, DPhil, School of History, The University, P.O. Box 363, Birmingham B15 2TT.
Wiener, Professor J. H., BA, PhD, Dept of History, City College of New York, Convent Avenue at 138th Street, NY 10031, U.S.A.
Wiener, Professor M. J., PhD, Dept of History, Rice University, Houston, Texas 77251, U.S.A.
Wilkie, Rev. W., MA, PhD, Dept of History, Loras College, Dubuque, Iowa 52001, U.S.A.
Wilks, Professor M. J., MA, PhD, Dept of History, Birkbeck College, Malet Street, London WC1E 7HX.
*Willan, Professor T. S., MA, DPhil, 3 Raynham Avenue, Didsbury, Manchester M20 0BW.
Williams, D., MA, PhD, DPhil, University of Calgary, Calgary, Alberta, Canada T2N 1N4.
Williams, Daniel T., BA, PhD, Dept of History, The University, Leicester LE1 7RH.
Williams, Sir Edgar (T.), CB, CBE, DSO, MA, 94 Lonsdale Road, Oxford OX2 7ER.
Williams, (Elisabeth) Ann, BA, PhD, 77 Gordon Road, Wanstead, London E11 2RA.
Williams, Gareth W., MA, MSc(Econ), MA, Dept of History, Hugh Owen Building, University College of Wales, Aberystwyth SY23 3DY.
Williams, Professor Glanmor, MA, DLitt, 11 Grosvenor Road, Swansea SA2 0SP.
Williams, Professor Glyndwr, BA, PhD, Dept of History, Queen Mary College, Mile End Road, London E1 4NS.
Williams, Professor G. A., MA, PhD, 66 De Burgh Street, Cardiff CF1 8LD.
Williams, J. A., MA, BSc(Econ), 44 Pearson Park, Hull, HU5 2TG.
Williams, J. D., BA, MA, PhD, 56 Spurgate, Hutton Mount, Brentwood, Essex CM13 2JT.
Williams, Patrick L, BA, PhD, 30 Andover Road, Southsea, Hants. PO4 9QG.

Williams, P. H., MA, DPhil, New College, Oxford OX1 3BN.
Williams, T. I., MA, DPhil, 20 Blenheim Drive, Oxford OX2 8DG.
Williamson, P. A., PhD, Dept of History, The University, 43/46 North Bailey, Durham DH1 3EX.
Willmott, H. P. MA, 13 Barnway, Englefield Green, Egham, Surrey TW20 0QU.
WILSON, Professor C. H., CBE, MA, LittD, DLitt, DLitt, DLitt, FBA, 1211 East Point Tower, 235 New South Head Road, Edgecliff, Sydney, NSW 2027, Australia.
Wilson, Sir David M., MA, LittD, FilDr, DrPhil, FBA, FSA, The Director's Residence, The British Museum, London WC1B 3DG.
Wilson, H. S., BA, BLitt, Dept of History, The University, Heslington, York YO1 5DD.
Wilson, R. G., BA, PhD, University of East Anglia, School of Social Studies, University Plain, Norwich NR4 7TJ.
Wilson, Professor T. G., MA, DPhil, Dept of History, University of Adelaide, Adelaide, South Australia.
Winch, Professor D. N., PhD, BSc(Econ), FBA, University of Sussex, Brighton BN1 9QN.
Winks, Professor R. W. E., MA, PhD, 648 Berkeley College, Yale University, New Haven, Conn. 06520, U.S.A.
Winstanley, M. J., BA, MA, Dept of History, Furness College, The University, Bailrigg, Lancaster LA1 4YG.
Winter, J. M., BA, PhD, Pembroke College, Cambridge CB2 1RF.
Wiswall, Frank L., Jr., BA, JuD, PhD, Meadow Farm, Castine, Maine 04421 U.S.A.
Withrington, D. J., MA, MEd, Dept of History, University of Aberdeen, Taylor Building, King's College, Old Aberdeen AB9 2UB.
Wokler, R. L., BA, MSc, MA, DPhil, 51 Hartington Grove, Cambridge, CB1 4AU.
Wong, John Yue-Wo, BA, DPhil, Dept of History, University of Sydney, N.S.W., Australia 2006.
*Wood, Rev. A. Skevington, PhD, 17 Dalewood Road, Sheffield S8 0EB.
Wood, Diana, BA, PhD, 7 Binswood Avenue, Headington, Oxford OX3 8NY.
Wood, I. N., MA, DPhil, School of History, The University, Leeds LS2 9JT.
Wood, Mrs S. M., MA, BLitt, Green Gables, Eardisley, Herefordshire HR3 6PQ.
Woolf, Professor, S. J., MA, DPhil, Dept of History, University of Essex, Wivenhoe Park, Colchester CO4 3SQ.
Woolrych, Professor A. H., BLitt, MA, DLitt, FBA, Patchetts, Caton, Lancaster LA2 9QN.
Wootton, Professor D. R. J., Dept of Political History, University of Victoria, PO Box 1700, Victoria, B.C., Canada V8W 2Y2.
WORDEN, A. B., MA, DPhil (*Literary Director*), St Edmund Hall, Oxford OX1 4AR.
Wordie, James R., MA, PhD, St. Andrew's Hall, Redlands Road, Reading, Berks. RG1 5EY.
Wormald, B. H. G., MA, Peterhouse, Cambridge CB2 1RD.
Wormald, C. Patrick, MA, 60 Hill Top Road, Oxford OX4 1PE.
Wormald, Jennifer, MA, PhD, St Hilda's College, Oxford OX4 1DY.
Wortley, Rev. Professor J. T., MA, PhD, DD, History Dept, University of Manitoba, Winnipeg, Manitoba, Canada R3T 2N2.

Wright, A. D., MA, DPhil, School of History, The University, Leeds LS2 9JT.
Wright, C. J., MA, PhD, 8 Grove Road, East Molesey, Surrey KT8 9JS.
Wright, D. G., BA, PhD, Dip Ed. 9 Victoria Park, Shipley, West Yorkshire BD18 4RL.
Wright, Professor E., MA, Institute of United States Studies, 31 Tavistock Square, London WC1H 9EZ.
Wright, Rev. Professor J. Robert, DPhil, General Theological Seminary, 175 Ninth Avenue, New York, NY 10011, U.S.A.
Wright, Professor Maurice W., BA, DPhil, Dept of Government, Dover Street, Manchester M13 9PL.
Wrightson, K., MA, PhD, Jesus College, Cambridge CB5 8BL.
Wrigley, C. J., BA, PhD, Dept of History, The University, University Park, Nottingham NG7 2RD.
Wroughton, J. P., MA, 6 Ormonde House, Sion Hill, Bath BA1 2UN.

Yale, D. E. C., MA, LLB, FBA, Christ's College, Cambridge CB2 3BU.
Yates, W. N., MA, Kent Archives Office, County Hall, Maidstone, Kent ME14 1XH.
Yorke, Barbara A. E., BA, PhD, King Alfred's College of Higher Education, Sparkford Road, Winchester SO22 4NR.
Youings, Professor Joyce A., BA, PhD, 5 Silver Street, Thorberton, Exeter EX5 5LT.
Young, J. W., BA, PhD, Dept of International History, London School of Economics, Houghton Street, London WC2A 2AE.
Young, K. G., BSc(Econ), MSc, PhD, (address unknown).
Young, Mrs Susan H. H., BA, 78 Holland Road, Ampthill, Beds. MK45 2RS.
Youngs, Professor F. A., Jr, 2901 South Carolina Avenue, New Orleans, Louisiana 70118-4391, U.S.A.

Zagorin, Professor P., PhD, Dept of History, College of Arts and Science, University of Rochester, River Campus Station, Rochester, NY 14627, U.S.A.
Zeldin, T., MA, DPhil, St Antony's College, Oxford OX2 6JF.
Zeman, Zbynek A. B., MA, DPhil, St Edmund Hall, Oxford OX1 4AR.
Ziegler, P. S., FRSL, 22 Cottesmore Gardens, London W8.
Zutshi, P. N .R., MA, PhD, Corpus Christi College, Cambridge, CB2 1RH.

ASSOCIATES OF THE ROYAL HISTORICAL SOCIETY

Abela, Major A. E., MBE, 21 Borg Olivier Street, Sliema, Malta.
Addy, J., MA, PhD, 66 Long Lane, Clayton West, Huddersfield, HD8 9PR.
Aitken, Rev. Leslie R., MBE, 36 Ethelbert Road, Birchington, Kent CT7 9PY.
Ayrton, M. McI., 134 Iffley Road, Hammersmith, London W6 0PE.
Ayton, A. C., BA, Dept of History, The University, Cottingham Road, Hull HU6 7RX.

Baxendale, A. S. OBE, BA, MA, Hon MA, 164 Tolmers Road, Cuffley, Herts, EN6 4JR.
Begley, M. R., 13 Adelaide Avenue, King's Lynn, Norfolk PE30 3AH.
Birchenough, Mrs F. J., 6 Cheyne Walk, Bramblefield Estate, Longfield, Kent.
Bird, E. A., 29 King Edward Avenue, Rainham, Essex RN13 9RH.
Blackwood, B., FRIBA, FRTPI, FSAScot, DipTP, Dip Con Studies, FSAI, FRGS, FRSA, Ebony House, Whitney Drive, Stevenage SG1 4BL.
Bottomley, A. F., BA, MA, Eversley School, Southwold, Suffolk IP18 6AH.
Boyes, J. H., 129 Endlebury Road, Chingford, London E4 6PX.
Bryant, W. N., MA, PhD, College of St. Mark and St. John, Derriford Road, Plymouth, Devon.
Bussey, G. R., 64 Pampisford Road, Purley, Surrey CR2 2NE.
Butler, Mrs M. C., MA, 4 Castle Street, Warkworth, Morpeth, Northumberland NE65 0UW.

Cairns, Mrs W. N., MA, Alderton House, New Ross, Co. Wexford, Ireland.
Carter, F. E. L., CBE, MA, FSA, 8 The Leys, London N2 0HE.
Cary, Sir Roger, Bt, BA, 23 Bath Road, London W4.
Chandra, Shri Suresh, MA, MPhil, MBA, B½ Havelock Road Colony, Lucknow 226001, India.
Chappell, Rev. M. P., MA, St. Luke's Vicarage, 37 Woodland Ravine, Scarborough YO12 6TA.
Clifton, Dr Gloria C., BA, 55 The Ridgway, Sutton, Surrey SM2 5JX.
Cobban, A. D., 11 Pennyfields, Warley, Brentwood, Essex CM14 5JP.
Condon, Miss M. M., BA, 56 Bernard Shaw House, Knatchbull Road, London NW10.
Cooksley, P. G., 4 Ellerslie Court, Beddington Gardens, Wallington, Surrey SM6 0JD.
Cowburn-Wood, J. O. BA, MEd, The Dolphins, 131 King Edward Road, Onchan, Isle of Man.
Cox, A. H., Winsley, 11a Bagley Close, West Drayton, Middlesex.
Creighton-Williamson, Lt-Col. D., 6 Old School Close, Hartley Wintney, Hampshire RG27 8HQ.

d'Alton, Ian, MA, PhD, 30 Kew Park Avenue, Lucan, Co. Dublin, Ireland.
Daniels, C. W., MEd, Culford School, Bury St Edmunds, Suffolk IP28 6TX.
Davies, G. J., BA, PhD, FSA, 16 Melcombe Avenue, Weymouth, Dorset DT4 7TH.

Davies, P. H., BA, Erskine House, Homesfield, Erskine Hill, London NW11 6HN.

Davis, J. M., BA, MA, MSc, 6 Ellerslie Court, Gladstone Road, Crowborough, East Sussex TN6 1PL.

Davis, Virginia G., BA, PhD, Dept of History, Westfield College, Kidderpore Avenue, London NW3 7ST.

Downie, W. F., BSc, CEng, FICE, FINucE, MIES, 10 Ryeland Street, Strathaven, Lanarkshire ML10 6DL.

Dowse, Rev. I. R., 23 Beechfield Road, Hemel Hempstead HP1 1PP.

Edgell, The Revd H. A. R., SB, StJ, Horning Vicarage, Norwich NR12 8PZ.

Elliott, Rev. W., BA, 8 Lea View, Cleobury Mortimer, Kidderminster, Worcs. DY14 8EE.

Enoch, D. G., BEd, MEd, Treetops, 14 St David's Road, Miskin, Pontyclun CF7 8PW.

Filletti, The Hon. Mr. Justice J. A., LlD, BA, 6 Balluta Buildings, St Ignatius Street, St Julian's, Malta.

Firth, P. J. C., 59 Springfield Road, London NW8 0QJ.

Fitzgerald, R., PhD, BA, 32 Kynaston Road, Enfield, Middlesex EN2 0DB.

Foster, J. M., MA, 3 Marchmont Gardens, Richmond, Surrey TW10 6ET.

Franco de Baux, Don Victor, KCHS, KCN, Flat 2, 28 St Stephen's Avenue, London W12 8JH.

Frazier, R. Ll., BA, Dept of History, The University, Nottingham NG7 2RD.

Freeman, Miss J., 5 Spencer Close, Stansted Mountfitchet, Essex.

Granger, E. R., Bluefield, Blundall Road, Blofield, Norfolk NR13 4LB.

Green, P. L., MA, 9 Faulkner Street, Gate Pa, Tauranga, New Zealand.

Grosvenor, Ian D., BA, 69 Church Road, Moseley, Birmingham B13 9EB.

Gurney, Mrs S. J., 'Albemarle', 13 Osborne Street, Wolverton, Milton Keynes MK12 5HH.

Guy, Rev. J. R., BA, Selden End, Ash, nr Martock, Somerset TA12 6NS.

Hall, P. T., Accrington and Rosendale College, Sandy Lane, Accrington, Lancs. BB5 2AW.

Hamilton-Williams, D. C., BSc, SRN, MRSH, 6 Faraday Avenue, East Grinstead, West Sussex RH19 4AX.

Hanawalt, Professor Barbara A., MA, PhD, Dept of History, University of Minnesota, Minneapolis, MN 55455, U.S.A.

Hawkes, G. I., BA, MA, PhD, Linden House, St Helens Road, Ormskirk, Lancs.

Hawtin, Miss U. G., BA, PhD, FSAScot, FRSAI, Honey Cottage, 5 Clifton Road, London SW19 4QX.

Hendrie, A. W. A., BA, ACP, Sandy Ridge, Amberley Road, Storrington, West Sussex RH20 4JE.

Hillman, L. B., BA, 18 Creswick Walk, Hampstead Garden Suburb, London NW11 6AN.

Hoare, E. T., 70 Addison Road, Enfield, Middlesex.

Hodge, Mrs G., 85 Hadlow Road, Tonbridge, Kent.

Hope, R. B., MA, MEd, PhD, 5 Partis Way, Newbridge Hill, Bath, Avon BA1 3QG.

Jackson, A., BA, 14 Latimer Lane, Guisborough, Cleveland.

James, T. M., BA, MA, PhD, 36 Heritage Court, Boley Park, Lichfield, Staffs. WS14 9ST.
Jarvis, L. D., Middlesex Cottage, 86 Mill Road, Stock, Ingatestone, Essex.
Jennings, T. S., GTCL, The Willows, 54 Bramcote Road, Loughborough LE11 2AS.
Jermy, K. E., MA, MIM, FISTC, AIFA, FRSA, FSA, 5 Far Sandfield, Churchdown, Gloucester GL3 2JS.
Jerram-Burrows, Mrs L. E., Parkanaur House, 88 Sutton Road, Rochford, Essex.
Johnston, F. R., MA, 15 Lon Y Waun, Abergele, Clwyd LL22 7EU.
Johnstone, H. F. V., 119 Kingsbridge Road, Parkstone, Poole, Dorset BH14 8TL.
Jones, Rev. D. R., BA, MA, Chaplain's Office, St George's Church, HQ Dhekelia, British Forces Post Office 58.
Jones, Dr N. L., Dept of History & Geography, Utah State University, UMC 07, Logan, Utah 84322, U.S.A.

Kadish, Sharman I. DPhil, 126 Broadfields Avenue, Edgware, Middlesex HA8 8SS.
Keast, W. J., MPh, BA, Ziba View, 39 St George's Road, Barbican, East Looe, Cornwall.
Keir, Mrs G. I., BA, BLitt, 17 Battlefield Road, St Albans Herts. AL1 4DA.
Kennedy, M. J., BA, Dept of Medieval History, The University, Glasgow G12 8QQ.
Kilburn, T., BSocSc, MA, Pineacres, Grove Lane, Hackney, Matlock, Derbyshire DE4 2QF.
Knight, G. A., BA, PhD, DAA, MIInfSc, 17 Lady Frances Drive, Market Rasen, Lincs. LN8 3JJ.

Land, N., BA, DPSE(History), FRSA, FRGS, FCollP, 44 Lineholt Close, Oakenshaw South, Redditch, Worcs.
Leckey, J. J., MSc(Econ), LCP, FRSAI, Vestry Hall, Ballygowan, Co. Down, N. Ireland BT23 6HQ.
Lee, Professor M. du P., PhD, Douglass College, Rutgers University, New Brunswick, NJ 08903, U.S.A.
Lewin, Mrs J., MA, 3 Sunnydale Gardens, Mill Hill, London NW7.
Lewis, J. B., MA, CertEd, FRSA, 93 Five Ashes Road, Westminster Park, Chester CH4 7QA.

McDowell, W. H., MA, MSc, BA, 13 Saughtonhall Avenue, Edinburgh EH12 5RJ.
McErlean, J. M. P., MA, PhD, Dept of History, York University, Downsview, Ontario, Canada M3J 1P3.
McIntyre, Miss S. C., BA, DPhil, 10 Sandymount Road, Walsall, West Midlands.
McKenna, Rev. T. J., P.O. Box 979, Queanbeyan, NSW 2620, Australia.
McLeod, D. H., BA, PhD, Dept of Theology, The University, P.O. Box 363, Birmingham B15 2TT.
Metcalf, D. M., MA, DPhil, 40 St Margaret's Road, Oxford OX2 6LD.
Mileham, Major P. J. R., MPhil, 16 Grovely View, Wilton, Wiltshire SP2 0NA.
Munson, K. G., 'Briar Wood', 4 Kings Ride, Seaford, Sussex BN25 2LN.

Nagel, Rev. Dr. L. C. J., BA, Trinity House, Bluntway, Horsham, Sussex RH12 2BL.
Newman, L. T., MSc, DIC, CEng, 60 Hurford Drive, Thatcham, Newbury, Berks. RG13 4WA.
Noonan, J. A., BA, MEd, HDE, St Patrick's Comprehensive School, Curriculum Development Centre, Shannon, Co. Clare, Ireland.

Oggins, R. S., PhD, Dept of History, State University of New York, Binghamton 13901, U.S.A.
Osborne, Irving M., BEd, Adv.DipEd, FRSA, FRGS, FCollP, 169 Goodman Park, Slough SL2 5NR.

Pam, D. O., 44 Chase Green Avenue, Enfield, Middlesex EN2 8EB.
Paton, L. R., 49 Lillian Road, Barnes, London SW13.
Paulson, E., BSc(Econ), 11 Darley Avenue, Darley Dale, Matlock, Derbyshire DE4 2GB.
Perry, E., FSAScot, 11 Lynmouth Avenue, Hathershaw, Oldham OL8 3 ES.
Perry, K., MA, 14 Highland View Close, Colehill, Wimborne, Dorset.
Powell, Mrs A. M., 129 Blinco Grove, Cambridge CB1 4TX.

Raspin, Miss A., London School of Economics, Houghton Street, London WC2A 2AE.
Rees, Rev. D. B., BA, BD, MSc(Econ), PhD, 32 Garth Drive, Liverpool L18 6HW.
Reid, N. H., MA, c/o Cayman Islands Museum Office, Government Admin. Building, George Town, Grand Cayman, British West Indies.
Rendall, Miss J., BA, PhD, Dept of History, University of York, Heslington, York YO1 5DD.
Richards, N. F., PhD, 376 Maple Avenue, St Lambert, Prov. of Quebec, Canada J4P 2S2.
Roberts, S. G., MA, DPhil, 23 Beech Avenue, Radlett, Herts. WD7 7DD.
Rosenfield, M. C., AB, AM, PhD, Box 395, Mattapoisett, Mass. 02739, U.S.A.
Russell, Mrs E., BA, c/o Dept of History, King's College London, Strand, London WC2R 2LS.

Sabben-Clare, E. E., MA, 4 Denham Close, Abbey Hill Road, Winchester SO23 7BL.
Sainsbury, F., 16 Crownfield Avenue, Newbury Park, Ilford, Essex.
Scannura, C. G., MA, 1/11 St Dominic Street, Valletta, Malta.
Scott, The Rev. A. R., MA, BD, PhD, Sunbeam Cottage, 110 Mullalelish Road, Richhill, Co Armagh, N. Ireland BT61 9LT.
Sellers, J. M., MA, 9 Vere Road, Pietermaritzburg 3201, Natal, S. Africa.
Shores, C. F., ARICS, 40 St Mary's Crescent, Hendon, London NW4 4LH.
Sorensen, Mrs M. O., MA, 8 Layer Gardens, London W3 9PR.
Sparkes, I. G., FLA, 15 Orchid Close, Dairy Hill, Halesworth, Suffolk IP19 8ES.
Starr, C. R., 63 Abbey Gardens, London W6 8QR.
Stearn, R. T., MA, PhD, 15 Chilton Road, Kew, Richmond, Surrey TW9 4JD.
Sygrave, I., BA, PGCE, MCollP, 52 Burgoyne Road, Haringey, London N4 1AE.

Teague, D. C., ARAeS, MIMM, 52 Beresford Street, Stoke, Plymouth PL2 3AL.
Thomas, D. L., BA, Public Record Office, Chancery Lane, London WC2A 1LR.
Thompson, L. F., Colne View, 69 Chaney Road, Wivenhoe, Essex.
Tracy, J. N., BA, MPhil, PhD, 239 George Street, Fredericton, N.B., Canada E3B 1J4.
Tudor, Victoria M., BA, PhD, 33 Convent Close, Hitchin, Herts. SG5 1QN.

Vardon, T. J., MA, 5 Bankfield Drive, Leamington Spa, Warwicks. CV32 6BQ.

Waldman, T. G., MA, 620 Franklin Bldg./I6, University of Pennsylvania, Philadelphia, Pa. 19104, U.S.A.
Walker, J. A., 1 Sylvanus, Roman Wood, Bracknell, Berkshire RG12 4XX.
Wall, Rev. J., BD, MA, PhD, 10 Branksome Road, Norwich NR4 6SN.
Ward, R. C., BA, MPhil, 192 Stortford Hall Park, Bishop's Stortford, Herts. CM23 5AS.
Warren, Ann K., PhD, Dept of History, Case Western Reserve University, Cleveland, Ohio 44106, U.S.A.
Warrillow, E. J. D., MBE, FSA, Hill-Cote, Lancaster Road, Newcastle, Staffs.
Weise, Selene H. C., PhD, Rte. 1, Box 1206, Keeling, VA 24566, U.S.A.
Welbourne, D. J., 57 West Busk Lane, Otley, West Yorkshire LS21 3LY.
Westlake, R. A., 53 Claremont, Malpas, Newport, Gwent NP9 6PL.
Whittaker, Rev. (Rtd) G. H., MA, 1 Ash Grove, Ilkley, West Yorkshire LS29 8EP.
Wickham, David E., MA, 116 Parsonage Manorway, Belvedere, Kent.
Wilkinson, F. J., 40 Great James Street, Holborn, London WC1N 3HB.
Williams, A. R., BA, MA, 5 Swanswell Drive, Granley Fields, Cheltenham, Glos. GL51 6LL.
Williams, C. L. Sinclair, ISO, The Old Vicarage, The Green, Puddletown, nr Dorchester, Dorset.
Williams, G., FLA, 32 St John's Road, Manselton, Swansea SA5 8PP.
Williams, P. T., FSAScot, FRSA, FFAS, Copper Beeches, Boynford Road, Holywell, Clwyd, North Wales.
Wilson, A. R., BA, MA, 80 Apedale Road, Wood Lane, Bignall End, Stoke-on-Trent ST7 8PH.
Windrow, M. C., West House, Broyle Lane, Ringmer, nr Lewes, Sussex.
Winterbottom, D. O., MA, BPhil, Clifton College, Bristol BS8 3JH.
Wood, A. W., A.Dip.R, 11 Blessington Close, London SE13 5ED.
Woodall, R. D., BA, Bethel, 7 Wynthorpe Road, Horbury, nr Wakefield, Yorks. WF4 5BB.
Worsley, Miss A. V., BA, 3d St George's Cottages, Glasshill Street, London SE1.

Young, Assoc., Professor M. B., BA, MA, PhD, Dept of History, Illinois Wesleyan University, Bloomington, Illinois 61701, U.S.A.

Zerafa, Rev. M. J., St Dominic's Priory, Valletta, Malta.

CORRESPONDING FELLOWS

Ajayi, Professor J. F. Ade, University of Ibadan, Ibadan, Nigeria, West Africa.

Bédarida, Professor F., Institut d'histoire du temps present, 44 rue de l'amirral mouchez, 75014 Paris, France.
Berend, Professor T. Ivan, Hungarian Academy of Sciences, 1361 Budapest V, Roosevelt-tèr 9, Hungary.
Bischoff, Professor B., DLitt, 8033 Planegg C., Ruffini-Allee 27, München, West Germany.
Boorstin, Daniel J., MA, LLD, 3541 Ordway Street, N.W., Washington, DC 20016, U.S.A.
Boyle, Monsignor Leonard E., OP, Biblioteca Apostolica Vaticana, Vatican City, Rome, Italy.

Cipolla, Professor Carlo M., University of California, Berkeley Campus, Berkeley, Calif. 94720, U.S.A.
Constable, Giles, PhD, School of Historical Studies, The Institute for Advanced Study, Princeton, NJ 08540, U.S.A.
Crouzet, Professor F. M. J., 6 rue Benjamin Godard, 75116 Paris, France.

Duby, Professor G., Collège de France, 11 Place Marcelin-Berthelot, 75005 Paris, France.

Garin, Professor Eugenio, via Francesco Crispi 6, 50129 Firenze F, Italy.
Gieysztor, Professor Aleksander, Polska Akademia Nauk, Wydzial I Nauk, Rynek Starego Miasta 29/31, 00–272 Warszawa, Poland.
Glamann, Professor K., DPhil, DLitt, The Carlsberg Foundation, H.C. Andersens Boulevard 35, 1553 København, V, Denmark.
Gopal, Professor S., MA, DPhil, Centre for Historical Studies, Jawaharlal Nehru University, New Mehrauli Road, New Delhi-110067, India.
Guenée, Professor Bernaerd, 8 rue Huysmans, 75006 Paris, France.

Hanke, Professor L. U., PhD, E8 Amity Pl., Amhurst, MA 01002, U.S.A.

Inalcik, Professor Halil, PhD, The University of Ankara, Turkey.
Inglis, Professor K. S., DPhil (History Dept) The Research School of Social Sciences, The Australian National University, GPO Box 4, Canberra, ACT 2601, Australia.

Klingenstein, Professor Grete, Institut fur Geschichte, Universitat Graz, Heinrichstrasse 26, A-8010 Graz, Steiermark, Austria.
Kossmann, Professor E. H., DLitt, Rijksuniversiteit te Groningen, Groningen, The Netherlands.
Kuttner, Professor S., MA, JUD, SJD, LLD, Institute of Medieval Canon Law, University of California, Berkeley, Calif. 94720, U.S.A.

Ladurie, Professor E. B. LeRoy, Collège de France, 11 Place Marcelin Berthelot, 75005 Paris, France.

Leclercq, The Rev. Dom Jean L., OSB, Abbaye St-Maurice, L-9737 Clervaux, Luxembourg.

McNeill, Professor William H., 1126 East 59th Street, Chicago, Illinois 60637, U.S.A.

Maruyama, Professor Masao, 2–44–5 Higashimachi, Kichijoji, Musashinoshi, Tokyo 180, Japan.

Michel, Henri, 12 Rue de Moscou, 75008 Paris, France.

Morgan, Professor Edmund S., Department of History, P.O. Box 1504A Yale Station, New Haven, Conn. 06520-7425, U.S.A.

Peña y Cámara, J. M. de la, Avenida Reina, Mercedes 65, piso 7-B, Seville 12, Spain.

Slicher van Bath, Professor B. H., Gen. Fouldesweg 113, Wageningen, The Netherlands.

Thapar, Professor Romila, Dept of Historical Studies, Jawaharlal Nehru University, New Mehrauli Road, New Delhi-110067, India.

Thorne, Professor S. E., MA, LLB, LittD, LLD, FSA, Law School of Harvard University, Cambridge, Mass. 02138, U.S.A.

Van Houtte, Professor J. A., PhD, FBA, Termunkveld, Groeneweg, 51, Egenhoven, Heverlee, Belgium.

Verlinden, Professor C., PhD, 3 Avenue du Derby, 1050 Brussels, Belgium.

Wang, Professor Juefei, Dept of History, Nanjing University, China.

Wolff, Professor Philippe, Edifici Roureda Tapada, 2ª,7, Santa Coloma (Principality of Andorra), France.

Woodward, Professor C. Vann, PhD, Yale University, 104 Hall of Graduate Studies, New Haven, Conn. 06520, U.S.A.

Zavala, S., LLD, Montes Urales 310, Mexico 10, D.F., Mexico.

TRANSACTIONS AND PUBLICATIONS

OF THE

ROYAL HISTORICAL SOCIETY

The publications of the Society consist of the *Transactions*, supplemented in 1897 by the *Camden Series* (formerly the Camden Society, 1838–97); since 1937 by a series of *Guides and Handbooks* and, from time to time, by miscellaneous publications. The Society also began in 1937 an annual bibliography of *Writings on British History*, for the continuation of which the Institute of Historical Research accepted responsibility in 1965; it publishes, in conjunction with the American Historical Association, a series of *Bibliographies of British History*.

List of series published

The following are issued in collaboration with the distributor/publisher indicated:

Annual Bibliography of British and Irish History	
From 1989	Oxford University Press
Bibliographies of British History	
All except 1485–1603, 1714–1789	Oxford University Press
1485–1603, 1714–1789	Harvester Press
Camden Series	
Old Series and New Series	Johnson Reprint
Third and Fourth Series*	Boydell and Brewer
Guides and Handbooks	
Main Series*	Boydell and Brewer
Supplementary Series*	Boydell and Brewer
Miscellaneous titles	Boydell and Brewer
Studies in History	
All titles	Boydell and Brewer
Transactions of the Royal Historical Society	
Up to *Fifth Series*, Vol. 19	Kraus Reprint
Fifth Series, Vol. 20 onwards*†	Boydell and Brewer
Writings on British History	
Up to 1946	Dawson Book Service
1946–1974	Instititute of Historical Research

Members' entitlements

Fellows and Subscribing Libraries receive free copies of new volumes of series marked*.

Corresponding Fellows, Retired Fellows and Associates receive free copies of new volumes of this series marked†.

Terms for members' purchase of individual titles are listed below.

Methods of Ordering Volumes

Institute of Historical Research—an invoice will be sent with volume.

In all other cases pre-payment is required. If correct price is not known, a cheque made payable to the appropriate supplier, in the form 'Not exceeding £ ' may be sent with the order. Otherwise a pro-forma invoice will be sent.

LIST OF TITLES ARRANGED BY DISTRIBUTOR

BOYDELL & BREWER

Address for orders: P.O. Box 9, Woodbridge, Suffolk IP12 3DF.

Camden Third Series: All titles now available; a list can be sent on request. Prices range from £19.50 for original volumes to £35 for the largest reprinted volumes. (£14.62–£26.25 to Members).

Camden Fourth Series: The following titles are available price £15. (£11.25 to Members) unless otherwise indicated:

1. Camden Miscellany, Vol. XXII: 1. Charters of the Earldom of Hereford, 1095–1201. Edited by David Walker. 2. Indentures of Retinue with John of Gaunt, Duke of Lancaster, enrolled in Chancery, 1367–99. Edited by N. B. Lewis. 3. Autobiographical memoir of Joseph Jewell, 1763–1846. Edited by A. W. Slater. 1964. £35.00.
2. Documents illustrating the rule of Walter de Wenlock, Abbot of Westminster, 1283–1307. Edited by Barbara Harvey. 1965.
3. The early correspondence of Richard Wood, 1831–41. Edited by A. B. Cunningham. 1966. £35.00.
4. Letters from the English abbots to the chapter at Cîteaux, 1442–1521. Edited by C. H. Talbot. 1967.
5. Select writings of George Wyatt. Edited by D. M. Loades. 1968.
6. Records of the trial of Walter Langeton, Bishop of Lichfield and Coventry (1307–1312). Edited by Miss A. Bearwood. 1969.
7. Camden Miscellany, Vol. XXIII: 1. The Account Book of John Balsall of Bristol for a trading voyage to Spain, 1480. Edited by T. F. Reddaway and A. A. Ruddock. 2. A Parliamentary diary of Queen Anne's reign. Edited by W. A. Speck. 3. Leicester House politics, 1750–60, from the papers of John second Earl of Egmont. Edited by A. N. Newman. 4. The Parliamentary diary of Nathaniel Ryder, 1764–67. Edited by P. D. G. Thomas. 1969.
8. Documents illustrating the British Conquest of Manila, 1762–63. Edited by Nicholas P. Cushner. 1971.
9. Camden Miscellany, Vol XXIV: 1. Documents relating to the Breton succession dispute of 1341. Edited by M. Jones. 2. Documents relating to the Anglo-French negotiations, 1439. Edited by C. T. Allmand. 3. John Benet's Chronicle for the years 1400 to 1462. Edited by G. L. Harriss. 1972.
10. Herefordshire Militia Assessments of 1663. Edited by M. A. Faraday. 1972.
11. The early correspondence of Jabez Bunting, 1820–29. Edited by W. R. Ward. 1972.
12. Wentworth Papers, 1597–1628. Edited by J. P. Cooper, 1973.
13. Camden Miscellany, Vol. XXV: 1. The Letters of William, Lord Paget. Edited by Barrett L. Beer and Sybil Jack. 2. The Parliamentary Diary of John Clementson, 1770–1802. Edited by P. D. G. Thomas. 3. J. B. Pentland's Report on Bolivia, 1827. Edited by J. V. Fifer, 1974.
14. Camden Miscellany, Vol. XXVI: 1. Duchy of Lancaster Ordinances, 1483. Edited by Sir Robert Somerville. 2. A Breviat of the Effectes

devised for Wales. Edited by P. R. Roberts. 3. Gervase Markham, The Muster-Master. Edited by Charles L. Hamilton. 4. Lawrence Squibb, A Book of all the Several Offices of the Court of the Exchequer (1642). Edited by W. H. Bryson. 5. Letters of Henry St John to Charles, Earl of Orrery, 1709–11. Edited by H. T. Dickinson. 1975.

15. Sidney Ironworks Accounts, 1541–73. Edited by D. W. Crossley. 1975.
16. The Account-Book of Beaulieu Abbey. Edited by S. F. Hockey. 1975.
17. A calendar of Western Circuit Assize Orders, 1629–48. Edited by J. S. Cockburn. 1976.
18. Four English Political Tracts of the later Middle Ages. Edited by J.-Ph. Genet. 1977.
19. Proceedings of the Short Parliament of 1640. Edited by Esther S. Cope in collaboration with Willson H. Coates. 1977.
20. Heresy Trials in the Diocese of Norwich, 1428–31. Edited by N. P. Tanner. 1977.
21. Edmund Ludlow: A Voyce from the Watch Tower (Part Five: 1660–1662). Edited by A. B. Worden. 1978.
22. Camden Miscellany, Vol. XXVII: 1. The Disputed Regency of the Kingdom of Jerusalem, 1264/6 and 1268. Edited by P. W. Edbury. 2. George Rainsford's *Ritratto d'Ingliterra* (1556). Edited by P. S. Donaldson. 3. The Letter-Book of Thomas Bentham, Bishop of Coventry and Lichfield, 1560–1561. Edited by Rosemary O'Day and Joel Berlatsky. 1979.
23. The Letters of the Third Viscount Palmerston to Laurence and Elizabeth Sulivan, 1804–63. Edited by Kenneth Bourne. 1979.
24. Documents illustrating the crisis of 1297–98 in England. Edited by M. Prestwich. 1980.
25. The Diary of Edward Goschen, 1900–1914. Edited by C. H. D. Howard. 1980.
26. English Suits before the Parlement of Paris, 1420–36. Edited by C. T. Allmand and C. A. J. Armstrong. 1982.
27. The Devonshire Diary, 1759–62. Edited by P. D. Brown and K. W. Schweizer. 1982.
28. Barrington Family Letters, 1628–1632. Edited by A. Searle. 1983.
29. Camden Miscellany, Vol. XXVIII: 1. The Account of the Great Household of Humphrey, first Duke of Buckingham, for the year 1452–3. Edited by Mrs M. Harris. 2. Documents concerning the Anglo-French Treaty of 1550. Edited by D. L. Potter. 3. *Vita Mariae Reginae Anglie*. Edited by D. MacCulloch. 4. Despatch of the Count of Feria to Philip II, 1558. Edited by S. L. Adams and M. J. Rodriguez-Salgado. 1983.
30. Gentlemen of Science: Early correspondence of the British Association for the Advancement of Science. Edited by A. W. Thackray and J. B. Morrell. 1984.
31. Reading Abbey Cartularies, Vol. I. Edited by B. R. Kemp. 1986.
32. The Letters of the First Viscount Hardinge of Lahore to Lady Hardinge and Sir Walter and Lady James 1844–1847. Edited by Bawa Satinder Singh. 1986.
33. Reading Abbey Cartularies, Vol. II. Edited by B R. Kemp. 1987. £19.50.
34. Camden Miscellany, Vol. XXIX: 1. Computus Rolls of the English Lands of the Abbey of Bec (1272–1289). Edited by Marjorie Chibnall. 2. Financial Memoranda of the Reign of Edward V. Edited by Rosemary Horrox. 3. A collection of several speeches and treatises of the late Treasurer Cecil. Edited by Pauline Croft. 4. John Howson's Answers to Archbishop Abbot's Accusations, 1615. Edited by Nicholas Cranfield

and Kenneth Fincham. 5. Debates in the House of Commons 1697–1699. Edited by D. W. Hayton. 1987. £19.50.

35. The Short Parliament (1640) Diary of Sir Thomas Aston. Edited by Judith D. Maltby. 1988.
36. Swedish Diplomats at Cromwell's Court, 1655–1656. Edited by M. Roberts. 1988.
37. Thomas Starkey: A Dialogue between Pole and Lupset. Edited by T. F. Mayer. 1989.
38. Minutes of the Rainbow Circle, 1894–1924. Edited by M. Freeden. 1990.
39. Camden Miscellany, Vol. XXX: 1. The Hospitallers' Western Accounts, 1373/4 and 1374/5. Edited by Anthony Luttrell. 2. William Latymers' Chronickille of Anne Bulleyne. Edited by Maria Dowling. 3. The Letters of Richard Scudamore to Sir Philip Hoby, September 1549–March 1555. Edited by Susan Brigden. 4. The Undergraduate Account Book of John and Richard Newdigate, 1618–1621. Edited by Vivienne Larminie. 5. Captain Henry Herbert's Narrative of his Journey through France with his Regiment, 1671–3. And: Ane Account of Our Regements Marches from the Winter Quarters to ther Entrance in France. Edited by John Childs. 6. Lord Cutts's Letters, 1695. Edited by John Childs. 7. George III and the Southern Department: Some Unprinted Royal Correspondence. Edited by Ian R. Christie. 8. John Robinson's 'State' of the House of Commons, July 1730. Edited by Ian R. Christie. 1990. £19.50.

INDEX to AUTHORS
in Transactions of the Royal Historical Society
Series 1–5

Aberdare, Lord, (Henry A. Bruce): The Value of Historical Studies. Inaugural Address of the President.
Old Series, Vol.VII, pp.384–394, 1878.

Ackers, B. St. John: Historical Notes on the Education of the Deaf.
Old Series, Vol.VIII, pp.163–171, 1880.

Adamson, J.S.A.: The Baronial Context of the English Civil War. Alexander Prize Essay, 1989.
Fifth Series, Vol.40, pp.93–120, 1990.

Addison, Paul: The Political Beliefs of Winston Churchill.
Fifth Series, Vol.30, pp.23–47, 1980.

Ady, Cecilia Mary: Materials for the History of the Bentivoglio Signoria in Bologna.
Fourth Series, Vol.XVII, pp.49–67, 1934.

Allan, Alexander Stewart: Historical Notices of the Family of Margaret of Logy, Second Queen of David the Second, King of Scots.
Old Series, Vol.VII, pp.330–361, 1878.

Amery, Leopold C.M.S.: The Constitutional Development of South Africa.
Fourth Series, Vol.I, pp.218–235, 1918.

Andrew, C.M.: The French Colonialist Movement during the Third Republic: the Unofficial Mind of Imperialism.
Fifth Series, Vol.26, pp.143–166, 1976.

Anscombe, Alfred: The Pedigree of Earl Godwin.
Third Series, Vol.VII, pp.129–150, 1913.

Anscombe, Alfred: Prégent de Bidoux's Raid in Sussex in 1514, and the Cotton MS. Augustus I(i), 18.
Third Series, Vol.VIII, pp.103–111, 1914.

Anscombe, Alfred: The Historical Side of the Old English Poem of 'Widsith'.
Third Series, Vol.IX, pp.123–165, 1915.

Armstrong, Charles Arthur John: The Inauguration Ceremonies of the Yorkist Kings and their Title to the Throne.
Fourth Series, Vol.XXX, pp.51–73, 1948.

Arnold, Isaac N.: Abraham Lincoln.
Old Series, Vol.X, pp.312–343, 1882.

Ashley, Percy: The Study of Nineteenth-Century History. [Plea for study of Europe, and Britain in relation to it, since 1815.]
New Series, Vol.XX, pp.133–147, 1906.

Cunningham, William: 'Walter of Henley'.
New Series, Vol.IX, pp.215–221, 1895.
Cunningham, William: Chiefly on Gray's Inn and Lord Bacon.
Presidential Address.
Third Series, Vol.IV, pp.1–20, 1910.
Cunningham, William: Principally on national institutions in England and Scotland, including the game of golf.
Presidential Address.
Third Series, Vol.V, pp.1–20, 1911.
Cunningham, William: The Family as a Political Unit [in Scotland and England].
Presidential Address.
Third Series, Vol.VI, pp.1–17, 1912.
Cunningham, William: The Guildry and Trade Incorporations in Scottish Towns.
Presidential Address.
Third Series, Vol.VII, pp.1–24, 1913.
Curran, Minnie Beryl: The Correspondence of an English Diplomatic Agent in Paris, 1669–1677 [William Perwich].
New Series, Vol.XV, pp.131–150, 1901.
Cussans, John Edward: Notes on the Perkin Warbeck Insurrection.
Old Series, Vol.I, pp.61–77, 1872.
Cust, Sir Edward: Es-Sukhra, the Locked-up Stone of Jerusalem.
Old Series, Vol.II, pp.15–31, 1873.
Cuvelier, Jean: British and allied archives during the war. Series II. Belgium.
Fourth Series, Vol.III, pp.28–39, 1920.

d'Alton, Ian: Southern Irish Unionism: A Study of Cork Unionists, 1884–1914.
Alexander Prize Essay, 1972.
Fifth Series, Vol.23, pp.71–88, 1973.
Darwin, J.G.: The Fear of Falling: British Politics and Imperial Decline since 1900.
Fifth Series, Vol.36, pp.27–43, 1986.
Davenport, Frances G.: The Decay of Villeinage in East Anglia.
New Series, Vol.XIV, pp.123–141, 1900.
Davies, Alun: The New Agriculture in Lower Normandy, 1750–1789.
Fifth Series, Vol.8, pp.129–146, 1958.
Davies, Godfrey: The Whigs and the Peninsular War, 1808–1814.
Fourth Series, Vol.II, pp.113–131, 1919.
Davies, James Conway: The Despenser War in Glamorgan, 1321.
Third Series, Vol.IX, pp.21–64, 1915.
Davies, Kenneth Gordon: The Origins of the Commission System in the West India Trade.
Alexander Prize Essay, 1951.
Fifth Series, Vol.2, pp.89–107, 1952.
Davies, Ralph R.: Kings, Lords and Liberties in the March of Wales, 1066–1272.
Fifth Series, Vol.29, pp.41–61, 1979.

Haines, Herbert: France and Cromwell.
New Series, Vol.V, pp.147–156, 1891.
Hall, Hubert: The Imperial Policy of Elizabeth, from the State Papers, Foreign and Domestic.
New Series, Vol.III, pp.205–241, 1886.
Hall, Hubert: The National Study of Naval History. II. New Methods of Research.
New Series, Vol.XII, pp.95–101, 1898.
Hall, Hubert: Some Elizabethan Penances in the Diocese of Ely.
Third Series, Vol.I, pp.263–277, 1907.
Hall, Hubert: The Sources for the History of Sir Robert Walpole's Financial Administration.
Third Series, Vol.IV, pp.33–45, 1910.
Hall, Hubert: British and allied archives during the War. England.
Fourth Series, Vol.II, pp.20–23, 1919.
Hall, Hubert: A Discussion on the Exploration of Anglo-American Archives.
Fourth Series, Vol.XVI, pp.55–68, 1933.
Hamilton, Walter: The Origin of the Office of Poet Laureate.
Old Series, Vol.VIII, pp.20–35, 1880.
Hampson, Norman: Francois Chabot and his Plot.
Fifth Series, Vol.26, pp.1–14, 1976.
Hanham, H.J.: The Problem of Highland Discontent, 1880–1885.
Fifth Series, Vol.19, pp.21–65, 1969.
Hanna, Alexander John: The Role of the London Missionary Society in the Opening Up of East Central Africa.
Fifth Series, Vol.5, pp.41–59, 1955.
Hannay, Robert Kerr: British and allied archives during the War. Scotland.
Fourth Series, Vol.II, pp.23–26, 1919.
Harcourt, Leveson William Vernon: The Two Sir John Fastolfs. [Sir John of Caistor or Sir John of Nacton?]
Third Series, Vol.IV, pp.47–62, 1910.
Harding, Alan: The Origins and Early History of the Keeper of the Peace.
Alexander Prize Essay, 1959.
Fifth Series, Vol.10, pp.85–109, 1960.
Harding, Alan: The Origins of the Crime of Conspiracy.
Fifth Series, Vol.33, pp.89–108, 1983.
Hargreaves, John Desmond: From Strangers of Minorities in West Africa.
Fifth Series, Vol.31, pp.95–113, 1981.
Harris, George: Materials for a Domestic History of England.
Old Series, Vol.II, pp.142–157, 1873.
Harris, George: Domestic Everyday Life, Manners, and Customs in the Ancient World.
Old Series, Vol.II, pp.393–438, 1873.
Harris, George: Domestic Everyday Life, Manners, and Customs in the Ancient World.
Old Series, Vol.III, pp.1–74, 1874.
Harris, George: Domestic Everyday Life, Manners, and Customs in the Ancient World.
Old Series, Vol.IV, pp.364–415, 1876.

Morgan, William Thomas: Some Attempts at Imperial Co-operation during the Reign of Queen Anne. [I.e. in American and West Indian colonies.]
Fourth Series, Vol.X, pp.171–194, 1927.
Morgan, William Thomas: Economic Aspects of the Negotiations of Ryswick.
Fourth Series, Vol.XIV, pp.225–249, 1931.
Morison, Margaret Cotter: A Narrative of the Journey of Cecilia, Princess of Sweden, to the Court of Queen Elizabeth.
New Series, Vol.XII, pp.181–224, 1898.
Morison, Margaret Cotter: The Duc de Choiseul and the Invasion of England, 1768–1770.
Third Series, Vol.IV, pp.83–115, 1910.
Morrell, William Parker: The Transition to Christianity in the South Pacific.
Fourth Series, Vol.XXVIII, pp.101–120, 1946.
Morrill, John: The Religious Context of the English Civil War.
Fifth Series, Vol.34, pp.155–178, 1984.
Morris, John Edward: Mounted Infantry in Mediaeval Warfare. [Including 'Comparative table of county levies', 1322, 1337–1338 and 1338.]
Third Series, Vol.VIII, pp.77–102, 1914.
Murray, Kathleen Maud Elisabeth: Faversham and the Cinque Ports.
Fourth Series, Vol.XVIII, pp.53–84, 1935.

Neale, John Ernest: The Commons' Journals of the Tudor Period.
Alexander Prize Essay, 1920.
Fourth Series, Vol.III, pp.136–170, 1920.
Nelson, Janet L.: 'A King across the Sea': Alfred in Continental Perspective.
Fifth Series, Vol.36, pp.45–68, 1986.
Newton, Arthur Percival: The Establishment of the Great Farm of the English Customs.
Fourth Series, Vol.I, pp.129–156, 1918.
Nicholls, J.F.: The Early Bristol Charters and their Chief Object.
Old Series, Vol.I, pp.88–95, 1872.
Nicholls, J.F.: The Free Grammar School of Bristol, and The Thorns, its Founders.
Old Series, Vol.I, pp.204–217, 1872.
Nipperdey, Thomas: Mass Education and Modernization: the Case of Germany 1780–1850.
Prothero Lecture, 1976.
Fifth Series, Vol.27, pp.155–172, 1977.
Norgate, Kate: The Alleged Condemnation of King John by the Court of France in 1202.
New Series, Vol.XIV, pp.53–67, 1900.

Obolensky, Dimitri: Nationalism in Eastern Europe in the Middle Ages.
Fifth Series, Vol.22, pp.1–16, 1972.
O'Day, Rosemary: The Ecclesiastical Patronage of the Lord Keeper, 1558–1642.
Proxime accessit, Alexander Prize Essay, 1972.
Fifth Series, Vol.23, pp.89–109, 1973.

Palmer, J. Foster: The Saxon Invasion and its Influence on our Character as a Race.
New Series, Vol.II, pp.173–196, 1885.
Palmer, J. Foster: The Celt in Power: Tudor and Cromwell.
New Series, Vol.III, pp.343–370, 1886.
Palmer, J. Foster: Spola. Easter Day in Rome, 1849. A Link in the Chain of Italian Unity.
New Series, Vol.V, pp.177–203, 1891.
Palmer, J. Foster: Development of the Fine Arts under the Puritans.
New Series, Vol.V, pp.205–228, 1891.
Palmer, John Joseph Norman: The Anglo-French Peace Negotiations, 1390–1396.
Alexander Prize Essay, 1965.
Fifth Series, Vol.16, pp.81–94, 1966.
Pantin, William Abel: The General and Provincial Chapters of the English Black Monks, 1215–1540.
Alexander Prize Essay, 1927.
Fourth Series, Vol.X, pp.195–263, 1927.
Pares, Richard: The Manning of the Navy in the West Indies, 1702–1763.
Fourth Series, Vol.XX, pp.31–60, 1937.
Pares, Richard: George III and the Politicans.
Fifth Series, Vol.1, pp.127–151, 1951.
Parker, Geoffrey: Why did the Dutch Revolt last eighty years?
Fifth Series, Vol.26, pp.53–72, 1976.
Parsloe, Charles Guy: The Growth of a Borough Constitution: Newark-on-Trent, 1549–1688.
Fourth Series, Vol.XXII, pp.171–198, 1940.
Parsloe, Charles Guy: The Corporation of Bedford, 1647–1664.
Fourth Series, Vol.XXIX, pp.151–165, 1947.
Pearl, Valerie: The 'Royal Independents' in the English Civil War.
Fifth Series, Vol.18, pp.69–96, 1968.
Pearson, Charles Buchanan: Some Account of Ancient Churchwarden Accounts of St. Michael's, Bath. [With Extracts, from 1379.]
Old Series, Vol.VII, pp.309–329, 1878.
Pearson, Charles Buchanan: Notice of the Register and Churchwardens' Account Book which belonged to Knebworth, Herts, preserved in Dr. Williams' Library. (Extracts, 1596–1609.)
Old Series, Vol.VIII, pp.230–241, 1880.
Pelham, Henry Francis: A Chapter in Roman Frontier History.
New Series, Vol.XX, pp.17–47, 1906.
Pelling, Henry: The Early History of the Communist Party of Great Britain, 1920–1929.
Fifth Series, Vol.8, pp.41–57, 1958.
Pennington, Arthur Robert: The Emperor Frederick II of the House of Hohenstaufen.
New Series, Vol.I, pp.133–157, 1884.
Penson, Lillian M.: The Making of a Crown Colony; British Guiana, 1803–1833.
Fourth Series, Vol.IX, pp.107–134, 1926.

Plucknett, Theodore Frank Thomas: The Impeachments of 1376.
Presidential Address.
Fifth Series, Vol.1, pp.153–164, 1951.
Plucknett, Theodore Frank Thomas: State Trials under Richard II.
Presidential Address.
Fifth Series, Vol.2, pp.159–171, 1952.
Plucknett, Theodore Frank Thomas: Impeachment and Attainder. [In Fourteenth and Fifteenth Centuries.]
Presidential Address.
Fifth Series, Vol.3, pp.145–158, 1953.
Plumb, John Harold: The Organization of the Cabinet in the Reign of Queen Anne.
Fifth Series, Vol.7, pp.137–157, 1957.
Poland, Sir Harry Bodkin: Mr. Canning's Rhyming 'Despatch' to Sir Charles Bagot. [With Extracts from other correspondence concerning the Anglo-Dutch commercial negotiations of 1826.]
New Series, Vol.XX, pp.49–60, 1906.
Pole, Jack R.: The New History and the Sense of Social Purpose in American Historical Writing.
Fifth Series, Vol.23, pp.221–242, 1973.
Pollard, Albert Frederick: The Authenticity of the 'Lords' Journals' in the Sixteenth Century.
Third Series, Vol.VIII, pp.17–39, 1914.
Pollard, Sidney: Reflections on Entrepreneurship and Culture in European Economies.
Fifth Series, Vol.40, pp.153–173, 1990.
Porter, Harry Culverwell: The Nose of Wax: Scripture and the Spirit from Erasmus to Milton. [Interpretations of Scriptures by English Theologians.]
Fifth Series, Vol.14, pp.155–174, 1964.
Postan, Michael Moissey: The Chronology of Labour Services.
Fourth Series, Vol.XX, pp.169–193, 1937.
Powell, Edgar: An Account of the Proceedings in Suffolk during the Peasants' Rising in 1381.
New Series, Vol.VIII, pp.203–249, 1894.
Powell, Edward: Arbitration and the Law in England in the Late Middle Ages.
Alexander Prize Essay, 1982.
Fifth Series, Vol.33, pp.49–67, 1983.
Powell, Frederick York: The *École des Chartes* and English Records.
New Series, Vol.XI, pp.31–40, 1897.
Power, Eileen Edna Le Poer: On the Need for a New Edition of Walter of Henley.
Fourth Series, Vol.XVII, pp.101–116, 1934.
Powicke, Frederick Maurice: A Discussion on the Modern Methods for the Study of Medieval History and their Requirements. Modern methods of Medieval Research.
Fourth Series, Vol.XVI, pp.45–53, 1933.